INSIDERS' GUIDE® SERIES

D1268323

INSIDERS' GUIDE®
NORTH CAROLINA'S
SOUTHERN COAST
AND WILMINGTON THIRTEENTH EDITION

ZACH HANNER, PAMELA WATSON,
REBECCA PIERRE & KATE WALSH

Published and Marketed by:
By The Sea Publications, Inc.
P.O. Box 4368
Wilmington, NC 28406
(910) 763-8464

Insiders' Guide®
is an imprint of
The Globe Pequot Press

THIRTEENTH EDITION
1st printing

Copyright ©2006
by By The Sea Publications, Inc.

Printed in the United States
of America

All rights reserved. No part of this
book may be reproduced in any form
without permission, in writing, from the
publisher, except by a reviewer who
wishes to quote brief passages in connection with a review in a
magazine or newspaper.

Publications from the Insiders' Guide®
series are available at special discounts for bulk purchases for sales
promotions, premiums or fundraisings.
Special editions, including personalized covers, can be created in large
quantities for special needs. For more
information, please write to:

By The Sea Publications
P.O. Box 4368
Wilmington, NC 28406
or call (910) 763-8464

Cover Photos: Peter Doran

photo: Peter Doran

~ Just 5 Minutes from the Beach! ~

Uplifting, Unique & Unusual

Find traditional, splashy abstracts, hand-blown glass, earthy raku', sculpture, realism, hand-cut gems & jewelry and much, much more. Enjoy the Gallery and its many wonderful artists!

© Seuss Enterprises 2006

THE Gallery RACINE

452.2073
www.racinecenter.com

Fun, Funky, & Friendly

Come in Anytime. Our Creative Staff is Here to Help. A Large Variety of Pottery. Daily Classes. Thursday Ladies Night. Family Sundays. Group Rates. Birthday Parties. Team Building Events. We Ship Everywhere. All Ages Welcome!

Firebird
Paint Your Pottery Studio
203 Racine Drive ▪ Wilmington
(Within Racine Center, across from Home Depot)
Summer Hours ▪ 7 Days ▪ Thursdays til 9pm

Table of Contents

Directory of Maps

Thank you
to our Advertisers...

...for another great year on the Southern Coast!

Wilmington and the Southern Coast

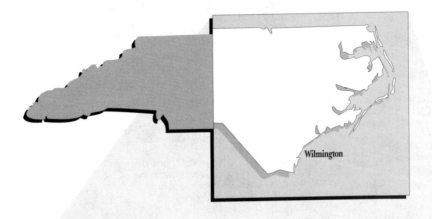

Wilmington

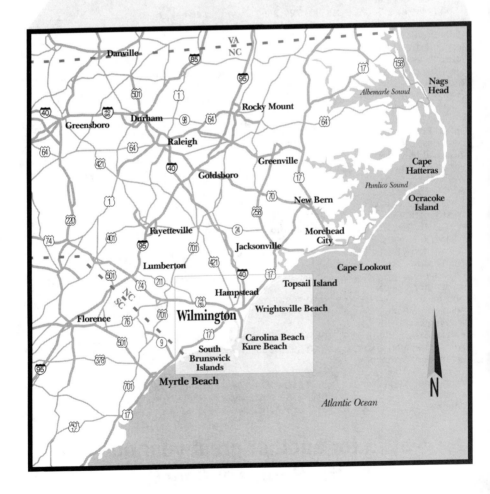

Topsail Island To Calabash

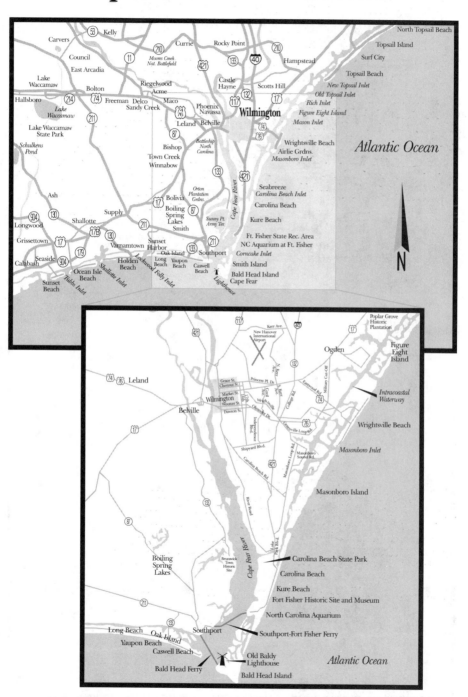

Downtown Wilmington

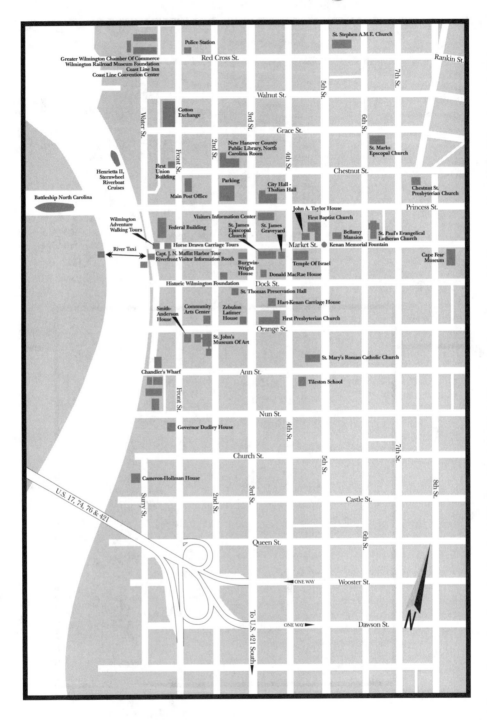

PREFACE

Welcome to the 13th edition of the Insiders' Guide® to North Carolina's Southern Coast and Wilmington. We think you'll find this book to be the most reliable and comprehensive collection of information, facts, tips and advice available for the southern coastal region extending from Topsail Island to the South Carolina border.

Inside this book you'll find recommendations on where to hear a symphony, charter a dive boat or shop for antiques. You'll find out where to rent a Jet-Ski, take a yoga class, buy original artwork, avoid traffic snarls, volunteer your time for a good cause, store your boat, locate emergency medical care or repair your bike. You'll also get invaluable information on how to plan an entire wedding on the southern coast. Those relocating here will find the chapters on Real Estate, Retirement, Healthcare, Commerce and Industry, and Schools and Childcare especially helpful when getting to know their new hometown.

This guide is not merely a checklist of things to do or places to go. Rather, it is designed to give you a sense of the character of the region and its offerings. We've tried to include information that will prove useful not only to short-term visitors, but also to newcomers who plan to stay awhile. Even longtime residents and natives may gain new perspectives about the people, places and events that have shaped this coastal area.

Keep in mind that you'll also find us on the Internet at www.insiders.com/wilmington. There you can view each and every chapter in this book in its entirety, plus find bonus information and chapters that we don't have room for in this book, such as pet-friendly accommodations and a complete homeowner's guide. You'll also find a link to www.insiders. com, where you can investigate other locales in the Insiders' Guide® series. On our website you will find our e-mail address: Please send us your questions and comments. We'd love to hear from you!

ABOUT THE AUTHORS

Zach Hanner

Zach Hanner is a graduate of the University of North Carolina at Chapel Hill with a major in performance studies. A former editor at citysearch.com, Zach has contributed to Durham's *Independent Weekly*, the Wilmington *Star-News*, the Myrtle Beach *Sun-News* and a number of other music and entertainment-related publications.

A professional actor as well, Zach has worked in the Wilmington and New York areas for the past 14 years, appearing in *Forrest Gump*, *The Patriot*, *Domestic Disturbance*, *Black Knight* and *Runaway Jury* as well as numerous commercial and television projects. He writes and directs children's theater for Wilmington's Journey Productions and is an active contributor to the Cucalorus Film Festival.

Ukulele player and front man for Wilmington's Hawaiian band Da Howlies,

Zach also plays bass in the surf guitar band The Noseriders. An avid surfer, both styles of music complement his love for the ocean. Zach lives on the gorgeous Intracoastal Waterway with his wife, Dagmar and their son Beck. Their dogs Violet and Maestro provide endless entertainment and their bothersome cat Veronica does not.

Pamela Watson

Zach Hanner

Pamela Watson

Pamela Watson is a freelance writer who has written travel articles, news, sports and features for more than 28 years. Her articles and columns have appeared in PC Magazine, *Reader's Digest*, *Private Clubs Magazine*, *Celebrate Northwest Arkansas Magazine*, *Wrightsville Beach Magazine*, *Greater Wilmington Business*, the Wilmington *Star News* and numerous other local, regional and national magazines and newspapers. Her travels have taken her from the Tower of London, to the gold mining towns of the California foothills, to hiking in Waimea Canyon on the island of Kaua`i. Having lived in seven states and three countries, she is delighted to call North Carolina home. She especially enjoys history and historical travel destinations, eco-tourism, the beach, the mountains and wine. Pamela is the author of two travel books, *Carolina Wine Country, The Complete Guide* (a journey through the vineyards and wineries of North and South Carolina), and *99 Fun Things To Do In Columbia and Boone County* (a delightful romp through the history and hidden mysteries of the heart of mid-Missouri). She is also a contributor to *Forgotten Missourians Who Made History* and *Exploring Columbia*. Pamela lives in Wilmington with her English-born husband Nick, and a house full of unfinished photo albums.

in 1992. Her writing has been published in periodicals including the Pelican Post, the Independent, and most recently in *Attaché Magazine*, the in-flight magazine for USAirways. Her experience writing award-winning poetry brings discipline, an economy of words and vivid descriptions to her work. Her first book of poetry, *A Mystery of Moon*, was published in the spring of 2005.

Kate Walsh

Kate Walsh

Kate Walsh loves to travel. Her adventures include bicycling from Paris to the Mediterranean, swimming in the Amazon River with pink dolphins, and studying pastry and chocolate in France. Kate produced and directed educational television programming for 20 years while working with the University of North Carolina, the University of South Carolina and the University of Wisconsin and she is currently pursuing her master of fine arts degree in creative nonfiction. Kate has lived in Surf City for 13 years.

Rebecca Pierre

Rebecca Pierre

Rebecca Pierre has years of experience in business writing, including package labeling, job descriptions and procedures, personnel, volunteer and resident newsletters, personnel and volunteer handbooks, employee surveys and a weekly column on volunteerism in a local daily newspaper. Rebecca began writing freelance after she moved to Oak Island

ACKNOWLEDGMENTS

Zach Hanner

Covering an area as wide and diverse as southeastern North Carolina is no easy feat and I'd like to thank all those that make this publication run so smoothly. I've enjoyed writing for the Insiders' Guide and I've met some interesting people and discovered a number of wonderful new things about my hometown. I wish to thank my wife, Dagmar, for all her love and endless support.

Pamela Watson

It's amazing, sometimes, how life takes you places! Wanting to be closer to our granddaughter brought us to Wilmington. Wanting to write about this wonderful area brought me to the Insiders' Guide.

Online writing has been a new experience for me, the original paper person, and helping to launch a new data tracking system for the company has been a challenge. Thank goodness Production Manager Melissa Stanley and Editor Molly Harrison were standing nearby with life preservers every time I started to sink. Whenever I had questions about the area or the new system, they were there with the answers. Thanks, ladies.

Thanks, too, to Publisher Jay Tervo for giving me the chance to be part of this terrific publication and its super staff. To my fellow writers who let me peek over their virtual shoulders to read their copy and learn the ropes, many thanks. Everyone has been warm and welcoming, which made an already fun job so much easier. I couldn't have done it without you.

Rebecca Pierre

I am pleased to be working with the other writers, the editor, the publisher, the production manager and everyone involved in the publication of the Insiders' Guide. Though some of their faces remain anonymous to me, each individual's contribution -- and there are many -- is equally important and is recognized as such. The teamwork is tremendous. The book itself, in addition to being a guide for residents, prospective residents and vacationers, has proven to be a source of information which has had the effect of touching people's lives in delightful and unexpected ways. I am proud to be a part of this effort.

Kate Walsh

I want to thank the entire staff of the Insiders' Guide for their generosity and great humor. I especially want to thank Jay Tervo for his vision, Molly Harrison for her patience, and Tom Jones for his kindness. Terry Meyer made my life easier this year by insisting I get high-speed Internet access -- thank you Terry. I have enjoyed meeting the island's newest entrepreneurs and seeing old friends again. This year Topsail Island offers more shopping, more dining and more things to do than ever before. Come to Topsail for a day and you might just stay forever.

Sink your toes into sand on the southern coast.

photo: Peter Doran

GETTING HERE, GETTING AROUND

Tourists and newcomers to North Carolina's southern coast will find it relatively easy to get around in the area, which consists of four coastal counties: New Hanover, Brunswick, Pender and Onslow. The city of Wilmington makes up most of New Hanover County, geographically the second smallest but among the fastest growing of North Carolina's 100 counties. Wilmington's population is around 95,000 and New Hanover County's is about 177,000.

Pender County, bordering New Hanover county on the north, includes the southern half of Topsail Island (Surf City and Topsail Beach), Hampstead and Burgaw. Primarily rural, Pender County was founded in 1875 and is the state's fifth largest county in area.

The northern half of Topsail Island is in Onslow County, which includes the coastal towns of Swansboro, Holly Ridge and Sneads Ferry. The City of Jacksonville, Camp Lejune Marine Base and Hammocks Beach State Park on Bear Island (accessible only by boat or ferry) are also in Onslow County.

Brunswick County, across the Cape Fear River to the west of New Hanover County, is quite unique in that its beaches face the Atlantic Ocean to the south. These beaches, on barrier islands between the ocean and the Intracoastal Waterway, stretch from the South Carolina state line to the historic fishing village of Southport. Bald Head Island is approximately four miles from Southport at the mouth of the Cape Fear River where it meets the ocean. Bald Head Island can be reached only by boat or the Bald Head Island Ferry, which does not transport vehicles.

BY LAND

Maps

To help you find your way around the Cape Fear area, a variety of maps are available at various locations, including visitors centers and chambers of commerce. The Guide Map, published by the Cape Fear Coast Convention & Visitors Bureau, 24 N. Third Street, (910) 341-4030 or (800) 222-4757, is good for the downtown Wilmington riverfront and historic district and includes information on attractions outside the city. Many other maps and brochures for the Cape Fear area are also available at the Wilmington Chamber of Commerce, 1 Estell Lee Place (just north of the Best Western Coast Line Inn at the west end of Nutt Street), (910) 762-2611. The Chamber of Commerce has extensive relocation data, community maps, a newcomer's guide and helpful information for students coming to the local colleges and universities. The Oak Island Recreation Center has maps of Oak Island, and the Welcome Center in Southport can help you with maps of that area.

Roadways

Although Wilmington lacks a freeway system (part of its relaxed charm, perhaps), navigating the area is fairly easy. Many streets and roads are being widened and improved to handle the increasing traffic flow of tourists and new residents.

Dr. Martin Luther King Jr. Parkway, on the north side of town, runs from Eastwood Road to N. Third Street, and is a quick way to get from one side of town to the other. It also connects to U.S. Highway 117, which then goes to U.S. Highway 421 west of the river, where it meets U.S. Highway 17 from the south. The route serves as a bypass for traffic from both the south headed north to I-40, and the north and the west headed for the beaches.

Market Street (U.S. Highways 17 and 74) is the main east-west route to and from downtown. Just east of College Road, Market crosses Eastwood Road, which on the north

CertifiedFirst.com

You planned to

Now what?

Thankfully, there's the CertifiedFirst™ Network. Now, no matter what happens to your car, you can count on the autobody repair specialists in the CertifiedFirst Network to take care of it. From the smallest scratch to the biggest dent, we'll get your car looking and performing like the day you drove it off the lot. So you can get back on the road. With confidence. **Consider it done.™**

NORTH BRUNSWICK COLLISION CENTER
9739 Blackwell Rd., Leland, NC 28451, PHONE: 910-371-3224
www.northbrunswickcollision.com

©2001 PPG Industries

3

side of Market turns into Martin Luther King Parkway. Go south on Eastwood to proceed to Wrightsville Beach. Market Street continues northeast as U.S. 17 N. to access the northern beaches. U.S. Highway 76 from the west takes a southerly route through Wilmington along Oleander Drive, a major shopping thoroughfare. At its western end, Oleander crosses Wrightsville Avenue, and then becomes Military Cut Off, which then crosses Eastwood and extends north past several shopping plazas, to end at N. Market Street.

From the north, Interstate Highway 40 (I-40) ends on the north side of Wilmington and becomes N.C. Highway 132, which is College Road, the main north-south route through the city. College Road continues south until it ends at U.S. Highway 421 (Carolina Beach Road), which continues south through Monkey Junction to Pleasure Island, where Carolina Beach and Kure Beach are located. U.S. 421 ends at the southern tip of Pleasure Island, the location of the state ferry to Southport.

The beaches of Brunswick County can be accessed either by taking U.S. 17 South from Wilmington and using the various feeder roads, or by taking the ferry from Fort Fisher on Pleasure Island to Southport and using N.C. Highways 133 and 211 until N.C. 211 merges with U.S. 17 South.

Wilmington, one of the few deep-water ports on the southeastern seaboard, is about 50 miles from the South Carolina state line. We've listed a few distances and driving times below to give a feel for how easy it is to get here.

DRIVING DISTANCES TO WILMINGTON

Raleigh, N.C.: 127 mi. — 2 hrs.

Charlotte, N.C.: 197 mi. — 4 hrs.

Asheville, N.C.: 310 mi. — 6 hrs.

Charleston, S.C.: 170 mi. — 3 hrs.

Columbia, S.C.: 210 mi. — 4 hrs.

Washington, D.C.: 375mi. — 7 hrs.

Atlanta, Ga.: 416 mi. — 8 hrs.

Nashville, Tenn.: 622 mi — 9 hrs.

New York, N.Y.: 618 mi. — 9 hrs.

Cleveland, Ohio: 750 mi. — 14 hrs.

INTERSTATES AND HIGHWAYS

For those wanting to take a really long drive to get here, Wilmington is linked to Barstow, California, via 2,554 miles of Interstate Highway 40, the longest interstate highway in the nation. The final leg from Raleigh to Wilmington, while scenic, is devoid of towns or distractions. Get some coffee before you start, and gas up because there are no gas stations or service plazas adjacent to the highway. There are a number of towns several miles off I-40, but they tend to roll up the sidewalks early, so be prepared to run this leg without stopping if you are traveling at night. However, there is one rest area about 55 miles north of Wilmington, where fast food and gas are nearby — Exit 364, Clinton/Warsaw.

From the south, U.S. Highway 17 roughly parallels the Atlantic Ocean shore, but is a number of miles inland, so there are no views of the ocean. If you aren't stopping in Myrtle Beach, you can avoid the congestion of U.S. 17 by taking the 6-lane bypass, S.C. Highway 31. Pick it up west of U.S. 17 at either S.C. Highway 544 or U.S. Highway 501 and breeze through the 25 miles to where it ends at S.C. Highway 9. When you exit, go east, following the signs back to U.S. 17 at Little River, South Carolina. Travel north and you'll cross the state line into North Carolina. Just off U.S. 17 on N.C. 179 is Calabash, famous for it's seafood restaurants.

Continuing north on U.S. 17 you'll reach Supply, North Carolina. Here you have the option of taking N.C. 211 into Southport, a historic fishing village at the mouth of the Cape Fear River. From Southport, you can take N.C. 133 or N.C. 87 north to rejoin U.S. 17 or take the state ferry to Fort Fisher on Pleasure Island. On U.S. 421 north of the ferry dock are Fort Fisher State Historic Site, Fort Fisher State Recreation Area and the North Carolina Aquarium, the largest of the state aquariums.

From the west, U.S. 74 from Charlotte and Interstate 20, becoming U.S. 76 from Columbia, South Carolina, merge near Whiteville and continue toward Wilmington. They junction with U.S. 17 just west of the N.C. 133 north exit to the USS North Carolina Battleship Memorial. The majority of these roads are easy-to-drive, four-lane highways through gently rolling countryside and coastal plains.

METRO AREA STREETS

Wilmington's unusual geographical configuration of being situated more or less on a tapering peninsula between the Atlantic Ocean and the Cape Fear River results in a layout of streets that does not follow any sort of orderly pattern one might find in an inland city. Downtown Wilmington is the only part of the city where blocks are laid out in a standard north/south, east/west arrangement. As a result, getting around for the tourist or newcomer is best accomplished by following route numbers whenever possible.

Because the city has no expressway system, city streets must carry all of the traffic flow. Surprisingly, even without freeways, traffic moves fairly well except during rush hours or heavy shopping periods, and even then, only a few streets are involved in the congestion.

Traffic from the west on U.S. Highways 17, 74 and 76 enters Wilmington via the Cape Fear Memorial Bridge, a very high, platform-type lift bridge that allows large ocean-going vessels to navigate up the Cape Fear River to the industrial area north of town. From downtown, the routes split, with U.S. 17 and 74 following the main drag, Market Street, on a more or less easterly direction through the city. U.S. 76 meanders toward the ocean on Dawson Street, then Oleander Drive, Wrightsville Avenue and finally Eastwood Road as it rejoins U.S. 74 and continues into Wrightsville Beach. U.S. 17 continues in a northeasterly direction on Market Street and provides access to Figure Eight Island and the Topsail Island beaches on its way to Pender and Onslow Counties plus Jacksonville and Camp Lejeune.

Traffic from the north on I-40 flows onto College Road, N.C. Highway 132, the main north/south route through Wilmington. College Road crosses Market Street and Oleander, then ends at Monkey Junction where it joins with Carolina Beach Road (U.S. 421) coming southeast from downtown. Carolina Beach Road continues south to Pleasure Island (Carolina Beach and Kure Beach).

Not only are Market Street, Oleander Drive and College Road the most heavily traveled streets in Wilmington, they also have the greatest concentration of commercial establishments. Restaurants, strip malls and shopping centers proliferate on all three thoroughfares, with the largest mall, Westfield Shoppingtown Independence, being located on Oleander Drive at Independence Boulevard. If you're heading for Wrightsville Beach, be aware that delays can occur at the drawbridge on U.S. 74 and 76 going onto Harbor Island. Once there, U.S. 74 heads to the north end of Wrightsville Beach and U.S. 76 goes to the south end.

Bike Routes

The Cape Fear area is blessed with a flat landscape and predominantly well-maintained roads, which makes touring the coastal plain by bicycle very pleasurable. However, there are few dedicated independent biking and hiking paths and trails. Bicycle facilities link many of the area's popular attractions.

About 4 feet of roadway on each side of U.S. Highway 421 on Pleasure Island is marked off and identified as a bike path for about 4 miles from north of Kure Beach to the ferry dock at Fort Fisher. This segment connects the N.C. Aquarium at Fort Fisher, the Fort Fisher State Historic Site and Fort Fisher State Park. The path will eventually connect with one partially completed that starts at the state boat launch area on Snow's Cut just east of Bridge Barrier Road in Carolina Beach. The entire 16-mile round trip route, known as the Pleasure Island Pedal Route, will connect Carolina Beach State Park with the Fort Fisher Ferry Terminal.

Also, 4-foot-wide bike lanes run along each side of River Road from U.S. 421 just north of Snow's Cut Bridge to Greenfield Lake on the south side of downtown Wilmington. This pleasant trip of 10.5 miles (one way) offers beautiful views of the Cape Fear River. A new benefit for pedaling visitors to downtown is the installation of more bicycle

If you're up for a casual, enjoyable bicycle ride, load your bike onto a carrier and travel to one of our popular state parks or beach communities. Why not bicycle on Pleasure Island or take the Fort Fisher-Ferry to Southport for a tour of this charming village? Take your bike via ferry and spend the day on Bald Head Island.

In some places, even a bicycle is too fast for the pace of life.

photo: Peter Doran

racks, designed by a local artist, throughout the downtown area. All Wave Transit buses are equipped with racks to carry two bicycles (no extra charge). For information on this program, call (910) 343-0106 or go to www.wavetransit.com/Services.htm#Bikes

A number of other bike routes using city streets and county roads have been developed, and maps for them are available, showing cyclists how to get around town on roads that match their traffic-handling skills. Roads are designated as neighborhood streets, local commuting streets, busy through-routes or touring routes. Parks, schools, public buildings and other points of interest are indicated. The maps show a complete street index and a park matrix that indicates the facilities available at each location. To obtain Wilmington bike maps, contact the City of Wilmington, Transportation Planning Department, P.O. Box 1810, Wilmington, NC 28402; (910) 341-3258. The map is also available for viewing online at www.ncdot.org/Transit/Bicycle/Maps/Maps_Urban.HTML, click on maps and then urban maps. Additional bike route information and helpful links can

be found at the Bicycle Advisory Committee website www.bikewilmington.com

The River-to-Sea Bike Route stretches from Riverfront Park at the foot of Market Street in Wilmington to Wrightsville Beach, a ride of just over 10 miles. This is a somewhat informal route used mostly by locals. Maps are available from the City of Wilmington, Transportation Planning Unit, P.O. Box 1810, Wilmington, NC 28402 or by calling (910) 341-3258. (See our chapter on Sports, Fitness and Parks.)

Some state-funded bicycling routes pass through Wilmington and along the neighboring coast using existing streets and roadways. They're marked by rectangular road signs bearing a green ellipse, a bicycle icon and the route number.

The Ports of Call Route, N.C. Bike Route 3, is a 319-mile seaside excursion from the South Carolina border to the Virginia line. Approximately 110 miles of it are along the southern coast, giving access to miles of beaches and downtown Wilmington.

The Cape Fear Run, N.C. Bike Route 5, links Raleigh to Southport. This 166-mile route crosses the Cape Fear River twice and intersects the Ports of Call.

Obtain free maps and information from the North Carolina Division of Bicycle & Pedestrian Transportation, 1552 Mail Service Center, Raleigh, NC 27601-1552; (919) 733-2804. Although the maps are updated regularly, be ready to improvise when it comes to information on campgrounds and detours. Detailed information, maps and map order forms are available online at www.ncdot.org/transit/bicycle/.

Brunswick County, which is essentially rural with small towns, has many biking opportunities on lesser-traveled roads through the countryside, in the towns and residential developments. In addition, there is a designated route of 32 miles from the historic fishing village of Southport to Orton Plantation and Brunswick Town Historic Site. A 3-mile segment of paved shoulder bike paths has recently opened from the state ferry dock to downtown Southport. At the Oak Island Recreation Center, you can obtain a pocket-sized booklet of bicycle trail maps. In it you will find 11 maps, including text description and trail length, with names like Heron Loop, Crab Dock Loop and Scenic Walkway Loop. Bald Head Island features an eight-mile loop trail that includes Old Baldy Lighthouse. This island is accessible only by private ferry from Southport; the fare is $15 per person plus $15 per bicycle for a round trip. Primarily residential with fine beach homes, Bald Head Island has a unique maritime forest and an excellent marina. No automobiles are permitted, so golf carts and bicycles are popular modes of travel.

Pender County has no designated bicycle routes or trails, but the area is primarily rural, with many lesser-traveled roadways available for bike touring.

In Onslow County there are two designated bicycle-touring routes: the Richlands Loop Bicycle Route and the Jacksonville City to the Sea Route. The Richlands route can be 50 or 20 miles, depending on your preference. The route is marked by green and white bike route signs. The terrain is level, and all roads are paved. The Jacksonville trip takes you from the Jacksonville Mall to Hammock's Beach State Park. This route intersects with the Ports of Call Route. Brochures and information can be obtained from Onslow County Tourism or Onslow County Parks & Recreation, 1244 Onslow Pines Road, Jacksonville, NC 28540; (910) 347-5332, www.co.onslow. nc.us/parks.

Local Buses

WAVE Transit Authority
1110 Castle St., Wilmington
(910) 343-0106

WAVE Transit Authority operates the Wilmington-area public bus lines and offers a variety of services. The adult one-way fare is $1.00. The fare is 50¢ for handicapped individuals with a Medicare card and seniors older than 65. Transfers are free. Children younger than 5 ride free when accompanied by a paying adult. Kindergarten through grade 12 students pay 50¢; high school students must show student ID. UNCW students and faculty with valid IDs ride free. Drivers do not carry change, so have your exact fare ready when you board the bus.

WAVE Pass Price List:

Passes are sold from the buses and the office.

7-day Adult	$10.00
7-day Reduced	$ 5.00
31-day Adult	$40.00
31-day Reduced	$20.00

Buses run from 6 AM until about 9:30 PM weekdays. On Saturdays, some routes may start later; on Sundays buses run 9:30 AM to 6 PM. There is no service on Thanksgiving Day, Christmas Day, New Year's Day, Easter Sunday, Memorial Day, July Fourth, Labor Day and Martin Luther King Jr. Day. All buses are handicapped accessible.

WAVE Routes:

Route 1: East Wilmington - Long Leaf Park

Route 2: Marketplace - UNCW

Route 3: Oleander Shopping Centers

Route 4: Eastwood Road - Mayfaire

Route 5: New Hanover Regional Medical Center

Route 6: Westfield Shoppingtown Independence and Long Leaf Mall, UNCW - downtown Wilmington; this connects with a shuttle which runs from Long Leaf

Mall to Lowe's Home Improvement at Monkey Junction.

• The Castle Hayne shuttle runs from Castle Hayne to downtown Wilmington

• The Brunswick Connector runs from the Leland area to downtown Wilmington

WAVE Transit Authority also offers Paratransit Service to meet the needs of the elderly, disabled and other special populations. Services include Travel Training, the Taxi Travel Voucher Program for the visually impaired and Dial-A-Ride Transportation or DART. DART is a curb-to-curb service with specially equipped vans that can accommodate both wheelchairs and semi-ambulatory passengers. Service is available Monday through Saturday from 6 AM to 8 PM and Sunday 9:30 AM to 6 PM. The fare is $1.50 one way and exact change is required. A personal care attendant may ride free of charge. Call (910) 343-0106 for an appointment at least 24 hours, but preferably four or five days, in advance and speak with the ADA contact person.

UNCW shuttle and fixed route services are free to all UNCW students and faculty who show a valid UNCW identification card. Four Seahawk Shuttles (blue, yellow, green and red) run within and around the campus area continuously Monday through Thursday from 7 AM to 9:30 PM and Friday from 7 AM to 6:30 PM.

The Wilmington Public Transit Guide, which contains a map and a table of schedules, is available at the Visitors Information Center, 24 N. Third Street in Wilmington, and on buses. For more information call the WTA at (910) 343-0106 Monday through Friday from 8 AM to 4:30 PM or TDD at (910) 763-9011, or stop by the WTA office at 1110 Castle Street, between 11th and 12th streets. A complete and detailed listing of route maps, schedules and information is available on the website: www.wavetransit.com.

Brunswick Transit System, Inc.
Dial-A-Ride
(910) 253-7800, (910) 754-2764
(877) 754-2764, TTY - (800) 855-2764

Brunswick County's Dial-A-Ride program provides safe, reliable and efficient non-emergency transportation throughout Brunswick County for those who either cannot or do not drive. Even for those who do, it can be a

handy service. At a cost of $1.50 to $5 one way, the service is definitely more affordable than other available services, and the vans are quite comfortable. All that's necessary is a little planning as reservations are required 48 hours in advance.

Long-Distance Bus Lines

Long-distance bus service to Wilmington is provided by **Greyhound**, (910) 762-6073, (800) 231-2222, and **Carolina Trailways**, (910) 762-6625, at the Wilmington bus terminal, 201 Harnett Street between N. Third and N. Front streets. Hours are 8:30 to 11 AM, 1 to 4:30 PM, and 8 to 9 PM. When phoning this location, use either local number, as one agent handles both bus lines; the toll-free number for Greyhound provides helpful recorded information and centralized service but is not local.

Trolley

Front St. Free Trolley
WAVE Transit Authority, 1110 Castle St., Wilmington
(910) 343-0106

A fun way to see the riverfront area and some of the shops is to take the Front Street Free Trolley in downtown Wilmington. A single trolley runs continuously from 7:30 AM to 9:20 PM Monday through Friday, 11 AM to 9:20 PM on Saturday and 11 AM to 6 PM on Sunday. Trolley stops are marked along the route, which goes along Front, Water and Second streets, and you can look for the trolley to stop approximately every 20 minutes. A route map, schedule and information are available on the website: www.wavetransit.com.

Taxicabs, Shuttle Vans and Limousines

In the areas of Wilmington, Wrightsville Beach, Carolina Beach and Kure Beach, taxis, shuttles, sedans and limos abound. Some companies provide strictly taxi service, some provide limousine, sedan or shuttle van service, and some companies provide a combination of some or all services. Within the city, taxi fares are uniform at $1.40 plus 30¢ per each one sixth of a mile plus $1.50 surcharge; outside city limits, fares are a set rate depending on destination; for example, fares from the airport to downtown or the beaches are usually on a flat fee basis. Some of the many available services are listed below. You can find others in local phone books.

WILMINGTON

A Capital Style Limo, Sedan, Van & Bus Service, (800) 948-6170 (Raleigh)

A & K Limo Services, (910) 790-3128

Azalea Limousine Service, (910) 452-5888

Beach Buggy Taxi, (910) 792-0232

Classic Limousine Service, (910) 793-8843

Coastal Limousine & Transportation, (910) 232-4645

Coastal Yellow Cab, (910) 762-3322 or (910) 762-4464

Dolphin Taxi, (910) 228-8294 or (800) TAXICAB (829-4222)

Kat's Taxi, (910) 763-5003 or (910) 763-5014

Lett's Taxi, (910) 343-3335
Lett's Limousine Service, (910) 343-4161

Pleasure Island Taxi, (910) 458-2222

Port City Taxi Inc., (910) 762-1165 or (910) 762-5230

Prestige Limousine Service, (910) 799-4484

Ray's Let's Roll Taxi Service, (910) 233-5164 or (910) 681-1110

WRIGHTSVILLE BEACH

X-tra Cab, (910) 798-5888

BRUNSWICK COUNTY BEACHES

In Brunswick County the following services are available. Easy Way and Southern are primarily airport shuttle by reservation

and Ace does airport runs and trips; A-1 is a limousine service.

A-1 Transport, (910) 269-1214

Ace Cab Co., (910) 278-5248, (910) 279-9799

A & E Cab, (910) 278-9100

Easy Way Transport Service, (910) 579-9926

Handy Taxi, (910) 443-8456

Oak Island Cab, (910) 278-6373, (910) 754-2515

Southern Hospitality, (910) 457-4949

ONSLOW COUNTY/TOPSAIL AREA

In Onslow County, the following cab and limo services are available, primarily out of Jacksonville.

A - 1 Taxi, (910) 353-0365

Chico's Cab, (910) 346-1900

Diamond Limousine Service, (800) 840-4070

Dynamic Cab, (910) 347-5757

Limousines 'R' Us, (910) 938-2486

Tarheel Taxi, (910) 455-2222

Yellow Cab, (910) 353-1111

Car Rentals

Along with the national chains and independent car rental services listed here, several new car dealerships also lease cars long-term.

Alamo & National Car Rental, Wilmington International Airport, (910) 762-8000 or (910) 762-0143, (800) 227-7368

Avis Rent A Car, Wilmington International Airport, Main Terminal, Wilmington, (910) 763-1993, (800) 831-2847

Enterprise Rentals, Reservations (800) 736-8222; 1930 Castle Hayne Road, Wilmington, (910) 772-1560; 4911 Market Street, Wilmington, (910) 350-0435; 5601-B Market Street, Wilmington, (910) 799-4042; 1437

South College Road, Wilmington, (910) 397-9110;

Capital Ford, 4222 Oleander Drive, Wilmington, (910) 790-0421; 3722 Carolina Beach Road, Carolina Beach, (910) 791-8201; 4019 Long Beach Rd., Oak Island, (910) 454-8943

Hertz, Wilmington International Airport, (910) 762-1010, (800) 654-3131

Thrifty Car Rental, Wilmington International Airport, (910) 343-1411, (800) 847-4389

Triangle Rent A Car, 4124 Market Street, Wilmington, (910) 251-9812, (800) 643-7368

BY AIR

Airports

Wilmington International Airport is the prime entry point for most people flying into the greater Wilmington area. Myrtle Beach International Airport in South Carolina is nearly the same distance from Shallotte as the Wilmington airport (about 40 miles), so visitors traveling by air to or from the Calabash and South Brunswick Islands areas might do well to check flight availability via Myrtle Beach. Those traveling to or from Oak Island, Southport, Pleasure Island or points north will find Wilmington International Airport easier to use. Small aircraft destined for Brunswick County can use Brunswick County Airport, just outside Southport.

Wilmington International Airport (ILM)
1740 Airport Blvd., Wilmington
General Information (910) 341-4125
Administration Offices (910) 341-4333

Wilmington International is an entirely modern facility, complete with baby-changing areas accessible to dads. Yet it has plenty of that charm peculiar to small airports. The recently renovated and expanded airport fronts 23rd Street, 2 miles north of Market Street, and by car is within 10 minutes of

For the latest New Hanover County public transportation schedules, go to WAVE Transit Authority at www.wavetransit.com

downtown Wilmington and about 20 minutes of Wrightsville Beach.

Two airlines serve the airport: the Delta connection to Atlanta, (800) 282-3424, and USAirways, (800) 428-4322. Short-term parking rates are $1 per half-hour, with a maximum 24-hour charge of $12. Long-term parking costs $1 per hour, with a maximum charge of $7 per day. Fifteen minutes of free parking is available in both parking areas.

Brunswick County Airport (KSUT)
4019 Long Beach Rd., Southport
(910) 457-6483

The Brunswick County Airport, named "The South's Best Airport" by readers of The Southern Aviator Magazine in 2005, is a fast-growing, full-service airport located on the mainland side of the Oak Island Bridge and is especially convenient to Bald Head Island and the Southport-Oak Island area. It has 24 hour glide slope lights and a 4,300-foot paved runway which can handle general aviation aircraft from the lightest to fairly sizable jets. The airport is in the process of lengthening it to 5,500 feet with the addition of a full-length parallel taxiway. It supports instrument approaches (GPS, NDB).

There are now 30 T-hangars and six commercial hangars with more planned. Services provided include: flight instruction, rental aircraft, a full-service aircraft repair facility on the field (Oak Island Aviation), and a state-of-the-art computerized fueling system. With a fuel purchase, you receive one free overnight tie-down. In addition, there is a full-time skydiving and sight-seeing operator, and during the summer months banner towing along the beaches is available. The terminal houses airport operations, Creative Real Estate, Enterprise Rent-A-Car and a Bait and Tackle Shop. There is also a computerized weather graphics station and an Automated Weather Observation System with real-time aviation weather available at (910) 457-1710.

Myrtle Beach International Airport (MYR)
1100 Jetport Rd., Myrtle Beach
General Information (843) 448-1589

The Myrtle Beach International Airport is convenient for those residents or visitors in the extreme southern coastal area. It is serviced by the following airlines: Atlantic Southeast Airlines (ASA) and Comair, which are part of the Delta Connection, a group of strong regional carriers that work together to give more passengers access to the Delta Air Lines network, (800) 282-3424; AirTran (seasonal), (800) 247-8726; Continental Airlines, (800) 525-0280; Spirit Airlines, (800) 772-7117; USAirways, (800) 428-4322; Hooters Airline, (888) 359-4668; Northwest (seasonal), (800) 225-2525; and United Express, (800) 241-6522.

Myrtle Beach International Airport is in the midst of a $200 million expansion that will include a new commercial airline terminal complex. The terminal will have 14 gates with passenger boarding bridges and will accommodate aircraft ranging from commuter jets to wide-body aircraft such as a B747. Other additions and enhancements include a food court, new parking lots and rental-car facilities, and improvements to fueling facilities and infrastructure. The project is scheduled for completion in between 2007–08.

Short-term parking rates are first 15 minutes free, 75¢ for each 20 minutes after that; the maximum for each 24 hours is $21. No overnight parking. Long-term parking is $2 for up to four hours, with a maximum of $8 for the first 24 hours, then $7 for each additional day. Economy parking is $6 for the first 24 hours and $5 each day after that. Take advantage of the free shuttle bus service between the terminal and the economy lot; buses run approximately every five to seven minutes.

Air Charters, Rentals, Leasing

If you're looking for a place to charter, rent or purchase a small aircraft, you can do it here. If your plane needs servicing or refueling, you can have it done here. If you want flight instruction, you can get it here. All the companies listed below are based at Wilmington International unless otherwise noted; not all services are provided by each company, but their staffs are knowledgeable and will assist you in finding whatever you need. (See also our section on Flying in the chapter Sports, Fitness and Parks.)

Air Wilmington, maintenance, service, charters, leasing, flight training, (910) 763-0146

Aero Service Inc. South, flight training, maintenance, transient services, (910) 763-8844

Aero Service Inc. North, transient services only, (910) 763-8898

BY SEA

Most boaters coming to the Cape Fear region do so via the magnificent Intracoastal Waterway (ICW), although some use that big puddle offshore, the Atlantic Ocean. Extending 3,000 miles along the Atlantic coast from Boston to Key West, the ICW provides protection from the open sea, along with a multitude of marinas and harbors. In North Carolina, the ICW follows a path behind a nearly continuous string of barrier islands from Virginia to South Carolina. See our chapter of Marinas and the Intracoastal Waterway for detailed information.

Ferries

Southport–Fort Fisher Ferry
(910) 457-6942, (800) 368-8969

North Carolina's ferry system actually began in the 1920s with a private tug and barge service crossing Oregon Inlet on the Outer Banks. Other private ferries subsequently developed that were subsidized by the state during the 1930s and '40s. In the late '40s and '50s, the state began purchasing the private ferry companies, and today the North Carolina ferry system has seven ferry routes, 24 ferries and over 400 employees. More than 1.1 million vehicles and more than 2.5 million passengers are transported every year over five bodies of water.

The Southport-Fort Fisher ferry service is not only a mode of transportation that saves miles of driving, but also one of the least expensive scenic tours. On the approximately 30-minute cruise, the ferry provides a panoramic view of the mouth of the Cape Fear River above Southport. On the Brunswick County side, huge yellow cranes mark the Military Ocean Terminal at Sunny Point, the largest distribution center in the country for military supplies. Other sights include Old Baldy, North Carolina's oldest lighthouse on Bald Head Island; Price's Creek Lighthouse, which guided Confederate blockade runners through New Inlet during the Civil War; and the Oak Island Lighthouse, the nation's brightest. (For information on tours and attractions, see our Attractions chapter.)

The Fort Fisher ferry terminal on Pleasure Island is near the southern terminus of U.S. 421 on the right. The Southport terminal is on Ferry Road, just off N.C. 211, about 3 miles north of town. During summer months, you need to get to the terminal at least 20 minutes before departure, on holiday weekends, 30 minutes. This ferry is extremely popular with visitors; capacity is limited to about 36 cars.

Departure Times:

* Winter only: 1/1 to 5/22 and 9/5 to 12/31

** Summer only: 5/23 to 9/4

Departs Southport	Departs Fort Fisher
5:30 AM	6:15 AM
7:00 AM	7:45 AM
7:45 AM*	8:30 AM*
8:30 AM	9:15 AM
9:15 AM	10:00 AM
10:00 AM	10:45 AM
10:45 AM	11:30 AM
11:30 AM	12:15 PM
12:15 PM	1:00 PM
1:00 PM	1:45 PM
1:45 PM	2:30 PM
2:30 PM	3:15 PM
3:15 PM	4:00 PM
4:00 PM	4:45 PM
4:45 PM	5:50 PM
6:15 PM	7:00 PM
7:45 PM**	8:30 PM**

Fares:

Pedestrians, $1

Bicycle & Rider, $2

Motorcycles, $3

Vehicle and or combination less than 20 feet, $5

Vehicles or combinations in excess of 20 feet up to 40 feet, $10

Vehicles or combinations greater than 40 feet to 65 feet maximum, $15

Annual Pass, $100 in cash

Call in advance if ferrying larger vehicles. Rates and schedules are subject to change. For information about the Southport-Fort Fisher Ferry only, call (910) 457-6942 or (800) 368-8969. For statewide and individual ferry information call (800) BY-FERRY (293-3779) or go to the website www.ncferry.org

Bald Head Island Ferry
Foot of W. Ninth St., Southport
(910) 457-5003, (800) 234-1666

The ferry between Southport and Bald Head Island is strictly for passengers. Travel on the island is by foot, bicycle or electric cart — no passenger cars are allowed. An individual, round-trip ferry ticket is $15 for adults and $8 for children ages 3 through 12. Children age 2 and younger ride free. In Southport, the ferry terminal is at Indigo Plantation at the foot of Ninth Street. It departs on the hour from 8 AM to 10 PM, except at noon, seven days a week. Ferries leave Bald Head Island every hour on the half-hour, except at 11:30 AM. Ferry parking in Southport costs $5 or $7 per day depending on which lot you use.

On North Carolina's southern coast, you can watch the sun rise over the Atlantic Ocean.

photo: Peter Doran

⊙ AREA OVERVIEW

The wonderful history, culture and economy of North Carolina's southern coast would not exist without the area's proximity to the water. While the ocean gets top billing in terms of geographical attractions, it was the existence of a relatively narrow river that gave rise to successful European settlement here. The Cape Fear River, a deep, often fast-moving body of water, begins at the confluence of the Haw and Deep rivers near Greensboro, meanders through Fayetteville and empties into the Atlantic Ocean 200 miles south of its source. With a compelling history and dangerous reputation, the Cape Fear River has always been a major influence on the formation and evolution of the city of Wilmington, 30 miles upstream from the open ocean.

The Cape Fear River

For centuries Native Americans had this area to themselves, until European settlers came. In 1524, when Italian explorer Giovanni da Verrazzano took his French-financed expedition into an unknown river in a wild place, he ushered in a new historical period that would slowly lead to European development of the area.

Verrazzano wrote glowingly of the area in his journal: "The open country rising in height above the sandy shore with many faire fields and plaines, full of mightie great woods, some very thicke and some thinne, replenished with divers sorts of trees, as pleasant and delectable to behold, as if possible to imagine." Despite the explorer's enthusiastic description, very little happened in terms of development at that time.

Initially Queen Elizabeth I had paved the way for colonization of the area by decreeing that the British had a right to conquer and occupy land not actually possessed by any Christian prince or people. Later, in 1629, Sir Robert Heath, attorney general for King of England Charles I, was granted a large area of what is today named Carolina. Neither Heath nor his heirs did anything to develop the area, so in 1663, Charles II granted the area as a reward to eight men who were called the Lords Proprietors.

Members of the Massachusetts Bay Colony, led by William Hilton, attempted to colonize the Cape Fear region in 1663. Their effort failed, and the following year, a new settlement ventured into the region. A group of English settlers from Barbados, led by John Vassal, established a settlement in 1664. By 1667, that settlement was abandoned because of a disagreement with the Lords Proprietors who backed another settlement, Charles Town, farther south on the west bank of the river. That effort failed in 1667 because of hostile coastal Indians, pirates, weak supply lines, mosquitoes and other problems that drove the residents south, where they founded the City of Charleston in South Carolina. Perhaps one of the greatest reasons for failure was, ironically, the very river that sparked interest in settlement.

In 1879 settler George Davis in James Sprunt's Chronicles of the Cape Fear River vividly described part of the problem with settlement caused by the river:

"Looking to the cape for the idea and reason of its name, we find that it is the southernmost point of Smith's Island — a naked, bleak elbow of sand, jutting far out into the ocean. Immediately in front of it are the Frying Pan Shoals, pushing out still farther, twenty miles, to sea. Together, they stand for warning and for woe; and together they catch the long majestic roll of the Atlantic as it sweeps through a thousand miles of grandeur and power from the Arctic toward the Gulf. It is the playground of billows and tempests, the kingdom of silence and awe, disturbed by no sound save the sea gull's shriek and the breakers' roar. Its whole aspect is suggestive, not of repose and beauty, but of desolation and terror. Imagination can not

The Official Tourism Agency for New Hanover County

Your Live Tourism Specialist

Available at Visitor Information Centers

The Historic New Hanover County Courthouse
24 North Third St *(the corner of Third & Princess Sts)*
Wilmington

The Riverfront Booth
(the foot of Market Street at Water St)
Wilmington

Visitor Center at the
Pleasure Island Chamber of Commerce
1121 North Lake Park Blvd
Carolina Beach

Wrightsville Beach Visitors Center
305 West Salisbury St
Wrightsville Beach

2006 Official Visitor's Guide
Historic Wilmington · Kure Beach · Carolina Beach · Wrightsville Beach
AN OCEAN, A HISTORIC RIVERFRONT TOWN AND THE STORIES THEY TELL
www.capefearguide.com · 866-534-0R...

Call for hours and information, Cape Fear Coast Convention & Visitors Bureau
1-866-842-5895 • 910-341-4030 • CapeFearVacation.com

adorn it. Romance cannot hallow it. Local pride cannot soften it."

The Town of Brunswick was founded by disgruntled English settlers from South Carolina on the west bank of the river in 1726, but it withered away as more strategically located Wilmington, on the high east bank, began to prosper. There river rafters would stop to trade at a place called the Dram Tree.

Establishing Wilmington says a lot about the tenacity of the successful settlers who managed to tame what was apparently a very wild place. They understood, as do their descendants, that the river presented more opportunities than obstacles and whatever it took to settle the area was worth it. Positioning the City of Wilmington on a bluff created a port relatively safe from storms. Later, it also proved to be a protective barrier against invaders from England during the Revolutionary War and Union troops during the Civil War.

The Cape Fear River was a profitable area for trading goods such as tar, turpentine and pitch, but sailors disliked coming here. The waters were dangerous to navigate and the residents viewed sailors as unsavory. In fact, by statute of the time, tavern keepers, retailers of liquor or keepers of public houses were not permitted to give credit to seamen, and seamen were not permitted to be kept, entertained or harbored by any resident longer than six hours. In addition, Wilmington did not and would not have sewage or drainage systems for years to come. As a result, diseases prevailed, such as small pox and malaria, and there were few doctors, the first of whom, Armande de Rossett, did not arrive until 1735. It was with trepidation and dread that seamen sailed into the river's waters, and that is how the river got its foreboding name.

Wilmington: The Port City

Previously called New Liverpool, New Carthage, New Town and Newton, Wilmington was settled in 1729. That same year, St James Parish was founded and still exists today as St. James Episcopal Church at the corner of Third and Market streets. The name of the city was finally decided when Gov-

A stroll on Wilmington's Riverwalk puts you in tune with the music of the Cape Fear River.

photo: Cait, student of DREAMS Center for Arts Education

ernor Gabriel Johnston took office. He was so excited and thankful for the prestigious appointment that he named the city after the man who gave him the job — Spencer Compton, Earl of Wilmington.

The City of Wilmington was incorporated in 1740 and continued to grow and prosper. During part of the 1700s, Wilmington also functioned six times as the seat of government for North Carolina, because at that time the Colonial Assembly moved about, usually being located where the governor lived or where the legislators met.

In keeping with its English heritage, many streets in Wilmington, such as Red Cross, Castle, Walnut, Chestnut, Princess, Market, Dock, Orange, Ann, Nunn, Queen and Church streets, are named after streets in Liverpool, England.

Wilmington flourished as a major port, shipbuilding center and producer of pine forest products. Tar, turpentine and pitch were central to the economy, and lumber from the pine forests was a lucrative economic resource. At one time, Wilmington was the site of the largest cotton exchange in the world. The waterfront bustled with steam ships crowding together to pick up or unload precious cargo.

Involvement in the American Revolutionary movement began for Wilmington in 1765, when the British Parliament passed the Stamp Act. Reaction and vigorous resistance were immediate and colorful, with much of the activity taking place at night and emanating from the taverns. Eventually, the Stamp Officer was intimidated into composing a letter of resignation, whereupon the residents gave him three cheers, carried him about the town on a chair and treated him to the finest

> *If you're coming to the Cape Fear Coast as either a new resident or a tourist, plan on bringing only about half as many clothes as you think you'll need. The area is very relaxed and laid back, and you'll find most business and many professional people are wearing sports clothes. Khaki pants and a sports shirt will get you by just about anywhere. During the lengthy warm season, shorts and a polo shirt are the uniform of the day and are acceptable almost anywhere, including restaurants.*

liquors. Subsequently, the colonists refused to receive the stamps from the British and forced the officials to abandon the use of stamps. In 1775 residents signed a pledge supporting the Continental Congress.

The city became involved in the Revolutionary War when Loyalists battled the Patriots 20 miles north at Moore's Creek on February 27, 1776. Although outnumbered, the Patriots won this battle, but in 1781 British forces captured the city and held it under the command of Major James Henry Craig. Later that year, Craig was joined by General Charles Cornwallis, who stayed in the Burgwin-Wright House at the corner of Third and Market streets. Across the street, the British Cavalry occupied St. James Church, using it as a riding school. The British troops were later withdrawn from Wilmington when Cornwallis surrendered at Yorktown October 19, 1781.

Following the Revolutionary War, Wilmington prospered greatly, both socially and as an important trading center. Numerous estates and plantations flourished on the outskirts, and many fine homes were built in the city. However, during the early 1800s the city floundered because of poor roads, few bridges, swamps surrounding the city, inadequate medical and sanitation facilities and navigation problems on the Cape Fear River. With the advent of steam power, railroads and navigational improvements to the river, Wilmington again began to prosper, and by 1840 was the largest city in the state. Thalian Hall, which currently houses the oldest continuously operating little theater company in the United States, was built in 1855 and has since been restored.

During the Civil War, Wilmington was the Confederacy's most important port. Fort Fisher and the Cape Fear River were home to many blockade runners who brought materials in from England and the Caribbean islands. Built in 1861, Fort Fisher was the last fort to fall to the Union army.

After the war, cotton, rice, peanuts, lumber and naval stores helped Wilmington regain its trading force. A sizable black middle class developed, and Wilmington became home to the state's first black lawyer and black physician. In 1866 the town officially became a city. However, by 1910 Wilmington lost its identity as the state's largest city when inland cities grew due to the development of the tobacco and textile industries.

During World War I, a thriving shipbuilding industry developed and cotton exports peaked. The Great Depression of the 1930s hit Wilmington hard and the city declined. However, World War II brought a rebirth of local shipbuilding, and 243 ships were built. In 1945 the North Carolina Legislature created the State Port Authority, which enabled the transformation of the shipyards into a modern port facility. In 1947 Wilmington College was established, later becoming the University of North Carolina at Wilmington.

Over the years, much of Wilmington's growth had been facilitated by a strong railroad industry, which eventually consolidated into the Atlantic Coast Line Railroad, a major employer in the city. Unfortunately, in 1955 the Atlantic Coast Line closed their offices and moved to Jacksonville, Florida, dealing a severe blow to Wilmington. A major effort was undertaken to bring diversified industry to the area, and by 1966 Wilmington had begun to rebound and was designated an "All American City."

The famous World War II battleship, *North Carolina*, was brought to the city in 1961 and berthed on the west side of the river across from downtown, providing a magnificent backdrop for Wilmington's Riverfront area. During the 1970s, a strong revitalization effort began in the downtown area, which, coupled with an intense preservation undertaking in the large historic district, resulted in a renewed and exciting central city.

In the 1980s the city saw another upswing as major companies, such as Corning Inc. and General Electric moved in, encouraging other diverse companies, including Applied Analytical Industry and Takeda Chemical Products, to call Wilmington home. Pharmaceutical Product Development, now PPD, became a homegrown Wilmington success story. (See our Commerce and Industry chapter.) A major film studio grew here, currently known as Screen Gems Studios, and many movies have been made in the area, earning Wilmington the nickname "Wilmywood."

The downtown revitalization effort in the mid-1980s did much to bring Wilmington into prominence. The successes of Chandler's Wharf Shops, The Cotton Exchange and

CLOSE-UP

Welcome to "Wilmywood"

Over the past 20 years, the Wilmington Film community has developed into an area completely equipped to take on any project, whether it be a big-budget motion picture or a small indie flick. TV's long-running *Matlock* series, starring Andy Griffith, was filmed here, as were TV's *American Gothic*, many commercials, music videos and industrial films.

At the heart of this phenomenon is EUE/Screen Gems Studios, a 32-acre complex on N. 23rd Street. Some of the studio's eight sound stages — totaling more than 100,000 square feet — are among the largest in the East. And you've probably seen the backlot several times on screen, although you probably thought you were looking at the streets of New York City, New Orleans, Beirut, Detroit or Bucharest.

The spark that ignited Wilmington's steadily burning film industry came in 1983 when Stephen King's *Firestarter* was filmed at the studios, then owned by Dino DeLaurentis. Carolco Pictures (makers of the Terminator films) bought the studio in 1989, then EUE/Screen Gems in 1996. Wilmington's ideal weather, its variety of locations, accessibility to transportation and low labor costs offer the film industry an effective formula for success.

So it's not surprising that many Wilmingtonians have film experience. Local musicians performed in *The Radioland Murders*. Local dancers went Stomping at the Savoy. Scores of locals earn their livings as "techies." Hundreds more work as on-screen extras. At least one Wilmington city councilman may be seen in TV commercials.

State-of-the-art recording studios serving the film industry also thrive around town. It's not unusual to see major Hollywood celebrities frequenting local restaurants and clubs while they're in town for a shoot. By the way, fees collected for film permits go toward downtown beautification projects.

Just a glance at the following sample of movies and TV shows made in and around Wilmington (the list is always growing) makes it clear why Wilmington has earned the nickname "Wilmywood":

28 Days, A Soldier's Daughter Never Cries, Against Her Will: The Carrie Buck Story, Alan and Naomi, Betsy's Wedding, Billy Bathgate, Black Dog, Blue Velvet, Crimes of the Heart, The Crow, Dawson's Creek, Domestic Disturbance, Dream a Little Dream, Empire, Everybody Wins, Fall Time, Golden Years, Justice and a Small Town: The Sandra Prine Story, Lolita, Margaret: A Burning Passion, The Member of the Wedding, Noble House, One Tree Hill, Out of Carolina, Raw Deal, Simple Justice, Sleeping With the Enemy, The Squeeze, A Stoning in Fulham County, Summer Catch, To Gillian on Her 37th Birthday, Too Young the Hero, Truman Capote's One Christmas, Tune In Tomorrow, Virus, When We Were Colored, Windmills of the Gods, and *Year of the Dragon.*

And who could forget *Amos & Andrew, Bad With Numbers, Cannibal Vampire*

Films are shot on location throughout the southern coastal region.

photo: EUE/Screen Gems Studios

Schoolgirls from Outer Space, Cyborg, Date with an Angel, The Exorcist III, Fire-starter, King Kong Lives, Little Monsters, Loose Cannons, The Lost Capone, Super Mario Bros., Teenage Mutant Ninja Turtles, Teenage Mutant Ninja Turtles II: The Secret of the Ooze, Weeds and *Weekend at Bernie's.*

ONE TREE HILL

After *Dawson's Creek* ran its course and wrapped production in Wilmington, producers Greg Prange and David Hartley began shopping around for another teen drama property. Enter, *One Tree Hill*, the story of a group of small-town teens who clash with their parents, get into trouble and revel in the usual high school she-nanigans.

Chad Michael Murray portrays Lucas Scott, a loner who returns to his mother's hometown and has trouble fitting in at his new high school. As it turns out, Lucas biological father, Dan Scott (Paul Johansson), is still in town. Dan's son Nathan (James Lafferty) is the star of the Tree Hill basketball team, and the two bump heads when Lucas makes the squad. But when they discover they're half-brothers, the tension twists even tighter.

One Tree Hill also stars Sophia Bush, Bethany Joy Lenz and former MTV vee-jay Hillarie Burton. It's immensely popular among the teen set and is approaching its fourth season on the WB. You can often spot the stars of the show out and about in Wilmington and they're very approachable and down-to-earth.

SURFACE

Producers Jonas and Josh Pate grew up in Raeford, N.C., and used Wilmington as the location for their first feature film, *The Grave*. So when they chose a loca-tion for their new sci-fi series on NBC, the Port City was a shoo-in. *Surface* follows the lives of three separate characters whose fates become intertwined due to the emergence of a new, monstrous species of vertebrate.

Lake Bell plays scientist Laura Daughtery, a marine biologist who discovers gigantic lizard-like creatures on the ocean's floor. Jay R. Ferguson is Rich, a family man that becomes obsessed with the creatures when one kills his younger brother, and Carter Jenkins is a teenage boy who finds one of the critters and raises it from an egg.

As each character uncovers new secrets about the creatures, they find them-selves being hunted by a rogue government agency determined to silence their discovery. But what exactly are the monster's real origins?

Surface is a very creative show that has proven the fact that Wilmington can double for nearly any location. They've utilized the film industry infrastructure quite well and will hopefully continue to aid in keeping local crews and actors busy.

The Coastline Convention Center encour-aged other establishments to set up shop. Restaurants, clothing stores, art galleries and antiques shops soon lined the streets. The flourishing nightlife adds a trendy setting to Wilmington, and the streets in the downtown area are quite safe. Throngs of tourists and residents alike stroll about until late in the evening.

Downtown Wilmington remains the historical core of the community and is still in many ways the neighborhood that defines the region. Suburbs may flourish, but there is something fascinating about the historic homes and buildings downtown, with their intimate proximity to the river. Both visitors and residents are affected by a sense of lingering ghosts. Important events happened here, in places that are still standing — places that have not been obscured by modern architecture or lost in the trends of a constantly changing American culture. Home to the county's seat of government for more than 250 years, this urban area has been on the forefront of historic changes.

The best perspective on Wilmington's rich and colorful history can be found at the Cape Fear Museum, 814 Market Street, (910) 341-4350, where the unique format allows visitors to walk through time in chronological order. (See our Attractions chapter.)

NEW HANOVER COUNTY

Wilmington in the 21st Century

Today the Wilmington area and its adjacent rural/suburban counties are experiencing substantial growth as both tourists and potential residents discover the desirability of vacationing and living in North Carolina's Southern Coast. An influx of retirees, many of them from the Northern states, has helped to make Wilmington a much more cosmopolitan city than one would expect in the heart of Dixie. Younger families, escaping from the stress of larger cities and looking for a more relaxed way of living and better quality of life, also have contributed to the population surge.

One of the keys to success in any central-city area is the presence of residents — a core group of people who do not leave for the suburbs at the end of the workday. Wilmington, blessed with a beautiful and extensive Historic District, made up of approximately 230 city blocks, has many full-time residents living in the downtown area. As more of the city's older homes are restored, and condominiums and townhouses are added (see our Real Estate chapter), both the Historic District and the downtown population will continue to grow.

A stroll through the Historic District reveals beautifully restored homes and commercial buildings, many of them antebellum, lining the shaded streets. A number of buildings bear plaques indicating their age: red

for 75 to 100 years and black if the structure is more than 100 years old. Magnificent and stately live oaks that retain their leaves all year are draped with Spanish moss. Azaleas and oleanders abound, and many of the homes have extensive gardens, some of which are opened to the public during the Azalea Festival in the spring, Riverfest in the fall, the History-Mystery tours at Halloween and Old Wilmington by Candlelight in December (see our Annual Events chapter). A leisurely walk through the Historic District is an adventure in history, and guided walking tours are available. For those who prefer to ride, there are horse-drawn carriages and trolley tours, both narrated (see our Attractions chapter).

With excellent shopping, outstanding restaurants, antiques to be discovered and a view of the river wherever you go, downtown Wilmington flourishes more every year. In the past ten years, the Cape Fear River has become a second focal point of the city's booming tourist industry, vying for tourist attention with the nearby beaches. Downtown hotels, inns, bed and breakfasts, shops and restaurants situated on its banks enjoy brisk business all year long. The Riverwalk offers an added dimension of entertainment and there is docking space available for private boats. A new convention center, marina and hotel will be built soon at the north side of downtown.

Aside from being a center of government for the city and New Hanover County, downtown Wilmington is also the center of the cultural arts scene. Thalian Hall, the oldest community theater tradition in the United States, presents many wonderful productions, both musical and dramatic. The Community Arts Center is constantly enhancing the arts scene by offering classes and sponsoring productions for adults and children. Numerous theater groups are active throughout the year. Downtown Wilmington also boasts many art galleries, music shops and the Cape Fear Museum (see our Attractions and The Arts chapters). The popularity and charm of this area has attracted many retail stores, financial institutions and entertainment and dining establishments. Something's always happening downtown.

MINI STORAGE

HIGH TECH, STATE-OF-THE-ART SECURITY

- Commercial
- Personal
- Wide Driveways
- On-Site Live-In Manager
- Boat Storage
- Clean and Well-Lighted
- Low Monthly Rates
- Open 7 Days
- Boxes & Packaging Supplies
- Outside RV/Boat Storage
- Monthly Pest Control
- Air Conditioned & Heated Space Available

WE ACCEPT DELIVERIES
2 LOCATIONS

mrstoreitonline.com

ONLY MINUTES FROM ANYWHERE IN WILMINGTON

392-8100
791-2323

901 Shipyard Blvd.
Toll Free 888-658-1523

6947 Market St.
Toll Free 888-608-2323

During the day, downtown Wilmington is quaint and charming, but at night it comes alive in a whole new way. Dance clubs, jazz bars, local and touring musicals, venues for rock 'n' roll, rhythm and blues and more can be found in the 55-block area of the downtown commercial district (see our Nightlife chapter). Perhaps the best thing about downtown Wilmington — and something that separates it from the rest of the city and nearby communities — is its pleasant and fascinating walkability. The Riverwalk, with its view of the Battleship North Carolina moored on the western shore, is a great place to stroll, grab a hot dog from a street vendor, listen to free music, and watch the river traffic that ranges from freighters to yachts to ski boats. The Riverwalk is about 7/8 of a mile in length and stretches from just north of the Coast Line Convention Center to south of Chandlers Wharf. Complete with wide patio-style areas and pocket parks with benches, the Riverwalk offers spectacular views of the river, especially at night.

Greater Wilmington

Over the last few years, the city of Wilmington and the surrounding area have experienced a tremendous building boom. Shopping centers now boast national chains such as Target, Barnes & Noble, Wal-Mart, Lowe's, Hecht's, Dillard's, Sears, JC Penney, Kohl's, Home Depot and others, all of which have enhanced the region's shopping choices considerably. Many upscale and specialty stores have also appeared throughout the area (see our Shopping chapter).

With all this new growth and the continuing popularity of the area, Real Estate is a lively business. "Plantations," gated communities and neighborhoods are developed so quickly that natives have been heard to say they occasionally get lost because of the changing landscape. However, in spite of the rapid growth, new housing in the area still remains quite affordable (see our Real Estate chapter).

Wilmington remains the educational hub of the southeastern North Carolina coast, with the University of North Carolina at Wilmington and Cape Fear Community College within its boundaries. Miller-Motte Business College and a branch of Mount Olive College are also in Wilmington (see our Higher Education and Research chapter).

The city holds the distinction of being the cultural center for not only this corner of the state, but also the whole North Carolina coastline. Performances by touring and home-based theater, dance and music companies enliven the local stages of Thalian Hall Center for the Performing Arts downtown and Kenan Auditorium and Trask Coliseum on the campus of UNCW. Writers, artists and musicians are evident in abundance. The Louise Wells Cameron Museum of Art is a showcase of regional and international artists (see our The Arts chapter).

The film industry lends an exciting opportunity for spotting the occasional celebrity or just watching the process of making movies. For many years, filmmaking accounted for a significant portion of the local economy; it still has the potential for growth because of Wilmington's well-established film industry infrastructure. The cornerstone of the local film industry, EUE/Screen Gems Studios, is complemented by a seasoned crew base, an active regional film commission and a large talent pool. Since the first movie filmed here in 1983 (Dino DeLaurentiis' Firestarter) Wilmington has been home to more than 300 movies and seven television series, including Matlock and Dawson's Creek and currently, One Tree Hill and Surface. Stars spotted in recent years include Bruce Willis, Richard Gere, Katherine Hepburn, Alec Baldwin, Kim Basinger, Mathew Modine, Sharon Stone, Patrick Swayze, Julie Harris, John Travolta and Anthony Hopkins. Linda Lavin, Broadway star and a woman known affectionately as "Alice" from the '70s TV series, lives downtown and works closely with the Community Arts Center. Pat Hingle, a Hollywood character actor for many years, lives in Carolina Beach and is still active in the film scene.

As North Carolina's principal deep-water port, the North Carolina State Port at Wilmington and some of the industrial complexes north of downtown host hundreds of ships and barges from many nations every year. The river recently has been dredged and deepened so that larger cargo ships and some of the cruise ships can now dock in Wilmington.

Statistical Data

As the second smallest of the state's 100 counties, New Hanover County encompasses only 199 square miles, most of which is the City of Wilmington. The county's 2005 population of 177,692 reflected a growth of 33.3 percent since 1990. Wilmington alone saw her population increase to nearly 95,000 in 2005, making it the larger of the two major Wilmingtons (the other one is in Delaware).

The largest industrial employer in the county is General Electric, with nearly 1,800 employees making nuclear fuel assemblies and aircraft engine parts. Corning, producing optical fibers, and International Paper, which produces pulp and paperboard, are two other major industrial employers. Recent years have seen an influx of pharmaceutical companies as well, and in 2004 Verizon Wireless opened a 1,200-employee call center here. By workforce, the largest is service at 27 percent, followed closely by retail trade at 24 percent, reflecting the influence of tourism in the area. The total workforce is roughly 83,000, of which well over 5,000 are directly attributable to travel and tourism, while about 10 percent of the workforce is in manufacturing. New Hanover County enjoys a 3.3 per cent unemployment rate.

Because of the Wilmington area's popularity and recent growth, educational facilities have been growing in number and reputation. Cape Fear Community College has two campuses that offer classes for degree seekers, continuing education and personal enrichment to 27,000 students annually. The University of North Carolina at Wilmington has been ranked as one of the 10 best regional public universities in the South by U. S. News & World Report for the past eight years, and is ranked seventh for 2005-06. The 661-acre campus is among the fastest-growing universities in the 16-campus UNC system. UNCW offers 71 undergraduate degree programs, 24 graduate degree programs and a marine sciences program that was recently ranked fifth-best in the world (see our Higher Education and Research chapter). Enrollment in 2005 topped 11,500.

The public school system prides itself on innovation. There are 37 schools in the New

A busy port, a place of commerce, a city with a past and a future — Wilmington is all this and more.

photo: Peter Doran

Running the Blockades:
Wilmington's Pivotal Role in the Civil War

Shortly after the beginning of the Civil War, in April of 1861, President Lincoln issued proclamations establishing blockades of Southern ports in the states of Virginia, North Carolina, South Carolina, Georgia, Florida, Alabama, Louisiana, Mississippi and Texas.

The purpose of the blockade was to cut off supplies to the Confederacy, principally from Great Britain, and curtail the export of cotton to finance the war. The seceding Southern states had little in the way of manufacturing to produce consumer goods or munitions and other items to maintain an army and wage war. England had the industrial capability to produce what the South needed, and the South had the cotton sorely needed for British textile mills.

When Lincoln established the blockade, he had little in hand to back up the decree. With more than 3,000 miles of coast from Texas to Virginia, the North had only about 35 modern vessels capable of enforcing the blockade. The Southern states were in worse shape. The Confederate Navy had virtually no ships, and only one shipyard, Norfolk, Virginia, was capable of building vessels of any size. All ships under construction at Norfolk at that time were destroyed by Union forces except for the Merrimac, which burned to the waterline but was salvaged and rebuilt later. However, the Confederacy seized a number of ships of various sorts in Southern ports and outfitted them mostly as privateers and gunboats to prey on Union commerce and harass Union ships and shore facilities.

Although the federal government called the Civil War an insurrection or rebellion rather than a war, a blockade was internationally considered an act of war. The blockade, coupled with the Confederacy's distinct geographical area and organized government, gave basis for Queen Victoria of England to issue a proclamation of neutrality concerning the hostilities between the Government of the United States and the Confederate States of America. Britain's neutrality was cheered by the South because it gave recognition to the Confederacy as a legitimate government.

This engraving from Le Monde portrays a Federal ship attacking a blockade runner off Fort Fisher.

photo: Lower Cape Fear Historical Society

The Union began building ships as rapidly as possible to enforce the blockade. The South, without effective shipyards and the means to equip and armor ships, had representatives in England contracting for the construction of warships and promoting merchant ship trade between England and the Confederacy. Although officially neutral, the British government tended to look the other way, partly because they were in sympathy with the Confederacy and partly because England sorely needed cotton. Export of cotton from the South to England in the first two years of the war dropped from 816 million pounds to 6 million pounds. As a result, textile mills had closed and two million people were out of work and starving.

Because of the blockade, Union ships were allowed to board merchant ships bound for the South and seize the vessels and their cargos as prizes. However, if the ships were en route to a neutral destination, they could not be seized. Consequently British ships began heading for Nassau, Bermuda and Havana. From there, they sailed to Charleston, Savannah and Wilmington, only three days and five or six hundred miles away, at much less risk of exposure to Union warships.

Another advantage of going to ports like Nassau was that cargos could arrive in large, deep-draft freighters from England and then be transferred to the small, fast, shallow draft, dark-colored, low-profile boats known as "blockade runners." Piloted by experts and departing the Bahamas only at night, the blockade runners could elude the Union ships, which had to remain well offshore in deeper water.

During the early stages of the war, Union forces concentrated their blockading efforts on the larger ports of Charleston, Savannah and New Orleans. Wilmington, the largest city in North Carolina at the time with about 10,000 residents, flourished as a result of the highly successful efforts of the blockade runners. With good rail service into Virginia, and General Lee's forces, Wilmington was instrumental in keeping the Confederacy operating.

Wilmington turned out to be a very difficult port for the federal ships to blockade. The city is about 25 miles up the Cape Fear River from the Atlantic Ocean, and access to the river is tricky, hence the Cape Fear name. Even though the Union vessels eventually numbered about 40, they were unable to intercept most of the sleek, dark blockade runners slipping through the treacherous waters on very dark nights without lights.

Federal ships attempting to enforce the blockade at Wilmington had to contend with several obstacles. The two entrances to the river were through shallow channels widely separated by Smith's Island and Frying Pan Shoals extending for miles into the ocean. Consequently, the Union had to maintain two blockades, and it took several hours going around the shallow shoals to get from one blockade to the other. Confederate signal stations on shore signaled to the incoming blockade runners which entrance was more lightly guarded.

As the war progressed, the blockades closed down all the Southern ports except Wilmington, which became the sole lifeline for supplies to the Confederacy. However, in January of 1865, Fort Fisher fell to a major Union assault, and the city of Wilmington was captured and held. The supply line was cut, and the fate of the Confederacy was sealed.

Overall, the Wilmington blockade runners were highly successful, with three-fourths of them getting through during the course of the war. Only about 130 vessels were sunk, captured or wrecked.

Hanover County Public School System, organized as kindergarten through 5th grades, 6th through 8th, and 9th through 12th, with an estimated 22,000 students and a mean student/teacher ratio of one teacher to 25 pupils. All classrooms are connected to the Internet. (See our Schools and Child Care chapter.)

With the mild climate, recreational opportunities abound in the area. Golf courses, playable year round, can be found throughout the area, with at least ten in New Hanover County and about 35 in Brunswick County, many of which are residential golf communities. Most county and municipal parks contain baseball and soccer fields along with tennis courts. The area's many miles of coastline, rivers and sounds offer a wide variety of fishing, watersports, and boating activities, and quite a few harbors, marinas and yacht clubs are available.

Wrightsville Beach

Wrightsville Beach is a special place for both the resident and the visitor and is quite unlike the commercial beaches that often come to mind when one thinks of the coast. There is no carnival atmosphere — no Ferris wheels or gaudy displays of beach merchandise (well, maybe just one that locals try hard to overlook), no bumper boats, no arcade. Instead, Wrightsville Beach is primarily an affluent residential community that has its roots in Wilmington. For over a century, the 5-mile-long island has been a retreat from the summer heat for Wilmington residents whose families have maintained ownership of beach homes there for generations.

Wrightsville Beach was incorporated in 1899 as a resort community. The Tidewater Power Company built a trolley system from downtown Wilmington to the beach, providing the only land access to the island until 1935. The company, which owned the island, was interested in development and built the Hotel Tarrymore in 1905 to attract visitors and revenue. Later named The Oceanic, this grand hotel burned down in 1934, along with most structures on the northern half of the island. Lumina, a beach pavilion, was also built by the Tidewater Power Company to attract visitors

On the site of the current Oceanic Restaurant at the south end of the beach, Lumina offered a festive place where locals gathered for swimming, dancing and outdoor movies. The building was demolished in 1973.

The Carolina Yacht Club, the first large structure on the island, was built in 1856 and is the second oldest in the country, after the New York Yacht Club. Development of the beach continued steadily until 1954 when Hurricane Hazel, a monster storm, came ashore and wreaked devastation on the island's homes and buildings. Hazel also shoaled the channel between Wrightsville Beach and adjacent Shell Island.

Developers, seeing an opportunity for expansion, filled in the remaining water and joined the islands together. Today, the area is the site of the Shell Island Resort Hotel, numerous condominiums and large homes. In the aftermath of two hurricanes in 1996, the resort hotel found itself precariously close

to an advancing inlet. Shell Island's condominium owners wanted to erect a seawall to save their property from the encroaching sea, but the state denied them permission to do so. North Carolina has very strict laws regarding seawalls because of their negative impact on the rest of a beach. In 2002, the inlet was dredged and moved north toward Figure Eight Island, thereby, for the time being, reducing the threat to Shell Island.

Today's Wrightsville Beach is a very busy and prosperous place. Because of its popularity with both residents and tourists, there is almost no available land for sale. The area is still a stronghold of long-term residents who summer in family homes built to catch the ocean breeze. The permanent residential population is about 3,000, but that figure swells considerably in the summer.

With a land mass of nearly a square mile, this island manages to maintain its charm despite an increasing influx of visitors. Surprisingly, brisk commercial development in the form of marinas, restaurants, the Blockade Runner Resort Hotel, the Holiday Inn Sunspree Resort and other services has not seriously changed the residential orientation of the island and its very clean beaches. Lifeguards oversee the safety of swimmers in the summer season, and the beach patrol keeps an eye on the area to make sure laws are obeyed. Alcohol and glass containers are not allowed on the beach. If you have questions, just ask one of the friendly lifeguards.

Boaters, sun worshippers, swimmers, surfers and anglers will find much to appreciate and enjoy about the setting. Public beach access points, liberally sprinkled along the shoreline, make a day in the sun a free experience for daytrippers — with the notable exception of parking.

Insiders know the island is extremely crowded during peak summer weekends and are inclined to leave those times for visitors. On in-season weekends, visitors are wise to arrive before 9:30 AM and bring plenty of quarters for the parking meters. (A quarter buys 15 minutes.) Or you can try your luck at finding a rare non-metered parking space. Rates on side street parking are hourly (and enforced) from 9 AM to 6 PM, but there is no charge before or after these times. Winter visitors enjoy free parking from November to March.

It's tempting, but don't make the mistake of parking at business locations or at private homes. Parking lots at area restaurants and hotels are vigilantly guarded, and residents are not inclined to allow unknown cars to occupy their driveways. Towing is very strictly enforced in no-parking zones.

Opportunities for water-related sports and entertainment are plentiful on Wrightsville Beach. Some of the most luxurious marinas along the North Carolina coast are clustered around the bridge at the Intracoastal Waterway and offer a full range of services (see our Marinas and Intracoastal Waterway chapter).

Charter boats, both power and sail, are available in abundance. Diving, Jet Ski rentals, windsurfing, parasailing, kayaking and sailing lessons are there for the asking (see our Watersports chapter). Bait, tackle, piers and more than enough advice on the best way to fish are all easy to find (see our Fishing chapter). Visitors who bring their own boats will appreciate the free boat ramp just north of the first bridge onto Harbour Island, the island between the mainland and Wrightsville Beach.

A visit to Wrightsville Beach, whether for a day or for a vacation, is bound to be a pleasant experience that will be repeated time after time. The island is wonderfully walkable, and you can find everything you need for a comfortable and memorable vacation almost any time of the year.

Figure Eight Island

Figure Eight Island, just north of Wrightsville Beach, is a private, very exclusive, oceanfront resort community. This island is, in the most extreme sense, a highly restricted residential island of 406 expensive homes. It's a favorite hideaway for stars and political bigwigs who want privacy when they're visiting the area. Former Vice President Al Gore and family, for example, have enjoyed vacationing here since 1997.

The development includes a yacht club, a marina, tennis courts and a boat ramp. The island is connected to the mainland by a causeway bridge, and a guard will let you onto the island only if you've called ahead to someone on the island, such as a friend or a real estate agent, and are on the list at the gate.

There are no commercial enterprises here, just pure beautiful beaches for the vacationer looking for some R&R and peace and quiet. The celebrity orientation of the island does not mean regular folk can't rent homes and enjoy a private vacation. In fact, the island is very hospitable to vacationers and welcomes guests to its uncrowded shores. To contact real estate companies on or near Figure Eight Island for rental information (some of the larger Wilmington real estate companies may also handle properties on this exclusive island), see our chapter on Weekly and Long-Term Rentals.

Masonboro Island

South of Wrightsville Beach and north of Carolina Beach is Masonboro Island. Barren of any development, Masonboro Island is the last and largest pristine barrier island remaining on the southern North Carolina coast. This 8-mile-long island, with an Atlantic Ocean beach on its eastern shore and marshes on its western shore facing the Intracoastal Waterway, is accessible only by boat. If you are fortunate enough to have a shallow-draft boat, just look for a spot to approach among the reeds — probably alongside other boats — and tie a meaningful line to the shore with your anchor because, as in all areas of the Cape Fear region, the tides have wide fluctuation. If you tie up at high tide, you may have a tough job getting off the sand if you try to leave at low tide.

The island, consisting of about 5,000 acres, has about 4,300 acres of tidal salt marshes and mud flats and only about 600 acres of beach. Although parts of the island belong to private landowners, no development is allowed. Masonboro is a component of the North Carolina Coastal Reserve and the National Estuarine Research Reserve. The island is home to gray foxes, cotton rats, a variety of birds, river otters and several species of aquatic life; it is an important nesting site for the beautiful and famous loggerhead sea turtles. You can spot the island by the large number of pleasure craft clustered on the Masonboro Sound side. If you want to be alone, pass by this gathering and look for small passages farther south on the island.

Access is only limited by the draft of your boat and how easily you can push it off when you run aground. Gather your gear and hike a short way to the ocean side, where it's a special pleasure to take a picnic and relax on the uncrowded beach. There are no facilities so be prepared to rough it. If you make the trip in the fall, be sure to take along insect repellent because the yellow flies can be extremely annoying. For more information on Masonboro Island, see the following chapters: Attractions, Camping and Higher Education and Research (North Carolina National Estuarine Research reserve).

Monkey Junction

At the southern end of College Road (N.C. Highway 132) where it joins with Carolina Beach Road (U.S. Highway 421), you'll find an area that has been rife with heated controversy in recent years. Known as Monkey Junction, this rapidly expanding area has experienced enormous growth both commercially and residentially, some of it fairly upscale. A faction of residents, especially ones more recently moving into the area, feel that the name "Monkey Junction" does not convey the image they'd like to have for their community. They prefer "Myrtle Grove," which is an area east of Monkey Junction.

Ever sensitive to the desires of their customers, the U.S. Postal Service dutifully changed the name of their postal station in the area from Monkey Junction to Myrtle Grove. However, the New Hanover County commissioners, ever sensitive to the desire of most residents of the county to preserve our historical heritage, have officially designated the area as Monkey Junction, and have erected signs to that effect.

The name Monkey Junction harkens back to the 1920s when the bus to Carolina Beach stopped at this intersection. An enterprising gas station nearby featured live monkeys as an attraction to draw customers from the bus. When the driver stopped, he announced, "Monkey Junction," and that's how it has been known ever since.

Carolina Beach

Carolina Beach, just 30 minutes from downtown Wilmington by car, is on a narrow slip of land between the Cape Fear River and the Atlantic Ocean. Separated from the mainland by the Intracoastal Waterway (Snow's Cut), the island is called Pleasure Island.

Established in 1857, when Joseph Winner planned the streets and lots for the 50 acres of beach property he had purchased, the island's only access then was by water. In 1866 a steamship began carrying vacationers down the Cape Fear River to Snow's Cut and a small railroad took them the rest of the way into Carolina Beach. In later years, a high-rise bridge was built over Snow's Cut connecting the island with the mainland.

A drive through Carolina Beach reveals a pleasant 1950s-style beach town of modest cottages, increasingly more upscale single-family dwellings and an abundance of three- and four-story condominiums. The town also has a movie complex, grocery stores, drugstores, beach shops and boutiques, numerous restaurants, both upscale and simple, hardware and variety stores, an ABC store and even bait shops. The beachfront motels, including several vintage motor courts, offer a welcome blast from the past. If you were a kid during the '50s and your parents took you on vacation to the beach, this was the kind of place you probably remember. Some of the best beachfront lodging values are offered here. The nostalgia is free.

Carolina Beach underwent a dramatic transformation during the 1990s. Once considered a wild party spot, it is currently evolving into a heavily residential community dedicated to creating a wholesome family environment. Recent years have seen the cultivation of improved services, pleasant landscaping, attention to zoning and tangible citizen action to make Carolina Beach an attractive visitor destination. With a fair amount of relatively inexpensive land still available on the island, home construction is booming.

The busy central business district is centered around an active yacht basin containing a large number of charter fishing boats and large excursion boats. The nearby Boardwalk area is currently undergoing revitalization and rebuilding in conjunction with the oceanfront Courtyard by Marriott Resort Hotel, which opened in 2003, and several mixed-use condo/retail projects planned and underway.

Anglers love Carolina Beach. The surf promises wonderful bounty all year long, and there are plenty of tackle shops and piers as well as the opportunity to experience deep-sea fishing from the sterns of a number of charter boats berthed in the municipal yacht basin. Several annual fishing tournaments are based on the abundance of king mackerel, and you can pay a nominal entry fee for a chance to reap as much as $50,000 for the winning fish.

At the northernmost end of the island, the beach is open to four-wheel-drive vehicles. While there is a certain allure to driving right off the street onto the sand of this expansive space, don't do it if you are in a two-wheel-drive car. Without the right tires, it's even possible to get stuck in the sand in a four-wheel-drive vehicle.

Carolina Beach also offers one of the few state parks in the region. For a modest fee, you can camp and enjoy the wonders of nature. The Venus's flytrap, a carnivorous plant that eats insects, is abundant in the park. This plant, a relic from pre-human existence on the planet, grows naturally within a 60-mile radius of Wilmington. A sizable marina is also located in the park.

Away from the seasonal bustle at the center of the city, Carolina Beach is a quiet community of about 5,000 year round residents. That number jumps three to five times at the peak of the vacation season. The community is growing in appeal to both locals from Wilmington and newcomers from other areas for two big reasons: it isn't crowded yet and it's affordable. Many a Wilmingtonian has given Wrightsville Beach over to visitors for the summer in the past few years and turned to Carolina Beach for a quiet spot on the sand.

Kure Beach

To the south, Carolina Beach merges into the town of Kure Beach. Kure Beach (pronounced "CURE-ee") is a younger community. Development began in the 1870s when Hans Andersen Kure moved from Denmark and bought large tracts of land in the middle of the island. Apparently, things moved slowly because Kure Beach wasn't incorporated until 1947.

Today Kure Beach is overwhelmingly residential, dotted with modest cottages, new upscale houses and a number of beach motels. Several condominium buildings cluster together in one area, but there is little in the way of tall buildings. In fact, new structures may not be built taller than 35 feet. At the center of town, a popular fishing pier extends well out over the ocean and there are several restaurants. A charming boardwalk with benches extends north along the beach and is lighted at night.

Once upon a time, some of the best real estate deals could be found in Kure Beach, but today this sleepy beach town is fast growing in popularity and price. Two of the newest developments, Kure Beach Village and Beachwalk, feature homes and town homes along with tennis courts, pools and clubhouses.

You won't find a lot of amusement park–style entertainment here, although there is an arcade. There is very little in the way of shopping. A permanent population of 1,500 residents makes for a very close community, but Kure Beach's small size should not lead visitors to think they're out in the boondocks. The town maintains its own municipal services and fire protection, and a local planner describes the community as being "like any big city, only smaller."

Kure Beach will remain small because it is completely surrounded. The Fort Fisher State Recreation Area and Historic Site are on the south side, and the U.S. Government owns the west side as part of a buffer zone for the military terminal at Sunny Point across the Cape Fear River. Carolina Beach borders the town on the north. Of course, the Atlantic Ocean forms the east border.

Fort Fisher

To the south of Kure Beach are the Fort Fisher State Historic Site and Fort Fisher State Recreation Area. The Historic Site, amidst twisted live oaks on the west side of U.S. Highway 421, was the largest of the Confederacy's earthwork fortifications during the Civil War. It fell to Union forces in 1865, cutting off the last of the Confederacy supply lines from the sea. During World War II, as an arm of Camp Davis to the north, it became an important training site for anti-aircraft and coastal artillery defenses and a large airstrip was located there. An extensive, newly expanded visitors center offers guided tours.

The Recreation Area on the east side of U.S. 421 has 4 miles of wide, unspoiled beach, a visitor center with bath house, a snack bar and restrooms (see our chapter on Sports, Parks and Fitness).

The North Carolina Aquarium at Fort Fisher is North Carolina's largest aquarium, with many dramatic exhibits and featuring a huge shark tank and half-acre freshwater conservatory (see our Attractions chapter).

At the southern end of U.S. 421 is the Fort Fisher–Southport Ferry, possibly the best $5 cruise in the world. See our Getting Around chapter for information about the ferry. Across the road is a public boat launch area that is popular for windsurfing, parasailing, kiteboarding, kayaking and fishing. All in all, these southernmost beaches of New Hanover County from Carolina Beach to the southern tip of Pleasure Island offer 7.5 miles of very pleasant vacationing and living.

BRUNSWICK COUNTY BEACHES

Bald Head Island

Four miles off the coast of Southport and the mainland, at the mouth of the Cape Fear River, is the island of Bald Head. The island is easily identifiable in the distance by the Bald Head Island Lighthouse. Built in 1817 and retired in 1935, the lighthouse is cataloged as the oldest lighthouse in North Carolina.

Once a favorite hiding spot for pirates such as Blackbeard and Stede Bonnet, Bald Head Island is now an affluent residential and resort community of about 220 year-round residents. It can only be reached by the island's private ferry or by personal boat. The island is graciously open to the public, and the summer population can reach from 4,000 to 6,000, with visitors renting vacation homes and playing golf (see our Golf chapter for course information).

It is probably safe to say this is one of the most unspoiled beach and maritime forest ar-

eas on the North Carolina coast. The island's natural beauty is protected, despite residential development as well as a few commercial amenities such as a restaurant, bed and breakfast inns, general store with deli, marina, golf course, specialty store, and golf cart and bike rental business.

The island has 14 miles of beaches, dunes, creeks and forests. The 2,000 acres of land are surrounded by 10,000 acres of salt marshes. The owners have deeded nearby Middle Island and Bluff Island to the state and The Nature Conservancy. The Bald Head Island Conservancy, a nonprofit organization, was formed to ensure that the unique natural resources of the island are maintained and preserved.

Turtle nesting on Bald Head Island accounts for 50 percent of all turtle eggs laid in North Carolina. The Sea Turtle Program, featured on public television, protects and monitors these wonderful creatures. There is an Adopt-a-Nest Program that pairs concerned humans with turtles in an effort to protect the nest and encourage the hatchlings toward the sea. Studies in which female turtles were tagged have revealed that pregnant turtles return to the same site to lay eggs every other year. Due to the many species of birds found on the island, the Audubon Society conducts an annual count here as part of its national program.

Something quite special about the island is the absence of cars. Gasoline-powered engines, with the exception of security and maintenance vehicles, are not allowed. The residents and visitors who rent homes all drive electric carts or ride bicycles. The resulting lack of noise pollution and exhaust fumes is one of the finest features of the place.

A visitor can come for the day by private ferry service from Indigo Plantation in Southport. The cost is $15 round trip. Day parking in Southport is $5 or $7 depending on the lot you choose. For a longer stay, there are many rental units on the island. The cost, compared to rental on much of the mainland, is slightly on the upper end, but so is the experience for the visitor who wants to really get away from it all in quiet style.

Despite Bald Head Island's private status, the welcome mat is always out for visitors.

Picture Perfect in Any Season!

Southport - Oak Island Area Chamber of Commerce

Caswell Beach · Oak Island · Bald Head Island
Southport · Boiling Spring Lakes · St. James

Welcome Center

4841 Long Beach Road
Southport, NC 28461

8:30 - 5:00 Monday-Friday (Year Round)
9:00 - 4:00 Saturday (March-November)

Chamber of Commerce

SOUTHPORT · OAK ISLAND AREA

Call
800-457-6964
for our new
Vacation & Residents Guide

www.southport-oakisland.com

The lighthouse can be toured for a small fee. The well-appointed marina welcomes transients.

Southport

Southport is a quaint, seaside town that offers numerous restaurants, antiques shops and historic sites. Along the west side of the Cape Fear River's mouth, Southport is reachable by both ferry and scenic highway. Leaving Wilmington, take the Cape Fear Memorial Bridge and hang a fast left onto N.C. Highway 133 just off U.S. Highways 17, 74 and 76. If you miss it, you can also take N.C. Highway 87, although the N.C. 133 route is very beautiful and offers several attractions, including Orton Plantation, Brunswick Town and the Progress Energy Nuclear Plant with its Brunswick Plant Energy Center. For information on the ferry route and schedule, see our Getting Around chapter.

The city of Southport is steeped in history. This coastal community saw the establishment of North Carolina's first fort in 1754: Fort Johnston. A small community of river pilots, fishermen and tradespeople grew up around the fort. In 1792 the town of Smithville was created. In 1808, Smithville became the county seat of Brunswick County. For the remainder of the century, the town made plans to link rail service with the existing river traffic to make the community a major southern port, and the city was renamed Southport.

The town was one of the first areas in the state to celebrate the Fourth of July and is widely regarded as the Fourth of July Capital of North Carolina. History records that in 1795, citizens gathered at Fort Johnston and observed a 13-gun military salute to the original 13 states. In 1813, a Russian warship anchored in the harbor fired a 13-gun salute, and it was on this Fourth of July that fireworks were used for the first time to close the celebration. In 1972, the Fourth of July Festival was chartered and incorporated as the official North Carolina Fourth of July Festival, and it has become a tremendously popular four-day event for residents and visitors.

Southport, listed on the National Register of Historic Places, is ranked by both Rand McNally and Kiplinger as one of the most desirable places in the United States to retire.

But Southport is great fun even for just a daytrip. History buffs will especially appreciate a visit to Southport for its beautiful old homes and historic cemeteries. Be sure to check out some of the better known historic spots. The Captain Thompson Home, for example, offers visitors a glimpse into the life of a Civil War blockade runner.

The literary set will enjoy a visit to the Adkins-Ruark House where author Robert Ruark lived as a young boy with his grandfather. One of Ruark's novels, The Old Man and the Boy, gives readers insight into Southport life years ago.

Southport's live oak–lined streets, charming architecture, quaint shops — most notably an abundance of antiques shops — as well as year-round golf, boating and fishing create an enormously pleasant environment. This is the place for people who genuinely want to kick back and enjoy beautiful coastal scenery. With a year-round population of nearly 2,600, there's still plenty of elbow room. If you fall head over heels for Southport and decide to make a permanent move, keep in mind that its charm also means that the town includes some of the area's most exclusive homes.

Leave the car — parking is free — and just walk around until you discover shops, restaurants and views that please you. It's an extremely casual community that invites visitors to pause and savor a slow pace of life that is fast disappearing in nearby Wilmington.

Oak Island

Just across the water from Bald Head Island and Southport is Oak Island, a narrow strip of land that includes Caswell Beach and the Town of Oak Island.

Caswell Beach is the site of Fort Caswell, a military stronghold that dates from 1827. Fort Caswell is now owned by the North Carolina Baptist Assembly and welcomes visitors of all denominations each year. The community has some summer homes, but the area has mostly permanent residences. The year-round population is 443, but up to 1,200 people can be staying on this part of Oak Island in the summer. Be sure to check out the Oak Island Lighthouse, which has guided seafarers since 1958. In 2003 it was

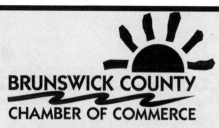

BRUNSWICK COUNTY
CHAMBER OF COMMERCE

Creating a premier place to live, work and play!

For more information contact us at 1-800-426-6644
or visit us online at www.brunswickcountychamber.org
4948 Main Street, Post Office Box 1185
Shallotte, North Carolina 28459

Coastal Communities
Residential & Commercial Real Estate

Coastal Communities
www.coastalcommunitiesrealty.com

4555 Fountain Dr.
Wilmington, NC 28403
(910) 395-4770
(888) 395-4770

3270 Holden Beach Road
Holden Beach, NC 28462
(910) 842-3190
(877) 752-0151

formally declared surplus by the General Services Administration of the U.S. Government and was deeded to the town. Plans are in the works for use of the lighthouse and the five acres of oceanfront property deeded along with it for the public in perpetuity.

As the name implies, Oak Island is famous for its beautiful live oak trees. Recreational areas include a championship golf course, 65 beach-access points, a picnic area on the Elizabeth River estuary system, a few restaurants and motels, and three fishing piers. With a population of nearly 7,300, Oak Island offers a quiet respite for a peaceful family vacation. For the most part, a visitor will enjoy renting a house for an extended vacation. In fact, vacation rental is the liveliest business here, with more than a dozen rental companies operating on Oak Island.

Holden Beach

Of the three islands in the group known as the South Brunswick Islands, Holden Beach is the longest and the largest. Stretching 11 miles along the Atlantic Ocean, the island is a jogger's paradise. Approximately 900 year-round residents call Holden Beach home. Visitors will find a host of opportunities for assimilating themselves into this exceedingly quiet family community. The beach and the sea are the central attractions in this town, which prides itself on a serene quality of life.

Ocean Isle Beach

Ocean Isle Beach is the center island, offering 8 miles of beach with a total resort experience: restaurants, specialty shops, public tennis courts, access to all watersports, and a water slide. This beach has the only high-rise hotel on the South Brunswick Islands. There is an airport that makes getting to Ocean Isle accessible by air, but don't expect to see commercial jets at this relatively small facility. Home to slightly 425 full-time residents, Ocean Isle welcomes visitors to a peaceful place.

Sunset Beach

Sunset Beach, described as a diminutive island gem, is only 3 miles long. Despite its size, this island experienced a 150 percent population increase between 1990 and 1997, with a current year-round population of more than 2,000 residents. Because it is reached by a one-lane pontoon bridge, making it the only island without a high-rise bridge in Brunswick County, there is sometimes a bit of a wait to get to Sunset in the high tourist season. However, the island is well-worth the wait. This bridge will probably be replaced by a high-rise someday, if the Department of Transportation has its way, but that discussion has been going on for years. Islanders like their bridge the way it is because it tends to keep traffic levels down.

Although this island is residential in character, it is a great choice for a family vacation. Some of the best bargains in vacation rentals are here, and the visitor who wants a quiet coastal place will do very well to book a house on this beach. As with all of the beaches on the southern coast, quality golfing is available on the mainland. For fishing enthusiasts, there is a full-service pier. Sunset Beach also offers a special delight — a walk to Bird Island at low tide.

Bird Island is completely untouched by development. A walk through the shallow inlet at low tide is easy for adults as well as children. There are frequent informal guided tours, announced by posters attached to street markers on the beach, so it's easy to hook up with locals who are pleased to share their knowledge of the island. The environment is purely natural and deeply comforting, where people of the 21st century can experience life as it was before the development of the land. In order to keep it this way, in 2002 the state of North Carolina purchased the island and dedicated it as the state's 10th Coastal Reserve Program site. Through this purchase, nearly 1,200 acres of wetlands, marsh and beaches are preserved for use by endangered species, including sea turtles and some species of sea birds. The island will be managed for use as an outdoor laboratory for research and education as well as traditional uses through a cooperative effort by the Division of Coastal Management, the Bird Island Preservation Society and an appointed Bird Island Local Advisory Committee.

Calabash

Calabash, home of numerous delicious Calabash-style seafood restaurants, sits on the banks of the Intracoastal Waterway. Restaurants abound and deep-sea fishing boats are docked in town, waiting to take you on the adventure of your life. Though small, with little more than 1,300 year-round residents, Calabash is abutted on the north by the town of Carolina Shores, a residential-only community.

Shallotte

The town of Shallotte serves as the hub for services for Brunswick County's beach communities. In fact, it is perhaps best-known as the commercial center of the county. Because of its mainland location and island proximity, Shallotte offers residents and visitors the convenience of larger-town living and services. This is the place in Brunswick County where you will find shopping malls with nationally known stores. The Brunswick County Chamber of Commerce is headquartered in Shallotte and can provide any information you may need about the South Brunswick Islands and the inland area. The town has a year-round population of approximately 2,000.

PENDER AND ONSLOW COUNTIES

Greater Topsail Island Area

Topsail Island is a 26-mile-long barrier island approximately 40 minutes north of Wilmington. The island is located in both Onslow and Pender counties and consists of three towns, North Topsail Beach, Surf City and Topsail Beach. The two mainland towns of Sneads Ferry and Holly Ridge complete the section known as the Greater Topsail Area. The area is a friendly place, offering a nice balance between residents and visitors and busy and quiet times. It's a place where nature at its finest can still be enjoyed.

Two bridges allow access to the island, a swing bridge in Surf City and a high-rise bridge connecting Sneads Ferry to North Topsail Beach. A single main road runs parallel to the ocean along the length of this narrow island, with side streets running from the ocean to the sound or Intracoastal Waterway. In a few instances on the wider parts of the island, you will find an additional smaller street or two running parallel to the ocean. There is only one traffic light on the whole island strand.

Topsail's summer population swells up to 35,000, as compared to the 3,500 year-round residents, consisting mostly of retirees. The convenient location between the cities of Jacksonville and Wilmington makes Topsail a desirable place to live. Residents here enjoy a quiet lifestyle on the beach.

Hampstead, our wonderful little wide spot in the road, is quickly becoming a destination community for many who choose to flee the hustle and bustle of the crowded city to seek the simpler, quieter lifestyle the gracious Southern coastal area offers.

GREATER HAMPSTEAD CHAMBER OF COMMERCE
Visit our website: www.hampsteadchamber.com
Phone: 910-270-9642 • 800-833-2483
Email: hampsteadcoc1@bellsouth.net

North Topsail Beach, the northernmost town, is a residential community with oceanfront resort condominium complexes and rental cottages. With only two restaurants and a pizza shop, North Topsail Beach's visitors depend on Surf City or Sneads Ferry for most of their shopping and entertainment. Surf City, located on both the island and mainland, is in the center of the island. It is the commercial hub with an array of restaurants and retail establishments. A variety of vacation rental homes, condominiums and motels are also found here, along with the most year-round residents. Topsail Beach, on the southern end of the island, is accessible only through Surf City. It is a quieter area with year-round homes, rental cottages, motels and condominiums complementing a small downtown shopping area.

Topsail Island is a small place with a big history. From the early Indians and explorers in the 1500s to pirates, the Civil War Era, World War II and Operation Bumblebee to the present, much has been documented about the Topsail area. This history can be found in the Missiles and More Museum on Channel Boulevard in Topsail Beach.

Local residents are protective of their environment. This is particularly evident in the Topsail Turtle Project and the Karen Beasley Sea Turtle Rescue and Rehabilitation Center, both run solely by volunteers. Many of the volunteers locate and monitor loggerhead turtle nests until the young turtles hatch and make their way to the sea, while others maintain the center and care for sick and injured sea turtles until they have been rehabilitated and returned to the ocean. A visit to the Turtle Hospital, as it is affectionately known, is a real highlight of a Topsail Island vacation.

On the mainland, Sneads Ferry and Holly Ridge offer more choices for entertainment, dining or shopping. Sneads Ferry is a small village where shrimping and fishing are a way of life. In recent years, however, the area has continually grown and developed into a community of upscale housing developments and shopping centers along the main highways. Holly Ridge boasted a large population during World War II when Camp Davis was established as an Army coastal artillery and

DDT–Outlet

3 Locations to Serve You!
Hampstead, Wilmington,
Sneads Ferry

MUST STOP

Huge Selection of In Stock Inventory

Complete
Custom
Packages
Available!

"Custom Ordered Sofas"

1000's of Fabrics
to Choose From
Leather Sofas
Quick Shipments

Large Selection of Wicker Furniture & All Weather Wicker

Interior Design Services Available

Large Selection of Outdoor Furniture

Come
See Us For All
Your Upholstered
Furniture, Tables
& Chairs,
Barstools, Nautical
Items, & More!

LARGEST

Selection of Nautical
Gifts & Accessories
in North Carolina!

We Carry a
Complete
Line of
Mattresses

Call Toll Free 1-877-954-6367 • Local 910-329-0160
www.DDTOUTLET.com

We Ship
Anywhere

Main Location
21740 Hwy. 17 North, Hampstead, NC
South of Holly Ridge, North of Hampstead

Open 7
Days a
Week

DDT 2

896 Route 210, Sneads Ferry, NC
(Near Four Corners)

DDT Outlet

7222 Market St., Wilmington, NC
(Formerly Pinehurst Pottery) (910) 686-0338

anti-aircraft training base. The town is now a quiet place enjoyed by longtime residents who find pleasure in the friendly services of locally owned restaurants, retail stores and service businesses.

AREA CHAMBERS OF COMMERCE

Chambers of commerce are great resources for gaining an understanding of the big picture in terms of a community's business, educational, entertainment and institutional flavor. Although these organizations are not generally in the tourism business, they have brochure racks filled with information of interest to the visitor, newcomer and even the longtime resident who just wants to know what's going on. Staff members are always courteous and interested in providing information to visitors.

Brunswick County Chamber of Commerce
4948 Main Street, Shallotte,
(910) 754-6644, (800) 426-6644
www.brunswickcountychamber.org

Burgaw Area Chamber of Commerce
100 W. Freemont Street Burgaw,
(910) 259-9817

Greater Hampstead Chamber of Commerce
15444 U.S. Highway 17, Hampstead Village Center, Hampstead,
(910) 270-9642, (800) 833-2483
www.hampsteadchamber.com

Greater Topsail Area Chamber of Commerce & Tourism
Treasure Coast Landing, 13775 N.C. Highway 50, Suite 101, Surf City,
(910) 329-4446, (800) 626-2780

Greater Wilmington Chamber of Commerce
1 Estell Lee Place, Wilmington,
(910) 762-2611

Myrtle Beach Area Chamber of Commerce
1200 N. Oak Street, Myrtle Beach, SC 29577,
(843) 626-7444, (800) 356-3016;
South Strand Office, 3401 U.S. 17 Business S., Murrells Inlet, SC 29576 (843) 651-1010.

North Brunswick Chamber of Commerce
151 Poole Road, Leland,
(910) 383-0553, (888) 383-0553

Pleasure Island Chamber of Commerce, (Carolina and Kure Beaches)
1121 North Lake Park Boulevard,
Carolina Beach,
(910) 458-8434

Southport-Oak Island Area Chamber of Commerce
4841 Long Beach Road S.E., Southport,
(910) 457-6964, (800) 457-6964
www.southport-oakisland.com

Wrightsville Beach Chamber of Commerce
315 Salisbury Street, P.O. Box 466,
Wrightsville Beach, NC 28480,
(910) 256-8116, (800) 232-2469

Beautiful vistas await you on the southern coast.

photo: Peter Doran

HOTELS AND MOTELS

The beach areas of North Carolina's southern coast have been a haven for tourists for many years, and even though resort hotels, efficiency apartments and motel lodgings are plentiful, don't count on getting a room without a reservation if your plans include the summer months, the Azalea Festival in the spring, or holiday weekends.

Full-service resort and business hotels are strategically located in desirable areas such as Wilmington's riverfront and nearby beaches. In smaller towns such as Topsail, Surf City and Oak Island, lower-priced oceanfront motels are more common. In Wilmington, the "motel strip" is primarily on Market Street west of College Road, and College Road itself, south of Market Street. You can find motels of every price range, from the budget Motel 6 to the pricier Hilton Riverside.

In addition to a major oceanfront hotel and numerous in-town motels, Carolina Beach teems with cozy family-run motels concentrated along Carolina Beach Avenue North within a half-mile of Harper Avenue. Kure Beach offers a similar strip of pleasant motels along U.S. Highway 421 in the center of town. There are no hotels or motels on Figure Eight Island or Bald Head Island. On Bald Head Island, daily accommodations are limited to two large bed and breakfast inns (see our Bed and Breakfasts and Small Inns chapter). Some rental homes are available for stays as short as a weekend (see our Weekly and Long-Term Vacation Rentals chapter).

No matter what type of accommodations you desire, plush or plain, city or beach, large or small, you'll be able to find a motel or hotel to satisfy your needs in the southern coast area. This chapter deals only with traditional hotel and motel accommodations. For other accommodation options, see our chapters on Bed and Breakfasts and Small Inns, Weekly and Long-Term Vacation Rentals and Camping.

PRICE CODE

Since prices are subject to change without notice, we provide only price guidelines based on double-occupancy, per-night rates during the summer (high season). Our codes do not reflect the 7 percent state/county and 1 to 6 percent room occupancy taxes (taxes may vary by county or municipality). Most establishments offer lower rates during the off-season. Always confirm rates and necessary amenities before reserving.

It may also be beneficial to inquire about corporate, senior citizen, AAA or long-term discounts even when such discounts are not mentioned in our descriptions. Most establishments accept major credit cards, and some accept personal checks when payment is made well in advance.

$	$75 or less
$$	$76 to $120
$$$	$121 to $150
$$$$	$151 and up

Wilmington

Baymont Inn & Suites $-$$
306 College Rd., Wilmington
(910) 392-6767, (800) 926-1139

Whether you're coming to Wilmington on business or for a family vacation, the Baymont Inn & Suites offers travelers top-quality accommodations and exceptional service at reasonable rates. With a AAA 3 diamond rating, and backed by a 110 percent customer satisfaction guarantee, your stay is sure to be relaxed and enjoyable. The 134 guestrooms feature many amenities including a coffeemaker, alarm clock, iron and ironing board, hair dryer, pillow-top mattresses, and in-room movies on-command.

Start the morning with a complimentary deluxe continental breakfast of fruits, cereal, assorted breads and muffins, hot waffles,

WRIGHTSVILLE BEACH
NORTH CAROLINA

Casual *Elegance*

spectacular *Ocean* views!

Enjoy an unforgettable getaway at North Carolina's premier oceanfront resort!

Oceanfront at
Wrightsville Beach, N.C.

Holiday Inn
SunSpree Resort

www.wrightsville.sunspreeresorts.com

910.256.2231 local • 877.330.5050 toll free • 910.256.9208 fax
1706 N. Lumina Ave. • Wrightsville Beach, NC 28480

306 South College Rd.
Wilmington, NC 28403
Phone: (910)392-6767
Fax: (910)392-2144

juice, milk and fresh coffee. All day long, you can enjoy complimentary fruit, hot beverages and fresh baked cookies. Take advantage of free wireless high-speed Internet access, concierge service and 24-hour free access to Gold's Gym and Health Spa Club. The Baymont Inn & Suites, next to Outback Steakhouse, is convenient to Corning Glass, DuPont, General Electric and UNCW and is within walking distance of several popular restaurants and two shopping centers.

Best Western Coastline Inn $$-$$$$
503 Nutt St., Wilmington
(910) 763-2800

Located in historic downtown Wilmington on the east bank of the Cape Fear River, the Best Western Coastline Inn offers first-rate accommodations along with beautiful views and exceptional service. All of their 53 rooms are non-smoking. Choose from rooms with two double beds, queen beds with queen sleeper sofa or executive suites, each having free high-speed wireless Internet access. Other in-room amenities include a 25-inch color television with cable and HBO, free local calls and long distance access, coffee/tea maker, iron, ironing board, desk/work area and hairdryer.

Wake up to a complimentary continental breakfast delivered to your door. On weekdays, enjoy a complimentary copy of USA Today newspaper as well. An exercise facility is on the premises and a business center has computer, printer, fax and copier

available. The hotel has ample free parking, a 24-hour front desk, safe deposit boxes and an elevator for your safety and convenience. Catering, meeting and banquet facilities are also available.

Comfort Suites of Wilmington $-$$$
4721 Market St., Wilmington
(910) 793-9300, (800) 221-2222

Comfort Suites of Wilmington is conveniently located between scenic Wrightsville Beach and Wilmington's downtown historic district. Each of the 73 deluxe suites features iron/ironing board, hair dryer, coffee maker, microwave, refrigerator, cable television and high-speed Internet. In addition, you get free local phone calls on two -ine telephones with voice mail and dataports. Suites have either two double beds or one king-sized bed. Both smoking and non-smoking suites are available.

The hotel has an indoor fitness facility and a business center. All guests are afforded a complimentary deluxe continental breakfast every day and a free USA Today newspaper Monday through Friday. Same-day laundry service is also available Monday through Friday.

Courtyard by Marriott $$
151 Van Campen Blvd., Wilmington
(910) 395-8224

This 128-room hotel offers comfortable accommodations especially suited to the business traveler. Rooms include large work desks, iron and ironing board, cable selection with pay movies, high-speed wireless Internet, coffee makers and voice mail. Rollaways and cribs are available, as are dry-cleaning service (except Sundays), self-service laundry facilities and an onsite fitness center. The attractive courtyard features a pool, whirlpool spa and gazebo. A moderately priced breakfast buffet (free for kids 3 and younger) is served daily from 6:30 to 10 AM weekdays and 7 to 11 AM on Saturday and Sunday. The hotel also has meeting and banquet space available.

The Greentree Inn $
5025 Market St., Wilmington
(910) 799-6001
www.greentreenc.com

The family tradition of warmth and hospitality has graced Wilmington's Green-

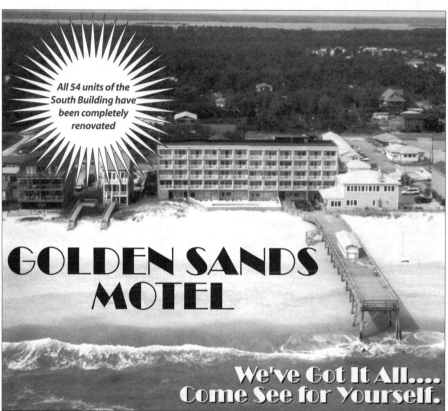

All 54 units of the South Building have been completely renovated

GOLDEN SANDS MOTEL

We've Got It All....
Come See for Yourself.

- Single, double & split double rooms for extra privacy
- Balconies offering sweeping waterfront view
- Color cable TV, refrigerator, & microwave
- Award-Winning Restaurant • Enjoy Year-Round Swimming, Indoor & Out
- Enclosed patio, walking pier, and Tiki Bar
- 2 Pools, Elevator • Conference & Banquet Tables
- Handicapped Rooms and Accessibility
- Fully Stocked Gift Shop • 64 New Oceanfront Rooms
- And of course...our special brand of southern hospitality

**P.O. Box 759 • U.S. Highway 421 South
Carolina Beach, NC 28428
(910) 458-8334
www.goldensandsmotel.com**

43

GREENTREE INN

123 spacious rooms
color tvs with cable & HBO
Free Local Calls
Children under 18
stay free

Complimentary
Continental Breakfast
Non-Smoking Rooms
Swimming Pool & Sun Deck
Corporate Rates

5025 Market Street
Wilmington, NC 28405
910-799-6001
www.GreentreeNC.com

tree Inn since its opening in 1972. The classic 1970s architecture features a second-floor, wrap-around balcony. All rooms have exterior entrances allowing easy access from your car. Located in the midtown section of Wilmington, the inn is conveniently situated just 6 miles from Wrightsville Beach and 4 miles from Wilmington's downtown Historic District.

The Greentree Inn provides excellent amenities for the price, which explains its popularity among families and business travelers alike. Boasting 123 clean and spacious rooms, Greentree's features include color TV with remote, free cable, 60 channels and free HBO. Free local phone calls, complimentary continental breakfast, an outdoor swimming pool and sundeck are some of the services that bring back satisfied visitors season after season. The Old Chicago restaurant and Lily's Banquets are on the property as well. Greentree offers king deluxe rooms, rooms with two queen beds or two standard beds, non-smoking rooms and accessible accommodations. A limited number of pet-friendly rooms are available with a non-refundable deposit required.

Hampton Inn - Medical Park $$-$$$
2320 S. 17th St., Wilmington
(910) 796-8881
www.hamptoninn-medicalpark.com
This award-winning Hampton Inn is located within the Medical Park area, practi-

cally across the street from the New Hanover Regional Medical Center and just minutes from historic downtown Wilmington and area beaches and attractions. It features 85 rooms with 14 suites in an all-interior property. The meeting space, which seats up to 65 people theater style, is perfect for medical conferences and corporate occasions. Amenities include an outdoor swimming pool in a well-landscaped setting, a fitness center on the property as well as a free full membership to Capital Fitness Spa Health Club just around the corner.

The Hampton Inn rooms have on-demand movies, refrigerators and wet bars, coffee makers, hair dryers, irons and ironing boards. Each room also provides free high-speed wireless Internet access, voice mail and dataport hook-ups. In addition, the hotel offers a 50-item complimentary continental breakfast, a business center and outstanding customer service. In 2005, the Hampton Inn Medical Park received the Lighthouse Award recognizing its placement in the top 2 percent of all Hampton hotels. A hospital shuttle is available to guests.

Hampton Inn Wilmington $$
5107 Market St., Wilmington
(910) 395-5045
Hampton Inn Midtown has 118 tastefully appointed rooms, each featuring wireless high-speed Internet, dataports, an iron and ironing board, hair dryer, cable TV with HBO, and a coffee maker. Upgraded rooms include the King Study and rooms with micro-fridges. Valet laundry is available during the week. Guests receive free passes to the Spa Health Club, and there's an on-site outdoor pool that's open from April through September. The hotel offers a meeting room accommodating up to 30 people with wireless high-speed Internet access. Local phone calls are free.

Ideally located, Hampton Inn is just 4 miles from Wrightsville Beach, 2 miles from Wilmington's Historic Downtown and less than a mile from UNCW. The hotel is within walking distance of several popular restaurants and shopping venues. Hampton Inn offers many packages for holidays, special events, shoppers and golfers. Group dis-

MEDICAL PARK

*Stay at Wilmington's newest Hampton Inn,
serving the region's fine medical facilities
and all of scenic, historic Wilmington*

For Your convenience

• We're Expanding...more rooms in 2007
• Great Location between the beach & Historic
downtown
• Free Wireless internet available in rooms & lobby
• Complimentary deluxe continental breakfast
• Upgraded rooms, featuring the "Cloud Nine" bed
experience

2320 South Seventeenth St. Wilmington, N. C.
For Reservations: 910.796.8881 • Fax: 910.796.8882
1.800.HAMPTON® www.hamptoninn-medicalpark.com

100%
HAMPTON
We guarantee high quality accommodations,
friendly & efficient service and clean,
comfortable surroundings.

For Reservations Call:
910.796.8881

counts are available for booking ten rooms or more.

Hilton Wilmington Riverside $$$-$$$$
301 N. Water St., Wilmington
(910) 763-5900, (800) 445-8667

Situated on the Riverwalk and overlooking the Cape Fear River, the Hilton is Wilmington's largest hotel and conference center. The hotel features 274 newly renovated guest rooms, each with a dual-line telephone with voicemail and dataport, high-speed Internet access, hair dryer, ironing equipment, coffee maker, On-Command Movies, HBO, WebTV and Nintendo.

The Hilton's Poolside & Cabana Bar, complete with ceiling fans and palm trees, is a great place for a sunset cocktail. Spencer's is the hotel's fine restaurant serving grilled steaks and seafood. The hotel's River Club Lounge and its fitness room are both popular. With 20,000 square feet of meeting and banquet facilities, the hotel offers 19 meeting rooms, including the Grand Ballroom, accommodating up to 600 people with food ser-

vice. Located in the heart of historic Wilmington, this property is convenient to more than 50 shops and restaurants, all within walking distance, and is only 3 miles from Wilmington International Airport.

Holiday Inn Express Hotel & Suites $$
160 Van Campen Blvd., Wilmington
(910) 392-3227,
(800) HOLIDAY (465-4329)

Customer-focused, well-maintained and tastefully decorated, this hotel provides a wide range of services and amenities. For a modest price, you can have top-notch lodging, from king and double-bed rooms to two-room executive or whirlpool suites. All rooms include ironing equipment, coffee makers, voice-mail telephones, dataports, free high-speed Internet access and cable TV with premium networks, HBO, Pay-Per-View movies and Nintendo.

Enjoy your complimentary deluxe continental breakfast by the fireplace in the cozy living room-style lounge or while relaxing next to the outdoor pool. Hotel amenities also include an exercise room, coin-operated laundry, airport shuttle and complimentary daily newspaper. The hotel boasts a comfortably furnished executive boardroom and several meeting rooms suitable for up to 150 people. Audiovisual equipment is available for rental, and catering can be arranged.

Centrally located, the 131-room Holiday Inn Express Hotel & Suites is convenient to Wilmington's business districts, downtown and Wrightsville Beach. Within walking distance are major restaurants, Wal-Mart Super Center and several shopping plazas.

Howard Johnson Express Inn $-$$
3901 Market St., Wilmington
(910) 343-1727

This one-story, 80-unit motel offers a variety of comfortable smoking, non-smoking and handicapped-accessible rooms to meet the needs of most travelers. Choose from standard rooms with one king or two double beds, home office rooms with upgraded amenities, or efficiencies that have kitchenettes. All have private bath, color TV with cable and free HBO, telephone and voicemail, dataport and coffee maker. Many rooms also come with a microwave and small refrigerator. There's no charge for local phone calls, and a complimentary continental breakfast is served from 6:30 to 10 AM daily. Children up to age 16 stay free in the same room with adults. Long-term rates are available. The Howard Johnson Express Inn is located 3 miles from downtown Wilmington, 7 miles from Wrightsville Beach and 3.5 miles from Wilmington International Airport.

Innkeeper Inn $-$$
5345 W. Market St., Wilmington
(910) 799-4292

Conveniently located at College Road and Market Street, the Innkeeper Inn offers 95 all-interior king and double guest rooms in a pleasant two-story hotel. Amenities include free USA Today newspaper on weekdays, cable TV with HBO, free high-speed wireless Internet access throughout the hotel, complimentary breakfast bar from 6 to 10 AM each day and an outdoor pool open seasonally. A business center with high-speed Internet access, fax, copier and dataport phones makes this a great stopover place for working travelers. The Innkeeper Inn is pet-friendly, too. A number of popular restaurants are close by, and UNCW is just a short drive, as are many local points of interest.

Jameson Inn $$
5102 Dunlea Ct., Wilmington
(910) 452-5660, (800) 526-3766

Promising "A Perfect Stay...Every Time," the Jameson Inn hospitality family believes each guest deserves a clean, comfortable, high-quality room and exceptional customer service. This inviting white-columned, colonial-style property has 67 rooms including doubles, kings and suites. Their premium rooms feature microwaves, refrigerators, coffee makers and recliners. Among the many amenities are free deluxe continental breakfast, free local calling, free weekday newspaper, as well as spacious work stations, ironing equipment, and 25-inch TV with cable and HBO in every room. Free wireless high-speed Internet, a fitness center, pool and meeting room make this hotel popular with business travelers and families alike.

MainStay Suites $-$$$
5229 Market St., Wilmington
(910) 392-1741
www.mainstaywilmingtonnc.com

This Gold Hospitality Award-winning MainStay Suites is a well thought out, comfortable, attractive alternative to traditional hotel lodging. Whether you're in town on business or on vacation, you can call this your home away from home for as long as you like. Accommodations available to meet your needs include king singles, two-bedroom suites and many choices in between. Thoroughly modern, every suite features its own central heating and air system and complete kitchen facilities, including full-size refrigerator with ice maker, two-burner electric stove, microwave, toaster, coffee maker, dishwasher, dishes, utensils, pots, even dishtowels and potholders. Other in-room amenities include cable TV, phones, high-speed Internet access, ironing equipment, hair dryer and shower organizer. A guest laundry is available, as are a fitness room, business center with high-speed Internet access, adjacent seasonal pool and an enclosed courtyard complete with grills for guest use. Convenient to shopping and restaurants, Main Stay Suites is only minutes from area beaches, historic downtown and Wilmington International Airport.

If It's Fun, It's Nearby.

SLEEP INN
BY CHOICE HOTELS

FREE High-Speed &
Wireless Internet!

- SEVEN Time Gold Hospitality Award Winner
- Continental Breakfast
- In-Room Coffee
- Outdoor Pool
- Free Local Calls
- Meeting Room
- Fitness Center
- 100% Satisfaction Guarantee
- Microwave & Refrigerator Available

MainStay Suites
BY CHOICE HOTELS

- Gold Hospitality Award Winner
- Newest All-Suite Hotel
- Full Kitchen
- Continental Breakfast
- Nightly & Weekly Rates
- Business Center
- Pool & Gas Grills
- Laundry Facilities

Beach 4 Miles
Historic District 3 Miles
Restaurants 1/2 Block

Sleep Inn
5225 Market Street
Wilmington, NC 28480
910-313-6665 • 866-SLEEP-99

MainStay Suites
5229 Market Street
Wilmington, NC 28480
910-392-1741

Riverview Suites at Water Street Center $$$
106 N. Water St., Wilmington
(910) 772-9988

Riverview Suites at Water Street Center, located across the street from and operated by the Hilton, offers 65 well-appointed suites overlooking the Cape Fear River. Each suite boasts a walk-out balcony, kitchen area, washer/dryer, pull-out sofa, cable television, hair dryer, ironing equipment, coffee maker and just about the most fantastic view in all of downtown Wilmington.

Sleep Inn $-$$
5225 Market St., Wilmington
(910) 313-6665,
(866) SLEEP-99 (753-3799)

This seven-time Gold Hospitality Award–winning hotel is located less than a half-mile west of the Market Street I-40 overpass. Sleep Inn offers 104 inside-corridor rooms with either queen-sized or two double beds. All rooms come complete with oversized showers, key-card security locks, cable TV, high-speed Internet access, coffee makers, irons and ironing boards. To make your stay more comfortable and pleasurable, Sleep Inn offers a fitness room and seasonal outdoor pool. A copier, fax machine and meeting room are available for guest use, as well as wireless Internet access in the lobby. A complimentary continental breakfast is offered every morning, and hot beverages are available free all day in the lobby lounge.

Suburban Extended Stay Hotel $
245 Eastwood Rd., Wilmington
(910) 793-1920

Ideally situated between I-40 and Wrightsville Beach, this 107-room establishment is just 3 miles from the beach and 10 minutes from downtown Wilmington. Since each room features a kitchen, the Suburban Extended Stay Hotel is a great choice for nightly or long-term visits and other special needs. Other amenities include free high-speed Internet access, dataport hookup, cable TV (including HBO), free local calls and voice mail. The hotel features daily maid service, a conference room, a copier and fax machine that guests can use, plus an outdoor pool, barbecue grills and a basketball court. Handicapped-accessible rooms are also available.

Wilmington Quality Inn $-$$
4926 Market St., Wilmington
(910) 791-8850

Newly renovated and centrally located to attractions, beaches, UNCW, the airport and Historic Downtown, the Wilmington Quality Inn offers travelers both comfort and affordability. Each of the 120 spacious guestrooms has a coffee maker, iron and ironing board, hair dryer, cable TV, telephone with free local calls, and free wireless high-speed Internet access. The hotel is within walking distance of several restaurants and serves a free deluxe continental breakfast every morning. A refreshing dip in the outdoor pool will revive

101 OVERSIZED GUEST ROOMS INCLUDING JACUZZI SUITES AND EXECUTIVE SUITES

ALL ROOMS INCLUDE:

- Wi-Fi Internet & Hi-Speed Internet (T-1 Line)
- Two Phones (1 Cordless) With Voice Mail & Conference Calling
- Cable TV with 25" Color TV & Free HBO
- Microwave, Refrigerator & Coffee Maker
- Iron/Ironing Board, Hair Dryer & Safe
- Web TV, Nintendo 64 & On Demand Movies

100% Smoke FREE

SERVICES/FACILITIES

- Free Deluxe Continental Breakfast Buffet
- Free 24 Hour Business Center
- Meeting Room & Executive Board Room
- Outdoor Pool, Spa & Fitness Center
- Manager Reception Mon-Thurs.

Wilmington's Finest...Great Location!
At I-40 And US 17 Exit

Satisfaction guaranteed!

WINGATE INN
BUILT FOR BUSINESS®
(for reservations only call: 866-395-7011)
www.wingateinns.com

5126 Market St. (Hwy. 17) Wilmington, NC 28405

you after a day of shopping or beach combing, and you can enjoy your complimentary USA Today newspaper while you sip coffee from the lounge. Bring Fido and Fluffy. Pets are welcome.

The Wilmingtonian $$-$$$$
101 S. Second St., Wilmington
(910) 343-1800, (800) 525-0909

The Wilmingtonian comprises five buildings with 40 unique non-smoking suites, plus dining rooms, conference and meeting rooms as well as a large ballroom. The buildings, dating from 1841 to 1994, are surrounded by extensive gardens and ponds with courtyards and balconies. The famed de Rosset House, built in 1841, features sweeping views of the Cape Fear River and offers a fascinating glimpse into the past. Its six luxurious suites are historically decorated yet equipped with modern conveniences, such as gas log fireplaces, large whirlpool tubs and separate showers. The signature suite, the Cupola, offers exquisite views of the city and breathtaking sunsets. Amenities for all suites include kitchen or wet bar, refrigerator, coffee maker, microwave, toaster, VCR and DVD. Complimentary high-speed Internet is available throughout the hotel.

The Wilmingtonian's dining room, located at the nearby private City Club and referred to as "the very best in gourmet dining" by Wilmington Magazine, is a great choice for corporate events and weddings and is accessible to guests of the inn. The hotel is just

two blocks from the Cape Fear River and within walking distance of area restaurants, galleries, antiques stores and shopping. The beaches are just a short drive away.

Wingate Inn Wilmington $-$$$
5126 Market St., Wilmington
(910) 395-7011, (866) 395-7011
www.wingateinns.com

"Built for Business" is Wingate Inn's slogan, but vacationers say it was also built for leisure. This outstanding, smoke-free hotel has the amenities, facilities and service every traveler requires, backed by a 100 percent satisfaction guarantee. Conveniently located to area attractions, beaches, golf, airport, shopping and historic downtown, the hotel offers an uncommon oasis of comfort. Just minutes from Wilmington International Airport, the hotel offers complimentary shuttle service.

Wingate Inn's oversized guest room selections include Jacuzzi Suites, Executive Suites, Deluxe Kings and Deluxe Doubles, all on interior corridors. The rooms are not only tastefully appointed and thoughtfully arranged, they're also functional. Each offers separate areas for sleep and work, free high-speed wireless and T1 Internet access, refrigerator, microwave, hairdryer, iron, ironing board, coffeemaker and electronic safe. Rooms are equipped with two phones and voice mail. The desk phone has two lines, a speaker, dataport and conference-call capabilities. In-room TV offers more than 65 free cable channels, including HBO.

For business travelers, the complimentary business center is complete with computer, laser printer, fax and copier. Copies and faxes are free for guests. There's also an Executive Boardroom and a larger meeting room available for your conference requirements.

Whether you decide to lounge by the outdoor pool or take advantage of the well-equipped fitness center and spa, you're sure to find a way to relax and unwind. Read your complimentary USA Today or watch the news on their 62-inch big-screen TV while enjoying a nutritious complimentary breakfast from the 42-item buffet. The hotel hosts a guest appreciation reception Monday through Thursday evenings, with complimentary wine, beer, soft drinks and snacks.

Wrightsville Beach and Vicinity

Blockade Runner Beach Resort $-$$$$
275 Waynick Blvd., Wrightsville Beach
(910) 256-2251, (800) 541-1161

Located in the heart of this beautiful barrier island, the Blockade Runner Beach Resort is one of the premier oceanfront resort hotels in Wrightsville Beach. Everything you need for a perfect vacation can be found within minutes of your room. When it comes to fun, this hotel has it all. At the harborside water center, you'll find complete services for sailing, fishing, kayaking, surfing, diving and eco-tours. Several championship golf courses are nearby, and shuttle service to tennis courts is available.

Families with children ages 4 to 12 will appreciate Sandcamper's, a supervised children's program that includes indoor crafts and games, plus beach, pool and island excursions and evening activities. You'll find a complete fitness center including a whirlpool and dry sauna. Looking for a massage after a long day? The hotel will schedule one for you. During the warm months, they also offer oceanfront yoga.

The Blockade Runner's outdoor patio bar provides casual dining with a spectacular view overlooking manicured gardens and the waters of the Atlantic Ocean. Enjoy an unforgettable dining experience and feel the ocean breeze while dining on the dinner deck at the award-winning East Restaurant. There are nightly features including a sushi bar, wine tastings and fresh local seafood and lobster. The award-winning Sunday Jazz Brunch includes a variety of local favorites and entertainment.

All rooms are either ocean or harborfront with queens or king bedding. The newly renovated oceanfront balcony section, The Terrace, offers additional amenities such as high-thread-count linens, plasma TVs and bathrooms with marble throughout, granite countertops and rainforest showers, all with a magnificent view of the oceanfront gardens.

Standard in each room is a refrigerator, coffee maker, hairdryer, ironing equipment and luxurious bathrobes. Other amenities include room service, Sundry Shop, complimentary safe-deposit boxes and a shuttle service around the island. For the business traveler, the Blockade Runner's Executive Club offers discounted room rates, free local calls, incoming fax service and high-speed wireless Internet connections. Conference and banquet facilities are available. Corporate rates are offered year-round.

Carolina Temple Apartments Island Inn $$
550 Waynick Blvd., Wrightsville Beach
(910) 256-2773

Built by the Temple family in the early 1900s, Carolina Temple Apartments consists of two historic plantation-style cottages. The property runs from the soundside of the island to the ocean, yet the buildings are set back like a well-kept secret. The inn was once Station 6 along the Wrightsville Beach trolley line (ask to see the old photos), and the pride with which the place is run is evident everywhere. Both buildings are classics with central hallways, spacious, breezy wraparound porches furnished with large rockers and the occasional well-placed hammock. A high sun deck overlooking the ocean and louvered outer doors to each of the 16 apartments gives a Caribbean feel. The apartments are not large but they are beautifully maintained, comprising one-, two- and three-room air-conditioned suites with private baths, ceiling fans and fully equipped kitchenettes.

The apartments are perfect for couples and families (up to six people). The decor is

Stay in an oceanfront hotel and you can enjoy surf fishing before and after breakfast.

photo: Peter Doran

tropical, with luminous beach colors and Caribbean-style folk art. The dune-front patio, surrounded by palms and oleander, is a cool, shaded place to relax. Rentals from June through August mostly require a one-week minimum, but split weeks sometimes become available. The inn closes in winter. This is an excellent bargain relative to the area. Extras include a small sound-side beach perfect for toddlers, a laundry facility, complimentary morning coffee, sound-side docking facilities and cribs.

Harbor Inn $$-$$$$
701 Causeway Dr., Wrightsville Beach
(910) 256-9402, (888) 507-9402

Situated where Banks Channel meets the Causeway Bridge, Harbor Inn offers something for everyone. Private balconies overlooking the harbor are just the place to relax with your morning coffee to plan a day on the water or at the beach. Except for the handicapped-accessible suite, which sleeps four, each tastefully appointed suite sleeps up to six people and features a fully equipped kitchenette with microwave, mini-fridge, coffee maker and stove/oven. The living room area has a dining table and comfort-

able furniture enhanced by a picture-perfect water view. Other amenities include individually controlled heat and air conditioning, daily maid service, linens, kitchen utensils, pots/pans, cable TV and toiletries. All of the rooms are non-smoking, however smokers may use their private balcony to smoke at any time.

Harbor Inn has a dock that can accommodate boats up to 25 feet, which makes this a very popular spot for boaters to vacation. Add to all this a beautiful outdoor swimming pool and you have the recipe for a great experience. Weekly rates are available.

Holiday Inn SunSpree Resort $$-$$$$
1706 N. Lumina Ave., Wrightsville Beach
(910) 256-2231, (877) 330-5050
www.wrightsville.sunspreeresorts.com

This award-winning, oceanfront resort hotel has an elegant yet casual Caribbean-like atmosphere that makes you feel relaxed and comfortable, whether you're visiting for fun, on business or attending a convention. As you enter the expansive oceanfront lobby, you're greeted by two blue and gold macaw parrots, one of the hotel's main attractions. The oceanfront Verandah Cafe Restaurant serves breakfast, lunch and dinner plus a popular Sunday Brunch Buffet. Gabby's Lounge with live entertainment Thursday through Saturday evenings, is ideal for that pre-dinner cocktail and appetizer or late-evening nightcap. In season Lazy Daze Pool Bar and Grill provides tropical drinks and good eats without leaving the comfort of your lounge chair. A market/gift shop is available for those forgotten items, and there's an ATM on site as well.

The resort offers a complimentary, supervised children's program for ages 4 to 12. The KidSpree is a dedicated children's activity room complete with games, toys, Nintendo and videos. A video arcade, beach playground, volleyball court and fitness center with state-of-the-art equipment give you lots of ways to exercise and have fun. Five recreational pools, including one in the indoor atrium, two whirlpools, and a poolside bar and grill offer total enjoyment whatever the weather.

Most of the 184 guestrooms have verandas with views of either the ocean or the sound and the Intracoastal Waterway. Whirlpool suites or rooms are also available. All rooms have microwave, refrigerator, coffee maker, ironing equipment, hairdryer, in-room safe, two dataport phones with voice messaging, complimentary coffee, in-room movies and Nintendo video games. The hotel has high-speed wireless Internet access, which is complimentary to all guests. A two-level covered parking deck is available, and guest parking is complimentary.

The hotel's conference center, with 8,500 square feet of meeting/conference space, features the 4,100-square-foot Lumina Ballroom, designed after the original Lumina Pavilion at Wrightsville Beach, dating from the early 1900s. An executive boardroom, smaller oceanfront meeting rooms and a business center make the hotel an ideal choice for business meetings, conventions and the corporate traveler.

Landfall Park
Hampton Inn & Suites $$-$$$$
1989 Eastwood Rd., Wrightsville Beach
(910) 256-9600, (877) 256-9600

Ranked number 1 in the world for 1999 and 2001, this hotel is definitely a cut above. The moment you walk into the lodge-style lobby of this property, you sense the quality. The free-standing stone chimney above a two-sided gas fireplace is surrounded by oversized rattan chairs and a plush sofa on one side and by the handsome Eagle Bar Lounge on the other.

With 90 traditional rooms and 30 apartment-style suites, the inn provides high-end amenities, complete with bell staff. It's just minutes from the beach and next door to one of the area's best restaurants, Port City Chop House. All suites feature a full kitchen with a microwave, stove, dishwasher and refrigerator. The Signature Suite provides "celebrity" accommodations, with a double-sided fireplace, entertainment center and two-person whirlpool bath. Executive one- and two-bedroom suites are enticing to movie-production staff and other business travelers seeking high quality. Desk and complimentary high-speed Internet access are standard. The Landfall Park Hampton Inn serves an upscale, 18-item continental breakfast from 6 to 10 AM daily and provides valet service on weekdays. A dedicated boardroom and large meeting room with standing space for 120 are suitable for corporate retreats or small receptions. Of special interest are the large kidney-shaped pool set in a lush garden landscape, a fitness room, a 24-hour suite shop, rattan rocking chairs on a colonnaded porch (a great place for breakfast) and the Gazebo Bar in summer. Landfall Park is on the mainland, less than a half-mile from the drawbridge, and one mile from the beach.

Sandpeddler Motel & Suites $$-$$$$
15 Nathan St., Wrightsville Beach
(910) 256-2028, (800) 548-4245

Sandpeddler Motel & Suites, located across the street from the Oceanic Pier & Restaurant, offers contemporary one-bedroom, one-bath condominium-style suites with a kitchenette. Each suite offers a private balcony with a great ocean view. All units sleep up to four people with one queen bed in the bedroom and a queen sleeper sofa in the living room. The Sandpeddler offers an outdoor swimming pool, laundry facilities, linen service and access to email, voice mail, a copier, a fax machine and a printer. Sandpeddler is 40 yards from the beach and within walking distance of many shops and restaurants.

Located just minutes from Carolina Beach, Historic Downtown Wilmington and the University of North Carolina at Wilmington

AMERI-STAY
INN & SUITES

Ameri-Stay Inn & Suites

5600 Carolina Beach Road
Wilmington, NC 28412
(910) 796-0770 (toll free) 800-961-STAY
www.ameristay.net

Shell Island Oceanfront Suites $-$$$$
2700 N. Lumina Ave.,
Wrightsville Beach
(910) 256-8696, (800) 689-6765

In Wrightsville Beach, overlooking 3,000 feet of pristine white sand beaches, this family-friendly resort hotel offers 160 oceanfront suites, each with a magnificent view of the Atlantic. Each beautifully decorated suite can sleep from four to six people and includes a bedroom, one and a half bathrooms, and a combination living room/dining room/kitchenette. The kitchenette includes refrigerator, microwave, stove top, coffee maker and blender. You will love having morning coffee or afternoon cocktails on your own private balcony.

Hotel amenities include Shelly's oceanfront restaurant and bar, an outdoor pool, an indoor heated pool, a hot tub, a fitness room, bicycle rentals, a sand volleyball court, a gift shop and laundry facilities. Plenty of parking is available under the covered deck.

Also ideal for meetings, conventions, weddings and social gatherings, Shell Island

Sand is a fact of life down here. We actually love and treasure it, but it can be a nuisance. Don't expect to go home without at least a little of the stuff in your suitcase or ground into your car's floor mats — no matter how vigorously you vacuum them!

has more than 6,000 square feet of meeting space with an ocean-view ballroom. What better way to relax and unwind at the end of a day-long meeting than to have the beach just a few steps away? Golf packages, shopping, fine dining, riverboat cruises, ghost tours or a stroll through the historic district are great ways to complement your event. Experience the tranquility of Shell Island Oceanfront Suites, where the road ends and the beach begins.

Summer Sands Suites $$$-$$$$
104 S. Lumina Ave., Wrightsville Beach
(910) 256-4175, (800) 336-4849

This comfortable, newly renovated 32-suite efficiency motel sits in the heart of Wrightsville Beach within a short walk of restaurants, shopping, laundry facilities and the strand. Rooms are ideal for two adults and two kids. Suites feature sleeping accommodations for up to four people, with a queen-sized bed in the bedroom and queen-sized wall bed in the living room. In addition, the suites offer a kitchen, dining area and private balcony with spectacular views of the island. The outdoor pool is open in the summer. Two handicapped-accessible suites are also available.

Carolina Beach and Kure Beach

Ameri-Stay Inn & Suites $-$$$
5600 Carolina Beach Rd., Wilmington
(910) 796-0770, (800) 961-STAY (7829)
www.ameristay.net

The 65-unit, three-story Ameri-Stay Inn & Suites is centrally located on U.S. Highway 421 South in the Monkey Junction area. Just a few miles from the beaches of Pleasure Island, the Fort Fisher Historic Site, state parks and the North Carolina Aquarium, this family-friendly hotel is a great place to put down temporary roots while visiting area attractions or playing a round or two of golf at one of the many nearby courses. Only 7 miles from UNCW and 8 miles from historic downtown Wilmington, this inn rates high on convenience. Ameri-Stay Inn & Suites is within walking distance of restaurants and shopping, too.

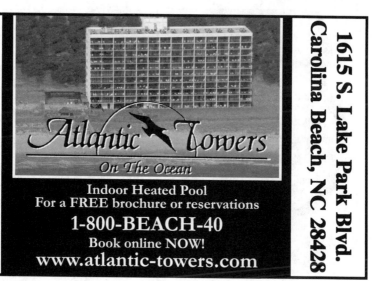

Oceanfront Condos with Balconies,
1 or 2 Bedrooms, Fully Furnished,
Oceanfront & Heated Enclosed Pools,
Video Game Room, Conference Room

1615 S. Lake Park Blvd.
Carolina Beach, NC 28428

Atlantic Towers
On The Ocean

Indoor Heated Pool
For a FREE brochure or reservations
1-800-BEACH-40
Book online NOW!
www.atlantic-towers.com

Guests can choose from standard king, double-bed and whirlpool suites, all featuring free cable TV with HBO, free local calls and free high-speed Internet access. Other in-room amenities include a coffee maker, an iron and ironing board, a hair dryer and a safe. Some rooms have a wet bar, microfridge or recliner. A complimentary continental breakfast is served every morning, and guests may enjoy complimentary fresh-baked cookies in the evening. Maybe you'd like to take a swim in the large indoor pool or lounge around it while watching the kids. A meeting room that accommodates up to 70 people is available too.

Atlantic Towers   **$-$$$$**
1615 S. Lake Park Blvd., Carolina Beach
(910) 458-8313,
(800) BEACH-40 (232-2440)
www.atlantic-towers.com

This 11-story establishment offers attractive, well-kept condominium suites with separate bedrooms and full kitchens. Each suite accommodates up to six guests. All 137 condos are oceanfront, and each has a telephone, cable TV, private balcony, an exterior terrace entrance, maid service and elevator service. The outdoor pool deck is in view of the ocean and stands beside a gazebo — a perfect place for a picnic. For cool evenings, there's an indoor heated pool in full view of the ocean. High-speed Internet access is available. Inquire about the Club Room, which

is suitable for corporate retreats, reunions and other special occasions.

Beachside Inn   **$-$$**
616 S. Lake Park Blvd., Carolina Beach
(910) 458-5598

For families, the Beachside Inn is just the ticket! Homey, comfortable and cheerful, each room is furnished differently, with a variety of arrangements available. Choose from single, double, king-size and combinations to meet your needs, including some two-room suites. Amenities in each unit include microwave, refrigerator, phone and 27-inch color TV with cable. Guests can stroll a short

ALPHIN CHEEK'S
BLUE MARLIN
Apartments *and* Cottage

Oceanfront &
Ocean View Apartments

Great Place for Families
& Friends

- **Family Owned &**   • **Kitchens**
  Operated   • **Central Heat & Air**
- **Daily Minimums &**•   **Individual Hot**
  Weekly Rates   **Water Heaters**
- **Private Bedrooms**   • **Linens Furnished**
- **Cable Color TV**   • **No Pets**
                           • **Wireless Internet**

PO Box 101 • Kure Beach, NC 28449

(910) 458-5752
For more information, check out our web site:
www.blue-marlin.com

DRY DOCK
family motel

Rooms & Efficiency
Apartments
Color Cable TV w/ Remote
Refrigerators/Microwaves

2 Large Pools
BBQ Grills & Picnic Tables
Daily Maid Service

P.O. Box 586
Hwy. 421 & Fayetteville Ave.
Carolina Beach, NC 28428
910-458-8346 • 888-518-8835

for you. The Columbus Motel's quaint charm and convenient location make it especially appealing to folks who don't want to be driving all over the place to have their vacation needs met. Here you'll find comfort, a big blue pool, and old-fashioned, down-home atmosphere. Within walking distance are the beach, shopping, the Boardwalk and good places to eat. The motel offers 18 rooms on two levels, each with a view of the pool.

Courtyard by Marriott $$-$$$$
100 Charlotte Ave., Carolina Beach
(910) 458-2030, (800) 321-2211

The 10-story Carolina Beach Courtyard by Marriott boasts 144 ocean-view rooms with private balconies. In each beautifully decorated room, amenities include complimentary high-speed wireless Internet access, coffee station, mini refrigerator, hair dryer, desk with chair and dataport. Suites also include a separate living area with wet bar and microwave. The hotel offers a large variety of the latest video games and pay-per-view movies.

A luxurious focal point of the hotel is a custom-designed oceanfront outdoor pool and tropical plaza featuring a sunbathing deck with direct beach access, an outdoor café with live music during the summer and staff to deliver cool beverages poolside. The indoor pool and hot tub are open year round, and an extensive exercise room and guest laundry facility are also available. For your beach enjoyment, kayaks, surfboards, body boards, bikes, beach chairs, umbrellas and other items are available to rent during the season.

The upscale hotel lobby is spacious, bright and attractive and features a lounge where guests may purchase a wide selection of beverages. Easily accessible are a computer center with high-speed Internet access and a Market Place that sells sundries, snacks, gifts and beverages. The Carolina Beach Courtyard by Marriott offers a full-service restaurant, the Seaside Grill, which is open every day serving a lavish breakfast buffet, lunch and dinner. Room service is available. A 3,300-square-foot ballroom can handle groups up to 300 and can be divided into three spacious rooms for smaller events or conventions.

distance to the beach or enjoy cooling off in the inviting pool located adjacent to the lovely flower-filled courtyard. Four separate cottage-style buildings house 18 rooms, both smoking and non-smoking. Beachside Inn is one of the best values on Pleasure Island.

Blue Marlin Apartments
and Cottages $$-$$$$
318 Ft. Fisher Blvd., Kure Beach
(910) 458-5752
www.blue-marlin.com

A wonderful place for families and friends to relax in a home-like apartment or cottage, the Blue Marlin is just a few steps from the beach and miles away from daily cares. Amenities include fully equipped kitchen facilities with basic dishes and utensils, central heat and air, color cable TV, private bath, telephone and high-speed wireless Internet. You'll appreciate having your own hot water heater, and bed linens and bath towels are furnished for your convenience. Apartments sleep from two to seven persons, depending on the unit, and the beach house sleeps five to eight. Apartments 1 through 4 were recently fully remodeled. The Bait and Tackle Shop has T-shirts, souvenirs, rafts, gifts and a small line of groceries in addition to fishing gear.

Columbus Motel $-$$
213 Cape Fear Blvd., Carolina Beach
(910) 458-5281

If you're looking for a clean, friendly, reasonably priced family motel, this is the place

Dry Dock Family Motel   **$-$$**
300 S. Lake Park Blvd., Carolina Beach
(910) 458-8346
www.insiders.com/wilmington/
wwwads/drydock/drydockindex.html

Here's a family-oriented, moderately priced motel within walking distance of the beach, amusements, Carolina Beach Lake, restaurants and shopping. Newly remodeled in 2004, the Dry Dock has a variety of accommodations to meet your needs — from single rooms to efficiency apartments. A spacious two-bedroom unit is great for families with kids. All units have a private bath with tub/shower, cable TV, air conditioning, microwave, refrigerator, and coffeemaker with complimentary coffee daily. One of the motel's two sparkling pools is equipped with a diving board. Picnic tables and barbecue grills for use by guests are on site, too.

Oceanfront • Rooms and Efficiencies
Heated Pool and Jacuzzi
Oceanfront Pool • Family Oriented

Sea Ranch Motel
OCEAN FRONT MOTEL www.visitsearanch.com
800-849-8977
910-458-8681

Golden Sands Motel   **$$ -$$$**
1211 S. Lake Park Blvd., Carolina Beach
(910) 458-8334
www.goldensandsmotel.com

You couldn't ask for more — immaculate, comfortable, spacious and attractive accommodations with a fantastic oceanfront location. Each of the 115 tastefully decorated rooms is air conditioned and has a refrigerator, microwave, telephone, coffee maker, iron, sofa and cable TV. A great feature is the split design offered in many of the rooms: two queen beds separated by a half wall, which is perfect for families with children or two couples staying together.

Hotel guests can choose from queen, king or efficiency-style rooms. Most face the ocean, and all have balconies or porches. On site is a popular seafood restaurant with tables out on the pier, where you'll also find a Tiki Bar. Golden Sands has a sparkling-blue outdoor pool, a year-round indoor pool and a great gift shop. Complimentary coffee is served in the lobby every morning starting at 6:30 AM. There is also a meeting room available.

Guy Johnson Motel   **$$**
235 Carolina Beach Ave. N., Carolina Beach
(910) 458-8105

Conveniently located one block from the boardwalk, next to the charter boat docks and across the street from the beach, this cozy motel has been a Carolina Beach fixture since the early 1940s, and family-owned since 1960. With a variety of amenities, the rooms and apartments are a boon to families, something for which the friendly owners pride themselves. Small kitchenettes are in the majority of rooms and the others have coffee makers, refrigerators and microwaves. Three rooms sleep up to four people. The remainder of the motel is apartments, which accommodate three to six people each. The rooms and apartments are exceptionally clean, and the staff even washes the bedspreads between guests. Other amenities include cable TV with HBO, rockers and lounge chairs on the street-side patios, and a refreshing outdoor pool.

Sandi Beach Inn   **$$$**
317 Fort Fisher Blvd. N., Kure Beach
(910) 458-5906

Ideal for a week at the beach with the kids or a relaxing weekend respite for you and that special person, Sandi Beach Inn is clean, comfortable, cozy and convenient. The six completely equipped mini-apartments are just a few steps from the ocean and not much farther to popular restaurants and Kure Beach Pier. Each two-room suite sleeps six and has a private bath with tub/shower, cable TV with HBO, water heater, heat, air conditioning, electric power supply and full-sized kitchen. Upstairs units have balconies with an ocean view. Off-season rates are available.

Seven Seas Inn
Oceanfront

910-458-8122

Rooms & Efficiencies	Non-Smoking Rooms
Interconnecting Units	Outdoor Grill
Two-Room Suites	Covered Picnic Areas
Ground Level Rooms	Guest Laundry Facilities
Limited Handicap Rooms	Ample Parking

Close To Restaurants - Kure Beach Fishing Pier - NC Aquarium

130 N. Fort Fisher Blvd. • P.O. Box 104
Kure Beach, NC 28449
Reservations: 866-773-2746
www.sevenseasinn.com

From here you're only a few steps away from everything you need for an unforgettable vacation. Each of the 16 comfortable rooms has air conditioning, refrigerator, microwave, dataport, 27-inch TV with cable and telephone. The motel's oceanfront location features a recreation area with pool, decks and outdoor showers. It's open year round. (Also see our chapter on Restaurants.)

Seven Seas Inn $$-$$$$
130 Fort Fisher Blvd., Kure Beach
(910) 458-8122, (866) 773-2746
www.sevenseasinn.com

The Seven Seas is a family-owned and operated inn on the oceanfront in Kure Beach, consisting of three buildings with oceanfront, ocean view and pool view. The inn has 32 clean, comfortable rooms in a variety of configurations that are remodeled and updated annually for the comfort of its guests. Large efficiencies, two-room efficiencies, interconnecting units and standard motel accommodations are roomy and equipped with twins, doubles, queen and king-sized beds. Non-smoking and limited handicapped rooms are available. All rooms have telephones, refrigerators, cable TV with complimentary HBO, and individually controlled air conditioning and heating units. The well-kept grounds include pool facilities with two shaded gazebos, a courtyard, a picnic area with a grill, benches and extensive landscaping. Small children, seniors and non-swimmers will appreciate a second three-foot-deep pool with seating all around. Restaurants, shops and the popular Kure Beach Fishing Pier are within a short walk of the Inn. When entering Kure Beach by the main road from the north (U.S. 421), look for Seven Seas Inn on the left with its many beautiful Agave plants.

Sea Ranch Motel $$
1123 S. Lake Park Blvd., Carolina Beach
(910) 458-8681, (800) 849-8977
www.visitsearanch.com

One of the most popular oceanfront motels on the beach, Sea Ranch offers both standard sleeping rooms and efficiencies, smoking and non-smoking. While most rooms have two full-sized beds, some singles with one full bed are available, as are some oceanfront efficiencies with queen beds. Every room has a refrigerator, television, telephone and air conditioning. Efficiency units have full kitchens that include stove, microwave, coffee maker, pots, dishes and silverware. Whether poolside or overlooking the ocean, these accommodations are clean, comfortable and inviting. An outstanding feature of the Sea Ranch Motel is its large heated pool and adjacent oversized Jacuzzi, which has room for 20. Both are located within a windowed brick enclosure. An oceanfront pool with a slide is great for small children as its depth ranges from just 2 to 6 feet. Guests may also enjoy a poolside gazebo. A relaxing retreat, the Sea Ranch has a wide sandy beach with private access walk.

SeaWitch Motel & Cafe $$-$$$
224 Carolina Beach Ave. N., Carolina Beach
(910) 458-8564

If you're looking for the ultimate in relaxation, superb dining, beach pleasures, pool and quality accommodations all in one spot, SeaWitch is just right for you. Forget driving.

Brunswick County Beaches

SOUTHPORT/OAK ISLAND

Blue Water Point Marina Resort $$
57th Pl. and W. Beach Dr., Oak Island
(910) 278-1230, (888) 634-9005

Located on the west end of Oak Island, this small, comfortable 28-room motel is especially convenient to boaters, while just across W. Beach Drive is a boardwalk to the beach strand. The motel offers rooms with waterway views, two double beds, showers, TVs and telephones. Various patios and sundecks provide a fine sunset view. The marina rents floating docks and boat slips with a water depth of 5 feet at mean low tide. (See our Marinas and the Intracoastal Waterway chapter.) City-owned boat ramps adjoining the marina are available to use for free. Other amenities include an adjoining restaurant and lounge (open from February 14 to November 1), a ship's store, a tackle shop and kayak rentals. Deep-sea fishing is available on two charter boats. (See our Fishing chapter). Sunset Cruises aboard the 60-foot head boat are offered as well. Call for reservations.

Captain's Cove Motel

- 42 Rooms
- Efficiency Apartments
- Color Cable TV
- Room Phones
- Pool
- Beach Access

SMALL PETS WELCOME!

Daily • Weekly
Long Term Rates

6401 E. Oak Island Dr. Oak Island, NC 28465

910-278-6026

www.realpages.com/captainscove

Captain's Cove Motel   **$-$$**
6401 E. Oak Island Dr., Oak Island
(910) 278-6026
www.realpages.com/captainscove

Captain's Cove, family owned and operated for 30 years, is located on the main street in Oak Island. Rooms open out onto the central parking court and are surrounded by beautiful oak trees. All rooms contain refrigerators, microwaves and coffeemakers. Efficiency apartments are available in addition to the standard rooms. The great things about Captain's Cove are the quiet family atmosphere, the beach access, a pool in a sunny location and the fact that restaurants and shopping are within walking distance. Captain's Cove is small-pet friendly as well.

Hampton Inn   **$-$$$**
5181 Southport Supply Rd., Southport
(910) 454-0016,
(800) HAMPTON (426-7866)

A Circle of Excellence Award winner, the Hampton Inn Southport, which opened in June 2000, has been rated in the top 10 percent of almost 1,300 Hampton Inns by Hampton inn guests. It is conveniently located near two shopping centers, halfway between downtown Southport and Oak Island and less than a 10-minute drive from the Brunswick County Airport. Eighty home-like guest rooms are available, containing king or queen-sized beds, A/C, TV, coffee makers, hairdryers, dataports and voice mail. Some rooms contain a microwave and refrigerator as well. Available upon request are cribs, rollaway beds and refrigerators. Nonsmok-

ing and handicapped-accessible rooms are available. Continental breakfast is provided in the well-appointed dining area. The inn offers an outdoor pool, a fitness center and a business center with free high-speed Internet access. Group rates are available, and the meeting room seats up to 40.

The Inn at South Harbour Village   **$$$$**
5005 O'Quinn Blvd., Southport
(910) 454-7500, (800) 454-0815

The spectacular waterway views from the decks adjoining the nine suites in The Inn at South Harbour Village are reason enough to stay here, whether it be for a romantic getaway, a honeymoon or even a meeting. The view inside is lovely as well. A golden glow permeates the plush ambiance of every room. All suites contain a full kitchen; two have Jacuzzis, one has a bath and a half, and one has two baths and a family room as well as a living room. All guests receive a free round of golf on the South Harbor Golf Course, a lovely par-three executive course. Within walking distance you will find Joseph's Italian Bistro, a fantastic restaurant. Ask about extended stays.

Island Resort & Inn   **$$-$$$**
500 Ocean Dr., Oak Island
(910) 278-5644

With a direct private beach access and an oceanfront deck and gazebo, Island Resort & Inn provides lovely ocean views. The inn features single rooms that include refrigerators,

The quiet beaches of Brunswick County beckon travelers to stay a while.

photo: Peter Doran

microwaves, coffee makers and complimentary coffee, and apartments consisting of one or two bedrooms with full kitchens including stoves, refrigerators, microwaves and dishwashers. Island Resort offers a pool and a hot tub. Ask about wedding and anniversary packages.

Ocean Crest Motel $$
1417 E. Beach Dr., Oak Island
(910) 278-3333

The owners and staff of the Ocean Crest Motel will make you feel welcome from the moment you arrive, and repeat guests just keep coming back. The location is unique to Oak Island because Ocean Crest is located right on the beach, not across the street. The

Before entering that inviting pool, please shower or hose yourself thoroughly. Sand, soil and sunscreen are very detrimental to pool filters, liners, tiles and pumping equipment. Oily surfaces can harbor germs as well.

motel offers a swimming pool, guest laundry and an affordable gift shop with a line of tropical apparel, jewelry, T-shirts, hats, pool and beach towels. This 62-room motel is situated adjacent to a fishing pier and a restaurant, making it an ideal spot for vacation accommodations. Especially attractive is the "Stay for Seven - Pay for 5" special weekly rate available year round.

Ocean Crest Motel offers a room choice of oceanfront with or without a private balcony, as well as standard rooms which are not oceanfront. Regardless of the room you choose, you are literally steps away from the beach. The most requested rooms are oceanfront rooms so be sure to make your reservation early for those. All rooms are updated, airy and bright, reminiscent of the tropics. Each is equipped with a ceiling fan, most with two double beds (sorry, no queens or kings), air conditioning, small fridge, coffeemaker, expanded cable and free local calls. Most rooms also have a small table and chairs. A limited number of both ground level or handicapped-accessible rooms are also available. The motel also rents one spacious, multi-level, oceanfront townhouse on a weekly basis only. It sleeps eight, has two bedrooms, 2.5 baths, queen sofa-bed, private balconies, whirlpool bath and laundry. Please note that the "Stay for 7 - Pay for 5" rate does not apply to the townhouse.

Ocean Crest is a couples and family-oriented motel known for quiet getaways and family get-togethers. No pets are allowed. All guests must have a credit card in order to make a confirmed reservation and at check-in even if guests pay in cash. Guests must be a minimum of 25 years of age unless accompanied by a parent.

Riverside Motel $
103 W. Bay St., Southport
(910) 457-6986

This small, eight-room establishment situated on the waterfront between the Ships Chandler Restaurant and the Cape Fear Pilot Tower commands an excellent view of Southport's harbor and the mouth of the Cape Fear River where it meets the sea. Both Old Baldy and the Oak Island Lighthouse can be seen from this spot. The motel was totally renovated in 2002, and the cozy double-occupancy rooms are equipped with either two double beds or queen-sized beds, ceiling fans, microwave ovens, cable TV, refrigerators, coffeemakers and telephones (local calls are free). The location on the Riverside in the historic district is conducive to strolls through the scenic town for meals, shopping or sightseeing.

Southport Comfort Suites $-$$$
4963 Southport-Supply Rd., Southport
(910) 454-7444

At Southport Comfort Suites you will find the quality you have come to expect from Choice Hotels — and more. General Manager Brian Stone is especially proud of the upbeat employee attitudes in all service areas, which is evident as well in the number of return guests. Centrally located between Southport and Oak Island, this hotel is convenient to activities and events in both places. Standard amenities include full length mirror, pulsating shower head, curved shower rod, hair dryer, refrigerator, coffee maker, microwave, ironing equipment, high-speed Internet service, access to an exercise room and an outdoor pool in season. Available for a fee is local laundry service and a meeting room that

seats up to 45. The complimentary Deluxe Continental Breakfast, which includes bagels and waffles, can be eaten in the sit down dining area if you prefer. All veterans and active-duty military personnel are eligible for an active-duty military rate.

HOLDEN BEACH

Gray Gull Motel $
3263 Holden Beach Rd. S.W., Holden Beach
(910) 842-6775

This family-owned motel, the only one at Holden Beach, is very well-maintained and courteously run. Each of the 17 carpeted rooms has cable TV and a telephone as well as easy access to the outdoor pool and picnic tables. The Gray Gull is on the mainland side of the Intracoastal Waterway, just minutes from the beach. The office is in the hardware store next door, where anglers can also buy tackle. Cancellations require 24-hour notice.

OCEAN ISLE BEACH

Causeway Inn $-$$
12 Causeway Dr., Ocean Isle Beach
(910) 579-9001

The Causeway Motel has 35 very clean rooms. Each room is equipped with double beds, individual air conditioning and heat, telephones, refrigerators, microwaves and cable TV. There are three handicapped-accessible first-floor rooms. The outdoor pool and sun deck are close to the parking lot, and the beach is only 200 yards away. This family-oriented motel is also convenient to dining and entertainment, including mini-golf and the waterslide, much of it within walking distance.

The Islander Inn $$-$$$
57 W. First St., Ocean Isle Beach
(910) 575-7000, (888) 325-4753
www.islanderinn.com

The Islander Inn is an oceanfront family hotel that offers 70 beautifully appointed guest rooms recently renovated for your enjoyment. All oceanfront rooms have a private balcony from which to view spectacular sunsets. Rooms include your choice of two queen beds or one king-size bed. All rooms offer a wet bar and refrigerator, a microwave and in-room coffee service, a remote control 25-inch TV with HBO, a telephone with voice

OCEAN-FRONT, SOUTHERN HOSPITALITY

AAA 3 Diamond Rated

Oceanfront at
57 W. First Street
Ocean Isle Beach, NC 28469
TOLL-FREE 888-325-ISLE (4753)
910-575-7000 • fax: 575-7075

The Islander Inn

look for our specials:
www.islanderinn.com

Newly Renovated
Indoor Heated Pool & Jacuzzi
Outdoor Oceanfront Pool
Expanded Continental Breakfast
High Speed Internet
Pristine White Sand Beach

mail and complimentary high-speed Internet access. The Islander Inn offers an expanded continental breakfast daily in the pool side breakfast room. Guests can enjoy the outdoor oceanfront pool with a sun deck and an indoor heated pool with Jacuzzi. The recent addition of an exercise room will keep your routine in place while away from home. The Islander Inn also offers handicapped-accessible rooms. Inquire about AAA and AARP discounts and off-season rates.

Ocean Isle Inn $$-$$$
37 W. First St., Ocean Isle Beach
(910) 579-0750, (800) 352-5988

At Ocean Isle Inn you can gaze at the beautiful Atlantic from your private oceanfront balcony or experience the impressive view of the Intracoastal Waterway and scenic marshlands from a sound-view room. Activities are offered for every member of the family from fishing, to golfing, to relaxing by the pool.

For your added pleasure the Ocean Isle Inn has recently upgraded the facilities to include accommodations tastefully decorated with handmade teak furniture and beautifully tiled floors, new quilted-top plush beds and new interior décor with bright tropical colors. All rooms are air-conditioned and feature in-room coffee service, refrigerator, microwave, wet bar, hairdryer, color cable television, dataport phones with voice mail and high-speed wireless Internet access. In addition, Ocean Isle Inn offers daily housekeeping service, complimentary deluxe continental breakfast, a heated indoor pool and an ocean side pool, a Jacuzzi spa and a private beach access.

Proximity to Myrtle Beach and Wilmington make the Ocean Isle Inn an ideal location for your next business meeting or group. The Ocean Isle Inn features an oceanfront conference facility that can accommodate up to 60 people and can be split into a meeting room with adjacent breakout space. An on-site event director is available to assist you in planning your next big meeting or group outing. And speaking of groups, Ocean Isle Inn is a perfect location for that family reunion or beachside wedding you have been dreaming of. (See our Wedding Planning chapter.)

Oceanfront On Ocean Isle Beach

Relax in oceanfront luxury overlooking our breathtaking island beach, palm trees and lush subtropical gardens. Choose from deluxe rooms, one to three bedroom suites (complete with kitchens and livingrooms) and 4, 5 & 6 bedroom Resort Houses. Enjoy daily housekeeping, complimentary hot breakfast buffet, three pools (one indoor), whirlpool spas, exercise room, shuffleboard, bikes. The Garden Bar and the poolside Tiki Bar feature light dining and mixed beverages. Golf packages on over 100 of the Carolinas' finest courses. Ask about our Free Summer Golf!

Highest Rated (AAA) Accommodations on Ocean Isle Beach!

800-334-3581

Book online: www.TheWinds.com

Be sure to inquire about midweek Supersavers discounts during the off-season, weekly rates, and AAA and AARP discounts. Handicapped-accessible facilities and elevators are also available.

The Winds Oceanfront Inn & Suites **$$-$$$**
310 E. First St., Ocean Isle Beach
(910) 579-6275, (800) 334-3581
www.thewinds.com

This oceanfront resort is an excellent choice for its range of accommodations and prices. Studios, mini-suites, deluxe rooms, one- and two-bedroom suites, and resort houses with four, five or six bedrooms are all richly appointed and comfortable. Some of the resort houses have private, outdoor Jacuzzis, many accommodations have indoor whirlpools and kitchen facilities. The grounds are beautifully landscaped with 11 varieties of palm trees, banana trees and lush flowering plants nestled among meandering boardwalks and decks. A wide expanse of beach provides for such activities as sunning, castle building or searching for seashells.

The Winds has a heated pool indoors, two outdoor pools, two outdoor Jacuzzis, an exercise room, beach bocce, shuffleboard, volleyball, bike rentals and nearby tennis. The Garden Bar Restaurant serves a light menu featuring salads, sandwiches and fresh-baked pizza and mixed beverages, including margaritas and daiquiris. A complimentary hot breakfast buffet is served daily. Honeymoon and golf packages (available at more than 110 championship courses) are easily arranged. In addition, from June through August, free summer golf programs are available at over two dozen courses. Some rooms are handicapped accessible. Ask about special off-season packages.

SUNSET BEACH

The Sunset Inn **$$-$$$$**
9 North Shore Dr., Sunset Beach
(910) 575-1000, (888) 575-1001

The Sunset Inn opened its doors to the beauty of the saltwater marsh and island life in June 2000. The honey-colored hardwood floors in the entrance and living area shine softly in the light that filters through the large windows. Here, continental breakfast is served on a lace-covered table every morning from 8 until 10 AM, or you can choose to have your morning meal in the living room or in the privacy of your own room. There are 14 rooms, each with a different theme and decor. All rooms have a king-size bed, wet bar, refrigerator, love seat and private screened porch with rockers. The four grand rooms each have a Jacuzzi plus a shower in their private baths, and the 10 standard rooms have showers. One handicapped-accessible room and two connecting rooms are available. Come experience the quiet comfort for yourself. Special rates are available off season and weekdays. AAA discounts apply.

SHALLOTTE

Shallotte Microtel Inn & Suites **$-$$**
4646 East Coast Ln., Shallotte
(910) 755-6444

Strategically located in Shallotte, this brand-new, 62-room hotel provides a haven for business and vacation travelers alike. Beaches are 5 to 8 miles away, six top golf courses are within 5 miles, historic Wilmington is a short 25-mile drive away, and Myrtle Beach is 15 minutes to the south. Room amenities include dataports and free local calls, and there are non-smoking rooms. Coffee and tea service in the lobby, copy and fax service, and guest laundry on-site are some of Microtel's special features. Guests can plan their side trips over the free continental breakfast or by the outdoor pool.

Topsail Island Area

Breezeway Motel and Restaurant **$$**
636 Channel Blvd., Topsail Beach
(910) 328-7751, (800) 548-46949

This vintage, soundfront motel, with a restaurant on the premises, features amenities for the whole family, including a swimming pool, fishing pier and boat dock. The many returning guests continue to enjoy the beautiful scenery, sunsets and easy access to sandbars for swimming or shelling in the sound. The 47 rooms offer a choice of two double beds, a king bed or efficiencies, and many rooms have microwaves and refrigerators. All rooms have cable TV and daily maid service. An ice machine and complimentary coffee are offered in the office. See our Restaurants chapter for information about the Breezeway Restaurant.

The rich history of the area can be found everywhere.

photo: Cache, student of DREAMS Center for Arts Education

Island Inn $-$$
302 North Shore Dr., Surf City
(910) 328-2341, (800) 573-2566

The Island Inn, located directly across from the beach, has an oceanfront deck and chaise lounges on the beach. There is also a pool on the premises. Accommodations include 20 motel rooms, each with a refrigerator, microwave and coffeemaker. Island Inn is located within two blocks of downtown Surf City's restaurants, shopping and fishing pier. It's open April through October.

Jolly Roger Inn $-$$$
803 Ocean Blvd., Topsail Beach
(910) 328-4616, (800) 633-3196

The Jolly Roger is on the oceanfront, on the same premises as the Jolly Roger fishing pier and centrally located in downtown Topsail Beach — what more could a vacationer want? Jolly Roger Inn has 65 rooms that include bedrooms, efficiencies and suites, some with a kitchen. Open year-round, the inn offers daily, weekly and seasonal rates.

Queens Grant Condominiums $$-$$$$
926 N. Anderson, Topsail Beach
(910) 328-2468, (800) 326-0747

Queens Grant offers oceanfront and soundfront condominiums with your choice of two or three bedrooms. Units have a variety of amenities, including microwave ovens, washers and dryers, TVs, VCRs and phones. Located on the property are a swimming pool, hot tub, tennis court, boat dockage, fish-cleaning station, clubhouse and picnic/recreation area with grills. This is a pet-free, smoke-free environment with a two-night minimum stay.

Sea Vista Motel $-$$
1521 Ocean Blvd., Topsail Beach
(910) 328-2171, (800) 732-8478

Guests, many of whom return regularly, are considered friends at the Sea Vista Motel. The tradition of friendly service continues at this oceanfront motel that features large rooms, full-size appliances, cable TV, balconies and individually controlled air conditioning. Individual rooms are privately

Topsail Island

Holiday Inn

EXPRESS®
HOTEL & SUITES

1565 Highway 210, P.O. Box 1160
Sneads Ferry, NC 28460-1160
910-327-8282
1-800-HOLIDAY
www.hiexpress.com/sneadsferrync

FREE High-Speed Internet • FREE Deluxe Continental Breakfast

owned, so decor and furnishings vary. There are 17 rooms with refrigerator and microwave, eight efficiencies, five mini-efficiencies and two apartments. Golf packages, romantic getaways and family reunions are some of the services offered. Discounts apply for seniors and seven-day stays, and children younger than 12 stay free. Pets are allowed with a $30 surcharge. This motel closes for the winter and re-opens March 1.

St. Regis Resort $$-$$$$
2000 New River Inlet Rd.,
North Topsail Beach
(910) 328-4975, (800) 682-4882

This vacation resort offers condominium units with one to three bedrooms, all with two full baths, both oceanfront and ocean-view. Each unit is individually owned and is tastefully furnished. In addition to clean, un-crowded beaches, you'll find a fitness center, a sauna, steam showers, tennis courts, shuffleboard, and indoor and outdoor pools

---

i *In the event you have a health-care situation or emergency, we have 911 service in the area, excellent hospitals and a number of urgent-care centers. Your hotel or motel staff can assist you with transportation, if necessary, and can direct you to the closest provider. Also see our Healthcare chapter for a list of medical centers and hospitals.*

---

with a Jacuzzi. A small convenience store and pizza restaurant are on the premises. It's open year round.

Surfside Motel $-$$
124 N. Shore Dr., Surf City
(910) 328-4099, (877) 404-9162

Surf City's only oceanfront motel is conveniently located downtown within walking distance of restaurants, shopping and the fishing pier. The large deck is a great place to relax, enjoy the sun and listen to the soothing sounds of the ocean. The seven oceanfront rooms have microwaves and refrigerators. All 13 rooms have cable TV, heat and air conditioning.

Tiffany's Motel $-$$
1502 N. New River Dr., Surf City
(910) 328-1397, (800) 758-3818

Mention pride in ownership, and Tiffany's Motel immediately comes to mind. Owners Bob and Ann Smith continually work to upgrade this property and recently added a new section to bring their total to 37 rooms. All rooms have a refrigerator and microwave, and the new rooms also have coffee makers and hairdryers. The three pools and deck are a great place to relax and forget your cares. There are five wheelchair-accessible rooms with handicapped-accessible showers and bathroom rails. Tiffany's Motel offers special weekly rates, five-night packages and group rates.

**Topsail Island Holiday Inn Express
Hotel & Suites**   **$-$$$$**
1565 N.C. Hwy. 210, Sneads Ferry
(910) 327-8282, (800) 465-4329
www.hiexpress.com/sneadsferrync

Opened in 2001, this hotel has a large outdoor pool and a great room with a fireplace and wonderful scenic views of North Shore Golf Course Country Club and the Intracoastal Waterway. In-room amenities include refrigerators, free high-speed Internet access, coffee makers, irons and ironing boards, hairdryers, two-line speaker phones with dataports and color televisions. Out of a total of 68 rooms, there are 15 suites with king-size beds and pull-out sofas, refrigerators and microwave ovens. Some rooms have whirlpool tubs. Guests can enjoy a free deluxe continental breakfast bar featuring fresh fruit, cereals, pastries and assorted breads. Located on the golf course, this hotel is just a short drive over the high-rise bridge to North Topsail Beach. Seasonal rates apply. AAA and AARP discounts and government rates are available as well as wedding and golf packages and group rates. The hotel has an elevator, is ADA compliant and is open year round.

Villa Capriani Resort   **$$$$**
790 New River Inlet Rd., N. Topsail Beach
(910) 328-1900, (800) 934-2400

Relax in this beautiful oceanfront resort complex with the Atlantic Ocean at your door. Villas include one, two and three-bedroom units, either oceanfront or ocean-view. A picturesque multilevel courtyard features several swimming pools and a whirlpool. Tanning decks and a cabana offer a spectacular view of the ocean. The Sea Turtle at the Villa, the onsite restaurant, serves fresh seafood and Italian dishes. The Villa Capriani Resort is open year round. There is a seven-day minimum stay in high season.

BED & BREAKFASTS AND SMALL INNS

Even though we've entered the third millennium, technology has yet to produce a machine allowing us to travel backwards in time, back to the days of horse-drawn carriages, sitting on the porch, sipping mint juleps and watching passersby. Until technology catches up with our yen for bygone days, there are always bed and breakfasts or small inns to quench our thirst for romance and escapism.

Despite, or maybe because of, Wilmington's small-town charm, the area offers travelers outstanding bed and breakfasts plus a number of wonderful small inns. Most feature fabulous antiques and have unique, fascinating histories, decor and gardens. Some are as casual as a pajama party, while others are steeped in Victorian elegance. Several beach bed and breakfasts invite you to enjoy the ocean breezes, dine overlooking the sea, wade in the surf and stroll on the sand. You'll find quite a different feel here, one that is definitely easygoing and informal.

As a point of information, bed and breakfasts differ from small inns when it comes to serving food to guests. If you like a full, cooked breakfast served at a given time usually in a common dining area, a bed and breakfast is for you. On the other hand, an inn usually provides only a continental breakfast, if any at all. Some inns have kitchenette facilities so that guests may prepare their own morning meal; some have variations on the breakfast offering, but none serve a formal meal at an appointed hour. Another difference between an inn and a bed and breakfast is the location. An inn is almost always "in town" and may be associated with a pub, restaurant or have a bar on the premises. Not so with a bed and breakfast, though some offer a self-service refrigerator for wine and beer or soft drinks.

Wherever you choose to stay, your hosts surely will be knowledgeable about the area and can assist you with directions and in making reservations for shows, meals, charters and golf packages.

Bed and breakfasts and inns typically do not allow pets, smoking indoors or very young children unless by prior arrangement. Most establishments accept major credit cards and personal checks, especially for making payment in advance. Many charge a fee for cancellations, so be sure to ask about the policy. Also note that often they require a full weekend lodging, especially during the Azalea Festival in April and Riverfest in October (see our Annual Events chapter for information on these events).

PRICE CODE

Since prices are subject to change without notice, we provide only price guidelines based on per-night rates during the summer (high season). Guidelines do not reflect the 7 percent state/county and 1 to 6 percent room occupancy tax (taxes may vary by municipality or county). Some establishments offer lower rates during the off-season, but always confirm rates and necessary amenities before reserving. It may behoove you to inquire about corporate discounts even if they are not mentioned in our descriptions.

$	$75 or less
$$	$76 to $120
$$$	$121 to $150
$$$$	$151 and more

Wilmington

Camellia Cottage   **$$$-$$$$**
118 S. Fourth St., Wilmington
(910) 763-9171
www.camelliacottage.net

Standing on a brick-paved street four blocks from the river, Camellia Cottage is a richly appointed, high-peaked Queen Anne shingle home built in 1889. Once the home of

Camellia Cottage

BED & BREAKFAST

Friendly Luxury

Innkeepers: Paula Tirrito & Steven Skavroneck
Featuring A 3 Course Breakfast
Pets Welcome

118 S. Fourth Street at Cottage Lane
Wilmington, NC 28401
(910) 763-9171 • Fax: (910) 362-8791

Located in the Historic District • www.camelliacottage.net
1-866-728-5272

prominent Wilmington artist Henry J. MacMillan, it still houses some of his work. In fact, artwork abounds throughout Camellia Cottage, from murals on the wrap-around piazza to hand-painted fireplace tiles.

Camellia Cottage offers three spacious guest rooms and one suite, each with its own character. Queen-size, antique-style beds, private baths and gas-fired hearths are standard. Morning coffee is provided. A sumptuous three-course breakfast is served any time up until 10 AM. The parlor is always available to guests.

This charming bed and breakfast is within walking distance of many fine restaurants and shops. A short drive will take you to the beaches, Battleship North Carolina, Cameron Art Museum and North Carolina Aquarium. Winter rates and discounts for long-term stays apply.

Dragonfly Inn   **$$**
1914 Market St., Wilmington
(910) 762-7025, (866) 762-7025
www.dragonflyinn.com

"Comfortable, naturally" is the motto of this casual-style bed and breakfast. With its oversized chairs, natural decor and homemade goodies, Dragonfly Inn is indeed a home away from home. In all the bedrooms, guests will find fleece robes and slippers, homemade aromatherapy candles and homemade scented soaps, lotions and shampoos in the bathroom. The Spirit of the Sea room has a TV, CD player, phone and king-sized

bed topped with pillows. A fireplace with gas logs adds a touch of romance. The private bath continues the ocean theme with a seashell wreath and ocean pictures. A two-bedroom suite includes the Spirit of the Forest and the Spirit of the Earth rooms, however, each room can be rented separately. The Forest room includes a TV, CD player and queen-sized bed. The adjoining private bath with claw-foot tub and shower leads to the suite's private tree-top balcony. The Spirit of the Earth room, with Native-American decor, features a king-sized bed, gas fireplace, CD player, TV and phone.

Dragonfly Inn
Bed & Breakfast

1914 Market St. Wilmington, NC

"Comfortable, naturally"

Call us toll free at: 1-866-762-7025
Or visit us at: www.dragonflyinn.com

FRONT STREET INN

ENJOY BEAUTIFUL SUNSETS FROM THE BALCONY

TWELVE CHARMING SUITES

· SPA TUBS, BALCONIES, FIREPLACES
· ALL WITH: PRIVATE BATHS, WET BAR
· SOL Y SOMBRA BAR / BREAKFAST ROOM
· EXERCISE AREA, OFF STREET PARKING
· WIRELESS

215 SOUTH FRONT STREET
WILMINGTON, N.C. 28401
RESERVATIONS: (800) 336-8184

www.frontstreetinn.com

POLLY AND RICHARD SALINETTI
PROPRIETORS

The welcoming foyer, with a dragonfly stained-glass door, leads to the living room, decorated with comfortable furniture. A reclining chair that heats up and vibrates waits to sooth weary bodies after hours of shopping and touring. There are also books, games, a TV/VCR and DVD player, a gas fireplace and an antique piano. A full breakfast is served to guests in the dining room. The sitting area on the second floor offers refreshments and snacks. Hot coffee is brought to your door every morning, and homemade desserts are available in the evenings. Inquire about winter, senior, military, student and multi-day discounts.

Front Street Inn   **$$$-$$$$**
215 S. Front St., Wilmington
(910) 762-6442, (800) 336-8184
www.frontstreetinn.com

Front Street Inn greets guests with a natural, understated ambiance and Bohemian charm. The Inn features original art, hand-painted 14-foot high walls, maple floors and exposed brick. The 12 rooms and suites are named and decorated according to their inspirations, such as Claude Monet, Pearl S. Buck, Rudyard Kipling and Georgia O'Keeffe. They are beautifully appointed with every amenity a traveler would love, including private baths, waffle-weave robes, hand-milled soap, fresh flowers, wet bars, TVs, CD/DVD players, dataports and wireless high-speed Internet access. Some suites have large spa tubs, multi-jet showers and fireplaces; the Hemingway Suite also has a private balcony.

The European breakfast, served buffet-style all morning, offers a variety of healthful (or sinful) selections. Always you'll find coffee, fresh fruit, cold cuts, cheese, croissants, biscotti and muffins. Room service is available. The Sol y Sombra Bar, with its famous handmade cork bar, offers juices, waters, sodas, beer, wine, champagne and snacks. The game room and fitness area in the lower level are wonderful for small groups, family gatherings or informal business meetings. An intimate private dining room (with catering kitchen) and porch are available for private gatherings of up to 25 people. Polly and Richard Salinetti, along with their staff, will assist you with anything from restaurant reservations to special requests (how about chocolates, in-house massage, flowers or champagne?) They also offer spa and romance packages.

The Inn occupies the renovated Salvation Army building, the first in the Carolinas, built in 1923. It is up the hill from Chandler's Wharf and the Riverwalk with picturesque views from the second-floor balconies. Convenient

i *B&Bs and small inns range in style from Victorian elegance to beach casual. Some allow pets or children, but many don't. Be sure and ask their policy when making your reservation, and choose the style that best suits your needs.*

Graystone Inn

9 Luxurious Rooms

Named one of America's "Top 10 Most Romantic Inns" by American Historic Inns

AAA Four Diamond Award

910-763-2000
1-888-763-4773
100 S. 3rd St.
Wilmington, NC
28401
www.graystoneinn.com

Select Registry

off-street parking is provided. Children are welcome, but please, no pets.

Graystone Inn $$$-$$$$
100 S. Third St., Wilmington
(910) 763-2000
www.graystoneinn.com

This stately historic landmark is one of the city's most prestigious inns, its rich, spacious interior inviting guests to enjoy an ambience of relaxed elegance. Built in 1905–06, Graystone Inn was originally "The Bridgers Mansion." Extensive renovations during the late 1990s restored the home's turn-of-the-century magnificence and added modern-day conveniences.

The vast ground floor includes an incredible library paneled in Honduran mahogany furnished with comfortable chairs, a sofa and a game table. Here you can relax in front of the fireplace and enjoy your morning coffee or evening glass of wine. A full cooked breakfast is served each morning in the beautiful formal dining room featuring mahogany dining tables, English floral wallpaper, a fireplace and period antiques.

From the great entrance hall, a grand Renaissance-style staircase made of hand-carved oak rises three stories, culminating in the ballroom. Nine guest rooms offer the visitor varied luxury including private, en suite baths (several with claw-foot tubs), period antiques, fine pima cotton linens, towels and robes, telephone, WiFi and cable TV. Five of the rooms have fireplaces and four offer up-graded bathroom facilities such as separate one or two-person showers and claw-foot or champagne tubs. Three rooms have king-sized beds, while the rest offer queens. Room rates include a full gourmet breakfast and beverage service throughout the day. An on-site fitness room is available.

Outdoors, the garden and terraces are exquisite. Frequently used as a set for motion pictures and television, Graystone Inn is unquestionably one of the most impressive structures in Wilmington. The Inn's location is ideal for walking to all downtown attractions and is convenient to the Riverwalk with its popular restaurants and shops.

welcome to the
HOGE - WOOD HOUSE
bed & breakfast

407 SOUTH THIRD STREET
WILMINGTON, NC 28401
910-762-5299

WWW.HOGEWOODHOUSE.COM

Enjoy Exquisite Southern Hospitality at Wilmington's Most Elegant B&B!

- *Local Specialty and Gourmet Amenities*
- *Weekly Corporate Rates and Military Discounts* • *TVs, CD Players and Wireless Internet*

"Chosen As One of The Top 10 Romantic B&B's in America!"

MURCHISON HOUSE
—— *Bed & Breakfast* ——
Experience Exquisite Southern Hospitality

WWW.MURCHISONHOUSE.COM
910.762.6626
305 SOUTH THIRD STREET
WILMINGTON, NORTH CAROLINA, 28401

Graystone Inn makes a prestigious venue for first-class weddings, receptions, reunions, birthdays, meetings and other events for up to 150 people. Choose the dining room, sitting room, entire ground floor and veranda or ballroom for your special occasion.

**Hoge-Wood House Bed and Breakfast $$$
407 S. Third St., Wilmington
(910) 762-5299
www.hogewoodhouse.com**

The Hoge-Wood House offers three upstairs guest rooms with private bathrooms. Each room has cable TV, VCR, DVD, telephone and high speed wireless Internet. There is also a refrigerator stocked with beverages and snacks. The Hoge-Wood House is exceedingly casual and comfortable. You'll

find fresh flowers and art throughout, and the downstairs parlor is cozy and inviting. The library, with its ceiling-high bookshelves, is ideal for relaxing with a good book or listening to music. It offers a supply of videos and DVDs, puzzles and an extensive collection of CDs, long-play records and seven-inch reel-to-reel tapes for your enjoyment.

The inn's affable proprietors, Page and Larry Tootoo (pronounced toe-toe), emphasize flexibility in their service. Page is a Registered Nurse who can easily accommodate special dietary needs. Full country breakfasts are served on seasonal ceramic and china dinnerware with silverware on a classic library table. (Tip: Larry makes a great pecan waffle and Page makes homemade syrups and jams.) Coffee lovers will appreciate the Kona coffee brewed daily.

Guest rooms are named for the Tootoo's children. Katherine's room offers a king-sized oak mission-style bed, while Leilani's room features a queen-sized cherry sleigh bed and a Jacuzzi. Joshua and Gabriel's room offers a queen-sized bed in a whimsical setting. Bicycles, fishing poles and a six-person deck-

i *After you choose that special B&B or inn, but before you book a reservation, always find out the cancellation policy. And be sure to find out the earliest and latest check in times, exact location and how to get there.*

ROSEHILL INN
BED & BREAKFAST

HISTORIC DOWNTOWN WILMINGTON

114 South Third Street
Wilmington, NC 28401
(800) 815-0250
(910) 815-0250
www.rosehill.com

••• Experience The Romance •••

side hot tub are available for guest use. The Hoge-Wood House is within walking distance of all downtown attractions and is one of the few bed and breakfast inns in Wilmington that offers off-street parking.

Murchison House　　　　　　**$$$$**
305 S. Third St, Wilmington
(910) 762-6626
www.murchisonhouse.com

This beautiful inn was selected from among thousands as one of the "2005 Top Most Romantic Inns of the Year" by American Historic Inns, Inc. Once the elegant home of David and Lucy Murchison, the structure was in decline for years before Sherry and Ron Demas purchased it in 1997. Using photographs to guide them, they lovingly brought the house back to life. Today this meticulously restored, 8,000-square-foot mansion, is filled with extraordinary antiques, art, furnishings and artifacts.

The five guest rooms are cozy, spacious and comfortable, each with sitting area and attached bath. Each of these richly colored bedchambers offers its own thermostat, telephone, wireless Internet connection, television, hair dryer, vintage linens, crystal and silver goblets.

Common areas on the first floor include sunny parlors, a butler's pantry, the chess room and a library with a full-sized billiards table. At 9 o'clock each morning, Bitsy, formerly a chef in Charleston, prepares a deluxe Southern breakfast, served in the formal dining room. Behind the house, the grounds have been beautifully landscaped and include a Koi pond with waterfall, fountains and a brick courtyard. Spacious porches overlook the garden so you can sit in a rocker with your coffee and bask in the morning sun or relax after a long day of sightseeing with a complimentary glass of wine.

Located in the heart of Historic Wilmington, Murchison House is convenient to shopping, restaurants, entertainment venues, theaters and, of course, the Riverwalk. This is a smoke-free, adult environment. Children younger than 12 and pets are not permitted.

Rosehill Inn Bed & Breakfast　　**$$-$$$$**
114 S. Third St., Wilmington
(910) 815-0250, (800) 815-0250
www.rosehill.com

Located in the heart of Wilmington's Downtown Historic District, the elegant Rosehill Inn provides a luxurious yet comfortable getaway that allows its guests to step into the past while still enjoying all of the modern amenities of today. The faithfully restored classic Greek Revival home, built in 1848, is tastefully adorned with oriental rugs, beautiful fireplaces with hand-detailed mantles and period antiques. It features a magnificent pulpit staircase with quarter-sawn white oak banisters, original inlaid oak floors and "egg and dart" mouldings. While appearing quite formal, this first-class bed and breakfast inn is genuinely warm and welcoming, as are its hosts, Laurel and Jeff Jones.

The Verandas

Voted
"Best in the South 2004"
by *Inn Traveler Magazine*

As Seen on HGTV's
"Fine Living" Program

SELECT REGISTRY.
DISTINGUISHED INNS OF NORTH AMERICA
MEMBER

Four Diamond
Award

202 Nun Street · Wilmington, NC
910.251.2212 · www.verandas.com

Each of the six quiet guest rooms has a private en-suite bath, fireplace (non-working), period writing desk, cable TV and fluffy spa bathrobes. Decorated in deep, rich colors, these rooms provide an unforgettable visual experience. The Heritage Room boasts a New Orleans–style iron gate bed. The Wedgwood Room, with its magnificent cherry four poster king-sized bed, is bright and cheery, decorated in a yellow and blue color scheme. The Regency Room features an elaborate iron bed and bathroom with inviting whirlpool tub. The Carolina and Tea Rose Rooms have bay windows with cozy sitting areas.

Early morning coffee service and a national newspaper start your day, followed by a full-service breakfast served in the spacious dining room, which boasts an impressive 17-foot dining table and crystal chandelier. Breakfast includes such delights as orange-almond French toast, "Beaujo" egg casserole, lemon-orange pancakes and a colorful fresh fruit plate.

The home's large wraparound porch is ideal for reading or relaxing. The Rosehill Inn's convenient location, only three blocks from the Cape Fear River, is a short romantic stroll to popular gourmet restaurants, charming shops and Riverwalk. According to Southern Living magazine, "This is no ordinary B&B; a stay at the Rosehill Inn is an experience not soon to be forgotten."

Tranquility Inn   **$$-$$$$**
119 N. Sixth St., Wilmington
(910) 251-7600, (866) 308-NCBB (6222)

Nestled among a bounty of azalea bushes and Carolina jasmine, Tranquility Inn is a fresh, new bed and breakfast that emphasizes health and life consciousness. Heart-healthy, vegetarian, well-balanced full breakfasts are served each morning in the beautifully appointed dining room or on one of the porches. Rest assured your special dietary needs can be accommodated.

The inn consists of three individual and uniquely decorated rooms and one two-bedroom suite, all with private baths, wireless Internet access, CD players and a deck or porch overlooking the garden and fishpond. Some rooms have a two-person jacuzzi tub or two-person rain shower. Owner Jenifer Gausman is dedicated to pampering her guests with personal attention to detail and tranquil accents in each room. Join her for complimentary morning yoga sessions.

In addition to morning yoga, in-room spa treatments are available at extra cost. These include aromassage, full body massage and mini facials.

Many packages are available — all are offered for two-night, double-occupancy guests and include Girls' Getaway offering massages, facials, Pilates and yoga classes plus special treats and other activities; Yoga for You, featuring morning yoga and special

C.W. WORTH HOUSE
A Bed & Breakfast
In the Victorian Tradition

*Celebrating over 20 Years of Hospitality
in Historic Wilmington*

412 South 3rd Street
Wilmington, NC 28401

(910) 762-8562
1-800-340-8559

www.worthhouse.com

breakfast plus evening yoga and meditation along with passes to a local yoga center; and Romantic Escape, with chocolate strawberries, floral arrangement, your favorite bottle of wine and two one-hour in room massages.

Tranquility Inn is located in Wilmington's historic district, four blocks to all that downtown has to offer, complete with horse-drawn carriages, free trolleys, amazing restaurants, shops and The Riverwalk.

Weekend accommodations are available for a minimum of two nights, and single-night accommodations are available during the week. Discount packages are offered for the business traveler, and Jenifer will be happy to arrange customized special packages for you. Relax, refresh and rejuvenate at Tranquility Inn.

The Verandas
"An Inn Second to Nun!" $$$$
202 Nun St., Wilmington
(910) 251-2212
www.verandas.com

With the look and feel of a luxurious European hotel, The Verandas is no ordinary B&B. Magnificently appointed with antiques and high-quality American, French and English reproduction furniture, original artwork and creative lighting, The Verandas will make you want to stay forever.

Owners Chuck Pennington and Dennis Madsen worked magic to restore the burned out mansion, which they purchased in 1995. Originally built in 1854 by shipbuilder Benja-

min Beery, the 8,500-square-foot home has a fascinating history. At various times it was a military hospital, apartment house, hotel, lodge hall, convent, boarding house, warehouse and refuge for vagrants. Today it is an award-winning, first-class bed and breakfast inn that has played host to numerous celebrities, and that stands within walking distance of the Riverwalk, Chandler's Wharf, fine restaurants and theaters.

Four large verandas give guests choice views of the charming gardens, historic neighborhood, downtown Wilmington and tree-lined streets. Spacious, tastefully decorated common areas invite guests to linger over complimentary wine in the evening, perhaps while listening to music played on a restored melodeon, or reading one of the intriguing coffee table books.

Each of the eight large corner guest rooms is different in character, and every one has a top-of-the-line mattress, hand-ironed sheets and cases, luxurious robes, candies and many extra special touches. Private, marble-floored bathrooms have soaking tubs, showers, custom-made soaps, lotions and shampoo. TVs with cable are discreetly hidden. Rooms also have high-speed Internet access, telephones, individual climate controls, and writing areas.

In the morning, French-pressed coffee and the same tea served at the White House accompany a homemade, four-course gourmet breakfast, which is served on the patio, or in the formal dining room with its exquisite crystal chandelier.

Not just for out-of-town visitors, tourists and corporate travelers, The Verandas is a place to consider when you're planning a special celebration, or when you just want to escape from the world for a couple of days. Chuck and Dennis are gracious, accommodating hosts who will do everything possible to ensure a relaxing, enjoyable retreat,

C. W. Worth House $$$-$$$$
412 S. Third St., Wilmington
(910) 762-8562, (800) 340-8559
www.worthhouse.com

Margi and Doug Erickson guarantee to provide a relaxing atmosphere for a memorable getaway. Built in 1893, the C. W. Worth House is a unique example of nineteenth-century English Queen Anne style and sixteenth-century French chateaux. This turreted house has a wide front veranda and elegant interior, which includes the original paneled foyer, antiques, a formal parlor with a Victorian-era pump organ and a comfortable study. A television/VCR is available in the study and in the third-floor sitting room. The seven guest rooms are spacious, and beds include four-poster and antique queen-size. Each guest room has a private bath, comfortable sitting area, ceiling fan, desk and telephone with dataport. Ask about the Azalea Room with its glassed-in veranda or the Hibiscus Room with its whirlpool bath and sitting area nestled in the corner turret. The entire house has central air conditioning.

A full gourmet breakfast, served by your hosts in the formal dining room includes special blend coffee, tea, juice, muffins and fresh fruit as a first course. The entree may be goat cheese and rosemary strata, eggs Florentine, artichoke/mushroom quiche or a baked banana-pecan pancake. A convenience for guests is a refrigerator on each floor, stocked with beverages and snacks. Outside, beautiful gardens highlighted with shade trees and brick walkways, a goldfish pond and a relaxing waterfall invite guests to linger a while. The C. W. Worth House is a nonsmoking inn. Children age 12 and older are welcome. Gift certificates, specials and packages are available.

If you're in Wilmington on business, you'll find all the conveniences you'll need and a quiet environment. Corporate rates are available Sunday through Thursday, as well as a fax, copier and dataport. C. W. Worth House is also equipped with high-speed wireless Internet access throughout the inn. Unlimited access is free for guests bringing their own equipment, but there is a $10 fee to rent a wireless network card. A desktop computer with Internet access is available to all guests in the third-floor living room.

Carolina Beach and Kure Beach

The Beacon House Inn
Bed and Breakfast $$-$$$$
715 Carolina Beach Ave. N., Carolina Beach
(910) 458-6244, (910) 458-7322,
(877) BEACON-6 (232-2666)
www.beaconhouseinnb-b.com

Originally a 1950s boarding house, The Beacon House Inn Bed and Breakfast is a reminder of a simpler life in days gone by. The decor features pine tongue-in-groove paneled walls, vintage photographs and memorabilia blended with modern amenities. Everything about the place says "relax and make yourself comfortable."

Air-conditioned guest rooms are decorated in different motifs and have paired doors, one being regular and one louvered to take advantage of hallway breezes while still offering privacy to room occupants. There are multiple options for rooms, including those with private baths, hall baths and shared suites. One guest room comes complete with a two-person air-jet whirlpool tub. A two-bedroom/bath suite is ideal for two couples traveling together or families with children. Full Southern breakfasts are served daily.

Three cozy, clean, cottages decorated in Caribbean themes are available for rent as well, offering two and three bedroom accommodations with fully equipped kitchens, linens, starter essential kits, satellite TVs and porches. Two of the cottages are pet friendly, and children are welcome in all three.

Custom packages are available, should you choose to rent the entire inn or the inn and cottages for a larger group, wedding or reunion. Private catering is also available on-site should you desire it. There are also special spa packages, and romance packages for that special occasion.

The Beacon House Inn is located in Carolina Beach, across the street from the ocean, close to the Boardwalk and a popular fishing pier. Endless outdoor activities can be found nearby. Golf opportunities are plentiful, and historic downtown Wilmington, the N.C. Aquarium at Fort Fisher and two great state parks are just minutes away.

Hidden Treasure Inn   **$$**
113 S. Fourth Ave., Kure Beach
(910) 458-3216

This delightful small inn, nestled under large shade trees, has a comfortable, down-home feel the minute you step through the gate into the garden. Each of the three non-smoking units is like your own little apartment. Take advantage of the gas grill, picnic table and patio for a casual cookout. Sun by the immaculate blue pool. Relax on the porch and enjoy gentle breezes. Or maybe you'd like to take a short stroll over to the beach. Hidden Treasures Inn's atmosphere of warmth and hospitality makes it a great getaway from the business of life. Hosts Matt and Nancy Salerno welcome their guests and make each one feel like a long-time friend. All units have air conditioning, cable TV, refrigerator, microwave and coffee maker, and the two efficiency kitchens are fully equipped. Linens, towels and daily maid service are included. Daily and weekly rentals are available.

Brunswick County Beaches

BALD HEAD ISLAND

Theodosia's Bed and Breakfast   **$$$$**
Harbour Village on Bald Head Island
(910) 457-6563, (800) 656-1812
www.theodosias.com

Be sure to schedule a stay at the island's first bed and breakfast inn. Theodosia's Victorian architecture is set against the Bald Head Island Marina, the Cape Fear River and island creeks and marshes. The decor in the 10-room inn is a blend of Victorian and West Indies motifs. Each room has a king, queen or double bed, its own luxurious bath, TV, VCR and telephone. Enjoy breath-taking vistas from your room's private balcony. The main-

Beacon House
Bed & Breakfast
& Cottages at the Beach

Weekly Rentals
Reunions • Weddings
Large Groups
Pet Friendly • A/C

715 Carolina Beach Ave North
Carolina Beach, NC 28428
Tel: 877.BEACON-6 / 910.458.6244
Fax: 910.458.9257
innkeeper@beaconhouseinnb-b.com
www.beaconhouseinnb-b.com

floor guest room is handicapped-accessible. Two rooms occupy the adjoining Carriage House.

Carson Lawrence, co-owner with her parents Gary and Pam Lawrence, manages the inn with a dedicated and professional staff, including an executive chef. Gourmet breakfasts and delightful baked goods are featured each morning at tables set for you. Hors d'oeuvres are served in the afternoon. Rooms come with complimentary golf carts and bicycles (the only means of transportation allowed on the island) and a temporary membership to the Bald Head Island Country Club.

The inn was named in honor of the daughter of America's most famous duelist, Aaron Burr. She disappeared off the North Carolina coast in 1812, and her ghost is said to fancy Bald Head Island these days.

SOUTHPORT/OAK ISLAND

The Brunswick Inn   **$$$$**
301 E. Bay St., Southport
(910) 457-5278

Since 1800 when it was built as the summer residence of Benjamin Smith, founder of Smithville (Southport) and tenth governor of North Carolina, this Federal-style mansion has looked out over the mouth of the Cape Fear River, The Intracoastal Waterway and the Atlantic Ocean. It served as summer residence for Governor Dudley as well. In 1856 the top two floors were rebuilt by Thomas

So close...but a world away
Bald Head Island

Theodosia's
Bed & Breakfast

Harbour Village
Bald Head Island, NC
800.656.1812 ~ 910.457.6563
www.theodosias.com

Bald Head Island Vacations
Resort Sales and Rentals
888.367.7091 ~ 910.457.1120
www.baldheadislandvacations.com

Meares, owner of Orton Plantation around the time of the Civil War. Seven years ago, Jim and Judy Clary purchased the building and went to work restoring it to its previous grandeur, including preserving the original heart-pine floors, the plaster ceiling moldings, the cathedral shaped pocket doors, the Southport Bows over the door and window casings, and the nine working fireplaces. Judy chose rich, vibrant colors that set off the spacious rooms and play up the interesting architecture. In the middle of the dining room stands a huge antique table, handmade in the mountains, above which hangs a crystal chandelier dropping from the second floor ceiling, through the rotunda. This is where the full, home-cooked, gourmet breakfasts, including homemade pastries, are normally served. Some mornings, though, breakfast is served in the cozy working kitchen in front of the fireplace.

Each beautifully decorated guest room has a private bath and contains a working fireplace for which the proprietors provide a Duraflame log. A well-stocked library, a parlor and an observatory, including telescope, are all available to guests. Afternoon hors d'oeuvres and wine are served, and guests are encouraged to spend some time on the veranda watching the passing scene.

You will be welcomed by Lizzie Lou, the Sunshine Girl (the resident cat). Don't be spooked by Tony, the whimsical resident ghost who sometimes makes his presence known. Tony was a harpist who played at the inn when balls were common occurrences. He drowned in a boating accident off Bald Head Island in 1882 and has made the inn his home since! More recently, Charles Bronson slept here. The Brunswick Inn was used in the making of several movies, including Summer Catch with Freddie Printz, Jr., The Wedding with Halle Berry, and Pirate Kids.

Lois Jane's Riverview Inn $$
106 W. Bay St., Southport
(910) 457-6701, (800) 457-1152

Owned and operated by fourth-generation descendants of the original owner, this beautifully restored 1892 home is near the old harbor pilot's tower and overlooks the mouth of the Cape Fear River. It is a quiet getaway within easy walking distance of Southport's restaurants, river walk, shops and

museums. Porches on the river side of the building are ideal for rocking away the time.

Two rooms with private baths and two with a shared bath have queen-size, four-poster beds and period furnishings that have been part of the home for years. The rooms to the front of the building have beautiful river views, and one room has its own entrance to the communal upstairs porch. Full Southern-style breakfasts are served daily in the dining room, and afternoon wine and cheese are additional touches. Special breakfast arrangements can be made with advance notice. Coffee is placed in the hallway outside the guest rooms each morning, and a small refrigerator is available. Ask about the separate deluxe efficiency apartment that is also available. Cancellations require a 72-hour notice for refunds.

Oak Island Beach House
Bed & Breakfast $$-$$$
4505 E. Oak Island Dr., Oak Island
(910) 278-1400, (800) 676-9593

If a list of your favorite book titles includes Treasure Island, The Shell Seekers, The Lighthouse Keeper or Beach Music, here is your chance to sleep in a room named after one of them – and decorated to suit. You will find these rooms at the Beach House Bed & Breakfast, the only and by default, the best B & B on Oak Island. The house was built by one of the first mayors of the town and has the distinction of being one of only five houses on the island to have survived Hurricane Hazel in 1954. All of the rooms have private baths and either king or queen-size beds. Lodging includes your choice of full or continental breakfast served in the dining room, afternoon snacks and complimentary soft drinks. You will find two large decks for lounging, a game room with TV, DVD, VCR, board games and a piano, and a cozy living room. Provided for your convenience are bicycles, beach toys, umbrellas and chairs, and picnic baskets. Personal services available are breakfast in bed upon request, laundry and reservations for dining and recreation in the area. Take advantage of the "stay for seven days and pay for only six nights" rate. Special packages are available for weddings, honeymoons, anniversaries and other celebrations. Special rates are available for a four-day minimum stay when all the rooms are rented by the same group. Golf or fishing weekend packages are available during the off-season. Beach House is closed between Thanksgiving and January 2 each year, and pets are not allowed.

HOLDEN BEACH

Crescent Moon Inn   **$-$$**
965 Sabbath Home Rd. SW, Holden Beach
(910) 842-1190, (877) 727-1866

This modern, family-friendly bed and breakfast inn, nestled on a 1.5-acre wooded lot, is only 1.5 miles from Holden Beach. Surrounded by carefully tended flower and herb beds, it is a large, white-brick building with a rear deck shaded by tall sycamore, birch, apple and pear trees. A screened porch is available for passing lazy afternoons. The decor is attractive and casual, full of earth tones and pastels, fiber rugs, wicker and rattan. The guest rooms have peaked ceilings with beams and skylights and are furnished with either king-sized, queen-sized or twin beds. Rooms are equipped with a ceiling fan, TV and VCR (a complimentary video library is available), and coffee is placed outside each room at 7:30 AM. Healthy continental breakfasts include home-baked goods to start your day. Beverages and snacks are available all day. The owners have arranged for guest parking at the beach at no additional cost. Add to this the proximity to the area's dozens of golf courses and easy access to both Wilmington and Myrtle Beach.

Heading south on U.S. Highway 17 from Wilmington, you turn left at the traffic light when you reach the intersection of U.S. 17 and N.C. Highway 211. Take the first right onto Stone Chimney Road. Continue 8 miles to Sabbath Home Road and turn right. Crescent Moon Inn will be on the left directly across

from the entrance to Sea Trace development. Ask about discount rates for four or more nights. A two-night minimum is required for stays during festival weekends and holidays.

Topsail Island Area

Bed & Breakfast at Mallard Bay   **$$**
960 Mallard Bay Rd., Hampstead
(910) 270-3363

Lodgings here include a roomy upstairs suite with a water view, four-poster bed, full private bath, sitting room with queen-size sofa bed and a TV/VCR. Laundry facilities are available at no extra cost. A full country breakfast is served on the weekends, and continental breakfast is offered on weekdays. Complimentary wine and cheese are served each afternoon. A canoe and kayak are available for a relaxing paddle in the waterway. A two-night minimum is required. This facility is within walking distance of Harbour Village Marina, close to local golf courses and only 15 minutes from the beach, restaurants and shopping.

The Pink Palace of Topsail   **$$-$$$**
1222 S. Shore Dr., Surf City
(910) 328-5114

Treat yourself like royalty at The Pink Palace, Topsail's only oceanfront bed and breakfast. These accommodations feature a comfortable living area with all the amenities, surrounded by three rooms adorned with tropical murals on the walls. All suites have access to a screened porch and three open air decks with a hot tub on the deck extension. Watch the sun rise from a relaxing rocker, hammock or swing.

The region has many buildings listed on the National Register of Historic Places.

photo: Peter Doran

VACATION RENTALS

There's just something about a visit to the coast that increases your overall feeling of well-being and recharges your batteries. The serene and scenic beaches surrounding the Wilmington area coax guests back year after year to refresh their relaxing skills and rejuvenate their energy levels. Thankfully for visitors from all over the world, the beaches of southeastern North Carolina feature a wide variety of agencies well equipped to connect you with a rental property to suit your needs. Ranging from the remote and picturesque locales on Topsail Island to the quiet seaside hamlets of the South Brunswick Islands, there are condominiums, townhouses, multi-bedroom homes and other lodgings designed to accommodate the vacationing couple, the business excursion or the family reunion.

If you're planning on spending more than just a couple of days on the southern coast, doing your research can result in getting your hands on the perfect spot and maybe even saving a few dollars. While the responsibilities may increase with renting a house, if your party is a big one, the advantages are numerous. The choice is yours. Do you want room service or would you rather be able to sleep late and make your own bed?

A long-term rental becomes your sanctuary during your stay at the beach, and the difference in comfort is fairly obvious. Who wouldn't prefer a living room with cable and stereo if you're bringing the entire family on vacation? Also, having a kitchen makes for a more communal atmosphere around mealtime, with guests being able to take advantage of items like fresh local produce and seafood.

ACCOMMODATIONS AND LOCATIONS

Do you prefer the sound side or the oceanfront? This is an important question to consider as rates for properties often increase with a stroll across the street toward the beach. While a beachfront home offers scenic views and an easy commute from your door to the waves, a different location, while just as convenient, might save you a bundle. If you have your own boat or are planning on renting one, a house on the sound might be perfect for you. While the sunrise over the Atlantic is breathtaking, the sunset over the sound is equally alluring.

During your stay, you can expect to have the basic appliances supplied by the owner of the property. Most rentals offer cable, telephone, heat and air, and come fully furnished. Dishes and cooking utensils are almost universally provided, but checking with your rental agency is always a good idea before setting out on vacation. Certain spots also offer activity centers such as gyms, swimming pools, tennis courts and numerous other forms of recreation.

More often than not, guests are required to supply their own sheets, towels, groceries, cleaning supplies and beach gear. Your rental agency should have a detailed checklist of items you will need during your stay. Almost anything too cumbersome to bring along (bicycles, kayaks, etc.) can be rented for a small fee. See our Sports, Fitness and Parks or Watersports chapters or ask your rental agency for details on which business offer these services.

A FEW RULES

There are a number of rules to follow when renting a beach home from a rental agency. The large majority of these properties are second homes for their owners, and renting them out means trusting their agency to choose responsible renters. Each agency has its own specific policies, and vacationing parties should make themselves aware of these policies and their consequences.

Nobody knows the coast better.

PRESENTING SOUTHEAST NORTH CAROLINA'S FINEST PROPERTIES

*A tradition of excellence in real estate
professionalism and customer service since 1976...
from Oak Island to Topsail.*

It's All Right Here!
*www.*intracoastalrealty*.com*

Listings, Virtual Tours
Area Information, Maps,
Local Weather and More!

Vacation and Long Term Rentals

Relax...we invite you to be our guest.

Our team of professionals will assist you in finding the perfect,
high quality property at Carolina , Kure and Wrightsville Beaches,
Figure 8 and Topsail Islands.
We offer a large selection of 1-7 bedroom cottages, condos and town homes.
Choose oceanfront, sound front or somewhere in between.

605 Causeway Drive, Wrightsville Beach
(910) 256-3780 or (800) 346-2463

Intracoastal
REALTY CORPORATION
Since 1976

1206 N. Lake Park Boulevard, Carolina Beach
(910) 458-2100

LEADING REAL ESTATE
COMPANIES *of* THE WORLD™

CHRISTIE'S
GREAT ESTATES

302 N. New River Drive, Surf City
(910) 328-0719 or (800) 753-2975

Call for a FREE rental brochure or book or go online today.
www.intracoastalrentals.com

CAROLINA BEACH · KURE BEACH · FORT FISHER

FOR THE BEST GUIDE TO
OUR AREA AND ALL IT HAS
TO OFFER, CALL US

UNITED BEACH
VACATIONS

· NORTH CAROLINA OCEANFRONT
· WIDE BEACHES
· SPACIOUS CONDOMINIUMS
· COTTAGES WITH UP TO 9 BEDROOMS

Call 1-800-334-5806 • www.unitedbeachvacations.com

Many area vacation homes require the minimum age of renters to be 21, however some extend that limit to 25, often excepting married couples under that age. Be sure to check with your particular agency prior to setting your heart on a vacation home. Large groups of young renters can often encounter resistance due to damage concerns. Large house parties are discouraged and many rental agreements prohibit them altogether, especially at the smaller, quieter beaches. Breaching this area of your contract can easily result in the forfeiture of your deposit and the instant termination of your rental agreement. The bottom line is being respectful of other people's property, privacy and peace and quiet.

While cleaning services may be offered upon checkout for a small fee, the agencies expect you to leave no trace of your visit. Oftentimes, a portion of your deposit goes to these services should you fail to leave things as you found them, and the agency is at liberty to determine these fees. As is expected,

you should treat your "home away from home" as though it was your own.

While most people own cell phones these days, the majority of area properties have a telephone for your use. Responsible use is expected and often agencies will block outgoing long distance calls to prevent abuse of phone service.

PETS

More often than not, rental properties aren't all that accommodating when it comes to our furry friends. There are some properties that allow pets, but those are exceedingly rare these days. If leaving your pet at home isn't a possibility, area kennels and "doggie daycare" services will look after your cherished companion. However, most towns have long since forbidden animals on the beach, especially in summer.

For a listing of Pet-Friendly Accommodations in the southern coastal area, see our online version of this book at www.insiders.com/wilmington/main-rentals.

Among those concerns should be the issue of fleas, as they present a major problem during the warms months. Fumigation and pest control will take a chunk out of your deposit, so please be conscious of your pet's condition. If you decide to roll the dice and ignore pet policies, some agencies will demand your immediate dismissal.

Before committing to a rental property, familiarize yourself with the location, especially with regard to your personal needs and preferences. Read pertinent chapters in this book, contact the local chamber of commerce or visitor information bureau, and chat with people at the agencies.

CONNECTING THE BEST OF WILMINGTON'S HISTORY, SPIRIT AND LIFESTYLE

IN ONE HOMETOWN NETWORK!

SALES • VACATIONS • LONG-TERM RENTALS

Wilmington Office
1601 S. College Rd.
Wilmington, NC 28403
(910) 395-4100
1-800-747-1968

Historic Downtown Office
106 N. Water St. Suite 112
Wilmington, NC 28401
(910) 772-1622
1-800-882-1622

Carolina Beach Office
1029 N. Lake Park Blvd.
Carolina Beach, NC 28428
(910) 458-8881
1-800-830-2118

Brunswick Office
1109 New Pointe Blvd., Suite 4
Leland, NC 28451
910-371-9937
877-370-9937

Network® **Call For A Free**
Real Estate **Relocation Package.**

www.networkwilmington.com

RATES

Prices fall in a wide range from $500 to $5,000 (or more) a week, depending on your choice of accommodation, location, luxury factor and season. Bald Head Island, Wrightsville Beach and Figure Eight Island are at the high end. Topsail, Carolina Beach, Kure Beach and the Brunswick Beaches (Oak Island, Holden Beach, Ocean Isle Beach and Sunset Beach) offer a broader array of less-pricey accommodations, but also have their share of high-end properties.

Most agencies require a deposit, and there are various stipulations in the agreement that you need to be familiar with. For example, a state/county tax of 7 percent and, depending on the location, a room tax ranging from 1 to 6 percent are added to the cost. Rental rates are subject to change without notice. Winter rates may be significantly less. A deposit of 50 percent is generally required to confirm reservations. Major credit cards are usually, but not always, accepted. Check with the individual rental agency for required methods of payment. Some accept personal checks provided they arrive 30 to 60 days in advance of your arrival.

RENTAL AGENCIES

This listing of rental agencies is a sampling of the many fine companies from which you may choose. We don't have room in this chapter to include them all. Select the beach of your choice and contact the area's chamber of commerce for the names of other rental companies (see our Area Overviews chapter for a list of local chambers of commerce). In Wilmington, the Cape Fear Coast Convention & Visitors Bureau, (910) 341-4030, is another helpful resource for finding other rental agencies.

Wilmington

Network Real Estate
106 N. Water St., Wilmington
(910) 772-1622, (877) 882-1622
110 New Point Blvd., Suite 4, Leland
(910) 371-9937, (877) 370-9937
www.networkwilmington.com

Network Real Estate offers a large, ever-expanding selection of premium vacation rentals in Carolina and Kure beaches, including oceanfront cottages and condominiums in a variety of price ranges. Amenities for most rentals include central air, major appliances, cable, outdoor decks and easy beach access. Additionally, Network's Historic Downtown Wilmington office offers new vacation rentals on the Cape Fear River across from the Battleship North Carolina as well as long and short term corporate rentals.

Riverview Suites at Water Street Center
106 N. Water St., Wilmington
(910) 772-9988

Riverview Suites at Water Street Center, located across the street from and operated by the Hilton, offers 65 well-appointed suites

WRIGHTSVILLE, CAROLINA, KURE BEACHES & GREATER WILMINGTON

SALES & RENTALS

Making Vacations Last A Lifetime!

Wrightsville Beach
910.256.3764 • 800.322.3764

Wilmington
910.799.2700 • 888.364.1307

Carolina & Kure Beaches
910.458.5658 • 800.994.5222

www.bryantre.com

Bryant
Real Estate
Established 1952

overlooking the Cape Fear River. The Riverview Suites is the only property on the Cape Fear River that offers walk-out balconies, kitchenettes, Tempurpedic beds and washer/dryers. The Riverview Suites is perfect for vacation and long-term corporate rentals. This property has one of the best views in town.

Wrightsville Beach and Vicinity

Bryant Real Estate
1001 N. Lumina Ave., Wrightsville Beach
(910) 256-3764, (800) 322-3764
www.bryantre.com

Offering vacation rental homes, condos and townhomes with locations from the ocean to the sound, Bryant Real Estate has been providing quality sales, rentals and property management services in the Wilmington, Carolina, Kure and Wrightsville Beach areas for more than 50 years. For year-round rentals, call (910) 799-2700. Daily, weekly and monthly rates are available in Wrightsville Beach, Carolina Beach and Kure Beach.

Bryant also has offices in Wilmington and Carolina Beach.

Holliday Vacations
2002 Eastwood Rd., Ste. 102, Wilmington
(910) 256-2911, (888) 256-2911
www.hollidayvacations.com

The friendly staff at Holliday Vacations specializes in Wrightsville Beach vacation properties, offering condominiums (some with pool and tennis facilities) and distinctive single-family homes. Ask about the free brochure for weekly, weekend and monthly rentals. They also offer long-term rental properties in Wilmington and Wrightsville Beach.

Intracoastal Realty
605 Causeway Dr., Wrightsville Beach
(910) 256-3780, (800) 346-2463
www.intracoastalrentals.com

This company has offered a great selection of properties on Wrightsville Beach since 1973, with a mix of single-family homes, old-style beach cottages and condominiums, featuring on-site swimming pools and tennis courts. A virtual tour of Intracoastal Realty's vacation rentals is available at their

VACATION RENTALS

website. Intracoastal also handles long-term rentals in Wilmington and Wrightsville Beach; call (910) 509-9700 or (800) 826-4428 for long-term rental information or visit their website for a complete list.

Station 1
95 S. Lumina Ave., Wrightsville Beach
(910) 256-3134
www.intracoastalrentals.com

With a view of the Atlantic Ocean from each of its 104 units, Station 1 offers weekly and monthly condominium rentals on Wrightsville Beach. This attractive complex, managed by Intracoastal Realty, includes 88 two- and three-bedroom condos and 16 three-bedroom townhouses. Amenities include a private tennis court, a seaside pool, laundry facilities and the use of bicycles. Each rental condo is fully furnished down to the linens and offers a spacious living/dining room, two baths and a fully equipped kitchen with dishwasher, microwave and coffeemaker. Townhouses include all of these features but offer three baths instead of two plus a fireplace and a garage.

Figure Eight Island

Figure Eight Realty
15 Bridge Rd., Wilmington
(910) 686-4400, (800) 279-6085

Figure Eight Realty boasts the largest vacation rental inventory on this exclusive, private island. They offer numerous homes on the ocean, sound, interior and salt marsh for those seeking a tranquil and private getaway. Located only minutes away from beautiful downtown Wilmington, Figure Eight Island offers vacationers both privacy and conve- nience. Should you decide to make the island your home or home away from home, Figure Eight Realty offers an experienced sales staff that will assist you with the purchase of island property.

Figure Eight Rentals
2413 Middle Sound Loop, Wilmington
(910) 686-4099, (800) 470-4099
www.waterfrontnc.net
www.figure8rentals.com

With a pristine beach undisturbed by thousands of tourists, those who vacation at Figure 8 appreciate the solitude and luxuri- ous accommodations available on the island.

BACHMAN REALTY
Bunnie Bachman, Owner/Broker, GRI, CRS, ABR
800-470-4099 | 910-470-4099 | bunbachman@aol.com
www.waterfrontnc.net

Figure Eight Island, Wrightsville Beach
& Intracoastal Waterway Properties
Vacation Rentals Available
www.figure8rentals.com

25 Years experience in waterfront
properties & Figure Eight Island

Whether you're planning a weekend getaway or a month long summer retreat, let Bunnie Bachman help you find the place that best suits your needs. With over 25 years of real estate sales and rental experience, Bunnie Bachman can dial in the ideal location for you and your family. Whether you have a party of four or forty joining you on vacation, bypass the masses and let Bunnie Bachman help! If you decide to look at purchasing a vaca- tion home or possibly making Figure 8 your home, Bunnie Bachman's 25 years of living on the island will be invaluable in helping you find your place in paradise.

HOLLIDAY Vacations

A Property Management Company

Vacation Rentals at Wrightsville Beach
Featuring Wrightsville Dunes,
Cordgrass Bay, Homes & More
Long - Term Rentals in Wilmington

2002 Eastwood Rd., Suite 102
Wilmington, NC 28403
910-256-2911   888-256-2911
Fax 910-256-6411
www.hollidayvacations.com

Carolina Beach and Kure Beach

Atlantic Shores Real Estate
9 S. Lake Park Blvd., Ste. A-3,
Carolina Beach
Rentals (910) 458-4975, (800) 289-0028
Sales (910) 458-5878, (877) 428-5878

Specializing in rental properties on Pleasure Island, Atlantic Shores Real Estate offers a variety of moderately priced comfortable accommodations including oceanfront and ocean-view condominiums with smoke-free and pet-friendly units available. They manage a variety of fully furnished oceanfront and ocean-view condominiums. Amenities include indoor and outdoor pools, tennis courts and recreation centers. Atlantic Shores rental properties are close to many area attractions.

Atlantic Towers
1615 S. Lake Park Blvd., Carolina Beach
(910) 458-8313, (800) 232-2440
www.atlantic-towers.com

Offering attractive one- and two-bedroom condominium units with oceanfront balconies, Atlantic Towers is situated right on the beach. The facility also includes both an outdoor pool and a heated indoor pool. Atlantic Towers offers nightly rentals and short-term and weekly rentals at discounted rates.

Blue Water Realty
1000 S. Lake Park Blvd., Carolina Beach
(910) 458-3001, (866) 458-3001 (toll free)
www.bluewaterrealtyinc.com

Blue Water Realty has properties that can accommodate groups large and small. In fact, they welcome large groups and will be happy to find just the rental that will make everyone happy and comfortable during their stay at the beach. A magnificent waterfront home, cottage, townhome or condominium complete with all of the amenities is just a toll-free phone call away. Blue Water Realty's staff is dedicated to making your vacation a pleasurable and memorable experience.

Bryant Real Estate
1401 N. Lake Park Blvd., Snow's Cut
Crossing, Carolina Beach
(910) 458-5658, (800) 994-5222
www.bryantre.com

Offering vacation rental homes, condos and townhomes with locations from the

Great for fishing, strolling or viewing, the area's many piers each have their own personality.

photo: Peter Doran

Welcome to Beautiful Carolina & Kure Beach
Vacation Rentals
Please View our Properties Online
or Call Us Toll Free 1-866-458-3001
www.bluewaterrealtyinc.com

Blue Water Realty & Investments Inc.
1000 S. Lake Park Blvd. • Carolina Beach, NC 28428
1-866-458-3001

ocean to the sound, Bryant Real Estate has been providing quality sales, rental and property management service in the Wilmington, Carolina Beach, Kure Beach and Wrightsville Beach area for more than 50 years. For year-round rentals call (910) 799-2700. Daily, weekly and monthly rates are available in Wrightsville Beach, Carolina Beach and Kure Beach. Bryant also has offices in Wilmington and Wrightsville Beach.

Bullard Realty, Inc.
1404 S. Lake Park Blvd., Carolina Beach
(910) 458-4028, (800) 327-5863

Bullard Realty, Inc. takes pride in an outstanding reputation by offering some of the finest vacation accommodations available. With more than 100 rentals on Carolina and Kure beaches, Bullard offers a choice of oceanfront, ocean-view and second-row with amenities such as indoor and outdoor pools, tennis facilities and recreation centers. Whether you want a cozy, one-bedroom condo for two or a six-bedroom, oceanfront vacation home for 17, Bullard Realty can help make your vacation dreams a reality.

Cabana Suites
31 Carolina Ave. N., Carolina Beach
(910) 458-4456, (800) 333-8499

Cabana Suites offers a Mediterranean flavor in the heart of Carolina Beach. The oceanfront complex consists of individually owned condos situated on a wide beach covered with white powdery sand. All units have a fully stocked kitchen.

Coastwalk Vacation Rentals
t/a Victory Beach Vacations
207 A, Fayetteville St., Carolina Beach
(910) 458-0868, (888) 256-4804

Choose from a variety of first-class, smoke-free accommodations for your hard-earned vacation, weekend getaway or off-season stay. Victory Beach Vacations is committed to excellence, with a friendly, patient staff that will help you select the perfect unit and arrange for all of your rental needs, including child care. Condos and houses are available with a wide variety of amenities — oceanfront, pools, harborfront with private piers and boat slips. Ask about their pet-friendly units.

Intracoastal Realty
1206 N. Lake Park Blvd., Carolina Beach
(910) 458-2100
www.intracoastalrentals.com

This company offers a great selection of vacation beach rentals in Carolina and Kure Beaches. From single-family homes, old-style beach cottages to condominiums, some properties have on-site swimming pools, boat docks and tennis courts. A virtual tour of Intracoastal Realty's vacation rentals is available at their website. Intracoastal also

Southern Retreats

MANAGED PROPERTIES
a Prudential Carolina Real Estate partner

Whether you're staying for a while or just a week, Southern Retreats has the ideal rental property for you! With offices ranging from Topsail Island to Calabash, we have prime locations on the numerous beaches, downtown Wilmington and everywhere in between.

877.454.0056 ▸ Carolina Beach, Wrightsville Beach
800.880.0455 ▸ Holden Beach, Ocean Isle Beach
Sunset Beach, Calabash
877.454.0055 ▸ Southport, Oak Island
866.798.0200 ▸ Topsail Island

Now you're heading in the right direction.

www.southernretreats.net

handles long-term rentals in the Carolina and Kure Beach areas and has offices in Wilmington and Wrightsville Beach as well.

Island Beach Rentals by Walker Realty
501 N. Lake Park Blvd. Carolina Beach
(910) 458-3388

With the Carolina and Kure Beach areas more popular than ever for those seeking a serene and relaxed vacation destination, why not let the team at Island Beach Rentals set you up in the perfect home for your summer getaway? Featuring a wide variety of condos, town homes and beach houses, you'll be able to find the ideal spot whether there are only two in your party or two dozen. With fantastic dining only a short trip from every location and plenty of activities for the entire family, Carolina and Kure beaches have become a popular alternative to the Wrightsville Beach madness. Tour the Fort Fisher historic site or take the kids to the Aquarium for an afternoon of ocean discovery. You'll have it all if you let Island Beach Rentals work for you.

Laney Real Estate Co.
140 Harper Ave., Carolina Beach
(910) 458-3739,(800) 235-9068

Laney Real Estate Co. is proud to announce its new location in Kure Beach. Sharon Laney brings years of experience as a customer-oriented business to the area. Laney's goal is to deliver personal service to each client in a friendly atmosphere. Rental properties are beautifully decorated and well maintained.

Network Real Estate
1029 N. Lake Park Blvd., Carolina Beach
(910) 458-8881, (800) 830-2118
www.networkwilmington.com

Network Real Estate offers a large, ever-expanding selection of premium vacation rentals in Carolina and Kure beaches, including oceanfront cottages and condominiums in a variety of price ranges. Amenities for most rentals include central air, major appliances, cable, outdoor decks and easy beach access. Additionally, Network's Historic Downtown Wilmington office offers new vacation rentals on the Cape Fear River across from the Battleship North Carolina as well as long- and short-term corporate rentals.

Palm Air Cottages
133 N. Ft. Fisher Blvd., Kure Beach
(910) 458-5269, (866) 458-5269

With one, two and three-bedroom cottages available (along with one oceanfront condo), Palm Air is an ideal getaway spot for couples or families. Located on gorgeous Pleasure Island, Palm Air is a short drive from historic Downtown Wilmington and a stone's throw from Fort Fisher and the Aquarium. A brief stroll reveals the beach close by, along with numerous shopping and dining alternatives. Hiking trails, fishing and boating opportunities are also nearby. While the

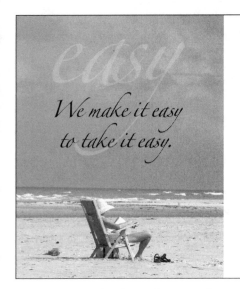

We make it easy to take it easy.

For a stress-free getaway for the entire family, Bald Head Island, N.C., is easy to reach and hard to beat. You'll ride a passenger ferry to a cape island with 14 miles of beaches, lush maritime forest and pristine marshes.

Call our Travel Specialists for details on great vacation getaway rates, including discounts on golf and recreation programs.

BALD HEAD ISLAND LIMITED
The Island Professionals

1-800-899-0359
retreattobhi.com

cottages possess the charm of years past, guests will find them completely equipped with all modern conveniences, such as cable television and full kitchens. A luxurious swimming pool is on site.

Southern Retreats
1025-B N. Lake Park Blvd., Carolina Beach
(910) 202-1430, (877) 454-0056
www.southernretreats.net

A partner of Prudential Carolina Real Estate, this property management company offers a variety of vacation and long-term rentals. Whether you're staying for a while or merely a week, Southern Retreats has the ideal rental property for you! Prime locations available on the beaches, downtown Wilmington and everywhere in between. Visit the website above for more information.

United Beach Vacations
1001 N. Lake Park Blvd., Carolina Beach
(910) 458-9073, (800) 334-5806
www.unitedbeachvacations.com

This large company manages fully furnished rental units, including condominiums, beach cottages, duplexes, townhomes and single-family homes on Carolina Beach, Kure Beach and Fort Fisher. Rentals are oceanfront, ocean-view and second-row properties. Some properties also offer amenities that include pools and tennis courts; many are in close proximity to the North Carolina Aquarium at Fort Fisher.

Brunswick County Beaches

BALD HEAD ISLAND

Bald Head Island Limited
5079 Southport Supply Rd., Southport
(910) 457-5002, (800) 432-7368
www.baldheadisland.com

This well-established company on pristine Bald Head Island has 100 rental properties, primarily single-family homes, distributed throughout seven island environments: maritime forest, marsh and creek, Harbour Village, golf course, West Beach, East Beach and South Beach. Each rental includes round-trip ferry passage and the use of at least one four-passenger electric golf cart for transportation around the island (cars are not permitted on Bald Head Island). Guests

If you are staying in an oceanfront house during the months of July - October, turn the outdoor lights off when possible. This is the turtle-hatching season and newborn loggerhead turtles usually hatch in the dunes at night. They make their way to the sea by following light reflected on the water. Lights on the houses can confuse them and cause them to go in the wrong direction.

Find your place by the sea.

www.RentOakIsland.com 800-909-RENT

Oak Island Accommodations 300 Country Club Drive Oak Island, NC 28465

renting through Bald Head Island Limited receive unlimited use of the business center located in the Chandler Building at Harbour Village. The company specializes in corporate retreats, weddings, family reunions and social gatherings for up to 200 people.

Bald Head Island Rentals, LCC
120 E. Moore St., Southport
(910) 457-1702, (800) 680-8322

Bald Head Island Rentals offers a large selection of luxury resort homes, cottages, villas and suites exclusively on Bald Head Island. Aiming to ensure a dream vacation on the island, their unique Five Star Guest

Services program includes accommodation and reservation services, concierge service, valet parking and guest departure services. Let Bald Head Island Rentals' experience and commitment to excellence make your vacation the best ever.

Bald Head Island Vacations
5003 O'Quinn Blvd., Ste. F, Southport
(910) 367-7091, (888) 367-7091

Dann and Gail Jackson have joined the Bald Head Island property management team. They are full-time residents on Bald Head Island. Together with Dann and Gail, owners Pam Lawrence and daughter, Carson, look forward to sharing more than 15 years of island experience with you. Real estate sales and vacation rentals are their business. They are committed to providing you with all the information you need to discover the many hidden treasures of Bald Head Island. Whether you are looking for a seaside retreat, a vacation getaway or the perfect retirement home, let them take care of you.

Old Baldy Associates
1105 N. Howe St., Southport
(910) 457-5551

Old Baldy Associates offers homes, villas and condos with two to five bedrooms in all areas on Bald Head Island from the creek to the oceanfront, golf course and maritime forest. Each fully furnished and well-equipped rental unit comes with a guest club

VACATION RENTALS OAK ISLAND, NC

Families love this unspoiled, treasured island with its 14 miles of beaches, three fishing piers and lots of local appeal.

Call us for information regarding this wonderful year-round vacation destination.

Coastal Vacation Resorts
P.O. Box 910 • Oak Island, NC 28465
910.278.5405 • 888.703.5469
www.coastalvacationresortsoakisland.com

ALAN HOLDEN VACATIONS

Generations of Family Vacations!

Alan Holden Vacations offers the largest selection of properties in the area.

128 Ocean Blvd. West
Holden Beach, NC 28462

Sales & Construction
Outstanding Agents
Outstanding Results.

Holden Beach
(800) 360-9770

Sunset Beach
(888) 414-7355

Calabash
(800) 765-3203

Oak Island
(866) 350-7653

www.AtTheBeachNC.com

1.800.720.2200
www.holden-beach.com
Vacations@AtTheBeachNC.com

membership, one or more golf carts, bikes, grills, beach chairs, linens and towels. Some units are pet friendly.

SOUTHPORT/OAK ISLAND

Coastal Vacation Resorts-Oak Island
5618 E. Oak Island Dr., Oak Island
(910) 278-5405, (888) 703-5469

The folks at Coastal Vacation Resorts take great pride in providing guests with the utmost in professional and personalized service. It is very important to them that your stay be a comfortable and enjoyable one. Here you will find a wide variety of rental options, whether you are searching for a long-term rental in a residential area or an oceanfront or waterway location for your special vacation. You will be sincerely welcomed to this lovely, family-oriented island and treated like family as well. Call for a free copy of the vacation guide or visit the website and book online.

Oak Island Accommodations, Inc.
300 Country Club Dr., Oak Island
(910) 278-6011, (888) 243-8132,
(800) 909-RENT
www.oakislandescape.com

Whether your interest is in deep-sea fishing, golf, kayaking through the waterways, or just lying back and enjoying the 14 miles of white sand and ocean waves, the staff at Oak Island Accommodations will make planning your vacation a breeze. Their collection of 650 charming oceanfront to sound-side cottages offers you selections from two bedrooms to 12 bedrooms, some with pet-friendly options. Visit their full-service website to make your choice online or call for a personal touch. Oak Island Accommodations offers linen and beach equipment rentals, concierge services and golf discounts for your convenience and pleasure.

Southern Retreats
4565 Long Beach Rd., Southport
(910) 202-1180, (877) 454-0055
www.SouthernRetreats.net

A partner of Prudential Carolina Real Estate, this property management company offers a variety of vacation and long-term rentals. Whether you're staying for a while or merely a week, Southern Retreats has the ideal rental property for you. Prime locations are available on the beaches, downtown Wilmington and everywhere in between. Visit the website above for more information.

HOLDEN BEACH

Brunswickland Realty
123 Ocean Blvd. W., Holden Beach
(910) 842-6949, (800) 842-6949

In business since the 1970s, Brunswickland Realty manages single-family cottages and larger homes. Accommodations are available on the oceanfront, second row, canal side, dunes and Intracoastal Waterway.

OCEAN ISLE BEACH

COOKE REALTORS®

Open 7 days a week
Internet bookings 24 hrs, a day
Great seasonal discounts
SALES • RENTALS • DEVELOPMENT

1-800-NC-BEACH
www.cookerealty.com

Coastal Vacation Resorts
131 Ocean Blvd. W., Holden Beach
(910) 842-8000, (800) 252-7000
www.coastalvacationresorts.com

This company, located on Holden Beach, (named one of the 38 Best American Beaches) specializes in premier vacation accommodations offering rentals to fit every lifestyle and budget. Oceanfront, second row, waterway canal and dune locations are available. Many homes offer amenities such as swimming pools, cabanas, tennis courts and an Intracoastal Waterway marina. Some have private pools. Bookings are available online, where you can view interior photos of the properties. Call for a free color brochure.

Hobbs Realty
114 Ocean Blvd. W., Holden Beach
(910) 842-2002, (800) 655-3367

Family owned and operated, Hobbs Realty manages 250 rental properties with expertise gained from 28 years in the business. Rentals are offered from the ocean to the waterway and everywhere in between. Just cross the bridge to the island, take the first left and you will find Hobbs Realty in the second office on the left. Check out the website for both interior and exterior views and to book online.

Alan Holden Vacations
128 Ocean Blvd. W., Holden Beach
(910) 842-6061, (800) 720-2200
www.holden-beach.com

This busy agency, the largest in the area, manages more than 300 rental properties on Holden Beach, from beach cottages and condominiums to luxury homes with private pools. Locations include oceanfront, canal and waterway, second-row and dune homes. Alan Holden will tell you "nobody knows the beach better than a Holden."

OCEAN ISLE BEACH

Cooke Realtors
1 Causeway Dr., Ocean Isle Beach
(910) 579-3535, (800) 622-3224
www.cookerealty.com

This well-established island realty company, on a family-oriented beach, offers 500 rental homes, cottages and condominiums from one to 12 bedrooms. Choose from oceanfront, second- and third-row, canalside, West End and Island Park locations.

Island Realty Inc.
109-2 Causeway Dr., Ocean Isle Beach
(910) 579-3599, (800) 589-3599

Island Realty is a family-owned company. Its staff takes a special interest in mak-

---

i *Most property management services offer you the option of having the rental unit cleaned following your visit. The charge is nominal and worth every penny, as you're just not going to feel like cleaning after you've had such a wonderful, relaxing vacation!*

ing sure that your vacation will be one to remember. The company has beach cottages, condominiums and villas available for rent. Whether on the oceanfront, waterfront or canal, there is a perfect location for everyone. Check out their website for more information.

R. H. McClure Realty Inc.
24 Causeway Dr., Ocean Isle Beach
(910) 579-3586, (800) 332-5476

R. H. McClure Realty, Inc. is a full-service realty brokerage that has been established on Ocean Isle Beach for more than 20 years. The large rental inventory includes oceanfront homes and condos, mid-island cottages and deep-water canal homes with individual private docks. Spring and fall discounts are available. Virtual tour and on-line bookings are available. Call for a free color vacation brochure.

Ocean Isle Beach Realty, Inc.
15 Causeway Dr., Ocean Isle Beach
(910) 575-7770, (800) 374-7361
www.oibrealty.com

Ocean Isle Beach Realty handles a variety of vacation rental needs, including single-family homes, condominiums and cottages. Rentals are available on the oceanfront, interior, canal and along the Intracoastal Waterway.

Sloane Realty Vacation Rentals
16 Causeway Dr., Ocean Isle Beach
(910) 579-6216, (800) 843-6044

Sloane Realty Vacations of Ocean Isle Beach and Sunset Beach provides vacationers with accommodations in privately-owned homes and condos on Ocean Isle Beach, Sunset Beach and the mainland golf courses. Whether a one-bedroom condo or a nine-bedroom home meets your needs, Sloane Realty Vacations has a premier selection to choose from. Call for a free brochure or book online. Winter rentals are also available.

Southern Retreats
120-1 Causeway Drive, Ocean Isle Beach
(910) 575-0290, (800) 880-0455
www.southernretreats.net

A partner of Prudential Carolina Real Estate, this property management company offers a variety of vacation and long-term rentals. Whether you're staying for a while or merely a week, Southern Retreats has the ideal rental property for you. Prime locations

The Islander Villas offer spectacular floorplans featuring 4 bedroom and 4 baths. These are the best Ocean Isle Beach has to offer.
15 Causeway Dr. • Ocean Isle Beach
(910) 575-7770 • (800) 374-7361
www.oibrealty.com

are available on the beaches, downtown Wilmington and everywhere in between.

Williamson Realty, Inc.
119 Causeway Dr. SW, Ocean Isle Beach
(910) 579-2373, (800) 727-9222
www.williamsonrealty.com

Among the area's largest vacation rental companies, Williamson Realty, Inc. offers more than 350 vacation homes and condos from oceanfront to soundfront. Well established since 1975, this company with its friendly professional staff will help you find that perfect beach rental for you and your family.

Vacation Rentals

Williamson Realty, Inc.

OCEAN ISLE BEACH

Oceanfront to soundfront cottages and condos. Enjoy beautiful sunrises as well as spectacular sunsets. Golf, fishing & shops nearby. Book your reservations online or call.

1-800-727-9222
www.williamsonrealty.com

FREE COLOR BROCHURE

Over 300 Vacation Homes on Beautiful Sunset Beach Island

Call for your free Rental Guide

**910-579-9000 or
1-800-331-6428**

**Visit us on the web at
www.sunsetvacations.com**

SUNSET
VACATIONS.

**401 S. Sunset Blvd.
Sunset Beach, NC
28468**

SUNSET BEACH

Carolina Golf and Beach Resorts
818 Colony Pl., Sunset Beach
(910) 579-7181, (800) 222-1524

Carolina Golf and Beach Resorts provides nightly and weekly golf and accommodations packages. Accommodations include one-, two- and three-bedroom condominiums on the Oyster Bay Golf Links and beach rentals on Sunset Beach.

Sea Trail Golf Resort & Conference Center
211 Clubhouse Rd., Sunset Beach
(800) 624-6601

Sea Trail Golf Resort & Conference Center is an excellent choice for your vacation, be it for a week or more than a month. Accommodations are in natural settings and you can choose from a guest room, a mini-suite efficiency or a spacious fairway villa. When you decide on a villa, you may have your choice of the Royal Poste, River Creek I & II, or Club Villa neighborhoods on the Dan Maples Golf Course. Also available are the newly built Champions, with one or two bedrooms and elevator access. Champion units are located on the Willard Byrd Golf Course.

There are three golf courses here, including the Rees Jones Golf Course (see our Golf chapter). Amenities provided by the Village Activity Center include an outdoor pool and whirlpool; the Oasis Pool Bar; an indoor pool and whirlpool; a weight room and cardiovascular theater with fitness classes including yoga, water yoga and water aerobics; a spa where you can get a soothing massage or a relaxing manicure or pedicure. The staff can

The area offers a wide variety of vacation rentals, from high-rise condos to cozy family beach cottages.

photo: Peter Doran

arrange for bicycling, deep-sea fishing, jet skiing, horseback riding or adventure cruising. Card games, board games and crafts are some of the available indoor activities. The activity center has an outdoor volleyball area and two tennis courts with racquet rentals. Especially for kids there is a pool, an activity room for arts and crafts, games, movies and weekly Kids Night Out parties.

Nearby communities offer a variety of entertainment at movie theaters, shopping centers and outlet malls, restaurants, dinner theaters and live shows.

The complimentary Sea Trail Shuttle is available to take you to the beach and throughout Sea Trail Golf Resort & Conference Center.

Sunset Properties
419 S. Sunset Blvd., Sunset Beach
(910) 579-9900, (800) 525-0182

This family-owned company, founded in 1988, handles the rental of more than 400 vacation homes and duplexes exclusively on Sunset Beach. Rentals run from Saturday to Saturday during the season. A minimum stay of two nights is required in the off season. Bookings are available online.

Sunset Vacations
401 S. Sunset Blvd., Sunset Beach
(910) 579-9000, (800) 331-6428
www.sunsetvacations.com

Sunset Vacations offers a wide assortment of attractive, single-family homes for rent throughout Sunset Beach, including oceanfront, canal, bayfront and inlet locations. They have beach homes to fit every style, location and budget, and you can book directly online. This is an experienced company with an extreme commitment to making your vacation just right.

Topsail Island

A Beach Place Realty
106 N. Topsail Dr., Surf City
(910) 328-2522, (877) 884-2522

Check it out before you check-in with A Beach Place Realty virtual tour. With online virtual tours of all their rental properties, your only surprise will be the fresh flowers Laura places in each cottage. In addition to this special touch, renters can be assured of

ACCESS *Realty*

Your Key to Coastal Living

1-800-TOPSAIL
2 Locations to Serve You!

513A Roland Ave. (beside post office)
*13480 Hwy 50/210
Surf City, NC 28445
910-328-4888

*opening this summer in the Surf City Gateway Plaza

friendly, efficient service for all their rental needs. A Beach Place Realty has single-family homes, duplexes and condominiums from one end of Topsail Island to the other. An added benefit includes quick repair service from the agency's own construction business.

Access Realty
513 Roland Ave., Surf City
13480 Hwy. 50/210, Surf City
(910) 328-4888, (800) 867-7245
www.accessthebeach.com

Access Realty is a full-service brokerage company that offers a variety of accommodations on Topsail Island, from oceanfront

Topsail Island

We'll get you there

Century 21 ACTION, Inc.
1.800.760.4150
century21topsail.com

Topsail Island

Beachfront Vacation Rentals & Sales
Condominiums • Townhomes • Beach Cottages

COASTLINE REALTY

Call for a free Vacation Brochure
(800) 497-5463 or (910) 327-7711
www.cbcoastline.com • rentals@cbcoastline.com

Located in the Topsail Way Shopping Center
965 Old Folkstone Road, Suite 108
Sneads Ferry, NC 28460

A Division Of

COLDWELL BANKER 🅱
Coastline Realty
Expect The Best.

An Independently Owned and Operated Member of
Coldwell Banker Residential Affiliates, Inc.

and soundfront homes to oceanfront condominiums with a pool and tennis court.

Jean Brown Real Estate, Inc.
522 N. New River Dr., Surf City
(910) 328-1640, (800) 745-4480
www.topsailbeaches.com

Jean Brown Real Estate, located in the heart of Surf City, has a friendly, qualified staff ready to assist vacationers or year-round renters in finding the properties that meet their needs. From the ocean to the sound and mainland locations, if Jean Brown Real Estate doesn't have the property required, they will try to find it elsewhere. Friendly, professional service can always be found at this agency.

Bryson and Associates, Inc.
809 Roland Ave., Surf City
(910) 328-2468, (800) 326-0747

Bryson and Associates have been serving the Topsail Island area for more than 20 years with a commitment to customer service. Prime rental properties are available on the oceanfront, second row, ocean view, soundfront, sound view and the canalfront. Queens Grant Condominiums are managed and rented through Bryson and Associates.

Century 21 Action, Inc.
518 Roland Ave., Surf City
200 North Shore Village, Sneads Ferry
(910) 328-2511, (800) 255-2233
www.century21topsail.com

In business for 34 years, Century 21 Action has two offices serving the Topsail area. With locations in Sneads Ferry and Surf City, Century 21 Action offers hundreds of the best vacation and long-term rentals. Oceanfront cottages to soundside condos, the staff at Century 21 Action will find the perfect fit for your coastal getaway.

Coldwell Banker - Coastline Realty
Topsail Way Shopping Center, 965 Old Folkstone Rd., Ste. 108, Sneads Ferry
(910) 327-7711, (800) 497-5463
www.cbcoastline.com

This company offers oceanfront vacation rentals that include condominiums (with swimming pools and tennis courts), townhomes, single-family homes, luxury oceanfront homes and beach cottages. They have numerous five-, six- and seven-bedroom homes as well as many long-term rentals.

Intracoastal Realty
302 N. New River Rd., Surf City
(910) 256-3780
www.intracoastalrentals.com

Intracoastal offers a great selection of vacation beach rentals in North Topsail, Surf City and Topsail Beach. You'll find the perfect single-family home, old-style beach cottage or condominium, many with on-site swimming pools and tennis courts. A virtual tour of Intracoastal Realty's vacation rentals is available at their website. Intracoastal also handles long-term rentals in the Hampstead and Topsail Island areas.

Island Real Estate by Cathy Medlin
The Fishing Village, Roland Ave., Surf City
(910) 328-2323, (800) 622-6886
www.topsailvacation.com

Build sand castles and memories as you let the vacation specialists of Island Real Estate provide that perfect beach rental for your family. This long-time veteran of real estate sales and rentals can provide you with anything from a ten-bedroom mega-house to a six-bedroom geodesic dome, to a one-or two-bedroom condo or townhome. If you · didn't find the perfect getaway, you didn't ask the vacation team at Island Real Estate about their 200 units.

Kathy S. Parker Real Estate
1000 N.C. Hwy. 210, Sneads Ferry
(910) 327-2219, (800) 327-2218

This full-service realty office has more than 100 long-term and vacation rental properties, primarily in the North Topsail Beach and Sneads Ferry areas. The rental specialists take pride in matching the renter with the right property. Homes or condominiums are offered for weekly, weekend or nightly rentals. This agency is open year round and offers 24-hour telephone service.

Sand Dollar Real Estate Inc.
Sand Dollar Village,
214 B North Topsail Dr., Surf City
(910) 328-5199, (800) 948-4360

Specializing in Topsail Island properties, Sand Dollar offers weekly or weekend

Topsail Realty, Inc.

We offer the greatest selection of vacation rental homes on southern Topsail Island.

712 South Anderson Blvd., Topsail Beach
(800) 526-6432   (910) 328-5241
www.topsail-realty.com

rentals from the oceanfront to the island's soundside. Rental properties include new homes and duplexes that boast up to eight bedrooms. Sand Dollar also handles property management.

Ward Realty Corp.
SALES • RENTALS • CONSTRUCTION

"Original Developers of Topsail Island"

800-782-6216 • 910-328-3221
www.wardrealty.com
e-mail: info@wardrealty.com
116 S. Topsail Dr., Surf City, NC

Southern Retreats
13567 N.C. Hwy. 50, Surf City
(910) 329-0200, (866) 798-0200
www.SouthernRetreats.net

A partner of Prudential Carolina Real Estate, this property management company offers a variety of vacation and long-term rentals. Whether you're staying for a while or merely a week, Southern Retreats has the ideal rental property for you. Prime locations are available on the beaches, downtown Wilmington and everywhere in between. Visit the website for more information.

Topsail Realty, Inc.
712 S. Anderson Blvd., Topsail Beach
(910) 328-5241 (800) 526-6432
www.topsail-realty.com

Bring the entire family, or make a quiet escape by yourself, to one of more than 200 vacation homes Topsail Realty offers for fulfilling, relaxing vacations on southern Topsail Island. For more than three decades, Topsail Realty has offered a variety of lodging, from homes for large families to two-bedroom cottages for quiet getaways. Locations vary from oceanfront to soundfront and include Serenity Point townhomes on the southernmost tip of the island. Topsail Realty is the only Topsail Island company that specializes exclusively in vacation rentals and property management in order to provide unsurpassed service for vacationers and homeowners.

Treasure Realty
Treasure Plaza, Ste. R, N.C. Hwys. 210
and 172, Sneads Ferry
(910) 327-4444, (800) 762-3961

Treasure Realty has specialized in vacation and long-term rentals in North Topsail Beach and Sneads Ferry for more than 15 years. The friendly staff has a combined 60-plus years of experience and holds an extensive inventory of oceanfront homes and condominiums as well as soundfront and mainland selections. Treasure Realty now features several of the largest rental homes on Topsail Island.

Ward Realty
116 S. Topsail Dr., Surf City
(910) 328-3221, (800) 782-6216
www.wardrealty.com

Ward Realty has more than 40 years experience in renting vacation cottages. With 200-plus cottages and condos, which range from luxury to budget, from oceanfront to soundfront, from the Topsail Inlet to the New River Inlet and the 26 miles of island in-between, Ward Realty has just the right vacation cottage for you.

Miles of shoreline offer opportunities to walk, dream and recharge.

photo: Peter Doran

⛺ CAMPING

North Carolina's southern coast provides a wealth of camping opportunities. Campgrounds nearest the beaches are generally RV towns with ample amenities, so if you'd like to take along the kitchen sink, you may as well take your electric bug-zapper too. But if you wear your home on your back and have the use of a small boat, leave the parking lot–style camping behind for the isolation of Masonboro Island. In the off-season, your only neighbors may be pelicans and rabbits.

Bicycle campers will find campgrounds about a day's ride apart except in the Wilmington vicinity, where campgrounds are less numerous. In any event, camping the southern coast is ideal for visitors on a budget, anglers who want to walk to the water each morning and anyone for whom recreation is re-creation.

Naturally, the highest rates at private campgrounds apply during the summer and holiday weekends. Tent sites are cheaper than RV sites. At most private grounds, weekly rates often discount the seventh day if payment is made in advance. Rentals by the month or longer are extremely limited from April to August. Some campgrounds offer camper or boat storage for a monthly fee.

As the Boy Scouts say, be prepared, especially for blistering sun, sudden electrical storms with heavy downpours, voracious marsh mosquitoes and insidious no-see-ums in summer. Temperatures in the region generally are mild, except for the occasional frost in winter. Average summer peak temperature is 88, average winter low is 36, and the overall yearly average temperature is 63. April and October average the least rainfall,

about 3 inches each, while July averages the most with nearly 8 inches. However, weather patterns can be a little unpredictable, so be prepared for rain in any season. Sunscreen is essential. Hats and eye protection are wise, and insect repellent useful.

For tent camping, a waterproof tent fly is a must, and a tarp or dining fly is handy when cooking. Pack longer tent stakes or sand stakes for protection against high winds. Stay abreast of weather reports, especially during hurricane season (June 1 through November 30), and always bring a radio. A lightweight camp stove and cook set will come in handy when restaurants aren't convenient and at the many campgrounds where fires are prohibited.

The primary creature hazards are poisonous snakes, which are prevalent in forested areas, and ticks, which have been known to carry disease. Beware of poison ivy, poison oak and poison sumac in brushwood and forests. Raccoons and other small nocturnal animals are seldom more than a nuisance, although rabid animals are occasionally reported in rural areas. Normally, the animals posing the greatest threat are human, which is why open fires and alcoholic beverages are restricted in most campgrounds.

For hikers or cyclists carrying packs, there are two noteworthy Wilmington retail outlets for equipment. In business for more than 50 years, **Canady's Sport Center**, 3220 Wrightsville Avenue, (910) 791-6280, is an excellent outdoor outfitter with a varied inventory. It's closed on Sunday. Another excellent source for equipment and outdoor clothing is **Great Outdoor Provision Co.** in Hanover Center, 3501 Oleander Drive, Wilmington, (910) 343-1648. It's open seven days a week. Your other choices for field gear are **Dick's Sporting Goods**, 816 S. College Road, (910) 793-1904, and the two **Wal-Mart Super Centers**, one at 5135 Carolina Beach Road, (910) 452-0944, and the other at 5226 Sigmon Road, (910) 392-4034, which are good

---

ℹ️ *All North Carolina state parks are wildlife preserves and prohibit the removal of any plants, rocks, animals or artifacts from their sites.*

Great people. Great camping.™

KOA at Wilmington, NC

- Free WiFi & cable TV
- Bark Park
- Cardio room
- New RV Wash
- Open all year
- Kamping Kabins®
- Clean restrooms and hot showers
- Large swimming pool
- Laundromat
- Full-service camp store
- Playground

7415 Market Street
Wilmington, NC 28411

Information: (910) 686-7705
Reservations: (888) 562-5699

www.wilmingtonkoa.com

choices for novices and tailgate campers. In Brunswick County, Wal-Mart Super Centers are located in Southport at 1675 N. Howe Street, (910) 454-9909, and in Shallotte, 4540 Main Street, (910) 754-2880.

We've provided here a list of the area's nicest, most popular camping destinations. (For information on children's summer camps, refer to our Kidstuff chapter.)

Wilmington

KOA at Wilmington
7415 Market St., Wilmington
(910) 686-7705, (888) 562-5699
www.wilmingtonkoa.com

Located five miles from Wrightsville Beach and 10 miles from downtown Wilmington, the Wilmington KOA is well situated for getting to all of the local attractions. The award-winning Wilmington KOA is one of the highest-rated campgrounds on the East Coast for cleanliness and friendly service. The tree-shaded grounds include a large swimming pool, a new children's playground, a soccer field, a giant chess set, a full-service camp store, more than 100 campsites (pull-through and tent sites) and full and partial hookups. This pet-friendly campground has clean, newly renovated restrooms, hot showers, laundry facilities and mail service. If you need a break from seeing the sights around town, the Wilmington KOA features Free Wireless Internet, a new RV Wash and an exercise room with cardio equipment. Rather than tent camping why not try the Wilmington KOA's charming heated and air-conditioned Kamping Kabins and Lodges. A convenience store and gas station are located at the entrance to the campground. Nightly, weekly and monthly rates are available, and reservations are accepted and recommended in the high season. The Wilmington KOA is open year round.

Masonboro Island

Accessible only by boat, Masonboro Island is the last and largest undisturbed barrier island remaining on the southern North Carolina coast. It is the fourth component of the North Carolina National Estuarine Research Reserve (see our Higher Education and Research chapter) and deservedly

so. This migrating ribbon of sand and uphill terrain, about 8 miles in length, is immediately south of Wrightsville Beach and offers campers a secluded, primitive experience in the most pristine environment on the Cape Fear coast. It is also used by anglers, bird-watchers, the occasional hunter, students and surfers (who prefer the north end). Everything you'll need must be packed in, and everything you produce should be packed out — everything!

Ninety-seven percent of Masonboro Island remains under state ownership and will always be accessible to visitors. Of the reserve's more than 5,000 acres, about 4,400 acres are tidal marsh and mud flats, so most folks land at the extreme north or south ends, on or near the sandy beaches by the inlets. Pitch camp behind the dunes only and use a cook stove; there is little or no firewood. While the North Carolina Division of Coastal Management hopes to limit its involvement with the island and preserve its traditional uses, it does prohibit polluting the island and camping on and in front of the dune ridge.

Wildlife is remarkable and fragile. During the warm months, Masonboro Island is one of the most successful nesting areas for loggerhead turtles, a threatened species. Piping plovers, also threatened, feed at the island in winter. Keep your eyes on the marshes for river otters and, at low tide, raccoons. Gray foxes, cotton rats and tiny marsh rabbits all frequent the small maritime forest. The marshes, flats and creeks at low tide are excellent places to observe and photograph great blue and little blue herons, tricolor herons, snowy and great egrets, oystercatchers, clapper rails and many other flamboyant birds. Brown pelicans, various terns and gulls, American ospreys and shearwaters all live on Masonboro, if not permanently then at least for some part of their lives. Endangered peregrine falcons are very occasional seasonal visitors.

We recommend plenty of sun protection and insect repellent, perhaps even mosquito netting in the warm months, and trash bags always. Keep in mind that some of the island is still privately owned, not only at the north end, but also throughout the island, and all of it is fragile. The University of North Carolina at Wilmington's Center for Marine Science Research is conducting an ongoing survey of

Sometimes, getting away from the bustle of the city is the best thing you can do for yourself.

photo: Peter Doran

visitor impact on the island and a continuing study of environmental changes caused by hurricanes and other natural forces. Visitors' behavior and scientific scrutiny together will have some influence on whether Masonboro Island becomes severely restricted, so responsible usage is paramount. For more information about Masonboro Island, see the Islands section in our chapter on Attractions.

Carolina Beach

Carolina Beach State Park
Dow Rd., Carolina Beach
(910) 458-8206

Once a campsite for Paleo-Indians, Colonial explorers and Confederate troops, Carolina Beach State Park remains a gem among camping destinations. Watersports enthusiasts are minutes from the Cape Fear River, Masonboro Sound and the Atlantic. The park offers a 42-slip marina with gas and diesel fuel and two launching ramps. Call (910) 458-7770 for the marina. Need we mention the great fishing? The park is a bird- and wildlife-watcher's paradise and home to lizards, deer,

snakes, rare frogs, carnivorous plants and occasionally alligators, opossums, gray foxes and river otters. (All plants and animals are protected within North Carolina State Parks and must not be collected or harassed.)

Six miles of hiking trails wind through several distinct habitats, including maritime forest, pocosin (low, flat, swampy regions) and savanna. Hikers on the Sugarloaf Trail pass over tidal marsh and dunes and along three lime-sink ponds. Cypress Pond, the most unusual, is dominated by a dwarf cypress swamp forest. Ranger-led interpretive programs deepen visitors' understanding of the region's natural bounty. Bikes are not allowed on any of the trails.

Dense vegetation lends the campsites a fair amount of privacy. Each site has a table and grill, and sites are available on a first-come, first-served basis (at a rate of $15 per site, per day or a senior citizen rate of $10 per day, per site for people 62 years of age and older). Two of the 83 campsites are wheelchair accessible. Drinking water and well-kept restrooms with hot showers are close by. There is a dump station for RVs, but

CLOSE-UP

A Meat-Eating Plant?
Meet the Venus Flytrap

Hide the chilluns and don't let the womenfolk outa yer sight! Well, maybe that's a bit alarmist – while North Carolina's carnivorous plant, the Venus Flytrap, does eat insects, it hasn't actually eaten any children or their mothers yet, but rumor has it that one did nibble on the nose of a curious kid who got too close. And some say one ate a very small Chihuahua once.

OK, maybe we made that up, but the Venus Flytrap is real, although there aren't many of them around, which is why you could be fined from $100 to $500 for removing one from state-owned or private lands without permission. While the carnivorous plants, which are native to this area, grow in the wild only in a 75-mile radius of Wilmington, they can be obtained legally from various plant nurseries that cultivate them.

Aside from eating meat, what's so unusual about this plant? Well, try to think of any plant you know of that moves very, very fast on its own without any outside help from the wind or animals. Got you there, didn't I? Consider the fact that this plant moves faster than the eye can see.

Venus's Flytrap, a carnivorous plant that eats insects, is abundant in Carolina Beach State Park. This plant, a relic from pre-human existence on the planet, grows naturally within a 60-mile radius of Wilmington.

To be exact, the Venus Flytrap's leaves change from their open, concave shape to their closed, convex, clamshell-like state in 100 milliseconds. That's 1/10 of a second – faster than the eye can blink. Scientists only recently have discovered that the plant, with the Latin name of Dionaea muscipula, performs this amazing speed-closing act by means of the slow storage of elastic energy followed by its fast release.

If fast closing were all there were to the plant's activity, it would be only semi-miraculous. However, this amazing plant manages to figure out what's good for it to eat and what isn't, which it sort of spits out. For example, if a twig or a leaf falls into the "trap," the leaves will close part way, and then reopen after 12 hours allowing the leaf or twig to fall out or be blown out by the wind.

The mysterious, bug-eating Venus Flytrap is found only in southeastern North Carolina.

photo: Carolina Beach State Park

So how does the Venus Flytrap figure out what's yummy and what isn't? Actually, the plant doesn't think too much about it – mostly because it doesn't have a brain to think with. The determination process is purely mechanical. Favorite treats to eat are spiders, flies, caterpillars, crickets and slugs.

On the inside surface of each pair of leaves are six stiff trigger hairs. If one of the trigger hairs is disturbed one time, nothing happens, but if two of the hairs are touched in close succession or one of the hairs is touched twice in rapid succession, the leaves instantly close – but not all the way. The two leaves close far enough that the spines on the edges of the leaves interlace, forming a cage-like trap that prevents anything inside from getting out.

If whatever is trapped inside the leaves doesn't move, the Venus Flytrap reopens after 12 hours to let the object out. But if whatever is inside continues to move about like a trapped bug or fly would, touching the trigger hairs, the plant realizes it's got a live one and closes the leaves tightly together, forming an airtight seal. Once that happens, it's all over for the bug – he's dinner for the next five to twelve days.

When the leaves close completely, the plant begins secreting acidic digestive juices, kind of like a human stomach does, to dissolve and absorb the soft tissue of the critter inside, leaving only the skeleton. Then the plant reopens, allowing the wind to blow the skeleton out. The number of times a pair of leaves can do this is very limited, however. When they're too pooped to close anymore, the leaves stay open, absorbing energy from the sun so that new pairs of leaves can develop. Eventually they die and fall off.

You might wonder why the Venus Flytrap enjoys snacking on bugs and insects. Well, the plants thrive in the sunny, wet bogs of the coastal area, but the bogs are so low in nutrients that the plants have to supplement their diets with the occasional succulent bug. However, if you buy a Venus Flytrap of your own and intend to feed it, remember that the plant doesn't like Big Macs or anything like that. Put hamburger inside the trap and it will die.

A bill currently pending before the North Carolina legislature would adopt the Venus Flytrap as The Official Carnivorous Plant of The State of North Carolina. Not many other states can have an official plant like that.

Curious about how the plant ended up with such an intriguing name? It's easy to understand how "Flytrap" might relate to its insect-catching abilities, but why "Venus?" According to the International Carnivorous Plant Society, the origin of the name is somewhat lurid. First studied in the 17th and 18th centuries, when women were often portrayed as temptresses greedy for power, botanists apparently found a parallel between capturing and digesting insects and certain aspects of female anatomy and behavior. Thus, the story goes that they named the plant after Venus, the pagan goddess of love and money.

There is some disagreement with regard to the correct spelling of the name. Carolina Beach State Park and the pending N.C. legislation use the term Venus Flytrap. Webster's Dictionary calls it Venus' Flytrap, and Botanical Society documents use both. So, take your pick.

no hookups. Unleashed pets and possession of alcoholic beverages are prohibited.

The park is 15 miles south of Wilmington, a mile north of Carolina Beach just off U.S. 421 on Dow Road. From Wilmington, make a right at the second stoplight after crossing Snow's Cut bridge. Stop by the Visitors Center at the park entrance for information, trail maps and brochures. You might want to spend some time at the Visitors Center exploring the interactive environmental-education exhibits, which include a computer program that explains prescribed burning, a quiz game on biodiversity, a Venus' flytrap puppet and a maze game from the perspective of an insect trying to maneuver through the park. (See our Sports, Fitness and Parks chapter for more information about Carolina Beach State Park.)

Brunswick County Beaches

SUNSET BEACH

KOA Kampground
7200 KOA Dr., Sunset Beach
(910) 576-7562, (888) 562-4240

KOA is a name that everyone recognizes as quality when it comes to camping, and this new facility provides that familiar camping experience to the South Brunswick Islands area. Only five miles from Sunset Beach and Ocean Isle Beach, the KOA offers RV campsites (including extra-long sites), tent sites, Kamping Kabins and a Kottage/Lodge. Sites include 30 AMP or 50 AMP service, cable TV and access to a Kamping Kitchen. DSL hook-up and wireless Internet are available, as are a swimming pool, horseshoe pits, a basketball goal, a volleyball net and fishing. Planned activities are offered on holidays and weekends. Amenities available with a small charge include LP gas, firewood and bicycles. Nearby amenities include three golf courses, area attractions and delicious Calabash seafood.

Ocean Aire Camp World Inc.
2614 Holden Beach Rd. SW
(N.C. Hwy. 130), Supply
(910) 842-9072

Open year round and located 2.5 miles from Holden Beach, this 133-site campground offers daily, weekly, monthly and annual rates. Amenities include 30-amp electricity, water and sewer, modern bath houses with tiled hot showers, laundry facilities, LP gas, security lights and a convenience store (open March through October). A large swimming pool, nine-hole putt-putt golf course, pool tables, video games, volleyball, horseshoes and a children's playground provide recreation options. Covered boat storage with monthly boat or camper storage rates is available.

SHALLOTTE

Sea Mist Camping Resort
4616 Devane Rd. SW, Shallotte
(910) 754-8916

Sea Mist's panoramic view of Shallotte Inlet and Ocean Isle Beach is enough to entice any camper, but the view is only one of the appealing amenities. Visitors love Sea Mist's pool, reputedly the largest in Brunswick County, with its shaded deck and picnic area. Volleyball, basketball and horseshoes are among the activities available. Use of the boat ramp carries no extra charge. This Woodall-rated resort is open year round and has 250 spacious RV sites with tables. Most have full hookups. The restrooms, bathhouse and coin-operated laundry facilities are clean, and the camp store is open from March 1 through November 30. Perhaps best of all, Sea Mist is only 10 minutes from the attractions of Ocean Isle Beach. Leashed pets are permitted. Daily and annual rates are available as well as boat storage for annual guests. Reserve early.

Sea Mist is at the Intracoastal Waterway opposite the east end of Ocean Isle Beach. Follow the blue and white camping signs along N.C. Highway 179 to Brick Landing Road and continue to the end of the pavement. Turn left onto Devane Road.

Topsail Island Area

Lanier's Campground
1161 Spot Ln., Surf City
(910) 328-9431, (877) 665-5347

This large, friendly campground is on the mainland side of the Intracoastal Waterway in Surf City. Full hookups, camper/pop-up and tent sites with recently added fire rings are available, some with shade. The interior roads are paved. Campground amenities include a swimming pool, pier, fish cleaning station, pay phones, picnic tables, a dump station, laundry facilities, limited groceries, a bath house, an arcade and a sandwich grill with hand-dipped ice cream. Horseshoes, beach bingo on Friday nights and Saturday afternoons, a children's playground, holiday activities and interdenominational church services are some of the activities offered in season at the campground. It's open year round.

Old Ferry Marina Campground
150 Old Ferry Rd., Sneads Ferry
(910) 327-2258

Old Ferry Marina Campground makes it convenient to camp and fish from the same property. A great place for a relaxing vacation, this campground is close enough to the beach for the sun worshiper. Returning campers claim they keep coming back because they enjoy the friendship of the owners and the other campers and fishermen. Full hook-ups are offered on a daily, weekly, monthly or seasonal basis. Besides fishing, amenities include a bath house.

Virginia Creek Campground
Watts Landing Rd., Surf City area
(910) 329-4648, (910) 329-3081

Virginia Creek Campground is located on a large tract of waterfront land that has been in the King family for 200 years. With pull-through sites, full hookups and tent sites, there is a spot for every camper. Amenities include a nearby boat ramp, hot showers, fishing, laundry facilities and convenience to restaurants, shopping and the beach. Virginia Creek Campground is pet friendly.

Inland

Holland's Shelter Creek
8315 N.C. Hwy. 53 E., Burgaw
(910) 259-5743

Holland's offers full RV hookups in a rustic setting along the river. If you don't have a recreational vehicle, Holland's also has cabins that provide the perfect balance between rustic atmosphere and comfort. Sleeping up to four persons, the cabins have heat, air conditioning and indoor plumbing. Canoe, kayak and paddleboat rentals are available for any size group from the solitary fisherman to family reunions or scout troops camping together. Holland's Shelter Creek Restaurant and General Store are located on the same property to make your camping trip complete. The campground is open year-round.

Lake Waccamaw State Park
1866 State Park Dr., Lake Waccamaw
(910) 646-4748

Lake Waccamaw, named after the region's tribal natives, is the largest of the Carolina bays and is 38 miles from Wilmington in Columbus County. It wasn't until the age of aviation that thousands of the elliptical depressions known as Carolina bays were noticed dotting the Carolinas' coastal plain. All the depressions are oriented along northwest-southeast axes. Locals came to call them "bays," referring to the abundance of bay trees — red, sweet and loblolly — that flourish there.

About 400,000 Carolina bays exist, ranging in size from a fraction of an acre to Lake Waccamaw's more than 9,000 acres. Some are lakes, but most are seasonal wetlands filled with fertile peat. Their origin is still a mystery. A hypothesis that an ancient meteor shower or explosion formed them collapsed under scrutiny. A widely accepted theory is that they were formed by strong winds blowing across a sandy landscape or shallow sea during the last Ice Age. Lake Waccamaw's shallow waters support 52 species of fish. Several species of aquatic animals living here exist nowhere else in the world.

The Visitor Center houses park offices, an auditorium where nature films are shown and an exhibit hall with interactive displays that highlight the lake and surrounding area.

Four nature trails — Lake Trail, Sand Ridge Nature Trail, Pine Woods Trail and Loblolly Trail — and the boardwalk provide memorable glimpses of the unique and diverse plant life here. Most trails begin from the Visitor Center or the picnic area. Among the many species of plants found here are the region's oldest stands of cypress trees, reindeer moss, turkey oaks and the rare Venus' flytrap.

Visitors planning to camp at Lake Waccamaw must be willing to rough it slightly. The camping area is undeveloped, with no more facilities than pit toilets, picnic tables and fire circles. Four primitive group campsites (no water) are available by reservation or on a first-come basis. Permits may be obtained at the Visitors Center, (910) 646-4748. Fees are $9 per site with $1 per person for groups of more than eight people. Reservations are for groups only and not intended for family campers. Trailer camping is not allowed.

The park is about 7 miles south of U.S. Highway 74/76. Highly visible signs along that route and along N.C. Highway 214 lead the way. Entrance to the park is from Bella Coola Road, which veers off State Road 1947.

⌘ RESTAURANTS

A bounty of mouthwatering, fresh-catch seafood figures prominently almost everywhere you dine along North Carolina's southern coast. These coastal waters yield consistently high-quality seafood, and just about every restaurant offers fresh daily seafood specialties that may include tuna, grouper, mahi-mahi, mackerel, triggerfish and shellfish, to name only a few. Talented local and transplanted chefs vie to create visually appealing entrees and bring innovative flair to seafood preparation. Fresh-catch entrees and specials are often available grilled, baked, broiled, blackened or fried.

This region's restaurants, particularly in the port city of Wilmington, reflect a rich international community in the choices of cuisine now available, including Thai, Indian, Chinese (including Szechuan), Greek, Italian, German, Japanese, Mexican, Jamaican, Caribbean and French.

Health-food enthusiasts are pleased by exciting vegetarian and organic dishes and products offered at numerous island restaurants and markets, including Lovey's Natural Foods & Cafe and Tidal Creek Foods Co-op.

Also represented throughout our area are a number of major restaurant chains, both national and regional, as well as the usual fast food options. Well-known pizza franchises — Domino's, Pizza Hut, Papa John's — offer delivery, and several area restaurants feature gourmet pizzas for the connoisseur.

FAVORITE LOCAL FOODS

Naturally, the traditional regional specialties make up the heart and soul of Southern coastal dining. The famous Calabash-style seafood is ever-present. It gets its name from the Brunswick County town to the south once heralded as the seafood capital of the world for having nearly 30 seafood restaurants within a square mile. Calabash style calls for seasoned cornmeal batter and deep frying and has become synonymous with all-you-can-eat. Calabash restaurants typically serve a huge variety of piping-hot seafood in massive quantities accompanied by creamy cole slaw and uniquely shaped, deep-fried dollops of corn bread called hush puppies.

Low-country steam-offs are buckets filled with a variety of shellfish, potatoes, corn and Old Bay seasoning. When fresh oysters are in season in the fall, oyster roasts abound. Crab meat is popular, and competition is stiff among restaurants boasting the best crab dip. Seafood chowder and chili are two other popular dishes put to the test in local competitions and cook-offs. New Year's Day dinners may include collards and black-eyed peas, symbolic of paper money and small change, to ensure prosperity in the year to come. Okra, sweet potatoes, grits, turnip greens, mustard greens and kale are also regional favorites. Hoppin' John, based on black-eyed peas and rice, is a hearty dish seen in many variations. Shrimp and grits is another favorite dish appearing in various incarnations from restaurant to restaurant. Boiled peanuts are popular snacks, frequently available at roadside stands, and nowhere does pecan pie taste better. Iced tea flows freely, in most places by the pitcher-full, and locals prefer it sweet.

Many North Carolinians enjoy good barbecue in all its variations — pork or beef, chopped or shredded, sweet or tangy — and the coastal regions are no exception. Many beach communities boast at least one barbecue restaurant hidden among the seafood restaurants — touting the best recipe, of course.

PLANNING AND PRICING

Reservations are generally not required unless your party consists of six persons or more, and many restaurants throughout the region don't accept reservations at all, especially during peak season. It wasn't very long ago that waiting time at most Wilmington

Come Home to Rossi's

All it takes is one taste - whether the delicate fish, the hearty veal or beef selections, tantalizing chicken choices, truly "al dente" pastas with their savory toppings - to recognize that here, EVERY dish is distinctively, deliciously, "a la Rossi." Crisp salads, crusty-topped breads, a fine wine list, two intimate, softly-lighted rooms as setting, the "Eighty-Eights" piano bar, with sparkling entertainment until 2 am - and oh, those desserts! all add to the evening's delight. And the service is the beach's best!

Come home to Rossi's...
the restaurant you've been waiting for.

Wilmington, NC
1125 Military Cutoff Rd.   910-256-8870

Rossi's

FINE
ITALIAN
CUISINE

The NORTH CAROLINA AQUARIUM at FORT FISHER

Come Sea Us!

You'll go *WILD* over our new
EXOTIC AQUATICS GALLERY!
Cuttlefish, Lionfish and Sea Snakes, Oh My!

- Dive programs twice daily
  - Feedings, 3pm daily
    - Sleepovers
      - Surfing
      - Camps
    - *Lots more!*

OPEN DAILY 9 - 5

1.910.458.8257 www.ncaquariums.com

restaurants was negligible. With the region's growing year-round visitor season, the wait has changed substantially for many restaurants. At most popular eateries in Wilmington, expect to find waiting lists throughout the summer, during festivals and on most holidays. Some restaurants have call-ahead seating, which allows you to place your name on the waiting list before your arrival. A call to the restaurant regarding their policy is recommended.

Restaurant hours are frequently reduced or curtailed in winter, although some restaurants close entirely for a month or more, especially in the beach communities. Most places serve later on Friday and Saturday nights than on weeknights, so call ahead to verify hours and reservations. You may also want to inquire about early bird specials and senior citizen discounts even if such information isn't included in our listings.

In keeping with the area's resort character and hot summers, dining here is generally very casual. While you might feel out of place wearing shorts at fancier restaurants such as The Pilot House or Caprice, casual dress is commonplace practically everywhere else. Wearing shorts or polo shirts during the summer, even at the better restaurants, may be the only practical way to end a very full day.

Most restaurants listed here accept major credit cards, and some will accept personal checks with an ID. We'll let you know which ones do not.

Coffeehouses are a welcome addition to the local landscape, particularly in Wilmington, so we've listed a number of the most popular spots at the end of the chapter. Often reflecting the communities in which they thrive, these southeastern North Carolina gathering places exhibit a definite artistic and coastal flair. Local artwork receives pride of place on many cafe walls in this culturally rich region. Warm and courteous friendliness is thrown in for good measure. All offer the standard array of coffeehouse beverages, from traditional espressos, lattes, cappuccinos and herbal teas to cool, sweet fresh fruit smoothies, with daily specials that are exquisitely exotic. Biscotti, muffins, scones and bagels, made fresh daily on the premises or at local bakeries, are traditional fare for area cafes.

110 BREWS
OLD CHICAGO®
PASTA & PIZZA

EAT. DRINK. BE YOURSELF.

5023 MARKET STREET WILMINGTON
PHONE: (910) 796.0644
FAX: (910) 796.0643

The Bakeries section at the end of this chapter lists outstanding establishments in the region. These talented and well-established bake shops also supply several local restaurants and eateries with delicious homemade breads and mouth-watering desserts.

PRICE CODE

The following price code is based on the average price for two dinner entrees only. For restaurants not serving dinner, the code reflects mid-priced lunch entrees for two. Dual codes indicate that lunch and dinner prices vary significantly. The price codes do not reflect the state/county 7 percent sales tax or gratuities.

$	Less than $15
$$	$16 to $25
$$$	$26 to $40
$$$$	More than $40

WHERE TO EAT

The southern coastal region, especially the Greater Wilmington area, presents an abundance of great places to eat. A complete listing of the region's restaurants and

You can find breakfast-all-day places, which serve meals complete with grits and biscuits, all over the southern coastal area.

"Yes...we're really from Brooklyn"

BROOKLYN PIZZA CO.
ogden commons shopping center
6932 Market Street • Wilmington, NC
395-5558 • 395-5106 • 395-5206
Serving: Pizza • Pasta
Calzone • Hot Sandwiches
DINE IN • CARRY OUT • DELIVERY

eateries could fill an entire book. This chapter offers a sampling of what's available in each area. If your favorite restaurant isn't listed here, it may be because it's among the many fine restaurants that are impossible to miss because of reputation or location. We've made a special effort to include the more out-of-the-way places that shouldn't be missed, along with some obvious favorites. Please keep in mind that restaurants may frequently change menu items, hours of operation or close after this book goes to press. Call ahead to verify information that is important to you.

Wilmington

Bijou   **$$$**
35 N. Front St., Wilmington
(910) 763-9545

Webster's defines "bijou" as "something delicate, elegant or highly prized," and this comfortable dining spot surely fits that description. Located a stone's throw from the Cape Fear River, Bijou offers outstanding French cuisine in a warm and cozy atmosphere. Bijou serves lunch and dinner and is even open for the late diner and those looking for a quiet spot to sip cocktails and chat. Their outdoor courtyard is perfect for couples or groups and is well suited to Wilmington's usually warm evenings. Dine on the finest in French comfort food from a menu that includes steaks, seafood dishes,

fresh breads and pastas and numerous other Gallic delicacies. With regular live entertainment and a banquet space available for private functions, Bijou is an elegant addition to Front Street dining.

Boca Bay   **$$$**
2025 Eastwood Rd., Wilmington
(910) 256-1887

Located between Wrightsville Beach and Wilmington, Boca Bay's covered outdoor patio, fountain and palm trees provide a relaxed, upbeat atmosphere. When you're hungry but not quite sure what you're in the mood for, this is the place to go. Boca Bay's tapas-style menu allows you and your companions to create your own dining experience by sharing a variety of specialties from around the world, served in smaller portions so you can enjoy several different yet complementary flavors in one meal. Of course, you'll want to complete your meal with one of Boca Bay's delectable desserts. Boca Bay is open every day for dinner, and in the spring and summer season they're open for Sunday brunch as well. Reservations are welcome.

Brasserie du Soleil   **$$$**
Lumina Station, 1908 Eastwood Rd., Wilmington
(910) 256-2226

Loosely translated as "Eatery of the Sun," the latest jewel in restaurateur Ash Aziz's crown is nestled in the heart of Lumina Station and continues his tradition of fine dining establishments. Featuring a delightful assortment of appetizers as well as a "make-your-own" salad option, the starters on the menu are top notch. Follow these with one of the sumptuous fish or steak entrees for a perfectly cooked main course. If you have any room left, the dessert list is superb and features the not-to-be-missed chocolate sampler. With a distinctive interior design, outstanding service and all the right peripheral touches (including a fantastic selection of wines, beers and cocktails), this spot will light up Lumina Station diner's palates year round.

Brooklyn Pizza Co.   **$$**
6932 Market St., Wilmington
(910) 395-5558

Craving real New York pizza? You'll find it at Brooklyn Pizza Co. The owner's father ran a pizza parlor in Brooklyn for decades, and the secret to delicious New York pizza has apparently been passed down from father to son. Besides the ultimate in NY pizza and a complete selection of tasty heroes, Brooklyn Pizza's menu also includes several pasta dishes, including the ever-popular Penne with Vodka Sauce – penne pasta with diced tomatoes, heavy cream, scallions and a dash of vodka. Chicken Marsala with Grilled Zucchini, Chicken Francese with Steamed Broccoli, and Fried Calamari are just a few of the entrees available. Brooklyn Pizza is open for lunch and dinner Monday through Saturday.

Caffe Phoenix   **$$-$$$**
9 S. Front St, Wilmington
(910) 343-1395

This downtown eatery has more than a decade on most other restaurants in the area. Offering the finest in Italian cuisine infused with many other influences, the Caffe Phoenix combines delicious food with a casual and comfortable environment. Numerous daily specials highlight the menu and garlic lovers won't be able to pass up the famous Caesar salad. Rotating art shows feature the finest of Wilmington's creative community and the renovated space has a fresh, updated feel. With a sidewalk café open in the warmer months for al fresca dining and a reputation as one of Wilmington's best places to be seen, this is one culinary experience you can't afford to miss.

Experience a Wilmington Classic

Innovative
Mediterranean Cuisine

Lunch • Dinner • Sunday Brunch
Private Catering for up to 80 guests

CAFFÈ PHOENIX

910.343.1395
9 South Front Street
Historic Downtown Wilmington

Wilmington, North Carolina

The Cape Golf and Racquet Club
Restaurant   **$$-$$$**
535 The Cape Blvd., Wilmington
(910) 794-5757

This unusual golf club restaurant overlooks the beautiful golf course at The Cape. After a full day on the course, visit the restaurant for some Southern hospitality and a menu filled with traditional favorites and house specialties. A formal banquet room is available for large parties. Or call the number above and ask about their custom catering. The restaurant is open daily for lunch and dinner and on Sunday for lunch only. Reservations are recommended.

Caprice bistro

A Bistro is a small, informal neighborhood restaurant, serving good food in generous portions at an affordable price. The ambience is friendly and unpretentious. The service is efficient and not intrusive. Ingredients usually come from the local market.

Caprice tries to recreate this concept...

10 Market Street
Wilmington, NC 28401
open 7 days per week from 5pm
www.capricebistro.com

Bon Appetit!
Thierry & Patricia Moity
910-815-0810

ONE SOUTH FRONT STREET
WILMINGTON
763-VINE

**Caprice Bistro: Restaurant
& Sofa Bar**   **$$-$$$**
10 Market St., Wilmington
(910) 815-0810
www.capricebistro.com

The setting is perfect. Historic downtown Wilmington's riverfront is within view, bricked streets lead to quaint boutiques, and a period horse-drawn carriage passes by regularly. Though lace curtains adorn the windows and white tablecloths drape the tables, Caprice Bistro's atmosphere is one of friendly, casual ease and, for those who have never experienced it, a glimpse of the charm and cuisine of an authentic French bistro. The hearty menu is traditional bistro fare served in generous portions at affordable prices. Your choices include a bounty of appetizers, entrees and classic desserts. Prepared with fresh ingredients and innovative style, this cuisine offers a full continental spectrum, from the homemade country pate, onion soup, steak au poivre, duck confit and profiterolles to an array of entrees featuring steak, seafood, poultry and game. The bistro's wine list offers European wines plus a good choice of American labels as well. Caprice Bistro's second floor is an intimate original sofa bar, perfect for relaxing with a martini or glass of wine. The full menu or simply appetizers and dessert is available in this beautifully appointed bar. The sofa bar is smoker-friendly. (The downstairs dining room is non-smoking.) Caprice Bistro opens nightly for dinner. The sofa bar remains open until 2 AM.

Chelsea's Downtown   **$$-$$$**
1 S. Front St, Wilmington
(910) 763-8463

A wonderful new addition to the heart of downtown, Chelsea's is the perfect place for light European fare and a perfectly paired glass of wine. Featuring examples of French, Italian and Spanish cuisine, the kitchen creates great panini sandwiches, sumptuous bruschetta and delicious salads on their tapas-style menu. With more than 40 wines by the glass and 150 different bottled varieties, Chelsea's also offers a full bar with a great selection of premium spirits and European beers. The restaurant's façade faces on to Front Street, providing some of the best people-watching in town. Enjoy the "Euro chic" atmosphere and impeccable service, and ask Douglas for a recommendation. Chelsea's is open for dinner nightly and stays open until 2 AM. Tuesdays through Sundays and is available for private luncheons.

Circa 1922   **$$$**
8 N. Front St., Wilmington
(910) 762-1922

Circa has become renowned for serving a tapas-style menu, which allows you and your companions to create your own dining experience by sharing several small plates of specialties from around the world. Or you can order individually by course. Each course is marked by the quality and exceptional service that makes this restaurant stand out from the rest. If you're looking to begin your meal with an appetizer, you may want to consider the crab and artichoke dip. Then it's on to an array of tempting choices for your main course. One excellent choice is the Filet Mignon Porto in Pastry, topped with Gruyere cheese and proscuitto ham and wrapped in a puff pastry served atop a tawny port wine sauce. Gauge your appetite for generously portioned, award-winning desserts. The bananas Foster will put you in a state of pure bliss, and the creme brulee is heavenly. The greatest part of Circa, aside from their appetizers, desserts and complete wine list, is the authentic 1922 atmosphere. You will expect F. Scott Fitzgerald to walk in the door before you leave. Circa opens nightly for dinner. Reservations are welcome.

The Copper Penny $-$$
109 Chestnut St., Wilmington
(910) 762-1373

If you're looking for a laid-back pub atmosphere with tastier fare than you'd be likely to find in a pub, you'll flip for the Copper Penny. Based on many of co-owner Christine Cadwallader's family recipes, including her dad's own award-winning chili, the menu has expanded significantly from the restaurant's early sandwich days. Each evening features a full entree selection including a steak, chicken and fish special, as well as nightly appetizers and soups. Definitely not your ordinary pub grub, The Copper Penny's comfort food pays homage to the old standard neighborhood bar and grill while upping the ante on its menu. The bar features 80 bottled beers, mostly American and mostly micro-brews. The Penny even offers monthly beer tastings to highlight new selections. Fourteen taps pour a wide variety of brews from ale to stout, and the extensive martini list is a nice way to kick off the night. Utilize The Copper Penny's catering service for your next affair or arrange to have your party thrown on the premises. This stately monument to the pub has a home-style feel that envelops you like a warm wool blanket in winter.

Deluxe $$-$$$
114 Market St., Wilmington
(910) 251-0333
www.deluxenc.com

Deluxe offers an aesthetically stimulating environment in a lively and casual atmosphere: eclectic decor of art deco, abstract expressionism and architectural formalism; paintings, wood sculpture and glasswork within a historic space under high ceilings with clean lines. It's a sublime and friendly environment for enjoying excellent New American style dinners, with the largest selection of fine wines in the region, and one of Wilmington's superior brunches. Dinner is memorable, with innovative offerings including French, Asian, Italian, New Southern, Low-country and Caribbean dishes that appeal visually while tempting the palate. One delicious example from a menu full of unique cuisine — pan-seared day boat grouper on

114 MARKET STREET
DOWNTOWN WILMINGTON
910•251•0333
Casual Upscale Dining
Wine Spectator
Award of Excellence
Reservations Suggested
www.deluxenc.com

lump crab potato hash with oven-roasted asparagus in fresh fennel-leek-smoked bacon vinaigrette, finished with béarnaise sauce. For brunch, the menu is equally attractive, with selections that include cinnamon pecan swirl French toast or apple-wood smoked salmon, served with melted white cheddar cheese, two poached eggs and topped with a mustard cream sauce. After dinner, sit back with a 20-year-old tawny or vintage port or a Grand Marnier flight, and you'll know why this cafe at the very heart of downtown is garnering a dedicated following.

Deluxe is open for dinner every evening and for Sunday brunch from 10:30 AM to 2 PM. Menu selections are prepared with a special emphasis on fresh local ingredients and exquisite plate presentation. Deluxe has achieved a Wine Spectator award of excellence four years in a row and the staff is dedicated to re-inventing fine dining styles for today's savvy gourmand.

Eddie Romanelli's $$
5400 Oleander Dr., Wilmington
(910) 799-7000

Eddie Romanelli's high-tone atmosphere is suffused with the richness of dark wood, red brick and comfortable banquette seating. The menu emphasizes American regional dishes, many with an Italian accent. Among the house specialties are an excellent crab dip and homemade 12-inch pizzas, some of which are unusual, such as the barbecued

An American Seafood Grill and Oyster Bar with Outside Dining in Historic Chandler's Wharf.

CAPE FEAR FOODS & SPIRITS

ELIJAH'S
RESTAURANT

910-343-1448
www.elijahs.com

OPEN SEVEN DAYS A WEEK ALL YEAR
Follow Market Street to The Cape Fear, Turn Left on Water Street,
Three Blocks to Chandler's Wharf

chicken pizza and Philly steak pizza. The menu offers a variety of appetizers (the pesto cheese toast is worth a try), sandwiches, salads with freshly made dressings and Italian baked specialties. Lunch and dinner menus are essentially the same, with dinner portions larger and served with a choice of soup or salad and a choice of potatoes or pasta. The popular bar adjoining the restaurant offers handsome sectional seating, and a late-night finger-food menu is served there. Menu and drink specials are offered every day. Eddie Romanelli's is open seven days a week.

Elijah's   **$$-$$$**
Chandler's Wharf, Water St., Wilmington
(910) 343-1448
www.elijahs.com

No one can say they've been to Wilmington until they've tried Elijah's crab dip. Directly on the Cape Fear River, Elijah's offers traditional low-country fare as well as such delights as oysters Rockefeller, the mouth-watering Shrimp and Scallops Elijah, and mahi fettucine. Elijah's is two restaurants in one — the oyster bar, which includes outdoor deck seating, and the enclosed dining room, with its more formal presentation of seafood, poultry, pasta and choice beef. Nautical artwork recalls the building's former incarnation as a maritime museum. The ambience is casual, and the western exposure makes it a great place for a sundown toast. Elijah's is open seven days a week year round and serves lunch, dinner and Sunday brunch.

Reservations are accepted only for parties of eight or more.

Elizabeth's Pizza   **$$**
4304 Market St., Wilmington
(910) 251-1005

Elizabeth's Pizza is locally owned and operated. Their friendly staff and great pizza make them one of Wilmington's most popular pizza places. Their pizza with its hand-tossed crust and all your favorite toppings is huge and always fresh. Sicilian style is also available. Elizabeth's has an extensive menu of sandwiches, pastas, strombolis and calzones. Elizabeth's is open every day for lunch and late dinner, until midnight.

Fat Tony's Italian Pub   **$$**
131 N. Front St., Wilmington
(910) 343-8881
250 Racine Dr., Wilmington
(910) 452-9000
www.fatpub.com

Founded on the simple joys of a good beer and a hearty Italian meal, Fat Tony's Italian Pub offers plenty of both. They have a selection of 24 draft beers, more than anywhere else downtown, and their menu is filled with generous helpings of fresh and flavorful Italian favorites. Begin your meal with any one of their yummy appetizers, including Pizza Chip Nachos topped with Spinach & Artichoke Hearts or Carolina Crab and Cheese, or try their lightly fried calamari. The huge, made-to-order pizza-dough breadsticks are stuffed with your choice of spinach and cheese, sun-dried tomato and goat cheese, or meatball and cheese. Craving New York–style pizza? Try any one of their specialty pizzas or calzones or select your own toppings. Or how about a pasta dish? Fat Tony's beef lasagna has received rave reviews, and the Pasta Tony (artichoke hearts, mushrooms and ricotta cream sauce baked with angel hair pasta and topped with mozzarella cheese) is another excellent choice. There are also lighter options, for those of you who are counting; try the Tony's Grilled Chicken Salad, Tortilla Pizza or Grilled Shrimp Caesar Salad — all tasty, complete meals. If through some miracle, or careful planning, you still have room for dessert, their homemade tiramisu is utterly divine. You can savor your meal in the comfortable indoor dining area or enjoy the coastal North Carolina breeze on one of the patios. The downtown location boasts a gorgeous view of the Cape Fear River. Fat Tony's Italian Pub is open Monday through Saturday 11 AM to 2 AM (the late-night menu is served 11 PM to 2 AM) and Sundays noon to midnight. Plan to visit Fat Tony's the first Saturday in November for their annual Chowdafest, with three types of incredible clam chowder. You can also try their new location on Racine between Eastwood and New Centre.

Fathoms Bistro $$-$$$
Lumina Station, 1900 Eastwood Rd., Wilmington
(910) 256-1254

Dining at Fathoms, whether indoors or on the patio in Tahitian gliders, is a casual affair with an emphasis on great food and a bright, cozy atmosphere. Local art and photography adorn the walls, and the menu features a coastal fusion cuisine highlighted by fresh-catch seafood, rotisserie and house-smoked meats, and local produce. The lunch menu features unique offerings in seafood, chicken and beef sandwiches, including the memorable Crab Melt sandwich. Heartier appetites will enjoy Fathoms' eclectic luncheon entrees. Dinner offerings include a great selection of mouthwatering appetizers, entrees and seasonal specials. Entrees feature seafood, beef, chicken, pasta and risotto, prepared with fresh herbs, vegetables and innovative sauces. With all ABC permits, Fathoms Bistro offers an eclectic wine list, including 20 pours by the glass, perfect for pairing with every meal.

Fat Tony's
ITALIAN PUB

• All ABC Permits
• Open 7 Days • Lunch & Dinner
FATPUB.COM
131 North Front Street • 343-8881
Historic Downtown Wilmington
250 Racine Drive • 452-9000
Near UNCW and the Beach

If brunch is just your style, Fathoms Bistro serves an appealing array of choices that reinvent traditional fare into tradition with flair. Omelets, egg dishes and griddle offerings are prepared with a variety of the freshest ingredients — seafood, smoked meats, vegetables and herbs — in the bistro's signature style. The Guest's Creation omelet allows your taste to follow your imagination with a variety of fresh ingredients. Brunch is available every Saturday and Sunday. Lunch and dinner are served daily year round.

Flaming Amy's Burrito Barn $
4002 Oleander Dr., Wilmington
(910) 799-2919

Looking for a tasty meal that will fill you up but won't empty your wallet? Flaming Amy's provides amazingly quick service and delicious, reasonably priced burritos, quesadillas and salads in a fun and lively setting. Their salsa bar will give you plenty of unique flavors to try, including a Pineapple Jalapeno Salsa. And if you're feeling daring, there's always the "Wall of Flame" which offers a wide variety of hot, hotter and super-hot sauces for you to sample (read the warning labels carefully before putting these sauces on your food as some are extremely potent). The burritos go way beyond beans and rice, to tasty combos such as The Big Jerk — a tortilla stuffed with rice, beans, cheese, Jamaican jerk chicken, roasted red peppers, sour cream and Pineapple Jalapeno Salsa. You can also customize your burrito with their selection of meats, veggies and toppings. For folks who want to hang out for a while, there are a pool table and some video games in the back. Flaming Amy's is open daily for lunch and dinner.

The Forks Restaurant $$
3151 S. 17th St., Wilmington
(910) 395-5999

The Forks Restaurant, located in the Louise Wells Cameron Art Museum, draws its name from the obvious nature of an eatery plus the location in south Wilmington and the two-day Civil War battle fought there. This 44-seat cafe features a menu offering contemporary regional Southern cuisine. Dine in the beautifully appointed cafe or venture out to the cafe's 50-seat sculpture court-yard. The Forks Restaurant is open for lunch Wednesday through Saturday from 11:30 AM until 2:30 PM and serves Sunday brunch from 11 AM to 3 PM. In conjunction with the museum's new Friday hours, the restaurant is open for dinner from 5:30 until 8:30 PM on Friday evenings.

Genki $-$$
University Landing, 419 S. College Rd. #26,
Wilmington
(910) 796-8687

The key to this authentic Japanese restaurant, owned and operated by Masauki and Reiko Augiura, is that every item is served fresh. The original flavors are tasted in every bite and aren't masked with heavy sauces or preservatives. Choose from tuna, eel, shrimp and California rolls and more, knowing that it's all low in calories and good for your health. You may watch Masauki make the rolls at the authentic sushi bar or sit in the aesthetically appealing dining room with a group of friends. Genki is open for lunch Tuesday through Friday and for dinner Tuesday through Sunday. Reservations are recommended.

Giorgio's Italian Restaurant $-$$
5226 S. College Rd., Wilmington
(910) 790-9954

Tucked away in a small shopping center near the Monkey Junction area of S. College Road, this family-friendly Italian restaurant is a huge hit with Insiders who suggest that you come hungry (even the lunch portions are huge). The atmosphere is cozy, with a friendly wait staff bent on making your dining experience a pleasure. Naturally, the food is the centerpiece, with a bountiful selection of salads, zuppas (that's soup for the uniniti-ated), appetizers and hearty pasta entrees with chicken, seafood, veal or sweet Italian sausage. Locals argue over their favorite dishes, but all are excellent choices. If you prefer something off the grill, try the Kansas rib eye or Roman pork tenderloin. The lunch menu offers slightly smaller versions of some dinner items plus a selection of create-your-own pasta dishes, a gourmet's choice of calzone entrees and Giorgio's signature sandwiches. Must-try sandwiches include the Italian sausage sub, Giorgio's muffaletta and the eggplant parmigiana sub. The restau-rant's small lounge area with full bar service is a cozy place to wait when the dining room is full. Giorgio's opens daily for lunch and dinner. While the portions are equally hearty at lunch, the price is very reasonable, as indicated by the dual price code listed above. Take-out services and party platters are avail-able.

Gumby's Pizza $$
1414-E S. College Rd., Wilmington
(910) 313-0072

Based on the cartoon character Gumby, who has the power to go inside books and become a part of the story, Gumby's Pizza will have you going inside this fun restaurant for more delicious pizza. Not only does this pizza feature fresh-made dough and the finest ingredients, but there are also Pokey sticks, pepperoni rolls, stromboli, calzones, wings, mozzarella sticks, cheese fries, salads, hot and cold sub sandwiches, rice bowls, low-carb melts pastas and carry out specials. For all the local partiers, Gumby's is open until 2 AM Monday through Wednesday, until 3 AM on Thursday, until 4 AM Friday and Saturday and until 11 PM on Sundays.

Heck of a Peck Oyster Bar $$
4039 Masonboro Loop Rd., Wilmington
(910) 793-2300

For steamed-oyster lovers nostalgic for the good old days of old-fashioned coastal oyster bars, Heck of a Peck Oyster Bar is a must. Two horseshoe-shaped bars, barstool seating and casual atmosphere create a friendly and companionable setting. Staffers take the work out of your meal by shucking your order in front of you at stainless steel sinks. Voted Best Oysters 2002 by Encore magazine's annual readers' poll, the restaurant's traditional fare isn't limited to fresh steamed oysters and the fixins — warm homemade cocktail sauce, cole slaw, steamed red potatoes and saltine crackers. Steamed shrimp, scallops, clams, crab legs and lobster tails are additional highlights. Located in southeast Wilmington at Masonboro Station, Heck of a Peck Oyster Bar is open daily for dinner with weekly specials Sunday through Thursday.

Hell's Kitchen $
118 Princess St., Wilmington
(910) 763-4133

Formerly a set for the locally filmed Dawson's Creek, Hell's Kitchen has fast become a popular downtown destination for good times among friends. This pub-style setting has a sinfully fun atmosphere so when you're feeling devilishly hungry, stop by and try something from their menu of pub sandwiches, burritos and nachos. Hell's Kitchen has a full liquor bar and offers a wide variety of draught and microbrew beers. Hell's Kitchen is open in the afternoon until closing at 2 AM.

Henry's Restaurant & Bar $$
Barclay Commons, 2508 Independence
Blvd., Wilmington
(910) 793-2929

Henry's is an exciting restaurant from the folks who created Eddie Romanelli's, The Oceanic and Bluewater. The cuisine is classic American fare created through high-quality, from-scratch cooking. The decor features beautifully hued stacked sandstone and hand-painted walls, a hand-painted ceiling and an awesome 100-year-old Brunswick-style tiger oak bar. Lunch possibilities range from generous salad selections (the grilled tuna and fresh spinach salad is a good choice) and cold deli sandwiches to luncheon plates (everything from roast beef and gravy to fresh catch) and hearty, two-handed sandwiches that come with your choice of a side item (12 sides to choose from). Start dinner with some of the best shrimp chowder in the region. Dinner menu highlights include hearty meal-size salads, sandwiches and generously portioned entrees, including pasta dishes, chicken, fresh seafood, prime rib and more. Insiders highly recommend Henry's awesome lump crab cake and the savory shrimp and grits. Sausage-stuffed pork chops and cashew-sesame-crusted grouper are just a few more favorites. The strawberry shortcake is made in-house and is better than Grandma's. Henry's bar offers all ABC permits with premium-pour liquors, eight draft beers and comfortable, upholstered banquettes for dining. Smoking is permitted in the bar area only.

Indochine: A Far East Café,
Thai & Vietnamese $$-$$$
Market St. at Forest Hills, 7 Wayne Dr.,
Wilmington
(910)-251-9229

You don't have to travel far to discover an exotic paradise. Just take a drive along Market Street and soon you'll discover Indochine: A Far East Café, serving Thai and Vietnamese specialties. The interior has a quiet, romantic ambiance, and in the outdoor dining area you'll find a serene garden setting with a Lotus Pond and soothing waterfall. The lunch menu offers a variety of Thai and Vietnamese rice and noodle dishes, soups, stews and salads. The dinner menu is filled with traditional Indonesian cuisine as well as house specialties, including the savory Grilled Salmon in Lemon Grass with Mango Salsa. All of Indochine's delectable and generously portioned dinner entrees may be paired with a suggested wine from their extensive list. Banquet facilities for parties of up to 60 people are also available. Indochine is open for lunch and dinner Tuesday through Saturday and on Sunday for dinner only.

Jackson's Big Oak Barbecue $
920 S. Kerr Ave., Wilmington
(910) 799-1581

A repeated winner of local magazine polls for the area's best barbecue since it opened in 1984, Jackson's is a family-run business fully deserving of the praise. The eastern North Carolina–style pork barbecue is moist and tangy, the hush puppies superior, and the friendly, knowledgeable staff is as hard-working as all get-out. The fried corn sticks are a specialty that should be a given with every meal, and if you're a fan of

Featuring a variety of
Organic & Natural Products

LOVEY'S

Natural Foods
and Cafe

Dine-In or Take-Out from our
Organic Specialty Salad Soup & Hot Bar
(featuring over 40 items)
Juice Bar • Cafe Menu • Organic Groceries
Wheat Free & Gluten Free • Vegan
Supplements • Health & Beauty Aid
Catering
Mon-Fri 9am - 7pm • Sat 9am - 6pm
Sun 11-5pm • 509-0331
Landfall Shopping Center • 1319 Military Cutoff Rd.

Brunswick stew, barbecue ribs and chicken, you won't be disappointed. The dining room is rustic and familiar, a good place to greet and meet. Jackson's is open for lunch and dinner Monday through Saturday. Contact the restaurant for large take-out orders (for up 200 people).

Jerry's Food, Wine and Spirits $$-$$$
7220 Wrightsville Ave., Wilmington
(910) 256-8847

Located just before the bridge over to Wrightsville Beach, Jerry's has been serving the finest in upscale cuisine for the past 11 years. Utilizing the freshest seafood, Jerry's offers gems like the Caribbean grouper, the stuffed flounder and Jerry's favorite, the grilled salmon. In the mood for something on the heartier side? Try the New Zealand rack of lamb or perhaps the mouth-watering Chateaubriand, served with a port wine and shitake mushroom sauce.

Featuring reasonably priced wines from your basic Hess Select Cabernet to high-end labels such as the Latour private reserve from Jerry's exclusive collection, the wine list has something for the novice to the seasoned connoisseur. Executive Chef Jason Godwin has honed his skills at other area restaurants and, along with sous-chef Steve Powell, plies his trade with the skill of a seasoned veteran. Open for dinner seven days a week, Jerry's ranks among the finest in Wilmington's upscale dining establishments.

Krazy's Pizza and Subs $
417 S. College Rd., Wilmington
(910) 791-0598

Krazy's Pizza and Subs has been family-owned and operated since 1986. With a loyal customer following, it offers a variety of Italian delights in a casual atmosphere with prices that won't strain your wallet. Best known for its "kreate your own" pizza, Krazy's has a wide range of toppings sure to please any palate. Or you can choose from their six specialty pizzas. Krazy's also serves up wonderful salads, including a Greek dinner salad. Don't miss their own tasty homemade Italian dressing. Not in the mood for pizza? Try the delicious homemade lasagna, veal parmigiana or baked ziti with meat sauce, either as an entree or a la carte. Appetizers, stromboli, calzones and a large selection of subs round out the menu at Krazy's. For the bambinos, a children's menu is available, plus a balloon clown provides free entertainment every Friday evening from 5:30 to 8:30 PM.

Lovey's Market $-$$
Landfall Shopping Center, Eastwood Rd.
and Military Cutoff Rd., Wilmington
(910) 509-0331
www.loveysmarket.com

If you're looking for a healthy meal made with entirely fresh ingredients, Lovey's is the perfect spot for a sit-down lunch or a quick take-out snack. This natural foods spot features a hot and cold bar that offers copious salad options as well as daily specialty items. With a variety of warm soups and beverages for the health conscious, Lovey's is ideal for those watching their diet. In addition to offering carrot and wheat grass juice at the Juice Bar, they even have an extensive selection of smoothies, made on the spot with only the freshest fruits. Vegans and vegetarians, this is the place for you! So if you're near the beach and have the urge for something that tastes great and is good for you, give Lovey's a try.

Luigi's $$
6612 Market St., Wilmington
(910) 798-0095

A little slice of Italy in an unlikely location, this bistro features authentic dishes with a little flair. Meals are prepared to order, so while they may take a little more time, it's comforting to know that your meal is coming to you fresh from the chef's hands. With

100% AUTHENTIC ITALIAN CUISINE
CASUAL DINING • RESERVATIONS SUGGESTED • CLOSED MONDAYS

DINE-IN • TAKE-OUT 6 DAYS A WEEK - 4-10PM

910-798-0095

6621 Market St. Wilmington
Across The Street From Harley-Davidson

fish, chicken, veal and pasta entrees that would delight any fan of Italian cuisine, this café brings the checked-tablecloth charm to Wilmington. Luigi's offers wine and beer and no smoking is allowed. Luigi's serves dinner Tuesday through Sunday.

Market Street Casual Dining $$
6309 Market St., Wilmington
(910) 395-2488

Market Street Casual Dining offers American, from-scratch cuisine heavily influenced by local fresh-catch seafood. This restaurant's comfortable, friendly atmosphere and extensive menu make dining a pleasure. The regular menu features a tasty variety of appetizers, soups, salads and entrees, but the nightly board specials are the draw, primarily because there are so many to choose from — six to eight appetizers and 14 to 20 entrees. A mouthwatering dilemma since all are innovative and skillfully prepared from the freshest seafood and produce available. Entrees also may include chicken, pasta and steak served with a choice of salad, grouper chowder or Manhattan clam chowder and, unless entree is served over pasta, a choice of baked potato, house potato, rice pilaf, French fries or mixed vegetables. The relaxed, friendly atmosphere invites lingering over coffee and dessert. Market Street Casual Dining has all ABC permits and serves beer and wine. Dinner is served nightly in-season. The restaurant is closed on Monday in the off-season. Reservations are not accepted.

NOFO Cafe & Market $
The Forum, 1125 Military Cutoff Rd., Wilmington
(910) 256-5565

Whether you're dining in for lunch, enjoying a late-afternoon snack or ordering from the deli case, NOFO Cafe & Market is a delicious choice in a casual setting. Luncheon choices include two daily specials and two homemade soups in addition to the regular menu of hearty deli sandwiches, meal-size salads and homemade desserts. Can't find a sandwich to your liking? Try it "your way" from a list of deli meats and salads, cheeses, breads, condiments and side items. If you're on the go for lunch, fax your order and they'll have it waiting for you. NOFO also offers an appetizing alternative menu for special diets, corporate lunch boxes, a take-out deli counter and catering. NOFO To Go features a daily menu of supper specials that are cooked and ready to pick up. Also check out the frozen food case for meal solutions. Sunday Brunch adds egg and breakfast entrees to the cafe's regular menu. NOFO is open for dinner, Monday through Saturday, with all ABC permits.

A colorful and appealing array of specialty foods awaits you in the market area attached to the deli. You'll find shelves of gourmet foods, condiments and sauces (many from North Carolina) in addition to mouthwatering imported chocolates, specialty teas and coffee beans, imported and domestic wine and much more. Gift baskets are a popular feature of the market. NOFO

paddys hollow
Restaurant & Pub

Chargrilled Steaks • Seafood
Gourmet Sandwiches & Large Salads
16 Premium Imported Draft Beers on Tap
Game Room

Seasonal Outdoor Dining
All ABC Permits
OPEN FOR LUNCH & DINNER
Mon.-Sat. 11:30 am-10:00 pm
Sun. 12:00 pm - 5:00 pm
Corner of N. Front & Walnut St.
in **The Cotton Exchange**
Downtown Wilmington • 762-4354

Always plenty of free parking

Cafe & Market opens at 10 AM seven days a week.

Old Chicago Pizza, Pasta & 110 Brews $-$$
5023 Market St., Wilmington
(910) 796-064

Like your neighborhood pub from by-gone days, Old Chicago Pizza, Pasta & 110 Brews offers great food, fun and friendship. Whether it's a quick lunch or dinner with the gang, there's always something happening at Old Chicago. Check out their daily draft and bottle specials. With 110 beers from all over the world, you're sure to find something new. You can even join their "World Beer Tour" and travel the world one beer at a time. Mondays, all day, you can get a "pizza and a pint for $5". For 30 years, Old Chicago has been known for the freshest Chicago-style pizza with made-from-scratch dough, but they also have great sandwiches, salads, calzones and burgers. Want your just desserts? Try their homemade cheesecake, Famous Big Cookie, or Kahlua® Hot Fudge Brownie. With a varied menu and great brews, you might want to make it your neighborhood hang out.

 Have local restaurants inspired you to try your hand at recipes for coastal cuisine? Check out the regional cookbook section at local bookstores.

P.T.'s Olde Fashioned Grille $
4544 Fountain Dr., Wilmington
(910) 392-2293
2420 S. 17th St., Wilmington
(910) 794-4544
1437 Military Cutoff Rd., Wilmington
(910) 256-8850

When you want a freshly grilled burger or chicken sandwich, forget the fast-food mills. Consistently voted Best Burger by Encore magazine's annual poll, P.T.'s can't be beat. Every menu item is a package deal that includes a sandwich (whopping half-pound Angus beef burgers, tender chicken breast, hot dogs, fresh roast beef, turkey and more), fresh-cut, spiced, skin-on French fries (or substitute a side salad) and a soft drink, refill included. Prices are low, and quality is high. You place your order by filling in an idiot-proof order form and dropping it through the window if you're eating on the outdoor deck. Order at the counter if you're eating inside. Your meal is prepared to order and ready in about 10 minutes — fast food that doesn't taste like fast food. P.T.'s also offers an alternative to beef with the lower calorie, low-fat Gardenburger. P.T.'s is west of S. College Road across from the south end of the UNCW campus. Or try their locations at the Progress Point Center on Military Cutoff Road or on South 17th Street in Wilmington. Take-out orders are welcome and may be habit-forming. P.T.'s is open daily until 9 PM and does not accept checks.

Innovations on Southern Regional Cooking in the Historic Craig House with Riverfront Deck.

THE PILOT HOUSE restaurant

OPEN SEVEN DAYS A WEEK ALL YEAR
Follow Market Street to The Cape Fear, Turn Left on Water Street,
Three Blocks to Chandler's Wharf

910-343-0200
www.pilothouserest.com

Paddy's Hollow Restaurant & Pub   **$$**
The Cotton Exchange, 10 Walnut St.,
Corner of Front and Walnut Sts.,
Wilmington
(910) 762-4354

Tucked away in the middle courtyard of the Cotton Exchange buildings, this narrow, intimate restaurant transports you back to friendly neighborhood pubs with an Irish flavor. Seating consists of high-backed wooden booths, tables and chairs or stools at the bar, where you can have a brew and a bite while catching up with the news, both televised and local. The lunch menu offers tasty appetizers, a soup du jour and grilled seafood, chicken or steak salads. Sandwich selections, featuring seafood, shrimp, prime rib and corned beef, are hearty and include a deli pickle slice and a choice of French fries, potato salad, pasta salad or fruit. In the mood for a burger? Paddy's 6 oz. Pub-burgers, cooked to order and accompanied by a pickle and french fries, are a real treat. In the intimacy of the high-backed booths and the subdued lighting, dinner at Paddy's can be a romantic affair. The dinner menu features the fresh-catch seafood prevalent in the Cape Fear area in addition to tasty beef entrees, specifically prime rib and New York strip, chicken and barbecued baby-back ribs. Check the board or ask your server for the daily lunch and dinner specials. Need some diversion? Check out Paddy's game room. Paddy's has all ABC permits, 16 tap handles for draft beer, and bottled beer and wine. Cigar and pipe smoking are not permitted. It's open for lunch and dinner Monday through Saturday and for lunch on Sunday.

The Pilot House   **$$-$$$**
Chandler's Wharf, 2 Ann St., Wilmington
(910) 343-0200
www.pilothouserest.com

The Pilot House is among the preeminent dining establishments downtown. Overlooking the Cape Fear River at Chandler's Wharf, the restaurant occupies the historic Craig House (c. 1870) and strives for innovations with high-quality Southern regional cooking. The wide-ranging dinner menu features sautéed and chargrilled seafood, beef and chicken, pan-seared duck, pasta and a delectable roster of appetizers. Daily lunch and dinner specials are equally tempting. Lunch selections include generous traditional and seafood salads, innovative sandwiches and entrees. You will see guests dressed in everything from Bermuda shorts to a shirt and tie. Lunch is more casual than dinner. The wine list is carefully chosen and well-rounded. The Pilot House features additional outdoor seating, weather permitting, and serves lunch and dinner seven days a week, year round, with brunch offered on Sunday. The addition of a newly renovated riverfront bar provides spectacular views of the Cape Fear River to go along with that cocktail. A children's menu is available. Reservations are recommended.

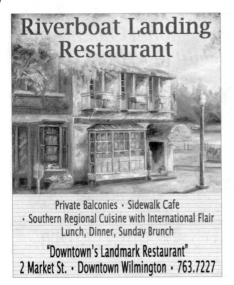

Riverboat Landing Restaurant

Private Balconies · Sidewalk Cafe
· Southern Regional Cuisine with International Flair
Lunch, Dinner, Sunday Brunch

"Downtown's Landmark Restaurant"
2 Market St. · Downtown Wilmington · 763.7227

Port Land Grille   **$$$**
Lumina Station, 1908 Eastwood Rd.,
Ste. 111, Wilmington
(910) 256-6056

This five-star restaurant alone is worth a trip to the coast. Port Land Grille knows the art of fine dining. The ambiance, indoors and out, offers an appealing sense of style with oversized tables draped with white tablecloths, black and white photographs of Old Wrightsville Beach, comfortable rooms with a view, exquisite service and, weather permitting, picturesque dining on the patio overlooking a landscaped pond at Lumina Station. Though the restaurant is reminiscent of the classy supper clubs of bygone eras, the food is its key to success.

Chef Shawn Wellersdick is renowned for his ability to transform quality ingredients into a meal of layered flavors and side dishes that rival the entree in taste and creativity. An excellent example is his version of mashed sweet potatoes (the secret involves scented vanilla beans). The menu includes meal-sized appetizers, especially when coupled with one of Port Land Grille's salads. A favorite is the crab cake nestled on a bed of buttered baby lima beans and served with an applewood-smoked bacon, fennel vinaigrette. The popular salad choice is characterized as a simple Southern salad — a chilled iceberg lettuce wedge with crisp bacon and bleu cheese dressing. Entrees feature fresh seafood and organically raised meats. Dessert is memorable, especially Port Land Grille's

signature coconut cake. This wonderful confection is seven layers of cake with a lemony filling, topped with a pistachio anglaise. The restaurant's award-winning wine list is almost exclusively American selections, especially small-production boutique wines. A popular spot for drinks and dining is the beautiful, well-stocked granite bar. Seating here overlooks the action in the open theater-style kitchen. The restaurant is completely non-smoking and, in addition to the main dining room, offers two private dining areas that seat 20 and 65 people, either of which is perfect for parties and corporate events. Open year-round, Port Land Grille serves dinner Monday through Saturday. Reservations are recommended, particularly on weekends, but walk-in guests are graciously accommodated.

Riverboat Landing Restaurant   **$$-$$$**
2 Market St., Wilmington
(910) 763-7227
www.riverboatlanding.com

Enjoy a panoramic sunset over the Battleship North Carolina from one of the nine intimate two-seater balconies that overlook the Cape Fear River. Downtown's landmark restaurant, the Riverboat Landing is located at the foot of Market and Water Streets nestled in a building that dates to the 1800s. A newly renovated interior decor complements the modern cuisine — an eclectic blend of Southern regional with French, Asian and Mediterranean influences. Enjoy selections from the expansive lunch menu, including traditional comfort food, as well as sandwiches from simple to sensational. Lunch is served Tuesday through Saturday. Sunday offers a special brunch menu, including the famous Eggs Chesapeake and quiche du jour. Blending a wide assortment of breakfast and lunch entrees, brunch offers selections to suit everyone's taste.

Dinner is served every night. Begin your evening with one of the unforgettable appetizers and a cocktail from the bar. Next, enjoy an elegantly prepared entrée from the unique and ever-changing dinner menu. A member of the professional staff will be happy to assist you in pairing a wine from an award-winning wine list. Remember not to leave without sampling some legendary desserts. From Chocolate Lava Pie a la mode to Creme Brulee Napolean, any of their enticing desserts will bring your meal to a sweet

Fine dining abounds in Downtown Wilmington.

photo: Peter Doran

conclusion. A children's menu is available upon request.

Roly Poly Rolled Sandwiches $
Cornerstone Center, 1616 Shipyard Blvd.,
Wilmington
(910) 796-0045
University Landing, 419 S. College Rd.
(910) 452-7772

Located in two convenient Wilmington locations — an active business corridor on Shipyard Boulevard, and at University Landing — Roly Poly puts the fun back into grabbing a quick bite. Their signature rolled sandwiches feature high-quality deli meats, cheeses, fresh veggies and homemade spreads in a huge soft-flour tortilla. The large array of choices range from the traditional to the innovative, or you can get creative with the "roll your own" option. Watching carbs? Ask for a low-carb tortilla with only five net carbs. Accompany your Roly choice with a soft drink and chips or a cup of delicious soup. Need to feed a large group? Party platters, catering and box lunches are available for meetings, seminars, picnics and other special events — corporate to casual. Call either location for details. Roly Poly is open for lunch and dinner daily and offers local weekday delivery with a $15 minimum.

Rossi's $$-$$$
1125 Military Cutoff Rd., Wilmington
(910) 256-8870

Wilmington's branch of Rossi's, sister restaurant to the famed Myrtle Beach eatery, continues in their fine traditions of "great service, great food and great entertainment" six nights a week. Rossi's features a full bar that also serves appetizers and entrees in addition to its full compliment of martinis. Live entertainment from the grand piano Tuesday through Saturday provides a cozy, parlor ambience for diners and cocktail enthusiasts alike. The menu offers a diverse selection of fare from a one-pound lobster tail to simple pasta dishes. The "Steer Butt," Rossi's version of Chateaubriand, comes highly recommended. In addition, the chef will gladly fulfill special requests from customers using whatever items are on the menu. Generous portions often find diners with take out for later. Rossi's features a ten-item children's menu providing a number of choices for the kids. They can also accommodate private parties by sectioning off one of the their three dining

123

rooms. The restaurant gives its last seating at 11 PM, with the bar serving appetizers until midnight.

Rucker Johns Restaurant and More $$
5564 Carolina Beach Rd., Wilmington
(910) 452-1212

Discover Rucker Johns, a local family favorite since 1992. Renowned for high quality and attention to detail, Rucker Johns' theme is casual and the service is serious. The made-from-scratch menu features an array of fresh salads, appetizers, sandwiches, burgers, hand-stretched grilled pizzas and unbeatable homemade soups. Entree choices include grilled chicken dishes, tender baby-back ribs, awesome prime rib, succulent steaks, tasty pastas and fresh seafood. Adjoining the oak-trimmed dining room is a horseshoe-shaped bar — the perfect place to enjoy live jazz on Saturday evenings or catch the big game. A second dining area is available for business luncheons and private parties. RJ's has all ABC permits and boasts a wine list with fine selections from around the world. Located in the Myrtle Grove Shopping Center at Monkey Junction, where Carolina Beach Road meets South College Road, RJ's is open for lunch

and dinner seven days a week, closing late on Friday and Saturday.

Salty's $$$
The Forum, 1125 Military Cutoff Rd., Wilmington
(910) 256-1118

Experience the sounds and tastes of Salty's and discover why it's already a Wilmington favorite. Four of the bestsellers on the menu are the Chilean sea bass, crab cakes, grouper and Salty's marinated filet — delicious! From swing and shag to fresh seafood and tender steaks, you and your friends will enjoy fabulous wines and live music in a casual yet sophisticated atmosphere with a little extra pizzazz. Salty's is open daily for dinner, and the lounge opens at 4 PM.

Terrazzo Pizzeria/Trattoria $$
Landfall Center, 1319 Military Cutoff Rd., Wilmington
(910) 509-9400

For a taste of authentic Italian cuisine, New York–style, Terrazzo is a must-visit. A cozy indoor atmosphere, outdoor patio seating, friendly service and a generous menu make dining here a pleasure. Terrazzo's delicious pizza menu offers everything — a wide

Wilmington's downtown features many inviting watering holes and eateries.

photo: Peter Doran

selection of toppings, including vegetarian, chicken, surf and turf choices, a white pizza and Terrazzo specialty pizzas. For a light snack, the large selection of tasty appetizers is a good choice. Lunch options include a daily special or generously portioned salads that make a great meal when coupled with the homemade soup of the day. Terrazzo's subs come hot or cold and are truly awesome. The Italian Delight entree choices feature homemade pasta dishes with fresh vegetables, meats and cheeses in delicious sauces and served with Ciabatta bread. Nightly dinner specials often include fresh local seafood. The restaurant serves beer and a huge selection of imported and domestic wines and will have a full bar by summer 2005. Terrazzo is open daily, Monday through Saturday, for lunch and dinner. Come early: This is a popular spot in the Wilmington-Wrightsville Beach area.

Texas Roadhouse $$
230 Eastwood Rd., Wilmington
(910) 798-1770

The Texas Roadhouse story is simple — legendary food with legendary service inspired by legendary folks! Everything here is made from scratch. Steaks cut by hand, award-winning ribs, grilled salmon, fried catfish, fresh-baked bread and delightful sides are all made from scratch with only the highest-quality ingredients. Leave room for dessert — Granny's Apple Classic, strawberry cheesecake and a Big Ol' Brownie. Every Tuesday night is Kids' Night, when kids get to enjoy games, crafts and lots of fun while you relax and enjoy your meal. Texas Roadhouse is open for dinner every day and serves lunch, Friday through Sunday only.

Tidal Creek Foods Co-Op $-$$
5329 Oleander Dr., Ste. 100, Wilmington
(910) 799-COOP (2667)
www.tidalcreek.coop

More than a grocery store, the co-op is a place to enjoy a delicious healthy meal or snack. The café offers many vegetarian and vegan delights. Have a cup of organic, freshly brewed, fair-trade coffee or tea. Or if you're in the mood for something cool, refreshing and really good for you, there's also a smoothie and juice bar, providing freshly squeezed fruits and vegetables. For an extra immune system boost, try a glass of their freshly pressed wheat grass. Café tables inside and out make this a perfect place for a healthy lunch with a friend or a group meeting. Hot dishes such as vegetable lasagna, stir fries, stews and pasta dishes provide a healthy, hearty meal. Also available are delicious sandwiches, such as eggplant parmesan, chicken curry wrap, or hummus and tofu wraps. Pair any of these sandwiches with a salad from their organic salad bar, antipasto or other side dishes and you have a complete lunch. Every day the cafe offers two seasonal soups that are always fresh and delicious. For dessert, there are cashew mint chocolate chip cookies, chocolate or carrot cakes, and a variety of biscotti. Deli platters are available by special order. Now located on Oleander Drive, Tidal Creek is across from Eddie Romanelli's restaurant.

Trolly Stop $
121 N. Front St., Wilmington
(910) 343-2999

Centrally located in historic downtown Wilmington, Trolly Stop serves a specially produced Smithfield all-meat dog, all-beef Sabrett dogs, no-carb veggie dogs and low fat/no-carb turkey dogs in a variety of taste combinations. Local favorites include the American (chili, mustard and onion), the Cape Fear (melted cheese and mayonnaise) and, naturally, the North Carolina (chili, mustard and cole slaw). Vegetarian and fat-free hot dogs are also available. Additional menu offerings are sweet Italian sausage, their unique Burger dog, a black bean salsa burrito, and nachos with toppings. Enjoy Hershey's ice cream at the downtown Wilmington and Southport locations.

Underground Sandwich Shoppe $
103 Market St., Wilmington
(910) 763-9686

Appropriately located "underground" on the corner of Market and Front streets in downtown Wilmington, this lively sandwich shop serves a variety of classic American choices that include everything from a grilled ham and cheese or Underground club sandwich to the Rueben and Piccadilly Philly. Their BLT is one of the best in town. Can't decide? Create your own with a choice of meats, cheeses, fixings and bread. Salads range from the house salad to their entree-size Italian chef salad. All sandwiches come with a drink and a side item. Try a glass of their fresh-squeezed lemonade on a hot coastal day. It's awesome! Underground also offers a selection of draft and bottled beers. The atmosphere is friendly and casual, and it's a great place to bring the family. The decor's theme suggests London's Underground Mass Transit system. An eye-catching mural, painted by local artist Chappy Valente, covers one wall of the restaurant and is thought to be one of the prime pieces of public art in downtown Wilmington. Underground is open daily.

Viet Bistro $-$$
149 S. College Rd., Wilmington
(910) 791-5208

Tucked away in the front corner of the Marketplace Mall, Viet Bistro is a simmering spot off the beaten path for many. But the restaurant's simple décor and minimalist aesthetic belie the wide variety of delicious dishes behind the kitchen door. Combining cuisines from the three distinct regions of Vietnamese geography, the menu offers the diner everything from sumptuous light fare such as summer rolls or seafood to spicy dishes that can easily clear your sinuses. Viet Bistro offers numerous vegetarian dishes as well as items prepared with rice vermicelli. A variety of soups are also available, most with pork or beef bases. A hidden treasure featuring some of the finest authentic Vietnamese food in town, Viet Bistro's food shines like a beacon.

Water Street Restaurant
& Sidewalk Cafe $$
5 Water St., Wilmington
(910) 343-0042

Housed in the Quince Building (1835), a former peanut warehouse on the riverfront, Water Street Restaurant can be quite romantic with its softly lit atmosphere evoking a bygone era in downtown Wilmington. The restaurant offers moderately priced, healthy meals all day, every day. Water Street's innovative dinner menu places emphasis on fresh-catch seafood, beef, a generous use of vegetables, delicious homemade dressings and daily soup specials (homemade, of course). Entrees include choice of Caesar or house salad and fresh-baked bread. For lunch, try the Water Greek Salad (toppings include tabouli, feta cheese, pepperoncini and sun-dried tomatoes), a black bean

burrito served with rice and a small green salad, or a host of sandwiches, from the 7 oz. Water Street burger to the Oyster Po-Boy. Their Portobello mushroom sandwich is an especially good choice. Sidewalk seating is in full view of the Cape Fear River, and live piano music is frequent. In fact, Water Street Restaurant is an attractive nightspot featuring live entertainment — jazz and Dixieland bands, flamenco guitar and more — Thursday through Sunday nights. Lot parking is available for the restaurant's patrons at the corner of Dock and Water streets.

Wilson's $$-$$$
4925 New Centre Dr., Wilmington
(910) 793-0999

Wilson's is a good choice for excellent food at a great value. Formerly known as Alleigh's, Wilson's still serves the same great all-you-can-eat buffets daily and has a variety of weekly lunch and dinner buffet specials. Choose from fresh seafood and hand-cut certified Angus beef or ribs, burgers, sandwiches and a Sunday brunch buffet. This 35,000-square-foot complex has everything from live bands, an outdoor Tiki Bar & Cafe and a Sports Bar with the most TVs in town, including a 200-inch big screen TV, to an intimate sofa lounge and a fun-filled Game Room. A late-night menu is available until 1 AM.

Wallace

The Mad Boar Restaurants $-$$$
111 River Village Pl., Wallace
(910) 285-8888

Just a 30-minute drive from Wilmington, The Mad Boar Restaurant offers three distinct dining options under one roof. The Mad Boar is a casual restaurant offering friendly service and a menu designed to please every member of the family, including appetizers, soup, salads, burgers and sandwiches. Dinner entrees feature steak, chicken and seafood. The Mad Boar is open daily for lunch and dinner. The Celtic Court banquet hall is an appealing setting for special events and corporate functions with seating for more than 300 guests. The River Dancer is a fine dining venue, offering the best wines and delectable creations. The Mad Boar restaurant is easily reached from the southern coast and Wilmington via

Interstate I-40 West. Take Exit 385, and then turn right.

Wrightsville Beach

Bluewater, An American Grill $$
4 Marina St., Wrightsville Beach
(910) 256-8500

Located just over the bridge on the Intracoastal Waterway, Bluewater is a sprawling two-story restaurant that offers great food with a panoramic view of the waterway that you won't want to miss. Open daily for lunch and dinner year round, Bluewater serves hearty American cuisine with a distinctly coastal flair in a tastefully nautical atmosphere. Lunch or mid-day snack choices include a dozen tasty appetizer selections (the hot crab dip is a must), numerous salad options, soups and chowder, sandwiches and generous lunch-size entrees. The coconut shrimp plate and the seafood lasagna are excellent choices, but the lump crab cake entree is incredible. Bluewater's dinner menu is equally generous in its choices and, while fresh-catch seafood is an obvious feature, the restaurant also excels with prime rib and steak entrees, chicken and barbecue baby-back ribs. Seating is available indoors on two floors, on a waterside patio downstairs and an intimate covered terrace upstairs. Bluewater has all ABC permits and serves a full range of imported and domestic wine and beer.

The Bridge Tender Marina
and Restaurant $$$
1414 Airlie Rd., Wilmington
(910) 256-4519

Located at the foot of the Wrightsville Beach drawbridge on historic Airlie Road, the Bridge Tender restaurant offers the finest steaks and seafood with a spectacular panoramic view of the Intracoastal Waterway. Since 1976, this fine casual dining establishment has earned their reputation for excellence through careful attention to detail, unparalleled cuisine and impeccable service. The Bridge Tender offers inside and outside dining with unobstructed views of the marinas, boats and waterway. The dinner menu offers a wide variety of appetizers and entrees along with several nightly specials. The lunch menu offers everything from sal-

ads and sandwiches to fresh seafood entrees. If you're in the mood for something lighter, visit the waterfront bar and deck to sample one of the unique appetizers such as oysters Rockefeller, crab and shrimp won-tons, sushi rolls or Asian-seared tuna. The Bridge Tender caters large and small events and is the perfect setting for a rehearsal dinner. The Bridge Tender serves lunch Monday through Friday and dinner nightly.

Causeway Cafe $
114 Causeway Dr., Wrightsville Beach
(910) 256-3730

Full of character and friendly service, Causeway Cafe offers possibly the best breakfast in Wrightsville Beach. Traditional made-to-order egg plates are hearty and standard fare. Choose from 15 different omelets, including the Carolina Blue Crab and Beefy Vegetable as well as traditional options, made from three eggs and cheese, served with hash browns or grits. Not in the mood for eggs? The giant specialty Belgian waffles, in nine mouthwatering flavors, malted pancakes and French toast are tasty alternatives. Lunch options include daily blackboard specials, sandwiches and salads dominated by fresh seafood. Subs, burgers, steak and other sandwiches are also good choices. A child'rens menu is available for children younger than 10. In-season and on weekends off-season, be prepared to wait for a table. It's worth the time spent on the covered front deck, and the folks at Causeway thoughtfully provide complimentary coffee. Open seven days a week for breakfast and lunch, Causeway Cafe is located near the drawbridge beside Redix beach store. They do not accept credit cards.

Dockside Restaurant $$
1308 Airlie Rd., Wrightsville Beach
(910) 256-2752

The view of the Intracoastal Waterway alone is worth a trip to Dockside. But if you're craving delicious and well-prepared local seafood, you'll also find the dining experience to be a mouthwatering adventure. The menu, not surprisingly, is dominated by fresh seafood. Broiled or fried (lightly coated with fine cracker meal) combination platters, snow crab legs, shrimp Creole and the popular Baja tuna are just a few of the dinner options. The seafood lasagna, a Dockside favorite, is definitely worth a try. Ask your server about the day's fresh catch, and check Dockside's special board for daily soup, sandwich, wraps and chef's specials. The lunch menu, available all day, is a generous listing of soups, salads, sandwiches and house specials, including broiled or fried seafood plates, served with french fries and cole slaw. Be sure to try the homemade Key lime pie. A children's menu is available. Dockside has all ABC permits, wine, and imported, domestic and draft beers. Seating is spectacular anywhere in the restaurant, but you have a choice of indoors with a view, on the outdoor deck along the ICW or outdoors under the canopy. Dockside is open daily for lunch and dinner.

King Neptune Restaurant   **$$**
11 N. Lumina Ave., Wrightsville Beach
(910) 256-2525

King Neptune has been in business since 1946, outlasting hurricanes and the competition, but not its appeal. From soups and chowders to steamers, platters and hearty specialties that include steaks, King Neptune focuses on seafood and does it well. The dining room is large and bright, decorated in Caribbean colors, with local art, beach umbrellas and photographs. The children's menu is unique in that it was selected and decorated by the third and fourth grades of Wrightsville Beach Elementary School. After dinner, the adjoining lounge is lively and offers perhaps the widest selection of rums on the Cape as well as an international selection of beers. King Neptune serves dinner seven days a week and offers senior citizen discounts. Free parking is available in the lot across the street.

Oceanic Restaurant   **$$-$$$**
703 S. Lumina Ave., Wrightsville Beach
(910) 256-5551

Few culinary experiences are as delightful as dining on the pier at the Oceanic, and there's nothing better than a pier table in the moonlight. By day, as pelicans and sea gulls kite overhead and the surf crashes below, you could be enjoying a chilled beverage, fresh blackened tuna or some of the region's most acclaimed crab dip. Should the weather turn angry, the Oceanic's three floors of indoor seating offer breathtaking panoramic views. The Oceanic offers a menu that is satisfying, delicious and dominated by fresh seafood.

From entree salads, seafood platters and specialties to chicken and steaks, the menu is quite varied and includes items for kids. Entrees include a variety of extras ranging from salads, seafood gumbo and heavenly she-crab soup to hush puppies, slaw, rice pilaf, vegetables, potatoes and confetti orzo. The Super Duper Grouper, pan-seared grouper in a crust of cashew nuts and sesame seeds served over celery mashed potatoes with roasted red pepper butter, is just one of the popular selections. Nightly specials feature fresh-catch seafood that can be grilled, sauteed, blackened or prepared with Cajun spices.

Full bar service, including domestic and imported beers, is available, and the juices used in mixed drinks are all squeezed fresh daily. Those seeking the perfect margarita should definitely stop here. The Oceanic also offers a generous wine list, with most available by the glass. The maritime decor features replicas of historic newspapers, the aerial photography of Conrad Lowman and a spectacular Andy Cobb sculpture of a huge copper grouper. Lunch and dinner are served daily. Parking is free for patrons; towing of all other cars is strictly enforced.

South Beach Grill   **$$**
100 S. Lumina Ave., Wrightsville Beach
(910) 256-4646

One of two restaurants given a four-star rating in this area, South Beach Grill offers exquisitely prepared fare in an exotic coastal ambience. The decor is marked by rich colors with fresh flowers on each table and dark wood tables and armchairs. The location, immediately south of the fixed bridge near the center of the beach, is convenient and overlooks Banks Channel, which is especially nice at sunset from the patio tables outside. Most important, meals are tasty, healthy and creative, emphasizing fresh-catch seafood, poultry and beef, plus burgers, sandwiches, wraps and an array of interesting appetizers, such as crabmeat nachos served on flour tortillas or South Beach's original fried pickles served with ranch dressing. All lunches include french fries or homemade potato chips; dinner entrees include a choice of house or Caesar salad. Lunch and dinner specials are offered daily. South Beach Grill has a children's menu and all ABC permits. Take-out orders are welcome. South Beach Grill opens for lunch and dinner daily. Reservations are accepted.

Trolly Stop $
94 S. Lumina Ave., Wrightsville Beach
(910) 256-3421

The Trolly Stop, a beach tradition since 1976, offers hot dogs in a surprising array of choices. How about a Surfers Hot Dog with cheese, bacon bits and mustard? Or go Nuclear with mustard, jalapeno peppers and cheese on your dog. Want something more traditional? The North Carolina Hot Dog is as Tarheel as they come with chili, mustard and cole slaw. Trolly Stop offers a specially produced Smithfield all-meat dog, all-beef Sabrett dogs, no-carb veggie dogs and low fat/no-carb turkey dogs Other popular items include a black bean burrito and nachos with toppings. The Wrightsville Beach location is open daily. Their other locations are open Monday through Saturday at 111 S. Howe Street in Southport, (910) 457-7017; and 103-A Cape Fear Boulevard in Carolina Beach, (910) 458-7557 (closed off-season); and in downtown Wilmington at 121 N. Front Street, (910) 343-2999.

Carolina Beach and Kure Beach

Barrier Island Restaurant $$
1140 N. Lake Park Blvd., Carolina Beach
(910) 458-5505

Barrier Island Restaurant is a local favorite, and as soon as you experience their friendly service you'll know why. Their moderately priced menu includes a variety of daily specials and delicious local seafood dishes. Try the fresh fried flounder or the tasty snow crab legs. Their great food will make you a regular customer. Barrier Island serves breakfast, lunch and dinner and is open year round.

Big Daddy's Seafood Restaurant $$
202 K Ave., Kure Beach
(910) 458-8622

A Kure Beach institution for three decades, Big Daddy's serves a variety of seafood and combination platters. In addition to seafood, the restaurant offers choice steaks, prime rib and chicken every day in a family-oriented, casual setting. Seafood can be broiled, fried, char-grilled or steamed.

Highlights of Big Daddy's menu include an all-you-can-eat salad bar; a large selection of seafood and beef entrees; special plates for seniors and children; and the sizable Surf and Turf (filet mignon and a choice of snow crab legs or char-grilled barbecue shrimp). An after-dinner walk along the nearby beach-front or on the Kure Beach fishing pier (both are a short block away) further adds to Big Daddy's appeal. The restaurant's interior, consisting of several rooms and a total seating capacity of about 500 people, comes as a surprise; it doesn't seem that big from the outside. Rare and unusual maritime memorabilia make for entertaining distractions. Entrance to Big Daddy's is through a colorful gift shop offering novelties and taffy. Patrons frequently make secret wishes and toss coins into the fountain there. Located at the only stoplight in Kure Beach, Big Daddy's has all ABC permits and ample parking in front and across the street. Big Daddy's is closed during the off-season (Thanksgiving through the beginning of March).

The Cottage Seafood Grill
& Coastal Cuisine $$
1 N. Lake Park Blvd., Carolina Beach
(910) 458-4383

The Cottage occupies a tastefully renovated 1916 beach cottage, which has been awarded historic plaques from the Federal Point Historical Society and the Wilmington Historic Foundation. The interior is modern, open and airy, preserving the several ground-level rooms as separate dining areas. An outdoor screened and covered deck, accompanied by a wonderful ocean breeze, makes al fresco dining a special pleasure. As a seafood grill, The Cottage features coastal cuisine at its finest. In addition to fresh-catch seafood, dinner offerings include chicken, beef and pasta. The lunch menu offers delectable sandwiches; a favorite is the Coastal Crabcake. Don't forget dessert at The Cottage; the flourless chocolate cake and the Key lime pie are favorites. The Cottage has all ABC permits and an extensive wine list. A children's menu is available. The Cottage is open year round Monday through Saturday

To avoid waiting in line at a popular restaurant, arrive before the 6:30 to 7:30 PM rush. Most are open for dinner by 5:30 PM.

for lunch and dinner. It is the perfect place for bridal functions and also offers on-site catering.

Deck House Casual Dining   **$$**
205 Charlotte Ave., Carolina Beach
(910) 458-1026

Deck House offers American, from-scratch cuisine heavily influenced by local fresh-catch seafood. The exterior reflects the building's history as a church, but the decor inside is tastefully nautical. The restaurant's regular menu features a tasty variety of appetizers, soups, salads and entrees, but the nightly board specials are the draw, primarily because there are so many to choose from — six to eight appetizers and 14 to 20 entrees. A mouthwatering dilemma since all are innovative and skillfully prepared from the freshest seafood and produce available. Entrees also may include chicken, pasta and steak served with a choice of salad, grouper chowder or Manhattan clam chowder and, unless entree is served over pasta, a choice of baked potato, house potato, rice pilaf, french fries or mixed vegetables. The relaxed, friendly atmosphere invites lingering over

coffee and dessert. The Deck House has all ABC permits and serves beer and wine. Dinner is served nightly in-season. The restaurant is closed on Monday in the off-season. Reservations are not accepted.

Hula Grille   **$$**
201 Oceanfront Boardwalk, Carolina Beach
(910) 458-8780

With a panoramic ocean view, outdoor deck and pier, great food and the ultimate in live beach music, Hula Grille is the newest place to kick back and relax in Carolina Beach. Their generous menu includes everything from specialty salads like the tuna Nicoise to succulent prime rib. Or try the always fresh, very local catch of the day. Daily dinner specials add to the already extensive menu. You may also want to sneak a peek at their dessert menu, which is filled with a rotating selection of yummy treats. And, of course, there's the music. Musical entertainment scheduled at the Hula Grille includes William 'Paco' Strickland playing classical Flamenco guitar softly in the background to add to your dining enjoyment. Or if you're in the mood for jazz, come by and sample the

Grab a slice or another snack from one of the southern coast's numerous late-night dining spots.

photo: Peter Doran

smooth vibe of Funkymandu. For beach music fans, the Hula Grille is the Carolina Beach venue for popular bands like the Band of Oz and the Craig Woolard Band. Call or visit the website for the complete schedule and ticket information. Offering a new and different dining experience that's sure to please both Carolina Beach regulars and first-time visitors, Hula Grille is open until 11 PM during the week and 2 AM on weekends.

Michael's Seafood Restaurant & Catering $$
1206 N. Lake Park Blvd., Carolina Beach
(910) 458-7761

Winner of the 2001 Restaurant of the Year Award (Wilmington Chamber of Commerce Small Business Coalition), Michael's is a popular locals' choice. Michael's dinner menu is available all day, and fresh seafood, either steamed or broiled, is the specialty here. Nothing is fried. Alternative menu options include a good selection of steak, chicken, pasta and pork chops. Michael's updates its menu seasonally and offers lunch and nightly specials. Lunch features the award-winning Captain M's Seafood Chowder, a homemade soup of the day and a variety of sandwiches. A children's menu is available. Enjoy the indoor dining area dominated by a 700-gallon aquarium of the staff's "pets," or outdoor dining on the deck with live entertainment on the weekends. The restaurant has all ABC permits and serves imported and domestic beer and wine. Off-site catering services are also available. Michael's is open for lunch and dinner daily year-round. The restaurant does not accept checks.

Mama Mia's Italian Restaurant $$
6 Lake Park Blvd., Carolina Beach
(910) 458-9228

Lace curtains adorn the front windows of this quaint Italian restaurant in the heart of Carolina Beach. The menu offers a variety of dining choices. Dominating the menu's continental specialties are seafood, chicken and veal prepared in traditional pasta dishes and served with homemade sauces. Chicken Parmigiana, seafood lasagna, veal Marsala and shrimp scampi are a few examples. Nightly specials, often with fresh seafood, are featured. Mama Mia's also offers soups, salads, homemade pizza and a large selection of sandwiches and subs. Everything is available for take-out and delivery is available

in the Carolina Beach area. A children's menu is available for children ages 12 and younger. Domestic and imported beer and wine are served. Open year-round, family owned and operated Mama Mia's serves dinner Sunday through Thursday and lunch and dinner on Friday and Saturday.

The SeaWitch Cafe $$
227 Carolina Ave. N., Carolina Beach
(910) 458-8682

The SeaWitch Cafe, located near Carolina Beach's oceanfront, features a menu rich in regional cuisine. Dine inside in the crisp setting or enjoy a leisurely meal on the covered wrap-around porch on the quarterdeck, which overlooks a beautifully landscaped courtyard. A bandstand in the corner of the courtyard offers an environment of wonderful entertainment showcasing some of the best bands around. This is the perfect spot for the ultimate seashore dining experience. If the same old fish recipes bore you, try the SeaWitch fish specialties, including catfish served fish-camp style, cedar plank salmon and a tuna steak with a wonderful ginger soy glaze. Fresh fish, such as yellow tail, tilapia and triggerfish, are popular choices. Seawitch also offers a variety of sandwiches, including Cajun prime rib, Beach Burger, oyster po' boy and the famous half-pound chargrilled burger. Among the salad selections, the Sea Witch Salad (roasted almond chicken salad and fresh fruit) is a favorite. Seawitch offers seafood platters, steaks, chicken, dinners for two and a variety of desserts to round out your meal. In season, the cafe serves lunch and dinner Monday through Saturday. Sundays, the island's favorite brunch is served from 11 AM to 3 PM. Available for all your catering needs, the SeaWitch will host rehearsal dinners, weddings, receptions and parties for up to 200 people. The adjoining Tiki Bar offers a full-service bar. Call for entertainment and special event updates and off-season hours.

Trolly Stop $
103-A Cape Fear Blvd., Carolina Beach
(910) 458-7557

Trolly Stop is centrally located in the heart of Carolina Beach and offers a custom produce Smithfield all-meat hot dog as well as all-beef Sabrett hot dogs to suit almost any whim. In addition, they offer no-carb vegetarian dogs as well as low fat/no-carb turkey dogs. Try the classic North Carolina dog with chili, mustard and cole slaw, the Snow's Cut (melted cheese and mayo) or the Carolina Beach (special sauce, mustard and onion). Vegetarian, all-meat and nonfat hot dogs are also available. Trolly Stop's menu includes sweet Italian sausage, their signature Burger dog, a black bean burrito and nachos with toppings. The Carolina Beach location closes during the winter months.

Brunswick County Beaches

BALD HEAD ISLAND

The Bald Head Island Club $$-$$$
Bald Head Island
(910) 457-7300

Open for lunch and dinner, Bald Head Island Club offers three venues to enjoy marvelous creations sure to please any palate. The executive chef's seasonal menus include a vast selection of seafood specialties, char-grilled steaks, pasta and delectable desserts prepared by the on-site pastry chef. Regional seafood and the freshest vegetables are hallmarks of the restaurant's cuisine. The wine list is extensive and offers premium vintages to complement each meal. On Thursday nights you can experience the Land and Sea Menu, featuring local seafood and succulent prime rib. Set in a building reminiscent of coastal New England, the elegant dining room is accented by a commanding ocean view. For those desiring a more relaxed atmosphere, the Club Lounge offers a full bar, dance floor and walls of windows enabling all diners to continually observe and absorb island life. Live entertainment on Friday and Saturday nights in season is a lounge feature not to be missed. Completing the dining options is the newly added Grill. Light and airy with walls that are kissed in color, this dining experience is heightened by the magnificent views of the island's award-winning golf course. A temporary membership, which is included in accommodation rates for all properties leased through Bald Head Island Limited, is required for Club dining. Reservations are requested.

The Maritime Market $
Maritime Way, Bald Head Island
(910) 457-7450

This is a deli and sandwich counter at the new Maritime Market grocery store. The well-prepared variety of sandwiches, salads and hot foods provides a delightful break while shopping. Some offerings include gourmet salads, taco salad, rotisserie chicken, stuffed Cornish game hens, meatloaf and wraps. The bright and spacious new market is located off Muscadine Wynd in the maritime forest area of the island.

River Pilot Cafe $-$$
Bald Head Island
(910) 457-7390

The remodeled River Pilot Cafe has the island's finest view of the Cape Fear River and serves breakfast, lunch and dinner in a more casual setting than the Club dining room. The menu emphasizes Southern cuisine in its use of regional seafood, fresh vegetables, meats and daily specials. The variety of offerings guarantees an enjoyable dining experience. Enjoy a late-night menu and your favorite cocktail in the adjoining River Pilot Lounge. In summer, the cafe serves the island's best breakfasts. It's also a superb vantage from which to view stunning sunsets while enjoying a meal or drink. The River Pilot is open daily for breakfast, lunch and dinner.

SOUTHPORT/OAK ISLAND

317 West Bay Waterway Steakhouse $$
317 West Bay St., Southport
(910) 457-0317

To enter the doors of 317 West Bay is to enter the casual elegance of black and white where the movie of everyday life on the Intracoastal Waterway and the mouth of the Cape Fear River unfolds before you from any seat in the house. From sailboats to yachts to ferries to looming container ships to flights of pelicans, seagulls and ibis to the joyful jumping of dolphins — it plays out in front of you scene after scene as you dine. On the walls of the dining rooms and the fully equipped bar you will see movie memorabilia from posters of films shot in Southport (A Walk to Remember, Domestic Disturbance, Patriot, Summer Catch, Divine Secrets of the Ya-Ya Sisterhood and more). Outdoor lovers can be served on the deck in season. Sports lovers can watch NASCAR races, golf games, football games and more on the 42" plasma screen TV while seated at bistro tables or at the bar. Favorites of the house include Oysters Rockefeller, 317 West Bay Crab Dip and prime rib. Don't miss Jumbo Scallop Scampi and Chicken & Shrimp Alfredo. All this can be accompanied by your choice of 27 wines by the bottle and 25 by the glass as well as West Bay's specialty drinks, domestic and imported beers and coffee drinks.

Bella Cucina $$-$$$$
5177 Southport-Supply Rd., Southport
(910) 454-4540

Beautiful Kitchen, indeed! Beautiful dining room, beautiful lounge, beautiful food. At Bella Cucina you will find Tuscan-style food made with recipes handed down in the family and using only the freshest ingredients, including herbs from a local farm, to achieve the subtle flavors. From Antipasto to Dolce, the dinner menu is filled with delicious selections such as: mussels with a spicy red sauce, Caesar salad, Tuscan chicken, Veal Parmesan, Shrimp Scampi, pasta, of course, and daily specials. Enjoy your meal with your choice of red or white wines by the glass or the bottle. Dessert is a must have with selections of homemade tiramisu, homemade cannoli or New York cheesecake. Follow that with coffee (including specialty coffees), tea or cordials.

For your convenience, Bella Cucina offers an early dining menu from 5 to 6 PM daily and a children's menu. Looking for the perfect place to celebrate a special occasion? The folks at Bella Cucina will be happy to help you. Stop at their Pizzeria next door, (910) 454-4357, for NY-style pizza, calzones, stromboli and hot and cold subs.

Dry Street Pub & Pizza $-$$
101 E. Brown St., Southport
(910) 457-5994

When you are driving into Southport, look for the water tower. Directly across the street you will find Dry Street Pub & Pizza. As you enter the building, you will see a large orange and green fish above your head and local art for sale on the pale yellow walls of this cozy restaurant with small tables and a bar. Oh, you're looking for food? But, of course! If it's lunch or a light dinner you want, then you have come to the right place. The

food is delicious and can be served with beer or wine if you prefer. You will find traditional and specialty pizzas with many toppings; tomato bread; crab dip; homemade soups; salads including chef, Greek, shrimp and Caesar; and a variety of sandwiches from ham and cheese to a chicken pita wrap to an Italian sausage sub; and homemade desserts. Daily specials are available as well. All this is served by John and Sheila Barbee and their friendly staff. They're open Monday through Friday for lunch and dinner and on Saturday for lunch.

Fishy Fishy Cafe $$$
106 Yacht Basin Dr., Southport
(910) 457-1881

Don't miss Fishy Fishy! Seafood can't get any fresher than coming from the boat that is docking right next door to the restaurant. Whether you arrive by land or by sea (and dock your boat in one of the slips provided), you will thoroughly enjoy the Caribbean flavor of the restaurant and the food. Grilled and blackened seafood are the specialties of the house, but pork, steak and colorful pasta dishes are available as well, cooked to perfection by chefs trained at the Culinary Institute in New York. Dine indoors where you can watch your food being prepared, or outdoors on either the covered or the open deck. Either place provides fantastic views of the Intracoastal Waterway. Fishy Fishy is the place to be for live music every Sunday during summer.

Latitudes Restaurant $
705 Ocean Dr., Oak Island
(910) 278-5747

Latitudes has attitude, there's no doubt about it! Margaritaville attitude that is. From the open indoor area with its sky blue walls to the covered deck, this oceanside restaurant and bar with its casual, laid-back atmosphere is inviting to fishermen from the pier next door as well as to beachcombers, swimmers, vacationers and locals. Latitudes opens daily at 11 AM for lunch and dinner with a menu that includes sandwiches (claiming the island's best burgers), baskets, steamed shrimp, wings, salads and, of course, sides. As well as soda, tea and coffee, available beverages include wine and domestic and imported beer. Come relax and breathe the

The southern coastal region offers tempting restaurants to suit everyone's tastes.

photo: Peter Doran

ocean air while you dine and don't forget to check out the live weekly entertainment.

Little Bits $
5902 E. Oak Island Dr., Oak Island
(910) 278-6430

In the area since 1975, Little Bits has become somewhat of a tradition on Oak Island. Those looking for a home-style breakfast or a light lunch whipped up before their eyes and served with a smile, find their way to Little Bits at the new location on the main street. There the owner, Little Bit, has transformed a small building into an American-style eatery with red and white decor and successfully incorporated the elegant fans and wall hangings from her native Vietnam in the scheme. Breakfast and lunch are served daily.

Live Oak Café $$$-$$$$
614 N. Howe St., Southport
(910) 454-4360

Live Oak Café, nestled under one of Southport's lovely old live oak trees, is housed in one of a row of three historic homes known as "The Three Sisters". Owner/Chef Sean Mundy and his wife, Jennifer Charron, spent seven months refurbishing the house to spectacular results. When you step inside the door, the original heart pine floors, the vibrant colors on the walls, the intimate dining rooms (there are three), the pub tables, beaded-board ceilings and the décor take you back to a simpler time. Friendly staff will greet you and treat you to superior customer service. During the season, you can be served on the screened porch as well and have your wine in the herb garden if you like. American nouveau cuisine using only the freshest ingredients is the basis for Sean's eclectic menu. From starters to entrees, you will find crab dip, Cajun-marinated fried alligator bites, low country gumbo, shrimp pasta, grilled rib eyes, herb-roasted pork chops and more. In addition, there is an excellent wine list with selections from Australia, California and Argentina, among others. Live Oak Café is open Tuesday through Saturday for dinner. Reservations are accepted.

Russell's Place Restaurant $
5700 E. Oak Island Dr., Oak Island
(910) 278-3070

Among Long Beach residents, Russell's Place is one of the most popular diner-style eateries for breakfast and lunch. No matter how crowded it gets, the food is served hot, fast and with a smile, and no one will rush you. Table-to-table conversation comes easily as folks dine on large omelets, flaky biscuits, pancakes and Belgian waffles for breakfast and entrees, sandwiches and burgers for lunch. Russell's Place is open daily for breakfast (served all day) and lunch. Take-out orders are welcome.

San Felipe Restaurante Mexicano $
4961-9 Long Beach Rd., Southport
(910) 454-0950

If your taste buds are set for authentic Mexican cuisine in an awesome array of mouth-watering choices, San Felipe is an excellent choice. Located in the Live Oak Village Shopping Center with enlarged dining room and expanded menu in 2005, San Felipe serves lunch and dinner daily in a lively and friendly atmosphere where regulars from as far away as Wilmington or Calabash sometimes partake of both meals in the same day. The decor is tastefully Mexican, and seating might be a cozy table or booths long enough to accommodate the whole family. San Felipe's made-fresh-daily traditional Mexican cuisine can be ordered in combinations or specialty entrees, with beef, chicken and seafood. The lunch-only options number more than 26. Another combination list offers 30 more. The menu boasts an appealing list of appetizers, vegetarian combinations, tasty Mexican desserts and a child's plate menu for children younger than 12. Regulars say that San Felipe has the best margaritas, regular and flavored, in town. The restaurant also has all ABC permits and serves Mexican and domestic beer. Ask about drink and lunch specials. Take out is available.

Sandfiddler Seafood Restaurant $$
1643 N. Howe St. (N.C. Hwy. 211), Southport
(910) 457-6588

With its high-pitched roof, plainly set tables and nautical decor, this large establishment offers rustic ambience and affordable low country cuisine. Lunch specials, served with hush puppies, slaw and fries, are low-priced. Landlubbers will find plenty of land food to choose from, including steaks and pit-cooked pork barbecue. Most of the regional seafood staples are available, including deviled crabs, fried fantail shrimp stuffed with crabmeat, and a good selection of combination platters. You can get take-out orders too. The Sandfiddler serves dinner year round and lunch every day in season except Saturday. Ask about prime rib specials on Fridays and Saturdays. Private dining facilities are available.

Trolly Stop $
111 S. Howe St., Southport
(910) 457-7017

Walking through historic Southport can work up an appetite, and Trolly Stop's long list of dogs is sure to appeal. Trolly Stop serves a specially produced Smithfield all-meat dog, all-beef Sabrett dogs, no-carb veggie dogs and low fat/no-carb turkey dogs. Choose from the Southport (topped with special sauce, mustard and onions), the Oak Island (tomato salsa, mustard and onions), the Old Baldy (plain, of course!) and everything in between. Vegetarian, all-meat and nonfat hot dogs are additional options. Trolly Stop also serves grilled sandwiches, sweet Italian sausage, a black bean burrito and nachos with toppings. The Southport and downtown Wilmington locations also serve Hershey's ice cream.

Turtle Island Restaurant and Catering $$-$$$
6220 E. Oak Island Dr., Oak Island
(910) 278-4944

Turtle Island Restaurant and Catering opened in November 2001, but the managers, far from being new to the business, have a wealth of restaurant experience among them. The decor is inviting, casual and tropical from the coral walls to the jungle print tablecloths to the tanks of tropical fish. A good variety of wines is available, and the menu is intriguing, including such items as Wings Over Oak Island and hot crab dip for appetizers. In addition to the entree specials, the restaurant serves Calabash-style seafood, pasta and sandwiches — and with such flair! Just wait until you see the work of art that is your meal. Visit on Wednesday night, Steam Night, for live music and specials on all steamed seafood items. Turtle Island opens Tuesday through Sunday at 5 PM. Come early or take advantage of call-ahead seating (reservations are available only for parties of six or more).

HOLDEN BEACH

Archibald's Delicatessen & Rotisserie $
2991 Holden Beach Rd. SW, Holden Beach
(910) 842-6888

We love the sandwiches and subs at Archibald's almost as much as the home-made desserts, and most people we meet around Holden Beach do too. The deli offers a modest menu of fine quality and value. Take the Richie's Roaster for instance — rotisserie chicken breast with provolone and garnish on a roll. Or Archie's B.L.E.S.T. — bacon, lettuce, egg salad, tomato on fresh honey-wheat toast. Pork ribs are another rotisserie specialty you'll want to try. You can design your own sandwich or sub or choose from a selection of excellent fresh salad plates and homemade soups. Sliced deli meats and cheeses, of a variety usually not seen outside the largest supermarket deli counters, are available to go. Many varieties of quiche are served, and fresh fruit pies are available in season. The screened-in patio is pleasant during mild weather. Archibald's serves lunch and, in high season, dinner in a comfortable, clean, casual shop, housed in a curious round building. The staff can put together party platters, complete dinners and cater your special occasion as well.

OCEAN ISLE BEACH

The Isles Restaurant $$$-$$$$
417 W. Second St., Ocean Isle Beach
(910) 575-5988

The Isles Restaurant, designed by North Carolina's own John W. Thompson, is a magnificent setting for your dining pleasure. Whether your preference is for an elegant luncheon or a gourmet dinner, The Isles is sure to please. Starters include catfish fingers as well as such favorites as oysters Rockefeller and hot crab dip. Follow that with Isles Signature She Crab Soup. Try the poached pear salad with pecans and Gorgonzola, blackened steak salad or Caesar salad. Then move on to pecan-encrusted salmon smothered in Frangelico cream liqueur, pan-seared scallops with fresh corn and tomatoes or the Jack Daniels ribs. And don't forget to leave room for dessert. The Isles offers an extensive wine list to give a special festivity to the meal. Martini lovers, don't miss the Martini Menu!

An oceanfront banquet facility that can accommodate more than 100 people is available for business meetings, reunions or weddings (see our Wedding Planning chapter). The room set-up can be configured to meet the needs of your function. Audio visual equipment is available. including a projector and wall-size screen that slides down.

Roberto's Ristorante $$-$$$
6737 Beach Dr., N.C. Hwy. 179,
Ocean Isle Beach
(910) 579-4999

Family owned and operated since 1985, Roberto's offers authentic Italian-American cuisine and brick-oven baked pizza. Open for dinner year-round, the menu also features salads, homemade Italian pasta favorites, fresh seafood, veal, char-broiled steaks and nightly chef's specials. Don't miss the homemade desserts. Menu items can be packaged to take out, and a children's menu is available. Roberto's has full ABC permits. Off-season, the restaurant opens for dinner Tuesday through Saturday. From Memorial Day through the summer months, dinner is served Monday through Saturday.

Sharky's Restaurant $
61 Causeway Dr., Ocean Isle Beach
(910) 579-9177

"It's feedin' time!" is the slogan at Sharky's Restaurant. Sharky's goal is to provide a family-oriented restaurant for people who enjoy good food and a relaxed atmosphere. They do it so well that in 2004, due to popular demand, they enlarged the seating area to accommodate more than 150 people. The food at Sharky's is well-priced and can be enjoyed on the enlarged screened deck (which is handicapped accessible) overlooking the waterway where you can watch the passing boats as you dine. There is plenty of parking or you can tie up your boat along the 150 feet of Sharky's dock — take a break from your boating and enjoy a good meal. Some customers fly into the airport, making Sharky's accessible by land, sea and air. Thoroughly casual and fun for everyone, Sharky's offers appetizers, salads, sandwiches, thin-crust pizza and dinner entrees that include steaks, pasta, seafood and daily specials. Occasionally, Sharky's hosts family-oriented holiday parties with music and plenty of food. The restaurant provides catering, free local delivery and has all ABC permits. It is open for lunch and dinner daily. For catering information contact Ray or Rob at the restaurant.

Sugar Shack $$
1609 Hale Beach Rd., Ocean Isle Beach
(910) 579-3844

Don't miss this place. The house specialty is a huge steak, marinated, slowly grilled and richly flavored. Sugar Shack features authentic Jamaican home cooking (yes, the chef/owner is Jamaican) in a colorful, intimate setting about a mile from the beach. Amid greenery, tropical artwork and floral table coverings, recorded reggae music adds a lively island feel most days, while live music is offered on weekends. Sugar Shack specializes in its own recipe for jerk seasoning. The flavorful jerk selections, served with a hot 'n' sweet sauce, anchor a small delightful menu that also includes Stamp & Go (a traditional spicy cod fritter), Brown Stewed Fish (slowly cooked red snapper) and a curried goat so tender it literally falls off the bone. Oh, and don't forget to try the award-winning baby back ribs! Nothing is too spicy for the average palate, but imported hot sauce is available if you want to hurt yourself. Some appetizers are enough for a meal, and the Jamaican Sampler is a good introduction. Other offerings include a grilled mango tuna, spiced-just-right crab fritters, homemade soups, great burgers and nightly specials, such as lightly fried coconut shrimp served with mango-pepper marmalade. Then you just need to top it all off with a luscious slice of homemade Key lime pie.

Guinness and Red Stripe beer are served. Take-out orders are welcome. Sugar Shack is one block south of Ocean Isle Beach Road, a few yards off N.C. 179. (Ocean Isle Beach Road intersects U.S. 17 about 3 miles east of Grissettown.) Sugar Shack is open nightly for dinner in summer and Tuesday through Saturday off-season. Live entertainment is featured on Saturday nights. Reservations are strongly suggested.

SUNSET BEACH

Crabby Oddwaters Restaurant and Bar $$
310 Sunset Blvd., Sunset Beach
(910) 579-6372

If the food weren't so darn good, this upstairs restaurant would still be worth a visit just to read the story of how it got its "damp and crawly name" (a story told in one easy-to-remember sentence of barely more than 400 words). This is a small, handsome restaurant with an enclosed deck overlooking a creek and a beautiful stained-glass mural of a beach scene beside the front door. The tables have holes in the center where you can pitch your shucked shells, and, despite the plastic utensils, the ambience and cuisine are high quality. Local seafood of all types is the focus, featuring a raw bar, some very interesting appetizers (Ever have alligator lightly dusted in Cajun spices?), wonderful nightly specials and tasty grilled foods, including soft-shell crabs. Delicious soups, such as she-crab, shrimp bisque and clam chowder, are available. A limited choice of landfood is offered. Entrees are served with fresh seasonal vegetables, a choice of rice or the potato of the day and sweet hush puppies. Full bar service is available, as are daily drink specials. Crabby Oddwaters is above Bill's Seafood on the mainland side of the pontoon bridge and is open for dinner nightly during the high season. It's closed December 1 through February 1.

Twin Lakes Restaurant $$
102 Sunset Blvd., Sunset Beach
(910) 579-6373

Many tables at Twin Lakes offer a panoramic view of the region's most picturesque watercourse and draw bridge. The restaurant stands rooted in the region's long-standing culinary tradition, having family connections to the earliest seafood days of nearby Calabash. With its tropical decor enhanced by palm trees outdoors, colorful table coverings and local art within, Twin Lakes is an attractive family restaurant that stays busy. The Twin Lakes featured menu, an astonishing 24 pages in length, includes meat and seafood specials that change nightly. Otherwise, seafood, beef, vegetables and pasta make up the bulk of a tasty and affordable menu. Entrees may be ordered fried, sauteed, grilled, broiled or blackened, and the seafood is never long out of the water. Seafood salads, stir-fry and pasta combinations are all nicely done. Irresistible desserts are available as well. Twin Lakes is open nightly for dinner.

CALABASH

Calabash Seafood Hut   **$**
1125 River Rd., Calabash
(910) 579-6723

Don't be surprised to find this tiny place with a line of customers stretching around the corner. It's that popular, as much for its low, low prices as for the food, which is as good as anywhere in Calabash. The seafood platters are huge, offering combinations of Calabash-style fish, shrimp, oysters, crab and scallops. Even the biggest appetites are satisfied with the daily lunch specials. Sandwich offerings include soft-shell crab in season. Children will enjoy many items that are not even on the children's menu. All meals are served with cole slaw, french fries and hush puppies. The atmosphere is clean and bright, and everyone is friendly. The Hut also serves dinner, and it does a brisk take-out business through the street-side window. The Hut is closed Mondays. Call ahead for take-out.

The Coleman's Original
Calabash Seafood Restaurant   **$$**
9931 Nance St., Calabash
(910) 579-6875

Seafood! Everything from oyster stew and teriyaki shrimp to stuffed flounder in hollandaise and soft-shell crabs — you will find it here. But if your taste buds are set for hamburger, chicken or steak, you can indulge them here as well. Coleman's is open every day for lunch and dinner year round, so take yourself down to the foot of River Road. There you will find other restaurants, but head for the one with its name up in lights. Coleman's is closed on Wednesdays.

Ella's of Calabash   **$$**
1148 River Rd., Calabash
(910) 579-6728

Ella's has been featured in Coastal Living magazine and in April of 2004 it was chosen for inclusion in Southern Living magazine's

special publication, Favorites, which features "204 Food Finds Across the Region". If you would like to know why — give Ella's a try. You will find that Ella's remains one of the stalwarts of Calabash, It stays open most of the off-season, and it's been doing so since 1950. Ella's draws patrons with good food, affordable prices and a casual, friendly atmosphere. Ella's offers a hearty lunch special that's a real bargain (choice of two kinds of seafood, plus slaw, hush puppies and fries). Steaks, chicken, oyster roasts (in season), mixed drinks and a children's menu are also available. Ella's is open daily for lunch and dinner. It is located midway between the waterfront and Beach Drive (N.C. Highway 179).

Topsail Island

Asahi   **$-$$**
124 N. New River Dr., Surf City
(910) 328-1121

Your choice on Topsail Island for Chinese or Japanese cuisine, Asahi offers a full sushi bar including nigirisushi, makizushi and temaki. Lunch specials and Bento box combinations are offered daily. Asahi offers free delivery for orders more than $10. Asahi is open every day for lunch and dinner, at least until 10 PM.

The Atlantis Restaurant & Lounge   **$$-$$$**
2000 New River Inlet Rd.,
North Topsail Beach
(910) 328-2002

The Atlantis experience starts on the ground floor of the St. Regis Resort. Guests enter a glass elevator and head straight to the seventh floor. Up top, ceiling-to-floor windows offer a one-of-a-kind view of Topsail Island's northern strand. Seafood, steaks and pasta are some of the prized menu items. A salad and choice of vegetable are provided with each entree. Cocktails and an extensive wine list and fine desserts are sure to please the palate. A children's menu is also available. The Atlantis is designed to handle large groups and is ideal for special events. The restaurant has full ABC permits, and reservations are recommended. The Atlantis is open during the summer season Tuesday through Sunday for dinner.

The Beach Shop and Grill $
701 S. Anderson, Topsail Beach
(910) 328-6501

Famous for its fresh-squeezed orange-ades, cheeseburgers and hot dogs, The Beach Shop and Grill has a full complement of breakfast offerings and a lunch menu that also includes great salads and club sandwiches. The signature dish here is crab cakes, but there is also a good selection of other seafood and steaks. Beer and wine are available, and you can eat in or take-out. Dinner is served only during the summer months of June, July and August.

The Blue Gecko $-$$
808 S. Anderson Blvd, Topsail Beach
(910) 328-1022

Here is a restaurant, bar, deli, gift shop and art gallery all in the same bright green building. The enjoyable lunch menu offers gourmet deli meats and cheeses, wraps and fresh salads. The buckets of fresh steamed local seafood are a real hit in the evening. The Blue Gecko makes dining at home hassle free with their great take-out food. Having the gang over for a day at the beach? The Blue Gecko caters too. You'll also find fun edibles and unique gifts for the gourmet home. The Blue Gecko is open all year.

Breezeway Restaurant $$
634 Channel Blvd., Topsail Beach
(910) 328-4302

Fresh, Southern-style seafood is the order of the day at the Breezeway, which is adjacent to the Breezeway Motel. Traditional fried, broiled, grilled or Cajun-spiced seafood is offered, along with selections of steak and chicken. Seafood lasagna and hot crab dip are specialties and the steamer bar serves up crab legs, lobster, oysters, clams and shrimp. Add a slice of chocolate pecan or Key lime pie, and the magnificent sunset view of Topsail Sound, and you have the makings of a wonderful dining experience. In business since 1949, the Breezeway has become a favorite with visitors and residents. The Breezeway is open nightly at 5 PM for dinner in the summer, spring and early fall. A children's menu and take-out service are available, as are wine and beer.

CRABBY MIKE'S

121 S. Topsail Drive
Surf City, NC
910-328-4331

- Chef Crafted Daily Lunch & Dinner Specials
- Seafood, Steaks, & Chicken
- Best Clam Chowder on the Island
- Only Salad Bar on the Island
- Beer & Wine

Open Daily for Breakfast & Lunch
7 am - 2 pm
Serving Dinner Tuesday through Sunday
5 - 9 pm
(Call for Off Season Hours)

Cindy's Oceanside Restaurant $-$$
102 N. Shore Drive, Surf City
(910) 328-3314

Right on the ocean and open every day, Cindy's is always a popular choice. Enjoy a leisurely breakfast of eggs, pancakes or waffles. The lunch menu features sandwiches, salads and daily lunch specials for $5.95. Dinner begins at 5 PM and the choices include steaks, seafood, chops and pasta. Great views, friendly service and located on the ocean in the heart of Surf City.

Clamdigger Restaurant $-$$
105 Sugar Ln., Sneads Ferry
(910) 327-3444

Looking for a hometown feel with a family-friendly atmosphere? Try the Clamdigger's lunch buffet offered Monday and Wednesday through Saturday. The menu items include sandwiches, chicken, seafood and made from scratch BBQ. Mother Shucker's Oyster Bar offers fresh oysters served raw, steamed, fried or grilled. Beer and wine are served, and a children's menu is available. The Clamdigger is open year-round but closes on Tuesday.

Crabby Mike's $-$$
121 S. Topsail Drive, Surf City
(910) 328-4331

The bright ocean-blue walls and splashes of lime green create a cool seaside vibe at Crabby Mike's. Mornings are filled with

139

Daddy Mac's
BEACH GRILLE

Oceanfront Dining • Elevator Access
Grilled Seafood • Steaks • Ribs • Pastas

108 N. Shore Drive • Surf City, NC 28445

910-328-5577

Jambalaya, tender Caribbean Crab Cakes, grilled seafood, tasty ribs, pasta and steaks. Daddy Mac's menu includes appetizers, soups, salads, sandwiches and daily specials. The full bar serves mixed drinks, domestic and imported beer and wine. A children's menu is also available. The restaurant has an elevator and is handicapped accessible. Daddy Mac's opens nightly at 5PM.

Dr. Rootbeer's Hall of Foam $
288 Fulchers Landing, Sneads Ferry
(910) 327-ROOT (7668)

Dr. Rootbeer's Hall of Foam, located in a vintage 1950s gas station near the waterfront in Sneads Ferry, sells root beer made from Jerome Gundrum's own recipe. Choose between old fashion fountain favorites like lime ricky, birch beer or sasparilla while listening to their 1953 Seeburg jukebox. With root beer floats, milkshakes and 16 flavors of hand-dipped ice cream, there are plenty of cool treats for everyone. Dr. Rootbeer also serves delicious sandwiches like his Dixie Pot Roast, chicken or tuna salad wraps, sweet Italian sausage and three different kinds of hot dogs, including foot-longs and his new Sweet Sassafras BBQ. Dr. Rootbeer's walls are covered with vintage root beer memorabilia that has been carefully collected for thirty-two years. Take home a six-pack of root beer and some root beer taffy or candy. Dr. Rootbeer's Hall of Foam is open all year.

Belgian waffles, eggs benedict, omelets and pancakes. At lunch the restaurant features homemade soups and chowders, great angus burgers, a full lunch menu and the island's only salad bar. In the evening, in addition to fried and grilled seafood, the chef cooks up unique seasonal specials and the Saturday night prime rib is a popular choice. Beer and wine is available. Crabby Mike's is open every day at 7AM, dinner is served Tuesday through Sunday in the summer and on weekends in the off-season.

Crab Pot $-$$
508 Roland Ave., Surf City
(910) 328-5001

Low-country and Caribbean cuisine are the specialty of the Crab Pot. Spicy seafood gumbo, jerk chicken and much more await the casual diner. Food can be picked up or enjoyed in the screened-in dining room or bar. A children's menu is available and the Crab Pot has a full bar. Shag lessons are offered on summer evenings. The Crab Pot is closed from Thanksgiving until March.

Daddy Mac's Beach Grille $$$
108 N. Shore Dr., Surf City
(910) 328-5577

This new oceanfront restaurant is already a favorite with locals. The restaurant's warm wood tones, terra-cotta and sage walls, ocean views and covered oceanfront deck create an instantly inviting atmosphere. Daddy Mac's serves up steaming bowls of Cajun

'EM 'R' Wings $
1016 Old Folkstone Rd., Sneads Ferry
(910) 327-0483

Appetizers, side orders, salads and sandwiches complement the specialty of the house — buffalo wings, served mild, medium or hot. This is a fun place to enjoy casual snacking, although meal choices of ribs or steak are available. Bar seating is separate from the dining room. Take-out orders are welcome. EM 'R' Wings has a full bar and is open all year.

Green Turtle Restaurant $$
310 Fulchers Landing Rd., Sneads Ferry
By water: New River Channel Marker 17
(910) 327-0262

The cafe on the bay overlooks the picturesque New River and specializes in seafood, steaks and pasta. The Green Turtle also offers fresh and creative entrees such as shrimp diablo, linguine pescatore, Cajun oysters and classic NY strip steaks. Enjoy your favorite cocktail while listening to the live entertainment. Family-friendly, the Green Turtle offers a children's menu. It's open daily, and reservations are suggested.

Holly Ridge Smokehouse Restaurant $
511-A U.S. Hwy. 17, Holly Ridge
(910) 329-1708

For breakfast, lunch or dinner, this well-known restaurant offers great home-cooked food. The specialty of the house is the slow-cooked barbecue, a favorite with eastern North Carolina barbecue lovers. A children's menu is available. Holly Ridge Smoke House is open year round but is closed Mondays.

Il Beauchaines $$-$$$
211 S. Topsail Dr., Surf City
(910) 328-1888

Shrimp and grits is a popular dish here, and the scallops and oysters are always a hit. The tantalizing menu also includes steak, chicken and pork dishes. Il Beauchaines has all ABC permits, and the upstairs dining room and bar overlook the beautiful Intracoastal Waterway. Homemade desserts and a children's menu are available. Il Beauchaines will also cater your private party. During the summer, reservations are strongly recommended. It's open Thursday through Sunday during the winter.

Indigo Marsh $$$$
602-B Roland Ave., Surf City
(910) 328-2580

Hand-trimmed chophouse-style steaks, creatively prepared fresh local seafood, a nice wine list and an extensive selection of spirits make Indigo Marsh a destination of delights. The back deck offers an outstanding view of the Intracoastal and is perfect for summer evenings. The restaurant also offers a specially priced Sunset Menu. They are open every day during the summer season and closed on Sunday in the winter. Reservations are recommended.

Island Delights $
312 N. New River Dr., Surf City
(910) 328-1868

Return to the 1950s and the days of the soda shop with a trip to Island Delights.

DR. ROOTBEER'S HALL OF FOAM

SNEADS FERRY
NORTH CAROLINA

KNOWN FAR & WIDE FOR OUR SECRET RECIPE ROOT BEER, CREAMY FLOATS, SHAKES, DIXIE POT ROAST BURGERS, SWEET SASSAFRAS BBQ, DOGS (LOADED) AND LOTS OF FUN!

288 FULCHERS LANDING ROAD • SNEADS FERRY, NC 910-327-ROOT (7668) • WWW.DRROOTBEER.COM

The eatery specializes in ice cream, milk shakes and sundaes as well as the expected selection of burgers, sandwiches and fries. Vacationing families enjoy returning here year after year for their evening ice cream treats. It's closed in the winter.

Long Island Pizza $-$$
610 N. New River Dr., Surf City
(910) 328-3156

Long Island Pizza offers much more than great pizza. The menu also offers pasta, broccoli or spinach rolls, calzones and stromboli. Beer and wine are available. You can eat in, take-out or have your meals delivered to your door. It's closed on Sunday and Monday and during the winter from Thanksgiving until March.

Lo-Re-Lei $
1019 Old Folkstone Rd., Sneads Ferry
(910) 327-0900

If you are hunting for a big juicy burger and a tall cold one head to Lo-Re-Lei's behind the big shark at Four Corners. Their daily lunch specials are $4.95 and include free iced tea. Try their Calabash-style seafood or hand-cut steaks. Join in on a mid-week Karaoke night, pool or dart tournament or kick it up a notch on weekends with live bands and drink specials, including chilled Jagermeister on tap. Lo-Re-Lei is open daily at 11 AM.

RESTAURANT & BAR

On Topsail Island at the corner
of Rts. 210 and 50,
1/4 mile east of the swing bridge

The Best in Seafood, Steaks & Pasta

Open at 5pm
Reservations and Take-Out orders accepted

404 Roland Avenue
Surf City, NC 28445
(910) 328-0010
Open Everyday Year Round

Mainsail Restaurant & Bar   **$$-$$$**
404 Roland Ave., (corner of N.C. Hwys. 210
and 50), Surf City
(910) 328-0010
www.bluemainsail.com

Mainsail Restaurant's well-balanced menu offers the tastiest foods to satiate even the most famished travelers, fishermen or golfers. Try the fresh grilled fish with a variety of savory sauces like spicy chipotle and creamy dill. Or try the Maryland crab cakes, steaks, pastas and homemade desserts. Enjoy the views from the Sunset Room while sampling the eclectic wine collection or a cocktail from the well-stocked bar. Reservations are recom-

mended, and take-out is accommodated. It's open daily, year round, for dinner.

Max's Pizza   **$-$$**
602A Roland Ave., Surf City
(910) 328-2158

Open year round, Max's is one of the island residents' favorite choices for wintertime dining on Topsail. This casual, friendly atmosphere spills over into the summer, when visitors blend with the local clientele to enjoy pizza, spaghetti, salads, burgers or hot-oven subs. Max's serves beer and wine. Take-out orders are welcome. It's closed on Wednesday during the off-season.

Mollie's Restaurant   **$-$$**
107 N. South Shore Dr., Surf City
(910) 328-0505
www.molliesrestaurant.com

Casual dining at its best, Mollie's offers a full breakfast menu, with additional specials to make the choice of a delicious meal even more difficult. Lunchtime patrons will find great salads and sandwiches on the menu in addition to Mollie's traditional daily luncheon specials. The crab melt sandwich, made from an old family recipe, is a once-in-a-lifetime experience. Mollie's has a full range of dinner meals, mostly fresh seafood, again with even more choices offered on the special board. Enjoy wine and imported or domestic beer with your meal. A children's menu and take-out are available. Mollie's is open year round, daily in season and closed on Tuesdays during the off-season.

New York Corner Deli   **$**
206 N. Topsail Dr., Surf City
(910) 328-2808

From da Bronx to da beach, this deli is the real thing. New York Corner Deli serves authentic deli sandwiches piled high with real New York City pastrami, salami and corned beef. Bite into their fresh rye bread, bagels and homemade salads or try a slice of their New York–style cheesecake and you will think you are in the Big Apple. The New York Deli serves the only lox and bagel plate you will find on the island. Diners can eat inside, outside at patio tables or call ahead for quick take-out. New York Corner Deli hosts and caters private parties and prepares take-home decorated deli trays and party sized hoagies.

- serving the Topsail area since 1987 -

Mollie's
CASUAL DINING   a fat tuna company

- FULL BREAKFAST MENU -
- GREAT SANDWICHES AND SALADS -
- FRESH LOCAL SEAFOOD -
- STEAKS, BURGERS, AND CHICKEN -
- PASTA SPECIALTIES -
- WINE AND BEER SELECTIONS -
- KIDS MENU -
- TAKE-OUT ALWAYS AVAILABLE -

open daily 7 am - 9 pm
closed Tuesday in the off season

107 NORTH SHORE DRIVE
SURF CITY, NC 28445
(910) 328-0505

www.molliesrestaurant.com

The restaurant is open Monday through Saturday from 7:30 AM to 7:30 PM and Sundays from 8 AM to 5:30 PM.

One Stop Seafood Restaurant   **$**
805 Roland Ave., Surf City
(910) 328-1986

If home-style cooking is your choice, you can't miss with One Stop. Try an omelet with their fabulous hash-brown casserole for breakfast. For lunch try their fried fish or country-style BBQ ribs with a slice of tomato pie or sweet potato casserole. One Stop offers an old-time beach atmosphere on the waterway. It is on the mainland side of the swing bridge and open year round.

Pepperoni's Restaurant   **$-$$**
2000 New River Inlet Rd.,
North Topsail Beach
(910) 328-4183

Hungry for some pizza? Pepperoni's Restaurant is a fun-filled Italian eatery located on the first floor of Building One in the St. Regis Resort. Toasted subs and handmade pizzas are Pepperoni's specialty. Thirsty? Pepperoni's offers a full beer and wine menu. Open seven days a week for breakfast, lunch and dinner, Pepperoni's offers family-friendly dining or take-out.

Pirates Cove   **$-$$**
316 Fulchers Landing Rd., Sneads Ferry
(910) 327-3395

Adjacent to Paradise Landing Marina, Pirates Cove offers seafood and pasta combinations, steaks and daily specials that include seafood from local boats. It's open year round for breakfast, lunch and dinner. Beer and wine are offered, and a children's menu is available.

Rick's   **$-$$**
510 Petes Way, (N.C. Hwy. 210),
Sneads Ferry
(910) 327-2300

Looking for a place to catch the game and enjoy a cold one? Head to Rick's where big screen TVs, tasty appetizers and cold beer make this destination a hole-in-one. When it's time for a full meal, try their pasta dishes, half-pound burgers, quesadillas and hand-cut steaks. And, of course, Rick's has a full bar.

"In The Heart of Surf City"

New York Corner DELI

206 N. TOPSAIL DRIVE SURF CITY, NC 28445
ONE BLOCK NORTH OF TRAFFIC LIGHT

BREAKFAST ALL DAY • DINING ROOM
• BOAR'S HEAD MEATS
• CATERING FOR ALL OCCASIONS

| CALL AHEAD FOR QUICK PICK-UP! (910) 328-2808 | FAX YOUR ORDER IN ADVANCE! (910) 328-2884 |

Riverview Cafe   **$-$$**
119 Hall Point Rd., Sneads Ferry
(910) 327-2011

The Riverview Cafe serves dinner plates heaped with your choice of fresh fried seafood, french fries, slaw and hush puppies. The waterfront location where you can watch the shrimp boats come in adds to this pleasurable experience. Visitors return year after year for a Riverview dinner, joining the locals who eat there on a regular basis. The bar is separated from the dining room and offers beer and wine. It's open year round for lunch and dinner.

Sears Landing Grill & Boat Docks   **$-$$**
806 Roland Ave., Holly Ridge
(910) 329-1312

Come by boat or car to this sound-side restaurant. Enjoy eating inside, on the porch or order take out. Choices include fresh grilled fish of the day, sandwiches, soft-shell crabs, peel-and-eat shrimp or the chef's famous beach hotdog or hamburger. Beer and wine are available. It's open for lunch and dinner. Sears Landing has deep-water access with boat slips available for rent by the day, week or month. Beer, soft drinks, water and ice can be purchased for your boat, trip to the beach or to just enjoy while rocking on the porch relaxing with a view of the Intracoastal Waterway.

Casual Dining & Catering
Children's Meals
Pub & Restaurant
Fine Wines, Domestic & Imports
Full ABC Permits
Live Music
4pm- Until

Skully's
Pub & Grub

718 South Anderson Boulevard
Topsail Beach, NC
910-328-3100

Skully's Pub and Grub   **$-$$**
718 Anderson Blvd., Topsail Beach
(910) 328-3100

Located in the heart of Topsail Beach, Skully's Pub offers great food in a fun atmosphere. The restaurant's homemade entrees include scampi, shrimp and crab au gratin, crab cakes, fried seafood and steaks. If you're in the mood for something lighter, try their homemade soups, salads or crab dip. Enjoy a shrimp, oyster or fish and chips basket, a delicious French dip or a burger. A children's menu is also available. Skully's pub offers a late-night menu, fine wines and spirits, imported and domestic beer, pool tables, a wide-screen TV and live entertainment. Skully's is open daily during the summer and is closed Mondays off-season. The pub opens at 4 PM and dinner is served from 5 to 10 PM.

HAMPSTEAD AREA

Mako's Raw Bar and Grille   **$-$$$**
55 Scotts Hill Loop Rd., Scotts Hill
(910) 686-9042

Mako's offers a wide variety of fresh seafood and a raw bar. Oysters on the half shell, steamed shrimp, mussels, clams, crab legs, seafood salads and the daily catch are just some of the offerings. Don't overlook their special crab cakes or soups that have proven to be favorites with the customers. Mako's also has a prime rib that is slow roasted in house. There are daily lunch specials and an evening special for each night. A full bar, a children's menu and take-out are available.

The Pasta Grille   **$-$$$**
513 Country Club Dr., Hampstead
(910) 270-2425

Specializing in pasta dishes, as the name indicates, The Grille treats diners to a variety of interesting dishes, including angel hair pasta with Shrimp a la Rosa, Penne with Chicken in Pesto or a selection of pizzas ranging from classic to Chicken a la Rosa or a grilled veggie pizza. There are daily early bird specials and a kids-eat-free special from 4 to 6 PM. Eat in the dining room, the bar or take-out. The Pasta Grille also has a small meeting room and a large banquet room that holds up to 120 people for special occasions. The bar opens daily at 3 PM and the restaurant at 4 PM for dinner. Reservations are accepted. A full bar and a children's menu are available.

BURGAW

Holland's Shelter Creek Restaurant   **$$**
8315 N.C. Hwy. 53 E., Burgaw
(910) 259-5743

Finish off a day exploring the countryside with a meal at Holland's. Known for their fresh seafood, Holland's offers hearty platters with everything from frog legs and catfish to oysters, shrimp and deviled crab platters. For those who prefer country cooking, the restaurant offers some of the area's best barbecue and pork chops. Dine in a rustic atmosphere with a view of the river, and relax with a cup of catfish stew or shrimp Creole. Holland's has beer and wine, seniors' specials and a children's menu. They are open year-round for lunch and dinner.

Coffeehouses

An interesting offspring of the traditional coffeehouse is the marriage of the cafe atmosphere and bookstores. The larger book superstores in Wilmington — **Barnes & Noble**, 322 S. College Road, and **Books-A-Million**, 3737 Oleander Drive — feature surprisingly cozy cafe settings that host cultural events, meetings and book discussion groups. The **Salt Shaker Bookstore and Cafe**, 705 S. Kerr Avenue, Wilmington, offers coffee and cafe-style food. A smaller, independent bookstore that features the twin delights of good coffee and good books is the **Quarter Moon books & gifts**, 708 S. Anderson Boulevard in Topsail Beach.

WILMINGTON

General Assembly
The Cotton Exchange, 303 N. Front St.,
Wilmington
(910) 343-8890

Located in The Cotton Exchange, this popular coffeehouse offers yummy pastries, fresh donuts, muffins and bagels to complement their fresh-roasted coffee, mocha shakes and specialty coffee drinks. Unique to the General Assembly is one of Wilmington's two scaled-down replicas of the Statue of Liberty. (The other is at a side entrance to Thalian Hall.) General Assembly is open daily.

Folks Cafe
1201 Princess St., Wilmington
(910) 362-1448
4023 Market St., Wilmington
(910) 762-9511

Owners Alan and Griselda invite you to join them at their neighborhood cafe where you'll enjoy delicious organic, fair-trade coffee, fresh sandwiches and bakery items, locally made ice cream, art by locals as well as Central American Folk artists, and music in a unique friendly atmosphere.

Port City Java
21 N. Front St., Wilmington
(910) 762-5282

Arboretum Center,
5917 Oleander Dr., Wilmington
(910) 792-9575

Barclay Commons,
2512 Independence Blvd., Wilmington
(910) 792-0449

Harris Teeter Cafe,
820 S. College Rd., Wilmington
(910) 796-0850

5621 Carolina Beach Rd., Monkey Junction
(910) 392-7746

Porters Neck Center,
8211 Market St., Wilmington
(910) 686-1033

Lumina Station,
1900 Eastwood Rd., Wilmington
(910) 256-0993

14280 US Hwy. 17, Hampstead
(910) 270-9833

113 N. Howe St., Southport
(910) 454-0321

Established in 1995, Wilmington's Port City Java now boasts seven locations in the Wilmington and Wrightsville Beach areas, one in Hampstead and one in Southport. Each is individual in decor and menu, from traditional coffeehouse fare to a luncheon

Local coffeehouses provide a place to relax and recharge your batteries.

photo: Peter Doran

menu of fresh garden salads and grilled panini (sandwich) specialties. Housing its own local roastery, Port City Java guarantees that your favorite coffee beverage is fresh daily. Try their non-java offerings, such as the Ghirardelli Hot Cocoa (a chocolate lover's dream) or the Oregon Chai Steamer, a ginger-honey spiced tea blend with steamed milk. If the heat of a coastal summer calls for something cool and refreshing, their Mocha Shake — chilled espresso, Ghirardelli chocolate and vanilla ice cream — is a popular choice. Or check out Port City Java's selection of fresh juices and pure fruit smoothies. Drive-through windows are open at the Porters Neck Center and Arboretum Center locations.

Wilmington Espresso Co.
24 S. Front St., Wilmington
(910) 343-1155

Wilmington Espresso Co. offers plenty of reading material such as magazines, local newspapers and books. The muffins and pastries are baked fresh daily, and all the usual specialties — espresso, cappuccino, lattes, tea and fruit smoothies — are served with a smile from the friendly staff. This shop serves all of your favorite coffeehouse fare in an intimate downtown setting. Windowed tables and rocking chairs situated right outside the front door beckon you to sit and relax. Also available at this location are whole gourmet coffee beans, coffeemakers and specialty teas.

CAROLINA BEACH

The Coffee Shop
108 Carolina Beach Ave. N.,
at the Boardwalk, Carolina Beach
(910) 458-2666

This authentic coffeehouse offers a tempting variety of hot and cold coffee drinks, all-fruit smoothies, pastries and ice cream in a comfortable atmosphere where folks can relax, talk, read or play board games. Owners Wendy and Steven Hughes have made The Coffee Shop a popular Boardwalk stopping place by adding a personal touch that's often missing in commercial establishments. Their friendly conversation and casual manner make everyone feel welcome. Just steps away from the beach, The Coffee Shop is open all year, though hours vary seasonally.

The Grind
308 S. Lake Park Blvd., Carolina Beach
(910) 458-6033

Warm and inviting, The Grind is Carolina Beach's most delightful casual gathering place. A variety of fresh coffees, fruit drinks, baked goods and beach snacks are served in a comfortable, bright, uplifting atmosphere Monday through Friday from 6:30 AM to 5 PM, Saturday from 7:30 AM to 5 PM and Sunday from 9 AM to 1 PM. A business center with broadband Internet access, wireless hot-spot, fax, printing and copy service are available adjacent to the sitting area. Owners Diane and David Lawn invite tourists and locals to stop in often. The Grind is located across from Carolina Beach Lake on the corner of Atlanta Avenue.

BRUNSWICK COUNTY BEACHES

Island Brews Coffee Shop & Cafe
1102 N. Howe St., Southport
(910) 454-0363

When you step inside the door of Island Brews you may think that their claim to fame is an easy, breezy, comfortable atmosphere. The gleaming floors, screened porch and separate area with cushy couch and chairs in front of a fireplace certainly give that impression. But stop and smell the coffee, try some of their special food and you will see there is more here than meets the eye. They have a special blend of espresso, flavored coffees and cappuccino as well as tea, smoothies, juices and more. Breakfast selections range from scones to breakfast burritos. Daily lunch specials include sandwiches, salads and even soup in a bread bowl. Don't leave without trying their exceptional desserts — take some with you. Cakes (like sour cream and coconut and seven-layer ultimate chocolate) are homemade locally. Croissants with fruit and cream cheese filling are baked on the spot. Or try the gourmet tiramisu cheesecake or New York cheesecake. Wireless Internet is available, private parties can be catered and be sure to ask about weekend entertainment. At Island Brews, it's not only about coffee.

The Flying Pig Coffeehouse
6006 Oak Island Dr., Oak Island
(910) 278-5929

Have you ever drawn a picture of a flying pig with your eyes closed? Well here's you chance. Rebecca and Steve Matson, own-ers of The Flying Pig Coffeehouse, offer this opportunity to all their customers and the results are in a book for all to see. This bright coffeehouse, with its eclectic furniture (for sale) made by Steve, is conducive to draw-ing, reading, writing or just enjoying a cup of coffee. There are newspapers and books available, from The Artist's Way to If Pigs Could Fly and Other Deep Thoughts. You can relax in the lovely tea garden adjacent to the coffeehouse if you prefer. Barrows tea, Chai, smoothies and other drinks are available. Try the specialties of the house: the frozen Arctic Pig or the hot Flying Pig. Ask about the monthly book club, poetry readings and weekend entertainment. The coffeehouse features the works of a different artist every month. There you will find paintings or wire sculptures among the many types of art from traditional to avant garde. Internet service, including wireless internet, is available to cus-tomers as well. The Flying Pig coffeehouse is open seven days a week.

Cappuccino By The Sea
3331 Holden Beach Rd., Holden Beach
(910) 842-3661

A friendly and inviting coffee shop in a converted house on the causeway, Cappuc-cino By The Sea is open year-round. Enjoying a 12th summer of business in 2005, this charming cafe features tables inside and out.

Local and regional newspapers, board games and a few books are available to peruse while savoring your favorite coffee or tea beverage and snack. Try a slice of scrumptious cake, homemade quick bread or some cookies. Cappuccino By The Sea also offers a line of gifts including body products, handmade mirrors and jewelry, Christmas ornaments, ce-ramic nautical dishes, windchimes, suncatch-ers, bathing suit wraps, ladies belts and hand-bags, potpourri, candles and coffee beans. Greeting cards and postcards are available. Gift baskets and birthday balloons can be shipped or delivered locally. Need local info? Owner Nancy Elwell can give you the low-down on everything from attractions to minor repair referrals. Check out the website. Internet service is provided as well.

Jumpin' Java Espresso Company
4635 Main St., Shallotte
(910) 754-5282

Comfy, casual, cheery and bright, this downtown Shallotte coffee shop, located on Main Street across from McDonald's, is a great place to stop and relax. In a hurry? Just use the drive-thru window. Either way you can enjoy hot or cold coffee and tea in any specialty you can imagine. Why not have some pastries, bagels or muffins with that? They are baked by a local professional chef. Do you prefer fruit smoothies? They've got them here.

The Fort Fisher ferry provides an easy shortcut between Fort Fisher and Southport.

photo: Peter Doran

Bakeries

WILMINGTON

Apple Annie's Bake Shop
University Square Mall, 837 S. Kerr Ave.,
Wilmington
(910) 799-9023
Landfall Shopping Center, 1319 Military
Cutoff Rd., Wilmington
(910) 256-6585

Boasting five generations of baking tradition, this award-winning bakery offers everything from bread to gourmet pastries. The goods are baked fresh daily on-premises with natural ingredients and no additives or preservatives. Long, windowed pastry cases display a wide range of the day's available goodies, including cakes, pies, cheesecakes, French pastries, cookies, biscotti, danish, muffins, assorted breads and rolls, cannoli, brownies and more. Wedding and special occasion cakes are their specialties. Holidays are especially festive at Apple Annie's, and they celebrate them all. Whether you want a heart-shaped Valentine's Day cake, spicy pumpkin pies for Thanksgiving or Challah bread at Rosh Hashanah, call the bakery for their holiday specials throughout the year.

Great Harvest Bread Co.
5327 Oleander Dr., Wilmington
(910) 793-2330

Some of the best breads in Wilmington can be found at Great Harvest. Their breads and pastries are baked fresh daily from high-protein whole wheat flour they mill themselves using no oils or preservatives. Selections vary with the season, but a typical week will feature 28 different breads plus muffins, scones, cinnamon rolls, cookies and seasonal pies. Stop by for a seasonal baking schedule that lists daily offerings. Christmas gift baskets of assorted breads are extremely popular and available from Thanksgiving to Christmas. These are great ideas for out-of-town gift-giving and are shipped from Great Harvest via UPS. At Easter, try the whimsical Honey Bunnies, a loaf of honey wheat bread made into a bunny shape. It's a delicious and fun addition to your Easter dinner menu. Limited seating is available if you'd like to enjoy coffee and a treat while making your selections. Firmly believing in the traditions of "the village bakery," Great Harvest contributes to the community in generous donations to area churches, non-profit organizations and local shelters.

Sweet & Savory Bake Shop & Cafe
1611 Pavilion Pl., Wilmington
(910) 256-0115

One of the area's premier wholesale/retail bakeries, Sweet & Savory supplies many local restaurants with fresh-baked breads and desserts. The bakery and cafe are located near the Wrightsville Beach bridge and just east of Plaza East shopping center. Dining in the cafe (seating is situated within the bakery) provides a unique experience as you watch

Brunswick County's copious marshland areas offer some wonderfully scenic views.

photo: Peter Doran

a working bakery in action. It comes as no surprise that the sandwich menu includes homemade breads. Sweet & Savory offers daily board specials that include fresh fish sandwiches, quiches, soups (chilled soups are offered in summer) and entree salads. The restaurant also offers an extensive breakfast menu with specialty sandwiches, omelets and other early morning delights. Vegetarian sandwiches and healthy, low-fat or low-carb selections are included on the menu. Catering is available. The bakery is open Sunday through Thursday until 9 PM and Friday and Saturday until 10 PM.

BRUNSWICK COUNTY BEACHES

Baked With Love
302 N. Howe St., Southport
(910) 454-0044

Obviously Lisa Botnick loves what she does (anyone who gets up at 2 AM to start baking must love it), and it shows in her product. Her specialties are Tapas-style pies and cakes, cookies, brownies and bread. She also bakes full-size pies, cakes and birthday cakes to order. But this is a bakery with a twist — imagine having lunch where you can smell the bread baking. Boar's Head brand meats and cheeses may fill the sandwiches

but the bread is baked in-house: Sourdough Bread, Rosemary Olive Oil Bread, Cibatta (try it with roast beef and Brie), Croissants (with turkey, bacon and cheddar) and whole-grain bread. She even carries bagels and lox. A kids menu is available, as are salads. You may even wish to try the quiche and side salad combo.

The French Bake and Pastry Shop
7290-10 Beach Dr., Seaside Plaza,
Ocean Isle Beach
(910) 575-0284

Robert, a native of Amsterdam and previous owner of an extremely successful restaurant, Chez Robert, which was situated next to the White House in Washington, D.C., has opened this wonderful classic patisserie Francaise. You know the moment you enter that this is no ordinary bakery. The decor is done in the traditional French yellow and blue colors with touches of white, and on the walls are Toulouse Lautrec posters and photos of the Eiffel Tower. Your nose will tell you as well — mmmm! Just smell those muffins, turnovers, pastries, rolls, croissants, eclairs, cream puffs, strudels, cheesecakes, baguettes and more. Robert bakes pies and cakes to order, as well as the most memorable wedding cakes ever.

ⓨ NIGHTLIFE

Along North Carolina's southern coastline, the term "nightlife" may have very different meanings to area natives and to visitors enjoying the sights. Plenty of residents spend summer nights away from the crowds by searching the beaches for loggerhead turtle nests and helping protect the ones they find. Others prefer the nights for fishing. Many youngsters enjoy surprising ghost crabs with their flashlights as the little critters (the crabs) make their nocturnal runs on the beach. Of course, there's little more romantic or peaceful than a leisurely stroll on the beach under a Carolina moon.

If going out on the town is more your style, area nightlife is primarily concentrated in Wilmington, with its numerous restaurants, nightclubs, bars and theaters. Outlying areas, especially the South Brunswick Islands, are famous for their quiet family atmosphere, but hot spots definitely do exist at Wrightsville Beach, Carolina Beach, Surf City and on Oak Island, particularly in summer.

Stroll the Riverwalk along Water Street and Front Street in downtown Wilmington. There are plenty of places along the way to pause for a toast or to hear live music. A horse-drawn carriage tour of downtown Wilmington is an exciting and informative introduction to the city too.

Billiards (see listings in this chapter) and bowling (see our Sports, Fitness and Parks chapter) are fun alternatives to the usual bar scene. Browsing our Attractions chapter will reveal more ideas — for instance, evening cruise opportunities on the Cape Fear River.

The last couple of years have brought a local resurgence of interest in jazz, blues and other musical genres, evident in the increasing number of restaurants and bars offering live music in the evenings, typically between Thursday and Sunday. Venues worth a visit for blues include The Rusty Nail and Water Street Restaurant.

Wilmington's busy theater scene, with Thalian Hall as its crown jewel, offers quality entertainment year round. In Brunswick County, the Odell Williamson Auditorium provides another venue for live performances and dramatic productions. Fans of classical music take note of area presenters that sponsor evening concert programs year round. See our chapter on The Arts for more information on both concerts and theatrical productions.

You will find some private nightclubs throughout the region. In order for an establishment to serve liquor, it must either earn the bulk of its revenue from the sale of food, or it must be a private club open only to members and their guests. Membership to most clubs is inexpensive, usually about $5 per year. At some venues, weekend visitors applying for membership should know that a three-day waiting period must elapse before you can become a full member, but it's easy to be signed in as someone's guest at the door.

What follows is a sampling and by no means the last word on the area's nightlife. At the end of the chapter is a section on movie theaters, for those whose nightlife tends toward the cinematic, and a section of a more literary persuasion.

NIGHTSPOTS

Wilmington

Bluepost Billiards
15 S. Water St., Wilmington
(910) 343-1141

Tucked away in the Jacobi Warehouse near the historic downtown Wilmington riverfront, this 5,000-square-foot billiards hall features a number of diversions — two 9-foot diamond pool tables, four valley blackcat tables, air hockey, ping pong, darts, foosball,

video games, and a video projector with a 10-foot screen. Worked up a thirst? They stock 54 brands of beers, including 14 on tap. Bluepost is open from 3 PM to 2 AM Monday through Friday and 2 PM to 2 AM Saturday and Sunday.

Break Time / Ten Pin Alley
127 S. College Rd., Wilmington
(910) 395-6658
www.breaktimetenpin.com

Wilmington's largest billiards parlor is also a popular bowling alley, sports bar and casual restaurant, serving sandwiches, burgers, soups, salads and more. Break Time possesses all ABC permits and has 29 top-quality pool tables, including coin-operated tables as well as regulation-size tables, 19 televisions, 24 lanes of bowling and arcade-style diversions. Neat attire is required; no tank tops. It's open 11 AM until 2 AM, and food service is available until closing.

Caprice Bistro: Restaurant & Sofa Bar
10 Market St., Wilmington
(910) 815-0810
www.capricebistro.com

Caprice Bistro's second floor is an intimate, original New York–style sofa bar, perfect for relaxing with a martini or glass of wine. The Caprice Martinis are amazing concoctions of the finest liquors and delectable ingredients. Their chocolate martinis will send you to chocolate-lovers' heaven, or try one of their seasonal martini specials, made with fresh fruit ingredients and garnished with locally grown herbs. During the early evening, the setting is romantic, with candlelight and soft music, but after 11 PM the music gets turned up a notch as the crowd gathers. This is the place to go in downtown Wilmington to enjoy an after-theater martini or dessert with friends. The sofa bar is open until 2 AM. Their full dinner menu is served until 11 PM, and appetizers and desserts are available until midnight. The sofa bar is smoker-friendly.

Chelsea's Downtown
1 S. Front St, Wilmington
(910) 763-8463

Looking for a place for cocktails but don't want to end up shoulder-to-shoulder with a crowd of twenty-somethings? Try Chelsea's, a pleasant alternative to the loud, brash nightlife found in many Wilmington

Open Daily
11AM - 2 AM

TEN PIN ALLEY

BREAK TIME
Sports Bar, Grille & Billiards

26 Pool Tables
24 Bowling Lanes
Darts Arena ★ Sports Arcade
Complete Pro Shop ★ Full Menu
Restaurant ★ 17 TV's

Marketplace Mall ★ 127 S. College Rd.
Wilmington, NC 28403
(910) 452-5455
www.breaktimetenpin.com

nightspots. Featuring a full bar and full menu service until 1 AM, this elegant corner club is the perfect stop for a pre-theater drink or a post-theater snack. With more than 150 wines from France, Italy, Spain, California, Oregon, Washington and North Carolina, you'll undoubtedly find a grape suited to your palate. Snag a table by the front window and enjoy hours of people watching. Open until 2 AM, Chelsea's is an ideal spot for those with refined tastes and late bedtimes.

Fat Tony's Italian Pub
131 N. Front St., Wilmington
(910) 343-8881
250 Racine Dr., Wilmington
(910) 452-9000
www.fatpub.com

A staple of Wilmington's downtown nightlife, Fat Tony's Italian Pub has a selection of 24 draft beers, more than anywhere else in town. One of the stops along the Haunted Pub Crawl, Fat Tony's has a house brew that's called the "Haunted Pub Brew" in honor of the ghosts (former guests of the Old Orton Hotel that burned down in the 1940s) who are said to linger here at the site of their old haunt. With Fat Tony's selection of beers on tap, big-screen TV and plenty of seats and pub tables, you won't want to leave either. Along with your beer, you can enjoy Fat Tony's late-night menu of Pizza Chip Nachos and New York–style pizza with all the toppings. There's also live music and an outdoor deck with a fabulous view of the river. Fat

Tony's Italian Pub is open until 2 AM Monday through Saturday and midnight on Sunday.

Hell's Kitchen
118 Princess St., Wilmington
(910) 763-4133

Formerly a set for the locally filmed TV show Dawson's Creek, Hell's Kitchen has fast become a popular downtown destination for good times among friends. This pub-style setting has a fun atmosphere so when you're feeling devilishly hungry, stop by and try something from their menu of pub sandwiches, burritos and nachos. Hell's Kitchen has a full liquor bar and offers a wide variety of draught and microbrew beers. Hell's Kitchen is open in the afternoon until closing at 2 AM.

Level 5 at City Stage
21 N. Front St., Wilmington
(910) 342-0272

Located on the top level of downtown's former Masonic temple, Level 5 has the best rooftop view in town. Summer nights locals and tourists alike mingle beneath the bar's massive awning and enjoy cool breezes off the Cape Fear River. Inside, a 250-seat theater boasts three comedy troupes Tuesday through Thursday and a six-month-long season of theater produced by the owners of the club. In the warm months, the bar features live music Thursday and Friday nights and house deejays on Saturday. Available for private parties, the theater/bar combination lends itself well to wedding receptions and fund-raising events.

Longstreet's Irish Pub
135 N. Front St., Wilmington
(910) 343-8788

Named after General Longstreet, a Civil War general portrayed by actor Tom Berenger in the film Gettysburg (Berenger was once part owner of the bar by the same name in this location), Longstreet's is a cozy basement pub in the Irish tradition, offering several draft and bottled beers, nightly beer specials, mixed drinks, Foosball, a jukebox and live music. The pub is located in what used to be the barbershop of the Old Orton Hotel, which was destroyed in a fire in the 1940s (and may still have a few ghostly guests). The Fat Tony's late-night menu is available at Longstreet's, so you can enjoy fabulous New York–style pizza along with your pint of Guinness (see the Fat Tony's writeup earlier in this chapter). Longstreet's is open Monday through Saturday until 2 AM and Sundays until midnight.

Marrz Theatre
15 S. Front St., Wilmington
(910) 772-9045

Voted Best Live Music Venue by Encore magazine, Marrz offers live music from national and regional bands on one of the largest stages in any area club. Show dates and times vary, so check the schedule at their website or call (910) 772-9045. A few of the national bands who have played at Marrz include Fuel, Collective Soul, Blue Oyster Cult, Ice-T and Edwin McCain. Marrz was also the set for the cult film Empire Records, and Katie Holmes made her singing debut on the Marrz stage in Dawson's Creek. Marrz has all ABC permits and offers full bar services, beer and wine, but no food service. Some seating is available. The second floor houses a game room and features a pool table, Foosball and other games. Ticket prices vary according to the band. Call the number listed above for prices and additional entertainment dates. Municipal parking is available directly behind the club.

Orton's Pool Room
133 N. Front St., Wilmington
(910) 343-8878

Billed as "America's Oldest Pool Room," Orton's is located in what was the basement space of the old Orton Hotel prior to its burning in the 1940s. The space is entirely renovated and, with 17 satellite televisions, it's a perfect place for catching a game. But it's the pool that keeps people coming to Orton's. Where else can you play on the very table used by the famed Willie Mosconi in 1953 to set a world billiards record of 365 consecutive balls? Take a trip downstairs and in to history with a game of pool at Orton's.

Rack `M Pub and Billiards
415 S. College Rd., Wilmington
(910) 791-5668

Pool prices at this club-style parlor are an affordable $2 per person per hour until 7 PM. From 7 PM to closing, prices are $3 per person per hour. Rack 'M is open every day from 3 PM until 2 AM and Saturday and Sundays noon until 2 AM. However, after 10 PM you must be age 21 or older to enter. You'll find it in the rear of the University Landing shopping center near Krazy Pizza & Subs.

Rum Runners: Dueling Piano Bar
21 N. Front St., Wilmington
(910) 815-3846

Rum Runners is an exciting new addition to downtown Wilmington. With its wildly tropical atmosphere, dining at Rum Runners will make you feel as though you're whiling away the hours on a Caribbean island. Then there is the high-energy show — two baby grand pianos played simultaneously (dueling pianos) by entertainers who encourage the audience to sing along with hit tunes from the '50s all the way up to the '90s. The staff also joins in once every hour with a song and dance routine, inviting more audience participation. The great food menu includes steak, specialty pizzas, chicken and fish dishes. Advance reservations are highly recommended for their popular dueling piano show. Rum Runners opens for dinner Wednesday through Sunday and the fun continues until 2 AM.

The Rusty Nail at Beatty's Tavern
1310 S. Fifth Ave., Wilmington
(910) 251-1888

Live blues and jazz enthusiasts won't want to miss this downtown Wilmington club's weekly line-up. The Blues Society of the Lower Cape Fear cuts loose on Tuesdays and the first Saturday of each month. Gary Allen's open mike is on Wednesdays. Thursdays features George's Bluegrass Jam. Various local bands play live on Friday and Saturday nights; call for a complete schedule. Beatty's Famous Jazz Jam is a Sunday-night tradition. This live-performance venue includes a state-of-the-art digital recording studio designed to capture some of the amazing music performed here. Open daily at 1 PM, Sundays at noon, the club has all ABC permits, serves beer and wine, offers bar specials and provides a sandwich menu. The Rusty Nail is a private club, but non-members can be signed in as guests. New members are welcome, and fees are reasonable, with several membership options available. Call the club for details. Located between Marstellar and Greenfield streets, the club boasts its own parking lot, a rarity in downtown Wilmington.

The Soap Box Laundrolounge
255 N. Front St., Wilmington
(910) 251-8500

The downstairs portion of The Soap Box features a sprawling space with couches, televisions, arcade games such as pool and foosball, and Internet access. These diversions prove useful when utilizing one of the numerous washers and dryers in the back, the only Laundromat located downtown. Upstairs lies a good-sized music facility that features some of the hottest local and regional bands for very reasonable cover charges. The downstairs bar is beer only but upstairs features all alcohol permits.

Water Street Restaurant & Sidewalk Cafe
5 S. Water St., Wilmington
(910) 343-0042

Water Street's relaxed, cozy atmosphere invites you to linger with a friend or loved one late into the night, any night of the week. The decor is colorful, somewhat rustic and warm. Sidewalk seating offers a view of the riverfront, and good food is always available. Water Street provides a musical venue for jazz, bluegrass and more with performances Thursday through Sunday.

Wilson's
4925 New Centre Dr., Wilmington
(910) 793-0999

With 35,000 square feet of space dedicated to great entertainment, great food and fun, Wilson's (formerly Alleigh's) corners the market on nightlife. This huge complex houses four distinct restaurants, a state-of-the-art virtual reality game room, banquet facilities and live entertainment Wednesday through Saturday.

The Tiki Bar & Cafe is an outdoor venue designed to resemble a tropical paradise. The Tiki Bar & Cafe features an extensively landscaped pond and fountain framed with tall fronds of bamboo. Tiki Bar patrons can enjoy tropical drinks, a raw bar and a Caribbean-

Check out weekend happenings with "Currents," the Star-News entertainment guide for movies, theater, nightlife, regional tourism and events, available to subscribers or in racks across the region.

Each weekend night downtown Wilmington is electric with live music of all types.

photo: Peter Doran

inspired menu Wednesday through Sunday starting at 5 PM (weather permitting).

The Sports Bar at Wilson's has the unique distinction of featuring 31 TVs, including the largest TV screen (200 inches) in Wilmington. In addition, The Sports Bar is one of only three venues in Wilmington to offer NTN Trivia, a tabletop electronic trivia game that enables customers to compete with teams across the country. Live bands perform Thursday through Saturday evenings, featuring everything from country and beach music to rock 'n' roll.

The Lounge at Wilson's offers an intimate, sofa bar setting with a 150-inch TV, dance floor and live music Wednesday through Saturday evenings.

And if games entertain you, check out Wilson's 7,200-square-foot Game Room featuring more than 120 games, including a roller coaster simulator and a 1920s Chicago-style shootout. Ask about their customer loy-alty reward program and their new, upscale prizes.

Wilson's truly has something for everyone and is open Sunday through Friday 11 AM to 2 AM and Saturdays 10 AM to 2 AM. A late-night menu is offered until 1 AM.

Wrightsville Beach

King Neptune's Pirate Lounge
11 N. Lumina Ave., Wrightsville Beach
(910) 256-2525

The Pirate Lounge in the King Neptune Restaurant is as lively as its proprietor, Bernard Carroll, who did the research to accurately identify all the pirate flags hanging in the room. It's the kind of decor you might expect of someone who'd rather be sailing, and, as a salt should, Carroll places some importance on rum. His "Rum Bar" features some 19 premium rums from around the world, including Gosling's and Appleton

Estate Jamaican Rum. Microbrewed and imported beers are always in stock, and an inexpensive Pub Grub menu offers plenty of quality munchies (available for take-out). The lounge is open every day and has all ABC permits.

Carolina Beach

Club Tropics
Ocean Plaza Electric Ballroom,
North End of the Boardwalk
(910) 458-7883

With a huge dance floor and live performances by the Radio Flyer Band every weekend, Club Tropics is the place to go if you feel like dancing the night away to some rock 'n' roll. Club Tropics is open year round every Friday and Saturday night from 8:30 PM to 2 AM, and the band hits the stage at around 10 PM.

Brunswick County Beaches

SOUTHPORT/OAK ISLAND

The Southport-Oak Island area is very much a family/fishing area. Nightlife is rather quiet: You will see long lines outside the movie theater in the evenings and find video stores quite busy. If your nighttime interests lie in the direction of music and entertainment, you will find a few places to go, some of which we've listed below.

49th Street Station Game Room and Bar
4901 E. Oak Island Dr., Oak Island
(910) 278-9811

If you are looking for a neighborhood bar where you can relax with a drink after work before you head home for dinner, then return later in the evening to socialize and play a game or two of pool, the Station is the one. Being a nicely refurbished old gas station, it is small, but large enough to hold the enthusiastic crowd that gathers for karaoke every Saturday night. The Station is also known for spearheading fund drives for persons suffering as as result of catastrophes or loss of income. Be it a cookout, a float in the Christmas Parade or a Poker run, they help

those less fortunate. Hours of operation are 11 AM until 2 AM, Monday through Saturday and noon until 2 AM on Sunday. Don't miss Friday night Retro Parties with a DJ providing the music.

Chasers Sports Bar & Grill
8520 E. Oak Island Dr., Oak Island
(910) 278-1500

Under new ownership, remodeled in 2005 and open seven days a week year round, Chasers remains a favorite place for locals to gather. There they can share an after-work drink, discuss their golf games and compare scores, socialize and get a good meal and drinks at affordable prices. The specialty is wings in a variety of flavors. Don't miss the sporting events, which you can watch on any of the five TVs from seating at the bar or any table in the room. While you are there, ask about Chasers Beach Club.

Concerts On The Coast
Franklin Square Park, corner of Howe
and E. West Sts., Southport
(910) 253-2672, (800) 222-4790

Supported by a grant from the Brunswick Arts Council and sponsored by the Brunswick County Parks and Recreation Department, the Southport Parks and Recreation Department and Security Savings Bank, this outdoor summer concert series features a variety of live bands playing in Franklin Square Park in the heart of historic Southport. This popular event is held June through September on Tuesday evenings from 6:30 until 8 PM. In case of rain, the concerts are held at the Centennial Center in Southport. Call for dates and schedule.

Duffer's Pub & Grille
928 Caswell Beach Rd., Oak Island
(910) 278-9299

Located on the second floor at the Oak Island Golf Club (see our Golf chapter), Duffer's Pub and Grille offers a spectacular view of the Atlantic Ocean on one side and the golf greens on the other. White linens on the tables in the dining/banquet room along with the flickering of candles set into the fireplace give an understated elegance to your dining experience. Duffer's offers a fully stocked bar featuring premium liquors and cordials, bottled and draught beer and a good wine list. Theme nights include Pasta

Night on Mondays, Wings Night on Tuesdays and Country Cooking on Wednesdays. Special events are held such as a Labor Day Party and bands on the large deck (weather permitting) or indoors. A banquet room is available for private parties. The bar is open every day from 11:30 until. Lunch and dinner are served daily.

HOLDEN BEACH

Concerts On The Coast
Intracoastal Waterway Stage, Jordan Blvd., Holden Beach
(910) 253-2672, (800) 222-4790

Supported by a grant from the Brunswick Arts Council and sponsored by the Brunswick County Parks and Recreation Department and the Greater Holden Beach Merchants Association, this outdoor summer concert series is a recent addition to the summer scene. The concerts feature live entertainment at the Intracoastal Waterway Stage on Jordan Boulevard, located near the base of the Holden Beach bridge, and are held on Sundays from 6:30 until 8 PM May through September. Call for dates and a schedule.

Paradise Cafe
102 Jordan Blvd., Holden Beach
(910) 842-4999

With ocean views from every seat inside or on the patio, the atmosphere at the Paradise Cafe invites you to kick back and relax Jimmy Buffet style. Open for lunch and dinner almost year round, the Paradise has daily specials to offer the freshest food available and a kids' menu to keep the little ones happy. Sit among the palm trees, tropical birds and local artwork hanging on melon-colored walls and enjoy appetizer's, burgers, pizza or hot sub. Of course, there is local seafood as well. Be sure not to leave until you have enjoyed a Paradise Sunset, the house drink. And remember, the Paradise has music on the patio week nights during the season — from country to beach music to pop.

OCEAN ISLE BEACH

Concerts On The Coast
Museum of Coastal Carolina, 21 E. Second St., Ocean Isle Beach (910) 253-2672, (800) 222-4790

Supported by a grant from the Brunswick Arts Council and sponsored by the Bruns-

wick County Parks and Recreation Department and the Ocean Isle Beach Property Owners Association, this outdoor concert series features live entertainment on the island in the Museum of Coastal Carolina parking lot. Concerts are held on Fridays from 6:30 until 8 PM May through September. Call for dates and schedule.

SHALLOTTE

Woodsong Concerts
The Village of Woodsong, 529 Sylvan St., Shallotte
(910) 253-2672, (800) 222-4790

Supported by a grant from the Brunswick Arts Council and sponsored by the Brunswick County Parks and Recreation Department and the Village of Woodsong, this outdoor concert series, new in 2005, features live entertainment at the gazebo. Call for date and time.

Topsail Island

SURF CITY

The Brass Pelican Tavern
2112 N. New River Dr., Surf City
(910) 328-4373

The Brass Pelican is a favorite private club for local residents and returning visitors who especially enjoy the large outdoor back deck. The membership fee is $5, and visitors can be signed in by a member. Entertainment is provided on Friday and Saturday nights with karaoke on Thursdays. Menu choices include deli sandwiches, appetizers and steamed seafood in the evening. Daily drink and food specials are offered.

Commodore Room
404 Roland Ave., Surf City
(910) 328-4331

This new upscale martini bar features a classic 40-foot polished wood bar with brass foot rails and trim. Sit back and enjoy your favorite martini or try their Topsail Lemonade before hitting the dance floor. It's open seven days a week with live music on weekends throughout the summer. The Commodore Room is located on the second floor, above the Mainsail Restaurant, and has its own entrance.

Crab Pot
508 Roland Ave., Surf City
(910) 328-5001

This down-home establishment has a take-out window and a casual screened-in dining room and bar. Crab Pot's "Shag Shack" is a favorite with folks who like beach music and shagging, the dance of the beach crowd. The Shack features entertainment by local disc jockeys and popular beach bands. No one is a stranger at the Crab Pot.

Gilligan's
N.C. Hwy. 50, Surf City
(910) 328-4090

Gilligan's is a private club with a membership fee of $5. Visitors for an evening can be signed in by a member. Featuring the largest dance floor in the area, Gilligan's has seasonal entertainment Wednesday through Sunday with karaoke and music for dancing. A shuttle service is always available. It's open daily year round.

Margarita's Bar & Grill
2111 N. New River Dr., Surf City
(910) 328-3066

Get ready to shag because the DJs here spin beach music on weekends. Feel the urge to belt out a tune? Margarita's hosts Karaoke nights ever Wednesday and Thursday. If you work up an appetite singing and dancing the night away, Margarita's dishes up the only late-night breakfast on the island, serving between 11 PM and 4 AM.

Squeaky's
1713 N. New River Dr., Surf City
(910) 328-1500

This bar has 5,000 square feet of fun, including a large dance floor, big screen TVs for big game and race days, walls of arcade games, pool tables, darts, DJs, Karaoke and bands. Enough said, Squeaky's has it all, including ABC permits. It is open every day at noon.

Surf City Wine & Cheese
602 N. New River Dr., Surf City
(910) 328-4111

Sometimes the best nightlife on Topsail Island can be grabbing a great bottle of wine and relaxing on the deck with friends. Surf City Wine and Cheese has an extensive variety on hand. Different wines are featured weekly and new lines are continually being added. Wine tastings are held from April to October, advance ordering for vacation convenience or a 10 percent discount on a case of wine are just some of the services offered. You will also find imported beers and wine-related gifts in this shop.

TOPSAIL BEACH

Beach Buggy of Topsail Island
Topsail Beach
(910) 620-3388, (910) 328-1375

Beach Buggy of Topsail Island's 15-passenger shuttle bus can be just what you need for a safe night out on the town, or for a Topsail Island tour, a group outing to a sporting event, bachelor party or anywhere you and your friends or family might wish to go together. Call the above numbers for information or reservations.

Skully's Pub and Grub
718 Anderson Blvd., Topsail Beach
(910) 328-3100

Located in the heart of Topsail Beach, Skully's pub offers a late night menu, fine wines and spirits, imported and domestic beer, pool tables, wide-screen TV and live entertainment. Pool tournaments are held every Wednesday night, and Thursdays are Surf Nights with surfing DVDs on the big screen and free drawings for surfing gear. Skully's restaurant makes homemade entrees including scampi, shrimp and crab au gratin, crab cakes, fried seafood and steaks. If you're in the mood for something lighter, try their homemade soups, salads, crab dip or sandwiches. Skully's is open daily during the summer and is closed Mondays off-season. The pub opens at 4 PM, and dinner is served from 5 to 10 PM.

SNEADS FERRY

Paradise Landing
318 Fulchers Rd., Sneads Ferry
(910) 327-2133

This nightclub has a Key West theme, complete with palm trees and a fantastic patio view. Lounging on the top deck with a strawberry daiquiri or drink of your choice gives the name "paradise" true meaning. Paradise Landing offers pool tournaments, music by North Carolina bands, dancing and horseshoes. Arrive by boat or car. Paradise

Landing is open seven days a week from 9 AM to 2 AM.

Movie Theaters

There are plenty of first-run theaters in the area, but films that are foreign, controversial or "artsy" have frustratingly short runs, if they run at all. It's a paradox, considering the number of films shot in Wilmington and the high level of local interest, but the situation is improving. The net number of screens from Wilmington to the South Carolina line is now 46. Carmike's 16-screen complex on Market Street features comfortable stadium seating in all screening rooms.

Most of the movie theaters in the region offer matinee showings every day during the summer, on holidays and weekends throughout the year at $5 per ticket on average. Full-price tickets typically cost $7.25. Discounted prices for seniors are also available at most theaters. Some area theaters now offer advance ticket sales ranging from the day of purchase to three days in advance.

WILMINGTON

A valuable film resource is **Cinematique of Wilmington**, a series that brings acclaimed foreign and classic films to town for three-day runs every other week (sometimes more often) to historic Thalian Hall, (910) 343-3664, at the corner of Chestnut and Third streets, in downtown Wilmington. Cinematique is a bargain at $7 a ticket. It's sponsored by WHQR 91.3 FM, the local public radio station. Show times are 7:30 PM Monday through Wednesday, but schedules may change to accommodate Thalian's stage schedule. You can receive Cinematique mailings by calling (910) 343-1640 or writing to Cinematique of Wilmington, 254 N. Front Street, Wilmington, NC 28401.

Hollywood East Cinema Grill, 4402 Shipyard Boulevard, (910) 792-1084, is an exciting new concept in movie theaters in Wilmington. Located at Long Leaf Shopping Center, Hollywood East offers intermediate run movies (a few weeks out of popular release) in an inviting, casual atmosphere with food and beverage service available. Hollywood East's menu consists of appetizers, sandwiches, handmade pizza, desserts and, naturally, popcorn. Beer and wine are served in addition to fountain drinks and bottled water. Prices range from $5 to $10 and the wait staff is unobtrusive during the film. The theater offers two screenings per film nightly, and seating in each of the three screening rooms is cabaret-style. The theater also accommodates private parties and sponsors corporate or sporting events. The ticket price, at $4, can't be beat. Ticket sales are cash only but Hollywood East accepts Visa, MC and Discover cards for food and beverage sales. Check movie schedules for Hollywood East at (910) 793-1234.

Carmike 16, 111 Cinema Drive, Wilmington, (910) 815-0212, with 16 screens, is enough of a development to require a street of its own (Cinema Drive), linking Market Street and Kerr Avenue. The stadium seats and leg room are the most generous in town, with the least possibility of an obstructed view.

Mayfaire 16, 900 Town Center Drive, Wilmington, (910) 256-0566, is an updated version of Market Street's facility situated centrally between Ogden, Wrightsville Beach and the Intracoastal community. You can expect to find at least one screen with something other than major blockbuster fare.

CAROLINA BEACH

Cinema 4, 1020 Carolina Beach Road, Carolina Beach, (910) 458-3444, is a cozy four-screen complex in the Federal Point Plaza shopping center next to Jubilee Amusement Park. This theater is a good choice if you relish the thought of a night at the movies away from long lines and Wilmington's traffic.

BRUNSWICK COUNTY BEACHES

Surf Cinemas, 4836 Long Beach Road SE, Southport, (910) 457-0320. Being situated south of the intersection of Long Beach Road and N.C. 211 (Southport-Supply Road), this four-screen theater is convenient to the entire Southport-Oak Island area. Please note

ℹ️ *Join the Cape Fear Contra Dancers, (910) 270-3363, and dance with the most friendly folks in town. Call for the current membership fee.*

that children younger than 2 years of age are not admitted.

Coastal Cinemas, 5200 Bridgers Road, Shallotte, (910) 754-7469, opened in the spring of 2003 with 10 screens and state-of-the-art digital surround sound. For your convenience and comfort it is handicapped accessible, includes high-back rocking seats, an expanded cafe area, and has a party room available for birthdays and group outings. Computerized ticketing allows advance ticket sales, credit card purchases and online purchase of tickets.

Literary Pursuits

With a strong and supportive arts community, writers of all kinds — novelists, playwrights, poets, screenwriters and journalists among them — flourish in the Lower Cape Fear region. Who couldn't be moved to rapturous prose by the breathtaking beauty of this coastal region or see opportunity in the overwhelming presence of the dramatic arts and the film industry. But the writing life is a solitary one, so it's no surprise that aspiring authors and poets seek out nightspots that satisfy twin desires: companionship and the need to share their work. Writers are naturally avid readers, so book discussion groups, poetry readings or a cappuccino with fellow writers are all part of the literary nightlife in coastal Carolina.

Barnes & Noble Booksellers
Mayfaire Town Center, Military Cutoff
between Eastwood Rd. and U.S. Hwy. 17 N.,
Wilmington
(910) 509-1880

The cafe at Barnes & Noble, a popular spot for both seasoned and would-be scribes, ensures there's enough caffeine at hand to chase the muse. Past events have included family-friendly poetry readings, writers group meetings and book clubs. Check B & N's monthly schedule for these and other literary events and local book-signings.

⊞ SHOPPING

If shopping is your passion, North Carolina's southern coast offers abundant opportunities to indulge it. The steady influx of retirees, a thriving golf industry, relocating businesses, active year-round tourism, booming commercial and residential development have brought with them a wide range of shopping options, from one-of-a-kind boutiques to national chain mega-stores. Whether your tastes lean toward the traditional, eclectic, funky or old-fashioned, you'll find what you're looking for here.

Today, few of the region's communities remain unaffected by this retail growth. Shopping centers, both large and small, abound in and around Wilmington and the adjacent beach areas, competing with each other to provide the best, most interesting goods and services. Hallmarks of the current retail development trend include aesthetically pleasing architecture, landscaped grounds, sculptured art, plentiful parking and upscale shops that rival those in any major metropolitan area. These multi-use commercial centers usually include restaurants, office space and service providers. Near Wrightsville Beach, Lumina Station, Landfall Shopping Center, Mayfaire Town Center and The Forum are excellent examples of this type of center and all are described in this chapter. The number of independently owned retail businesses continues to grow as well.

Primary business and shopping areas for the Port City include downtown Wilmington, the College Road area, Market Street, Oleander Drive, Monkey Junction and the Military Cutoff/Eastwood Road area adjacent to Wrightsville Beach, but don't hesitate to venture off onto side streets where you'll discover a host of shopping treasures. Wilmington also has the area's greatest concentration of superstores and discount chains, including Wal-Mart, Best Buy, Target, Sears, JCPenney, Home Depot, Petsmart, Sam's Club, Costco, Office Max and Stein Mart, in addition to the upscale Hecht's, Belk and Dillard's department stores.

As you explore the region's shopping options, you will notice that coastal North Carolinians love gourmet foods, wine, imported cheeses, hard-to-find herbs and spices, ethnic cooking and specialty bakeries. Local food markets and chain grocery stores, while not covered in this chapter, are abundant throughout the area and will stock or order new items at a customer's request.

This chapter contains a mere sampling of available shopping possibilities, including some of the unique, as well as the tried-and-true shops. These have been divided into easy-to-read sections for some of the major areas of Wilmington, the Wrightsville Beach vicinity and the coastal communities of Carolina Beach, Topsail Island, Southport-Oak Island and the South Brunswick beaches.

For the off-season visitor traveling to the beach communities, most of the stores and businesses included in this chapter offer year-round hours of operation. However, some reduce or limit these hours in the winter months so it's wise to call ahead to make sure the store will be open when you plan to visit.

Historic Downtown Wilmington

Step back in time while shopping along the streets of downtown Wilmington. Surrounded by the city's beautiful historic homes and museums, brick streets and serene waterfront, downtown provides a relaxed and unique shopping locale. Rare are the shoppers who aren't tempted to slow their steps in this tranquil setting. Personal service by business owners and a cozy, small-town atmosphere further add to the shopping experience.

Most of the stores concentrated along the streets of downtown Wilmington are

Local Scene

Distinct Shops, Dining & Services. Distinctly Wrightsville Beach.

Lumina Station offers the true essence and local escape that makes Wilmington and Wrightsville Beach such wonderful places. Here you will find shops and restaurants offered no where else. Join us to meet the merchants who deliver this personality to you. Take a stroll through our shopping village, and find yourself

LUMINA STATION
1900 EASTWOOD RD. SUITE 44
WILMINGTON, NC 28403 (910) 256-9956

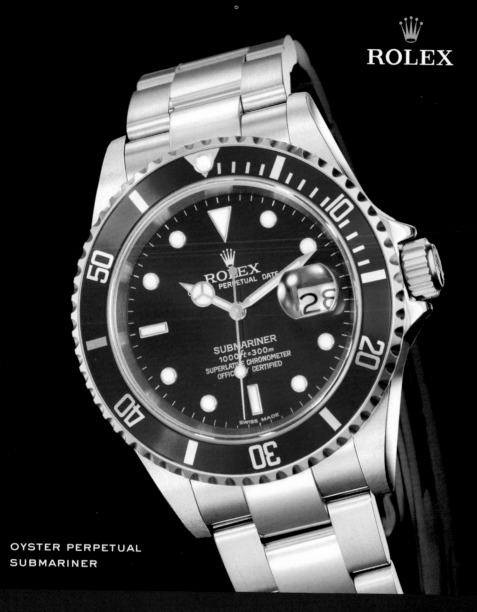

ROLEX

OYSTER PERPETUAL
SUBMARINER

REEDS *Jewelers*®

MAYFAIRE TOWN CENTER
910-256-2962

WESTFIELD SHOPPINGTOWN INDEPENDENCE
910-799-6810

OFFICIAL ROLEX JEWELER
ROLEX ♛ OYSTER PERPETUAL AND SUBMARINER ARE TRADEMARKS.

Blackburns Studio
Custom Interiors / Window Treatments

Monday thru Friday 9-5pm | 710 South 17th Street
Wilmington, North Carolina
910.763.4992 deedee@blackburnsstudio.com

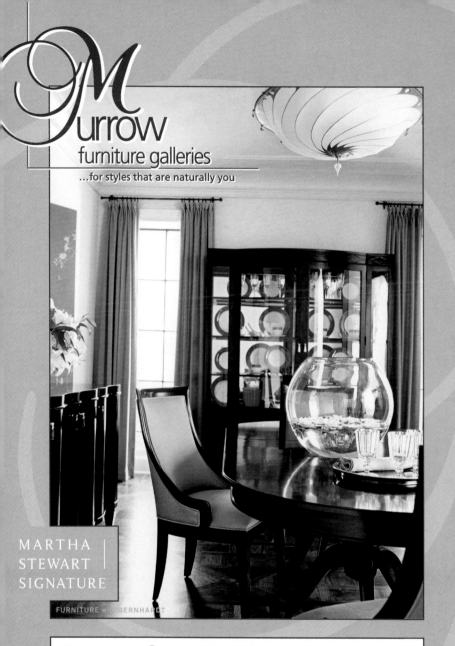

Murrow furniture galleries

...for styles that are naturally you

MARTHA
STEWART
SIGNATURE

FURNITURE with BERNHARDT

Competitive Discount Prices

45,000 sq. ft. of beautifully decorated showrooms filled with Bernhardt,
Henkle Harris, Century, Lexington, Drexel Heritage, Pennsylvania House,
Statton, Thomasville and more. Professional Interior Designers on staff.

We Ship Worldwide

3514 So. College Rd. • Wilmington, NC 28412 • (910) 799-4010
Hours: Monday-Friday 8:30-5:30, Saturday 9:00-5:30 • www.murrowfurniture.com

"If It's From Kingoff's... It's Guaranteed"

KINGOFF'S
JEWELERS

Wilmington's largest selection of fine quality jewelry since 1919

DOWNTOWN WILMINGTON
10 NORTH FRONT ST.
762-5219

THE FORUM
1119-B MILITARY CUTOFF RD.
256-4321

WWW.KINGOFFS.COM

Transform your home for less!

2 acres of...

- HOME DECOR
- FLORAL
- AREA RUGS
- LAMPS
- WICKER FURNITURE
- DECORATIVE GARDEN
- POTTERY

- WILMINGTON'S **BIGGEST** CHRISTMAS DEPT. (in season)
- FRAMED ART
- MIRRORS
- DINNERWARE / GLASSWARE
- ACCENT FURNITURE

AND MUCH MORE!

Transform your home for less!

potteryplus

www.gopotteryplus.com
910-791-7522
5744 Market St. • Wilmington
(Just 1/2 Mile North of the I-40 Overpass!)
MON-SAT 9am to 8pm • SUN 12pm to 6pm

VISA
MasterCard
DISCOVER

TM&©2006 LillyPulitzer®

palm garden
A Lilly Pulitzer® Signature Store
PREMIER

Landfall Center
1319A Military Cutoff Rd.
Wilmington
phone: 910-256-9984
toll-free: 888-650-3428
fax: 910-256-9920
www.shoppalmgarden.com

Lilly
PULITZER®

JUST WHAT YOU'D EXPECT FROM A STATE WITH 3,375 MILES OF SHORELINE AND WIND NEARLY EVERY DAY.

GREAT KITES.

With great kites comes our commitment to great service. We are the largest full service kite and kitesurf shop in the Cape Fear area. From expert advice to repairs and lessons with kites for all ages and skill levels. Plus windsocks, decorative flags, unique toys, flying toys, garden spinners, wind chimes, and much more.

Blowing in the **Wind**

BLOWINGINTHEWIND.COM

Learn about kitesurfing at our Wrightsville Beach location or at gokitesurf.com.

Downtown Wilmington inside the Cotton Exchange ○ 910.763.1730, (toll free) 888.691.8034 ○ 312 Nutt Street, Wilmington, North Carolina 28401
Wrightsville Beach next to Lighthouse Beer & Wine ○ 910.509.9989, (toll free) 888.509.9989 ○ 222 Causeway Drive, Wrightsville Beach, North Carolina 28480

independently owned and reflect the interests and tastes of their owners. You won't encounter rack after rack of the same items. Here you'll find art galleries, antiques shops, fine clothing, funky garb, beachwear, toys, gourmet items, CDs, wine, linens, glassware, candies, fine and costume jewelry, collectibles, books, home furnishings, scents, candles and more.

Part of the charm of this shopping district is its compact size and pleasant walkability. Park your car on the street, in one of several parking decks, or, if you're shopping at one of the retail/dining centers, park at no cost in their lots. Downtown is like an open-air mall with an astonishing selection of spots in which to pause and take in the beautiful scenery. Coffee shops, delicatessens, pubs, ice cream parlors, candy shops and full-service restaurants offer constant temptation to shoppers. Many restaurants have outdoor seating right on the sidewalk, a setup guaranteed to lure your weary feet to pause.

Downtown is anchored by two large centers, The Cotton Exchange, a shopping/dining/office complex at the northern end of the riverfront, and Chandler's Wharf at the southern end. The area between — Water Street, Front Street, Second and Third Streets and their cross streets — includes several busy city blocks lined with restaurants, galleries, banks, services and stores that offer a wide variety of shopping possibilities.

Antiques buffs, surrounded by the heady sense of southern coastal history, will find it impossible to bypass downtown Wilmington's pleasing variety of antique stores. (See our section on Antiques in this chapter.)

Blackbeard's Bryde
J. W. Brooks Building, 18 S. Water St., Wilmington
(910) 815-0660

The Cape Fear region's colorful pirate history inspired the name for this intriguing boutique offering the latest and best styles in women's clothing, along with very unusual jewelry, including one-of-a-kind pieces. Blackbeard's Bryde has fantastic candles, soaps, incense and a gift line that may leave you with smiles and giggles. With prices you'll love, this local secret is worth discovering. You'll want to visit again and again.

Blowing In The Wind
The Cotton Exchange, 312 Nutt St., Wilmington
(910) 763-1730, (888) 691-8034
www.blowinginthewind.com

Blowing in the Wind has plenty of kite-flying fun for everyone. As the area's largest full-service kite shop, with locations in downtown Wilmington and Wrightsville Beach at 222 Causeway Drive, (910) 509-9989, they carry a huge selection of colorful kites for all ages and skill levels, from easy-to-fly single line kites, delta kites and box kites, to controllable stunt kites and big show kites. Looking for a thrill? Try one of their Jet-Ski assisted kiteboarding lessons (read all about this exciting sport in the Watersports chapter). Blowing in the Wind in Wrightsville Beach is the area's only supplier of kiteboarding products and lessons. Be sure to check out the dazzling array of kites and explore their wide selection of windsocks, wind chimes, puzzles and wooden toys for kids.

Candles Etc.
Chandler's Wharf , 2 Ann St., Wilmington
(910) 763-1703

The largest Root Candle distributor on the East Coast, Candles Etc. has all 24 colors made by this upscale candle company, as well as brochures explaining the history. They are also the exclusive dealer for Wilmington Historic Prints. You'll want to browse for hours, but don't miss the fabulous view of the river from their deck.

Chandler's Wharf
22 Ann St. and 25 S. Water St., Wilmington

Overlooking the river at the corner of Ann and Water streets, Chandler's Wharf offers many appealing shopping opportunities. Created by Thomas Henry Wright Jr. in the late 1970s, it has evolved over time as a retail/dining complex, but part of it began as a ship's chandler in the 19th century. There was a maritime museum here in the 1970s and some marine artifacts are still scattered about the grounds, including an enormous anchor and other reminders of the complex's origins. Cobblestone streets, plank walkways, attractive landscaping and a gorgeous view of the Cape Fear River are some of the features that make shopping at Chandler's Wharf such a pleasant experience. The center is flourishing today with some of Wilmington's most delightful stores. It also boasts three of the city's most appealing restaurants, The Pilot House, The George and Elijah's (see our Restaurants chapter). Dining in any one of these is a pleasure heightened by the option of enjoying your meal on outdoor decks overlooking the river.

Some of the shops at Chandler's Wharf include **A Proper Garden**, (910) 763-7177, which has everything and more for the garden and gardener; **A. Scott Rhodes**, (910) 763-6616, a full-service jewelry store specializing in custom design and offering selections in fine diamonds, precious stones, local estate jewelry and designer pieces; **Arts Wilmington Gallery**, (910) 343-4370, which is owned and operated by the Wilmington Art Association and offers a fine selections of original art and gifts by local artists; **Candles Etc.**,(910) 763-1703, exclusive distributors of Root Candles and Wilmington Historic Prints; and **Romax Shoes**, (910) 763-8033, which sells quality shoes, accessories and jewelry.

The Cotton Exchange
321 N. Front St., Wilmington
(910) 343-9896

The site of the largest cotton-exporting company in the world in the 19th century, this collection of eight buildings overlooking the Cape Fear River was converted into a shopping and dining center in the early 1970s. Its renovation marked the beginning of the restoration of downtown Wilmington. Shoppers can enjoy a bit of history as they stroll the mall's tri-level space, where displays of cotton bales, weighing equipment and photographs tell the story of the center's evolution and about many downtown locations. Parking is free in the large lot for visitors of the complex.

The sampling of specialty shops listed below suggest the scope of shopping possibilities at The Cotton Exchange (all stores are within the complex bounded by Water and Front streets). **T. S. Brown Jewelry**, (910) 762-3467, specializes in loose gems, custom settings and handcrafted pieces. **The Celtic Shop**, (910) 763-1990, features imported Irish and Scottish clothing, Celtic music, jewelry, clan heraldry items, books, authentic Irish breakfast tea and many other gift ideas. **Kringles Korner**, (910) 762-7528, is the place to Christmas shop in downtown Wilmington, offering a variety of unique ornaments, nativities, angels and wonderful Christmas collectibles. **Occasions ... just write!**, (910) 343-9033, features social stationery and invitations, fine writing instruments, sealing wax, journals and desk accessories plus a large selection of cards. **Two Sisters Bookery**, (910) 762-4444, carries a surprisingly wide range of books, including ones of local interest, as well as cards and gifts. **Caravan Beads**, (910)343-0550, is a bead-lovers paradise offering classes and a venue for birthday parties. **The Candy Barrel**, (910) 762-3727, has homemade candies, fudge and taffy. **The Zoo**, (910) 815-3410, is a fun toy store featuring plush animals, Lionel and HO trains. Some other shops you'll find worth visiting are **General Assembly**, (910) 343-8890, for specialty coffee drinks and pastries; **The Sand Dollar**, (910) 763-6769, a delightful place to find shells, lighthouses and garden items; **Crescent Moon**, (910) 762-4207, for handcrafted stained and blown glass; **Down to Earth**, (910) 251-0041, an aromatherapy gift shop; **Hummingbird Station**, (910) 251-2566, for crafts, pottery and gift items; and **Cape Fear Footwear**, (910) 763-9945, which carries sandals, tennis shoes, Hushpuppies and handbags.

Gifts of Aloha, Ltd.
Hawaiian Specialty Gifts & Island Apparel

Hele Mei!
(Come See!)

130 N. Front Street
Wilmington, NC
www.alohagiftsnc.com

910.251.0201
next to downtown post office
Monday – Saturday 11am-6pm

wear, Originals by Maleka, the resident designer. Choose from island gifts to distinctive home decorator items for the island-inspired "hale" (home). Favorites include Kona coffee, chocolate macadamia nuts, silk and fresh flower leis, beauty products, perfumes, jewelry and a wide selection of Hawaiian CDs and DVDs.

Daughtry's Old Books
22 N. Front St., Wilmington
(910) 763-4754

In the heart of downtown Wilmington for more than 20 years, Daughtry's Old Books is a book-lover's haven. If you're searching for that long out-of-print treasure or something wonderful to read, this store is crammed from floor to ceiling with an estimated 30,000 titles, everything from the very rare to contemporary fiction. Looking for first editions? Daughtry's carries about 500 of them.

Gifts of Aloha, Ltd.
130 N. Front St., Wilmington
(910) 251-0201
www.alohagiftsnc.com

At Gifts of Aloha, Ltd., you'll almost feel the island breezes as you step through the door. Here you'll find everything Hawaiian, including Toni, the manager, who is a professional hula dancer of Hawaiian descent. This unique shop carries authentic resort, cruise and island apparel for men, women and children, including ever-popular Aloha shirts, as well as an exclusive designer line of women's

Island Passage Elixir
4 Market St., Wilmington
(910) 762-0484

Located near the waterfront at the end of Market Street, this charming boutique offers the latest in women's clothing fashions as well as a selection of personalized gifts, jewelry and shoes. Visit Island Passage's other shops: Island Passage at Lumina Station, 1900 Eastwood Road near Wrightsville Beach, (910) 256-0407; and Island Passage Riverside, (910) 457-4944, on Bald Head Island, which carries fun island resort wear

Shop for fresh regional produce, plants, herbs, cut flowers and seafood at the Riverfront Farmer's Market. An open-air market, set up along Water Street in downtown Wilmington, the Farmer's Market is held every Saturday (8 AM to noon) from mid-April through December. Every third Saturday arts and crafts are for sale by local artisans.

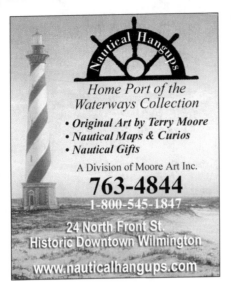

Home Port of the Waterways Collection

• *Original Art by Terry Moore*
• *Nautical Maps & Curios*
• *Nautical Gifts*

A Division of Moore Art Inc.

763-4844

1-800-545-1847

24 North Front St.
Historic Downtown Wilmington

www.nauticalhangups.com

of artistic maps depicting the coastal regions of the United States, and the original maps, hand-drawn and painted in oils by Moore, are the source of these unique and highly collectible prints, notecards and other items featured in the shop. Each map includes a poem, by the artist, about the region portrayed. Look closely and you'll find a hidden, good luck rabbit in each map. Nautical Hangups also carries nautical-themed gifts and accessories to complement Moore's art.

Rare Cargo
112 N. Front St., Wilmington
(910) 762-7636

Describing themselves as "purveyors of stuff you could probably do without," Rare Cargo's focus is on fun for all ages. Don't miss their eclectic selection of fun gifts, stationery, books, jewelry, cards and giggles. Winner of the 2006 Encore Reader's Choice Award for Best Gift Shop, as well as the Star News Readers Choice Award for Best Destination Downtown, Rare Cargo is definitely a Wilmington favorite.

and is your one-stop shop for everything you need to enjoy the traffic-free pleasures of the locale. They even have kayak, canoe, bicycle and golf cart rentals. A larger Bald Head Island location on Maritime Way, called Maritime Passage, (910) 454-8420, has a fabulous selection of clothing, shoes and accessories for men, women and children.

Return Passage
15 S. Water St., Wilmington
(910) 343-1627

In the Jacobi Warehouse, right around the corner from Island Passage Elixir is the latest Island Passage shop. Return Passage has deeply discounted merchandise from all of the other Island Passage locations, as well as gently worn items. They carry the hottest name brands and styles of once-worn clothing, and their inventory changes constantly. At Return Passage, you can trade in your gently worn clothing for cash or store credit that can be used at any of the Island Passage boutiques.

Kingoff's Jewelers
10 N. Front St., Wilmington
(910) 762-5219
www.kingoffs.com

Jewelers since 1919, Kingoff's offers a large selection of fine diamonds and colored stone jewelry in 18K and platinum, Tag Heuer watches and exciting gifts by Waterford Crystal. Guaranteed watch and jewelry repairs are done on the premises. Appraisals by four Guild Gemologists of the Diamond Council of America are also available. Kingoff's is the exclusive seller of the Old Wilmington Cup created in the early 1800s by Thomas Brown. This pewter cup is a favored gift among Wilmingtonians. For 87 years, their patrons know, "If it's from Kingoff's, it's guaranteed."

Ropa, Etc.
120-B S. Front St., Wilmington
(910) 815-0344

Ropa, Etc. is the area's exclusive retailer for such lines as Liz & Jane, Flax, Willow and Cut-Loose. This terrific shop also carries great makers such as Rico and Pure hand-knit sweaters, TSD, and Habitat. Ropa, Etc. is also known for its unique collection of hand-wrought American and European jewelry plus great accessories to complement any outfit. Fabric is easy care, with style and comfort guaranteed.

Nautical Hangups
24 N. Front St., Wilmington
(910) 763-4844, (800) 545-1847
www.nauticalhangups.com

Dubbed the "Home Port of the Waterways Collection," Nautical Hangups showcases the unique creations of local artist Terry Moore. The Waterways Collection is a series

Kingoff's Jewelers ... *Since 1919*

Wilmington's largest selection of fine quality jewelry

5 GUILD GEMOLOGISTS, DIAMOND COUNCIL OF AMERICA

WILMINGTON'S LEADING JEWELERS

10 N. Front St. - 762-5219
9-5:30 Mon - Fri, 10-4 Sat

1119-B Military Cutoff Rd. - 256-4321
10-5:30 Mon - Fri, 10-4 Sat

If It's From Kingoff's...It's Guaranteed"
www.kingoffs.com

The Old Wilmington City Market
119 S. Water St., Wilmington

The Old Wilmington City Market is a riverfront gem. This historic brick and stucco building, built in 1879, stretches a city block in width between Front and Water streets. From its humble origins as a vegetable market, this old world–style arcade with glass skylights throughout is now a shopping haven featuring art galleries and chic specialty shops including women's boutiques, T-shirts, hats, jewelry, fresh-cut flowers in season, plants, gardening supplies, handmade local soaps, unique exotic woods, imported goods and works by local artists. The market also features a relaxing seating area. Open year round, hours vary according to season.

Toms Drug Company
1 N. Front St., Wilmington
(910) 762-3391

This authentic, old-style drugstore has been a landmark in downtown Wilmington since 1932. Despite a serious face-lift in 1995, the store continues to have an old-Wilmington flavor and dedication to customer service. The complete pharmacy offers citywide delivery. Have questions? Just ask Dusty or any of the other friendly staff at Toms.

Twice Baked Pottery Painting Studio
6 Market St., Wilmington
(910) 632-6778

You can while away a few hours on a rainy day or after a stroll along the riverfront by stopping in the Twice Baked Pottery Painting Studio. Choose from a wide variety of items to create your own unique pottery piece. With more than 50 paint colors, as well as stencils, stamps and idea books, this is a fun place to forget your troubles and just get into a creative mood. Owner Angel Cody and her friendly staff are happy to provide assistance. Special events are presented monthly such as 'Girls Night Out' and wine tastings, so call for a schedule. Group rates are available for parties of six or more and you may bring your own food and drinks. The shop is closed on Monday and closes one hour early if there are no painters. Hours are seasonal.

Toms Drug Co.

Since 1932

Forget Something? Prescriptions, toothpaste, sunglasses, film, gift items?

Come See Us, We're Nice, We're Fun...

762-3391 • 1 North Front Street

Midtown Wilmington

Midtown Wilmington is defined as stretching from Historic Downtown Wilmington to the Wrightsville Beach vicinity.

OLEANDER DRIVE AREA

**Hanover Center
3501 Oleander Dr., Wilmington
(910) 392-3300**

Complementing Westfield Shoppingtown Independence mall directly across the street, this lively strip center was Wilmington's original shopping destination. Opened in 1956 before any other strip malls, it has been completely remodeled and remains a popular shopping venue. Listed below are merchants and businesses currently located in Hanover Center.

AAA Vacations, (910) 763-8446, offers vacation, travel and insurance services, plus it's a AAA Motor Club office. **Liberty Home Care**, (910) 815-3122, provides nursing, physical therapy and other social and home health aid. Four full-service banking centers with ATMs are **Bank of America**, (910) 251-5285; **BB&T**, (910) 313-2000, **RBC Centura**, (910) 772-8890, and **Cooperative Bank**, (910) 392-7894. **Wild Bird Centers**, (910) 343-6001, offers backyard nature products, garden accessories and seed for attracting birds. **Great Clips**, (910) 362-0054, is a moderately priced salon providing haircuts and permanents. **Great Outdoor Provision Company**, (910) 343-1648, carries outdoor clothing, equipment, footwear and accessories for fly fishing, backpacking, climbing and paddle sports. **Omega Sports**, (910) 762-7212, a running specialty store, offers sporting gear, apparel and shoes.

K & W Cafeteria, (910) 762-7011, serves some of the best food in town. **J. Michael's Philly Deli**, (910) 763-6466, is a great place

 For a shopping change of pace, spend the day in Southport. Stop for lunch at one of the great seafood restaurants overlooking the Waterway and the Cape Fear River. Ride the Southport-Fort Fisher Ferry. Relax on a swinging seat in the park.

for sandwiches and other deli fare for lunch and dinner. **Temptations Foods & Cafe**, (910) 763-6662, offers great lunch fare (soups, salads, sandwiches, quiche) plus gourmet treats, chocolates and sweets, North Carolina specialty foods, coffee, tea, wine and food gifts. **Harris Teeter**, (910) 343-4216, will take care of all your grocery shopping needs. **Eckerd Drugs**, (910) 763-3367, is a convenient and reliable pharmacy drugstore. For a quick, tasty meal, there's **Chick-Fil-A**, (910) 452-9399. Tropical Smoothie Café, (910) 343-1223, serves fresh fruit drinks, breakfast all day, sandwiches and light fare, and **Hardees**, (910) 791-5457, offers a great quick snack any time.

At **Stein Mart**, (910) 772-1533, you'll find upscale merchandise at discount prices, including clothing, shoes, gifts, linens and accessories. **Sterling House**, (910) 763-3656, is an inviting store offering gifts, jewelry, collectibles, home accessories, the full line of Vera Bradley luggage and handbags, Hallmark cards and fine stationery. **Picture This**, (910) 762-2780, offers arts, gifts and home decor items. **SAS Shoes**, (910) 772-9994, sells comfort shoes for men and women and the complete line of San Antonio Shoes. Extended sizes are available. **Shoe Shak**, (910) 772-9993, sells fashion footwear for adults in a wide range of sizes. They also carry handbags and jewelry. **Talbots**, (910) 313-1100, sells high-quality, classic clothing for women. **Tiny World**, (910) 251-8925, is a specialty store carrying fine children's clothing sizes preemie to 16.

Adjacent to the main block of Hanover Center is another strip of stores, Azalea Plaza, which is home to **Haverty's** furniture, (910) 791-3320, **Pier 1 Imports**, (910) 392-3151, **Books-A-Million**, (910) 452-1519, and **Office Depot**, (910) 392-9013.

**The Herb Shop
Oleander Oaks, 5725 Oleander Dr.,
Ste. B-8, Wilmington
(910) 452-HERB (4372)**

Owned and operated by a registered pharmacist since 1994, The Herb Shop has the right products for you. A broad range of vitamins, supplements, homeopathic remedies and herbal nutritionals are available. Numerous reputable product lines are featured as well as bulk herbs. You can also find a large variety of teas. Be sure to try some of their excellent smoothies and coffees. Free weight-control and health counseling are provided by qualified health professionals during store hours, which are Monday through Friday 10 AM to 6 PM and Saturday 10 AM to 3 PM.

Ivey Hayes Gallery
Originals and Fine Art Reproductions
Bradley Square, 5629 Oleander Dr., Ste. 114, Wilmington
(910) 794-9121

The Ivey Hayes Gallery is home to one of southeastern North Carolina's most beloved artists. A prolific painter, Ivey Hayes' love for painting began at an early age and has lasted more than 30 years. Drawing from personal experiences, Ivey uses bold, vibrant colors to express feeling and emotion, making each of his pieces come to life with its own distinct personality. Music, dance, coastal imagery, local and pastoral scenes of his native North Carolina are just a few of his subjects. His artwork has been exhibited throughout his home state, in Washington, D.C., Boston and New York as well as galleries and private collections in the United States.

Both original fine art and signed, limited-edition giclée prints are available. If you haven't yet experienced the vibrant paintings of Ivey Hayes, stop by and discover his award-winning art, inspired by life in North Carolina.

Perry's Emporium
Barclay Commons, 2520 Independence Blvd., Wilmington
(910) 392-6721, (800) 261-5705
www.perrysemporium.com

Walk through the leaded-glass doors of Perry's Emporium and step back into the 1890s. Twenty-eight antique floor cases hold one of the largest collections of estate pieces in the city, in addition to more contemporary styles of fine jewelry, loose diamonds and silver flatware. An additional 14 antique wall display cases showcase jewelry, art, fine china and crystal. Celebrating over a decade of service to the area, this 5,300-square-foot store is the largest retail jeweler in Wilmington. Perry's services include two full-service master jewelers, two graduate gemologists, lapidary services, jewelry repair and a bridal service. Appraisals are available for new, used and antique jewelry.

REEDS Jewelers
Westfield Shoppingtown Independence Mall, 3500 Oleander Dr., Wilmington
(910) 799-6810
Mayfaire Town Center, 926 Inspiration Dr., Wilmington
(910) 256-2962
www.reeds.com

REEDS Jewelers is a true American success story, having grown from one hometown store in Wilmington to a full-service jewelry retailer with 80 stores in 18 states. Founded in 1946 by Bill and Roberta Zimmer, REEDS Jewelers continues its tradition of excellence at Westfield Shoppingtown Independence and their new flagship store at Mayfaire Town Center.

REEDS Jewelers offers many exclusive lines of fine jewelry such as the Venus Diamond Collection. REEDS Jewelers is also an authorized distributor for prestigious designer brands such as Rolex, David Yurman, Tag Heuer, Omega, Armani, Fendi, Gucci, Michele Watch, Mikimoto, Penny Preville, Scott Kay and Tacori.

Serenity Place Gallery
Anderson Square, 4113 Oleander Dr., Ste. E, Wilmington
(910) 794-1944, (877) 509-2823

If you love the artwork of Thomas Kinkade, the "painter of light," Serenity Place Gallery is a must see. This small but elegant gallery is filled with Kinkade's breath-taking prints and limited-edition pieces. Gift items featuring the artist's distinctive style include beautiful coffee-table books, stationery, collector's plates, calendars, music boxes and more. Serenity Place is also an authorized Bradford dealer.

Tidal Creek Foods Co-Op
5329 Oleander Dr., Ste. 100, Wilmington
(910) 799-COOP (2667)
www.tidalcreek.coop

Since 1982, a commitment to providing the highest quality natural and organic foods, great customer service and ongoing consumer education has been central to the Tidal Creek philosophy. This community-owned cooperative food market takes pride in offering the most healthful foods and products available at the best possible prices. Their buyers look for organically produced foods

Cafe Open for
Lunch & Dinner
• Salad Bar
• Cafe
• Groceries
• Prepared Foods
• Organic Meats
• Dairy Products
• Bulk Grains, Beans, &
Snack Foods
• Personal Care
products
• Nutritional
supplements
• Herbal preparations
• Certified Organic
Produce Department

c o o p e r a t i v e
f o o d   m a r k e t
& Cafe

Wilmington's Source
for all things organic

www.tidalcreek.coop

910-799-2667
mon-sat 8-8 • sun 10-6
5329 oleander drive

residents, has more than 150 stores offering a wealth of shopping opportunities in an attractive and climate-controlled environment. Planning to "shop 'til you drop"? Strategically placed throughout the mall are groups of upholstered chairs (with a few coin-operated "massage chairs"). There's a 400-seat food court and 15 eateries. Sears, **JC Penney**, **Belk** and **Dillard's** department stores anchor this complex of trademark stores, independent shop owners and rented kiosk vendors. There are sporting goods shops, jewelry stores, software stores, shoe stores, specialty gift stores, fragrance and bath shops, music stores, home furnishing stores, an impressive range of apparel boutiques for the whole family ranging from infant-size to adult plus sizes, a full-service salon, nail care, banking services and much more.

Can't decide on the perfect gift? Gift cards, redeemable in any of the mall stores or restaurants where American Express is honored, are a good choice. The customer service center, located in the Dillard's wing, provides Kiddie Kruzzers, wheelchairs, gift cards, complimentary gift wrap, shopping bags, faxing and copying services and friendly assistance. Electric wheelchairs are also available and free. A family rest area, adjacent to the food court, offers co-ed children's bathrooms, changing stations, private nursing areas and the Disney Channel on TV. Westfield Shoppingtown Independence Mall is open daily.

UNIVERSITY AREA

Dance & Romance
University Landing, 419 S. College Rd.,
Ste. 14, Wilmington
(910) 793-2090

Whether you're planning a romantic evening alone with your sweetheart or the best bachelorette party ever, Dance & Romance has everything you'll need. Along with massage oils, lotions, lubricants, movies and adult toys, you'll also find the sexiest lingerie, swimwear and exotic dancewear, including beautiful gowns, adult costumes and Halloween costumes, hot leather goods, body hosiery and much more, all at competitive prices and in sizes ranging from extra small to 4X. This unique shop also has jewelry and shoes with heels from two to eight inches in clear, white, silver or black to accent any outfit.

from local growers, small farms and companies that share the co-op's high standards.

Among the offerings at Tidal Creek, shoppers will find fresh, natural organic foods, including certified organic produce, hormone-free dairy products, chemical-free and organic meats, local eggs, frozen prepared foods and desserts and a wide variety of packaged grocery items. Also available are organic bulk items (whole grains and flours, cereals, herbal teas, beans and pasta and natural snack foods are a few examples), health and beauty aids, aromatherapy oils, organic wines and microbrewery beers.

Tidal Creek features a deli and cafe, complete with an organic salad bar and a hot bar, numerous grab-and-go sandwiches and meals, baked goods, a fresh organic juice bar, coffee and smoothie bar. More than just a grocery store, the co-op is the place to enjoy a delicious, healthful meal or snack and keep up with the latest in the Wilmington healthy lifestyle community. While Tidal Creek is community owned and operated, you don't have to be an owner to shop there — everyone is welcome. Tidal Creek is across the street from Eddie Romanelli's restaurant on Oleander Drive.

Westfield Shoppingtown Independence Mall
3500 Oleander Dr., Wilmington
(910) 392-1776

Westfield Shoppingtown Independence Mall, known simply as "the mall" by area

Great deals can be found on everything from produce to souvenirs in the many outdoor markets.

photo: Gwynne Moore

McAllister & Solomon Books
4402 Wrightsville Ave., Wilmington
(910) 350-0189, (888) 617-7882

People who love vintage, rare or just plain hard-to-find books will relish a browse through McAllister & Solomon Books, just a block off S. College Road. They stock used and rare books, as well as a large selection of regional history books, in this well organized and appealing bookstore. Books are bought, sold or traded with about 25,000 titles in the store at any given time. Store specialties include local and North Carolina history, military history, world history, African Americana, genealogy, mystery fiction and literature. Looking for a particular title? Ask the staff about an Internet search. McAllister & Solomon has access to a database of millions of books daily through a computerized out-of-print search network.

New Balance Wilmington
29 Van Campen Blvd., Wilmington
(910) 332-2020

This locally owned, nationally known specialty store features a full line of New Balance and Dunham footwear, New Balance performance apparel and sport bags. The friendly and knowledgeable staff will ensure you have the proper fit and style for your athletic needs. You will find shoe sizes ranging from 5 to 20 and widths from 2A to 6E. The store is located in the Monk's Corner Shops near Cracker Barrel and the Wal-Mart SuperCenter.

Racine Center for the Arts
203 Racine Dr., Wilmington
(910) 452-2073
www.racinecenter.com

The Racine Center for the Arts is an exciting and unique addition to southeastern North Carolina's growing arts scene. This spacious, 22,000-square-foot building's two floors host a multitude of art forms, so whether art is your vocation or passionate interest, there is something to inspire you. On the first floor, here's what you'll find: The Gallery at Racine, which is a fine arts gallery showing the work of locally and nationally recognized artists including George Pocheptsov and Dr. Seuss; Blue Moon Showcase, an artisan gift and home furnishing co-op; and Picasso's Cafe, an indoor/outdoor eatery. Upstairs you'll find the Racine School of the Arts, a non-profit fine arts education program for children and adults (the school consists of four large studios including a full-service pottery studio). Also upstairs is Firebird, a paint-your-own pottery studio where you can learn many techniques includ-

Have fun, get some fresh air and shop, too. Many local merchants, artists and vendors have booths or tents at popular outdoor events such as Riverfest, Seafood, Blues & Jazz Festival, North Carolina Azalea Festival and Art in the Park (see our Annual Events chapter).

It's About Style.
sophisticated cork and hardwood floors

Sutton's Rugs & Carpets
3520 South College Road Wilmington, NC 28412 • 910-794-8100 • www.suttonrugs.com

ing mosaics. You can even stuff a critter, that is, make your own plush toy. Be sure to ask about group discounts and calendar specials.

SOUTH COLLEGE ROAD & MONKEY JUNCTION AREA

Fountaine Bridals & Formals
5202 Carolina Beach Rd., Ste. 11,
Wilmington
(910) 794-9959

Wilmington's oldest bridal shop, Fountaine Bridals & Formals is known for its large selection of fabulous gowns for weddings, proms and other formal occasions from size 2 to 28. They also have dresses for bridesmaids and mother-of-the-bride. Outfit every lady in your wedding party, including your flower girl. An exceptional line of bridal accessories includes handbags, shoes and jewelry. Their experienced staff provides full bridal consulting and alterations are done on the premises. Fountaine's also does gown preservation.

Island Appliance
5946 Carolina Beach Rd., Wilmington
(910) 790-8580
www.homeappliances.com/island

The Island Appliance showroom features appliances displayed in home-like vignettes. You can select from Whirlpool and Maytag to Thermador and Viking as well as many other brands. Their factory-trained technicians service most major brands. With low prices and free local delivery, Island Appliance is a great place to shop for all of your appliance needs.

Pine Valley Market
3520 S. College Rd., Wilmington
(910) 350-FOOD (3663)

Encore magazine's Reader's Choice Awards named Pine Valley Market the "Best Gourmet Shop in Wilmington" for 2004 and 2005. The store was also voted "Best Butcher" in 2005, and "Best Catering", "Best Butcher" and "Best Gourmet" for 2006. Pine Valley Market contains a dazzling selection of fine wines from around the world, a full-service butcher shop, and a wide array of gourmet delights. They also offer yummy custom-made and grilled sandwiches, burgers (including a low-carb burger) and fresh salads. With their selection of prepared foods, the Pine Valley Market is a great place to stop by after work to pick up a delicious gourmet meal for the whole family. Pine Valley Market also has catering menus available for breakfast/brunch, corporate breakfast and lunch, dinner, dessert and gourmet party platters to suit any gathering or special event.

Sutton's Rugs and Carpets
3520 S. College Rd., Wilmington
(910) 794-8100
www.suttonrugs.com

At Sutton Rugs and Carpets, it's all about style. From custom designed and manufactured area rugs and wall to wall carpeting to hardwood and other surfaces, Hobbs and Donna Sutton and their design team can help you with all of your floor covering needs. Locally owned and operated, this full service carpet and flooring gallery has everything you need to created beautiful floors.

MILITARY CUTOFF ROAD AREA

Landfall Shopping Center
Eastwood Rd. and Military Cutoff Rd., Wilmington

Just minutes from Wrightsville Beach, this retail, dining and service center is convenient to both downtown Wilmington and Wrightsville Beach. Landfall Shopping Center offers a full-day shopping experience for all your needs from gifts to apparel to home. It offers a boutique-style **Belk** department store, (910) 509-1323, plus many specialty stores and services. Here are some we recommend.

The Julia, (910) 256-1175, carries an exciting collection of upscale day and evening apparel, ever-changing and modern, yet classic. **The Seasoned Gourmet**, (910) 256-9488, is an exciting store for cooks and people who enjoy entertaining. **Apple Annie's Bake Shop**, (910) 256-6585, is a local favorite for the finest hand-made and hand-decorated desserts and cakes. Looking for a convenient, full-service florist? Landfall Center's **Something Special**, (910) 256-0020, is committed to quality and personal service. **Lovey's Market**,

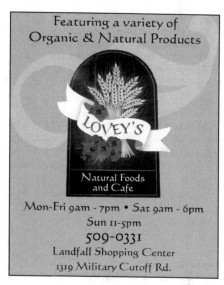

Featuring a variety of
Organic & Natural Products

LOVEY'S

Natural Foods
and Cafe

Mon-Fri 9am - 7pm • Sat 9am - 6pm
Sun 11-5pm
509-0331
Landfall Shopping Center
1319 Military Cutoff Rd.

(910) 509-0331, is a popular natural food store with a good selection of organic produce, a deli, a juice bar and a salad bar. The **Northeast Regional Library**, (910) 256-2173, a large branch of the New Hanover County Library, is open Monday through Saturday. **UNCW Executive Development Center**, (910) 962-3578, housed in the Northeast Regional Library, is a state-of-the-art meeting facility with 8,000 square feet of space accommodating up to 200 participants.

Lovey's Market
1319 Military Cutoff Rd., Wilmington
(910) 509-0331
www.loveysmarket.com

Lovey's is an ideal location for the discriminating shopper who prefers natural and organic goods. Featuring the finest in homeopathic and herbal supplements, vitamins, health and beauty aids for hair and skin and bulk grains, flour, beans and spices, the vibe at Lovey's is a friendly one. While the grocery section offers delicious produce and meat-free selections for the vegetarian and vegan customer, it also features free-range meats and poultry. Parents will appreciate their selection of baby food and other toxin-free items available for young children. All shoppers will enjoy the extensive hot and cold food bar. Lovey's can even bring their tasty treats to you through their catering service. Top off your visit with a delicious smoothie and you'll realize why Lovey's is such a hit with the locals.

Palm Garden
(A Lilly Pulitzer ™ Signature Store)
Landfall Shopping Center, Eastwood Rd.
and Military Cutoff Rd., Wilmington
(910) 256-9984
www.shoppalmgarden.com

Palm Garden is a paradise of Lilly Pulitzer™ apparel, shoes and accessories. Offerings include dresses, separates, golf and tennis wear and swimwear for ladies, as well as a wonderfully cheerful children's collection. You won't want to miss the matching shoes and accessories. If you're looking to brighten up your home, there is even a Lilly Pulitzer™ home collection. Shop at the Palm Garden and your home and wardrobe will bloom with color.

The Forum
1125 Military Cut-off Rd., Wilmington
(910) 256-0467

Providing shoppers with a sense of graciousness, The Forum is characterized by classical architecture and warmly colored Canadian sandstone, accented with arches, columns, pediments and balustrades. The Forum's shops are unique, upscale and carry a tempting selection of goods.

Charming boutiques offer a wide array of gifts, jewelry, wines, women's fashions and children's clothing. **Charlotte's**, (910) 509-9701, is an extraordinary gift and jewelry shop, with a diverse selection. **Ikebana Design**, (910) 509-1383, is an exceptional, full-service florist and gift shop. **NOFO Cafe and Market**, (910) 256-5565, offers an eclectic array of gifts, gardening accessories, home furnishings and books. **Oliver**, (910) 256-2233, sells high-fashion clothing and accessories for men and women. **Peanut Butter & Jelly**, (910) 256-4554, offers delightful gifts, clothing and accessories for children as well as Midnight Pickles maternity line. **Personal Touch**, (910) 256-8888, specializes in both ladies' apparel and fine designer jewelry. **Ropa, Etc.**, (910) 256-8733, offers women's clothing made of fine cottons and linens. **Tara Grinna Swimwear**, (910) 509-9999, is a specialty swimwear store.

Looking for high-end shops filled with antiques, imported furniture, art and home accessories? The Forum has one of the largest antiques importers in North Carolina, **Acquisitions, Ltd**, (910) 509-9366. **Interiors**, (910) 509-9598, includes two interior design firms and a retail shop selling European antiques and home accessories. **Spectrum Gallery**, (910) 256-2323, features art, glass and custom jewelry.

Upscale restaurants, cafés and bakeries offer a wide variety of excellent foods. (See our Restaurants chapter for more details.) **Salty's**, (910) 256-1118, specializes in gourmet seafood, beef, chicken and pasta. **Flavor Fusion**, (910) 256-6600, offers multi-cultural, infused cuisine. **Rossi's**, (910) 256-8870, is where you'll find fine Italian cuisine and a festive European environment, as well as **Eighty Eights**, (910) 256-8870, an elegant piano bar. For those who prefer a casual dining experience, the **NOFO Cafe and Market**, (910) 256-5565, offers an array of coffee drinks, delectable soups, salads, sandwiches and light fare. **Blueberry Hill Dessertery**, (910) 509-0700, serves an awesome selection of bakery treats, espresso and specialty coffee drinks.

Blue Hand Home
The Forum, 1125 Military Cutoff Rd.,
Wilmington
(910) 509-0088

This delightfully eclectic store's theme is "casual, chic and uncomplicated luxury." You're bound to find irresistible choices in furniture, including armoires, beds, dining rooms and original and reproduction pieces inspired by old world craftsmanship. Upholstered furniture is clad in rich chenille, damask, linens or leather. Make decorating a delight with cashmere throws, stylish lighting, scented Votivo candles and more. Professional interior design services, from blueprint to complete decoration, are available.

EyeTECH Optical Boutique
The Forum, 1119-D Military Cutoff Rd.,
Wilmington
(910) 509-0291

EyeTECH Optical Boutique offers an environment where clients feel comfortable experimenting with eyewear as an expression of their own personal style. Their slogan, "Art for Your Face," means just that for customers because this is a place where individuality is preeminent. EyeTECH Optical Boutique stocks a wide range of exclusive frame collections such as Prada, Lafont, Alain Mikli, Chopard and Cazal and they have more than 1,000 frames on display. Customized frames are also available in hand-carved wood and genuine horn.

Sports optics are a specialty, and EyeTECH Optical Boutique is a premium dealer for Oakley, Costa Del Mar, Rudy Project, Maui Jim and Rec Specs. All sports frames are available in prescription. They carry a huge inventory of sunglasses as well.

Definitely not a self-serve, one-size-fits-all shop, EyeTECH Optical Boutique strives to address the specific requirements of each individual. A second location is in The Theatre Building in Pinehurst, (910) 235-0291, so visit them at either one.

Ki Spa and Salon
The Forum, 1125 Military Cutoff Rd., Wilmington
(910) 509-0410
www.kispasalon.com

At Ki Spa, the philosophy is simple and timeless. They combine natural products, pure aromatherapy and healing techniques to promote total body renewal. Ki, the ancient Japanese word for energy, is incorporated into all spa treatments. Ki Spa offers a tranquil environment that's ideal for specialty and couples massage, body treatments, facials, peels, microdermabrasion, permanent hair removal, waxing, manicures (natural nails) and pedicures. For weddings, relax and rejuvenate your spirit with a package designed especially for you, your bridal party and your guests. Ki Spa "unlocks the energy of your mind, body and spirit."

Kingoff's Jewelers
The Forum, 1119-B Military Cutoff Rd., Wilmington
(910) 256-4321
www.kingoffs.com

Jewelers since 1919, Kingoff's offers a large selection of fine diamonds and colored stone jewelry in 18K and platinum, Tag Heuer watches and exciting gifts by Waterford Crystal. Guaranteed watch and jewelry repairs are done on the premises. Appraisals by four Guild Gemologists of the Diamond Council of America are also available. Kingoff's is the exclusive seller of the Old Wilmington Cup created in the early 1800s by Thomas Brown. This pewter cup is a favored gift among Wilmingtonians. For 87 years, their patrons know, "If it's from Kingoff's, it's guaranteed."

Ropa, Etc.
The Forum, 1121-D Military Cutoff Rd., Wilmington
(910) 256-8733

Experience the pleasure of fine cottons and linens and make dressing comfortable and fun. Ropa, etc. is the area's exclusive retailer for such lines as Liz & Jane, Flax, Willow and Cut-Loose. This terrific shop also carries great makers such as Rico and Pure hand-knit sweaters, TSD and Habitat. Ropa, etc. is also known for its unique collection of hand-wrought American and European jewelry plus great accessories to complement any outfit. Fabric is easy care, with style and comfort guaranteed.

Learning Express Toys
Progress Point, 1437 Military Cutoff Rd., Wilmington
(910) 509-0153
www.learningexpress.com

Learning Express Toys is a great place for kids and their parents because everything inside offers educational opportunities and fun at the same time. You'll find an extensive dress-up section, puzzles, science kits, books, games, yoyos (including Yomega), Playmobil, Corolle dolls, Thomas Trains, Groovy Girls, Manhattan Baby and Creativity for Kids.

Learning Express Toys carries Legos, puppets, electronics kits and K'nex plus a large selection of kites for kids of all ages, from easy-to-fly kites to sophisticated stunt models. In this 3,300 square feet of fun, perhaps the largest department is the art section. This popular area offers art supplies and activities to please all interests, ages and skill levels, from finger paints to a potter's wheel. Another sought-after feature of the store is the free personalizing offered. Items include clipboards, lap trays, beach totes and pails, piggy banks and more.

The store's huge Birthday Wish Bucket allows a child to register their wishes for birthdays, providing parents, grandparents and friends with an easy way to shop for gifts that are sure to light up a youngster's face. Other store services include a Baby Gift Registry, free gift wrapping, gift cards, UPS shipping and a Grandparents Discount Club. Discounts are also available to teachers and other professionals who work with children. If Learning Express Toys doesn't have a particular item, they promise to try and find it.

Mayfaire Town Center
Near the intersection of Eastwood Rd. and
Military Cutoff Rd., Wilmington
(910) 256-5131

Mayfaire is a wonderfully innovative place to shop. Designed to emulate the sense of community and friendly commerce found at the center of town, this shopping haven is one of those rare places where you can go with a shopping list and find everything you're looking for. There are more than 40 chain stores, specialty shops, salons and businesses at Mayfaire Town Center, providing a complete range of goods and services. You'll find **After Hours Formal Wear, Ann Taylor, Banana Republic, Barnes & Noble, Catherine's, Chico's, Claire's, Club O2 Fitness, Coldwater Creek, Cost Plus World Market, David's Bridal, EB Games, Glo Medspa, GNC, Hallmark, Hecht's, J. Jill, Jos. A. Bank, Kirkland's, Linens 'n Things, Liz Claiborne Shoes, Michaels, Nextel, Norwalk Furniture, Onestop Cellular, Pier 1 Imports, Pier 1 Kids, Portrait Innovations, Rack Room Shoes, Red Bank Wine, Reeds Jewelers, The Sharper Image, Talbots, Trade Secret, Williams-Sonoma, Ulta, Vanity** and much more. And when all of that shopping leaves you with an empty stomach, meet a friend for lunch at one of the tempting restaurants and cafes scattered throughout the center: **The Artisan Market and Café, Atlanta Bread Co., Cold Stone Creamery, Fox & Hound, Mama Fu's, Qdoba Mexican Grill, Red Robin Gourmet Burger, Romano's Macaroni Grill, Smokey Bones** and **Starbucks**. With ample free parking, convenient sidewalks and plenty of benches for resting tired feet, Mayfaire Town Center is definitely a shopper's paradise. After the day is done, you'll enjoy a flick at Mayfaire 16 Cinemas.

REEDS Jewelers
Mayfaire Town Center, 926 Inspiration Dr.,
Wilmington
(910) 256-2962
Westfield Shoppingtown Independence
Mall, 3500 Oleander Dr., Wilmington
(910) 799-6810
www.reeds.com

REEDS Jewelers is a true American success story, having grown from one hometown store in Wilmington to a full-service jewelry retailer with 80 stores in 18 states. Founded in 1946 by Bill and Roberta Zimmer, REEDS

Jewelers continues its tradition of excellence at Westfield Shoppingtown Independence and their new flagship store at Mayfaire Town Center.

REEDS Jewelers offers many exclusive lines of fine jewelry such as the Venus Diamond Collection. REEDS Jewelers is also an authorized distributor for prestigious designer brands such as Rolex, David Yurman, Tag Heuer, Omega, Armani, Fendi, Gucci, Michele Watch, Mikimoto, Penny Preville, Scott Kay and Tacori.

MARKET STREET AREA

Pottery Plus
5744 Market St., Wilmington
(910) 791-7522
www.gopotteryplus.com

Shopping at Pottery Plus is like having a warehouse of favorite things for your home and garden. The pallets of goods will delight the designer in you and wow your pocketbook, too! This two-acre bargain paradise features 12 decorated theme trees during Christmas plus all the silk greenery and ornaments to go with them. During our long spring season, the store is filled to the rafters with garden decor and great-looking outdoor furniture.

Wilmington Stone Garden
6955 Market St., Wilmington
(910) 452-1619

Wilmington Stone Garden, located at Military Cutoff and Market Street, should be your first stop when planning or beautifying your home or garden. Wander through an acre of stone or the showroom to select just the right materials for your home-improvement project. Cast stone statuary, ranging from the whimsical to the unique, are prominently displayed outside. If their great selection of birdbaths, benches, planters, urns and Charleston fountains doesn't inspire you, their Secret Garden will. Hidden behind a tall fence on the grounds, this inviting water garden is a delightful haven. Don't forget to browse the gift shop's eclectic selection of garden gifts, sculpture, beautiful polished stones, geodes and fossils. Wilmington Stone Garden is known to locals as a fun place to shop, and you can feel free to bring the kids. The store is open Monday through Saturday.

Wrightsville Beach

Blowing In The Wind
222 Causeway Dr., Wrightsville Beach
(910) 509-9989, (888) 509-9989
www.blowinginthewind.com
www.gokitesurf.com

Blowing in the Wind has plenty of kite-flying fun for everyone. As the area's largest full-service kite shop, with locations in Wrightsville Beach and downtown Wilmington at the Cotton Exchange, 312 Nutt Street, (910) 763-1730, they carry a huge selection of colorful kites for all ages and skill levels, from easy-to-fly single line kites, delta kites and box kites, to controllable stunt kites and big show kites. Looking for a thrill? Try one of their Jet-Ski assisted kiteboarding lessons (read all about this exciting sport in the Watersports chapter). Blowing in the Wind in Wrightsville Beach is the area's only supplier of kiteboarding products and lessons. Come check out the dazzling array of kites and explore their wide selection of windsocks, wind chimes, puzzles and wooden toys for kids.

Mott's Channel Seafood
120 Short St., Wrightsville Beach
(910) 256-3474

Since 1990, Motts has been providing fresh seafood to folks from its waterfront location at Wrightsville Beach. Whether you arrive by boat or by car, you'll find a large selection of fresh, first-quality seafood. They also offer an extensive selection of sauces and spices to help you prepare a great seafood meal. For anglers, they have live and frozen bait as well as ice for your catch.

Surf City Surf Shop
The Landing, 530 Causeway Dr.,
Wrightsville Beach
(910) 256-2265, (910) 256-4353 or
(910) 350-8666 (surf report)

In business for more than 25 years, Surf City describes the store as "a shop for surfers by surfers" and carries a large variety of surfboards. Whether you're into the classic boards — Hobie, Weber, Yater, Hansen and Velzy — or the newer shapes — Lost, Merrick, Rusty, HIC, Aftermath — Surf City has them all, as well as the clothing and accessories you'll need to hit the waves. Skateboarding gear is another feature of this lively store,

with a large selection of skateboard components, including decks and wheels, clothing and accessories, including the area's largest selection of sunglasses. Into snowboarding? Surf City offers some of the best snowboarding gear available, including boards, bindings, clothing and boots.

Wrightsville Beach Vicinity

Shopping options are limited, by design, on the largely residential Wrightsville Beach, but there's been an explosion of retail growth over the bridge on the mainland side. (All the stores in this section have a Wilmington address.)

Lumina Station
1900 Eastwood Rd., Wilmington
(910) 256-0900
www.luminastation.com

If you're shopping for local flavor, you'll find Lumina Station as satisfying as a day at the beach. Inspired by Lumina, the beloved Wrightsville Beach dance pavilion once central to the East Coast social scene, Lumina Station is so true to its historical roots that it won Coastal Living magazine's first-ever award for contextual design.

Beautiful landscaping, whimsical sculptures and storybook bridges complement the heavily wooded campus, making strolling the Station a very pleasant way to pass the time. Rocking chairs — the center's signature icon — are grouped here and there under deep overhangs, providing a shady place to rest, enjoy a cappuccino, or sit back and visit with passersby.

Fortunately, the shops, restaurants and business located here are just as unique as the setting. Local merchants own and operate virtually all of the establishments. You'll find some truly special offerings, from jewelry and books to art, gift items, home accents and clothing for the entire family. You can pamper yourself in the day spa, work out with a personal trainer and enjoy a fabulous meal in one of the restaurants, all without ever getting into your car.

Lumina Station cafés and restaurants provide something for everyone, from your morning coffee to fine dining. Start your day with fresh-brewed coffee from **Port City Java**, (910) 256-0993. Enjoy brunch, lunch or dinner at **Fathoms Bistro**, (910) 256-1254. For great steaks, visit **Chester's Steakhouse**, (910) 256-0995. Enjoy a relaxing cocktail at **The Dirty Martini**, (910) 509-2865, then go next door to have an exceptional meal at **The Port Land Grille**, (910) 256-6056, which features progressive regional American cuisine.

The following is a listing of the shops and services you'll find at Lumina Station. You'll also find warmth, friendliness and an authentic old Wrightsville Beach atmosphere. Overall, it's an experience you couldn't possibly have anywhere else. **Airlie Moon**, (910) 256-0655, is an eclectic, unique gift store offering one-of-a-kind products for the bed, bath and home. **Alligator Pie**, (910) 509-1600, is an amazing, one-of-a-kind children's boutique. For fine gifts, stationery and home accessories, stop by **Embellishments**, (910) 256-5263. An ideal place to help you complete your home with unique finishing touches would be **Finely Finished**, (910) 256-0777. For your one-stop boutique shopping experience with personalized service, you have to visit **Jennifer's**, (910) 256-6522. Intracoastal Realty, (910) 256-4503, is one of the area's most popular agencies for sales, vacation rentals and mortgage financing services. State-of-the-art equipment and personal training are both available at **Lumina Fitness**, (910) 509-9404. Swing into **Monkees**, (910) 256-5886, for the perfect shoes, contemporary ladies clothing and accessories. Whether you're looking for a unique baby gift, special birthday present or traditional wedding gift, you'll find it at **The Pink Petunia**, (910) 509-9940. For fine women's wear, check out **R. Bryan Collections**, (910) 256-9943. **S. Burke**, (910) 256-3311, invites you to discover a unique and beautiful selection of fine jewelry, home accessories and imaginative gifts. **Sito Chiropractic**, (910) 256-2655, offers family chiropractic care. You definitely don't want to miss **T.A.G. The Artists' Gallery**, (910) 509-2882, featuring fine art and master craft.

Alligator Pie
Lumina Station, 1900 Eastwood Rd.,
Wilmington
(910) 509-1600

Alligator Pie is truly a one-of-a-kind children's boutique, offering an amazing collection of clothes, toys, gifts and furnishings for children of all ages in a friendly atmosphere and one convenient location. Whether your tastes are traditional, trendy or somewhere in between, this unique and fascinating store is likely to have what you want. In clothing, the store offers the best of American and European brands for boys and girls from newborn to junior sizes, including Roxy, Quiksilver, Baby LuLu, Wes 'n Willy, Catimini, K.C. Parker, O'Neill, Billabong, Robeez and Zutano. Their collection includes play clothes, sleepwear, special occasion wear, shoes, outerwear and accessories. Pre-teen and junior size clothes are available in their loft, where you'll also find shoes, sandals, accessories and room decor for that trendy tween. Naturally, Alligator Pie offers only the hottest award-winning toys. Selections include crafts, puzzles, games, beach toys, dolls, art kits, dress-up, a great selection of large plush animals including cats, dogs, unicorns, horses and dinosaurs, "Board games for all ages" and much more.

Alligator Baby offers almost every item you could want for a baby, including beautiful blankets, silver rattles, developmental toys, cozy sleepwear and soft lovies. Equipment offered includes Britax car seats, Peg Perego high chairs and strollers, Petunia Pickle Bottom diaper bags and the new Bugaboo stroller. They also offer Mustela skin care products and great selection from which to choose for a baby registry.

Fountainside Fine Art Gallery
Lumina Station, 1900 Eastwood Rd.,
Ste. 44, Wilmington
(910) 256-9956
www.fountainsidegallery.com

Fountainside Gallery is one of Wilmington's leading destinations for fine art. Representing local, regional and national artists, Fountainside has a selection of art that will appeal to the serious collector as well as the casual art lover. The gallery regularly hosts exhibitions and educational demonstrations, inviting artists from across the U.S. to capture the beauty of the Cape Fear Coast. As well as placing art with residential customers, they work with corporate clients and design professionals. Come and enjoy the paintings, sculpture, glass and woodwork in the Fountainside's intimate, relaxed environment. You'll find the Fountainside Gal-

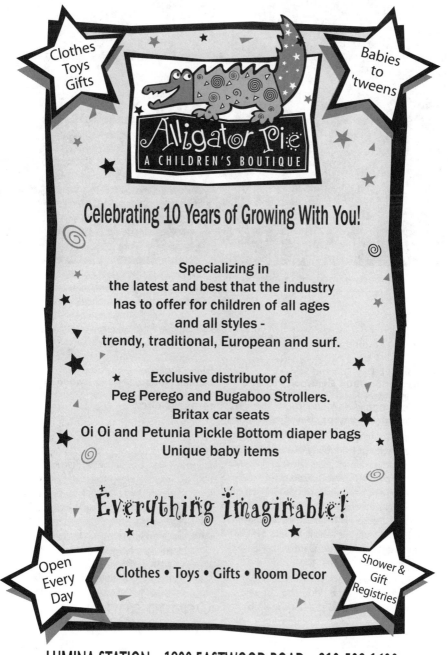

A variety of shopping experiences burst forth from renovated historic spaces.

photo: Peter Doran

lery on Eastwood Road before the Wrights-ville Beach Drawbridge in Lumina Station.

**Harbour Club Day Spa and Salon
Lumina Station, 1904 Eastwood Rd., Ste. 101, Wilmington
(910) 256-5020
www.harbourclubdayspa.com**

A spa where guests can relax and rejuvenate in a haven of tranquility, Harbour Club's team of highly trained professionals is dedicated to providing personalized beauty and body treatment programs. On its long list of outstanding services are such specialties as Haute Couture Body Wellness and Advanced Facial Treatments. Also available are facials, therapeutic massages, depilatory services, manicures and pedicures

Harbour Club offers a complete bridal service package for the bride and her wedding party, which includes a consultation to determine hairstyle with headpiece placement and cosmetic application, if desired. Their coordinator can also arrange delivery of catered food and beverages on the day of the booking. To soothe and polish the bride and groom before their big day, they

can choose from an array of facial and body treatments, hair, skin and nail options.

**Island Passage
Lumina Station, 1900 Eastwood Rd., Wilmington
(910) 256-0407**

Offering a colorful palette of artistically presented attire plus accessories for all ages, Island Passage is one of Wilmington's favorites. Don't miss their other stores at 4 Market Street in downtown Wilmington and their store on Bald Head Island near the marina — Island Passage Riverside, which carries fun island resort wear, (910) 457-4944. A larger Bald Head Island location on Maritime Way, Maritime Passage has a fabulous selection of clothing, shoes and accessories for men, women and children, (910) 454-8420.

Ogden and Porter's Neck

This section of Market Street, dormant until recent years, runs northward to Hampstead, Figure Eight Island and the Topsail Island area. Increased residential and commercial development has resulted in the rapid growth of shopping opportunities. Listed below are a few of the more well-established shops. (Most stores in this section have Wilmington addresses.)

The Canvas Goose
7976 Market St., Wilmington
(910) 686-9162

Celebrating 24 years in business in spring 2006, this quaint little shop sits in a charming, village-green-type setting. Inside you will find a wealth of collectibles and gifts, including Byers Choice Carolers, Churchill Weavers throws and Dept. 56 cottages and accessories. The Canvas Goose also offers a variety of garden and wind sculptures, garden accessories and distinctive handcrafted items including jewelry, ceramics and glassware from primarily American artists. UPS shipping and gift wrapping are available.

DDT-Outlet
7222 Market St., Wilmington
(910) 329-0160
www.ddtoutlet.com

If you're looking for furniture and accessories with a beach or nautical theme, you'll find them at the DDT Outlet. With more than 20,000 square feet of unique merchandise to chose from and services ranging from complete beach house and condominium packages to shipping your purchases back home, shopping in this great store is a must. Be sure to have plenty of time to browse displays of furniture, nautical gifts, wicker, barstools, pictures, yard ornaments, PVC furniture and more. Owners Tom and Niki Miller also offer a large, descriptive catalog to assist clients. If you need help in the selection of your furniture package, Niki is the expert, according to Tom. DDT is open seven days a week, year round.

Porters Neck Yoga & Spa
8044 Market St., Ste. A, Wilmington
(910) 686-6440
www.portersneckyogaspa.com

Escape to wellness, enhance your life. A full-service day spa, complete with hair and nail salon plus a yoga studio, Porters Neck Yoga & Spa is the perfect place to spend a morning or afternoon full of beauty, relaxation and bliss. The many spa services include a variety of massage therapies, couples massage, customized aromatherapy,

reflexology, restorative facials, body scrubs and treatments, all designed to put you in a state of blissful contentment. Looking for the perfect gift? Porters Neck Yoga & Spa has gift certificates and packages available as well. Hours are Monday through Friday 9 AM to 7 PM, Saturday 9 AM to 5 PM and Sunday 11 AM to 1 PM (yoga only).

Wild Birds Unlimited
7223 Market St., Wilmington
(910) 686-7210

This attractive and unique store, with a motto of "We bring people and nature together," is a must-visit for bird lovers, backyard gardeners and nature enthusiasts. Choose from a large variety of specialty seeds, suet, birdhouses, birdfeeders, nature books and gifts, garden items and much more. Wild Birds Unlimited also carries a selection of scopes and binoculars by Eagle Optics. Have questions? Everyone on staff is an expert, literally. Each employee has completed an in-depth course in ornithology through Cornell University.

Carolina Beach

Shopping on Pleasure Island — Carolina Beach and Kure Beach — is concentrated in Carolina Beach, a small, but rapidly growing family-beach community at the north end of the island. In addition to a number of chain "beach" stores (Wing's, King's, Blue Reef, etc.), Carolina Beach boasts a variety of year-round specialty shops, and more are added each year. Keep in mind that winter months mean shortened or limited hours for many retail businesses. Call ahead so you won't be disappointed by a "closed" sign.

When you want beachy stuff, shells, toys, towels, suits and souvenirs, you have to go to a beach store. From Topsail Island to Sunset Beach you'll find all kinds of locally owned shops filled with wonderful souvenirs and beach treasures. Some beach communities have popular chain stores like Wings and Kings, but for the most part, their stores reflect the local flavor.

Books in Time
915-C N. Lake Park Blvd., Carolina Beach
(910) 458-7973

Books in Time offers approximately 12,000 titles, primarily used paperbacks and hardcover books. Used paperbacks cost half of the cover price, and, when you're finished, you can trade it in for store credit. Used hardcover books are marked with a discounted price. Local artists and writers are given counter and wall space to display their work. There's even a complete line of greeting cards. Hours are Tuesday through Saturday from 10 AM to 6 PM and Sunday noon to 5 PM.

The Checkered Church Gift Shop
800 St. Joseph St., Carolina Beach
(910) 458-0211

Housed in a former Catholic church, this blue-and-white-checked building is filled with beach-related home-decor items, including pine furniture, prints, M.A. Hadley pottery, baskets, weather vanes, wind chimes, bird houses and the work of many local artists. Christmas items, many with a nautical theme, are available year-round. Also unique to The Checkered Church is a stunning 100 percent cotton afghan that portrays the Pleasure Island coastline and assorted wildlife found in the area. The Checkered Church truly is the little shop off the beaten path you always hope to discover.

Eccentric Cat
Snow's Cut Shopping Center, 1401 N. Lake Park Blvd., Carolina Beach
(910) 458-5810

Just past Snow's Cut bridge over the Intracoastal Waterway, you'll find the Eccentric Cat. Filled with pottery and fun stuff for your home decor, plus clothing, jewelry, handbags and other accessories, this shop offers a variety of unusual items. They also have a great selection of lounge wear and sleep wear. Dog lovers, don't feel left out; Eccentric Cat has some neat dog stuff too. Stop by and meet Oliver, their "salescat."

Frame Mart & Gallery
Pleasure Island Plaza, 1009 N. Lake Park Blvd., Carolina Beach
(910) 458-6116

Owner Scott Brown offers a full line of custom framing services, including pick up and delivery, in this combination art gallery and frame shop. In addition, Scott offers photo and frame restoration. Bring in a treasured piece for framing or select a favorite from the varied range of work from local, regional and national artists. Framed artwork is also available for purchase, and the shop carries the Harbour Lights lighthouses. Frame Mart & Gallery is open year-round, Tuesday through Saturday, or by appointment.

Island Colors
6 N. Lake Park Blvd., Carolina Beach
(910) 458-4674

Island Colors features a huge selection of comfortable, colorful Fresh Produce sportswear. With sizes from six months to 3X, there is something for everyone as well as coordinating swimwear and accessories. Gift certificates are available. It's open year round. Call for current hours.

Le Soleil
112 Cape Fear Blvd., Carolina Beach
(910) 458-2786

Le Soleil is a coastal lifestyle boutique offering upscale gifts, home decor and bath items. Featuring quality tees and lounge pants for women, men and kids, and Life is Good clothing and accessories, the shop also offers artwork, bath and body items, books, exclusive Soy Candles, cards and stationery, food specialties, gift baskets, kitchen accessories and pet gifts.

Linda's Fashions
201 N. Lake Park Blvd., Carolina Beach
(910) 458-7116

Linda's, open seven days a week year-round, has a wide assortment of ladies sportswear, dresses for special evenings on the town, jewelry, scarves and other accessories. You'll find resort wear made of comfortable, machine-washable material in stylish cuts and colors. Linda's Fashions is a favorite place to find top-quality ladies clothing at prices you can afford.

Peter Doran Fine Art Photography
740 Fort Fisher Blvd. N., Kure Beach
(910) 458-6893
www.peterdoranphotography.com

For over 30 years, Peter Doran has pursued his passion for photography, both academically and artistically. With a master's degree from the State University of New York at Buffalo, Peter has traveled extensively, photographing wonders of the world, both great and small. Bringing his eye and talent to the Cape Fear Coast, he now focuses exclusively on the wonders of our area. It is his photography that graces the cover and decorates the inside pages of this book. Peter specializes in matted and framed prints and his is the only local company offering high-quality, frame-able post cards of the area, 250 different scenes in all. His work is available for viewing and purchase in many of the fine galleries in this area.

Sterling Craft Mall
101 Cape Fear Blvd., Carolina Beach
(910) 458-4429

Located in a renovated 1920s building near the entrance of the Courtyard by Marriott in the heart of Carolina Beach, Sterling Craft Mall features more than 140 crafters offering everything from handmade clothes and hand-carved wooden toys to pottery and stained glass. Six artists working in assorted media are also highlighted. Five huge cases of handcrafted sterling silver jewelry will tempt you, and the low prices are impossible to resist. It's open on Friday and Saturday.

Unique Boutique
207 S. Lake Park Blvd., Carolina Beach
(910) 458-4360

Originally built as a guest cottage for a larger home, the Unique Boutique carries one-of-a-kind ladies sample clothing at wholesale prices from boutiques in various cities around the country. Additionally, clothing, shoes, hats, jewelry, accessories and swimwear are featured.

The Yankee Trader
1009 N. Lake Park Blvd., A-3,
Carolina Beach
(910) 458-0097

Look for unusual and one-of-a-kind nautical gifts at The Yankee Trader. Bestsellers are the stoneware oil-lamp lighthouses as well as canvas Maine bags, N.C. lighthouses, authentic model ships, Lefton Lighthouses and more. Known as the island's Christmas shop, the store carries Snowbabies and North Pole Village by Department 56, Margaret Furlong angels, Boyd's Bears, limited-edition Pipka

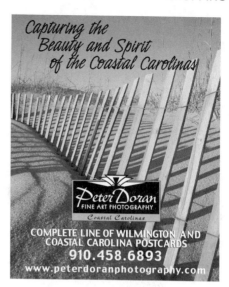

Capturing the Beauty and Spirit of the Coastal Carolinas

Peter Doran
FINE ART PHOTOGRAPHY
Coastal Carolinas

COMPLETE LINE OF WILMINGTON AND COASTAL CAROLINA POSTCARDS
910.458.6893
www.peterdoranphotography.com

Santas, Willow Tree angels, Newport collection of scrimshaw, Cape Fear throw, Mercury glass ornaments and other limited-edition collectibles.

Brunswick County Beaches

SOUTHPORT/OAK ISLAND

The quaint charm of Southport and the quiet of Oak Island's small, coastal community belie the area's growth. Recent increases in residential and commercial construction and development, plus the opening of Wal-Mart on N.C. Highway 211 between the two communities, herald a changing era for this region, and the growing number of year-round retail businesses is a reflection of this trend.

Some of the shops listed here are found within an easy walk in Southport's picturesque historic district. Leave the car parked on the street and enjoy a leisurely stroll along the town's waterfront and main thoroughfare, particularly Howe and Moore streets. You'll find gift and jewelry shops, restaurants, art galleries, clothing stores and a maritime museum. If you're interested in antiques markets, see the Southport listings in the Antiques section at the end of this chapter.

Angelwing Needle Arts
507 N. Howe St., Southport
(910) 454-9163

Angelwing is a charming needle arts shop with a great big reputation. The shop stocks such a wide range of quality supplies, kits and accessories for needlepoint, counted thread, crewel embroidery, counted cross stitch, knitting, crochet and quilting that customers come from as far away as Raleigh to shop there. Knitting and stitching groups meet in the evenings on a regular basis to receive inspiration and moral support from each other and from the staff. Finishing services are available as well.

Blue Crab Blue
4310 Long Beach Rd., Southport
(910) 454-8888

Wonder where the locals shop? Discover this quaint boat-builder's cottage near the Oak Island Bridge and you will find it brimming with handcrafted pottery, jewelry, stained glass, metal work, watercolors and other gift ideas. It is a treasure trove of specially commissioned, exclusive and one-of-a-kind arts all at affordable prices. Owner Barbara Donahue supports local and regional artists and selects each piece with an eye for detail and quality of craftsmanship. Pottery pieces, including raku, ceramic and coiled, range from artistic to utilitarian to whimsical. The hand-crafted jewelry is of excellent quality and design, made of sterling silver, sea glass and genuine stones. There's much more to see and, with year-round hours, this friendly shop is a must-visit. In addition, every purchase leaves the shop carefully and beautifully packaged. Shipping is available. After-hours appointments to see the collection are welcomed.

Books 'n Stuff
4961-11 Live Oak Village Shopping Ctr.,
Long Beach Rd., Southport
(910) 457-9017

With more than 18 years in the Oak Island-Southport area, bookstore owner Susan Warren meets the reading needs of residents and visitors alike all year long. Her store carries more than 40,000 previously read paperbacks, a large section of books on tape and CD, and hundreds of new, discounted books as well as collectible books. Not sure what you want? Susan's extensive knowledge of books and authors will ensure that you leave with just the right ones. When you're finished, trade in for credit and save on the next one. Journals, address books and book accessories are available as well.

Cape Fear Jewelers
102 E. Moore St., Southport
(910) 457-5299

Serving as Southport's jeweler since 1985, Cape Fear Jewelers boasts a large selection of 14K gold nautical jewelry, including the original Bald Head and Oak Island lighthouse charms. There you will find a wide selection of fine diamonds, gemstone jewelry, silver jewelry and brand-name watches. Conveniently located in historic downtown Southport, this full-service store offers watch repair, onsite jewelry repair and appraisals as well.

Good Ship Lollipop
108 E. Moore St., Southport
(910) 457-5034

Fondly known as Grandma's Paradise, Good Ship Lollipop well deserves its nickname. In fact, you will find a line of Camp Grandma products here, including door mats, cookie jars, flags and more. The store carries adorable clothing in sizes newborn to 6X. There are hand-knit sweaters, hats and mittens, bathing suits with matching flip flops, girls dresses with matching hats and — not to be missed — astronaut raincoats! Christening, dedication and baptism items are available as well as handmade crib quilts, Boo Boo Bunnies, Tooth Fairy Pillows, picture frames, Baby Gund and Stephan stuffed animals, colorful clocks that can be made to order by a local artist — anything your heart desires to spoil your grandchild.

Howe Street Purveyors
600-602 N. Howe St., Southport

Stopping at this shopping center on the way to downtown Southport or on the way out again is an excellent choice. **papaya island**, (910) 457-0256, offers comfortable clothing for you and your family in colors that will make you happy. **Cat on a Whisk**, (910) 454-4451, is a perfect spot to find food-related gifts — from gadgets to gourmet foods. What's more, N.C. products are featured here. **Bermuda Bay**, (910) 457-1030, is the place to shop for coastal clothing for men and women. **Live Oak Deli & Catering**, (910) 454-8104, serves lunch Monday through Saturday offering Boar's Head Brand meats and cheeses, salads available by the pound and fresh locally baked desserts.

Olde Southport Village Shoppes
1102 N. Howe St., Southport

You are sure to find something to please at this collection of shops made up of refurbished old N.C. buildings. Crickett's Cottage, (910) 201-4056, carries an eclectic mix of seashells, jewelry, gifts and antiques. At **The Prissy Parrot**, (910) 523-1203, you can indulge yourself in the tanning bed and purchase new clothing and jewelry. **A Taste of Home**, (910) 457-0713, carries clothing and gifts as well. At **Duck Duck Goose**, (910) 454-0643, you will find hand-painted items such as mailboxes, glassware and gourds as well as handmade aprons, pillow cases and more. Stop for tea and light fare in **The Pink Palace Tea Room and Gift Shoppe**, (910) 454-8385, where cottage-style furniture, vintage linens, teapots and accessories are for sale. Beginning and advanced One Stroke and Tole Painting classes are taught at **Rambling Rose**, (910) 457-7644, and here you can purchase hand-painted windows, furniture and gift items. Stock up on candles, lotion and spa wear at **Scents-abilities, Smelly Stuff for the Bath, Body and Home**, (910) 523-0587. Indulge your sweet tooth at **Brunswick Candy Company**, (910) 457-6543, where you will find Lollipop Trees, fudge and candies with local names like "Oak Island Snappers." Don't leave without visiting the **Village General Store**, (910) 448-0188, to stock up on antique "usefuls", homemade jellies, dried apples, walking sticks and more.

Ropa, Etc.
417-C N. Howe St., Southport
(910) 454-8833

Are you ready for something new and exciting? Then you're invited to experience the pleasure of fine cottons and linens, which make dressing comfortable and fun. Ropa, etc. is the area's exclusive retailer for such lines as Liz and Jane, Flax, Willow and Cut-Loose. This terrific shop also carries great makers such as Rico and Pure hand-knit sweaters, TSD, Habitat, CLICK and Kiko. Ropa, etc. is also known for its unique collection of jewelry from makers around the world

plus great accessories to complement any outfit. Sizes range from extra small to extra large and fit a variety of shapes. Ropa, etc. has two other locations to serve you: 120-B S. Front Street, Wilmington, (910) 815-0344, and 1121 Military Cutoff Suite D, Wilmington, (910) 256-8733.

Waterfront Gifts & Antiques
117 S. Howe St., Southport
(910) 457-6496

When Southport Insiders need to buy a gift, Waterfront Gifts is often their first stop. This shop, near the waterfront at the end of Howe Street, is known for distinctive gifts for all occasions, including jewelry, greeting cards, distinctive accessories, antiques, wall and table-top sculptures, books on local and regional history and a large selection of nautical gifts.

HOLDEN BEACH

Lowell's Bookworm
3004 Holden Beach Rd. SW, Holden Beach
(910) 842-7380, (877) 720-7199

L. Bookworm is a delightful place to satisfy your reading hunger. Whether you want easy beach reading or more stimulating literature, you're likely to find it here. If not, Lowell's will gladly special order it for you. They carry a good selection of new fiction, nonfiction, bestsellers, children's books and paperbacks. Used books are sold and traded; check with the store for trade-in rates. Photocopying and fax services are available. While browsing, be sure to look through the extensive regional and local history room.

OCEAN ISLE BEACH

Silver Coast Winery
6680 Barbeque Rd., Ocean Isle Beach
(910) 287-2800

If you're looking for that special gift for any occasion, Silver Coast Winery offers unique items for every taste. From beautifully handcrafted wine glasses and wine serving accessories, to kitchen items, glassware, even Christmas ornaments, you'll find a wide variety from which to choose. Need a gift basket? They will be happy to create one for you with items of your choice from the shop. Browse the art gallery (see Shopping - Galleries) featuring local artists for something really different, and don't forget a bottle or two of their award winning wines. The shop is open during regular winery hours (see our Attractions chapter).

SUNSET BEACH

Golf Cart Outlet, Inc.
7102 Ocean Hwy. W., Sunset Beach
(910) 579-8070

The Golf Cart Outlet is a remanufacturing company with a most unusual product. Here you will find golf carts converted into Street Carts (street legal golf cars). If you are looking for the perfect hunting buggy, look no further. You will find Lift Kit Carts at the Golf Cart Outlet as well. These all-terrain golf carts sport 22-inch knobby tires and a large cargo bed along with other options. Neighborhood carts, which can go as fast as 25 mph, and passenger shuttles are available, as are many custom options to suit your needs.

The Village at Sunset Beach
Corner of N.C. Hwys. 179 and 904,
Sunset Beach

This attractive shopping center brings a number of amenities — a Food Lion grocery store, a gas station, a bank, restaurants and retail stores — to the Brunswick Island communities. Specialty shops include **J. Huffman**, (910) 579-9998, a ladies' fashions and accessories boutique, and The **Blue Heron Gallery**, (910) 575-5088, an excellent choice for eclectic art and gifts. **The Pelican Bookstore**, (910) 579-8770, is a cozy place to browse for new and used titles, gifts or books highlighting local interests. Copies, UPS shipping and a fax service are available at The Pelican. Great finds in used clothing can be had at **Bloomin'deals Consignment**, (910) 575-4848. **Sunset Gourmet Cafe & Coffee Bar**, (910) 575-6759, is new in 2006. **EDGE Professional Training Fitness Studio**, (910) 471-4500, occupies second floor space.

CALABASH

Callahan's of Calabash Nautical Gifts
9973 Beach Dr., Calabash
(910) 579-2611, (800) 344-3816

Don't leave Calabash without a stop at Callahan's. The building is a huge sprawling structure that actually houses several departments under one roof, so plan for a long visit. Calabash Nautical Gifts, the store's namesake, has everything nautical you can

imagine plus a large selection of gifts, gold and silver jewelry, homemade candy and fudge, a complete card shop and much more. St. Nick Nacks Christmas Shop, the holiday (Christmas, Easter, Halloween) collectibles area of the store, boasts nearly three million ornaments. If you're a collector, this is a must-stop destination. You'll find generous selections of Christopher Radko ornaments, Seraphim Classic angels, Precious Moments, Snowbabies, Department 56 Villages and others. In yet another area of this sprawling store, you'll discover Pea Landing Mercantile. This area of Callahan's features mouthwatering fudge and homemade candy, gourmet foods, cookbooks with a coastal flair, and accessories for home or garden. Worn out from all this shopping? The benches on the building's covered wraparound porch are a great place to rest tired feet.

Reflections Stained Glass
947 Carter Dr., Calabash
(910) 575-3503

Pati Lewellyn started working in stained glass as a hobby more than 16 years ago. She found that the choice of glass and supplies was limited and dreamed of opening her own shop one day. Nine years ago she did just that, and you will find more glass and supplies in her shop than just about anywhere on the East Coast. In addition to selling pattern books, glass, grinders, saws and a complete line of supplies and tools, Pati gives classes in the shop. She teaches an "angel" class for beginners, which takes only an hour or so to do, as well as classes in the basics, cutting and grinding, lamp making, boxes, panels and anything else you might want to learn. Classes are taught one-on-one by appointment. People have come from as far as Murrells Inlet and Wilmington for classes and from Rocky Mount, Virginia and even Ireland for purchases. Custom work and group demonstrations are available.

Victoria's Ragpatch
Ragpatch Row, 10164 Beach Dr. SW,
Calabash
(910) 579-2015

This elegant shop is actually two boutiques at one location. The first floor is overflowing with a wide selection of upscale apparel for ladies and children, including shoes and accessories. The upstairs studio offers everything you need for entertaining or furnishing your home — linens, furniture, lamps, dinnerware, art and accessories. Step into the adjacent kitchen for tasty samples of assorted dips, soups, tea, coffee and pies. Gift baskets and gift wrapping are available. Victoria's Ragpatch has a second, smaller shop located on the Causeway at Ocean Isle Beach, (910) 579-3158.

The YardBird Emporium
10138 Beach Dr. SW, Calabash
(910) 575-5455

Proprietor Mary Keefe is a storehouse of knowledge about birds and squirrels, their feeding habits and their habitats. (Hint: Attaching a bluebird house to a tree is not the best or safest location as snakes and squirrels can easily get to the bluebird babies.) Proof of her knowledge can be seen in the bluebirds feeding on the porch of her shop and flying around the buildings. In addition to all kinds of supplies, such as hummingbird feeders, bird houses, squirrel feeders, field guides, bluebird nesting boxes and poles, yard ornaments, etc., The Yard Bird carries Coles Specialty Feed such as raw peanuts, safflower seed, special feeder and premium seed mixes as well as Droll Yankee and Duncraft and Vari-Craft products.

Topsail Island

Barefoot Child
The Fishing Village, 409 Roland Ave., Surf City
(910) 328-1887

Every child deserves to feel special with a gift of clothing or toys from this adorable boutique filled with "Little Baby Pretty Things." Owner Cathy Medlin has stocked the shelves with whimsical and fun to play with toys. Barefoot Child is open daily.

Beach Furniture Outfitters
520 New River Dr., Surf City
(910) 328-4181

Whether you need furnishings to completely set up housekeeping or just one special accent piece, Beach Furniture Outfitters has choices for every taste and pocketbook. Its specialty is contracting to fully furnish and equip a beach home or condominium, but don't overlook the single items available to

D's Interior Design
Furniture Gallery
featuring Traditional & Resort Furnishings

Hardwood, Ceramic, Carpet, Vinyl, Laminate, Custom Plantation Shutters, Blinds, Window Treatments, Wallpaper, Fabrics, Accessories, Unique Gifts, & Jewelry

Creative Interior Design
by Donna Wells, Owner
Interior Designer/AAS

834 Hwy 210 Sneads Ferry, NC 28460
(910) 327-2166

complete your decorating scheme. Free set up and delivery are offered on the island. It's open daily except Sunday.

Bert's Surf Shop
310 N. New River Dr., Surf City
(910) 328-1010

A longtime favorite on the beach, Bert's has a full line of name-brand swimwear and sportswear for the whole family as well as footwear, beach T-shirts and sunglasses. It also offers a full line of sports equipment for sale, including skateboards and surfing gear. It's open seven days a week.

D's Interior Designs
834 N.C. Hwy. 210, Sneads Ferry
(910) 327-2166

This is the place to find everything you want for your home. D's Interior Design offers traditional and beach furniture, unique gifts and creative interior design items, including wallpaper, fabrics for custom bedspreads and window treatments, upholstery, carpet, vinyl, laminate floor coverings, art work and accessories. D's is also an authorized Yankee Candle Dealer. It's open Monday through Saturday.

Docksider Gifts & Shells
14061 Ocean Hwy. 50, Surf City
(910) 328-1421

Here you can have that special sharks' tooth you found on the beach wired into jewelry while you browse through this family-

DDT—Outlet

3 Locations to Serve you!
Hampstead, Wilmington, Sneads Ferry

Huge Selection of In Stock Inventory

Complete Condo Packages

Custom Ordered Sofas

Large Selection of Wicker Furniture & All Weather Wicker

Everything you need for your home in one place!

Come See Us For All Your Tables & Chairs, Upholstered Furniture, Barstools, Nautical Items, & More!

Interior Design Services Available

We Carry a Complete Line of Mattresses

Large Selection of Outdoor Furniture

LARGEST
Selection of Nautical Gifts & Accessories in North Carolina!

www.DDTOUTLET.com

Main Location
21740 Hwy.17 North, Hampstead, NC
(Between Hilltop BP and the Rt. 17/210 light)

We Ship Anywhere Open 7 Days a Week!

Call Toll Free
1-877-954-6367
Local **910-329-0160**

DDT 2 896 Route 210, Sneads Ferry, NC
(Near Four Corners)

DDT Outlet 7222 Market St., Wilmington, NC
(Formerly Pinehurst Pottery) (910) 686-0338

friendly beach store with more than 100,000 items. Fresh saltwater taffy, shells, wind chimes, Thirstystone coasters, books, paint sets, postcards and T-shirts fill every inch of this store. Be sure to check out the Docksider's new Family Fun Center featuring video games, snacks and a playland. The Docksider is open daily.

East Coast Sports
The Fishing Village, 409 Roland Ave., Surf City
(910) 328-1887

East Coast Sports carries a full line of sports clothing including Columbia, Bimini Bay and Sperry Topsiders. In addition to clothing, you can find everything you could ever want or need for inshore or offshore fishing, including a professional staff to answer all your questions. East Coast is open year round.

The Fishing Village
409 Roland Ave., Surf City
(910) 328-1887

The Fishing Village is a nice collection of shops, conveniently located in Surf City. Built

in a reproduction fishing village style and centrally located overlooking the Intracoastal Waterway, the village offers an interesting alternative when vacationers want to get off the beach for an afternoon.

The Gift Basket
702 S. Anderson Blvd., Topsail Beach
(910) 328-7111

Serving the area since 1973, The Gift Basket is best known for its line of fine jewelry, but there is much more. The Gift Basket also features an impressive line of tide and nautical clocks and precision weather instruments. The Gift Basket is open every day.

Iron Pelican Emporium
110 N. New River Dr., Surf City
(910) 328-1616
www.ironpelican.com

Iron Pelican Emporium offers a wide selection of truly unique merchandise. You can find a nice selection of dressy sportswear for women, cute shoes, vintage and contemporary purses and hats, accessories and fabulous jewelry. The Iron Pelican also has collectible and antique glassware, ceramics and dishware, including vintage cookie jars. This is a great place to shop for yourself or someone special. It's open daily in season, with limited winter hours.

Island Traders
311 S. Topsail Dr., Surf City
(910) 328-1004

Daily shipments of new merchandise assures shoppers a surprise each time they visit Island Traders. Name brand and catalog clothing at 40 to 70 percent below retail for guys and gals makes this a good place to stock up on golf, casual and school clothing.

Island Treasures
627 S. Anderson Blvd., Topsail Beach
(910) 328-4487

The treasures in this shop are many and varied. In the clothing department, one can choose from casual clothes for women, such as the popular Cotton Connection line. Their "Topsail Time" T-shirts and sweatshirts are favorites for the entire family. Island Treasures carries a surprisingly wide array of gifts that include wonderful nautical prints, lamps, flags, windsocks, a full line of sunglasses, hats and beach supplies. There are also wooden toys from Melissa & Doug and cuddly over-sized stuffed animals to amuse and intrigue the younger set. The shop is open daily from Easter through September, with reduced winter hours.

Mea's Jewelry and Gifts
Treasure Coast Square,
208F N. River Dr., Surf City
(910) 328-0920

Looking for that special decorating item for your home or garden? Mea's has a selection of collectible lighthouses, accessories, flags, rugs, art candles and dishware. In addition to high-quality decorating items and specialty furniture, the store offers a wide variety of jewelry and watches, decorative beach bags, hats and other gift selections. In winter, hours are cut back.

Mystic Treasures Jewelry
121 S. Topsail Dr., Surf City
(910) 328-6300

This new shop carries gorgeous sterling silver, 14K and 18K gold and platinum jewelry. All of their jewelry is designed and handcrafted by local and regional artists. Mystic Trea-

Iron Pelican

WOMENS CLOTHING & ACCESSORIES

ANTIQUES

GIFTS

COLLECTABLES

EMPORIUM

110 NORTH NEW RIVER DRIVE
SURF CITY, NORTH CAROLINA 28445

TEL (910) 328-1616   FAX (910) 328-3407

open daily 9 - 6
sunday 11 - 5

WWW.IRONPELICAN.COM

sures also offers custom-designed jewelry and repairs. They are open seven days a week during the summer and are closed Mondays during the winter months.

Pastimes Toys and Gifts
Treasure Coast Plaza, 208D N. New River Dr., Surf City
(910) 328-2737

This quality toy store offers a wide selection of fun and educational toys to capture the imagination. Whether the interest is puzzles, science, games, arts and crafts or construction, the appropriate toy can be found on these well-stocked shelves. Pastimes is a great place for grandparents and parents to find the special gift. It ranks high on the list of unique specialty shops on Topsail Island. It's open daily.

Quarter Moon books & gifts
708 S. Anderson Blvd., Topsail Beach
(910) 328-4969, (910) 328-2300,
(800) 697-9134

Offering fascinating pages and gifts to enchant, Topsail Island's bookstore, Quarter Moon, offers a good range of hardcover and paperback books and an excellent selection of stationery, greeting cards and note cards. Quarter Moon's kids section has great books for all ages. The expanded gift selection includes pajamas, robes, slippers, sandals, lots of beach bags and hats. There are gifts for all occasions and many turtle-related items. A selection of smoothies, cappuccino or coffee drinks can be enjoyed in the outside seating

Boats resting in quiet harbors make for a lovely view in many coastal towns.

photo: Peter Doran

area, or inside if you choose. It's open year round.

Radio Shack
**1950 N.C. Hwy. 172, Ste. A., Sneads Ferry
(910) 327-1478
13741 Ocean Hwy. 50, Ste. B., Surf City
(910) 329-5000**

Specializing in consumer electronics, these conveniently located Radio Shacks have the parts and pieces you may have forgotten to bring on vacation with your electronic equipment. Radio Shack carries a good inventory of replacement batteries, battery packs, prepaid phone cards, flashlights and alarm clocks. They are open Monday through Saturday.

Spinnaker Surf Shop
**111 N. Shore Dr., Surf City
(910) 328-2311**

Spinnaker's is Surf City's location for surf and skate brands such as Quiksilver, Billabong, Rip Curl, Rusty, Lost, Volcom, Hurley and O'Neill. The store also has a large selection of girls' surf brand apparel, swimsuits and accessories. This great surf shop carries designer eyewear such as Oakley, Electric and Dragon; shoes and sandals by DC, DVS, QS/Roxy, Reef, Rainbow and Globe; and novelty gifts. The Spinnaker Arcade down below offers dozens of traditional games including pool tables, foosball and video games;

it's a cool place out of the sun. Looking for surfboards to buy or rent? Spinnaker's has a large selection. It's open daily, year round (but it's closed Tuesdays in the winter).

Starfish Distinctive Gifts & Treasures
**14210 N.C. Hwy. 50, Ste. B, Surf City
(910) 328-5500**

This new gift shop is wall-to-wall cute and filled with the irresistible. Between their gorgeous line of silver metalware serving pieces, fun Nora Fleming cake plates and platters and other unique items for the home, the Starfish is a great place to shop for that perfect wedding or hostess gift. There is a nice selection of lotions and candles, including Caswell-Massey baby and spa products, beautiful seashell soaps and Camille Beckman's Mango Beach spa line. Starfish also features paintings by local artists, jewelry and pirate toys for kids. The shop offers complimentary gift-wrapping, and shipping is available.

Surf City Florist
**106 N. Topsail Dr., Surf City
(910) 328-3238**

Fresh flowers for special occasions are not all you'll find in this delightful shop. Also check out their balloons, plants and stuffed animals. Local flower delivery is available. Surf City Florist is open every day but Sunday.

Topsail Art Gallery
& Frame Shop

"Where Every Piece Is a Treasure"

Take home a piece of Topsail Island

Topsail Photos

ART POTTERY GLASS & MORE

121 South Topsail Dr. Surf City, NC 328-2138

Mystic Treasures
Jewelry

Proudly supporting american artists

121 S. Topsail Drive, Surf City NC 910-328-6300

Surf City Shopping Center Gift Shop
Corner of Roland Ave. and Topsail Dr.,
Surf City
(910) 328-0835

Bathing suits and casual wear for the whole family plus a variety of other vacation and beach items can be found here. Since this store is connected to the IGA grocery store, the merchandise in the grocery store, such as sunscreen, toiletries, magazines and paperback books, complements the items in the gift shop, allowing a great opportunity for one-stop shopping. It's open daily in the summer season and closed Tuesdays in the winter.

Surfside Sportswear and Gifts
314 N. New River Dr., Surf City
(910) 328-4141

A year-round favorite with residents, Surfside offers the most complete line of women's clothing on the island. The racks are always filled with bathing suits, casual wear and party attire in a wide variety of sizes and in styles for the young and not-so-young. In addition to clothing, Surfside has a great shoe selection, an assortment of jewelry,

glassware and decorating items. It's open daily year round.

Topsail Art Gallery
121 S. Topsail Dr., Surf City
(910) 328-2138

If you are searching for a gorgeous coastal photograph, watercolor, print or painting, Topsail Art Gallery is the area's premier location. American artists are highlighted here and they have a wide variety of originals and reproductions from local, regional and nationally known artists. The gallery offers unique gift items, blown glass, ceramics and great hand-crafted metal sculptures, copper fountains and birdbaths. An on-site frame shop can custom-frame any selection. The gallery is open year round. Owners Mike and Judy Hendy pride themselves on their ability to fill customers' special requests.

The Topsail Island Trading Company
201 New River Dr., Surf City
(910) 328-1905

The Topsail Island Trading company carries a variety of gourmet items, specialty gifts, a line of fine causal clothing for the whole family, plus jewelry and accessories. While browsing you may detect a delicious aroma — that's the famous homemade fudge you've been hearing so much about. With more than 50 flavors to choose from it's really hard to make a choice, yet it's impossible to leave the Trading Company without a box or bag of fudge in hand. Topsail Island Trading Co. is open daily.

HAMPSTEAD

DDT-Outlet
21740 N.C. Hwy. 17 N., Hampstead
(910) 329-0160
www.ddtoutlet.com

If you're looking for furniture and accessories with a beach or nautical theme, you'll find it at the DDT Outlet. With more than 20,000 square feet of unique merchandise to chose from and services ranging from complete beach house and condominium packages to shipping purchases back home, shopping in this great store is a must. Be sure to have plenty of time to browse displays of furniture, nautical gifts, wicker, barstools, pictures, yard ornaments, PVC furniture and more. Owners Tom and Niki Miller also offer a large, descriptive catalog to assist clients. If you need help in the selection of your furniture package, Niki is the expert, according to Tom. DDT is open seven days a week, year round.

The Flower Basket of Hampstead
14361 U.S. Hwy. 17 N., Hampstead
(910) 270-4141, (877) 607-7615

If you love having beautiful floral arrangements in your home, whether for entertaining or "just because," this is the place to shop. The Flower Basket maintains an extensive inventory of fresh-cut flowers. The shop also carries a selection of green houseplants, fine gifts, quality candles and a variety of plush animals. A full-service florist, The Flower Basket staff can help with wedding bouquets, special orders and funeral arrangements.

My Front Porch Gifts & Collectibles
224 Hampstead Village Dr., Hampstead
(910) 270-1177, (888) 302-2955

This eclectic gift shop has so much variety that you can spend an entire afternoon browsing. There are garden items, wind chimes and flags, baby gifts, wedding gifts, Heritage Lace curtains and linens, gourmet foods, hunting gear, golfing and nautical items, men's attire, women's fashion items, a year-round Christmas room and more. My Front Porch is also the home of Carolina Peanut products with freshly made peanut butter and boiled peanuts daily. Open Monday through Saturday from 10 AM to 5 PM year round, My Front Porch offers complementary gift wrapping and is a UPS shipper location.

Antiques

HISTORIC DOWNTOWN WILMINGTON

Antiquers can spend days exploring Wilmington's varied antiques stores, which span the spectrum in size, price and quality. Park the car along Front Street, adjacent streets or in a downtown parking deck and set off on foot to discover infinite treasures. Or head to the New Castle Antiques District on Castle Street between 5th and 7th streets, an area undergoing revitalization. Start your shopping day with breakfast or take a break for lunch at one of the District's many eateries such as Halls at 5th and Castle, a neighborhood favorite since 1920, or Jester's Java inside the Newcastle Antique Center.

To guide you through the more than 250,000 square feet of Wilmington's antiques and collectibles stores, pick up a copy of *A Guide to Greater Wilmington Antique Shops* leaflet at any of the antiques stores listed in this chapter. It is compiled by the Greater Wilmington Antique Dealers Association and contains a map with brief descriptions of about 35 shops and dealers. Unfortunately they can't all be included here, so put on your walking shoes, pick up the map and venture out into the past.

Adams on Castle
606 1/2 Castle St., Wilmington
(910) 251-2224

Adams on Castle houses a wide range of antiques, including period furniture, nautical artifacts, fine art, china, crystal and silver. Appraisals are available by owner Charles Adams, a veteran appraiser for more than 30 years in Wilmington.

The Ivy Cottage

A Wonderful Treasure Hunt! Hundreds Of New Items Every Day!

Wilmington's Finest Consignment Shop

Antiques • Classic Furniture • China, Crystal and Silver • Oriental Carpets • Fine Jewelry • Lamps & Mirrors • Light Fixtures
Over 20,000 Square Feet!

910-815-0907   www.threecottages.com
3020-3030-3100 Market Street • Wilmington • Mon-Sat 10-6 • Sunday 1-5

Antiques of Old Wilmington
25 S. Front St., Wilmington
(910) 763-6011

Established in 1982, this store has been in the same location longer than any of the city's antiques shops. Antiques of Old Wilmington specializes in antique lighting fixtures, mahogany furniture, china, silver and glassware.

Eddies Antiques & Collectibles
127 N. Front St., Wilmington
(910) 342-0026

Eddies holds an eclectic assortment of furniture, silver, rugs, jewelry, china, crystal and much more. You can browse for hours. It's open Monday through Saturday from 9 AM to 5 PM.

Michael Moore Antiques
539 Castle St., Wilmington
(910) 763-0300

Located in the New Castle Antiques District, this shop features 3,200 square feet of antique furniture, glassware and sterling silver. Michael Moore Antiques is partnered with the Antique Emporium, which special-izes in lamps, light fixtures, glass shades and offers a large selection of parts for lamps and light fixtures.

Newcastle Antique Center
606 Castle St., Wilmington
(910) 341-7228

You'll find a huge selection in the New-castle Antique Center. This upscale antiques mall represents about 30 dealers of antique wicker, fine furniture, Heisey glass, porcelain, silver and more. Shop at your leisure, then take a break and refuel at Jester's Java, a coffee shop and cafe located right in the mall. The Newcastle Antique Center is open Monday through Saturday from 10 AM to 5 PM and Sunday 1 to 5 PM. Jester's Java is closed on Sunday.

MIDTOWN WILMINGTON

The Ivy Cottage
3020, 3030 & 3100 Market St., Wilmington
(910) 815-0907
www.threecottages.com

The Ivy Cottage is Wilmington's premiere furniture and home accessory consignment shop, consisting of three buildings with more than 20,000 square feet in all. Each of the buildings is filled to overflowing with antiques, classic furniture, china, crystal, silver, oriental carpets and fine jewelry. There are also two large garden areas with outdoor furniture, fountains, planters, fencing, gazebos and wrought iron decorative pieces. Hundreds of new items arrive daily. Spend a few hours or a couple of days! You'll probably never see the same thing twice. The Ivy Cottage is a wonderful treasure hunt! Hours are Monday through Saturday from 10 AM to 6 PM and Sunday from 1 to 5 PM. Call for winter hours.

SOUTH COLLEGE ROAD AND MONKEY JUNCTION AREA

While a large number of antiques stores are clustered in downtown Wilmington and the New Castle Antique District, there are other opportunities for antiquing around the region. Listed below are additional shops in Wilmington and the rest of the region.

Betty B's Trash To Treasure
6333-B Myrtle Grove Rd., Wilmington
(910) 798-0633

If you love to stroll through antiques, collectibles and memorabilia, you'll love Betty B's. This store is filled with just about everything, including estate jewelry, small furniture, linens, an impressive collection of china and glassware, books and much more. You can also have porcelain and china restored here.

SOUTHPORT /OAK ISLAND

Magnolia Gifts & Antiques
301 N. Howe St., Southport
(910) 457-4982

Visitors to this pristine shop will find a large selection of gifts, decorative accessories and jewelry on the first floor. An attractively arranged second floor features antiques, garden gifts, silk and dried floral arrangements and more.

Northrup Antiques Mall
111 E. Moore St., Southport
(910) 457-9569

Antiques shoppers will delight in the 38 antiques and collectibles dealers housed under one roof in historic downtown Southport.

Throughout this one-stop-shopping, two-story building, shoppers will find a variety of unique gifts. The possibilities for found treasures include antique furniture and accessories, sterling silver, Slow Blue, antique toys, glassware, linens, porcelain, books, Civil War artifacts, Byers Choice Carolers and nautical treasures. Don't miss the specialty candles by A. I. Root. Original artwork by local artists is featured and sold exclusively in this shop.

Southport Antiques
105 E. Moore St., Southport
(910) 457-1755

Quality antiques and consignments are a specialty of this store. Look for antique furniture, quilts, art, rugs, porcelain, nautical items, glass, folk art, silver, jewelry, linens and more. Need a personal property appraisal for insurance or estate purposes? This service is available at Southport Antiques.

TOPSAIL ISLAND

Old Chapel Antiques
322 Sneads Ferry Rd., Sneads Ferry
(910) 327-2060

A selection of oak, mahogany and cherry furniture and oak fireplace mantels are just some of the pieces you will find at Old Chapel Antiques. The owners, the McLaughlins, look for unusual and hard-to-find items for their shop. From Depression glass to comic books to a large collection of Hot Wheels cars and Precious Moments, you can find almost anything and everything here. Call the above number for hours or an appointment.

BURGAW

Burgaw Antiqueplace
101 S. Wright St., Burgaw
(910) 259-7070

If you're a serious shopper, you won't want to miss this place. There are 50 dealers located in 15,000 square feet. It's known as the largest antique mall in eastern North Carolina. The list of items is endless but includes dishes, glassware, pottery, furniture, silver, primitives and jewelry. With an antique furniture refinisher on the premises, furniture can be purchased and restored all in one place. If you wish to do your own refinishing, they also have a booth selling refinishing supplies. There are two appraisers on site that are available by appointment. Deliveries are available. To add to your shopping pleasure, try some of their fresh fudge sold on the premises. Burgaw Antiqueplace is open daily.

Furniture

HISTORIC DOWNTOWN WILMINGTON

Carolina Furniture
315 Red Cross St., Wilmington
(910) 762-4452

This family-owned business has been a Wilmington landmark since 1922 and is the only full-service furniture store in the downtown area. It offers home furnishings for every room in the house, most major household appliances, TVs and DVDs, stereos and more. The store takes pride in offering its customers reasonable, everyday prices and an affordable in-store financing plan. Customer parking, a plus in downtown Wilmington, is available.

UNIVERSITY AREA

Rose Bros. Furniture
421 S. College Rd., Wilmington
(910) 791-1110
5128 Oleander Rd., Wilmington
(910) 791-3471

Since 1953, family-owned Rose Bros. Furniture has been a Wilmington institution. Here you can find quality home furnishings, fine bedding and accessories at affordable prices, with such name brands as Ashley, Broyhill, Bassett, La-Z Boy, Sealy Posturepedic, Stearns & Foster and Simmons Beautyrest. Hallmarks of Rose Bros. Furniture are exceptional customer service, knowledgeable staff, flexible financing and professional decorating support.

SOUTH COLLEGE ROAD AND MONKEY JUNCTION AREA

Murrow Furniture Galleries
3514 S. College Rd., Wilmington
(910) 799-4010
www.murrowfurniture.com

Since 1979, family owned and operated Murrow Furniture Galleries has been serving the Cape Fear region with quality home furnishings at discount prices. It's all here, from

Get Inspired.

Everyone's got their own design ideas. That's why I love working with Norwalk. With thousands of fabrics and hundreds of styles designed to inspire, you can get custom furniture that's just right for you. And their professional design consultants will help you pull the whole look together.

You furnish the idea. Norwalk will furnish the rest.

Candice Olson
Interior Designer and host of Divine Design

Mayfaire Town Center
Wilmington, NC
910-256-7919

NORWALK®
THE FURNITURE IDEA

norwalkfurnitureidea.com

contemporary design to traditional elegance, set in a world of extraordinary style.

Their 66,000-square-foot gallery showcases hundreds of top-quality name brands such as Drexel Heritage, Thomasville, Bernhardt's Martha Stewart, Henkel Harris, and Lexington's Tommy Bahama and Liz Claiborne collections. They also have the largest selection in southeastern North Carolina of lamps, artwork, accessories and unique accent items from all over the world.

Murrow's staff of interior design professionals will help you make the perfect choices for your home, from a single piece to a complete turn-key design project. Whatever your home-furnishing desires, Murrow Furniture has just what you need.

MILITARY CUTOFF ROAD AREA

Blue Hand Home
The Forum,
1125 Military Cutoff Rd., Wilmington
(910) 509-0088

This delightfully eclectic store's theme is "casual, chic and uncomplicated luxury." You're bound to find irresistible choices in furniture, including armoires, beds, dining rooms and original and reproduction pieces inspired by old world craftsmanship. Upholstered furniture is clad in rich chenille, damask, linens or leather. Make decorating a delight with cashmere throws, stylish lighting, scented Votivo candles and more. Professional interior design services, from blueprint to complete decoration, are available.

Norwalk - The Furniture Idea
Village at Mayfaire, Wilmington
(910) 256-7919
www.norwalkfurniture.com

Looking for something fresh and new in home furnishings? The design experts at Norwalk - The Furniture Idea will help you create custom furniture and decor that suits your personal style. This family owned and operated company offers design solutions and custom, upholstered furniture made to your specifications. Their professional design team offers personalized service. They'll even come to your home and measure, draw floor plans and help you blend your new furniture and accessories with those you already have. You'll get exactly what you want. With more than 1,000 fabrics and 100 furniture styles to choose from, it's easy to find just the right combination to suit your style. Once you've made your selections, your furniture will be custom made to your order and delivered to your home in 35 days.

Norwalk has been making custom upholstered furniture since 1902. Now they've team with designer Candice Olson for some "divine designs." This trend-setting store is the only one of it's kind in Wilmington and well worth a visit.

MARKET STREET AREA

The Master's Touch
Dutch Square Industrial Park,
300 Old Dairy Rd., Wilmington
(910) 799-4545

Serving the Wilmington area's furniture needs since 1978, The Master's Touch showroom, open Monday through Friday, features fine furniture from original antiques to reproduction and contemporary pieces. They are especially noted for repair and beautiful restoration services of elegant originals to simple sentimental pieces. Winning the title of "Top 125 Craftsmen in North America" by Fine Woodworking magazine and featured in the March 2005 issue of Southern Living magazine, The Master's Touch is now well known for specialty carving and original designs of American art pieces being considered for the White House.

Featured in the Raleigh News & Observer, their hand-carved duck, turkey and geese calls are truly works of art and are carved from a variety of hardwoods. They can be custom-designed to feature the image of a hunter's favorite dog or the hunter's initials. Collectible boxes for displaying these unique masterpieces are also available.

SOUTHPORT

Mangoes
619C N. Howe St., Southport
(910) 454-8000

Step into a tropical paradise right in downtown Southport. You will find beautifully hand-crafted furniture of mahogany and cane with a relaxed, West Indies feel included in the line carried by this exotic shop. Holley Rogers, shop owner, imports much of her merchandise from Egypt, India and Honduras and blends the furniture with exquisite gifts and accessories. Lamps, paintings, bookends and more, featuring monkeys, palm trees and even camels await you. The staff is available to visit your home and help you with decorating ideas.

Galleries

HISTORIC DOWNTOWN
WILMINGTON

American Pie
113 Dock St., Wilmington
(910) 251-2131

This is a delightful shop of contemporary American crafts and folk art. Here you'll discover some of the most unusual arts and crafts in the Southeast. About 100 American artists are represented and their work includes handmade furniture by Sticks, hand-blown glass, unusual jewelry, hammered metals, ceramics, one-of-a-kind handmade books and hand-carved whistles.

Fidler's Gallery and Framing
The Cotton Exchange, Nutt St., Wilmington
(910) 762-2001

The collections found here include limited-edition pieces, fine-art posters and originals from a wide range of local, regional, national and international artists. These artists include Timberlake, Mangum, Wysocki, Landry, Wyeth, Kunstler and many more.

THE GOLDEN GALLERY

The Gallery for regional imagery.

910-762-4651 • The Cotton Exchange • www.thegoldengallery.com

Among the many and varied subjects are florals, wildlife, seascapes and the Civil War. Professional custom framing is also available. Housed within the gallery, Wrigley's Clocks offers a selection of timepieces such as wall, mantel and floor (or grandfather) clocks. Wrigley's services what it sells with authorized factory repairs as well as all other makes of clocks. They even make house calls.

The Golden Gallery
The Cotton Exchange,
307 N. Front St., Wilmington
(910) 762-4651
www.thegoldengallery.com

The Golden Gallery is truly a family affair. Mary Ellen Golden's original watercolors and prints depicting Wilmington landmarks and southeastern North Carolina scenery are well-known and sought after among visitors and residents alike. Husband John Golden, songwriter and storyteller, is noted for his songs about coastal Carolina's legends, folklore, characters and events. CDs of these ballads and sea songs, including the Civil War era "The Fall of Fort Fisher," and "Colonial Songs and Scottish Ballads" featuring "The Battle at Moore's Creek" are available at the gallery. His most recent CD is "Hatteras Memories," featuring original songs of lighthouses, coastal life-saving stations and the brave people who ran them. Fine-art photography and illustrations of local landmarks are son John W. Golden's specialty, and many of his black and white and color prints are on display. Mary Ellen has been painting in watercolor since 1975

and has been in the Cotton Exchange since 1977. Her techniques and tips are featured in a video, Watercolor Can Be Easy, created by Mary Ellen and Wilmington artist Eloise Bethell. It's available for sale in the gallery.

New Elements Gallery
216 N. Front St., Wilmington
(910) 343-8997

A downtown Wilmington arts destination since 1985, this award-winning gallery features a wide range of contemporary and traditional works in oil, watercolor, acrylic and mixed media. Decorative and functional pieces in glass, ceramics, fiber and wood are also featured, as well as handcrafted jewelry. A sampling of the artists at New Elements Gallery include Claude Howell, Dorothy Gillespie, Bruce Bowman, Robert Irwin, Kyle Highsmith, Nancy Tuttle May, Sally Bowen Prange and Dina Wilde-Ramsing.

OLEANDER DRIVE AREA

Serenity Place Gallery
Anderson Square,
4113 Oleander Dr., Ste. E, Wilmington
(910) 794-1944, (877) 509-2823

If you love the artwork of Thomas Kinkade, the "painter of light," Serenity Place Gallery is a must see. This small but elegant gallery is filled with Kinkade's breath-taking prints and limited-edition pieces. Gift items featuring the artist's distinctive style include beautiful coffee-table books, stationery, collector's plates, calendars, music boxes and more. Serenity Place is also an authorized Bradford dealer.

UNIVERSITY AREA

The Gallery at Racine
203 Racine Dr., Wilmington
(910) 452-2073
www.racinecenter.com

Located in the Racine Center for the Arts, this gallery is a welcoming and comfortable place for art enthusiasts of all ages. The Gallery at Racine exhibits one-of-a-kind artwork by local and nationally renowned artists with an eclectic collection of artwork in a variety of styles and price ranges, including sculpture, oils, watercolor, acrylics, pottery, raku, blown glass printmaking and more. Special shows are highlights at the gallery, and exhibits change every six to eight weeks. The Gallery features the work of thirteen-year-old child prodigy, George Pocheptsov; the unique driftwood and copper sculptures of local artist Shaw Lakey; the limited-edition reproductions of Dr. Seuss; and many more. The Gallery at Racine also sponsors the non-profit Racine School of the Arts, which provides fine art and clay classes, workshops and camps for all ages and skill levels in a positive setting. Contact the gallery for more information and class schedules.

Walls Fine Art Gallery
2173 Wrightsville Ave., Wilmington
(910) 343-1703

Exhibiting fine original oil paintings — many painted by nationally respected artists — in a 3,000-square-foot gallery, owners David Leadman and Nancy Marshall, painters themselves, use their more than 60 years of experience to consult with clients to help them make the best selection. They'll even simplify the selection process by bringing art to your home. Walls offers the finest hand-carved and gilded frames suitable for artwork from contemporary abstract to 12th-century icon.

SOUTH COLLEGE ROAD AND MONKEY JUNCTION AREA

Artworks Fine Art Gallery
5226 S. College Rd., Ste. 6, Wilmington
(910) 392-6545

The only fine art gallery and framing location in the Monkey Junction area, Artworks

Gallery displays original fine art in a wide variety of media (oils, pastels, acrylics, watercolors, mixed media, photography, ceramics, pottery and glass). Artworks Fine Art Gallery has something to suit every art lover. Artists represented are locally, regionally, nationally and internationally renowned. Owner Gloria Ezzell, a designer with 30 years of experience, can assist you with every decorating need. She and her staff can help you choose the perfect work of art, and with their professional, onsite framing services, they can guide you in your framing choices. The end result will be a comfortable and gorgeous home that is truly a work of art. Come "expose yourself to fine art"!

MILITARY CUTOFF ROAD AREA

Fountainside Fine Art Gallery
Lumina Station, 1900 Eastwood Rd., Ste. 44, Wilmington
(910) 256-9956
www.fountainsidegallery.com

Fountainside Gallery is one of Wilmington's leading destinations for fine art. Representing local, regional and national artists, Fountainside has a selection of art that will appeal to the serious collector as well as the casual art lover. The gallery regularly hosts exhibitions and educational demonstrations, inviting artists from across the U.S. to capture the beauty of the Cape Fear Coast. As well as placing art with residential customers, they work with corporate clients and design professionals. Come and enjoy the paintings, sculpture, glass and woodwork in the Fountainside's intimate, relaxed environment. You'll find the Fountainside Gallery on Eastwood Road before the Wrightsville Beach Drawbridge in Lumina Station.

Spectrum Gallery
The Forum II, 1121 Military Cutoff Rd., Wilmington
(910) 256-2323, (888) 233-1444

Spectrum Gallery offers an exciting collection of handcrafted jewelry, original fine art, pottery and art glass. Local and regional artists, working in a variety of media, including watercolors, oils, pastels and multimedia, are featured in an ever-changing collection of original art. The gallery's art-glass collection represents glassblowers from North America. Gallery owner, Star Sosa is an award-winning jewelry designer, specializing in custom jewelry in silver, gold and platinum.

SOUTHPORT/OAK ISLAND

ArtShak Studio, Gallery and Sculpture Garden
822 N. Howe St., Southport
(910) 457-1757, (910) 457-0374

The ArtShak has moved to a new location — and what a shack! Thom Seaman, sculptor, and Linda Platt, artist, began their adventure in Southport in 1997 in a small wooden building with no heat, determined to live their dream of making a living doing what they love. After upsizing twice they have finally built a space worthy of their work. The front section of the U-shaped building encompasses the gallery. The ceiling soars to 20 feet with 14 windows lining the top, allowing ambient light to enter. Here you will find paintings and painted glassware including windows from Linda's creative hands. By commission she paints furniture in all its personalities from impressionistic to funky to just cool — whatever your taste requires. Thom's striking metal sculptures also inhabit this area. The free-standing, wall-hung sculptures and mobiles are made from aluminum, brass, copper and steel, and some are finished with textures, patinas or paints. You will find art by potters, fabric artists and other painters as well. The wings of the U are private areas including studios. A sculpture garden is in the center. Developed around three venerable live oaks, which were lovingly left standing by the planning and construction of the building, the garden includes a waterfall fountain and pond to complement the gorgeous flowering plants. You can see why Thom says they have created an environment, not a business. In addition to the art in the gallery, Thom and Linda accept commissions for custom designs, including murals. Thom says, "If we design it together, you will love it forever."

Franklin Square Gallery
130 E. West St., Southport
(910) 457-5450

Since 1979 Franklin Square Gallery has been operated by the nonprofit Associated Artists of Southport. It is housed in an impressive century-old historic building in the heart of Southport directly behind Franklin Square Park. The association is responsible

FOUNTAINSIDE
fine art gallery
LUMINA STATION
1900 EASTWOOD RD SUITE 44
WILMINGTON, NC 28403 • 910-256-9956

Rick McClure "Summer Rentals" 26" x 30" oil on canvas

OFFERING ORIGINAL FINE ART & SCULPTURE
MAJOR CREDIT CARDS ACCEPTED
DELIVERY & SHIPPING AVAILABLE
WWW.FOUNTAINSIDEGALLERY.COM

for maintaining and operating the gallery and a pottery studio located on the grounds behind it. The City of Southport provides the buildings and maintains the exteriors. The expectation was that the artists would create and maintain an important cultural center and, indeed, they have. In addition to the workshops, classes and competitions provided by the association, the gallery features paintings and pottery of its members, the annual exhibit of the Oak Island Quilters challenge squares, the annual Brunswick County Photography Contest sponsored by the Brunswick County Parks and Recreation Department, and artwork of the students of the Brunswick County Public School System. All paintings and pottery in the gallery are available for sale to the public.

Ricky Evans Gallery and Southport Picture Framing Company
211 N. Howe St., Southport
(910) 457-1129

The Ricky Evans Gallery features his lighthouse paintings in addition to a series of paintings of historic Southport landmarks and a coastal waterfront series. Don't miss the "Lighthouse Room" which features all the lighthouses of the lower Cape Fear and includes note cards with views of the Oak Island Lighthouse done by local artists. Proceeds from these and other items are donated to the Friends of the Oak Island Lighthouse for use in preserving this historic landmark. Original paintings, watercolors and limited-edition posters are available as well.

In addition to numerous private art galleries, southeastern North Carolina also features great art displays in public spaces.

photo: Ashley, student of DREAMS Center for Arts Education

In other rooms of the quaint old house that houses the gallery, you will find paintings, pottery, stained glass, metal sculptures and more, all the work of local artists, on display and for sale. Custom picture framing is available, and the gallery is open year round. Tucked on the south side and to the rear of the gallery, Spencer Pottery is a must stop. It is a small pottery shop and working studio where classes can be scheduled as well.

OCEAN ISLE BEACH

Silver Coast Winery
6680 Barbeque Rd., Ocean Isle Beach
(910) 287-2800

"Most works of art, like most wines, ought to be consumed in the district of their fabrication," declared British author Rebecca West. At Silver Coast Winery, you can sample and purchase both local wine and local art in the winery's on-site gallery. Featuring the works of Michael Rigsbee, Rusty Hughes,

Justine Ferreri and others, the gallery focuses on the area's talent in ever-changing exhibits. The light and airy hall with its soaring ceiling allows artists the space for imaginative display, so you'll never know what you'll find there. The gallery is open during normal winery hours (see our Attractions chapter).

SUNSET BEACH

The Blue Heron Gallery
The Village at Sunset Beach,
Corner of N.C. Hwys.179 and 904,
Sunset Beach
(910) 575-5088

The Blue Heron is an elegant gallery that features breathtaking artwork from a variety of American artists, including talented local artists. The owner chooses wisely, so be prepared to browse at length through an impressive collection of fine blown glass, pottery, sculpture, handcrafted jewelry and other visual art in a variety of media. Whether your taste is for the whimsical, traditional, modern, functional or avant garde, you can indulge it at The Blue Heron Gallery.

CALABASH

Sunset River Marketplace
10283 Beach Dr. SW, Calabash
(910) 575-5999

"A gallery of art and unique creations" is the way Ginny and Joe Lassiter refer to this, their retirement enterprise, which opened in 2002. And such it is. You can feel the positive energy radiating throughout the gallery as you move from display to display enchanted by what you see. You will find paintings, pottery, sculpture, jewelry, beautiful functional items and items whose function it is to be beautiful, all meticulously crafted and thoughtfully displayed by talented local artists from the Carolinas. In addition, the marketplace provides classes and workshops in a variety of genres, including painting in various media and styles, basket making, pottery and photography. Framing is done on the premises as well.

TOPSAIL ISLAND

Seacoast Art Gallery
203 Greensboro Ave., Surf City
(910) 328-1112

Sandy McHugh is the artist in residence at this homey little gallery. Sandy's artworks depict her pleasure of returning to the beach. Many of her watercolors are local beach scenes, and her humor is evident in her sketches of beach birds with captions underneath. Stop in and visit with Sandy during the summer months only.

Topsail Art Gallery
121 S. Topsail Dr., Surf City
(910) 328-2138

If you are searching for a gorgeous coastal photograph, watercolor, print or painting, Topsail Art Gallery is the area's premier location. American artists are highlighted here and they have a wide variety of originals and reproductions from local, regional and nationally known artists. The gallery offers unique gift items, blown glass, ceramics and great hand-crafted metal sculptures, copper fountains and birdbaths. An on-site frame shop can custom-frame any selection. The gallery is open year round. Owners Mike and Judy Hendy pride themselves on their ability to fill customers' special requests.

👥 ATTRACTIONS

Known to generations of visitors for beautiful, family-friendly beaches and waterways, North Carolina's southern coast also offers a multitude of attractions that have more to do with history than geography. The rich historic legacy of Wilmington and the surrounding communities manifests itself in museums, monuments, churches, grand old residences and other structures that speak eloquently of the past. However, there is little doubt that the proximity to the sea lends a distinct resort quality to this culturally vibrant region.

With the advent of a new trend in vacationing known as heritage tourism, visitors are searching for more than long days on the beach in coastal destinations. What is heritage tourism? This concept addresses the desire of modern visitors to explore sites and attractions that make history come alive and provide the ability to experience life as it was once lived in that area. Historic sites such as the Battleship *North Carolina*, Thalian Hall, Brunswick Town, Fort Fisher, Penderlea Homestead and Topsail Island's Assembly Building convey specific eras and events as no textbook or commemoration can.

Downtown Wilmington's historic legacy and related attractions are integral to the identity of the Cape Fear region. This port city's historic district has a colorful past and is the most varied single attraction in the area, easily explored on foot, by boat, trolley or horse-drawn carriage.

By 1840 Wilmington was the largest city in North Carolina. Nicknamed the Port City by residents, it was on a par with other great Southern ports such as Charleston, Galveston and New Orleans. But when the Atlantic Coast Line Railroad company pulled out of Wilmington in the 1960s, the city went into such a rapid decline that even its skyline was flattened by the demolition of several buildings and railroad facilities on the north side of town. Downtown was nearly deserted until a core of local entrepreneurs revitalized and restored their hometown. In 1974 downtown Wilmington became the state's largest urban district listed in the National Register of Historic Places. Many of the images of Wilmington's past are preserved in the North Carolina Room at the New Hanover County Public Library's main branch at 201 Chestnut Street, throughout The Cotton Exchange and at Chandler's Wharf in downtown Wilmington. Likewise, the Cape Fear Museum and the Wilmington Railroad Museum interpret the region's history in far-reaching exhibits. Combined with a variety of tour options (listed in this chapter), these places are excellent resources for interpreting what you see today or exploring the rich history preserved here.

This region is so rich in history it would be impossible to list every historical attraction in a book this size. However, preserving and sharing the rich historic bounty is such a point of pride with Insiders that visitors won't fail to notice clearly marked areas of interest as they explore the region. For example, as you travel neighboring Brunswick County to such places as Southport's Old Smithville Burial Ground, stay alert for other sites with similar stories to tell, such as Southport's old Morse Cemetery on W. West Street and the John N. Smith Cemetery on Leonard Street off Herring Drive. Memorials are so abundant you may miss the one at Bonnet's Creek (Moore Street north of downtown Southport), at the mouth of which "Gentleman Pirate" Stede Bonnet used to hide his corsair. (This and many other sites are on the Southport Trail, listed in this chapter.)

Naturally, many attractions are typical of the seashore: excellent fishing, fine seafood dining, the many cruise opportunities. No beach resort would be complete without water slides, go-cart tracks or batting cages, and we've got plenty of those. These amusements, as well as miniature golf, movies and bowling, are concentrated along our most heavily traveled routes. Just keep your eyes open; you can't miss them. In Wilmington,

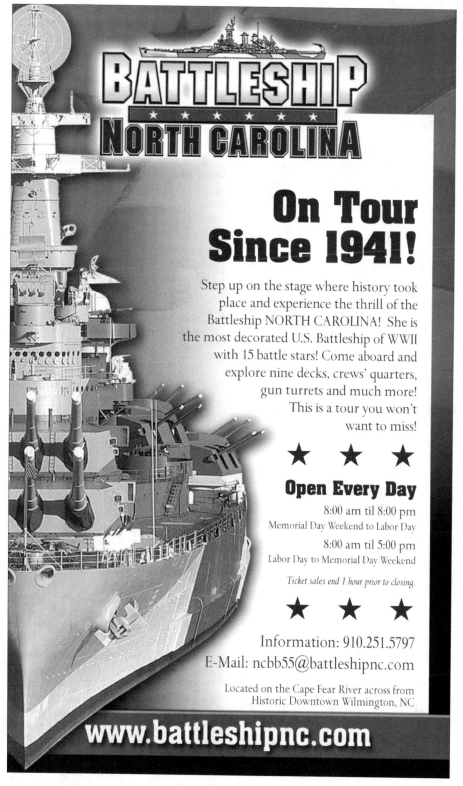

BATTLESHIP
NORTH CAROLINA

On Tour Since 1941!

Step up on the stage where history took place and experience the thrill of the Battleship NORTH CAROLINA! She is the most decorated U.S. Battleship of WWII with 15 battle stars! Come aboard and explore nine decks, crews' quarters, gun turrets and much more! This is a tour you won't want to miss!

★ ★ ★

Open Every Day

8:00 am til 8:00 pm
Memorial Day Weekend to Labor Day

8:00 am til 5:00 pm
Labor Day to Memorial Day Weekend

Ticket sales end 1 hour prior to closing.

★ ★ ★

Information: 910.251.5797
E-Mail: ncbb55@battleshipnc.com

Located on the Cape Fear River across from
Historic Downtown Wilmington, NC

www.battleshipnc.com

Oleander Drive east of College Road is the predominant amusement strip, having several more attractions than listed here. North of Ocean Isle Beach, Beach Drive (N.C. Highway 179/904) is another strip with its share of go-carts, miniature golf and curiosities. Around Southport, check out the rapidly expanding Long Beach Road area between Southport and Oak Island. Topsail Beach and Surf City share the limelight as Topsail Island's two centers of attractions. It would be redundant to list every enterprise — they're opening faster than we can list them, and you're bound to stumble across them as you gravitate toward each community's entertainment center.

Reasons to explore Wilmington and the southern coast don't fade with the end of summer heat and sun. The "shoulder" or off-season has gained in vitality since the mid-1990s, except in some of the smaller beach communities. Mild temperatures, reduced rates, the boom in the region's golf courses and year-round activities convince the off-season visitor that southeastern North Carolina is a great place to relax.

It would be difficult to overstate the importance of the region's gardens, for which North Carolina is rightly famous. The fact that the North Carolina Azalea Festival, in which garden tours are focal, is based in Wilmington makes a strong case for the southern coast's horticultural significance. The spectacular 100-year-old Airlie Gardens, containing 67 acres of gardens and 10 acres of lakes, is a must-see for gardening enthusiasts. Annual and perennial plantings are well-supported public works. The gardens at Orton Plantation near Southport are simply spectacular in springtime.

In this chapter we describe many of the area's prime attractions, followed by a brief section on the southern coast's islands. Wilmington's attractions are grouped into three subsections: Downtown Wilmington, Around Wilmington and Outside Wilmington. Within each section, attractions are listed alphabetically.

Visitor Information

Information to supplement this guide can be obtained at several locations:

Cape Fear Coast Convention & Visitors Bureau, 24 N. Third Street, (910) 341-4030, in the 1892 courthouse building

Visitors Information Booth, by the river at the foot of Market Street in Wilmington

Public libraries, especially New Hanover County's main branch at Third and Chestnut streets in Wilmington

Southport Visitors' Center, 113 W. Moore Street in Southport, (910) 457-7927

Greater Topsail Area Chamber of Commerce, Treasure Coast Landing, 13775, Suite 101, N.C. Highway 50 in Surf City, (910) 329-4446 or (800) 626-2780

Of course, all the area's chambers of commerce are helpful; see our Area Overview chapter for a list.

Downtown Wilmington

Battleship North Carolina
Cape Fear River, Wilmington
(910) 251-5797
www.battleshipnc.com

Without question, the Battleship *North Carolina* is the centerpiece of the Wilmington Riverfront. A majestic symbol of this country's hard-earned naval victories in World War II, the Battleship is a must-see attraction. Enshrined in a berth on Eagles Island across the Cape Fear River from historic downtown Wilmington, this awesome vessel is dedicated to the 10,000 North Carolinians of all the armed services who gave their lives during World War II.

Commissioned in 1941, the 45,000-ton warship wields nine 16-inch turreted guns and carries nickel-steel hull armor 16 to 18 inches thick. The USS *North Carolina* Battleship survived a direct torpedo hit in 1942, a tribute to the strength of its construction. In fact, the "Immortal Showboat" is known for the relatively small number of casualties it suffered during the war.

The Battleship *North Carolina* came to its present home in 1961. It took a swarm of tugboats to maneuver the 728-foot vessel into its berth, where the river is only 500 feet wide. After much effort and tribulation, the city of Wilmington gained a majestic and irreplaceable piece of history that continues to provide visitors with an enlightening journey into the past.

The 'turtle bridge' section of Greenfield Lake's 4-mile walking loop is a perfect spot for quiet contemplation.

photo: Peter Doran

You can drive to it easily enough, but using the river taxi is more fun. (See the write-up for Capt. Maffitt Sightseeing Cruise below.) You can absorb all the Battleship *North Carolina* has to offer at your own speed and see what is most interesting to you with a self-guided tour that takes you to more than nine decks. Included are the crew's quarters, galley, sick bay, gun turrets and exhibits that reveal the heart of this World War II battleship, including new visual displays with first-person accounts of daily life aboard the battleship. These individual stories help bring history to life, capturing the imaginations of children and adults alike, who may have only read about World War II in textbooks. More features to check out are the engine room, the plotting rooms, radio central, the Admiral's Cabin, the bridge and combat central. Don't miss the Kingfisher float plane, one of the last of its kind to survive, located on the stern of the Battleship's main deck. Plan on taking at least two hours to enjoy the tour.

Spend some time in the visitors center, where you can view the fascinating displays related to the Battleship *North Carolina*, its place in WWII history, as well as the memorabilia and personal belongings of the people who lived and worked on board. On your way out, don't forget to visit the Ship's Store, a gift shop filled with Battleship *North Carolina* souvenirs and gifts with a nautical or military theme. Ample parking adjoins the berth, and Battleship Park includes a sheltered picnic area. Please note that only the visitors center and the main deck of the Battleship are wheelchair accessible.

Tours cost $9 for those ages 12 and older and $4.50 for children ages 6 through 11. Children 5 and younger get in free. The cost is $8 for seniors 65 and older as well as retired and active-duty military personnel. The Battleship is open every day. From Memorial Day weekend to Labor Day, hours are 8 AM to 8 PM. From Labor Day to Memorial Day weekend, hours are 8 AM to 5 PM. Ticket sales end one hour before closing. There is no extra charge for unscheduled appearances by old Charlie, the alligator who makes his home near the Battleship at the river's edge.

Bellamy Mansion Museum
503 Market St., Wilmington
(910) 251-3700

The assertion that the Bellamy Mansion is Wilmington's premier statement of prewar opulence and wealth is impossible to contest. ("Prewar" here refers to the War Between the States, a.k.a. the Civil War, the War of Northern Aggression, the Late Unpleasantness.) This four-story, 22-room wooden palace completed in 1861 is a classic example of Greek Revival and Italianate architecture. Its majesty is immediately evident in 14 fluted exterior Corinthian columns. Most of the craftwork is the product of both free and enslaved African-American artisans, some of whom, it is said, were granted their freedom on the steps of this very building.

Before plans were set to renovate and restore the mansion in 1972, it hadn't been lived in since 1946. Volunteer guides are sure to point out the glassed-in portion of a wall left unrestored to illustrate the extent of a 1972 fire set by an arsonist. That event was linked to the disfavor in which the Bellamy Mansion had been held by some locals, who saw it as a symbol of slavery, which further legitimizes the mansion's value as a historic and cultural landmark. The mansion's museum exhibits embrace regional architecture, landscape architecture, preservation and decorative arts. The museum hosts multimedia traveling exhibits, workshops, films, lectures, slide shows and other activities. Ongoing and painstaking restoration qualifies Bellamy Mansion as an important work in progress. Behind the mansion, the newly rebuilt carriage house opened to the public in late spring 2001 and houses the visitors center, gift shop and mansion offices. Adjacent to the carriage house, the Bellamy Mansion slave quarters show a rare example of urban slave housing. Future renovation plans include this unique five-room, two-story brick dwelling.

Bellamy Mansion Museum is open to the public Tuesday to Saturday 10 AM to 5 PM and Sunday 1 to 5 PM. Tours, both guided and self-guided, begin at the carriage house with a brief film on the mansion's history and preservation efforts. Please note that the last guided tour begins at 4 PM. Admission is $7 for adults and $3 for children ages 5 through 12. Children younger than 5 enter free of charge. Friends of the Bellamy Mansion are admitted free. Call ahead for group rate information.

Burgwin-Wright House and Garden
224 Market St., Wilmington
(910) 762-0570

When Lord Charles Cornwallis, still in danger of a Rebel pursuit, fled to the coast after the Battle of Guilford Court House in central North Carolina in 1781, he repaired to Wilmington, then a town of 200 houses. He lodged at the gracious Georgian home of John Burgwin (pronounced "bur-GWIN"), a wealthy planter and politician, and made it his headquarters. The home, completed in 1770, is distinguished by two-story porches on two sides and seven levels of tiered gardens. The massive ballast-stone foundation remains from the previously abandoned town jail. A free-standing outbuilding houses the kitchen and a craft room and is located behind this beautifully preserved Colonial home. Monthly demonstrations of open-hearth cooking are held here on a Saturday (call for schedule).

The Burgwin-Wright House, currently owned by the National Society of the Colonial Dames of America in the State of North Carolina, is one of the great restoration/reconstruction achievements in the state, and visitors may peruse the carefully appointed rooms and period furnishings.

Admission is $7 for adults and $3 for children. Children younger than 5 are admitted free. Group tours are available by appointment. The museum is open Tuesday through Saturday 10 AM to 4 PM, with the last tour at 3 PM on all days.

Colonial Christmas is a special event at the house during the second weekend in December. The house is filled with the music of the 1700s and decorated for the holiday season with greenery and fruit, while the art of open-hearth cooking is highlighted. There are performances by dancers in full colonial costume and demonstrations of colonial weaving/tapestry in the craft room and you can even take a peek in to the old jail's dungeon. And for history buffs, a colonial surgeon demonstrates surgery as it was performed on the battlefield. Admission for Colonial Christmas is $10.

Cape Fear Museum
814 Market St., Wilmington
(910) 341-4350
www.capefearmuseum.com

For an overview of the cultural and natural histories of the Cape Fear region from prehistory to the present, the Cape Fear Museum, established in 1898, stands unsurpassed. A miniature re-creation of the second

Open 9AM-5PM Tuesday through Saturday
1-5PM on Sunday

Open seven days a week
Memorial Day through Labor Day

Located at 814 Market Street
in historic downtown Wilmington

Where the
Lower Cape Fear
story begins.

910.341.4350
www.CapeFearMuseum.com

Visit the Museum Store!

battle of Fort Fisher and a remarkable scale model of the Wilmington waterfront, c. 1863, are of special interest. The Michael Jordan Discovery Gallery (which includes a popular display case housing many of the basketball star's personal items) is a long-term interactive natural history exhibit for the entire family. The Discovery Gallery includes a crawl-through beaver lodge, Pleistocene-era fossils and an entertaining Venus's-flytrap model you can feed with stuffed "bugs." Children's activities, concerts, special events, and ac-claimed touring exhibits contribute to making the Cape Fear Museum not only one of the primary repositories of local history, but also a place where learning is fun.

The museum is open Tuesday through Saturday 9 AM to 5 PM and Sunday 1 to 5 PM. During the summer season (Memorial Day through Labor Day), the museum is open Mondays from 9 AM to 5 PM. Admission is $5 for adults, $4 for seniors and students with valid ID, $4 special military rate with valid military I.D.; and $1 for children ages 3 through 17. Children younger than 3 and Cape Fear Museum members are admitted free. Admission is free to all New Hanover County residents on the first Sunday of each month. Groups of 12 or more may be eligible for a discount on admission fees and should contact the museum for details. Cape Fear Museum is disabled accessible and offers an interesting, well-stocked gift shop for visitors.

Cape Fear Serpentarium
20 Orange St., Wilmington
(910) 762-1669

Featuring more than 100 species of snakes, most of them poisonous, the Serpen-tarium boasts the largest collection of ven-omous snakes in the world. Owner Dean Ripa is a major breeder of the South American bushmaster, the world's longest pit viper and the rarest of venomous snakes. He claims to be the world's first and only breeder capable of having the blackhead bushmaster repro-duce in captivity. In addition to 37 bushmas-ters, the Serpentarium also houses gaboon vipers, king cobras, Australian taipans, a 23-foot python, black mambas, a Nile croco-dile and a 6-foot monitor lizard. The Serpen-tarium is open daily 11 AM to 5 PM. Winter months, it is closed on Tuesdays. Hours are subject to change, so call ahead. All tickets are $7. Group tours are available and school groups are welcome.

Capt. J.N. Maffitt Sightseeing Cruise
Riverfront Park, Foot of Market St.,
Wilmington
(910) 343-1611, (800) 676-0162
www.cfrboats.com

Named for Capt. John Newland Maf-fitt, one of the Confederacy's most suc-cessful blockade runners, the *Capt. Maffitt* is a converted World War II Navy launch affording 45-minute sightseeing cruises with live historical narration along the Cape Fear

ATTRACTIONS

River. Cruises set out at 11 AM and 3 PM daily from Memorial Day to Labor Day. Off-season weekend cruises are available from May 1 to Memorial Day and from Labor Day to mid-November. Cruise tickets are $11 for adults and $5 for children ages 2 to 12. The *Capt. Maffitt* is available for charter throughout the year, and it doubles as the Battleship River Taxi during the summer. No reservations are necessary, and it runs on the quarter-hour from Wilmington's riverfront to the Battleship *North Carolina* and on the hour and half-hour for the return trip except at 11:30 AM and 3:30 PM during the sightseeing cruise times. River taxi fees are $3 per person and free for children younger than 2.

Chandler's Wharf
225 S. Water St., Wilmington
(910) 343-9896

More than 100 years ago, Chandler's Wharf was crowded with mercantile warehouses, its sheds filled with naval stores, tools, cotton and turpentine and its wharves lined with merchantmen. A disastrous (and suspicious) fire in August 1874 changed the site forever. In the late 1970s, Chandler's Wharf became an Old Wilmington riverfront reconstruction site, a positive turning point for downtown revitalization.

Today much of the flavor of the 1870s remains, and Chandler's Wharf is again a business district, or, more accurately, a shopping and dining district. Two historic homes transformed into shops stand on the cobblestone street, beside wooden sidewalks and the rails of the former waterfront railway. The original ship chandler warehouse has been converted into popular boutiques and galleries; a pictorial history of Wilmington is displayed there.

Elijah's and The Pilot House restaurants overlook the Cape Fear River, and the Riverwalk provides a delightful waterside stroll that connects Chandler's Wharf with the rest of downtown. (See our Restaurants and Shopping chapters.)

 Sacred Spaces: Architecture and Religion in Historic Wilmington by Walter H. Conser Jr. is an excellent resource for studying Wilmington's historic churches.

Chestnut Street United Presbyterian Church
710 N. Sixth St., Wilmington
(910) 762-1074

This tiny church, built in 1858 and originally a mission chapel of First Presbyterian Church (see below), is a remarkable example of Stick Style, or Carpenter Gothic, architecture. Its exterior details include decorative bargeboards with repeating acorn pendants, board-and-batten construction, a louvered bell tower (with carillon) and paired Gothic windows. When the congregation, then slaves, formed in 1858 under the auspices of the mother church, the chapel was surrendered by the mother church to the new, black congregation, which purchased the building in 1867. The congregation's many distinguished members have included the first black president of Biddle University (now Johnson C. Smith University), the publisher of Wilmington's first black newspaper, a member of the original Fisk University Jubilee Singers, the first black graduate of MIT, and North Carolina's first black physician.

First Baptist Church
411 Market St., Wilmington
(910) 763-2471

Even having lost its stunning 197-foot, copper-sheathed steeple to Hurricane Fran in 1996, First Baptist was still Wilmington's tallest church. For years this tower, the taller of the church's two steeples, had been known to visibly sway even in an average wind. The steeple's repair was completed in early 1999.

Being literally the first Baptist church in the region, this is the mother church of many other Baptist churches in Wilmington. Its congregation dates to 1808, and construction of the red-brick building began in 1859. The church was not completed until 1870 because of the Civil War, when Confederate and Union forces in turn used the higher steeple as a lookout. Its architecture is Early English Gothic Revival with hints of Richardson Romanesque, as in its varicolored materials and its horizontal mass relieved by the verticality of the spires, with their narrow, gabled vents. Inside, the pews, galleries and ceiling vents are of native heart pine.

Sunday School classes occupy an equally interesting building next door on Fifth Street, the Sidbury House, which exhibits such classic Italianate elements as frieze vents and brackets, and fluted wooden columns. The church offices are located in the Taylor House next door on Market Street.

First Presbyterian Church
125 S. Third St., Wilmington
(910) 762-6688

Visiting clergymen held services occasionally to Presbyterians in Wilmington in the 1700s. The First Presbyterian Church was organized in 1817. This congregation continues to have among its members some of the most influential Wilmingtonians. The Rev. Joseph R. Wilson was pastor from 1874 until 1885; his son, Thomas Woodrow Wilson, grew up to become slightly more famous. The church itself, with its finials and soaring stone spire topped with a metal rooster (a symbol of the Protestant Reformation), blends Late Gothic and Renaissance styles and is the congregation's fourth home, the previous three having succumbed to fire. During the Union occupation, the lectern Bible was stolen from the third church, which burned on New Year's Eve 1925. The stolen Bible was returned years later to become all that remains of the sanctuary.

Today, intricate tracery distinguishes fine stained-glass windows along the nave as well as the vast west window and the chancel rose. The 1928 E. M. Skinner organ, with its original pneumatic console, is used regularly. Handsomely stenciled beams, arches and trusses support a steep gabled roof. To one side is the Kenan Chapel, with its transverse Romanesque arches. The education building behind the sanctuary is quintessential Tudor, complete with exterior beams set in stucco, wide squared arches, casement windows with diamond panes, interior ceiling beams and eccentric compound chimneys. Having undergone major renovation in the early 1990s, First Presbyterian is an impressive sight. Its carillon can be heard daily throughout the historic district.

Ghost Walk of Old Wilmington
Market St. at the Riverfront, Wilmington
(910) 794-1866

Visitors and locals alike enjoy this nightly walking tour of the area around downtown Wilmington. The tour meets year round by the Riverfront at the foot of Market Street. Hours are: April 1 through October 31 nightly at 8:30 PM, plus Tuesday through Saturday at 6:30 PM; November and March, Tuesday through Saturday at 6:30 PM; December, January and February, Thursday through Saturday at 6:30 PM. Special Halloween times vary and you're advised to call ahead. Cost is $12 for adults, $10 for seniors, students and military, free for children ages 6 and younger. Tours for groups of 15 people or more can be arranged year round; please call ahead.

Haunted Pub Crawl
Downtown Wilmington
(910) 794-1866

Partake in an evening of spirited adventure on a journey to Wilmington's most wildly haunted pubs. Revel in the seamy red-light district of yore and uncover startling truths of life in an 18th-century port city. From the disreputable obsession of the merry wench, "Gallus" Meg, to the barbarous haunts of a notorious madman, this is a fun-filled night of levity and libations. Reservations are required. The tour begins at 7:30 PM. Nights vary; call the number above for the most current schedule. The Haunted Pub Crawl is a great way to add some excitement to a special event or party, or to just get together with some friends for a scary good time. Group tours for 10 or more adults can be arranged year round. Cost is $15 per adult.

Horse-Drawn Trolley & Carriage Tours
Market St. between Water and Front Sts., Wilmington
(910) 251-8889

See historic downtown Wilmington the old-fashioned way — by horse-drawn carriage or trolley. This half-hour tour in a fringed-top surrey (open-air trolley) is narrated by a knowledgeable driver wearing 19th-century garb. The personable driver offers interesting anecdotes about the historic mansions and waterfront along the way. At busy times such as Azalea Festival and Riverfest, horse-drawn tours are especially popular.

Don't miss the memorable seasonal events, including the romantic horse-drawn Valentine ride in a French evening coach, an Easter Bunny–drawn ride, the Halloween Ghost Trolley ride, the Thanksgiving Turkey–drawn ride, or the Caroling by "Reindeer" Christmas ride. Carriage rides are also available for weddings, private parties and other special occasions. Call the number above for reservations and rates.

Seating is on a first-come, first-served basis. From April through October, tours operate Tuesday through Saturday from 10 AM to 10 PM and Sunday 11 AM to 4 PM. In November, December and March, the carriages roll Friday and Saturday 11 AM to 10 PM and Sunday 11 AM to 4 PM. During January and February, call for hours. Expect to pay $11 for adults and $5 for children age 11 and younger; rates are subject to change without notice, however.

Henrietta III
Docked at S. Water St at the foot of Dock St., Wilmington
(910) 343-1611, (800) 676-0162
www.cfrboats.com

This elegant, refurbished riverboat is a large, three-level, paddle-free vessel with a capacity for 600 guests. In fact, the Henrietta III is so spacious that it can accommodate three events — wedding parties, dinner cruises, themed cruises, etc. — at once. Cruise the Cape Fear River in style on this beautiful riverboat with a variety of options that include a 90-minute narrated sightseeing cruise, narrated lunch cruise, dinner dance cruise and more. Most cruises are available from April through December, while others only go out during the summer season. Rates vary according to the type and length of the cruise. Prepaid reservations are required for cruises that include meals. The *Henrietta III* also offers special events cruises throughout the year. Contact Cape Fear Riverboats at the phone numbers above for more information on current rates, cruise schedules and special events cruises. The riverboat's elevator makes all decks handicapped accessible. The *Henrietta III* is U.S. Coast Guard–approved.

Oakdale Cemetery
520 N. 15th St., Wilmington
(910) 762-5682

When Nance Martin died at sea in 1857, her body was preserved seated in a chair in a large cask of rum. Six months later she was interred at Oakdale Cemetery, cask and all. Her monument and many other curious, beautiful and historic markers are to be found within the labyrinth of Oakdale Cemetery,

Wilmington's first municipal burial ground, opened in 1855.

At the cemetery office, you can pick up a free map detailing some of the more interesting interments, such as the volunteer firefighter buried with the faithful dog that gave its life trying to save his master, and Mrs. Rose O'Neal Greenhow, a Confederate courier who drowned while running the blockade at Fort Fisher in 1864. Amid the profusion of monuments lies a field oddly lacking in markers — the mass grave of hundreds of victims of the 1862 yellow fever epidemic. The architecture of the monuments, the Victorian landscaping and the abundance of dogwood trees make Oakdale beautiful in every season. The cemetery is open from 8 AM to 5 PM daily. Oakdale Cemetery office hours are Monday through Friday 8:30 AM to noon and 1 to 4:30 PM. Admission is free.

The Riverwalk
Riverfront Park, along Water St., Wilmington

The heart and soul of downtown Wilmington is its riverfront. Once a bustling, gritty confusion of warehouses, docks and sheds — all suffused with the odor of turpentine — the wharf was the state's most important commercial port. Much has changed today. Now you can experience Wilmington's charm and historical continuity by strolling The Riverwalk. Dining, shopping and lodging establishments line the walk, and live entertainment takes place at the small Riverfront Stage on Saturday and Sunday evenings from June to early August. Check with the Visitors Information Booth at the foot of Market Street for schedules. The third Sunday of each month from 4 to 7 PM in the spring and summer months, Riverfront Park is the site of the Sundown Shindig, a street fair with merchants, food vendors and entertainment with the Cape Fear River sunset serving as a lovely backdrop for the festivities.

Immediately to the north, schooners, pleasure boats and replicas of historic ships frequently visit the municipal dock. Coast Guard cutters and the occasional British naval vessel dock beyond the Federal Court House; some ships allow touring, especially during festivals. Benches, picnic tables, a fountain and snack vendors complete the scene, one of Wilmington's most popular.

St. James Episcopal Church and Burial Ground
25 S. Third St., Wilmington
(910) 763-1628

St. James is the oldest church in continuous use in Wilmington, and it wears its age well. The parish was established in 1729 at Brunswick Town across the river (also see St. Philip's Parish, below). The congregation's original Wilmington church wasn't completed until 1770. It was seized in 1781 by Tarleton's Dragoons under Cornwallis. Tarleton had the pews removed, and the church became a stable. The original church was taken down in 1839, and some of its materials were used to construct the present church, an Early Gothic Revival building with pinnacled square towers, battlements and lancet windows. The architect, Thomas U. Walter, is best known for his 1865 cast-iron dome on the U.S. Capitol. A repeat performance of pew-tossing took place during the Civil War, when occupying Federal forces used the church as a hospital. A letter written by the pastor asking President Lincoln for reparation still exists. The letter was never delivered, having been completed the day news arrived of Lincoln's assassination. Within the church hangs a celebrated painting of Christ (Ecce Homo) captured from one of the Spanish pirate ships that attacked Brunswick Town in 1748. The sanctuary also boasts a handsome wood-slat ceiling and beam-and-truss construction. Church offices are in the McRae House, built in 1900 from a design by Henry Bacon, who also designed the Lincoln memorial in Washington, D.C.

The cemetery at the corner of Fourth and Market streets was in use from 1745 to 1855 and bears considerable historic importance. Here lies the patriot Cornelius Harnett, remembered for antagonizing the British by reading the Declaration of Independence aloud at the Halifax Courthouse in 1776. He died in a British prison during the war. America's first playwright, Thomas Godfrey, is also memorialized here. The cemetery once occupied grounds over which Market Street now stretches, which explains why utility workers periodically (and inadvertently) unearth human remains outside the present burial ground. This burial ground is also a

favorite spot on the History-Mystery Tour in October (see the Annual Events chapter for a description). Visitors are welcome to take self-guided tours of the church on weekdays between 9 AM and early afternoon when services are not underway.

St. Marks Episcopal Church
600 Grace St., Wilmington
(910) 763-3292

Established in 1869, this was the first Episcopal church for blacks in eastern North Carolina, and it has conducted services uninterrupted since that time. The building (completed in 1875) is a simple Gothic Revival structure with a buttressed nave and octagonal bell tower. All visitors are also welcome to attend worship services on Sunday. Please check local Saturday newspapers orcall the church at the number listed above for the schedule.

St. Mary's Roman Catholic Church
412 Ann St., Wilmington
(910) 762-5491

Numerous historical writers have referred to this Spanish Baroque edifice (built 1908-11) as a major architectural creation, often pointing out the elaborate tiling, especially inside the dome, which embraces most of this church's cross-vaulted interior space. The plan of the brick building is based on the Greek cross, with enormous semicircular stained-glass windows in the transept vaults, arcade windows in the apse and symmetrical square towers in front. Over the main entrance, in stained glass, is an imitation of Leonardo da Vinci's Last Supper. A coin given by Maria Anna Jones, the first black Catholic in North Carolina, is placed inside the cornerstone.

St. Paul's Evangelical Lutheran Church
12 N. Sixth St., corner of Sixth and Market Sts., Wilmington
(910) 762-4882

Responding to the growing number of German Lutherans in Wilmington, North Carolina's Lutheran Synod organized St. Paul's in 1858. Services began in 1861 as the Civil War broke. Construction came to a halt when the German artisans working on the building volunteered for the 18th North Carolina Regiment and became the first local unit in active duty. The building was occupied and badly damaged by Union troops after the fall of Fort Fisher in early 1865. Horses were stabled in the building and its wooden furnishings were used as firewood.

The completed church was dedicated in 1869, only to burn in 1894. It was promptly rebuilt. There have been several additions and renovations since. Today the building is remarkable for its blend of austere Greek Revival elements outside (such as the entablature, pediments and pilasters) and Gothic Revival (such as the slender spire, clustered interior piers and large lancet windows). Also notable are its color-patterned slate roof and copper finials and the gently arcing pew arrangement. The removal of paneling during renovations in 1995-96 uncovered beautiful stenciling on the ceiling panels and ribs in the vestibule, nave and chancel.

Temple of Israel
1 S. Fourth St., southeast corner of Fourth and Market Sts. Wilmington
(910) 762-0000

The oldest Jewish temple in North Carolina, this unique Moorish Revival style building was erected in 1875–76 for a Reform congregation that was formed in 1872. Its two square towers are topped by small onion domes, and the paired, diamond-paned windows exhibit a mix of architrave shapes, including Romanesque, trefoil and Anglo-Saxon arches. Another notable feature is a magnificent chandelier, brought to the United States from Landau, Germany. Believed to be more than 500 years old, the chandelier was originally lighted by oil, later by candles and finally by electricity. The Pilcher-Tracker organ, constructed in 1901 and restored in 1990, is one of only three such organs known to still be in operation. When the Front Street Methodist Episcopal Church was destroyed by fire in 1886, the Temple of Israel congregants offered their building as a substitute

until a new church could be erected. The offer was accepted and the Methodists met in the Temple for a little more than two years. During the week, you may stop by the office at 9 S. Fourth Street between the hours of 9 AM and noon to request a viewing of the temple's interior.

Thalian Hall/City Hall
310 Chestnut St., Wilmington
Center Box Office (910) 343-3664,
(800) 523-2820

Since its renovation and expansion in the late 1980s, the name has been, more accurately, Thalian Hall Center for the Performing Arts. And yes, it does share the same roof with City Hall. Conceived as a combined political and cultural center, Thalian Hall was built between 1855 and 1858. During its first 75 years, the Hall brought great national performers and some surprising celebrities to its stage: Lillian Russell, Buffalo Bill Cody, John Philip Sousa, Oscar Wilde and Tom Thumb, to name a few. That tradition continues. Full-scale musicals, light opera and internationally renowned dance companies are only a portion of Thalian Hall's consistent, high-quality programming. Today the center consists of two theatres — the Main Stage and the Studio Theatre — plus a ballroom (which doubles as the city council chambers). With its Corinthian columns and ornate proscenium, it's no wonder Thalian Hall is on the National Register of Historic Places. Private and group tours are offered Monday through Friday by appointment and include the main theatre, backstage, the studio theatre, ballroom, gallery and City Hall. Contact Thalian Hall's administrative offices, (910) 343-3660, to schedule a tour and for tour rates. A self-guided tour is also available from noon to 6 PM Monday through Friday and from 2 to 6 PM on Saturday. Admission for the self-guided tour is $1.

The best deal in historic Wilmington is the Passport tour ticket. Tour Bellamy Mansion Museum, the Burgwin-Wright House and the Zebulon Latimer House for $18, a $3 savings. The ticket may be purchased at any one of these locations and is good for one week after purchase.

Wilmington Adventure Walking Tour
Riverfront Park,
Foot of Market St., Wilmington
(910) 763-1785

For the past eighteen years, lifelong Cape Fear resident Bob Jenkins (the man with the straw hat and walking cane) has been leading the Wilmington Adventure Walking Tour, speaking passionately and knowledgeably about his hometown. Expounding upon architectural details, family lineage and historic events, Bob whisks you through 250 years of history in about two hours. You'll see residences, churches and public buildings. Tours begin at the flagpole at the foot of Market Street at 10 AM and 2 PM daily, weather permitting, April through October. Cost is $10 for adults and $5 for children ages 6 to 12. Children younger than 6 go along for free. Although no reservations are required, it's best to call ahead, especially in summer. Off-season, November through March, group tours are by advance reservation only.

Wilmington Children's Museum
Corner of Second and Orange Sts., Wilmington
(910) 254-3534

The goal at this multi-faceted museum is to "stimulate children's imagination, curiosity and innate love of learning" through play. Climb aboard their pirate ship, experiment in the science lab or make a special souvenir in the art room. You can count on the Children's Museum for fun, affordable, educational, play-centered programs both children and their adult friends are sure to enjoy. They have art and science programming all day, every day. Toddler Time is on Fridays from 9 to 10:30 AM. To learn more about what's offered, check out the Kidstuff chapter.

Wilmington National Cemetery
2011 Market St., Wilmington
(910) 815-4877

In 1866-67, immediately after the Civil War, the United States Congress enacted legislation to create national cemeteries to honor and protect the remains of U.S. soldiers who fell in battle or died of disease.

The Wilmington National Cemetery was established in 1867 on five acres of land about a mile east of downtown. The cemetery originally contained the remains of more than 2,000 Union soldiers, many of whom died at Fort Fisher and were later interred here. More than 1,300 are unidentified; many are black, identified as U.S.C.T. (United States Colored Troops) or U.S. Col. Inf. (United States Colored Infantry). Markers with round tops indicate known burials, and stones with flat tops indicate unknowns; nearly all are government issue. Since the Civil War period,

The Bellamy Mansion is a lovely example of the historic architecture of downtown Wilmington.

photo: Peter Doran

the Wilmington National Cemetery has received the remains of Americans through the Vietnam conflict. The cemetery no longer has room for additional deceased soldiers; however, spouses and family members of soldiers already interred there may still be buried near their loved one. Visitors interested in finding a specific grave may use the locator at the entrance of the cemetery. Grounds are open daily from 7:30 AM to 5 PM.

Wilmington Railroad Museum
501 Nutt St., Wilmington
(910) 763-2634

The dramatic transformation that Wilmington underwent when the Atlantic Coast Line Railroad closed its corporate offices in the late 1960s is clearly borne out by this museum's fine photographs and artifacts. Beyond history, the Railroad Museum is a kind of funhouse for people fascinated by trains and train culture. For the price of admission, you can climb into a real steam locomotive and clang its bell for as long as your kids will let you. Inside, volunteers will guide you to exhibits explaining why the 19th-century Wilmington & Weldon Railroad was called the "Well Done" and that the ghost of beheaded flagman Joe Baldwin is behind the Maco Light — at least one volunteer claims to have seen it.

Ask about the museum's "Memories" book in which visitors are encouraged to share their favorite train memories; it includes entries by celebrities who have visited Wilmington. The museum building was the railroad's freight traffic office and is listed on the National Register of Historic Places. Visitors can run the model trains in the enormous railroad diorama upstairs, which is maintained by the museum's model train committee. Downstairs, the children (both young and not so young) will enjoy the Lionel trains and a small scale HO model, and on the first floor lies a new, unique HO scale train set worth approximately $10,000. Also on the second floor is the hands-on children's corner.

Adult programming, children's workshops, model train workshops, an Annual Train Show in October and group discounts are available. The museum also invites you to conduct your birthday parties on its caboose;

the rental fee includes souvenirs and a tour of the museum.

March 15 to October 14, the museum is open Monday through Saturday from 10 AM to 5 PM and Sunday from 1 to 5 PM. October 14 to March 14, it's open Monday through Saturday from 10 AM to 4 PM. The museum is closed New Year's Eve, New Year's Day, Easter Sunday, Thanksgiving, Christmas Eve and Christmas Day. Admission fees are $4.50 for adults, $4 for military personnel and senior citizens 60 and older, and $2.50 for children ages 2 to 12. Children younger than 2 are admitted free.

Wilmington Trolley Company
Dock and Water Sts., Wilmington
(910) 763-4483
www.wilmingtontrolley.com

Located near the Henrietta III at the foot of Dock Street, the Wilmington Trolley offers a 45-minute guided tour of historic downtown Wilmington over a course of about 8 miles. Available daily, April through October, the tours leave on the hour from 10 AM to 5 PM. There are some evening tours available during the summer months, with the last tour leaving at 8 PM. Fees are $11 for adults and $5 for children ages 2 to 12. Call ahead for evening and off-season tour availability.

Zebulon Latimer House
126 S. Third St., Wilmington
(910) 762-0492

This magnificent Italianate building, built by a prosperous merchant from Connecticut, dates from 1852 and is remarkable for its original furnishings and artwork. The house boasts fine architectural details such as window cornices and wreaths in the frieze openings, all made of cast iron, and a piazza with intricate, wrought-iron tracery. Behind the building stands a rare (and possibly Wilmington's oldest) example of urban slave quarters, now a private residence. What sets the Latimer House apart from most other museums is the fact that it was continuously lived in for more than a century, until it became home to the Lower Cape Fear Historical Society in 1963. It has the look of a home where the family has just stepped out.

The Historical Society is one of the primary sources for local genealogical and historical research. For information on membership, write to 126 S. Third Street, Wilmington, NC 28401. The Society's archives are housed at the Latimer House and are available to the public Monday through Friday from 10 AM to 4 PM.

The Latimer House is open Monday through Friday from 10 AM to 4 PM and Saturday noon to 5 PM. The last guided tour is conducted a half-hour before closing. Admission is $7 for adults and $3 for students. Children 5 and younger are admitted free. Walk & Talk Tours, which require reservations, encompass about 12 blocks of the historic district and last two hours, are given for $9 every Wednesday and Saturday at 10 AM.

Around Wilmington

Airlie Gardens
300 Airlie Rd., Wilmington
(910) 798-7700

Enjoy the pleasures nature has to offer, smell the roses, admire the azaleas, gaze at the camellias and stand in the shade of the 450-year-old Airlie Oak while visiting this quintessential Southern garden. Wander at your leisure along curving paths and walkways in this lush natural setting and note the bounty of flowering vines — honeysuckle, jasmine, wisteria — and the maritime forest of trees native to the region — live oaks, cedars, pines and wax myrtles. Need a rest? Benches are plentiful, so "set a spell," as they say here in the South.

In the early 1900s Airlie Gardens was designed in a post-Victorian European style showcasing plants for all four seasons — azaleas in spring, magnolias and live oaks in summer, camellias in the fall and winter. Statuary, pergolas and fountains grace the gardens. Bordered by Bradley Creek and salt marshes, these beautiful 67-acres support two freshwater lakes that attract swans, ducks, geese, herons, egrets and more.

From January 15th through March 15th the gardens are open Tuesday through Saturday from 9 AM to 5 PM. From March on the gardens are open Tuesday through Sunday from 9 AM to 5 PM. Admission is $5 for adults and $3 for children 12 and younger. Admission is free for members. Individual

memberships cost $25 and include half price admission to the Airlie Concert Series. New Hanover County residents are admitted free the second Saturday of each month.

EUE/Screen Gems Studios Tour
1223 N. 23rd St., Wilmington
(910) 343-3500

They don't call Wilmington "Hollywood East" for nothing, and Screen Gems Studios, the biggest film production facility outside of Los Angeles, is the prime reason. At the head of the entire operation is Frank Capra, Jr., filmmaker in his own right and son of the legendary film director who brought us such classics as It's A Wonderful Life, Mr. Smith Goes To Washington, It Happened One Night and many more.

Screen Gems offers a one-hour walking tour, featuring a variety of sights depending on the level of production activity. As activity on the lot changes, so do the tours. Regular highlights are the sets from the popular television series One Tree Hill, old movie sets and props in Soundstage 1, a video overview of Screen Gems' history in the studios' screening room, a question-and-answer session and more. Cameras are permitted in designated areas.

Tours are offered Saturdays at noon and 2 PM. Group tours are available year round by reservation. Arrive 10 minutes before the hour. Admission is $12 for adults, $8 for seniors and $5 for children younger than 12.

Greenfield Lake and Gardens
U.S. 421 S., at the intersection of Third St. and Carolina Beach Rd., Wilmington

In springtime the colors here are simply eye-popping. In summer the algae-covered waters and Spanish moss are reminders of the days when this was an unpopulated cypress swamp. In winter the bare tree trunks rise from the lake with starkness. Herons, egrets and ducks are regular visitors, as are hawks and cardinals. The 5-mile lake-view drive is a pleasure in any season, and there's a paved path suitable for walking, running or cycling around the entire lake. Greenfield Lake is 2 miles south of downtown Wilmington along S. Third Street. In summer months, eco-tours of the lake are available upon request through Cape Fear River Watch; call (910) 762-5606 for more information. (See more about Greenfield Lake in our chapter on Sports, Fitness and Parks.)

Jungle Rapids Family Fun Park
5320 Oleander Dr., Wilmington
(910) 791-0666

This self-contained amusement magnet includes the only true water park in eastern North Carolina plus more game attractions than a family could exhaust in a week. The quarter-mile-long Grand Prix GoKart track features bridge overpasses, banked turns, timing devices and one- and two-passenger cars. Children less than 56 inches tall must ride with licensed adult drivers.

The Waterpark includes six excellent slides — the Sidewinder, which is a half pike, plus the four-tube slide called the Volcanic Express. Floating the Lazy River, which encircles the water park, is great for a relaxing bask. Lifeguards are always on duty, and there are plenty of lockers, lounges, tables and umbrellas.

Also worthwhile are a wonderful wave pool, the Kiddie Splash Pool (with four kiddie slides), jungle-themed miniature golf, "The Rock" climbing wall, the adrenaline-pumping Alien Invader Laser Tag, the high-tech arcade featuring more than 100 games ranging from the classic to state-of-the-art, and the air-conditioned Kids Jungle (Wilmington's largest indoor playground, for children ages 8 and younger).

Jungle Rapids caters kids' parties on site. They also offer on-site meeting and function rooms (the largest accommodating 200 people). The Big Splash Cafe and Pizzeria offers an ample menu during park hours.

The Waterpark opens Memorial Day weekend and is open daily from 11 AM to 7 PM. The Dry Park attractions are open at 10 AM; 1 PM on Sunday off-season. Call for off-season hours. Also see our Kidstuff chapter.

Louise Wells Cameron Art Museum
3201 S. 17th St., Wilmington
(910) 395-5999

The only art museum within 150 miles of Wilmington, the Louise Wells Cameron Art Museum is located in a new, 42,000-square-foot facility on the corner of S. 17th Street and Independence Boulevard. The Cameron Art Museum features a permanent collection focusing on North Carolina art, tempo-

rary exhibitions, a sculpture court, Civil War defensive mounds on the museum's campus, an expanded gift shop, The Forks restaurant and more. (See our Arts chapter for more information.)

Museum hours are 10 AM to 5 PM Tuesday through Saturday and 10:30 AM to 4 PM Sunday. Admission is $7 for adults, $15 for families and $2 for children ages 5 to 18. Children younger than 5 and museum members are admitted free. Admission is free on the first Sunday of every month.

New Hanover County
Cooperative Extension Arboretum
6206 Oleander Dr., Wilmington
(910) 452-6393

This 7-acre teaching and learning facility is the only educational arboretum in southeastern North Carolina. Nature and garden enthusiasts will discover 33 gardens. The arboretum was formally opened in 1989 and is still in the midst of development. These gardens rank among the finer theme gardens in the area. Boardwalks and paths wind through a profusion of plants, grasses, flowers, trees, shrubs, herbs and vegetables, and there is plenty of shaded seating. Several sections, such as the Herb Garden with its variety of medicinal, culinary, fragrance and tea species, are sponsored by local garden clubs. Other themed gardens include the Rose Garden's Heritage roses, a hands-on Children's Garden and the Aquatic & Bog Gardens, some of the largest in the state. The arboretum also has an Ability Garden, which helps physically and/or mentally challenged individuals learn about and experience the joys of gardening. Working in cooperation with the N.C. State University Cooperative Extension, the arboretum also offers community services and educational programs on a variety of skill levels up to Master Gardener courses.

The arboretum assists commercial and private horticultural enterprises and helps residents create attractive home landscapes. This last mission is served by their plant clinic and the Garden Hotline, (910) 452-6393, where volunteer master gardeners field questions about horticulture from 9 AM to 5 PM. The arboretum also sponsors and hosts seminars, classes and workshops. Some of the programs offer certificates upon completion. Need a special gift for a gardener? Don't miss

WWW.TREGEMBOANIMALPARK.COM

- **10 ACRES OF EXOTIC ANIMALS**
- **OVER 80 DIFFERENT TYPES OF ANIMALS**

5811 CAROLINA BEACH RD WILMINGTON, NC 28412

910-392-3604

TREGEMBO ANIMAL PARK

the delightful variety of gifts and gardening books (their specialty) available at The Potting Shed gift shop, (910) 452-3470, in the Reception Center. The shop is open from 10 AM to 4 PM Monday through Friday.

Admission to the arboretum is free. Donations are welcome and much needed. Funding is primarily by individual and corporate sponsors, volunteers, fund-raising events and local garden clubs. Volunteer docents lead tours on request during Extension office hours from 8 AM to 5 PM Monday through Friday. Self-guided tours are permitted daily from dawn to dusk. (The gates are closed but not locked during this time.) Enter the grounds from Oleander Drive (U.S. Highway 76) immediately east of Greenville Loop Road and west of the Bradley Creek bridge. And, yes, the arboretum is available for weddings.

Tregembo Animal Park
5811 Carolina Beach Rd., Wilmington
(910) 392-3604
www.tregemboanimalpark.com

Formerly known as the Tote-Em-In Zoo, Tregembo Animal Park will delight and amaze kids of all ages. Carrying on a family tradition that goes back more than 50 years, the Tregembos have expanded and updated the zoo to create habitats for their animals from around the world. There are some of the familiar zoo favorites like Jashan the white tiger, a lion named Simba and Ben the bear, along with some exotic new additions including a giraffe, a zebra and a group of ring-tailed lemurs that reside on their very own Lemur Island. Kids will have a great time exploring the park, feeding the ducks and goats, and watching the amusing primate antics of the monkeys. Tregembo Animal Park is a fun place to spend an afternoon with the kids (or grandkids). Their large gift shop is filled with seashells, nautical items, T-shirts, toys and souvenirs. Tregembo Animal Park is open from 9 AM to 5 PM daily and closes during the winter season. Ticket prices are $8 and for adults, $7 for seniors 55 and over and $6 for kids ages 2 to 12. Group rates are available for school groups, but please call in advance.

Outside Wilmington

Cape Fear River Circle Tour
Southport-Fort Fisher Ferry, U.S. Hwy. 421,
south of Kure Beach
(910) 458-3329 (Ft. Fisher),
(910) 457-6942 (Southport),
(800) 368-8969

A Circle Tour brochure is available at the ferry, the Cape Fear Coast Convention & Visitors Bureau, 24 N. Third Street, Wilmington, (910) 341-4030, and visitor information racks throughout the area. It directs you around a loop that includes a ride on the Fort Fisher/ Southport ferry and connects Wilmington, Pleasure Island, Southport and eastern Brunswick County. The circle tour will bring you to seven major attractions (free unless otherwise noted): Battleship North Carolina (fee),

Orton Plantation Gardens (fee), Brunswick Town/Fort Anderson, Southport Maritime Museum (fee), Progress Energy's Brunswick Nuclear Plant, North Carolina Aquarium (fee) and Fort Fisher Civil War Museum. Total time for driving is about two hours, which includes about 30 minutes riding the ferry. The brochure provides information on the attractions and ferry schedule.

Historic Poplar Grove Plantation
10200 U.S. Hwy. 17, Wilmington
(910) 686-9518 Ext. 26

This 1850 Greek Revival house and the 628-acre plantation were supported by as many as 64 slaves prior to the Civil War. Today, costumed guides lead visitors through this lovingly restored mansion and recount the plantation's history. Skills important to daily 19th-century life, such as weaving, smithery and basketry, are frequently demonstrated, and visitors are invited to walk the estate's grounds and view the plantation's outbuildings, including a tenant house, an outdoor kitchen and more.

Poplar Grove, dedicated to preserving the plantation's heritage, maintains a busy schedule of classes and demonstrations throughout the year. Annual events include Halloween hayrides, the Down Home Antiques Fair, an Herb and Garden Fair, Baskets of Summer, Arts in These Parts, and a Christmas Open House. Check out the Annual Events chapter for detailed descriptions or call the Poplar Grove plantation offices, (910) 686-9518, Ext. 26.

Listed on the National Register of Historic Places, Poplar Grove Plantation is 9 miles outside Wilmington on U.S. 17 at the Pender County line. A gift shop, playground, picnic area, restaurant and wedding and party facilities are located on the grounds. Poplar Grove Plantation is open to the public Monday through Saturday 9 AM to 5 PM and Sunday noon to 5 PM. Please note that the last guided tour of the plantation house is at 4 PM daily. Fees for the guided house tour are $8 for adults ($6 each for groups of 15 or more), $7 for seniors, $5 for students ages 6 to 15 and free for children 5 and younger. Poplar Grove will be closed for Easter, Thanksgiving and from December 16 through February 1; call for Christmas hours. Parking is plentiful, and access to the estate's grounds and outbuildings are free.

Wrightsville Beach

Wrightsville Beach Museum of History
303 W. Salisbury St., Wrightsville Beach
(910) 256-2569

The Wrightsville Beach Museum is housed in the Myers cottage, one of the oldest cottages on the beach (built in 1907). The museum opened its doors in May 1995. The museum presents beach history and lifestyles through permanent exhibits featuring a scale model of the oldest built-up section of the beach, photos, furniture, artifacts, a slide show and recorded oral histories, plus rotating exhibits on loggerhead turtles, surfing, the Civil War, shipwrecks, hurricanes and beach nightlife at such bygone attractions as the Lumina Pavilion. The museum is open Tuesday through Friday 10 AM to 4 PM, Saturday noon to 5 PM and Sunday 1 to 5 PM. Admission is $3. Children younger than 12 are admitted free with an adult. The museum is wheelchair accessible. Upon crossing the drawbridge, bear left at the "Welcome to Wrightsville Beach" sign; the museum is on the right near the volleyball courts beyond the fire station.

Wrightsville Beach Scenic Cruises
Waynick Blvd., Wrightsville Beach
(910) 350-2628

In the warm season, a cruise aboard the 40-foot pontoon vessel along the calm Intracoastal Waterway affords a fine view of the landscape and wildlife of the tidal environment. Nature excursions to Masonboro Island are guided by a marine biologist. One-hour

When you're going to take the Southport-Fort Fisher Ferry, be sure to arrive early — at least 20 minutes — during the tourist season. The ferry is quite popular and fills quickly. Snacks and drinks are available and there's plenty of room to wander while you wait. When feeding the gulls while you're on the ferry, do so from the stern (back end); the other passengers will appreciate that, and the captain will fuss at you if you don't!

harbor cruises, shuttles to Masonboro Island and sunset cruises are other highlights. Walk-ons are accepted, but reservations are required for the narrated nature excursions. Call for in-season cruise and excursion schedules and off-season charters and small-group excursions. Motor boats and a 40-foot motor yacht are available for rental.

Carolina Beach and Kure Beach

Fort Fisher-Southport Ferry
U.S. Hwy. 421, south of Kure Beach
(910) 457-6942

More than transportation, this half-hour crossing is a journey into the natural and social history of the Cape Fear River. You'll have excellent views of Federal Point, Zeke's Island and The Rocks from the upper deck. On the Southport side, you'll spot historic Price's Creek Lighthouse at the mouth of the inlet. The crew is knowledgeable, and the cabin is air-conditioned. When traveling between Southport and New Hanover County, timing your trip to the ferry schedule makes getting there half the fun. (See our Getting Here, Getting Around chapter for schedules.)

One-way fees are $1 for pedestrians, $2 for bicycle and rider, $3 for motorcycles, $5 for vehicles from 20 feet or less, $10 for vehicles 20 to 40 feet, $15 for vehicles 40 to 65 feet. The ferry can be part of a wide-ranging, self-directed car-and-foot Circle Tour that includes seven attractions and museums in Wilmington, Southport and Pleasure Island. See our listing for the Cape Fear River Circle Tour in the Outside Wilmington section of this chapter.

Fort Fisher State Historic Site
U.S. Hwy. 421, south of Kure Beach
(910) 458-5538

Fort Fisher was the last major Confederate stronghold to fall to Union forces during the War Between the States. It was the linchpin of the Confederate Army's Cape Fear Defense System, which included forts Caswell, Anderson and Johnston and a series of smaller batteries. Largely due to the tenacity of its defenders, the port of Wilmington was never entirely sealed by the Union blockade until January 1865. The Union bombardment of Fort Fisher was the heaviest naval demonstration in history up to that time. During the war, the fort, which stretched for 1.5 miles, was the largest and strongest earthen fort in the Confederacy.

Today, the Department of Cultural Resources operates and maintains the remains of Fort Fisher as a State Historic Site. The property boasts scenic easements of both the Cape Fear River and the Atlantic Ocean. A quarter-mile tour trail surrounds the archaeological remains of the Confederate fort. Exterior exhibits, a reconstructed palisade fence and a partially restored gun emplacement enhance historic interpretation.

The tour trail encircles the Western Bastion, including the partially restored Shepherd's Battery, which boasts a fully functional reproduction of a rifled and banded 32-pounder cannon. This huge gun is the only one in the nation said to be fired on a regular basis. On the north side of the fort, re-created palisades will be of interest to Civil War buffs. Because Fort Fisher is an archeological site, metal detectors are prohibited.

Following your visit to the fort, walk across U.S. Route 421 to the Cove, where you'll find a live oak–lined area overlooking the ocean; it's a great place for a relaxing stroll by the ocean. Swimming here is discouraged because of dangerous currents and underwater hazards. However, miles of unspoiled beaches are available immediately to the south at Fort Fisher State Recreation Area, complete with bathhouse showers, visitors center and concession stand. (See Sports, Fitness and Parks.)

Highlights of the Fort Fisher Historic Site's renovated visitors center include an upgraded theater, an enlarged gift shop, disabled-accessible restrooms, a free 15-minute audiovisual program chronicling the history of the fort, a museum and a state-of-the-art, 16-foot fiber optic map. An eight-minute narrative accompanying the map narrates the final Battle of Fort Fisher. Civil War enthusiasts will especially enjoy the expanded exhibits, dioramas, artifacts and an informative audio program. The surrounding grounds, including The Cove and earthworks, are open to the public and are available for tour daily.

The site, about 19 miles south of Wilmington, was once commonly known as Federal Point. The ferry from Southport is an excel-

CLOSE-UP

The Three
Cape Fear Lighthouses

The first lighthouses built on North Carolina's southern coast were a series of beacons installed along the 25-mile stretch from the mouth of the Cape Fear River to Wilmington. Lighthouses like Campbell Island Light, Orton's Point Light, Upper Jetty Light and the lightship at Horseshoe Shoal have all disappeared. Price Creek Lighthouse is the only one of this original series that stands today.

Price Creek Lighthouse

Price Creek Lighthouse, erected in 1849, was the last lighthouse built in the original series. Originally there were two beacons standing next to each other at this site: a 20-foot circular brick structure and a wooden structure on top of a keeper's brick house. During the Civil War, the keeper's house was used as a Confederate States Signal Station and the beacons were a means of communication between Fort Fisher and Fort Caswell. In the hands of the Confederate States Signal Corps, the beacons served military and civilian blockade runners.

The wooden tower was seriously damaged between the late 1800s and early 1900s and eventually disintegrated. The brick beacon still stands, though it was damaged during the Civil War when the Confederate forces damaged or destroyed all beacons to prevent Union forces from safely navigating the river.

The Price Creek Lighthouse is located on private property on the west bank of the Cape Fear River, about two miles above Southport. It can be seen clearly in the distance from aboard the deck of the Southport/Fort Fisher Ferry while in the mouth of the Southport Harbor. At this writing, Price Creek Lighthouse cannot be toured, but some discussion about making it available to the public is being held.

Bald Head Island Lighthouse

The 1817 Bald Head Island Lighthouse, known as "Old Baldy", was not the first beacon to stand on Bald Head Island. The first was the 1795 Bald Head Island Light Station — actually the first lighthouse structure built in North Carolina. The first light station, however, was built too close to the water, was plagued with erosion problems and was torn down by 1810.

In 1817 the 109-foot-tall Old Baldy was built of bricks coated with cement on the outside. Inside it has a ground floor of brick and a stone floor in the lantern room while the rest of the floors are Carolina yellow pine. It still has the original 12" by 14" double glazed windows from Boston.

Old Baldy is one of three lighthouses in the Cape Fear region.

credit: Jay Tervo

Because of the limited range of its lens, the Bald Head Island Lighthouse was not useful for warning ships away from Frying Pan Shoals which extend over 30 nautical miles out into the ocean. In 1854 Congress voted to place a lightship on the shoals. When the Cape Fear Lighthouse, a 150-foot steel skeleton structure, was built on the shoals in 1903, Old Baldy was downgraded to a low-intensity non-blinking light.

The Bald Head Island Lighthouse was discontinued in 1935, but from 1941 to 1958 the structure housed a radio beacon to guide ships in low visibility. With the construction of the Oak Island Lighthouse in 1958, the Cape Fear Lighthouse was dismantled and the radio beacon was removed from Old Baldy.

On self-guided tours of Old Baldy, which is now an historic site, you can climb all the way to the top. A small climbing fee is charged at the museum next door and the funds are used for preservation of the structure. Or you can arrange to participate in the Bald Head Island Historic tour by calling Ann Mills at (910) 457-7481.

Oak Island Lighthouse

Constructed in 1958, the present Oak Island Lighthouse was one of the last lighthouses built in America and is the last manually operated lighthouse in the world. It was not the first beacon on Oak Island. As in the case of the Price Creek Lighthouse, there were originally two beacons on Oak Island, part of the series of navigational lights designed to guide ships to the harbors of Brunswick Town and Wilmington.

The original beacons were meant to be situated to allow approaching ships to line them up to help with navigation, but they were not properly placed. Both lights were destroyed during the Civil War. They were rebuilt in 1879, but the front beacon was seriously damaged by a hurricane in 1893, and their use was discontinued the following year.

The present lighthouse is 153 feet high with an 8-inch thick reinforced concrete base anchored with 24 pipe pilings filled with concrete to 67 feet below ground. This design allows the tower to sway about three inches in a 100 mile per hour wind. The tower itself is concrete with color compounds mixed into it to keep it from ever needing painting.

The 11-foot-tall aluminum lantern on top arrived by water from Portsmouth, Virginia, and was put into place by two Marine helicopters. The 4,000-watt, aero-beam lights can be seen 24 miles out to sea. A second bank of lights is used as backup. With 2,500,000 candlepower, it is one of the most powerful lighthouses in the world. Its characteristic flash pattern is four flashes every ten seconds.

Members of the U.S. Coast Guard act as light keepers and climb the 120 narrow metal steps to the platform and a 14-rung metal ladder to the lantern room for weekly inspections. A metal box attached to a shelf with a pulley is used to haul tools, lamps and other supplies to the top of the tower. From the base of the tower, the light is switched on each evening 30 minutes before sunset and off each morning 30 minutes after sunrise.

In 2003, because the service provided by the lighthouse, though it is useful, is no longer considered vital, the National Park Service and the U.S. General Services Administration approved the gift of the lighthouse to the town of Caswell Beach. This transfer ensures that the lighthouse will remain in local control with proper preservation. The Town of Caswell Beach has formed the Friends of the Oak Island Lighthouse (FOIL). The members of the group have built a handicapped accessible walkway over the dunes and a viewing platform across the street from the lighthouse and overlooking the five acres of beachfront which was included in the transfer of the lighthouse property.

lent and time-saving way to get there from Brunswick County. From April through September, the visitors center is open Monday through Saturday 9 AM to 5 PM and Sunday 1 to 5 PM; winter hours, November through March, are Tuesday through Saturday 10 AM to 4 PM (closed Sunday and Monday). For more information, guided tour schedules or to inquire about group tours, call the phone number above. Admission is free but donations are appreciated.

North Carolina Aquarium at Fort Fisher
900 Loggerhead Rd., Kure Beach
(910) 458-8257
www.ncaquariums.com

The North Carolina Aquarium at Fort Fisher continues to grow, even after completing a size-tripling renovation in 2002. Sea snakes, lionfish, cuttlefish and an octopus are among the new exhibits of 2005. Located on the ocean, east of U.S. 421 and south of Kure Beach, (15 miles south of Wilmington), the facility is one of three state-owned aquariums on the North Carolina coast. Visitors begin with a huge freshwater conservatory, and then move toward a quarter-million-gallon ocean tank, experiencing along the way a variety of fascinating exhibits. The journey is like a trip down the Cape Fear River, beginning with a Piedmont waterfall, continuing along creeks, swamps, estuaries and beaches, and finishing in the open ocean beyond the river's mouth. Altogether, 2,600 creatures are on exhibit. It's open daily 9 AM to 5 PM except Christmas, New Year's and Thanksgiving days. Admission is $8 for adults, $7 for seniors, and $6 for ages 6-17. The aquarium also hosts many fun events, classes and programs for all ages. See our Kidstuff chapter for a more detailed description of this exciting attraction.

Wheel Fun Rentals
107 Carolina Beach Ave. N., Carolina Beach
(910) 458-4545
Lake Park Blvd. and Atlanta Ave.,
Carolina Beach
(910) 458-4545

Tired of sunbathing? Want to add some excitement to your trip to the beach? Try exploring Carolina Beach in a Deuce Coupe, surrey or Chopper from Wheel Fun Rentals. The Deuce Coupe is a covered bicycle built for two, allowing couples to pedal side-by-side (great idea for a date). Equipped with lights, the four-wheeled covered Surrey can seat up to six adults and two children, making it perfect for a family or group outing. Or for those who prefer to go it alone, the Chopper offers a sleek and stylish way to pedal along the boardwalk. Don't have any beach gear? Wheel Fun Rentals has everything you could need for a day at the beach, from surfboards and boogie boards to beach umbrellas, chairs and sand toys. Or try their Lake Park location where you can rent paddleboats and kayaks, and spend a quiet afternoon paddling on the lake. Wheel Fun Rentals is open every day from 9 AM to 10 PM (weather permitting). Call to book parties or special events.

Brunswick County Beaches

BALD HEAD ISLAND

Bald Head Island Historic Tour
Departure from Indigo Plantation,
W. Ninth St., Southport
(910) 457-5003

This guided-tour package may be the most convenient way for a daytripper to get to know Bald Head past and present. The three-hour tour, provided year round, begins with a 10 AM ferry departure and includes visits to Old Baldy Lighthouse, the Smith Island Museum of History and Captain Charlie's Station. Put into service in 1817, Old Baldy is the state's oldest standing lighthouse, the second of three built on the island to guide ships across the Cape Fear Bar and into the river channel. The tour fee ($40 per adult, $35 per child 12 and younger — subject to change) includes the round-trip ferry ride, the island tour and an $8 voucher toward the purchase of lunch at the River Pilot Cafe. Tour guests return to Southport by ferry at 2:30 PM. Reservations are required and can be made at the above number. For more information, you may call (910) 457-7481. You must arrive at the departure site by 9:30 AM for the 10 AM departure. If you prefer to linger on the island after the tour, ferries to Southport run every hour on the half-hour. Remember to dress appropriately for the weather and wear comfortable shoes as the tour requires walking.

SOUTHPORT/OAK ISLAND

The Chapel of the Cross at St. Philip's
E. Moore and Dry Sts., Southport
(910) 457-5643

Southport's oldest church was in continuous use until Easter Sunday 2004, when St. Philip's dedicated a new 350-seat church on property across the street. The new church has the traditional clapboard look on the exterior, a bell tower and carillon. The Chapel of the Cross at St. Philip's is a beautiful clapboard church erected in 1843, partly through the efforts of Colonel Thomas Childs, then commander of Fort Johnston, one block east. It stands beside Southport City Hall. Within the chapel flies nearly every flag that has flown over the parish since 1741, including Spanish and English.

The building exhibits Carpenter-style Greek Revival elements, particularly evident in the pediments and exterior wooden pilasters, as well as English Gothic details. Entrance is made through the small, square tower, with its louvered belfry, simple exterior arcading and colored-glass lancet windows. The church's side windows of diamond-paned clear glass flood the sanctuary with light, illuminating the handsome tongue-and-groove woodwork on the walls and ceiling. It's a beautiful, quiet place that remains open 24 hours a day for meditation, prayer or rest as well as being available for funerals, weddings, healing services and other religious forums. Guidelines are available for those interested in using the chapel for religious purposes.

Environmental Overlook Trails
3003 E. Oak Island Dr., Oak Island
(910) 278-5518

If you like wandering and looking for wildlife, these trails are for you. The Butterfly/Hummingbird Garden is located on the trail behind the Recreation Center at 3003 E. Oak Island Drive. There are elevated platforms overlooking the path, including indigenous trees and flowers and plants that attract butterflies and hummingbirds. A trail to the west side of the Recreation Center leads into the rainforest area, where the wetlands can be

viewed from elevated platforms. At the east end of 31st Street (next to the Recreation Center) is Tidal Waves Park, where you will find a small picnic shelter near the floating dock, which can be used for launching canoes and kayaks. Canoe/kayak trail maps are available at the center. The Environment Crossover crosses the Davis Canal, giving an elevated view of the canal and the wetlands on either side. The trail winds through the trees to the other side of the island, and a crossover walk leads to the ocean side and gives a closer view of the salt marsh. Wildlife, such as snakes, raccoons deer, and various birds, make their appearances here.

The Town of Oak Island has also purchased land at the west end of Oak Island, where they are preserving the dunes. A wooden walkway has been constructed on which you can wander through the dunes and stop at overlook points where you may chance to see red fox, black snakes, fiddler crabs, loggerhead sea turtles, raccoons or several species of shorebirds.

Fort Caswell
Caswell Beach Rd., Caswell Beach
(910) 278-9501

Considered one of the strongest forts of its time, Fort Caswell originally encompassed some 2,800 acres at the east end of Oak Island. Completed in 1838, the compound consisted of earthen ramparts enclosing a roughly pentagonal brick-and-masonry fort and citadel. Caswell proved to be so effective a deterrent during the Civil War that it saw little action. Supply lines were cut after Fort Fisher fell to Union forces in January 1865, so before abandoning the fort, the Caswell garrison detonated the powder magazine, heavily damaging the citadel and surrounding earthworks. What remains of the citadel is essentially unaltered and is maintained by the Baptist Assembly of North Carolina, which owns the property. A more expansive system of batteries and a sea wall were constructed during the war-wary years from 1885 to 1902. Between the Tuesday after Labor Day and the Friday before Memorial Day, Fort Caswell is open for self-guided visits Monday through Friday 8 AM to 5 PM and Saturday 8 AM to noon. Admission is $3 per person.

The Grove
Franklin Square Park,
E. West and Howe Sts., Southport

Shaded by centuries-old live oaks and aflame with color in spring, this is a park to savor — a place in which to drink in the spirit of old Smithville. The walls and entrances that embrace The Grove were constructed of ballast stones used in ships more than 100 years ago. Set back among the oaks, stately Franklin Square Gallery was once a schoolhouse and then City Hall and now is an art gallery displaying art in several media. The park is a place to indulge in local legend by taking a drink of well water from the old pump — a draught that is sure to take you back to a simpler time.

Keziah Memorial Park
W. Moore and S. Lord Sts., Southport

A shady little park with a gazebo, benches and a partial view of the waterfront, Keziah Park is notable for its uncannily bent live oak. Estimated to be 800 years old, the tree is called the Indian Trail Tree after the legend that it was curved while a sapling by ancient natives who used it to blaze the approach to their preferred fishing grounds beyond. It later rooted itself a second time, completing an arch.

North Carolina Maritime
Museum at Southport
116 N. Howe St., Southport
(910) 457-0003

Read "Gentleman Pirate" Stede Bonnet's plea for clemency, delivered just before he was hanged; view treasures rescued from local shipwrecks; see a 2,000-year-old Indian canoe fragment; inspect the fine details of nearly 100 hand-built ship models; learn about hurricanes, sharks' teeth, shrimping nets and much more in one of the region's newest and most ambitious museums. Many of the exhibits are hands-on, and a Jeopardy-style trivia board is a favorite of history buffs of all ages. The museum boasts an extensive maritime research library and video collection and is within walking distance of Southport's restaurants and shopping. Hours are 9 AM to 5 PM Tuesday through Saturday. Admission is $2 for adults age 16 and older, $1 for seniors (62 and older) and free for children younger than 16. Ask about periodic special exhibits and lectures.

Old Brunswick Town State Historic Site/
Fort Anderson
8884 St. Philips Rd. SE, off N.C. Hwy. 133,
Southport
(910) 371-6613

At this site stood the first successful permanent European settlement between Charleston and New Bern. It was founded in 1726 by Roger and Maurice Moore (who recognized an unprecedented real estate opportunity in the wake of the Tuscarora War, 1711-13), and the site served as port and political center. Russelborough, home of two royal governors, once stood nearby. In 1748 the settlement was attacked by Spanish privateers, who were soundly defeated in a surprise counterattack by the Brunswick settlers. A painting of Christ (Ecce Homo), reputedly 400 years old, was among the Spanish ship's plunder and now hangs in St. James Episcopal Church in Wilmington. At Brunswick Town in 1765, one of the first instances of armed resistance to the British crown occurred in response to the Stamp Act. In time, the upstart, upriver port of Wilmington superseded Brunswick. In 1776 the British burned Brunswick, and in 1862 Fort Anderson was built there to help defend Port Wilmington. The earthworks of Fort Anderson are 100 percent intact and one of the best examples of earthworks that exist today. Occasional church services are still held in the ruins of St. Philip's Church.

Admission to the historic site is free and open to the public all year, Tuesdays through Saturdays from 10 AM until 4 PM. The site is closed on most major holidays. From Wilmington, take N.C. 133 about 18 miles to Plantation Road. Signs will direct you to the site (exit left) that lies close to Orton Plantation Gardens. The site's visitors center offers a gift shop, a research library, an exhibit hall, a 14-minute slide presentation on the history of Old Brunswick Town, staff offices and handicapped accessibility.

Old Smithville Burial Ground
E. Moore and S. Rhett Sts., Southport

"The Winds and the Sea sing their requiem and shall forever more. . .". Profoundly evocative of the harsh realities endured by Southport's long-gone seafarers, the Old Smithville Burial Ground (1804) is a must-see. Obelisks dedicated to lost river pilots, monuments to entire crews and families who lived and died by the sea, and stoic elegies memorialize Southport's past as no other historic site can. Many of the names immortalized on these stones live on among descendants still living in the area.

Orton Plantation Gardens
Off N.C. Hwy. 133, Southport
(910) 371-6851

Orton Plantation represents one of the region's oldest historically significant residences in continuous use. The family names associated with it make up the very root and fiber of Cape Fear's history. Built in 1725 by the imperious "King" Roger Moore, founder of Brunswick Town, the main residence at Orton Plantation underwent several expansions to become the archetype of old Southern elegance. It survived the ravages of the Civil War despite being used as a Union hospital after the fall of Fort Fisher. Thereafter it stood abandoned for 19 years until it was purchased and refurbished by Col. Kenneth McKenzie Murchison, CSA.

In 1904 the property passed to the Sprunt family, related to the Murchisons by marriage, and the plantation gardens began taking shape. In 1915 the family built Luola's Chapel, a Doric structure of modest grandeur available today for meetings and private weddings. The gardens, both formal and natural, are among the most beautiful in the east, consisting of ponds, fountains, statuary, footbridges and stands of cypress. The elaborately sculpted Scroll Garden overlooks former rice fields. Elsewhere are the tombs of Roger Moore and his family. The best times to visit Orton Plantation are from late winter to late spring. Camellias, azaleas, pansies, flowering trees and other ornamentals bloom in early spring; later, oleander, hydrangea, crepe myrtle, magnolia and annuals burst with color. Bring insect repellent in the summer. If you're lucky, you may catch a glimpse of Buster, the 10-foot gator who has lived in the lagoon near the house for many years. He's been known to sun himself in front of the gardens. Touring the gardens takes an easily paced hour or more.

The gardens are open every day. From March through August hours are 8 AM to 6 PM and from September through November hours are 10 AM to 5 PM. Admission is $9 for adults, $8 for seniors, $3 for children ages 6 through 16 and free for children younger than

6. Group rates are available. Orton Plantation is off N.C. 133, 18 miles south of Wilmington and 10 miles north of Southport. Nearby are the historic sites of Brunswick Town and Fort Anderson.

Priority Sailing
606 W. West St., Southport
(910) 454-4479

David and Carolyn Pryor, retired professors and sailors extraordinaire, offer customized adventure cruises aboard the 52-foot cutter, Carolina Gale, providing opportunities to sail on the Atlantic Ocean and Cape Fear River. Up to six sailors of various skill levels may participate in the operation of the sailboat or just sit back and relax. The captains provide information on history, marine life and ecology as well as sailing knowledge and skills. Morning, Afternoon or Sunset Cruises sail the Atlantic Ocean along Oak Island, Bald Head Island or up the Cape Fear River along Battery Island and the Southport shore. There are also Full Moon Cruises and Weekend Cruise packages. The dinghy, Cats Paw, can be used for exploration or trips to shore. The Pryors provide sailing instruction as well (see our Watersports chapter). Because Priority Sailing is affiliated with the non-profit organization Priority Human Services, your sailing adventure helps to promote child, youth and family development.

Progress Energy -
Brunswick Plant Energy Center
8520 River Rd., N.C. Hwy. 87, Southport
(910) 457-6041

Have you ever wondered exactly how electricity is produced by nuclear energy? Of course, nuclear power plants are off limits to the general public, but in the Visitors Center you can see a model of the Southport plant, watch it operate and listen to the audio recording explaining the process.

Do you know that one million gallons of water per minute flow through the cooling units of the power plant in Southport? You will find exhibits that show the methods used for keeping sea turtles from entering the intake canal and for screening fish and other sea creatures where the water enters the plant, sending them down the "slide for life" to a holding pond and returning them to their natural environment.

Topsail Island's
Karen Beasley Sea Turtle Rescue
and Rehabilitation Center

A late-night walk along the strand on Topsail Island becomes an amazing and humbling experience for a local couple. When their flashlight beam shines on a strange marking in the sand, they follow the trail to an astonishing sight. A 350-pond Loggerhead sea turtle is at the dune line digging sand with her flippers.

A sea turtle hatchling
—
photo: Courtesy of Karen Beasley Sea Turtle Rehabilitation Center

Being Insiders, they know exactly what to do: turn off the light, take the dog back to the truck and call the "Turtle Lady," as Jean Beasley is affectionately known on the island. Beasley is Director of Topsail Island's Karen Beasley Sea Turtle Rescue and Rehabilitation Center, a nonprofit, all-volunteer center dedicated to saving and rescuing sea turtles and educating the public about these marvelous creatures. Within moments Beasley arrives and begins intervention on behalf of the turtle. She removes obstacles that might impede the turtle's movement and sits quietly to observe and protect the turtle without disturbing it from its ancient rite of passage.

Sea turtles are prehistoric creatures, having swum in the oceans as many as 115 million years ago. A turtle may live to 100 or more years of age. They ritually return year after year to their coastal nesting area to lay their eggs beneath the sand. As many as 120 eggs are buried and the mother then lumbers back into the breaking surf and disappears, repeating this four to five times a summer.

Only one of thousands of hatchlings may survive to adulthood. The hatchling must dig itself out of the sand, turn towards the ocean and navigate its way down the beach and into the surf. It must overcome hostile circumstances like tire ruts in the sand, litter and especially lights. The baby turtles attempt to make their primal journey to the sea at night to avoid natural predators, but often the beaches are no longer dark but lighted by resort and residential development. In an undeveloped, moonlit setting the ocean would be lighter than the land and the hatchling instinctively would move toward the light.

Jean Beasley and her band of volunteers have worked tirelessly to educate people to turn off outside lighting in hatching season. The education process had been so effective that one of the island's largest resort condominium complexes, the St. Regis, has agreed to turn off the lights along their section of beachfront.

Despite these inroads, humans continue to be the most caustic factor in the endangerment of sea turtles. While many people point their fingers at commercial fishing as the culprit, Beasley is quick to point out that we all play a role in the degradation of the marine environment. Recreational boating is a major cause of impact injury to sea turtles. But the litter like Styrofoam cups, plastic bottles, plastic six-pack rings, cigarette butts, abandoned fishing lines and nets are all deadly to sea turtles, who either ingest them or becomes entangled in them and drown. Long-line hooks offshore, set nets, as well as toxins from agriculture, farming and landscaping run-off also endanger marine life.

The Topsail Island Turtle Project began several years ago when local resident Karen Beasley committed her efforts to save the endangered sea turtle. After Karen's death from cancer, the torch was passed to her mother, Jean Beasley. Since the early 1990s the project has grown to include a turtle hospital, an interns' house, scores of volunteers and growing international recognition as a sea turtle haven and expert resource. With no paid staff, including Beasley, and interns who receive only housing with no stipend, it is immediately apparent that dedication, compassion and hard work are what run the center.

Funded primarily by private donations that range from school kids' coins to major gifts of several thousand dollars, the project puts 100 percent of donations to work for the turtles. Grants are sought for specific programs, like satellite tagging recently made possible by a large corporate grant. The satellite-tagging program will study the relatively unknown migratory patterns of sea turtles. Five of the world's seven species of sea turtles have been found in the waters off Topsail Island.

The turtle hospital is cramped, humid and smells of the ocean. Several plastic tanks of varying sizes house the "patients." CJ, one of the most well-known patients here, had the biggest tub. CJ was a Loggerhead who was at least 50 years old. He came ashore on Ocean Isle in October of 2002 and was observed struggling in the surf for several days to the dismay of volunteers who could not capture him. He finally washed ashore in an emaciated state covered with leeches and barnacles. With eyes sunken in and barely enough flesh left to cover his bones, he was brought to the turtle hospital. Beasley speculated that he was too large to escape through the turtle excluder device that commercial fishing boats have on their drag nets. If a sea turtle aspirates water it will become what's known as a floater. Unable to dive or hunt for food, it will eventually starve to death, and this is probably what would have happened to CJ if he had not been rescued. With tender care at the turtle hospital, CJ regained his strength and grandeur. His release back into the ocean was an emotional and triumphant act of closure for those who so lovingly nursed him back to health. Turtle releases on Topsail Island often draw crowds of spectators who share in the feel-good moment of glory.

Jean Beasley,
"The Turtle Lady"
—
photo: Courtesy of Karen Beasley Sea Turtle Rehabilitation Center

The Karen Beasley Sea Turtle Rescue and Rehabilitation Center is at 822 Carolina Boulevard in Topsail Beach. For more information call (910) 328-3377, visit their website at www.seaturtlehospital.org or see the write-up in our Attractions chapter.

Other exhibits include explanations of used fuel storage, how to read an electric meter, stationary bikes which you can pedal to see how much electricity you can generate, a mini theatre where you can watch videos about the industry, and more. The exhibits are open during various times, so it's best to call (910) 457-6041 for more information and for a listing of phone numbers. The center is closed on holidays and weekends. Tour of the exhibits is self-guided, and admission is free. Programs, presentations and guided tours are available for school and civic groups with advance arrangements.

Southport Trail
(910) 457-7927

This two-mile-long walking tour links 25 historic landmarks, among them the tiny Old Brunswick County Jail and the Stede Bonnet Memorial. Architectural beauty abounds along the route, revealing Queen Anne gables, Southport arch and bow, and porches trimmed in gingerbread. The free brochure describing this informal, self-guided chain of discoveries can be obtained at the Southport Visitor Center, 113 W. Moore Street (where the tour begins) Monday through Saturday from 10 AM to 5 PM in summer. Off-season, call for information at (800) 388-9635.

St. Philip's Parish
Old Brunswick Town State Historic Site, off N.C. Hwy. 133, north of Southport
(910) 371-6613

After St. James Episcopal Church left Brunswick Town in favor of the rival port of Wilmington, the Anglican parish of St. Philip formed in 1741. In 1754 it began building a brick church at Brunswick, the seat of royal government in the colony. After struggling with finances and a destructive hurricane, the church was finally completed in 1768, only to be burned by the British in 1776 (the colony's first armed resistance to the Stamp Act occurred nearby at the royal governor's residence).

Today, all that remains of St. Philip's church, the only Colonial church in southeastern North Carolina, is a rectangular shell — 25-foot-high walls, 3 feet thick — plus several Colonial-era graves (some of which are resurfacing with time). The ruin's round-arched window ports are intact and suggest Georgian detailing, but little solid evidence exists about the building's original appearance beyond some glazing on the brick. Three entrances exist, in the west, north and south walls, and three, triptych-style windows open the east wall.

Services are still held held periodically within the ruins. The body of North Carolina's first royal governor (Arthur Dobbs) is reputed to have been interred at St. Philip's, as he requested, but it has never been identified. St. Philip's Episcopal Church in Southport (see previous listing) was named after the Colonial parish to perpetuate its memory. (Also see the listing for Old Brunswick Town State Historic Site.)

Trinity United Methodist Church
209 E. Nash St., Southport
(910) 457-6633

Built c. 1890 for a total of $3,300, this church is the third to occupy this site. Today the building features two of the area's best stained-glass windows (at either side of the sanctuary); handsome, diagonally paneled walls; and a beaded ceiling (i.e., finished with narrow, half-round moldings) finished by a 15-year-old carpenter. Emblazoned across the original front-transom window is the abbreviation "M.E.C.S." (Methodist Episcopal Church, South) a remnant of the days when the church was split from its northerly brethren due to the Civil War. The clapboard exterior includes Shingle-style detailing, a cedar-shingled roof and a gabled bell tower. Trinity Church stands at the corner of N. Atlantic Avenue, east of the Fire Department and across the street from the Post Office.

Waterfront Park
Bay St., foot of Howe St., Southport

At the end of Howe Street, you'll come upon this breezy little park and take in the breathtaking scene at the convergence of the Intracoastal Waterway, the Cape Fear River and the Atlantic Ocean. From the swings overlooking the waterfront you can see Old Baldy Lighthouse and Oak Island Lighthouse (the brightest in the nation). Gone are the pirate ships and menhaden boats, but the procession of ferries, freighters, barges and sailboats keeps Southport's maritime tradition alive.

Stroll or cycle the Historic Riverwalk trail, an easy 0.7-mile scenic route that meanders from the City Pier, past the fisheries and the small boat harbor, and culminates at a 750-foot boardwalk with benches and handrails over the tidal marsh near Southport Marina. Leave your bike in the rack and walk on to the gazebo for an unbroken view of the Intracoastal Waterway and the ship channel. It's a restful, romantic place where the only sounds you're likely to hear are the cawing of crows and the clank of halyards.

Winds of Carolina Sailing Charters
Southport Marina, foot of W. West St., Southport
(910) 278-7249, (910) 232-3003, (910) 457-1162

The Winds of Carolina offers four customized daily trips along the Oak Island shoreline aboard the 37-foot, twin-cabin sloop *Stephania*. The Morning Sail leaves at 9:15 AM. The Afternoon Sail leaves at 1 PM, and lunch baskets are available for this excursion at an additional cost. (The morning sail is $53 per adult and the afternoon sail is $55 per adult, $30 for children 12 and younger). The Sunset Sail ($55 per person, $30 for children) leaves at 5:30 PM (time is adjusted to coincide with the time of sunset) and includes a fruit and cheese appetizer tray. The Moonlight Sail ($55 per person, $30 for children — four people minimum for this cruise) departs at 9 PM on the five days prior to and after a full moon. Call for sailing dates. Off-season (December, January and February) trips include the Morning Sail, departing at 10:30 AM and the Sunset Sail at 3 PM. The Winds of Carolina operates year round and they are more than happy to accommodate your schedule.

All trips last three hours and are under the command of a USCG-licensed captain and a first mate. Each includes narration of points of interest and history of Oak Island, complimentary beverages and fresh towels for sun worshiping on the forward decks. Guests are welcome to take the helm while under sail. Space is limited to six passengers, and reservations are required. Half-day and full-day private custom charters are available.

Have a honeymoon, birthday or engagement celebration coming up? Book the overnight Boat & Breakfast to sleep on the boat and have your breakfast delivered to your cabin in the morning. For romanticism and privacy the Boat & Breakfast is limited to one couple per night at $125 per couple.

OCEAN ISLE BEACH

Museum of Coastal Carolina
21 E. Second St., Ocean Isle Beach
(910) 579-1016

Standing on the ocean floor would be a wonderful way to experience the marine environment up close. Visitors to this museum can do the next best thing — walk through The Reef. This largest natural seascape diorama in the Southeast is home to life-sized models of sharks, dolphins, game fish, octopus and crustaceans. The remains of a shipwreck, dating from about 1800, rest on the simulated sea floor. Elsewhere, Civil War artifacts, tidal exhibits, a display of shark jaws, a Green Swamp wildlife habitat exhibit and other artifacts and exhibits bring the natural history of the Coastal Carolinas to life. View live snakes and learn about sea turtles as well.

The Shore holds a 500-gallon Touch Tank stocked with sea stars, whelks, horseshoe crabs, sea anemones, spider crabs, hermit crabs, an assortment of fish and more.

Fall, winter and spring hours are Fridays and Saturdays from 10 AM to 4 PM and Sundays from 1 to 4 PM. Children's programs and touch tank feedings are held on Saturdays. The museum hosts an Evening Lecture Series, marsh walks, beach walks and intertidal pool walks. School groups and other visits are available during weekdays by appointment only.

Summer hours are Mondays, Tuesdays and Thursdays from 10 AM until 8:30 PM; Wednesdays, Fridays and Saturdays from 10 AM until 5 PM; and Sundays from 1 to 5 PM. Afternoon children's programs are held at 3:30 Mondays through Fridays. Evening programs include sea turtle information programs at 7 PM on Mondays and Tuesdays and a live snake program on Thursday evenings at 7 PM. Seating is limited for summer evening programs, and seats fill fast. Arrive an hour early to get a seat pass and tour the museum before the program begins.

Silver Coast Winery
6680 Barbeque Rd., Ocean Isle Beach
(910) 278-2800

Who would expect to find a winery just 15 minutes inland from the beach? Not just any winery, mind you, but an upscale, commercial vineyard and production facility situated on 40 acres, surrounded by dense, Carolina woods; a winery that has been winning gold, silver and bronze medals for their wines since opening in May of 2002. The folks at Silver Coast Winery invite you to sample wines in the tasting room, tour the winery and learn about wine making. Their wine shop includes a large selection of award winning wines and gifts (see our Shopping chapter), and the art gallery offers an eclectic display of art from local artists. Plan a private party, corporate event, or wedding (see our Wedding Planning chapter), or just enjoy a picnic lunch in the breezy gardens. They also host a variety of special events each month throughout the year (see our Annual Events chapter). During January and February, opening hours are Wednesday through Sunday from noon to 5 PM. March through December hours are Monday through Saturday 11 AM to 6 PM and Sunday from noon until 5 PM.

SUNSET BEACH

Ingram Planetarium
7625 High Market St.,
The Village at Sunset Beach, Sunset Beach
(910) 575-0033

The Ingram Planetarium is named for Stuart Ingram, founder of the Museum of Coastal Carolina. The planetarium boasts a state-of-the-art facility with a 40-foot dome theater. Programs change seasonally but always include the ever popular "The Sky Tonight." Check the website for special sky events, telescope clinics and other activities such as Mars Parties in late October and early November 2005.

The Astronomy Club meets the third Sunday of each month at 7 PM. A holiday program, Season of Light, runs from Thanksgiving weekend through the last weekend in December.

Fall, winter and spring hours are 3 to 7 PM on Thursdays through Saturdays with shows on the hour. Telescope viewing is available with light and weather permitting. Summer programs begin at 1 PM with children's programs and crafts in the Paul Dennis Science Hall followed by star shows in the theater on the hour from 2 to 7 PM Tuesdays through Saturdays. Additional summer programs include a live snake program on Tuesday evenings and a sea turtle information program on Wednesdays. The Paul Dennis Science Hall has hands-on science, math and astronomy exhibits. The gift shop is a veritable storehouse of fun, educational gifts and decorative gift ideas. School groups and other groups are scheduled during the week by appointment only.

CALABASH

The Hurricane Fleet
Deep Sea Fishing Center
Hurricane Fleet Marina, Calabash
(843) 249-3571, (800) 373-2004

The Hurricane Fleet Deep Sea Fishing Center is located in the middle of the "seafood capital of the world," where shrimp are a very large part of the catch. Have you ever wondered just how and where the shrimp are caught? Why not take a cruise on the 90-foot Hurricane II, which engages working shrimp boats while their crews explain shrimping along the Carolinas. You will see dolphin and sharks feed on the by-catch as the nets are pulled only a few feet from the bow of the Hurricane II. Most popular among all ages is the Dolphin Adventure Cruise. Cost is $21 for adults and $18 for children 11 and younger. Known for their deep-sea fishing experiences, the Hurricane Fleet has an open party boat for half-day and Gulf Stream fishing, with prices ranging from $39 to $79. Their fleet of sport-fishing vessels is available for private charter for inshore, offshore and Gulf Stream fishing for tuna, dolphin and wahoo. All fishing cruises include bait, tackle, rod and reel and fishing license. All vessels are U.S. Coast Guard approved. Call for additional information, cruise schedules, rates and reservations.

Topsail Island and Vicinity

Beach Buggy of Topsail Island
Topsail Beach
(910) 620-3388, (910) 328-1375

Beach Buggy of Topsail Island's 15-passenger shuttle bus can be just what you need for a safe night out on the town or for a Topsail Island tour, a group outing to a sporting event, bachelor/bachelorette party or anywhere you and your friends or family might wish to go together. Fully licensed and insured, Beach Buggy of Topsail Island also provides shuttle service to the Wilmington and Jacksonville airports. Call the above numbers for information or reservations.

Buccaneer Cruises
111 N. New River Dr, Surf City
(910) 546-TOUR (8687)

The Buccaneer, Surf City's newest cruise vessel, offers sightseeing, sunset and party cruises. Sightseeing cruises provide the opportunity to see dolphins, osprey and other wildlife as you cruise by Blackbeard's old hideout. Cruise times are 1, 3 and 5 PM Monday through Saturday. Sunset cruises offer time to relax and view Topsail's spectacular sunsets; they depart at 7 PM. Cost for either cruise is $10 per person, with kids younger than 12 paying $6 and kids younger than 5 riding free. Party Cruises, featuring live bands, DJs and local entertainment, are on a scheduled basis with theme nights, including a Southern-style BBQ cruise, shrimp cruise, Jimmy Buffet cruise and more. Prices are $15 or $20 per person depending on the cruise. No one younger than 21 years old is permitted on the Party Cruise. Reservations are not required. To guarantee space, stop at the dock to purchase tickets in advance.

Camp Lejeune Marine Corps Base Tour
Back Gate Base Entrance, N.C. Hwy. 172, Sneads Ferry
(910) 451-7433

In 1999 the U.S. Marine Corps instituted a self-guided tour of Camp Lejeune, home of East Coast "expeditionary forces in readiness." The tour was designed to take visitors from pre-Colonial America to the edge of technology on the base that serves the largest single concentration of Marines anywhere in the world. A printed tour guide with map, directions and a complete narrative of the 25 points of interest can be picked up at the Main Gate base entrance on N.C. Highway 24 in Jacksonville. The tour is well-marked by large white signs and can start at any specific point of interest. Depending on how much you choose to visit, a tour can range from one or two hours to a half or full day.

The legacies of Marines past are witnessed on the tour. The Montford Point and N.C. Veteran's Cemeteries are located near Camp Johnson. These two sites are the final resting places for veterans and families from the Civil and Revolutionary wars. Other points of interest include early historical spots, specific buildings, military equipment (both U.S. and captured pieces) and off-base historical locations. The tour is free, but can be closed down at any time for security purposes. For more information, call the number above.

Dorothy's Harbor Tours
720 Channel Blvd., Topsail Beach
(910) 545-RIDE(7433)

Cruise Topsail Sound and the Intracoastal Waterway in Topsail Island's tour boat, Dorothy. With seating for 28 people, this craft offers regularly scheduled daytime and sunset cruises every day from April through September, bringing you a fantastic opportunity to watch dolphins frolicking, osprey's nesting and many other joys of nature. Private charters are available. Tickets, at a cost of $12 per person, are available on site. Call

for tour departure times. No food or drinks are available, but you can bring your own.

Karen Beasley Sea Turtle Rescue and Rehabilitation Center
822 Carolina Blvd., Topsail Beach
(910) 328-3377
www.seaturtlehospital.org

While the primary purpose of this facility is the care and rehabilitation of injured sea turtles, it is open on a limited basis for the public to view and learn about this program aimed at protecting the endangered species. The center is open during the summer months on Monday, Tuesday, Thursday, Friday and Saturday from 1 to 4 PM. (Arrival close to 3 PM will not guarantee admission if there is a line of folks waiting.) The center is not open to the public at other times of the year and may close in the summer without notice for emergencies. Due to the popularity and the limited size of this facility, arrival 15 minutes before opening is suggested. No calls for reservations are accepted. Visitors can expect to see large loggerhead turtles, green sea turtles or the rare Kemp's Ridley and learn the history and problems each has endured, plus more about their treatment and predicted release. Donations are appreciated.

Missiles and More Museum
Assembly Building, 720 Channel Blvd., Topsail Beach

The Missiles and More Museum offers a tour through the history of the Topsail Island area. It begins with the early settlers and takes you through Blackbeard the Pirate to the time of World War II, when Topsail Island became part of the training ground for Camp Davis. It continues with artifacts from Operation Bumblebee, part of the nation's early space program, and the invention of the ramjet engines that were assembled here on the island and used to propel the Talos and Terrier rockets. Other displays include a history of each local town and the Ocean City Beach area. Video footage of Operation Bumblebee and World War II activities are shown as part of the museum tour. The museum is run by volunteers and is open April through October on Monday, Tuesday, Thursday, Friday and Saturday from 2 to 4 PM. For large groups, or to visit during the remainder of the year, call the Greater Topsail Area Chamber of

Commerce and Tourism at (910) 329-4446 to schedule a private showing with a docent.

Sea Turtle Nest Sitting
(910) 470-2880

Lucky vacationers walking on the beach between July and October might spot the signs of a turtle nest about to hatch. Turtle project volunteers prepare the nesting area and beach for the emerging turtles by creating runways and clearing the area of obstacles. At night, volunteers sit these nests and wait for the actual hatching. When visitors and/or residents come upon a roped-off nest that has been prepared with runways, they are welcome to join volunteers in this awe-inspiring experience. However, survival of the baby turtles requires patience and a willingness to follow instructions on the part of the spectators and participants. For volunteer information on nest sitting please call (910) 470-2880.

Shellabrations
(910) 328-5341

Shellabrations offers private, group or individual shell-identification walks along the beaches of Topsail Island. Shelling expert Pat Crist will guide your tour in areas where the most shells can be found at a particular time, or the area of your choice. There is a charge of $6 per hour for each person, with children younger than 5 coming along for free. Reservations are required.

Triple J Stables
120 Lake Haven Dr., Sneads Ferry
(910) 327-0577

Triple J Stables is a new attraction in the Topsail Area and offers trail rides and riding lessons. Guided trail rides are by appointment and should be reserved at least one day in advance. The stables are open seven days a week. Summer day camp is also available.

Turtle Talks
Location TBA
(910) 328-3377

Each Thursday afternoon at 4 PM between Memorial Day and Labor Day, an educational talk is given on the lifestyle and habits of the loggerhead turtle and how the Topsail Turtle Project is working to protect this endangered species. Questions are welcomed, and the presentation is geared to all age levels. Admission is free, and reservations are not required.

Other Islands

MASONBORO ISLAND

Evidence suggests that the first stretch of continental American coastline described by a European explorer may have been the beach now called Masonboro Island. The explorer was Giovanni da Verrazzano, the year, 1524. During the Civil War, Masonboro's beaches were visited by the destruction of three blockade runners and one Union blockader.

Before 1952 Masonboro was not an island but was attached to the mainland. In that year Carolina Beach Inlet was cut, giving Carolina Beach its boom in the tourist fishing trade and creating the last and largest undisturbed barrier island remaining on the southern North Carolina coast — 8-mile-long Masonboro Island. Made up of 5,046 acres, of which 4,300 acres are tidal salt marshes and mud flats, Masonboro is now the fourth component of the North Carolina National Estuarine Research Reserve, the other three being Zeke's Island, which lies south of Federal Point in the Cape Fear River (see listing below), Currituck Banks and Rachel Carson Island, the latter two being farther north.

Most impressive is the island's profusion of wildlife, some abundant and some endangered, in an essentially natural state. Endangered loggerhead turtles successfully nest here, as do terns, gulls, ghost crabs and brown pelicans. Their neighbors include gray foxes, marsh rabbits, opossums, raccoons and river otters. Several types of heron, snowy egrets, willets, black skimmers and clapper rails forage in the creeks and mud flats at low tide. The estuarine waters teem with 44 species of fish and a multitude of shellfish, snails, sponges and worms. Its accessibility to UNCW's marine biology program, among the world's best, makes Masonboro an ideal classroom for the study of human impact on natural habitat. More information on Masonboro Island and barrier island habitats may be obtained through UNCW's Center for Marine Science, (910) 962-2470.

Masonboro island is a peaceful place where generations of locals have fished, hunted, sunbathed, swum, surfed, camped and sat back to witness nature. Small wonder Masonboro Island has always been close to locals' hearts. Accordingly, the Coastal Management Division of the North Carolina Department of Environment, Health and Natural Resources administers the island with as little intrusion as possible. Camping, hunting and other traditional activities pursued here are allowed to continue, albeit under monitoring intended to determine whether the island can withstand such impact. So far, so good.

If you don't own a boat and can't rent one for getting to Masonboro, refer to the listing for Turtle Island Ventures in the Rowing and Canoeing section of our Watersports chapter, or see the listing for the Blockade Runner Scenic Cruises in this chapter.

ZEKE'S ISLAND

You can walk to this island reserve in the Cape Fear River and you need not walk on water. Simply drive down by the boat ramp at Federal Point (beyond the ferry terminal) and wait for low tide to allow you to walk The Rocks, a breakwater first erected in 1873 that extends beyond Zeke's Island for just more than 3 miles. You can go by boat if keeping your feet on the tricky rocks isn't your idea of fun. This component of the North Carolina National Estuarine Research Reserve consists of Zeke's Island, North Island, No-Name Island and the Basin, the body of water enclosed by the breakwater, totaling 1,160 acres. The varied habitats include salt marshes, beaches, tidal flats and estuarine waters. Bottle-nosed dolphins, red-tailed hawks, ospreys and colonies of fiddler crabs will keep you looking in every direction. Fishing, sunbathing and boating are the primary pursuits here, and hunting within regulations is allowed. Bring everything you need, pack out everything you bring, and don't forget drinking water!

KIDSTUFF

here's no limit to the wonderful imagination and limitless energy of kids. They want to know everything from "Why is the sky blue?" and "How come Santa's handwriting looks like yours?" to "What's for dinner?" and "What is there to do around here anyway?" Now that's one question you can easily answer. There really is no better place to visit or to raise a family than along North Carolina's beautiful coast. Being near the ocean means you'll find numerous water activities to engage in. And this area cherishes its history and fosters the arts, so there are many exciting educational activities too. Among a parent's greatest area resources for entertaining kids are the various museums, which offer classes and workshops in arts and crafts, and the North Carolina Aquarium at Fort Fisher, which also offers classes and workshops as well as outdoor activities. Opportunities for adolescents to learn boating skills, participate in gymnasium and team sports and take part in many other activities, both physical and cerebral, exist with the various parks and recreation departments throughout the area. To contact these resources, see the listings in our chapters on Watersports and Sports, Fitness and Parks. Information on child care can be found in our Schools and Child Care chapter.

For this chapter, we've tried to ferret out some of the participatory activities that are easily overlooked as well as the bare necessities of kidstuff to balance the ubiquitous consumer-oriented offerings. Keep in mind that many of the activities listed here are not strictly for kids; conversely, many attractions and activities listed in other chapters are not exclusively for adults. Be sure to comb other chapters (especially Attractions) for great kidstuff ideas. Each section in this chapter deals with a type of activity or interest: Amusements (including hobbies and toys), Animals, Arts, Birthday Parties, Eats, Exploring Nature, Farms, Getting Physical, Getting Wet, Going Mental (for inquisitive minds), Go Fish, Holidays and Summer Camps.

Amusements

This section is designed for children who enjoy spending their free time engaging in a favorite hobby. From comics or baseball card collecting, video game playing, airplane building to toy shopping, you've come to the right place.

Adam's Memory Lane Comics
5751 Oleander Dr., Wilmington
(910) 392-6647

Stocking one of the area's largest inventories of comic books (new and old), collections and supplies, Adam's Memory Lane is an essential stopover for comics fans. Adam's claims to have the best collection of vintage comics in southeastern North Carolina. Also stocked are Yo-Gi-Oh! game cards, Comic Shop exclusive action figures, old toys and other oddities. You'll find the shop in the Philips' Azalea Plaza a short distance west of the Greenville Loop Road intersection. Memory Lane is open Monday through Saturday noon to 6 PM and Sunday from 1 to 4 PM.

Firebird Ceramic Studio
Paint-Your-Own Pottery
Studio and Art Supplies
Racine Center for the Arts, 203 Racine Dr., Ste. 205, Wilmington
(910) 452-2073

Firebird is a full-service, paint-your-own pottery studio in a delightfully cheerful atmosphere. They provide a large selection of bisque ware with a wide variety of colors and effects. All you need to provide is your creativity. Studio assistants will glaze and fire your piece for you. Just visiting Wilmington? Firebird will ship the finished pottery to your home. You can also try your hand at mosaics and glass painting with their qualified staff to assist you. This is a great activity for birthday parties, ladies' nights

Come Over & Play!

You'll find our selection & service unsurpassed!

Learning Express is dedicated to delighting kids and making their dreams come true through innovative and engaging play. Our unique toys encourage creativity, curiosity and long lasting fun.

Learning Express Toys

www.learningexpress.com

...Always the perfect toy

Learning Express Advantages

UNIQUE Selection · EXPERT Service · B-DAY Gift Registry · Gift Wrap FREE · Personalized FREE · VIP Frequent Buyer

Progress Point · 1437 Military Cutoff Rd. · 509-0153

out, couples nights, bridal showers, kids-only hours or just an afternoon out. Come and experience the fun of painting your own pottery. Art supplies and kits are also conveniently available.

The Game Giant
419 S. College Rd., Unit 40, Wilmington
(910) 790-0154
6792 Market St., Wilmington
(910) 793-4263

Specializing in used video games and game systems, The Game Giant buys games for cash and accepts trade-ins for store credit, the amount of which varies according to the condition of, and demand for, the individual game. The Game Giant is in University Landing, across from Rockola Cafe on S. College Road (north of Oleander Drive).

Hungate's Arts, Crafts & Hobbies
Westfield Shoppingtown Independence Mall, 3500 Oleander Dr., Wilmington
(910) 799-2738

Hungate's stocks an impressive inventory of art supplies, including stretched canvas. In addition to a huge assortment of model trains, planes and automobiles, the store carries rockets, toys, puzzles, novelties, miniature collectibles and books. This is a store for kids of all ages.

Learning Express Toys
Progress Point, 1437 Military Cutoff Rd,
(corner of Military Cuttoff and Eastwood)
Wilmington
(910) 509-0153
www.learningexpress.com

Learning Express Toys is among those rare places that capture kids' imaginations with high-quality alternatives to the run-of-the-mill products. Interactive and entertaining, the store succeeds in making learning fun for kids from infancy through early adolescence. The staff includes toy experts with broad knowledge of the products, which translates into excellent service. Learning Express Toys is organized in sections geared to particular interests, such as Whiz Kids (learning games and books for boys and girls), Science & Nature (including electronics and nature projects), Let's Pretend (fantasy dress-up), Great Beginnings (for infants and toddlers) and Transit (including Thomas and Darda race tracks). This is the place to find that volcano your child needs for the diorama. Ask about professional discounts, free personalizing, free gift wrapping and

Some activities for kids on rainy days: paint-your-own pottery, bowling, movies, skating, museum classes, library story times, the North Carolina Aquarium at Fort Fisher or one of the many other indoor attractions found in our Attractions chapter.

Birthday Wish Buckets. Their mission is to help you find the perfect toy.

Pastimes Toys
Treasure Coast Square, 208-D N. New River Dr., Surf City
(910) 328-2737

Pastimes Toys offers a great variety of toys, most with educational value, for children of all ages and skill levels. You'll find games, books, crafts and puzzles for a special for a rainy day and everything you need for a good time on the beach or outdoors in the sunshine. Owners Doug and Sherry Mewborn have years of experience and can help shoppers select the perfect item to stimulate or enhance a child's special interest.

Ten Pin Alley
127 S. College Rd., Wilmington
(910) 452-5455
www.breaktimetenpin.com

This 24-lane bowling alley has plenty of fun opportunities for kids. There's a youth league that bowls every Saturday afternoon from 12:30 to 2 PM. Ten Pin Alley is filled with arcade games to add to the fun. Call for more information about joining the youth leagues.

Toys R' Us
4510 Oleander Dr., Wilmington
(910) 791-9067

The inevitable hunt for a child's toy may well lead you to this gargantuan chain toy store near the intersection of S. College Road.

U.S. Trolls
2305 Market St., Wilmington
(910) 251-2270

Children of all ages will enjoy troll dolls handmade by Helena, Minna and Johannes Kuuskoski. The trolls are really cute; some are furry, and all are for sale. Hear troll stories as you shop. Written description simply doesn't do this place justice. Make sure to check out this store that has many unique and exciting things to see. There's parking in the rear of the building, with an easy exit to 23rd Street.

Animals

Despite the growing population of this region, it's not so hard to spot glimpses of nature here and there. In fact, it is not uncommon to witness hawks, ospreys and turkey vultures taking lunch breaks within Wilmington city limits. Deer are frequently sighted in outlying areas at dusk. And watching dolphins cavort mere yards offshore can be endlessly entertaining. To be truly among animals, especially of the petting or feeding-by-hand variety, also check Ashton Farm, listed in the Summer Camps section of this chapter, and Greenfield Lake, listed in our Attractions chapter.

Hugh MacRae Park
Oleander Dr., east of S. College Rd., Wilmington

Hugh MacRae Park is a quiet respite nestled between acres of trees right in the middle of busy Wilmington. Children love this park for the picnics, walks and many sights to see. The resident wildlife at the duck pond provides wonderful educational entertainment for children year round. Ducks march around the pond frequently, quacking as they go, especially when the park employees put out their weekly feed or when visitors offer bread. You'll often find ducks sleeping in the shade on warm afternoons. From the footbridge traversing the pond you get an excellent view of the many frogs, snapping turtles — from newborns to moss-backed elders — and fish that live beneath the water lilies. Some of the carp are of astounding size. Frogs are easiest to spot on the ground on damp mornings. Also look for spider webs, often quite large, among the bushes, but stay on the paths to avoid poison ivy. Plenty of shade trees and a gazebo invite picnicking. Be sure to bring your own beverages as there is no drinking water available at the pond. Park restrooms and playgrounds are on the premises.

North Carolina Aquarium at Fort Fisher
900 Loggerhead Rd., Kure Beach
(910) 458-8257

The North Carolina Aquarium at Fort Fisher is located on the ocean, east of U.S. 421 and south of Kure Beach, (about 15 miles south of Wilmington). Since its reopening in 2002, the Aquarium has continued to add fascinating exhibits, the most recent of which is Exotic Aquatics, added in 2005. Cuttlefish, lionfish, sea snakes, reef fishes, and an octopus are all included in this, the only exhibit that does not showcase indigenous animals.

With it's 235,000-gallon saltwater tank, fascinating displays, interactive exhibits and half-acre freshwater conservatory, the Aquarium features "The Waters of the Cape Fear," following the river from the Piedmont to the Atlantic Ocean. About 2,600 freshwater and saltwater creatures are on exhibit. Featured in the Coastal Waters Gallery are seahorses, a baby loggerhead sea turtle and an indoor salt marsh exhibit. The Aquarium is open daily 9 AM to 5 PM except Christmas, New Year's and Thanksgiving days.

All three North Carolina aquariums offer programs for people of all ages to learn more about aquatic life. The variety at the Fort Fisher facility includes everything from quickie "creature features" to half-day camps and workshops. Many activities require reservations and a nominal fee, but others are free with Aquarium admission.

Everyday visitors may encounter impromptu learning opportunities such as "smart-cart" presentations or "creature features" around the touch-pool, the alligator exhibit or the moray eel cave. Videos about everything from sharks to shrimp are shown daily in the auditorium. Divers, using underwater sound equipment inside the Cape Fear Shoals tank, answer questions on a wide range of topics twice a day. And at 3 PM daily, you can watch Aquarium staff feed some of the animals. Educators are on-hand to field questions.

Tregembo Animal Park
5811 Carolina Beach Rd., Wilmington
(910) 392-3604
www.tregemboanimalpark.com

Formerly known as the Tote-Em-In Zoo, Tregembo Animal Park will delight and amaze kids of all ages. Carrying on a family tradition that goes back more than 50 years, the Tregembos have expanded and updated the zoo to create habitats for their animals from around the world. There are some of the familiar zoo favorites like Jashan the white tiger, a lion named Simba and Ben the bear, along with some exotic new additions including a giraffe, a zebra and a group of ring-tailed lemurs that reside on their very own Lemur Island. Kids will have a great time exploring the park, feeding the ducks and goats, and watching the amusing primate an-

Travel the town with ease when you catch the Wave.

photo: Ashley, student of DREAMS Center for Arts Education

tics of the monkeys. Tregembo Animal Park is a fun place to spend an afternoon with the kids (or grandkids). Their large gift shop is filled with seashells, nautical items, T-shirts, toys and souvenirs. Tregembo Animal Park is open from 9 AM to 5 PM daily and closes during the winter season. Ticket prices are $8 and for adults, $7 for seniors 55 and over and $6 for kids ages 2 to 12. Group rates are available for school groups, but please call in advance.

Arts

There's no better way to open a child's eyes to all the hidden beauty of the world than through the arts. Engaging in painting, music, dance and drama is also a terrific way to build a child's self-esteem and sense of community. Checking with the various parks and recreation departments in your area can be rewarding, since many of them offer art classes. Facilities hosting such activities are the Community Arts Center (see later entry), the Martin Luther King Jr. Center, 401 S. Eighth Street, (910) 341-7866, and the Derrick G. S. Davis Center in Maides Park, 1101 Manly Avenue (north of Princess Place Drive), (910) 341-7867. The latter two are administered by the Wilmington Recreation Intervention Division and offer free after-school activities that include arts and crafts. Wilmington also has an abundance of dance schools catering to young children.

Community Arts Center
120 S. Second St., Wilmington
(910) 341-7860

This city-owned facility offers an annual July Arts Camp for school-age children. It includes four one-week sessions of hands-on creative fun in practically every medium imaginable, such as painting, music, dance, acting and writing. Offerings change, so call for current information and register early. In addition to the Arts Camp, the Community Arts Center offers classes for children in dance, music and acting during the school year. Some adult classes are open to young adults ages 13 through 17 with permission of the instructor.

The Thalian Association, (910) 251-1788, the nation's oldest theatre tradition, manages the center. The Thalian Association Children's Theatre stages performances by young casts during the school year. Studio and theater space is also available for rental.

Dreams Center for Arts Education
515 Ann St., Wilmington
(910) 772-1501
www.dreamswilmington.org

The Dreams Center for Arts Education is a non-profit youth development organization that offers free art programming to the Wilmington area's most marginalized youth. Classes are free of charge for children ages 8 to 17 and provide a structured after-school atmosphere. From 3:30 to 6:30 PM, Monday through Friday, participants have the options of studying visual arts, drama, music, dance, creative writing, photography and graphic design. In addition to their regular after-school activities, the program features a three-week intensive arts camp where kids can develop their skills even further. Serving over 500 children each week at over 20 locations, Dreams helps kids focus on their creative side and provides a safe environment for expression.

Racine Center for the Arts
203 Racine Dr., Wilmington
(910) 452-2073
www.racinecenter.com

A great place to enjoy the arts with your family, the Racine Center welcomes folks of all ages to visit this multi-faceted facility. Classes and camps offer opportunities to learn pottery making, painting, printmaking, drawing, music, drama and other fine arts. All teachers are professional artists who love to teach within this warm, inviting atmosphere. Check out the wonderful galleries full of truly unique pieces at all price levels. Dine in the center's peaceful sculpture garden or check out items you'll find once in a Blue Moon.

Poplar Grove Historic Plantation
10200 U.S. Hwy. 17 N., Wilmington
(910) 686-9518

Every spring, Poplar Grove Historic Plantation and the Pender County School System sponsor "Arts in These Parts," an exhibit of student artwork. An opening-day reception with refreshments is open to the public. Call for details.

Westermark Voice Studio
Sara Graham Westermark, Soprano
620 Cobblestone Dr., Wilmington
(910) 233-1323
www.sarawestermark.com

Sara Graham Westermark, a classically trained singer with a master's degree in Voice Performance from the University of Missouri-Columbia, offers affordable voice lessons for children of all ages. Lessons can be recorded on a CD, which is a wonderful tool for practice sessions at home. Sara is an active singer in this region, appearing as a soloist with the Wilmington Symphony Orchestra, Southeastern Oratorio Society, Wilmington Oratorio Society, UNCW Concert Choir, UNCW Opera Scenes and other area organizations.

Sara has taught private voice lessons for more than ten years in addition to working with elementary singing groups. She also teaches music and voice at Cape Fear Community College. Give your child the gift of Sara's instruction and the benefit of her years of experience.

The Wilmington School of Ballet and Creative Art Center
3834 Oleander Dr., Wilmington
(910) 794-9590

This is Wilmington's only school dedicated to classical ballet. It emphasizes the fundamental basics of being a disciplined ballerina. Ballet and modern dance classes are available for ages three to adult. Their innovative program for preschoolers (ages 3 through 5) utilizes movement, props, music and imagery games to encourage learning the joy of dance; they don't focus on the discipline of ballet until the child is mature enough. Beginning at age 6, training begins to take on more of the academic structure of a ballet class. Levels progress in a planned, sequential manner, each building on the previous level. Pre-professional training offers students the opportunity to study daily, preparing them for professional dance careers. The school offers a Broadway-based tap and jazz program for ages three and older. Children from infant to four years old can participate in the parent/child music classes, which feature both Kindermusik and music together.

Serious students who take four or more dance classes a week can audition for "The

Wilmington Ballet Company," a nonprofit, in-house youth ballet company. Also, the program offers the Wilmington Broadway Company, which allows students age 8 and older additional performance opportunities in the tap and jazz disciplines. The Wilmington School of Ballet participates in many outreach programs, including scholarships and summer camps for underprivileged youths.

The Field Studio
3173 Wrightsville Ave., Wilmington
(910) 251-8988
www.fieldstudio.biz

The Field Studio offers private vocal instruction by Liz Field and private piano instruction by Steve Field. Both are classically trained, professional musicians with master's degrees in their respective areas.

Steve has more than 15 years of experience teaching piano privately. He has been on faculty at the University of Connecticut and the University of Memphis. He maintains a performing career doing recitals, accompanying and conducting throughout the country. Steve has a passion for passing on his knowledge, experience and love of the piano to anyone who has a desire to learn. Steve offers private piano lessons for kids ages 6 and older.

Liz has been teaching voice since 1987 to students at all levels. A Lyric Coloratura Soprano, Liz is in demand as a soloist and as a leader of her Vocal Enrichment Seminars for Choral Singers. She truly loves helping children find their true voice and experience the joy of singing. Liz offers singing lessons for girls ages 11 and older and boys ages 15 and older. At the Field Studio, they make music seriously fun!

Girls Choir of Wilmington
205 Dover Rd., Wilmington
(910) 799-5073

Formed in 1997, this community-based choral ensemble has approximately 100 girls enrolled. Girls ages 9 and older perform a variety of classical, folk, sacred, secular and popular music. The members learn teamwork, discipline, musicianship and community service through the concerts and activities.

Wilmington Academy of Music
3830 Oleander Dr., Wilmington
(910) 392-1590

The academy is a private school, founded in 1987, that offers a full range of music instruction in voice, piano, guitar, harp, violin, viola, cello, percussion, trumpet, trombone, clarinet, saxophone, flute, tuba, oboe, bagpipe and more for students of all ages. Theory, orchestration, arranging and other classes are available. Traditional, Suzuki and jazz techniques are the methods of choice. Weekly private lessons and monthly group lessons, recitals and master classes are offered. The academy offers a variety of ensembles for weddings, receptions and special events, featuring the combined talents of faculty members and experienced local musicians. Drama classes will be offered in the near future. Call for details.

Brunswick School of Dance
920 Ocean Hwy. W., Supply
(910) 754-8281, (910) 754-6106

Housed in a remodeled country store since 1982, Brunswick School of Dance, now in its 24th year, specializes in teaching children age 3 and older the basics of movement and strives to build self-esteem and confidence. Class size averages 12 to 14 students. Most classes take place in the afternoon Monday through Thursday, but there are morning classes for preschoolers. Round-trip van pickup service is available. Styles taught to older students include ballet, tap, jazz, pointe and lyrical. Adult classes include tap and jazz. Ask about the Liturgical Dance Group,

which performs to Christian music at worship services in the area. The school is convenient to most of the South Brunswick Islands. In May of each year all students participate in a recital in Odell Williamson Auditorium at Brunswick Community College.

SOLA – School of Learning and Art
216 Pine Grove Rd., Wilmington
(910) 798-1700

SOLA offers something for creative children of all ages and abilities. Among the many wonderful programs are the following:

SOLA's Pre-School is a program for 3- to 5-year-olds, offering a curriculum balanced with school preparatory academics, fine arts and developmental skills. Morning Half Day is from 8:30 AM to 12:15 PM. Space is limited, so call for wait list information.

SOLA's After Pre-School Art Program is held from 1 to 3 PM or from 1 to 5 PM. Drop-ins are welcome on a daily or weekly basis. This class is for 3- to 5-year-olds not registered for SOLA's morning pre-school. Students will experience a very relaxed class, plenty of fun and exploration with pottery, paint, glue and more. Think of it as a very artsy midday pre-school.

SOLA's After-School program offers classes in drawing, painting, mixed media, pottery and music. Also available is a non-traditional after-school care program for young artists ages kindergarten through fifth grade from 2:30 to 6 PM.

SOLA's Home School program can take care of the art and music instruction for your curriculum. Classes are designed to meet all media and cultural exposure across grade levels in a child-friendly art studio. Students are thoroughly immersed in the creative process. Parents are welcome to stay and play, too!

SOLA's Summer Camp for boys and girls puts the fun in summer camp; it features week-long sessions with age-appropriate groups and activities. Choose either Half Day Camp from 8:30 AM to 12:30 PM or Full Day Camp from 8:30 AM to 4:30 PM. Kids enjoy both indoor and outdoor activities. Messy, fabulous arts and crafts are an integral part of every day. Students create pottery on the wheel and by hand, make their own T-shirts, experience paint and glue in ways they never have before while building a variety of theme-based projects. Campers play with new and old friends in a home-like workshop and backyard environment. Teachers at SOLA don't just babysit, they rock the house. Signing up is "easy as pie in the face!"

Wilmington Children's Museum
116 Orange St., Wilmington
(910) 254-3534

The Children's Museum's mission is to stimulate children's imagination, curiosity and innate love of learning. Each visit here is an opportunity to explore, discover, create and imagine. Climb aboard the pirate ship, experiment in the science lab or make a special souvenir in the art room. You can count on the Children's Museum for fun, affordable, educational, play-centered programs both children and their adult friends are sure to enjoy! Art and science programming are offered all day, every day. Toddler Time on is held Fridays from 9 to 10:30 AM.

Birthday Parties

Gone are the days of simple birthdays with only presents and cake. Today's kids look forward to gatherings that include numerous physical activities from trampolines and gymnastics to skating and soccer. If you're looking for an extra-special place to give your child a memorable birthday party, look into these venues, offering colorful party rooms and various services. Some include the use of the arcades, games and more. And don't overlook your local bowling center; per-game prices for children younger than 12 are often discounted (see the Bowling section in our chapter on Sports, Fitness and Parks).

Carolina Beach Mini-Golf & Batting Cages
906 N. Lake Park Blvd., Carolina Beach
(910) 458-8888

For a change of pace, plan your child's birthday party at this beach town attraction. Let the kids practice their batting skills, play miniature golf or try out some of the many different arcade games. Everyone attending the party will get $1 off the regular price. A deck with tables is available, but you need to bring our own party fare; you can purchase ice cream and soft drinks in the arcade. Open seasonally every day from 10 AM until late evening, Carolina Beach Mini Golf is set in a

beautiful tropical environment with waterfalls, streams and mountainous terrain.

Coastal Tumblegym
220 Winner Ave., Carolina Beach
(910) 458-9490

Coastal Tumblegym hosts 90-minute birthday parties, usually on Saturday or Sunday afternoons (weekdays by special arrangement), featuring two certified professional instructors to lead the children in various physical activities. These may include mastering an obstacle course, playing on a trampoline, running relay races, working out on gymnastic equipment or traversing a 40-foot-long "Moon Walk" floor. Really popular is a 50-foot inflatable Seaweed Monster that's 12 feet high; inside is a slide and other fun stuff to climb on, over and under. Parents supply food and refreshments.

Firebird Ceramic Studio
Racine Center for the Arts, 203 Racine Dr.,
Ste. 205, Wilmington
(910) 452-2073

Located within Wilmington's premier arts facility, Firebird is a perfect place for a child's birthday party. Choose from a large selection of ceramic bisque and let the kids paint it their way. The friendly staff at Firebird Ceramic Studio will be happy to teach the kids some special effects if you wish. All birthdays include helium balloons, space for gifts and goodies, a commemorative plate or mug for guests to sign, and lots of laughs. They'll clear glaze the pieces and fire them for you. You can even choose to add a meal to the festivities at Picasso's Café, downstairs in the sculpture garden.

Jelly Beans Family Skating Center
5216 Oleander Dr., Wilmington
(910) 791-6000

Indoor roller skating can be a great way to celebrate birthdays, and Jelly Beans will provide everything you need for the party, including place settings, ice cream, refreshments, even the cake if you wish. A bonus is the host, who serves and cleans up afterward. Ask about other provisions, too, such as pizza (additional costs may apply). Choose among several skating sessions lasting two, three or four hours, depending on the day and time.

Jungle Rapids Family Fun Park
5320 Oleander Dr., Wilmington
(910) 791-0666

Jungle Rapids offers several birthday packages that vary according to age and price. Choose from packages that include go-carts, laser-tag (for older children), waterpark (seasonal), a climbing wall, video games or minigolf. Packages feature play time, a party in a private room with a host, pizza and soda.

Scooter's Family Skating Center
341 Shipyard Blvd., Wilmington
(910) 791-8550

Party time at Scooter's is a great time for kids. The birthday child receives a 30-day skating pass, special announcement and a Scooter's T-shirt. The party kids get a skating pass and rental skates (note that inline skates and speed skates cost $2.50). One slice of pizza per child and soda are provided; all you need to bring is a cake or cupcakes. The cost is $89 for up to 10 guests and $5 per additional child. Adult guests with the party are admitted free; if they wish to skate, they'll need to pay for their skate rental.

Ten Pin Alley
127 S. College Rd., Wilmington
(910) 452-5455
www.breaktimetenpin.com

Ten Pin Alley will provide everything you need for a happy bowling birthday party. All you have to bring is the birthday cake, the birthday boy or girl and a bunch of their friends (10 person minimum). The cost is $12 per child and includes one hour of bowling (two lanes per 10 kids), bowling shoe rental, four arcade game tokens for each child, your choice of pizza or hot dogs with chips, and drinks. The birthday child will receive a "Happy Birthday" bowling pin with balloons. Call ahead for further details and to make a reservation.

Wilmington Children's Museum
116 Orange St., Wilmington
(910) 254-3534

There are few birthday venues as educationally stimulating as the Children's Museum, where kids can pretend to be a pirate on a pirate ship, play dress-up with a variety of fun costumes, or get into any number of creative, artistic and entertaining activities with dedicated adult supervision. The museum's

Birthday Bash lasts 90 minutes and includes a party coordinator to assist you, a decorated party room, play time, Slime Time! (time to play with slimy stuff in the science lab), a Maraca Parade, and Flashdance (time to dance with a flashlight to some upbeat tunes), and at the end of the party each guest is given a Goodie Bag (containing a museum sticker, museum pencil and a pass for one free visit). You can also add-a- theme. Themes include: Pirates Ahoy!, It Glows!, Animal Alley and Mad Lab. The Wilmington Children's Museum stimulates children's imagination, curiosity and innate love of learning. Birthday parties cost $125 for non-members, $110 for museum members. There's an additional $10 charge for add-a-themes. The Children's Museum can accommodate parties of up to 26 people, with a maximum of 16 children. For more information or to book a party, call (910) 254-3534.

Wilmington Railroad Museum
501 Nutt St., Wilmington
(910) 763-2634

Conduct a birthday party on a real caboose at the Wilmington Railroad Museum. It's fun for the whole family: Thomas trains plus a hands-on play area for the younger ones, and a box car complete with hobos and a 1910 engine to climb aboard for children of all ages. While the kids are having a great time playing on the trains and going on a scavenger hunt, their parents can learn about the Atlantic Coast Line Railroad's fascinating history. Everyone will enjoy the large model train layouts and gift shop. So grab your engineer hat and railroad whistle, it's all aboard for a trainload of fun. The cost is $50 for members and $75 for non-members, which covers 10 children and 10 adults and includes a gift certificate to the gift shop for the birthday child. Each child gets a paper engineer hat and a plastic whistle.

Eats & Sweets

No discussion of kidstuff would be complete without something for the sweet tooth. By sweets we mean not only candy but also baked goods and ice cream. As you travel the coast, you'll be tempted by all manner of strategically placed retailers who will dulcify your day. What follows here are some of the kings and queens of confectionery, the barons of bonbon. Read on at the risk of your waistline. Your kids will love you for it.

WILMINGTON

Apple Annie's Bake Shop
Outlet Mall, S. College Rd., Wilmington
(910) 799-9023
Landfall Shopping Center, 1319 Military
Cutoff Rd., Wilmington
(910) 256-6585

Two locations mean that satisfying a sweet craving will seldom take you too far out of your way. Baking everything fresh daily, Apple Annie's offers a sumptuous array of cakes, cupcakes, pies, cookies, breads and plenty more. This is one of those shops in which the air itself is intoxicating. For birthdays and other special occasions, Apple Annie's offers extraordinary custom creations. Kids cakes are out of this world! Just give them a picture, drawing, photo or other image and turn a cake into a personal statement — they can put just about any image on your cake using a computer process and a sugar laser printer. They'll also make 3-dimensional characters for the top. (Outlet Mall is a short distance south of the UNCW campus, next to Dick's Sporting Goods.)

Kohl's Frozen Custard & Jumbo Burgers
92 S. Lumina Ave., Wrightsville Beach
(910) 256-3955
6931 Market St., Wilmington
(910) 452-2300
620 S. College Rd. Wilmington
(910) 799-1252
5658 Carolina Beach Rd., Wilmington
(910) 350-0051
1669 N. Howe St., Southport
(910) 457-0052

Not ice cream, but the more full-bodied custard is Kohl's claim to local fame. Whipping up homemade-style custard in vanilla and chocolate daily plus a special flavor of the day (sometimes two), Kohl's creates some mouth-watering concoctions with its custard. They also have great cheeseburgers and hot dogs. The Wrightsville Beach store is closed during winter months.

The Scoop Ice Cream & Sandwich Shoppe
365 N. Front St., Wilmington
(910) 763-3566

A short walk from Wilmington's riverfront in the Cotton Exchange, "The Scoop" is just the place to grab a hot dog, sandwich or salad and milk shake for an on-the-go meal. Better yet, stay awhile and partake of such sinful creations as banana splits and peanut-lovers sundaes. On those cool winter afternoons, stop in for a hot apple cider or cocoa and cookies. Especially popular in warm weather are the soda floats, including Egg Creams, Boston Coolers, Leap Frogs and Hobokens. Seating just outside the inviting shop offers an extremely pleasant shaded oasis in which to enjoy your lunch, snack or dessert in practically any season, but particularly on deliciously warm days. It's a fine stopover for the weary shopper.

Vic's Corn Popper
1616 Shipyard Blvd., Wilmington
(910) 452-2869

Popcorn in a sweets listing? You bet, especially if it's Vic's freshly made caramel corn. Vic's is an award-winning popcorn franchise, and you'll find more different kinds of popcorn than you may have ever seen before.

CAROLINA BEACH AND KURE BEACH

Squigley's Ice Cream & Treats
208 S. Lake Park Blvd., Carolina Beach
(910) 458-8779

With 4,050 flavors and taste sensations, this ice cream parlor offers something for everyone. They will make any flavor combination you desire, all that's required is imagination and a sweet tooth. A large board lists customers' favorite picks, such as cashews, Oreo and Butterfinger. You can also choose from ten toppings like blueberry, raspberry or peanut butter. Squigley's offers dozens of regular flavors for less daring folk. With lots of indoor and outdoor seating, Squigley's is a great choice for a tasty treat during the day or after dinner. It's open seasonally.

BRUNSWICK COUNTY BEACHES

Frosty's Ice Cream, Antiques and Shells
8600 E. Oak Island Dr., Oak Island

Heading for the beach? Why not take a refreshing break for ice cream? When you have crossed the bridge over the waterway and turned right at the light, keep your eyes peeled for the shops in the fourth block topped by the red-orange sloped roof. Nestled there is Frosty's. Inside you will find the yellow walls covered with fish net, shells and sea creatures, the ceiling and floor pale blue. Round tables and white sweetheart chairs evoke the atmosphere of an old-fashioned ice cream parlor. While the kids are slurping up sundaes, biting into banana splits or licking luscious cones dipped from their choices of 24 flavors, you can browse the antiques, seashells, starfish, metal art (don't miss the gecko on the ceiling) and collectibles, including John Deere, Coca Cola and Tom Clark Gnomes. Candy and drinks are available as well. It's open between late March and Thanksgiving.

Calabash Creamery
9910 Beach Dr., Calabash
(910) 575-1180

Do you know you can go to school to learn how to make ice cream? Greg and Kristi Hansen did just that. Now they make their "Distinctive Homemade Ice Cream" on the premises at the Calabash Creamery. It's so good the creamery was featured in the August 2005 edition of Southern Living magazine. You can watch how it's done either through the viewing window in the dining room or by watching their video.

You will find delicious flavors you never heard of before. Try Cowabash Crunch, Sweet Potato Souffle, Banana Pudding or Cantaloupe. Enjoy your choice from 24 flavors in the dining room while you listen to old-time player piano music at the drop of a quarter. Or "set a spell" in the rocking chairs on the wraparound porch. Banana splits and sundaes are served as well. Do you think you can finish the Kitchen Sink Sundae – 15 scoops of ice cream and six toppings of your choice, whipped cream and cherries?

Before you leave be sure to take advantage of a photo op with the mama and baby cows, Scoop and Dip.

TOPSAIL ISLAND & VICINITY

Dairy Queen
Krystal Plaza Shopping Center,
N.C. Hwy. 172, Sneads Ferry
(910) 327-1240
106 N. New River Dr., Surf City
(910) 328-3112

Ice cream, cupcakes, ice cream cakes, floats, sundaes and DQ's famous blizzards make it hard to choose a favorite. If ice cream isn't your choice, hot dogs, grilled chicken and barbecue sandwiches are also on the menu. The Sneads Ferry Dairy Queen is open year round with reduced hours in the winter months. The Surf City store closes in the winter.

Dr. Rootbeer's Hall of Foam
288 Fulchers Landing, Sneads Ferry
(910) 327-ROOT (7668)

Dr. Rootbeer's Hall of Foam, located in a vintage 1950s gas station near the waterfront in Sneads Ferry, sells root beer made from Jerome Gundrum's own recipe. Just one sip of his delicious ambrosia will transport you back to simpler times. Sit back and enjoy the free 1953 Seeburg jukebox, a root beer float, milkshake or other cool treat, including hand-dipped ice cream. This is more than a soda shop; Dr. Rootbeer's is a museum. The walls are covered with vintage root beer memorabilia that has been carefully collected for 32 years. Dr. Rootbeer also serves delicious sandwiches like the Dixie Pot Roast, chicken or tuna salad wraps and three different kinds of hot dogs, including foot-longs. Take home a six-pack of root beer. Dr. Rootbeer's Hall of Foam is open all year.

Exploring Nature

The most accessible, most affordable and most attractive sources of fun for kids on the southern coast are the same ones that draw adults in droves: the beaches and nearby waterways. So no matter what your kids' ages, get them down to the water, from Topsail to Calabash. Try a different beach now and then to pique their interest; there's a great difference in character from beach to beach.

Combining activities with beach visits may also be worthwhile. Driving a four-wheel-drive vehicle on the beach at the Fort Fisher State Recreation Area is a bouncy jaunt most kids love. The area offers pristine surf, calm tidal waters on the inland side suitable for toddlers, great fishing and, just minutes away, a fine Civil War museum and historic site. (See the Off-Roading section in our Sports, Fitness and Parks chapter.)

North Carolina's southern coast encompasses a wide variety of parks, giving kids plenty of room to run, play and explore. Venerable pine trees surrounded by beautiful flora and interesting fauna make these parks delightful places for families to spend time together. (See the Sports, Fitness and Parks chapter for a list of parks.)

Buccaneer Cruises
111 N. New River Dr, Surf City
(910) 546-TOUR (8687)

The Buccaneer, Surf City's newest cruise vessel, offers sightseeing cruises that kids will find interesting and fun. The cruises provide an opportunity to see dolphins, osprey and other wildlife as you cruise by Blackbeard's old hideout. Cruises cost $10 per person, with kids younger than 12 paying $6 and kids younger than 5 riding free. Reservations are not required. To guarantee space; stop at the dock to purchase tickets in advance.

Farms

A farm visit can provide children with a fascinating educational experience that's also a downright good time. From picking fruits and vegetables to learning about the care and feeding of farm animals, kids will enjoy the hands-on opportunities offered by the farms listed below.

Ashton Farm
5645 U.S. Hwy. 117 S., Burgaw
(910) 259-2431

Ashton Farm is 72 acres of historic plantation about 18 miles north of Wilmington. Owners Sally and Jim Martin provide children ages 5 through 12 with down-to-earth fun. Kids participate in farm life, sports with minimized competition, and nature. Among the activities are swimming, canoeing, horseback riding, softball, hiking, crafts, animal care, rodeos and archery. (Also see the Summer Camps section later in this chapter.)

Holden Brothers Farm Market
5600 U.S. Hwy. 17 W., Shallotte
(910) 579-4500

Bring the kids to pick strawberries and tomatoes in season. The fields and market are open from April 1 through Christmas and are 3 miles south of Shallotte.

Lewis Strawberry Nursery & Farms
6517 Gordon Rd., Wilmington
(910) 452-9659

Picking berries can be almost as much fun as eating them. In late spring, peaking in May, the strawberries at Lewis' Nursery ripen into succulent concentrations of juicy, deep-red sweetness that almost defy belief. Whether you and the kids pick them yourselves or buy them by the quart, this is a treat you'll want to repeat.

Lewis' Gordon Road location is popular with locals for their strawberries, blueberries and blackberries, with the added attractions of homemade ice cream, potted plants and flowers for sale. Lewis Farms is open to the public only from April through mid-July, Monday through Saturday from 8 AM to 6 PM and Sunday from 1 to 6 PM. Gordon Road intersects Market Street (U.S. 17) just south of the Military Cutoff Road intersection and N. College Road near the junction with I-40. Or Pick-Your-Own at their other location along Castle Hayne Road, near the General Electric facility; it's open Monday through Saturday 8 AM to 6 PM and Sunday 1 to 6 PM.

Getting Physical

Check our chapter on Sports, Fitness and Parks for information on field and team sports for children of school age. Included in this section are physical activities that either apply specifically to young children or are not covered in the sports categories.

Carolina Beach Mini-Golf & Batting Cages
906 N. Lake Park Blvd., Carolina Beach
(910) 458-8888

After school, weekends and vacation days are popular times for youngsters and teens to spend a few hours perfecting their batting skills, playing a few rounds of miniature golf or trying out some of the many different arcade games at this beach town attraction. Open seasonally every day from 10 AM until late evening, Carolina Beach Mini Golf is set in a beautiful tropical environment with waterfalls, streams and mountainous terrain.

City of Wilmington Sherriedale Morgan Boxing and Physical Fitness Center
302 S. 10th St., Wilmington
(910) 341-7837, (910) 341-7872

Administered by Wilmington Parks, Recreation and Downtown Services, the center welcomes children ages 8 and older to participate in fitness training and professionally supervised boxing. Fitness equipment includes treadmills, stationary bicycles, stair climbers, free weights, weight machines, jump ropes, heavy bags, boxing gloves and scheduled exercise classes, all this for a facility use fee of only $50 per year for Wilmington city residents and $80 for non-residents. Hours are Monday through Friday 9 AM to 8 PM and Saturday 10 AM to 2 PM. Junior Olympic boxing is available for ages 8 to 16; call for competitive boxing information and fees.

Fit For Fun
302 S. 10th St., Wilmington
(910) 341-4630

This program, sponsored by Wilmington Parks & Recreation Department, affords children from birth through 5 years the opportunity to play with parental involvement. The cost is $3.50 per child. Hours are Monday through Friday 9 AM to noon and 1 to 4 PM and Saturday 9 AM to noon.

Jelly Beans Family Skating Center
5216 Oleander Dr., Wilmington
(910) 791-6000

Roller skating can be family fun at its best and perhaps simplest, and Jelly Beans appeals especially to kids and their parents. Grown-ups may appreciate the Top-40 music on Thursday nights. The rink is a clean, well-kept place with a well-stocked pro shop providing rentals, sales and repairs. Also available is a snack bar and the Stuff Shop, which sells toys and novelty items. Jelly Beans also hosts skating birthday parties, has an after-school program and a summer day camp. Jelly Beans hosts its own in-line hockey league for kids 14 and younger (see the Sports and Fitness chapter for more details). It is near the intersection of Oleander Drive and Forest Park Road, 5 miles from downtown.

Skater's Choice
260 Sneads Ferry Rd., Sneads Ferry
(910) 327-2277

Skater's Choice offers roller skating Friday nights (7 to 10:30 PM), Saturday nights (6:30 to 10 PM) and Saturday afternoons (1:30 to 4 PM). Regular cost for evening skating is $5 and includes skates. The fee, including skates, for the matinees is $3. The charge to rent inline skates is $1 more. The

rink is available for parties on Saturday and Sunday. The snack bar sells popcorn, drinks and prepackaged sandwiches and snacks. Skater's Choice is open year round.

Topsail Beach Skating Rink
Anderson Blvd, Topsail Beach
(910) 328-2381

Located over the Topsail Beach Post Office, this rink is open on weekends from 7 to 10 PM in April and May. During the summer it's open nightly. The cost for admission and to rent skates is $5. Inline and traditional skates are available. Drinks and snacks are are sold at the concession stand

The Martin Luther King Jr. Center
401 S. Eighth St., Wilmington
(910) 341-7866

In the summer months, the Wilmington Recreation Intervention Division sponsors basketball for kids ages 6 to 17, divided into appropriate age groups. The center now offers Tae Kwan Do for kids as young as six, all the way up to adults. Other activities include field trips and games as well as a soccer league. The center has two seven-foot pool tables, bumper pool, Foosball, Ping Pong and air hockey. During the school year, the center is open Monday through Thursday for after-school homework time and games. Every second Friday the center features live entertainment in the afternoon.

Scooter's Family Skating Center
341 Shipyard Blvd., Wilmington
(910) 791-8550

Scooter's is the current name for this classic rink, founded in 1959. Once you pass through the door, however, you walk right into the 21st century, complete with disco lighting show, sound system, special glow-in-the-dark carpeting and black lighting throughout the entire rink. Scooter's is a full-service roller skating center with a complete pro shop, snack bar and lots of video games to round out your night of fun. Birthday parties and fund-raising events are more than welcome.

The rink is open Wednesday from 7 to 9 PM. On Friday night Scooter's skates from 7 to 11 PM; Saturday the rink is open from 1 to 11 PM with an all-day MegaSkate, an afternoon session from 1 to 6 PM and a night skate from

6 to 11 PM; on Sunday public skating is from 2 to 5 PM. For further information or to book a party, call the number listed above.

Wheel Fun Rentals
107 Carolina Beach Ave.
N. at the Boardwalk
Carolina Beach Lake Park,
corner of Lake Park and Atlanta
Carolina Beach
(910) 458-4545

Kids of all ages will love this. For a reasonable rate, the whole family can spend an hour or even a day riding Deuce Coupes, Choppers or Surreys. Popular anytime, and equipped with lights, four-wheeled covered Surreys come in two sizes, the large one can seat up to six adults and two children. Also available are cruisers, mountain bikes and tandems. For the water enthusiast, surfboard, boogie board, kayak, water bikes, paddle boats, beach chairs and umbrellas are also available. Owners Duke and Tracee Hagestrom promise a fun ride, no matter what you choose.

Getting Wet

As if the ocean weren't enough, this area offers plenty of other opportunities for kids to douse themselves, and some of them are downright thrilling, especially the water slides. One of the best is at the Jungle Rapids Family Fun Park, 5320 Oleander Drive, (910) 791-0666, in Wilmington. Most warm weather attractions are open seven days a week between Memorial and Labor days. Beyond these, kids can find places to get wet in our Watersports chapter or our Sports, Fitness and Parks chapter.

Go Fish

Buccaneer Cruises
111 N. New River Dr, Surf City
(910) 546-TOUR (8687)

Go shrimping like the pros on a Bubba Gump Shrimp Cruise. Learn how commercial shrimp boats operate. Have fun, catch fish and learn about exotic underwater marine life. The cost is $20 per person, and trips depart 9 AM and return at 11 AM. Call to find out the list of days when this trip is offered.

Captain Charlie's
Kids Fishing Tournament
Southport City Pier,
Waterfront Park, Southport
(910) 457-7923, (910) 457-7945

Held annually on the same weekend as the King Mackerel Tournament, the Kids Fishing Tournament fills the Southport Pier with junior anglers (up to age 16) while the senior anglers are out at sea. A joint effort of the Southport Recreation Department and the Southport Lions Club along with some retail sponsors, it is a big event for the kids, who bring their own rod and reel and bait. The first 100 kids receive a free T-shirt, and there are free hot dogs and drinks for everyone. There is a fish-bowl drawing for prizes throughout the tournament; the prize for the biggest fish is a rod and reel, and there are many other prizes donated by merchants. Best of all, this is a catch-and-release tournament — an environmental lesson for kids.

Children's Crab Derby
Old Yacht Basin, Southport
(910) 457-7923, (910) 457-7945

Have you ever seen a crab race? Sounds even better than a frog race, doesn't it? Bring your child (up to age 16), a small submergible basket or crab line and bait in early September and hope the tide is at its best for good crabbing! (But don't worry, a local commercial crabber usually stocks the yacht basin with some extras.) The children are divided into teams of two or three according to age. Prizes are given for the biggest crab and the most crabs caught in each age category.

Dorothy's Harbor Tours
720 Channel Blvd., Topsail Beach
(910) 545-TOUR (8687)

Take a child on an exciting fishing adventure aboard the Dorothy, Topsail's newest cruise boat. This 2-hour educational fishing excursion offers the opportunity to catch pinfish, pigfish and various other species while learning about the various types of underwater marine life. All gear is supplied. Children younger than 7 must be accompanied by an adult. The cost is $25 per person. Call for scheduled days. Trips are from 9 to 11:30 AM. Bring your own food and drinks (no alcohol, please).

Historians re-enact the Revolutionary War battle at Moore's Creek.

photo: Peter Doran

Going Mental

Babbage's
Westfield Shoppingtown Independence
Mall, 3500 Oleander Dr., Wilmington
(910) 791-8168

Babbage's carries a fine selection of video games, CD-ROMs and computer games in addition to its wide range of other computer software.

Books-A-Million
3737 Oleander Dr., Wilmington
(910) 452-1519

This book superstore adjacent to Office Depot hosts story hours with various themes and related activities for young children every Saturday at 3:30 PM. When the children's section is otherwise quiet, kids enjoy playing on the "train-car" benches. The locomotive houses a TV that shows ongoing children's

Fans of model trains can get on the right track with the Cape Fear Model Railroad Club, (910) 270-2696, which welcomes novices as well as experts.

programming or videos to keep kids entertained while their parents browse nearby.

Brunswick County Library
Margaret and James Harper Library,
109 W. Moore St., Southport
(910) 457-6237
Leland Library, 487 Village Rd., Leland
(910) 371-9442
G.V. Barbee Library, 818 Yaupon Dr.,
Oak Island
(910) 278-4283
Rourk Library, 5068 Main St., Shallotte
(910) 754-6578
Hickmans Crossroads Library, 1040
Calabash Rd., Calabash
(910) 575-0173

Story times, including books, music and crafts, for children ages 2 through 5 are offered at these Brunswick County public libraries at 10 AM on Monday at the Harper Library in Southport, Tuesday at the Leland Library and at Hickmans Crossroads Library in Calabash, Wednesday at the Barbee Library on Oak Island and Thursday at Rourk Library in Shallotte. Afternoon activities for school-age children from kindergarten up include stories and crafts and are held at 4 PM at Leland, Hickmans Crossroads, Oak Island and Shallotte on the same days listed above. The Brunswick County Libraries also host a summer reading program for school-age children. The six-week program involves weekly special guests and activities at the libraries. Participation in all library programs is free.

Cape Fear Astronomical Society
Bryan Auditorium at UNCW's Morton Hall, Wilmington
(910) 762-1033

Kids old enough to understand that those bright objects in the night sky are incredibly distant will appreciate the occasional sky observations, using members' telescopes, sponsored by the Astronomical Society to raise interest in membership. Viewing sessions are announced in the calendar of the Wilmington Star-News.

The public is also invited to the society's monthly meetings, which feature interesting films and presentations. Meetings take place on the first Sunday of each month (or the second, if delayed by a holiday) and are also announced in the newspaper. The society is open to everyone of any age, regardless of any astronomical knowledge.

In addition to the popular public viewing sessions, the society also undertakes periodic school talks and trips to planetariums. Membership has one prerequisite, if you could call it that: a sincere interest in astronomy and in learning more about it. Memberships cost $20 per year ($25 for families) and include the society's monthly newsletter, Cape Fear Skies, and the Astronomical League's quarterly publication, Reflector. Members can also get a reduced subscription rate to Sky and Telescope magazine.

Contact Ronnie Hawes, the club's president, at the society's mailing address, 305 N. 21st Street, Wilmington, NC 28405.

New Hanover County Public Library
Main Branch, 201 Chestnut St., Wilmington
(910) 798-6303
Carolina Beach Branch, 300 Cape Fear Blvd., Carolina Beach
(910) 458-5016
Myrtle Grove Branch, 5155 S. College Rd., Wilmington
(910) 452-6414
Northeast Regional Library, 1241 Military Cutoff Rd., Wilmington
(910) 256-2173

The Children's Rooms at these libraries are excellent resources for stimulating entertainment that isn't limited to story times. Activities are designed for children in three age groups. Toddler Time offers stories, songs and interactive finger plays just for babies ages 18 months through 3 years and their parents. Preschool Storytime may include films and is geared for ages 3 through 5. The Toddler and Preschool events are offered weekly on different days at the different library branches, giving you a choice of schedules. Book Break, offered during the summer, is a weekly storytime for children ages 6 through 10 that offers longer stories, read-alouds, activities and films. All programs are free and open to the public.

There's a Book Buddies Club for 4th through 5th graders and a new book club called Bookworms for 2nd through 3rd graders. Holiday programs include an annual selection of ghostly tales for Halloween and a Christmas crafts program that provides decorations for trimming library and family trees. Carolina Canines offers a program called "Paws for Reading," in which assist dogs are used for children to improve their confidence in reading aloud. Family programs may present history as related in song, African dance or readings by children's authors. Call the library's Youth Services office at the number above to inquire about schedules and registration, which may be limited for some workshops.

Fort Fisher Aquarium Outreach Program
Assembly Bldg., 720 Channel Blvd, Topsail Beach
(910) 329-4446

Touch and learn about sea creatures! This popular outreach program from the North Carolina Aquarium at Fort Fisher is a one-hour presentation on invertebrates held every Wednesday afternoon during July and August from 1 to 2 PM. Children enjoy the educational experience of touching and learning about sea creatures. A donation of $5 per family is requested. The Topsail Island Historical and Cultural Arts Council sponsors this event.

Quarter Moon Book Store
708 S. Anderson Blvd., Topsail Beach
(910) 328-4969

Quarter Moon has a great selection of books, puzzles and games for all ages. There is a large kids section with books for toddlers to teens. Much of the merchandise is selected for its educational value, and they carry many books about the beach and local environment.

Wilmington Children's Museum
116 Orange St., Wilmington
(910) 254-3534

The Children's Museum is a colorful, exciting space where kids up to age 12 can engage in activities that will enhance lifelong learning and creativity. Programs focus on the arts, science and technology, health and safety, mathematics, multicultural studies and the environment. In its storefront setting, the museum features a two-deck pirate ship complete with treasure maps and costumes; a fully stocked grocery store complete with shopping carts and cash registers that introduce basic math concepts. Kids of all ages enjoy the theater stage where they can become different personalities using a variety of costumes and props.

Kids love to visit the "Let's Go Lego" exhibit and create a masterpiece on the mosaic wall or build a racecar to race down the indoor track. Youngsters can learn about the different properties of sand by pouring and sifting. Then they can look over a collection of 300 sand samples from around the world. Check out the purple sand!

The Art and Science classrooms always have exciting programs designed to spark a child's curiosity and innate love of learning. Explore with microscopes in the computer lab or maybe learn about what makes stars twinkle at night. The Art Studio is designed to introduce children to a multitude of arts media and methods while enhancing the capacity for learning and creativity.

The Children's Museum relies heavily on volunteers and welcomes new participants. It is open Tuesday through Saturday from 10 AM to 5 PM and Sunday from 1 to 4 PM; it's open on Mondays as well during June, July and August, and most school holidays. Admission is $3.50 per person.

Holidays

The holidays are a special time for families. Be sure to check the local newspaper for details of specific events happening in the area, since the southern coastal region is known for going all out for every celebration. Christmas is filled with too many events to

mention, such as the Poplar Grove Christmas Open House

Poplar Grove Historic Plantation, 10200 U.S. 17 N., (910) 686-9518 Ext.26; the Island of Lights Festival, held at various locations in Carolina Beach and Kure Beach, (910) 458-7116; and the Christmas By-The-Sea Festival in Oak Island and Southport locations, (910) 457-6964. Check these and other holiday happenings in our Annual Events chapter. Listed here are some offerings grouped by holiday. Be sure to stop by or phone the Cape Fear Coast Convention & Visitors Bureau at 24 N. Third Street in Wilmington, (910) 341-4030, (800) 222-4757, for the latest Calendar of Events; you can also access it online www.cape-fear.nc.us.

EASTER

Easter Egg Hunt
Franklin Square Park
W. West and Howe Sts., Southport
(910) 457-7945

This citywide Easter egg hunt is held every year on a Saturday before Easter in Franklin Square Park, where there are plenty of hiding places. Nine hundred plastic eggs with prizes inside and 10,000 candy eggs are scattered throughout the park to the delight of the participating children.

Easter Egg Hunt at Hugh MacRae Park
S. College Rd., Wilmington
(910) 395-1940

Hosted by the Wilmington Jaycees for the past 29 years, the annual Easter egg hunt is a great time for some 3,000 youngsters ages 10 and younger. Volunteers place more than 10,000 hollow plastic eggs filled with candy in "hiding places." The participating children are divided into age categories and assigned specific hunting areas. When the horn sounds on the appointed day, bedlam ensues.

HALLOWEEN

Haunted Wilmington Walking Tours and Other Fun Things

Join some of the area's most renowned local actors and ghost hunters as they lead you through old alleyways and down dark streets on a journey into the depths of Old Wilmington. Meet the poor souls who still haunt our fine city. Hear tales, both past and present. The Ghost Walk of Old Wilmington conducts a nightly walking tour throughout the year. The tour meets year round by the Riverfront at the foot of Market Street. Hours are April 1 through October 31 at 8:30 PM, plus Tuesday through Saturday at 6:30 PM; from November 1 through March 31 the tours are Tuesday through Saturday at 6:30 PM. Special Halloween times vary. You're advised to call ahead, (910) 602-6055.

On the last Saturday and Sunday in October just before Halloween, the Bellamy Mansion, 503 Market Street, sponsors a weekend of fun ghost stories and legends and kid-friendly entertainment. You can visit many haunted, spooky homes. For ticket information call (910) 251-3700.

Poplar Grove Historic Plantation, (910) 686-9518, has more than 20 years of experience in the fine art of Halloween scariness. The Haunted Barn and Haunted Hayride are guaranteed to bring up some goose bumps, and all the little kids love the fun house. Professional rides and carnival games, tarot card and palm readings, colorful decorations and plenty of food are big draws, too. A costume contest, puppet show with handmade puppets and other fun stuff make a ghostly trip to Poplar Grove Historic Plantation a must for all ages.

Pumpkin carvers celebrate Halloween on the Riverwalk in downtown Wilmington.

photo: Gwynne Moore

The Wilmington Jaycees, (910) 395-1940, have as much fun as the kids do around Halloween. Watch the newspaper for dates and times to visit their famous Haunted House, which changes locations from year to year. Each room has a different theme and lots of fright-filled moments.

Trick-or-Treat Under the Sea
North Carolina Aquarium at Fort Fisher
900 Loggerhead Rd., Kure Beach
(910) 458-8257

Looking for a safe, family-oriented place to enjoy Halloween a little early? The aquarium provides safe, indoor trick-or-treating (at candy stations provided by local businesses). There are costume contests, crafts, storytelling and lots of aquatically themed Halloween fun. There is a modest admission fee, but kids three and younger are admitted free. Call the above number for exact date, time and further details.

KWANZAA

This seven-day African-American cultural celebration is observed yearly in the Wilmington area during the week between Christmas and New Year's Day. The word refers to the harvest's "first fruits." During the holiday, people use each day to meditate on one of the holiday's seven principles: umoja (unity), kujichagulia (self-determination), ujima (collective work and responsibility), ujamaa (cooperative economics), nia (purpose), kuumba (creativity) and imani (faith).

Edens Institute Inc., an organization that promotes African-American and multicultural heritage programs, has an annual Kwanzaa celebration that features food, music, a lighting ceremony, crafts for kids, African dancing and vendors. Watch for announcements in the Friday Currents section of the Wilmington Star-News. For information, call (910) 254-0708.

Public radio WHQR 91.3 FM, broadcasts its own Kwanzaa production, Season's Griot, created and performed by local storyteller and musician Madafo Lloyd Wilson together with other storytellers from around the country. This hour-long program is distributed nationally as a holiday special broadcast. Call for details and program times, (910) 343-1640.

CHRISTMAS

Christmas Lights at Kings Grant

The Kings Grant subdivision off N.C. Highway 132 (N. College Road), is a must-see for kids and adults during the weeks prior to Christmas. Each year, residents adorn their homes with an incredible array of lights and decorations, attracting caravans of people who turn off their headlights to view the spectacle in all its glory. Turn right onto Kings Drive, which is about 1.25 miles north of the Market Street overpass. Just follow the line of cars; you can't miss it!

Santa at Bellamy Mansion
503 Market St., Wilmington
(910) 251-3700

On the second Saturday in December, kids are invited to Bellamy Mansion to share Christmas wishes with Santa and have their picture taken. There are refreshments, along with arts and crafts and plenty of holiday fun. Call Bellamy Mansion at the above number for more details.

Santa Claus at Westfield Shoppingtown
Independence
3500 Oleander Dr., Wilmington
(910) 392-1776

Santa Claus arrives at the mall every year in mid-November and remains ensconced in winter glory until his midnight ride on Christmas Eve.

Summer Camps

Summer is the main anticipation of almost any school-aged child, but it can be tiring for parents, especially those who work, to invent fun, imaginative activities for their children day after day. Summer camps are a great antidote for this problem. The southern coast offers many different camps for you and your child to choose from. Day camps and sports camps (rather than overnight camps) are the norm in the southern coastal region. For sports camps, children must own basic personal equipment, including protective gear. Team items such as bats and balls are provided. Be sure to review our chapter on Sports, Fitness and Parks as well. Day campers generally need only swim suits, tow-

Wilmington Family YMCA Summer Camp

Pick from a variety of camps or combine camps for an all-day Y experience: *Day Camp, Kinder Camp, Sports Camps, Upward Bound Camp, Girls Summer Pageant, Stars on Stage or Kids Triathlon Camp.*

2710 Market Street, Wilmington, NC 28403
(910) 251-9622 www.wilmingtonfamilyymca.org

We build strong kids, strong families, strong communities.
A United Way Agency

els and sneakers to get the most out of their camp experiences.

An extremely useful publication, Summer Alternatives, lists dozens of summer activities for school-age children in our area. It is distributed in late April by the New Hanover County Schools and may be obtained free by calling the Community Schools office at (910) 254-4221, or you can pick one up at your child's school.

Ashton Farm Summer Day Camp
5645 U.S. 117 S., Burgaw
(910) 259-2431

Ashton Farm, established in 1975, is 72 acres of historic plantation about 18 miles north of Wilmington. Owners Sally and Jim Martin provide children ages 5 through 12 with down-to-earth fun. Kids participate in farm life, sports with minimized competition, and nature. Among the activities are swimming, canoeing, horseback riding, softball, hiking, crafts, animal care, rodeos and archery and more.

One-week sessions from June to August are available (daily with permission).

Discounts apply for additional weeks and/or additional children registered. The camp provides round-trip transportation to Wilmington, camper health insurance and drinks; children should pack their own lunches. Single-day camps have been added to coincide with teacher workdays.

Brigade Boys & Girls Club
2759 Vance St., Wilmington
(910) 791-4282

Serving area children since 1896, the Brigade Boys & Girls Club is a popular place for summer activities. Between the last day of school and the first day back, kids enjoy a wide variety of games, sports competitions of all sorts, reading, plus arts and crafts. The regular summer program runs Monday through Friday from 6:30 AM to 6 PM. Youngsters are divided according to age groups: 6 through 11 years and 12 to 18 years. A swimming pool with certified lifeguards makes this a great place to spend a hot summer day; some swimming instruction is available. Free breakfasts and lunches are provided.

Brunswick County Parks and Recreation Department
Building M, Government Complex, Bolivia
(910) 253-4357, (800) 222-4790

Activities at this camp include swimming, water parks, miniature golf, pottery creations and more. Participants meet at the Brunswick County Government Complex in Bolivia each morning of camp, which runs Monday through Friday from 9 AM to 5 PM. Day camp registration is subject to availability and is taken on a first- come, first-serve basis, starting in April (call for dates). Payment is expected at the time of registration.

Cape Fear Museum
814 Market St., Wilmington
(910) 341-4350
www.capefearmuseum.com

A variety of activities involving local history and nature are available to children ages 5 through 12 in half-day and full-day camps at the museum, five days a week from June through mid-August. Call weekdays between 9 AM and 5 PM for information and to register. (Also see our Attractions chapter.)

Carolina Coastal Adventures Camp
1337 Bridge Barrier Rd., Carolina Beach
(910) 458-9111

In July through August, week-long fun camps for kids include lessons in surfing, kayaking and fishing plus visits to the North Carolina Aquarium at Fort Fisher, hiking in the state park, and marsh exploration. When the weather doesn't cooperate, kids keep busy with games, crafts and videos with a marine science theme. Has your child developed an interest in kayaking, fishing or surfing? Try one of these week-long, in-depth programs; the Kids Coastal Kayak Discovery Camp provides kayaking adventures and information about kayak safety, the Captain's Fishing Camp takes kids on great fishing and learning adventures, the Surfing Beach Days Camp is a week filled with surfing, body-boarding, surf kayaking, surf fishing and beach ecology. There are some discounts available for early registration (March/April).

Emma Anderson Memorial Chapel Youth Program
1101 S. Anderson Blvd., Topsail Beach
(910) 328-1619, (910) 328-1532

This long-running program by the Emma Anderson Memorial Chapel has families planning their vacation around program dates. Daytime activities for children and youth ages 6 to 19 are offered Monday through Friday during the summer months. A schedule of events is prepared weekly, and activities can include beach volleyball, fishing on the pier, miniature golf, pizza parties, a cookout, basketball, volleyball, billiards, ping pong and more. Participants can come for one day or the whole program. There is no cost to attend this program, which often offers opportunities to include parents and other family members.

Girls Inc. Day Camp
1502 Castle St., Wilmington
(910) 763-6674

Girls Inc. offers half-day and full-day camps in Wilmington and Brunswick County from one week after school lets out for summer break until one week before school resumes. Activities include sports, crafts, swimming, computer classes, sewing, field trips, career exploration, science projects and cooking. Guest speakers are brought in from time to time. The Wilmington camp accepts girls from kindergarten to age 18. Call (910) 763-6674 for information and to register.

Jelly Beans Family Skating Center
5216 Oleander Dr., Wilmington
(910) 791-6000

Jelly Beans' summer day camp, for kids ages 5 through 12, is especially convenient (and affordable) because your child can just drop in for a single day at a time. While roller skating is a natural part of regular activities, Jelly Beans concentrates heavily on outdoor and educational field trips.

North Carolina Aquarium at Fort Fisher
Kure Beach
(910) 458-8257, (910) 458-7468

Aquarium summer camps promise learning and fun for youngsters in three age groups – 5 and 6 years old, 7 through 9 and 10 through 12. Schedule Monday through Friday from 8:30 AM to 12:30 PM, sessions are offered in June and July. Each group of 12 campers will enjoy age-specific, fun-filled outdoor activities, including crafts and programs that help kids understand and appreciate aquatic environments.

UNCW Athletic Department
601 S. College Rd., Wilmington
(910) 962-3233

UNCW sponsors day and overnight summer sports camps in baseball, softball, basketball, tennis, volleyball and soccer. These sessions give younger players a good foundation for the sports and emphasize fundamentals. Call for information early in the season, as these camps tend to be quite popular.

UNCW MarineQuest
601 S. College Rd., Wilmington
(910) 962-2386

The University of North Carolina at Wilmington's Division for Public Service and Continuing Studies invites kids to become part of MarineQuest, one of the most unique marine and environmental education programs in the country. MarineQuest encompasses a wide variety of marine and education programs for ages 6 through adult. For information about Summer by the Sea Camp (for kids ages 6 through 9), Coast Trek (ages 12 through 13), OceanLab (ages 14 through 15), Positively Reactive Chemistry Camp (ages 8 through 12), among others, call the information line at (910) 962-2386.

City of Wilmington Recreation Division
Adventure Pathways Summer Camp
302 Willard St., Wilmington
(910) 794-6003

For kids who truly enjoy challenging physical activities and like being on the move, the Adventure Pathways programs are just the ticket. Guaranteed not to be boring, the week-long excursions, held in June, literally go in three different directions. Sessions for boys and girls ages 10 to 14 include exploration, watersports, hiking, climbing and overnight camping. Space is limited. Fees range from $175 to $200; registration begins at the end of February and the deadline is May 6.

Wrightsville Beach Parks and Recreation Department
1 Bob Sawyer Dr., Wrightsville Beach
(910) 256-7925

Art Camp, Soccer Camp and Creative Performance Arts Camp are among the fun offerings for kids sponsored by the Wrightsville Beach Parks & Recreation Department. How about surfing or tennis lessons? Call for a brochure and more information.

Wilmington Family YMCA
2710 Market Street, Wilmington
(910) 251-9622
www.wilmingtonfamilyymca.org

YMCA summer day camps for tots to teens (from kindergarten through age 16) operate June through August on weekdays. The "Y" is open for daytime activities from 7:30 AM to 8 PM. Among the many fun things to do, kids can participate in pool swimming, indoor and outdoor sports, arts and crafts, reading, music and games. Field trips to the beach, local attractions and other kid-friendly places are popular. Stop by to register as spots are limited.

ⓘ THE ARTS

North Carolina claims a long and rich history in the arts, and the southern coastal region nurtures this heritage through a wide range of cultural opportunities. Wilmington, with its coastal and historical ambiance, competes as a major center for the visual and performing arts. The city's lively downtown area is the hub of arts organizations and activities for the region, and it lures musicians, painters, actors, writers, filmmakers, sculptors and dancers to the coffeehouses and cafes to discuss their crafts. On any given day year-round the community's calendar overflows with diverse and intriguing cultural events.

Residents and visitors to the southern coast find exciting entertainment showcased by the many established institutions devoted to the arts, including the Thalian Hall Center for the Performing Arts, Louise Wells Cameron Art Museum in Wilmington and the Odell Williamson Auditorium in Brunswick County. These institutions host nationally and internationally renowned artists, as well as local and regional talent.

In addition to a community already rich in theatrical talent, the film industry established a working movie studio in Wilmington in 1985. The studio attracts film production companies and professional actors to the area on a regular basis. Often, while working on location here, many of these actors — John Travolta, Sandra Bullock, Paul Newman, Linda Lavin and Pat Hingle, to name a few — share their expertise with local actors and thrill audiences with performances on area stages. Some, like Mr. Hingle and acclaimed actor Henry Darrow, choose to stay and become a part of the working arts community.

Cinematique, an ongoing showcase for "classic, foreign and notable films" is jointly sponsored by public radio station WHQR and the Thalian Hall Center for the Performing Arts. The films are shown in Thalian Hall, where the palpable history and opulence add an amazing mood to the screening. On occasion, capacity crowds have held a popular film beyond the normal Monday-through-Wednesday-night screenings.

Music is another vital part of the regional arts scene. Wilmington has its own symphony orchestra, a vibrant chamber music series, a regular concert series and dozens of ensemble groups ranging from professionals to enthusiastic amateurs. On a daily basis, local clubs and restaurants serve up a stimulating offering of live music from every imaginable genre.

Theater companies are plentiful and employ the talents of local writers, musicians and performers. There are several stages in town, including Thalian Hall, Kenan Auditorium and Trask Coliseum at the University of North Carolina at Wilmington, Citystage in the historic Masonic Temple downtown and the Scottish Rite Temple.

Touring companies regularly visit Wilmington, particularly during the Azalea Festival in the spring and Riverfest in the fall. Over the centuries, Wilmington has hosted such notables as Lillian Russell, Maurice Barrymore, Oscar Wilde and John Philip Sousa. Come closer in time and consider this diverse collection of performers: Al Hirt, Chet Atkins, Frank Sinatra, The Ciompi String Quarter, Judy Collins, Koko Taylor, Itzak Perleman, Roberta Flack, Reba McEntire, Kenny Rogers, Charlie Daniels, the Beach Boys and Ray Charles. In neighboring Brunswick County, audiences at the Odell Williamson Auditorium, located on the campus of Brunswick Community College, have thrilled to an equally impressive roster of performers, including The Tommy Dorsey Orchestra, Doc Watson, The Lettermen, Mike Cross, the Preservation Hall Jazz Band, Lee Greenwood, The Platters and The Glenn Miller Orchestra.

The visual arts occupy a prominent position in the cultural experiences of North Carolina's southern coast. In addition to several commercial art galleries, particularly

North Carolina Symphony

75th ANNIVERSARY

Grant Llewellyn invites you to celebrate with us a milestone of musical significance – the North Carolina Symphony's 75th Anniversary.

THE 75TH ANNIVERSARY CELEBRATION

Audiences from concert hall to concert hall all across North Carolina have experienced some of their deepest emotions while listening to music performed by the North Carolina Symphony.

Since the first concert in 1932, the orchestra has persisted in its service and commitment to North Carolina and through the decades, we have never stopped perfecting our musicianship, deepening our dedication to our art form, and believing in our power to enrich the lives of everyone we touch.

We invite you to join us in this loving celebration of our 75th Anniversary in Wilmington.

Raleigh · Chapel Hill · Durham
Wilmington · New Bern
Southern Pines · Fayetteville

Music Director Grant Llewellyn

Cape Fear Series

The North Carolina Symphony performs six concerts between September and May. All performances are held at Kenan Auditorium on the campus of UNC-Wilmington at 8pm.

Tickets

910.962.3500
800.732.3643
www.ncsymphony.org

Outdoor drama is a cultural attraction throughout southeastern North Carolina..

photo: Myke Wharff

in the Greater Wilmington area and Southport, the region has Louise Wells Cameron Art Museum, regarded as one of the finest art museums in the Southeast. Local artists also exhibit their work in area restaurants, coffeehouses and upscale shopping centers.

North Carolina's southern coast region is a rich environment for the arts, offering a variety of opportunities for both creating and enjoying the cultural arts. This chapter lists just a sampling of the arts scene in the region.

Museums, Performance Halls and Organizations

Acme Art Inc.
711 N. 5th St., Wilmington
(910) 763-8010

An avant-garde renovation of an old warehouse is the perfect home for this artist-owned and operated studio. The working environment zings electric with artists running their drills, welding with their blow-torches and dueling airbrushes on bold mats of color. The gallery space is upgraded with track lighting, and opening exhibits are warm and friendly.

Associated Artists of Southport
130 E. West St., Southport
(910) 278-5562, (910) 457-5450

Housed in historic Franklin Square Gallery in Southport, this nonprofit organization provides an increasingly rich environment for the growth and development of local visual artists. It is dedicated to the cultural enrichment of the community through education and the promotion of original art. In 2004 the association celebrated the 25th anniversary of its inception and the 100th anniversary of the Franklin Square Gallery building. Newly renovated, the gallery houses two floors of 2D and 3D exhibit rooms, a sales office, a classroom and the Brunswick Arts Council Room. There are regularly scheduled workshops in various media by recognized artists as well as judged exhibitions and competitions, all of which are open to the public. A national juried competition and exhibit is held each July in conjunction with the N.C.

The Wilmington Symphony Orchestra
Steven Errante, Conductor

Saturday, September 30, 2006
8:00 PM
GRAND OPENING
CONCERT
Keats Dieffenbach, *violin*
Sponsored by
Wilmington Gastroenterology Associates

Saturday, November 4, 2006
8:00 PM
MARY JO WHITE, *flute*
Sponsored by
Cooperative Bank

Saturday, December 2, 2006
8:00 PM
HOLIDAY CONCERT
UNCW Concert Choir,
Joe Hickman, *conductor*
Sponsored by **Plantation Village**

Saturday, February 17, 2007
8:00 PM
A CELEBRATION OF BLACK HISTORY MONTH
Joy Murrell, *soprano*
Marva Robinson, *soprano*

Sponsored by
International Paper Company

Saturday, May 5 , 2007
8:00 PM
OPERA SPECTACULAR
Nancy King, *soprano,*
Michael Rallis, *tenor*

Sponsored by
Prudential CRES
Commercial Real Esate

Subscriptions may be purchased by calling
Kenan Auditorium Ticket Office at (910) 962-3500 or 1-800-732-3643.
Single tickets can be purchased beginning Monday, August 21, 2006.

www.wilmingtonsymphony.org

Fourth of July Festival. Drawing and painting classes are held Monday through Friday in the upstairs studio. Pottery classes are conducted in the pottery studio behind the gallery. Painting and pottery classes for children of the community are conducted yearly and are partially funded by grants from the Brunswick Arts Council. Kids Day is a community fun day, free to the public, sponsored by the Associated Artists, Brunswick County Parks and Recreation Department and Southport Parks and Recreation Department. Association members serve as instructors, speakers and judges for local schools and organizations. Monthly meetings are held the third Monday of each month. Call for more information or a membership application.

Brunswick County Arts Council
P.O. Box 276, Supply
(910) 269-1552

Established in 1981, this nonprofit volunteer organization is Brunswick County's primary arts information and funding source. Arts funding is channeled to this group from the North Carolina Arts Council. With money received each year, the Brunswick Arts Council provides financial assistance to approximately 18 local arts groups through Grassroots Arts Program grants; sponsors community events such as Concert by the Sea; and publishes a directory of Brunswick County artists and art groups as well as sponsoring the Brunswick County Arts Council Art Show. This valuable resource for local arts information is available through the organization, the Southport-Oak Island Chamber of Commerce, (910) 457-6964, and the Brunswick Chamber of Commerce, (800) 426-6644. Membership in the council is open to all interested citizens. The Brunswick Arts Council offers a range of programs including cultural symposiums, programs for the classroom, bus trips to regional art venues, and more. The range of interests includes the visual arts — painting, pottery, sculpture, photography, woodworking, quilting and handwork — and the performing arts of music, drama and dance. The council offers individual grants to artists who are in need or have a special educational interest in pursuing their goals. President Dariel Bendin

invites anyone who is interested to attend monthly meetings held at Brunswick Community College on the first Monday of each month at 5:30 PM.

The Community Arts Center
120 S. Second St., Wilmington
(910) 341-7860

The Community Arts Center, formerly the Wilmington U.S.O., is a part of Wilmington's Parks and Recreation Department and is located in the center of historic downtown. Primarily a learning facility where anyone may go to take low-cost lessons in a full range of disciplines, the Community Arts Center also serves as a rehearsal space for most of Wilmington's community theatre groups. The Thalian Association community theatre manages the building for the city and has offices and rehearsal space within the center. For nominal fees, students of all ages can experience hands-on work under the direction of skilled local artists. In addition to workshops and classes, other programs include performances, concerts and fund-raisers, usually staged in the Center's Hannah Block 2nd Street Stage theatre area of the facility.

Oak Island Art Guild
P.O. Box 913, Oak Island
(910) 253-3101

The Oak Island Art Guild meets the second Friday of each month at the Oak Island Recreation Center. Experienced artists lead free workshops in a relaxed atmosphere. These are held monthly and are open to the public. Workshop topics include watercolor, oils, acrylic, pastel, pen-and-ink, batik, colored pencil, clay, collage, tile painting, glass painting, enameling, calligraphy, portraits, abstracts and more. Each year The Guild awards a $600 scholarship to a high school senior who is planning to major in an arts-related field. It donates arts books and videos to the local library and sponsors the Labor Day Arts and Crafts Fair. In cooperation with the Parks and Recreation Department, the Guild is involved in the Celebration of Oak Island and the annual Arts by the Shore, which is a judged art show held in the Oak Island Recreation Center.

Before I left the house this morning I...

Explored hybrids at the Detroit Auto Show.

Welcomed Miles Davis into the Rock + Roll Hall of Fame!

Discovered tips for healthier grocery shopping.

Explored theories about the solar system's origin.

WHQR is your station for NPR news.

We deliver local voices and global perspectives that take you beyond radio. We call it radio with vision.

WHQR 91.3 fm

Listen and See

On Air at 91.3 fm | **Online at** whqr.org
In Person at 254 N. Front Street, Downtown Wilmington

Odell Williamson Auditorium
**Brunswick Community College,
150 College Rd., Supply
(910) 755-7416, (800) 754-1050 ext. 416**

Built in 1993 by the citizens of Brunswick County for the educational and cultural enrichment of the community, this 1,500-seat, state-of- the-art facility on the campus of Brunswick Community College offers entertainment opportunities in the heart of Brunswick County. In its short history, this center for the arts has presented the talents of the North Carolina Symphony, the U.S. Marine Band, the Kingston Trio, Jerry Reed, the All American Boys Chorus, the North Carolina Shakespeare Festival, the Tommy Dorsey Orchestra, The Lettermen, Lee Greenwood, Pebo Bryson, a presentation of The Odd Couple starring Jamie Farr and William Christopher (Klinger and Father Mulcahey from the TV show M*A*S*H), and various national touring companies performing such classics as Death of a Salesman. The auditorium and lobby are available for private and public rental. The auditorium has a subscription season each year. For tickets or information about renting the facility call (910) 755-7416 or (800) 754-1050 ext. 416.

Louise Wells Cameron Art Museum
**3201 S. 17th St., Wilmington
(910) 395-5999**

The pinnacle of visual arts in southeastern North Carolina, the Louise Wells Cameron Art Museum opened its new state-of-the-art facility on April 21, 2002. Situated at the intersection of Independence Boulevard and 17th Street, this 42,000-square-foot museum was designed by renowned architect Charles Gwathmey, who characterizes the building itself as an abstract sculpture.

The Cameron Art Museum is the only American institution whose primary purpose is to collect, display, preserve and archive North Carolina art. This exceptional museum houses a stunning permanent collection of 18th-century to contemporary North Carolina art, including the works of such artists as Mary Cassatt, Minnie Evans, Claude Howell and Elisabeth Augusta Chant, in the 7,200-square-foot Permanent Collection wing. This wing, composed of 10 individual galleries, boasts much of the artwork owned by the museum itself. In addition to the permanent collection, six to eight changing exhibitions are presented each year in the Featured Exhibition wing located beneath the museum's signature pyramidal skylights. This area can be divided into as many as four individual exhibition spaces.

The Cameron Art Museum also features the Galleria, home to the museum's ceramic and decorative arts collections; a sculpture court; The Forks Restaurant; a reception hall; and the museum shop, which holds a special corner for children. Civil War buffs will enjoy the restored defensive mounds located on the museum grounds, once used by the Confederacy. Classes, workshops and community meetings are held in the Pancoe Art Education Center, also on the museum campus.

Museum hours are Tuesday through Saturday 10 AM to 5 PM and Sunday 10:30 AM to 4 PM. Admission is $7 for adults, $15 for families and $2 for children ages 6 to 18. Children younger than 5, active military and museum members are admitted free. Come on the first Sunday of each month and enjoy the museum during what is referred to as "pay what you can." Restaurant seating is available Tuesday through Sunday for lunch and on Sunday for brunch.

Thalian Hall Center for the Performing Arts
**310 Chestnut St., Wilmington
(910) 343-3660
Box Office: (910) 343-3664,
(800) 523-2820**

Built in 1858, this majestic performance center has gone through several restorations and, at this time, offers three performance spaces. Housed within are a 752-seat main theatre, the 250-seat Council Chamber and a 136-seat studio theatre. With a lively local performing arts community and the addition of touring companies, at least one of the spaces is in use each evening or afternoon. More than 35 area arts and civic organizations use the facility, and more than 450 performances and screenings in music, theatre, dance and film are presented each year. (See our Attractions chapter for more information.)

Waterway Art Association
**Calabash Fire House,
Persimmon Rd., Calabash
(910) 575-7981**

The Waterway Art Association was established in 1991 to "encourage artistic

passion

excitement

intimacy

IT HAPPENS HERE.

2006 - 2007 Season
Sunday Evenings at 7:30 pm
New Recital Hall, UNCW

October 22 Borromeo String Quartet
November 19 Degas Quartet
January 28 Ciompi Quartet
March 11 Amit Peled
May 13 Carolina Piano Trio

Chamber Music
WILMINGTON

Check us out at www.chambermusicwilmington.org

awareness and growth both on an individual as well as a community level." An important part of this mission is accomplished in the group's sponsorship of enrichment classes for elementary school children.

With the exception of December, meetings are held on the third Wednesday of the months of September through May at 1:30 PM. Meetings are followed by arts-related programs. Paint-ins are held every Wednesday. Members of all skill levels participate in a variety of activities such as professional workshops, outdoor sketching and painting sessions, trips to museums, plus lectures and exhibits. The association hosts a Memorial Day Exhibit, which is a juried show, and a Labor Day Show, an outdoor event.

Wilmington Art Association
Chandler's Wharf, 225 S. Water St., Wilmington
(910) 799-8598

Composed of professional and amateur visual artists and art enthusiasts, the Wilmington Art Association holds small art shows throughout the year and conducts an annual juried exhibition, the Spring Juried Art Show and Sale, held during the Azalea Festival activities in April. The WAA also holds meetings on topics of interest, sponsors frequent workshops, critiques, educational programs and special projects, and gives two scholarships to UNC-Wilmington art students annually. Meetings are held monthly September through June on the second Thursday evening of each month in the Pancoe Art Education Center at the Louise Wells Cameron Art Museum.

Music

Azalea Coast Chorus of Sweet Adelines
(910) 791-3846

Sweet Adelines, the female counterpart of the Society for the Preservation and Encouragement of Barbershop Quartet Singing in America (see Cape Fear Chordsmen, below), promotes and preserves the art of singing four-part harmony, barbershop style. The Sweet Adelines meet on Mondays at 7 PM at the Wrightsville Beach Baptist Church. Membership is open to all women who enjoy this original American style of music.

Blues Society of the Lower Cape Fear
(910) 350-8822

Founded by a small group of blues enthusiasts in 1988, the Blues Society of the Lower Cape Fear continues to be a mainstay of Wilmington's music community and is one of the most successful music societies in eastern North Carolina. The group offers musicians of all skill levels an opportunity to participate in the society's weekly jam sessions and annual events, including an exciting blues talent competition held the first weekend in November. The BSLCF also actively participates in state and local arts organizations and programs. Blues fans don't want to miss the annual Cape Fear Blues Festival held in July. (See Annual Events for more details.) The Cape Fear Bluesletter is available through membership in the society. Monthly membership meetings are held on the first Monday of the month at 7:30 PM. Musicians and blues enthusiasts can join the group's long-standing weekly jam session every Tuesday night from 8 PM until midnight (or later). BSLCF provides any professional equipment you may need; just bring your instruments. Call for meeting and jam locations.

Brunswick Concert Band
Southport
(910) 457-0861

The nonprofit Brunswick Concert Band is composed of volunteers from Brunswick, New Hanover, Pender and Horry counties who have been playing together for the past 16 years. No auditions are required, and volunteers who have at least a high-school skill level are invited to join, with the stipulation that members have their own instrument and can read music. The band plays a variety of music styles — Big Band, jazz, light classical, marches and show tunes — and conducts two formal concerts annually, a spring concert held in March or April and a Christmas concert. It also plays at a variety of festivals and events in the area, particularly the N.C. Fourth of July Celebration. Brunswick Concert Band is a member of the Association of Concert Bands. Weekly rehearsals are held on Tuesday evenings from 7 to 9 PM at the Progress Energy Brunswick Energy Center in Southport.

The Cape Fear Chorale
Patty Conner (910) 313-0516

The Cape Fear Chorale has been performing in the Wilmington area since the fall of 1998 and presents concerts in the fall and spring of each year. The director, accompanist and 44 singers all volunteer their time, talents and effort to provide quality choral music to the Cape Fear Region. New singers are welcomed at the beginning of each concert season.

Cape Fear Chordsmen
(910) 772-9967

This group is Wilmington's chapter of the Society for the Preservation and Encouragement of Barber Shop Quartet Singing in America. Members practice male four-part harmony singing weekly at 7:30 PM on Tuesday evenings at the College Acres Baptist Church in Wilmington. New members are welcome; call for more information and a concert schedule.

Chamber Music Wilmington
Azalea Station, Wilmington
Sharon Stone (910) 343-1079
www.chambermusicwilmington.org

Chamber Music Wilmington is a non-profit presenting organization that brings world-class chamber music concerts to the southeastern NC. Many of the artists and ensembles are North Carolinians who have gained critical acclaim on a national and/or international level.

Their 2006-07 evening series presents the Borromeo String Quartet, cellist Amit Peled and violinist Ara Gregorian, Duke's Ciompi Quartet, and the Carolina Piano Trio.

In addition to the evening subscription series, the organization also works in conjunction with area schools and educators to develop educational enrichment projects for young audiences. Chamber Music Wilmington offers family concerts including an Instrumental Petting Zoo, where children can touch and explore a variety of orchestral instruments with the help of a professional musician. These programs are designed to help parents and children explore the world of music together. Tickets are available by

The Field Studio
Private Piano & Vocal Instruction
We make music seriously fun!
Steve Field - Piano • 910-251-8988
Liz Field - Voice • 910-251-7797
3173 Wrightsville Ave.
Highwood Park Plaza • Wilmington, NC 28403

subscription or individually. The concerts fill quickly, so come early.

The Field Studio
3173 Wrightsville Ave., Wilmington
(910) 251-8988
www.fieldstudio.biz

The Field Studio offers private vocal instruction by Liz Field and private piano instruction by Steve Field. Both are classically trained, professional musicians with master's degrees in their respective areas.

Steve has 15 years of experience teaching piano privately. He has been on faculty at the University of Connecticut and the University of Memphis. He maintains a performing career doing recitals, accompanying and conducting throughout the country. Steve has a passion for passing on his knowledge, experience and love of the piano to anyone who has a desire to learn.

Liz has been teaching voice since 1987 to students at all levels. A Lyric Coloratura Soprano, Liz is in demand as a soloist and as a leader of her Vocal Enrichment Seminars for Choral Singers. She loves helping people find their true voice and experience the joy of singing. At the Field Studio, they make music seriously fun!

Girls Choir of Wilmington
205 Dover Rd., Wilmington
(910) 799-5073

Formed in 1997, this community-based choral ensemble has an enrollment of approximately 100 girls. Girls ages 9 and older perform a variety of classical, folk, sacred, secular and popular music. The members learn teamwork, discipline, musicianship and community service through the concerts and activities.

Harmony Belles
(910) 799-5850

Formed in 1986, this local women's group sings four-part harmony a cappella. Their performances for civic organizations, churches, nursing homes, educational programs in schools and at local events emphasize their philosophy of community service. Rehearsals are Tuesday evenings from 6:30 to 9 PM. Harmony Belles is open to new members; call for rehearsal location and membership information. The Belle Chords, a female quartet within the group, performs in a four-part harmony, barbershop style.

North Carolina Jazz Festival
Wilmington Hilton Riverside,
301 N. Water St., Wilmington
(910) 350-0250

This winter weekend festival is usually scheduled for the first weekend in February and features mainstream jazz performances by national and international stars. The main event is held at the Wilmington Hilton Riverside, and a preview program is given the day before. (See our Annual Events chapter.) Good luck getting tickets to the main event if you don't have a standing order for them because this is a hugely popular festival with fiercely devoted fans.

North Carolina Symphony
(910) 962-3500
www.ncsymphony.org

The Cape Fear Series of the North Carolina Symphony presents six concerts from September through May at Kenan Auditorium on the campus of UNC-W. For tickets, call Kenan Auditorium Ticket Office at (910) 962-3500 or (800) 732-3643.

Sea Notes Choral Society
(910) 278-5542

This nonprofit volunteer organization is based in Southport and serves Brunswick County. Membership in the chorus, whose numbers currently exceed 100, is open to all interested singers. Some choral experi-

ence would be useful, but no auditions are required unless you are applying to be a soloist. The group rehearses every Monday evening at 7 PM at the Trinity United Methodist Church in Southport. Concerts include a variety of music, from the Messiah to folk to gospel to pops. The chorus has a new director every season with three primary concerts annually — in the spring, on the Fourth of July and at Christmas. Members are asked to pay dues of $25 per year to supplement contributions and grants. All concerts are free, though donations are gratefully accepted.

Summer Sundays
Keziah Memorial Park, W. Moore
and S. Lord Sts., Southport
(910) 457-7927

Open-air concerts sponsored by the City of Southport and the Southport Visitors Center are held in the historic Keziah Memorial Park from Memorial Day weekend through Labor Day weekend on Sundays from 2 until 4 PM. Bring chairs, blankets, picnic baskets, kids, families and elders and enjoy music by local artists. Jazz, rhythm and blues, rock 'n' roll, bluegrass, show tunes, Big Band music and more assure something for everyone's taste and enjoyment.

Westermark Voice Studio
Sara Graham Westermark, Soprano
620 Cobblestone Dr., Wilmington
(910) 233-1323
www.sarawestermark.com

Sara Graham Westermark, a classically trained singer with a master's degree in Voice Performance from the University of Missouri-Columbia, offers affordable voice lessons for all ages. Each lesson is recorded on a CD, which is a wonderful tool for practice sessions at home.

Sara is an active singer in this region and has appeared as a soloist with the Wilmington Symphony Orchestra, Southeastern Oratorio Society, Wilmington Oratorio Society, UNCW Concert Choir, UNCW Opera Scenes and other area organizations. She has taught private voice lessons for more than ten years in addition to working with elementary singing groups. She also teaches music and voice at Cape Fear Community College. Give yourself, family member or friend the gift of Sara's instruction and the benefit of her years of experience.

WILMINGTON CONCERT ASSOCIATION

ALL PERFORMANCES AT KENAN AUDITORIUM, UNCW CAMPUS

OCTOBER 12, 2006

Nadja Salerno-Sonnenberg, *violin* & Anne-Marie McDermott, *piano*

Breathtakingly Daring and Original

NOVEMBER 10, 2006

The Tokyo String Quartet

"Breathing together" (Washington Post). All-Stradivarius instruments.

JANUARY 17, 2007

Bulgarian State Opera, with *Turandot*

Distinguished Singers, Impressive Chorus & Orchestra

FEBRUARY 22, 2007

Moscow Festival Ballet, with *Don Quixote*

Fiery, Classical Production

MARCH 6, 2007

Jonathan Biss, *piano*

"A huge talent — an extraordinary virtuoso" (Baltimore Sun).

Subscriptions and Tickets may be purchased by calling
Kenan Auditorium Ticket Office at (910) 962-3500 or 1-800-732-3643.

WILMINGTONCONCERT.COM

Westermark Voice Studio
Sara Graham Westermark, Soprano

Affordable voice lessons • Classically trained
Masters in Voice Performance • Record all lessons on CD

(910) 233-1323 or saraw@ec.rr.com

Wilmington Academy of Music
3830 Oleander Dr., Wilmington
(910) 392-1590

The Academy is a private school, founded in 1987, that offers a full range of music instruction in voice, piano, guitar, harp, violin, viola, cello, percussion, trumpet, trombone, clarinet, saxophone, flute, tuba, oboe, bagpipe and more for students of all ages. Theory, orchestration, arranging and other classes are available. Traditional, Suzuki and jazz techniques are the methods of choice. Weekly private lessons and monthly group lessons, recitals and master classes are offered. The academy offers a variety of ensembles for weddings, receptions and special events, featuring the combined talents of faculty members and experienced local musicians. Drama classes will be offered in the near future. Call for details.

Wilmington Choral Society
(910) 790-0382

This large, well-established chorus has been a presence in Wilmington since 1950. Attracting singers from Wilmington and the surrounding areas and from a cross-section

of ages and professions, the chorus prides itself on high-performance standards of classic choral selections and a wide variety of contemporary music. The group participates in three or four concerts annually. Members rehearse on Tuesdays from 7:25 to 9:30 PM at the Cape Fear Christian Church in Wilmington, and the organization is open to all interested singers. No auditions are necessary.

Wilmington Concert Association
(910) 763-4374

Established in 1929, Wilmington Concert Association brings four to five classical music and dance concerts of national and international prominence to Wilmington each year at UNCW's Kenan Auditorium. Performers in recent years have included the Alvin Ailey Repertory Ensemble, pianist Arcadi Volodos, Helikon Opera of Moscow, the Ballet du Capitole de Toulouse, Yo Yo Ma, Zurich Chamber Orchestra, Peter Schiekele and the Canadian Brass. Membership is open to everyone.

Wilmington Symphony Orchestra
4608 Cedar Ave., Wilmington
(910) 791-9262
www.wilmingtonsymphony.org

Founded in 1971, the Wilmington Symphony Orchestra is a cultural jewel in the Port City's crown, performing a series of concerts that enrich, entertain, and educate thousands of adults and school children throughout the year. The musicians are local amateur and professional instrumentalists, and gifted students and faculty who volunteer their time and talents. Musicians are selected each year by audition. The conductor, Dr. Steven Errante, is Professor of Music at UNCW. The Wilmington Symphony Orchestra also continues to serve the Cape Fear Region as a leader in music education through an extensive educational and outreach program that includes a Free Family Concert, the Wilmington Symphony Youth Orchestra and its Junior Strings Division, an annual Student Concerto Competition, and Artist-in-Residence Programs in area schools.

Helpful Art Gallery Guides for Wilmington and Southport-Oak Island are available at area galleries, chambers of commerce and visitor information centers.

Theater

Wilmington has a rich theatrical tradition that is continually expanding. Wilmington's Thalian Hall Center for the Performing Arts is home to the Thalian Association, the oldest

Wilmington's Premiere dramatic theatre company presents its 2006 season...

Jake's Women

Betrayal

Sight UNSEEN

10th Annual New Play Festival

MOBY DICK- Rehearsed

All Shows in Wilmington's Historic Thalian Hall
For More Information and Season Tickets:
www.BigDawgProductions.org

continuous community theater in the country, dating from 1788. The theater hosts professional and amateur productions on an almost nightly basis.

Several local theatrical companies present original and popular productions at such area locations as Kenan Auditorium at the University of North Carolina at Wilmington, the Scottish Rite Temple on 17th Street, and schools and churches. Additionally, Wilmington is on the circuit for touring dance companies, symphonies and musicals.

Big Dawg Productions
(910) 343-3664
www.bigdawgproductions.org

Dedicated to producing professional theater and cultivating excellence in the arts, this nonprofit theater company (in its eleventh year) performs five dramas and comedies per season at Thalian Hall Center for the Performing Arts. Other programs developed by the group include The New Play Festival, which showcases talented youth and adult playwrights, and the support of the development of talent through a technical internship

program. One production of each season is a classic work which is offered to local K-12 classes; past offering have included Dracula, Henry V and Moby Dick to be presented in 2006.

Level 5 at City Stage
21 N. Front St., Wilmington
(910) 342-0272

Whether you're in the mood for a serious drama, a musical or comedy, Level 5 at City Stage is the place to go in downtown Wilmington for great theater. Level 5 at City Stage offers an intimate theater setting where there are no bad seats! Adjacent to the theater, Level 5 contains a popular rooftop bar where you can socialize before and after the show. Ticket prices are reasonable, and the performances are Broadway caliber. Now entering its fourth season, Level 5 at City Stage has already made its mark on the Wilmington theater scene, so if you haven't seen a show there yet, come see what you've been missing. The Level 5 at City Stage theater group produces its own shows and provides a

THALIAN Community THEATRE

1788

presents

A Season of Firsts

All Wilmington Premieres!

CATS
October 5-15, 2006

OVER THE RIVER AND THROUGH THE WOODS
December 7-10, 2006

CROWNS
February 1-4, 2007

TUESDAYS WITH MORRIE
starring
Pat Hingle
March 15-18, 2007

Disney's
BEAUTY & THE BEAST
May 11-20, 2007

Thalian Hall Main Stage

TICKETS: (910) 343-3664

www.thalian.org • (910) 251-1788

rental facility for other local theater company performances and independent film screenings. If you need a good laugh, local comedy groups also perform here during the week. Call for schedule and ticket information.

Opera House Theatre
2011 Carolina Beach Rd., Wilmington
(910) 762-4234

A professional theater company presided over by artistic director Lou Criscuolo, this group stages five major productions and three experimental works each season in Thalian Hall. Guest artists and directors are featured frequently. Auditions are open.

Thalian Association
120 S. Second St., Wilmington
(910) 251-1788
www.thalian.org

Tracing its theatrical roots back to 1788, the Thalian Association is a volunteer performing group staging four full-scale productions yearly in Thalian Hall. The Thalian Association Children's Theatre (TACT) stages three productions a year in the Hannah Block 2nd Street Stage in the Community Arts Center in downtown Wilmington. Operating under the supervision of a volunteer board of directors, the Thalian Association stages two yearly fund-raising events, the Southern Coast Bluegrass Festival and the Orange Street Arts Festival, and seeks to involve volunteers in all its plays and activities.

Willis Richardson Players
(910) 763-1889

Established in 1974 and specializing in dramas by minority playwrights, the Willis Richardson Players perform several works per season of interest to all audiences.

Dance

The Wilmington area offers the broadest spectrum of experiences in dance classes. The following is only a sample.

Class Act Dance Company
(910) 452-4765

Class Act is a senior women's dance group that performs for local civic organizations, nursing homes, schools, churches and other community activities. Auditions for experienced dancers, 55 years and older, are held at any time. Rehearsals are held twice weekly at the New Hanover County Senior Center, Mondays from 11:30 AM to 1 PM and Fridays from 11:30 AM to 1 PM.

The Dance Cooperative
1209 Market St., Wilmington
(910) 763-4995

The Dance Cooperative consists of six dance professionals who are bound together by one common goal, to foster a link between professional dance artists and the community. Their mission is to nurture the dance community by providing affordable classes, rehearsal space and performance opportunities to those under-served artistically, culturally and economically in the greater Wilmington area. The Dance Cooperative currently has a program of classes for children and adults (drop-ins are welcome), and both an informal and formal performance series. Some scholarships are available for children who wish to take these classes. Once a month, The Dance Cooperative hosts special workshops led by master artists. Call (910) 763-4995 for more details and schedule information.

Theatre Dance Workshop
(910) 458-3302

Theatre Dance Workshop is a place where singing, dancing and acting all come together. Classes in the performing arts are available for adults and children ages 7 and older. The students are part of senior and junior companies that perform original choreography, scenes and songs from Broadway shows.

Writing

North Carolina Writers' Network
(919) 967-9540

North Carolina Writers' Network, based in Carrboro near Chapel Hill, is a vital resource for North Carolina writers. This well-established organization offers an extensive library and helps writers sharpen their skills in poetry, fiction, nonfiction, playwriting and technical writing through state-wide writer workshops. The North Carolina Writers' Network also provides information and submission guidelines for statewide and regional

competitions. The annual themed Fall Conference, hosted in alternating North Carolina regions, is a popular event for writers of all skill levels.

Playwrights Producing Company
(910) 799-5043

A nonprofit company supporting emerging North Carolina playwrights, this organization offers seminars and looks for scripts-in-progress, which are read by actors and critiqued by the volunteer audience. Readings of selected productions or original plays are a highlight of monthly meetings. Membership is open. Call for meeting dates, times and locations.

Crafts

Azalea Coast Smockers Guild
(910) 392-2696

This active group of needlewomen teaches smocking and heirloom sewing. Beginning as well as experienced smockers are welcome. Call for monthly meeting information.

Brunswick Quilters
Moose Lodge, Rt. 130, Shallotte
(910) 842-8474

This quilters group includes members from as far away as South Carolina and boasts more than 80 members. Meetings are held the second and fourth Tuesday of each

Celebrate Wilmington! and the Walk of Fame

Mount Rushmore has its presidents, Hollywood has a star-studded sidewalk and, since 1997, Wilmington has a Walk of Fame. Located behind the Cotton Exchange shopping center in historic downtown Wilmington, the Walk of Fame Plaza was created through the efforts of Celebrate Wilmington!, which is sponsored by the University of North Carolina at Wilmington. The main goal is to celebrate Wilmington's arts community and recognize those who have enriched the Cape Fear area.

Visitors to this small plaza on Nutt Street will find a graceful arbor with flowering vines and tubs of seasonal plants at the entrance. Tall, distinctive banners bearing the Celebrate Wilmington! emblem flap overhead in a breeze from the Cape Fear River waterfront nearby. Bronze benches provide a comfortable place to rest and view the eight-pointed stars that line the walkway, bearing the names of Walk of Fame honorees.

To be chosen for this honor, candidates must satisfy a specific criteria. Inductees are those people who have lived, worked and/or enriched the Wilmington/Cape Fear region and have attained national or international recognition in one of the following fields — the arts, business, education, literature, broadcasting/television/film, journalism, sports, science, medicine, the military, politics or government.

Current Walk of Fame honorees (in order and with year of induction) are:

1997 - Roman Gabriel A Wilmington native, Roman Gabriel played All-State football, baseball and basketball while at New Hanover High School and starred as a football quarterback at North Carolina State. He went on to a career in professional football as an NFL quarterback, playing for the Los Angeles Rams and the Philadelphia Eagles.

1997 - Minnie Evans A native of the Cape Fear region, Minnie Evans was a visionary artist who, without prior training, began to paint prolifically in middle age. Using whatever materials she could find, she painted vibrant and colorful pictures depicting the dreams and vision she experienced all of her life. A collection of her work hangs on permanent display in the Louise Wells Cameron Art Museum.

1998 - Hugh Morton The legacy that Hugh Morton leaves behind is as a preservationist, naturalist and photographer. He contributed much time and effort into preserving North Carolina history through his work on the Save The Battleship and Cape Hattaras Lighthouse projects. Morton is also an internationally recognized photographer whose work appeared in several well-known magazines, including Time and National Geographic.

1998 - Henry Bacon Though born in Illinois, Henry Bacon spent most of his life in Wilmington, designing the Confederate Memorial at Third and Market Streets and the estates of local families. He is most noted for his design of the Lincoln Memorial in Washington, D.C., for which he won international recognition and the highest honors of the American Institute of Architects. Bacon is buried in the Oakdale Cemetery, 520 N. 15th Street, Wilmington.

1999 - Frank Capra, Jr. Frank Capra, Jr. has been instrumental in the development of Wilmington's film industry. Internationally recognized as a filmmaker, Capra returned to Wilmington in 1996 to become president of EUE/Screen Gems

Studios. His earlier visit in 1983 resulted in the filming of Dino DeLaurentiis' movie, Firestarter, on location at Orton Plantation. Since his return, Capra has been tireless in his efforts to bring film production to the Cape Fear region and strengthen communication between the industry and the community. Capra participates in Wilmington's theater arts and teaches classes in the Film Studies Program at UNC-Wilmington.

1999 - Caterina Jarboro Born Katherine Yarborough in Wilmington, Caterina attended school here until, at age 13, she journeyed to New York to study music. During her illustrious career, she achieved international fame as a soprano and paved the way for other talented African-Americans in American opera. Caterina performed in many of the world's great opera houses, including Paris, Vienna, Warsaw, Madrid, Moscow and the United States. She also thrilled Wilmington audiences on two occasions by performing at the Academy of Music (Thalian Hall) and the Williston High School auditorium.

2000 - Althea Gibson Breaking through racial barriers throughout her career, tennis legend Althea Gibson achieved several "firsts" as an African-American athlete, especially a black female athlete, and won nearly 100 professional titles. In 1958, after retiring from professional tennis competition, she made golf history as the first African-American to earn an LPGA card. Althea's connection to Wilmington dates back to her move to the city as a young girl to train with Dr. Hubert Eaton, who discovered and mentored her. She trained on Dr. Eaton's regulation-size tennis court in downtown Wilmington, living with his family and attending Williston High School.

2000 - Robert C. Ruark, Jr. Robert Ruark, born and raised in Wilmington, graduated from New Hanover High School. He later earned fame and recognition as a journalist and, eventually, as a bestselling novelist. His books include Something of Value, Poor No More, Uhuru and The Honey Badger.

2001 - David Brinkley A Wilmington native for the first 21 years of his life, veteran journalist and news commentator David Brinkley got his start in print news with the Wilmington Morning Star. He went on to work for the United Press and NBC radio in the 1940s before turning to an emerging new medium called television. Brinkley, one of the first journalists on television, is credited as a pioneer in the field of broadcast news.

2001 - Charlie Daniels Hit country music singer/songwriter and Grammy winner Charlie Daniels has strong roots in the Cape Fear region. Born in Wilmington in 1936, Daniels grew up on Carolina Beach Road and still has family in the area. He received an honorary degree from UNC-Wilmington in 1996. Two of Daniels' most recognized songs include "The Devil Went Down to Georgia" and "The South's Gonna Do It Again."

2002 - Claude Howell Believing that the quality of Wilmington's light was unlike

Local celebrities are honored with a star on Wilmington's Walk of Fame

photo: Deb Daniel

that of any other place, Claude Howell explored the effect light has upon the objects and shapes of coastal living. He helped found the art department at Wilmington College, later the University of North Carolina at Wilmington, and left many serigraphs to St. John's Museum of Art. His collection is now housed in the Louise Wells Cameron Museum of Art.

2003 - Isaac ("Ike") Bates Grainger Banking and golf made good partners for a man who excelled at both. An executive of Murchison National Bank of Wilmington, North Carolina Bank & Trust Co. of Greensboro, Grainger joined Chemical Bank of NYC (now Chase Manhattan), where he was president from 1956-60, when he reached mandatory retirement age. At the same time he was rising through the ranks of the banking world, Grainger served as chairman of the joint rules committee of the U.S. Golf Association (USGA) and the Royal and Ancient Golf Club of St. Andrews. He was president of the USGA from 1954 to 1955 and received the USGA's Bob Jones Award for distinguished sportsmanship in golf in 1988. Living to be 104, Grainger was one of the oldest veterans in New Hanover County and the oldest member of the Cape Fear Golf Club, which hosts an annual golf tournament, the Isaac B. Grainger International Match Play Championship, in his honor.

2004 - Sonny Jurgensen Born in Wilmington, Sonny Jurgensen attended New Hanover H.S. and went on to a brilliant college football career at Duke University. Sonny began his NFL career playing for the Philadelphia Eagles and later became a record-setting quarterback for the Washington Redskins. In 1983, he was inducted into the Pro Football Hall of Fame.

2005- Don Payne Graduating from New Hanover High School in 1982, Don Payne went on to garner three Emmy awards as a writer for the hit Fox animated series, The Simpsons. Cape Fear Museum currently has a number of Payne's items of Simpson's memorabilia on display.

2006- Meadowlark Lemon Lemon's antics as the leader of the Harlem Globetrotters throughout the '70s and '80s, at the height of the group's popularity, made him beloved by basketball fans the world over. He continues working as a goodwill ambassador through his organization, Camp Meadowlark.

month with a business meeting at the first Tuesday meetings and teaching workshops or programs at the fourth Tuesday meetings. Visitors are always welcome. Members are invited to participate in monthly Block of the Month lotteries as well as Fat Quarter lotteries. One of the group projects is the making of Comfort Quilts, which are donated to the Brunswick County Sheriff's Department to be given to children involved in traumatic situations. The Brunswick Quilters will be hosting the next annual Meet the Quilters Day for area quilting groups in 2006. This event features a special speaker, Show and Tell, door prizes and time to visit.

Art museums and theatres often offer members free general admission and/or reduced rate tickets to special events. Becoming a member of the local museums and/or theatres you and your family visit frequently can often save you money in the long run, and it's a way of supporting the arts in your community.

Embroiderers' Guild of America (910) 686-4463

The Scotch Bonnet Chapter of the Embroiderers' Guild of America offers workshops, classes and other educational opportunities for everyone interested in the art of needlework. All skill levels and interests are welcome. Monthly meetings are held at 10 AM on the third Monday of every month from September through June at St. John's Episcopal Church.

Oak Island Beach Quilters
Oak Island Recreation Center, 3003 E. Oak Island Dr., Oak Island
(910) 842-8474

The Oak Island Beach Quilters is a sociable, friendly group that welcomes members, visitors and vacationers alike, from beginners to experts. The group meets every Wednesday from 10 AM until 3 PM with a business meeting on the second Wednesday of each month. These meetings include new techniques presentations, sharing of ideas and techniques, show and tell, and just working together on individual or group projects. Every year there is a quilting challenge that involves a theme, a particular color, fabric or shape or a combination of these. Challenge entries are displayed at Franklin Square Gallery in Southport (see the Galleries section of this chapter) where visitors can vote for their favorites. The group responds to national and world natural disasters, such as those in New Orleans and Mississippi in 2005, with charity quilts for the victims. They also donate Cognitive Quilts to nursing homes. These quilts are hung on the wall and used to stimulate discussions, which are therapeutic for patients with Alzheimers. The group maintains a lending library of quilting books and plans road trips to quilting stores and shows as well.

Oak Island Senior Center
5918 E. Oak Island Dr., Oak Island
(910) 278-5224

Classes are available in water color, oil and tole painting, basket weaving, chair caning, cooking, computer basics, cake decorating, needlework, bow making, and shell angels. Fees are $25 for members and $35 for non-members.

Port City Basketmakers
Poplar Grove Plantation, 10200 U.S. Hwy. 17 N., Wilmington
(910) 686-4868

Members of this group work to stimulate public interest in the art of basketry and to preserve the techniques of the craft. Workshops and seminars are available, and new members, from novice to advanced weavers, are welcome. Call for meeting dates and times.

Wilmington's Thalian Hall is the place to see a variety of arts performances.

photo: NC Department of Tourism

CLOSE-UP

Cape Fear's Celebrity Roster

Wilmington and the Cape Fear area have played well-known roles throughout the nation's history, but few people are aware of the famous and talented folks who once called this area home:

- Henry Bacon, *architect*
- David Brinkley, *TV journalist*
- Frank Capra, Jr., *motion picture filmmaker*
- John Cheek, *operatic baritone*
- Charlie Daniels, *country-rock musician*
- Sammy Davis, Sr., *stage performer*
- Edward B. Dudley, *first popularly elected governor of North Carolina*
- Mary Baker Eddy, *founder of Christian Science Church*
- Nelson Eddy, *singer*
- Minnie Evans, *visionary painter*
- Roman Gabriel, *NFL Player of the Year, 1969, L.A. Rams*
- Althea Gibson, *tennis champion (U.S. Open 1957-58, Wimbledon 1957-58, French Open 1956)*
- Thomas Godfrey, *first American playwright*
- Cornelius Harnett, *patriot of the American Revolution*
- William Hooper, *signer of the Declaration of Independence*
- Caterina Jarboro, *operatic soprano*
- Michael Jordan, *basketball star, Chicago Bulls*
- Sonny Jurgensen, *NFL Hall of Famer*
- Charles Kuralt, *TV commentator and author*
- Meadowlark Lemon, *basketball star, Harlem Globetrotters*
- Sugar Ray Leonard, *Olympic gold medalist boxer*
- Hugh Morton, *preservationist, naturalist and photographer*
- Robert Ruark, *author and safari hunter*
- Anna McNeill Whistler, *"Whistler's Mother"*
- Woodrow Wilson, *28th president of the United States*

The sun, sand and sea have drawn visitors to our shores for generations.

photo: Peter Doran

WEDDING PLANNING

"Yes, I do." These words are heard over and over again along the southern coast, from church sanctuaries to elegant halls to the surf's edge. No doubt about it, the wedding industry is thriving in New Hanover, Brunswick and Pender counties. While couples of all ages still opt for the traditional church ceremony, a growing number plan an outdoor wedding, choosing to tie the knot on one of the local beaches or in a garden. Interesting wedding/reception locations are abundant, from the Henrietta III Riverboat to the famous Orton Plantation and fabulous Louise Wells Cameron Art Museum.

In this chapter, we help guide you through the intricacies of planning a wedding in the southern coastal area, from applying for a license and choosing a magistrate or minister to hiring a caterer and photographer. We also provide you with information on locations, musicians, florists, formal wear, transportation and rental equipment. If you want someone else to handle all the necessary planning details, we suggest some popular wedding consultants. Be sure to look in our Salons & Day Spas chapter for some great gift ideas and beauty services for your special day. Planning a wedding can be a thrilling adventure. Our goal is to help you enjoy the experience.

Marriage Licenses

A North Carolina marriage license is a must. You may get the license in any county, but must turn it into the Register of Deeds in the county where the wedding takes place. This is very helpful for out-of-town couples coming to the beach area to be married, because they can get their license at home (if they live in North Carolina) and bring it with them.

Courthouses are open Monday through Friday but are closed on holidays. Hours vary, so phone ahead (Register of Deeds offices are listed below). Both parties must be present. Take with you three forms of identification — certified birth certificate, Social Security card and valid driver's license or DMV picture card ID. If a person has been divorced, the divorce decree must be recorded and in some instances, you'll be required to show a copy of the divorce decree itself. No blood test, physical exam or waiting period is necessary to obtain a marriage license, which costs $50 to $60 and is payable by cash only. In some instances, application forms are available online.

The license is valid for 60 days after being issued. Bring your marriage license to the wedding. Two witnesses must sign the license following the ceremony. The person who performs the ceremony is responsible for getting the license back to the Register of Deeds in the county in which you were married within 10 days. After you're married, the officiant or magistrate will issue you a marriage certificate.

REGISTER OF DEEDS OFFICES

New Hanover County Register of Deeds - Vital Records
24 N. 3rd Street, Room 103, Wilmington
(910) 798-4537 or (910) 798-7754
http://www.nhcgov.com/ROD/RODmarriage.asp

Brunswick County Register of Deeds
75 Courthouse Drive, Bolivia
(910) 253-2690, (877) 625-9310
http://rod.brunsco.net

Onslow County Register of Deeds
109 Old Bridge Street, Jacksonville
(910) 347-3451 http://co.onslow.nc.us/register_of_deeds

Pender County Register of Deeds
300 E. Fremont Street, Burgaw
(910) 259-1225 http://www.pender-county.com/Departments/rod

Wedding Locations

The Wilmington area is home to literally hundreds of churches, plus synagogues, a Muslim mosque and a Buddhist temple. Houses of worship often require that you have some affiliation if you are planning to use the facilities. Contact the person in charge and he or she will give you the specifics. Prepare to pay a fee for the use of the sanctuary as well as to compensate for services. It is customary to pay between $50 and $150 for ministerial services. See our Worship chapter or the yellow pages of local phone books for a list of houses of worship.

The area's pristine beaches, barrier islands and historic gardens make magnificent backdrops and are a huge draw for couples who are in love with nature as well as each other. Some opt for an informal ceremony on the beach where everyone can go barefoot, while others choose such venues as Airlie Gardens, the New Hanover County Arboretum or Orton Plantation. If an outdoor wedding appeals to you, keep in mind that southern coast weather can be unpredictable; always plan an indoor alternative. And remember to plan well in advance; at least a year out in many cases. You'll have a lot of competition for some locations and services.

For seaside weddings at Wrightsville Beach, you will need to apply for a special use permit, especially if you want to use the Wrightsville Beach gazebo. There's a fee for the permit based on the number of participants, and some regulations apply. Contact the Wrightsville Beach Parks and Recreation Department, #1 Bob Sawyer Drive, Wrightsville Beach, (910) 256-7925, for information and permits.

Contact the Pleasure Island Chamber of Commerce, (Carolina and Kure Beaches), 1121 N. Lake Park Boulevard, Carolina Beach, (910) 458-8434, for information regarding the many suitable island locations available for weddings. A permit and fee are required for use of the Carolina Beach Lake gazebo or other municipally owned facilities, but none is required for a beach ceremony. Remember, alcohol and glass containers are prohibited on the beach.

CONGRATULATIONS!

We will ensure that you are a radiant and tranquil bride!

We offer selections in:

• Hair Design • Full Service Salon
• Cosmetic Design • Full Nail Services
• Massage Therapy • Facials
• Hair Extensions

HARBOUR CLUB
DAY SPA and SALON

Lumina Station
1904 Eastwood Rd.
Suite 101
Wilmington, NC 28403
910-256-5020

www.harbourclubdayspa.com

WILMINGTON

Airlie Gardens
300 Airlie Rd., Wilmington
(910) 798-7700

A rare gem just moments from Wrightsville Beach, the lavish landscape of historic Airlie Gardens offers 67 acres of azaleas, camellias and some of the world's most exotic plants in a setting that can accommodate up to 300 guests. The Italian pergola, which provides a natural aisle leading down to the foot of one of two manmade freshwater lakes, is the most popular place to conduct the ceremony. Afterwards, most couples choose the famous Airlie Oak as the site for their reception. Please make reservations at least one year in advance.

Bellamy Mansion Museum
503 Market St., Wilmington
(910) 251-3700

Make your wedding a memorable occasion with an evening event at Wilmington's beautifully restored Bellamy Mansion (1859-1861). This magnificent landmark provides a breathtaking backdrop for ceremonies, receptions, rehearsal dinners and wedding photography. Ornate plaster work, original brass chandeliers, marble and slate mantles and elaborate Victorian-style carpets provide a truly Southern atmosphere. More than 5,000 square feet, including the two main floors of the house, the grounds and the porches, are available for your guests. Your caterer may work on the basement level. Centrally located in the heart of Wilmington's downtown historic district, the mansion enjoys a large on-site parking lot. This is an ideal location for a small wedding or larger reception, and your guests will enjoy the comfort and beauty of this antebellum treasure.

Cape Fear River Deck
**Chandler's Wharf, 2 Ann St., Wilmington
(910) 763-1703**

Fantastic views of the river create a romantic backdrop for your bridal luncheon, rehearsal dinner, ceremony and reception on the Cape Fear River Deck. Part of Riverwalk along the Cape Fear River, the Deck is the perfect location for a Wilmington wedding. Owners Michael Lambrix and Howard Brown have more than 25 years of event planning experience and will take care of the details while lighting the celebration with a variety of unique, upscale candles from Candles Etc. They work with Elijah's restaurant and the Pilot House for the catering. Never mind the weather, a tent will save the day.

Graystone Inn
**100 S. Third St., Wilmington
(910) 763-2000, (888) 763-4773
www.graystoneinn.com**

The historic Graystone Inn, with its turn-of-the-20th-century elegance, frequently hosts wedding receptions and events. Rest assured, your hosts will take every step possible to ensure your special day goes as planned. They have compiled a recommended list of only the finest caterers, florists, musicians and photographers to make your choices as worry-free as possible.

Don't forget gifts for the wedding party. For the bride's attendants a sterling silver pendant or make-up brush or gemstone earrings make lovely gifts. For the ushers a sterling silver business card holder, a fountain pen, or a sports watch will please. For the maid of honor and best man more special gifts are called for.

The grand Renaissance-style staircase, with its sweeping curves, provides a feeling of warmth and allows you to make a dramatic entrance to the ceremony. Your guests will have a commanding view of your wedding nuptials from the parlor and grand entrance hall. The beautiful ground floor contains 4,300 square feet of space, accommodating up to 150 guests. The dining room's magnificent 12-foot long mahogany table is perfect for a catered feast, or it can be the setting for an intimate dinner. Along with your wedding festivities, your guests will enjoy taking advantage of all that downtown Wilmington has to offer.

Henrietta III Wedding Cruise
**Cape Fear Riverboats, Wilmington
(910) 343-1611, (800) 676-0162
www.cfrboats.com**

For an event you'll never forget, choose the Henrietta III, a truly unique wedding and reception location. After exchanging vows on or off the boat, enjoy a leisurely cruise down the beautiful Cape Fear River with your sweetheart and wedding party. The Henrietta III can host weddings from four to 400 guests, with menus ranging from light hors d'oeuvres to an elegant four-course dinner. Plan ahead and book early.

Lily's
**5025 Market St., Wilmington
(910) 799-7617**

Lily's is a gracious 4,000-square-foot banquet hall located behind Wilmington's charming Greentree Inn. A great place for all of your bridal events, Lily's can accommodate up to 250 guests for a plated, sit-down meal and larger crowd for a cocktail reception. For your convenience, a separate Green Room is available for personal preparations, such as dressing the bride. Owners Jay and Lee Kapner will work with your choice of caterers and service suppliers to give you a day to remember.

Louise Wells Cameron Art Museum
**3201 S. 17th St., Wilmington
(910) 395-5999, ext. 1000**

For a wedding day enhanced by fine art and brilliant architecture, there's no experience in Wilmington like the beautiful environment at Louise Wells Cameron Art Museum. You can exchange your vows and hold your

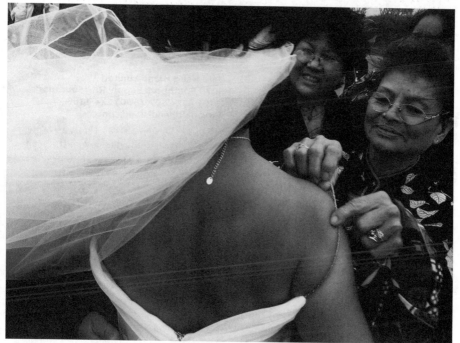

Friends and family help tie the knot.

photo: Peter Doran

reception indoors or on the lovely outdoor patio. Add exquisite catering by The Forks, the Cameron Art Museum's exclusive restaurant/caterer, and the success of your special day is assured. There's no aspect too great, no request that cannot be considered for your event. Their forte is private consultation, right to the last detail. For more information, contact the Museum at the number above.

St. Thomas Preservation Hall
208 Dock St., Wilmington
(910) 763-4054

Listed on the National Historic Register, St. Thomas Preservation Hall is staffed with courteous and helpful professionals who want your wedding day to run smoothly and be remembered with joy. This beautifully restored building, which dates back to 1846, was newly renovated in fall 2005, and is designed and fully equipped for rehearsal dinners, weddings and receptions for up to 250 guests. At St. Thomas, there are no restrictions imposed and no requirement to use an in-house service. You can choose any band, disc jockey, caterer, bartender or florist you desire, and your providers have all day to set

up and decorate at no extra charge. You can also take great satisfaction in knowing that all rental proceeds go to maintain and preserve part of Wilmington's history. An interesting side note is the fact that Father Tom Price, who was baptized and attended school in this building, is currently up for sainthood in the Roman Catholic Church.

The Wilmingtonian
101 S. Second St., Wilmington
(910) 343-1800, (800) 525-0909

The City Club at de Rosset, on the grounds of the historic Wilmingtonian, is the ideal location for a sumptuous wedding. This historic mansion epitomizes the architectural style of the old South and combines Southern charm with the very best in gourmet dining and service. This is the place to choose whether you're planning a true old-fashioned Southern wedding or a thoroughly modern event. They can even arrange for music, if desired. Weather permitting, plan to have both wedding and reception in the beautiful garden, where up to 300 people can be served, depending on the format. If it's rainy or cold, you'll find a gorgeous setting inside the

Wilmingtonian as well. All in all, The Wilmingtonian offers an atmosphere of elegance and refinement for your special day.

CAROLINA/KURE BEACH

Courtyard by Marriott
100 Charlotte St., Carolina Beach
(910) 458-2030, (800) 458-3606

The beautiful, 144-room Courtyard offers a full range of facilities and services for any size wedding. Banquet facilities offer seating for up to 250. This popular oceanfront hotel boasts a courteous, professional and very friendly staff. With the Atlantic Ocean as a dramatic backdrop, the Courtyard by Marriott is an ideal setting for the perfect wedding. Why not get married right on the beach?

North Carolina Aquarium at Fort Fisher
900 Loggerhead Rd., Kure Beach
(910) 458-8257, ext. 218
www.ncaquariums.com

The Aquarium's half-acre freshwater conservatory, 235,000-gallon saltwater tank featuring hundreds of sea creatures and dramatic exhibit galleries offer exceptional backdrops and romantic photo opportunities for your wedding ceremony. Exchange your vows before a colorful underwater display or amidst ferns and trees in the beautiful Cape Fear River Freshwater Habitat. You may choose the location that's just right for your dream wedding, whether large or small. The North Carolina Aquarium at Fort Fisher can accommodate up to 1,000 people, and up to 500 for a seated dinner.

BRUNSWICK COUNTY BEACHES
Bald Head Island

The Bald Head Island Club
Bald Head Island
(910) 457-7300

The Bald Head Island Club offers a variety of settings with breathtaking ocean views perfect for your special event. The four indoor, air-conditioned site options can beautifully accommodate a relatively intimate rehearsal dinner of 15, an extravaganza reception of 200 and anything in between. If you have always dreamed of celebrating under the stars, an outdoor tent site is available year-round. The attentive staff features on-site executive and pastry chefs ready to

cater to your every need. Club Event Planner Kiera Pridgen is available to assist you with planning and more. You can reach her at extension 106.

Bald Head Island Limited
5079 Southport-Supply Rd., Southport
(910) 457-7507, (800) 234-1666
www.baldheadisland.com

Idyllic Bald Head Island is an excellent choice for taking the plunge into the sea of matrimony. You can choose from various locations around the island such as the Shoals Club at East beach, the Harbourside Pavilion in Harbour Village or the Gazebo at Cape Fear Station located in the picturesque maritime forest. The elegant Shoals Club offers magnificent views of the Atlantic Ocean while the Gazebo's backdrop includes a lush green lawn and woodland paths. The Harbourside Pavilion's scenery includes an expansive marsh, the Cape Fear River and Old Baldy which is the oldest lighthouse in North Carolina. Other venues include the Association Center, private homes and of course anywhere along the island's 14-miles of pristine beach. The goal of the folks at Bald Head Island Limited is to indulge your taste, provide flawless service and make your event effortless.

Marsh Harbour Inn
21 Keelsen Row, Harbour Village
(910) 457-1702, (800) 680-8322

If you have always dreamed of a wedding by the sea, either open to the elements or under a canopy, come to the Marsh Harbour Inn, where you can honeymoon as well. Beautifully appointed guest rooms are available, as are 55 rental homes. A small reception (up to 30 people) can be held indoors if you wish. Catering is available through Fishy Fishy Cafe (see our Restaurants chapter), and the folks at the inn will be happy to assist you with a minister, the wedding cake and flowers.

Theodosia's Bed and Breakfast
Harbour Village, Bald Head Island
(910) 457-6563, (800) 656-1812

The 10 upscale guest rooms at Theodosia's and lovely rental homes on Bald Head Island are ideal places for wedding guests and honeymoons. Theodosia's can help plan your wedding ceremony, and catering for other special events is available as well.

The Village Chapel of Bald Head Island
105 Lighthouse Wynd, Bald Head Island
(910) 457-1183

This exquisite little chapel, nestled among flowers with a panoramic view of the marsh, is a nondenominational church. Services are held every weekend by visiting ministers. It is available for weddings of no more than 110 guests. The visiting minister may be available to officiate or you can provide your own minister. Weddings are limited to one per day and no weddings are performed during Easter week. Remember that you will need to arrange for ferry transportation and golf cart rental for all guests, as no vehicles are allowed on the island. If you think it would be fun to have a golf cart get you to the church on time, this would be one of the loveliest spots to tie the knot.

Southport/Oak Island

Southport Community Building
223 E. Bay St., Southport
(910) 454-0665

The Southport Community Building, owned and operated by the City of Southport, is available for rental and is a favorite setting for weddings and receptions. It is located at likely the loveliest spot in Southport — on a bluff overlooking the Cape Fear River and surrounded by ancient live oaks. The building offers a huge elegant reception room with honey-colored hardwood flooring, a fireplace, large windows providing panoramic views, a warming kitchen and a private conference room. Wedding ceremonies are held inside or outside on the wooden deck facing the Cape Fear River. Check out the website for more information.

Ocean Isle Beach

The Isles Restaurant
417 W. Second St., Ocean Isle Beach
(910) 575-5988

Why not have a lovely beachside wedding with music provided by the Atlantic Ocean and a backdrop of blue sky and brilliant sun? Or tie the knot in the glow of a magnificent North Carolina sunset. Then hold your reception at The Isles Restaurant oceanfront banquet facility, which is separate from the other dining areas, provides privacy for your event and can seat more than 100 guests. Your specialized menu will be prepared with the freshest of ingredients by the restaurant's excellent chefs and served by your own staff. The Special Events Coordinator can assist with all your wedding arrangements, including referrals to florists, for tuxedo alterations and to churches where a minister may be available to do the honors. (See the Receptions and Caterers section in this chapter.)

Ocean Isle Inn
37 W. First St., Ocean Isle Beach
(910) 579-0750, (800) 352-5988

The Ocean Isle Inn offers a perfect setting for a beachside wedding or wedding reception. Weddings can be performed in the oceanfront garden or directly on the beach. Banquet space is also available for up to 50 people, as are group rates for five or more rooms. And after your dream-filled day, you are invited to stay for your honeymoon. You will be more than pleased with the luxurious honeymoon package offered. Spacious and lovely accommodations, an abundance of amenities and an on-site event director make Ocean Isle Inn an ideal choice for your special day. (See the Wedding Planners section in this chapter).

Silver Coast Winery
6680 Barbeque Rd., Ocean Isle Beach
(910) 287-2800

If visions of a wedding in Tuscany fill your dreams, you don't have to travel far for the experience. Say your vows in the vineyard at Silver Coast Winery. A true vineyard and winery in the heart of Brunswick County, Silver Coast is nestled on 40 acres, surrounded by lush woods and just 15 minutes from the beach. Your guests can enjoy the spacious outdoor setting while sipping award-winning wines. Or you can choose the barrel room with its indoor waterfalls or the art gallery exhibiting works by local artists. For intimate affairs or larger groups, Silver Coast Winery is a unique setting for your special day. (For more information, see our Attractions chapter).

The Winds Oceanfront Inns and Suites
310 E. First St., Ocean Isle Beach
(910) 579-6275, (800) 334-3581
www.thewinds.com

The Winds offers a captivating beach setting for your wedding event. Creative honeymoon packages and catered receptions are available. Frolic in the ocean surf, swim in the heated pool, relax in the Jacuzzi spa, explore the island on bike rides, play tennis or golf and enjoy romantic dinners for two.

Sunset Beach

Sea Trail Golf Resort & Conference Center
211 Clubhouse Rd., Sunset Beach
(800) 624-6601

If you are looking for a romantic coastal setting for your wedding, be sure to check out Sea Trail Resort and Conference Center. Let their experienced staff handle all details to insure that your special day is unique and memorable. The lush gardens with a wedding gazebo overlooking lily ponds and the golf course is the perfect location to capture that feeling of romance. Locations abound,

from The Village Activity Center with private outdoor decks overlooking a tropical pool to a 9,600-square-foot, air-conditioned tent set amidst ponds, gardens and golf courses. The newly remodeled Jones/Byrd Ballroom with a 5,000-square-foot patio offers panoramic views of the beauty of Sea Trail. The Carolina Ballroom provides a formal setting that will overwhelm you with 10,000 square feet of function space and a 4,000-square-foot reception hall overlooking gardens and fairways.

The Sunset Inn
9 N. Shore Dr., Sunset Beach
(910) 575-1001

Weddings and/or receptions at the Sunset Inn are very special indeed. The experienced staff can make all the arrangements, and you can marry on the gazebo, on the beach or at the inn. The gorgeous natural setting has the marsh on one side and the ocean a block away on the front side. Accommodations are available for your guests as well as a Honeymoon Suite, complete with Jacuzzi, for the bride and groom.

TOPSAIL ISLAND

Assembly Building
720 Channel Blvd., Topsail Beach
(910) 328-4282

Enjoy a wedding at sunset on the porch of the historic Assembly Building or get married on the beach and host your reception in this nicely decorated and well-equipped large building that has room for more than 100 people, a band and a dance area. A kitchen is on site. Advance reservations are a must; restrictions apply and a donation is expected. Contact Sue Newsome for information and reservations.

The Atlantis Restaurant & Lounge
2000 New River Inlet Rd.,
North Topsail Beach
(910) 328-2002

More than 8,000 square feet, a seventh-floor view of North Topsail Beach and a dance floor contribute to the atmosphere of this island wedding destination. There's room for a band, 200 guests and plenty of photo opportunities. The Atlantis provides buffet and banquet services, and a complete menu is available on their website. Reservations are accepted year-round.

Dorothy Cruise Boat
720 Channel Blvd., Topsail Beach
(910) 545-7433

Create a custom wedding ceremony aboard the Dorothy as you cruise the Intra-coastal Waterway. Or choose to hold your bachelor or bachelorette party aboard this boat. Perhaps a sunset in the background is part of your dream. Capt. Dave will charter the boat for your special occasion and will work with you to make your event a very special occasion to be remembered.

St. Regis Resort
2000 New River inlet Rd.,
North Topsail Beach
(910) 328-0778

This impressive beach resort offers wedding opportunities on the beach or in their delightful gazebo. Onslow Hall is available for smaller receptions of 75 or less people, while the larger Pender Hall can accommodate up to 150. There are two bars and a dance floor in Pender Hall. Tables and chairs are provided in both halls. Clients must provide for their own caterer and bartenders.

Tiffany's Motel
1502 N. New River Dr., Surf City
(910) 328-1397, (800) 758-3818

Tiffany's has a great setting for your casual, beach wedding. Choose between a wedding on the elevated deck, by the pool or on the beach. Motel accommodations are available for wedding guests, and owners

Bob and Ann Smith will go out of their way to accommodate all your wedding needs.

Reception Facilities and Caterers

"A jug of wine, a loaf of bread and thee beside me..." Reception facilities in the Wilmington area offer as many choices as the mind can imagine. You can choose a location such as a hotel or restaurant that will provide the food and beverages, or engage a caterer for another setting. Our Restaurants chapter lists a number of excellent places that host wedding celebrations — everything from the bachelor's party and bride's luncheon to a rehearsal dinner or a full-blown reception.

If you'd prefer to host the reception in Wilmington's Historic District or in a romantic oceanfront house facing one of the many beaches, a caterer can provide all services while you enjoy the company of your guests. The caterer will also clean afterwards. For a catered function, expect to spend $20 to $50 or more per guest, depending upon your choice of menu and type of bar service.

WILMINGTON

Beau Rivage Resort & Golf Club
649 Rivage Promenade, Wilmington
(910) 392-9021, (800) 628-7080

An elegant, colonial-style clubhouse offers gracious formal banquet facilities accommodating up to 250, making this a perfect venue for wedding receptions and rehearsal dinners. Beau Rivage offers comfort, convenience, privacy and accessibility. The friendly, professional staff invite you and your guests to have a joyous, fun-filled, relaxed celebration. They will gladly work with your choice of Wilmington's finest caterers, florists and other suppliers. Whether your group is large or small, Beau Rivage is prepared to meet all your needs. For overnight guests, there are comfortable golf villas, outdoor swimming, tennis facilities and, of course, golf packages.

Caffe Phoenix
9 S. Front St, Wilmington
(910) 343-1395

Conveniently located in the heart of historic downtown, Caffe Phoenix is only a short stroll from any number of local wedding

Experience a Wilmington Classic

Innovative Mediterranean Cuisine
Lunch • Dinner • Sunday Brunch
Complimentary Parking
Private Catering for up to 80 guests
CAFFÈ PHOENIX
910.343.1395
Wilmington, North Carolina
9 S. Front Street • Historic Downtown Wilmington

venues. Their second floor space is reserved exclusively for private, catered events and can accommodate up to 85 guests. The third floor 2 bedroom apartment can also be utilized for pre-wedding rehearsal activities for local or out-of-town guests. Menus are made to order and showcase the skills of the restaurant's talented kitchen staff while a full beverage menu can be made available as well. The 150-year-old building's fully renovated space features beautiful heart pine floors, a fantastic view and parking just across the street. Enjoy your special day in a comfortable and warm environment just steps from the Cape Fear.

Elijah's
2 Ann St., Wilmington
(910) 343-1448
www.elijahs.com

Enjoy your special day at Elijah's restaurant, Wilmington's premier riverfront dining destination. The lounge area comfortably seats 50 and the main dining room approximately 120. Also, in conjunction with the Cape Fear River Deck (910) 763-1703, Elijah's can provide for an outdoor event for up to 100. Visit their website for pictures of the dining areas and to look at their menus.

To give everyone extra time to relax and prepare, hold the rehearsal dinner two nights before the big day rather than the night before.

WEDDING PLANNING

Jerry Rouse Catering
7220 Wrightsville Ave., Wilmington
(910) 256-8847

Jerry Rouse Catering will coordinate your catering needs for any number of guests. Their knowledgeable staff offers more than 37 years of professional experience and will happily assist you in selecting the most appropriate menu. Taking any dietary, religious or occasional need into consideration, Jerry's puts together an event for every desire with nothing left to chance. For your convenience, a complete list of wedding services is offered, such as tent set-up, shrimparoos, videography and music, to assure that your special day is memorable in every way.

Lily's
5027 Market St., Wilmington
(910) 799-6001

Lily's is a gracious 4,000-square-foot banquet hall located behind Wilmington's charming Greentree Inn. A great place for all of your bridal events, Lily's can accommodate up to 250 guests for a plated, sit-down meal and larger crowd for a cocktail reception. For your convenience, a separate Green Room is available for personal preparations, such as dressing the bride. Owners Jay and Lee Kapner will work with your choice of caterers and service suppliers to give you a day to remember.

Louise Wells Cameron Art Museum
3201 S. 17th St., Wilmington
(910) 395-5999, ext. 1000

The Forks, Cameron Art Museum's exclusive restaurant/caterer, has an expert staff who provide exceptional service for wedding events. Rehearsal dinners, bridal luncheons, engagement parties and fabulous receptions are all part of their repertoire. The Forks Restaurant is known for its creative approach to Southern dining. Add to that the luxury of

eating in a unique setting, and your guests will have a most memorable event.

Lovey's Market
Landfall Shopping Center, Eastwood Rd.
and Military Cutoff Rd., Wilmington
(910) 509-0331

If you've enjoyed the fresh, healthy, natural foods of Lovey's Market for lunch, you can bring that experience to your wedding menus. Lovey's offers the same delicious, fresh fruits, vegetables, salads, soups and beverages in their catering department. Owner Marie Parga and her professional catering staff can create the perfect rehearsal dinner, bridal luncheon or wedding reception. They will help you select just the right menu to complete your perfect day. Need flowers, a photographer or rental items? Marie can handle it all. For catering that's delicious and healthy too, call the catering professionals at Lovey's Market.

The Pilot House
2 Ann St., Wilmington
(910) 343-0200
www.pilothouserest.com

Enjoy your wedding day, rehearsal dinner, ceremony and reception at one of the most popular Cape Fear riverfront restaurants, located in the historic Craig House in Chandler's Wharf. Serving the finest in both traditional and innovative Southern cuisine for over 26 years, The Pilot House will serve approximately 100 guests in the casual elegance of the sunny dining room or outdoors on the covered patio.

Pine Valley Market
3520 S. College Rd., Wilmington
(910) 350-FOOD (3663)

Truly a one-stop shop for off-premise catering, Pine Valley Market will provide everything you need from setting up to cleaning up. From a romantic dinner for two to a full-scale party for 300 people, wine expert Kathy Webb and personal chef Christi Ferretti can handle it. Their specialty is intimate settings with a true gourmet flair. Whether you choose a brunch, dinner or cocktail reception, call this creative team to assist you with an event to remember. You'll love their party platters, accompaniments and entrees. Want vegetarian or low-carb selections? No

The duties of a best man include being an assistant to the groom and head of the groomsmen. He is also in charge of the bachelor party, getting the groom to the church, paying the officiant, signing the marriage license, holding the rings and giving a toast at the reception.

problem. What they don't do themselves, they can order for you, including specialty items such as wedding cakes and ice sculptures. You won't be disappointed!

Poplar Grove Plantation
10200 U.S. Hwy. 17, Wilmington
(910) 686-9518

If you're looking for someplace different to hold your service, reception and even your rehearsal dinner, historic Poplar Grove has a number of amenities suited to your needs. Parties can rent the Manor House, courtyard, gazebo, cultural arts center and even the entire grounds for their special day. Off the beaten path and an extremely popular destination, Poplar Grove has a cozy feel for celebrating one's nuptials.

Riverboat Landing
2 Market St., Wilmington
(910) 763-7227
www.riverboatlanding.com

Many marriage proposals have taken place on the nine two-seater balconies of this picturesque restaurant that overlooks the Cape Fear River. Owner Steve Kohlstedt says multiple family weddings have resulted from the restaurant's consistently high quality in both food and service. One couple who enjoyed a romantic balcony dinner, came back to renew their vows on their 20th wedding anniversary. The next year, they had a reception for one of their daughters and the following year, a rehearsal dinner was held for another family member! In over 20 years of business, the Riverboat Landing restaurant has hosted more than 1,000 wedding rehearsal dinners and an equal number of wedding receptions. The restaurant offers in-house catering for up to 110 people in its private banquet room and off-site catering for a maximum of 500. Catering services are fully customized with offerings of the finest seafood and steaks, hors d'oeuvres and buffets.

Wilsons Catering
4925 New Center Dr., Wilmington
(910) 793-0999 ext. 20

For creative cuisine, exquisite presentation and exceptional service, call Wilsons Catering. Their on-site event planner will help you chose your menu, either from

RIVERBOAT LANDING RESTAURANT

On-Premise Catering for up to 110 Guests
Off-Premise Catering for up to 500 Guests

2 Market St · Downtown Wilmington · 763-7227

their current selection of items or from your imagination. From rehearsal dinners to lavish receptions, Wilsons can accommodate your guests in their banquet rooms or at your chosen location, and will work with you to make sure every detail is perfect.

WALLACE

Mad Boar Restaurants
111 River Village Pl., Wallace
(910) 285-8888

The Celtic Court offers a unique atmosphere with seating for more than 300 guests. The Celtic Court has luminous alabaster chandeliers, a hand-carved mahogany bar, hand-painted gold leaf walls, an elevated stage, a dance floor and the latest in audio visual equipment. Offering fine cuisine, the Celtic Court is the perfect place for your rehearsal dinner or wedding reception.

WRIGHTSVILLE BEACH

King Neptune Restaurant
11 N. Lumina Ave., Wrightsville Beach
(910) 256-2525

King Neptune offers fabulous Caribbean seafood in a unique island atmosphere just steps away from the ocean dunes of Wrightsville Beach. Private banquet rooms for up to 35 guests are great for rehearsal dinners and small receptions. If you want to reserve the whole restaurant, the staff can accommodate up to 125 people.

CAROLINA BEACH AND VICINITY

The Cape Golf and Racquet Club Restaurant
535 The Cape Blvd., Wilmington
(910) 794-5757

This unusual restaurant overlooks the beautiful golf course at The Cape. Two formal banquet rooms are available for smaller groups, or the entire facility can be reserved to accommodate up to 150 guests. Their outstanding chef can customize your menu to make your special day memorable.

The Cottage Wine Bar & Grill
One N. Lake Park Blvd., Carolina Beach
(910) 458-4383

If you're looking for a truly outstanding, first-class event featuring excellent food prepared to perfection, this is the place. Owners Fred and Margaret Crouch and son Chris will go out of their way to assure your wedding parties are successful. The Cottage offers full-service for catering both on and off the premises, with special menus designed to highlight your occasion. This tastefully renovated 1916 beach cottage seats 52 inside and 40 on the enclosed deck. You can have a sit-down dinner, buffet, heavy or light hors d'oeuvres — even breakfast, if you choose.

Courtyard by Marriott
100 Charlotte St., Carolina Beach
(910) 458-2030 (800) 458-3606

This beautiful oceanfront hotel offers banquet facilities for up to 250 guests and boasts a courteous, professional and very friendly staff. A lovely, romantic environment, with the Atlantic Ocean as a dramatic backdrop, awaits you and your guests. The Courtyard by Marriott is an ideal setting for the perfect wedding.

North Carolina Aquarium at Fort Fisher
900 Loggerhead Rd., Kure Beach
(910) 458-8257, ext. 218
www.ncaquariums.com

For your wedding reception, consider the beautiful North Carolina Aquarium at Fort Fisher, situated on the Atlantic Ocean's picturesque shores. Greet your guests in the Cape Fear Conservatory atrium. Dine and dance in this romantic environment where seahorses gently sway and colorful fishes accent the underwater scenery. The Aquarium can accommodate up to 1,000 people, and up to 500 for a seated dinner. Contact the Special Events Coordinator, who will work with you to ensure a truly memorable occasion.

BALD HEAD ISLAND

Marsh Harbour Inn
21 Keelsen Row, Harbour Village
(910) 457-1702, (800) 680-8322

If you are planning an intimate indoor reception (up to 30 people) Marsh Harbour Inn is an excellent choice. You and your guests will thrill to the view of Bald Head Creek and the wide expanse of lovely natural marshland providing a beautiful backdrop for your auspicious occasion. Catering can be provided by the trained chefs at Fishy Fishy Cafe in Southport (see our Restaurants chapter), who will prepare your scrumptious repast just the way you want it using only the freshest ingredients. Lovely comfortable rooms can be reserved at the inn for you, your wedding party and guests or, if you prefer, there are 55 rental homes available on the island as well.

OAK ISLAND

Turtle Island Restaurant and Catering
6220 E. Oak Island Dr., Oak Island
(910) 278-4944

The folks at Turtle Island are happy to work with you in planning the menu and in presenting their luscious food in a way that makes it candy for the eyes. They will cater your wedding reception or rehearsal dinner on-site or off-site to meet your highest expectations. Turtle Island has all ABC catering permits.

OCEAN ISLE BEACH

The Isles Restaurant
417 W. Second St., Ocean Isle Beach
(910) 575-5988

An oceanfront banquet facility with glorious views of the Atlantic Ocean and fantastic sunsets is available for your wedding reception at The Isles Restaurant. Food is prepared by the excellent restaurant chefs and served by your very own staff in the private dining area, which seats more than 100 guests. Drinks, including Champagne, are available as well.

Silver Coast Winery
6680 Barbeque Rd., Ocean Isle Beach
(910) 287-2800

Your reception can have an old world feel in a true vineyard and winery in the heart of Brunswick County. Silver Coast Winery is nestled on 40 acres, surrounded by lush woods and just 15 minutes from the beach. Your guests can enjoy the spacious outdoor setting while sipping award-winning wines. Or perhaps the barrel room with its indoor waterfalls, or the art gallery exhibiting works by local artists, would better suit your nuptial needs. For intimate affairs or larger groups, Silver Coast Winery is a unique setting for your special day. (For more information, see our Attractions chapter).

TOPSAIL ISLAND AND VICINITY

The Atlantis Restaurant & Lounge
2000 New River Inlet Rd.,
North Topsail Beach
(910) 328-2002

The Atlantis has a fabulous view of the ocean and can handle up to 200 guests. They offer a variety of pasta, steaks and seafood in a buffet or banquet setting. An extensive wine list coupled with specialty cocktails and tasty appetizers will keep wedding guests smiling. A separate smoking lounge and bar provides an eye-in-the-sky view of the sand and surf. Inside, on the dance floor, the lucky couple will undoubtedly remember their first dance as moonlight filters through ceiling-to-floor windows.

JC's Catering
212 N.C. Hwy. 210, Holly Ridge
(910) 347-7566

From a formal sit-down dinner with china and silver to one of their famous pig-pickings on paper plates, JC's Catering has it all. Choose from seafood, steak or JC's delicious barbecue with salads, vegetables and/or heavy hors d' oeuvres. A minimum of 50 meals is required for JC's to travel to the location of your choice with everything needed to feed the wedding reception guests.

Mainsail Restaurant & Bar
404 Roland Ave., Surf City
(910) 328-0010
www.bluemainsail.com

Unlike any other place on Topsail Island, the Commodore Room is a great place to hold wedding receptions, anniversary parties or holiday parties. Enjoy a drink at the cherry wood bar or dance the night away on the dance floor. The Commodore Room offers a tasty selection of wonderfully prepared appetizers, entrees and desserts. They offer either sit-down affairs or buffet-style dinners. Let the experienced staff take care of all your reception or party needs. The Mainsail Restaurant Commodore Room also caters off-site, full service or simple party platters.

Pasta Grille
513 Country Club Dr., Hampstead
(910) 270-2425

Part of the Olde Pointe Golf and Country Club Complex, the Pasta Grill offers outstanding food and drink for any and all wedding functions. There are three separate rooms, ranging from the intimate grill to the Osprey Room, which can seat up to 150 people. The Pasta Grill provides an excellent venue for engagement parties, bridal showers, luncheons, rehearsal dinners and wedding receptions. The quaint gazebo overlooking the clubhouse pond is the perfect spot for romantic toasts and photo opportunities.

Skully's Catering
718 S. Anderson Blvd., Topsail Beach
(910) 328-3100

Meat trays, vegetable trays and hors d'oeuvres are the specialty of this catering crew, but they would love to work with you to design a custom menu for your wedding, rehearsal party or any function you might have coming up. For on-site catering, the dining room of their restaurant, Skully's Pub & Grub at the same address, can be rented. If you have your own venue in mind, they'll happily cater off-site. Give owner Sharon Jordan a call at the above number and discuss your catering needs.

Cakes

Because your wedding is a reflection of your individual style, you'll want your cake to fit into the theme, satisfying both the eye and the taste buds. The Southern Coast has outstanding bakeries and individuals who prepare gorgeous cakes. Since they are too numerous to mention all of them here, we've listed a few of our favorites.

WILMINGTON

Apple Annie's Bake Shop
University Square Mall, 837 S. Kerr Ave.,
Wilmington
(910) 799-9023
Landfall Shopping Center, Eastwood Rd.
and Military Cutoff Rd., Wilmington
(910) 256-6585

Apple Annie's wedding cakes are customized to delight your palate. Each tier is like a torte with four layers of cake and three layers of filling. For your wedding events, Apple Annie's can provide gourmet cakes, cookies, pastries and fine breads. All of their baking is done on the premises and their cakes are handmade and decorated with loving care. Each is scrumptious and perfect every time.

Danny's Pastry Shoppe
2323 S. 17th St., Wilmington
(910) 392-0009

With more than 40 years in the bakery business, Danny Danek can create just about any cake design you can imagine, including duplicating photos or magazine pictures. He's even made a four-foot tall pagoda cake and provided the cake for Donald Duck's 50th birthday celebration at the White House. He uses real buttercream icing and offers an ample selection of fillings.

Sweet & Savory Cafe and Bake Shop
1611 Pavilion Pl., Wilmington
(910) 256-0115

Kimber Herring decorates her wedding cakes with an exquisite buttercream frosting or an assortment of different icings. Nothing comes out of a can! Luscious rolled fondant and edible flowers are intertwined to please your eyes and taste buds. Kimber, husband Dave and a very experienced staff will cater for 50 to 500 people.

If you and your spouse-to-be are paying for your own wedding, consider using a separate credit card specifically to pay wedding expenses. It's a good way to keep all your wedding transactions in one place, and if you have a billing dispute, the credit card company can help you out.

SOUTHPORT

Barb's Midtown Deli
4346 Long Beach Rd., Southport
(910) 457-4600

Barb's Midtown Deli is known in the area for its bakery products, and when it comes to wedding cakes, they are extremely helpful. You can bring in a picture of a cake you like, choose one out of several books available in the deli, or custom design your own. In any case, you will receive a delicious and beautiful result. Barb's also provides hors d'oeuvres and catering.

OCEAN ISLE BEACH

The French Bake and Pastry Shop
Seaside Plaza, 7290-10 Beach Dr.
Ocean Isle Beach
(910) 575-0284

Robert Williams, a native of Amsterdam and retired from Chez Robert, his very own famous restaurant in Washington, D.C., now owns and runs this French patisserie. He bakes custom-designed wedding cakes using irresistible ingredients that will delight you and all your guests. Having a beach wedding? Ask for his special cake decorated with white chocolate seashells.

PENDER COUNTY

Angie's Cake Creations
25101 U.S. Hwy. 421, Willard
(910) 619-7172

Using her great-grandmother's recipe, Angie creates her exquisite Signature Cake generously spread with snow-white buttercream icing and decorated to the bride's wishes. Reasonably priced, beautiful and fresh, Angie's wedding creations are sure to bring raves.

Wedding Accommodations

For hotels and motels in Wilmington and North Carolina's Southern Coast, check out our Hotels and Motels chapter. Also look through the Bed & Breakfast and Small Inns chapter. For a listing of those accommodations that specialize in hosting wedding parties, visit our Premier Wedding Accommodations page at www.insiders.com/

wilmington. There's also a listing of Honeymoon accommodations online.

Wedding Officiants

North Carolina law requires that wedding ceremonies be conducted by an ordained minister or a magistrate. A boat captain can't do the trick anymore! The state has replaced its former justice of the peace system with court-appointed magistrates. These officials may perform wedding services, but they are often severely limited as to times and places they can accommodate, and they do charge a fee.

If you want to be married by a minister, most major religions are represented in Wilmington (see our Worship chapter). An extensive listing, by denomination, is available in local phone books. Many denominations require a special counseling period, and some have specific requirements regarding re-marrying divorced persons. The following interfaith ministers are among those on the North Carolina coast who can make your wedding ceremony memorable.

4 Winds and 7 Seas
Sunset Beach
(910) 575.8171

Assuring you a relaxed, romantic, spiritual wedding celebration any season of the year, at the time and place of your choosing, 4 Winds and 7 Seas will work with you to make this moment be as powerful as your feelings, with words strong enough to last a lifetime. Reverend Don Towne will join two souls in marriage, renewal or commitment no matter the weather. You can expect courtesy, sensitivity, respect for your privacy, acceptance of your religious or spiritual views and consideration of your individuality.

A Wedding Minister, Penelope Morningstar
Wilmington
(910) 791-7200

Reverend Penelope Morningstar is an interfaith minister who has been officiating weddings since 1994. She will help you create a beautiful ceremony and officiate your wedding at the location of your choice. If you are not a member of a local church or are marrying outside your faith, Reverend Morningstar can offer you the blessing and guidance of an ordained minister. Whether you are plan-

ning to be married on the beach, on a cruise boat, in the park, at a hotel, in your home or anywhere in the greater Wilmington area, with Reverend Morningstar's help, it will be a sacred moment to treasure for a lifetime. Premarital counseling is available but is not required.

Bridal Registries

The Wilmington area offers a wide variety of stores at which the bride and groom may register for gifts. Here are some favorites.

Bed, Bath & Beyond, 352 S. College Road, Wilmington, (910) 784-9707

Belk, Westfield Shoppingtown Independence, 3500 Oleander Drive, Wilmington, (910) 392-1440; Shallotte Crossing, 130-1 Shallotte Crossing Parkway, Shallotte. (910) 755-0939

Dillard's, Westfield Shoppingtown Independence, 3500 Oleander Drive, Wilmington, (910) 796-3300

Fisherman's Wife, 1425 Airlie Road, Wilmington, (910) 256-5505

Hecht's, Mayfaire Town Center, 940 Inspiration Drive, Wilmington, (910) 256-2115

JC Penney, Westfield Shoppingtown Independence, 3500 Oleander Drive, Wilmington, (910) 392-1400

Pier 1 Imports, 3741 Oleander Drive, Wilmington, (910) 392-3151

Mayfaire Town Center, 6885 Main St, Wilmington, (910) 509-2950

Victoria's Ragpatch, Inc., 10164 Beach Dr., SW, Calabash, (910) 579-2015; 117 Causeway Drive, Ocean Isle Beach, (910) 579-3158

Florists

Flowers are the symbol of both romantic and devoted love. The Wilmington area is home to an amazing showcase of artistic florists who will make your most fanciful

Keep in mind travel and comfort needs of your guests when choosing a location for your wedding. Be sure to include written directions and maps with your invitations.

floral dream come true. Here are just a few big bloomers.

WILMINGTON

Azalea Coast Florist
713 N. Fourth St., Wilmington
(910) 815-0102, (910) 763-5558,
(800) 858-6426

Sheila McNamee and her exceptionally talented staff create custom designs for all occasions. Your wedding flower arrangements, centerpieces and bouquets will be perfect for your perfect day.

Ikebana Design and Accessories
The Forum, 1125 Military Cutoff Rd. Ste. S, Wilmington
(910) 509-1383

Master Ikebana specialists Bonnie Burney and Ruth Lees offer the most exotic wedding arrangements we've ever seen. They also have gourmet baskets, a wide variety of gifts, home and wedding accessories such as ring-bearer pillows and flower-girl baskets. For floral excellence, consult with these ladies or any of their professional staff.

Sophia V. West Florist, Inc.
8086 Market St., Wilmington
(910) 686-0496

With 40 years of wedding experience, the experts at Sophia V. West Florist will create any type design that meets the bride's taste. Please schedule an appointment for your free, very personal consultation; have your date, time, dress colors and favorite flowers in mind. It helps to leave the planning a little open-ended for that last-minute flower that might be just perfect for the wedding bouquet. Plant rentals are available.

CAROLINA BEACH

Marshall Gardens
1230 N. Lake Park Blvd., Carolina Beach
(910) 458-3292

Jan Marshall and her talented floral assistants strive to make each woman's wedding dream come true. Limited only by the imagination, they can create just about anything you want from shell bouquets to Hawaiian leis. Because they have an on-site nursery, live plants, palms and exotic flowers

are available to rent, as are gazebos, arches and arbors. Marshall Gardens specializes in weddings held on the beach, on cruise boats or where ever your heart desires.

BRUNSWICK COUNTY BEACHES

Brunswick Town Florist
4857 Long Beach Rd., Southport
(910) 457-1144

Brunswick Town Florist offers free bridal consultations by appointment. Experience in weddings on the beach, at Orton Plantation, on Bald Head Island and in Wilmington are proof of the flexibility of this florist. Owners Catherine Bayley and Don Baker work personally on every wedding serviced through their shop. They can accommodate any style of wedding and are especially talented in custom designs.

Calabash Florist, Inc.
10009 Beach Dr., Calabash
(910) 579-7837, (888) 566-1497

The folks at Calabash Florist can provide you with floral decorations in a church or indoor reception area as well as an outdoor setting such as a garden. They are willing to work with any budget and can provide invitations, guest books, engraved knives, and rental of candelabra and arches.

Coastal Florists & Gifts
4729 Main St., Shallotte
(910) 754-6200

As well as creating floral decorations any way you want them, these talented people can refer you to the best place to have your wedding cake made, and where you might find a director to help you put all the details together and make your wedding a smooth-running event.

Expressions Florist & Gift Shoppe
2920 Holden Beach Rd., Holden Beach
(910) 842-9717

Housed in a 100-year-old building, this shop advertises "Designs of Distinction." The owner, Barbara Gray, offers free wedding consultation offering suggestions and tips to make things run smoothly and beautifully. Whether you are planning a beach wedding or a church wedding, contemporary, Victorian or traditional, she can custom-design your flowers to the style of your wedding dress, making for a unique and beautiful look while working within your budget. She also makes flowers for wedding cakes. Rentals available include a spiral candelabra, a seven-branch candelabra and candle arches.

Southport Florist
313 N. Howe St., Southport
(910) 457-5177

Located near downtown Southport, Southport Florist can fill all your basic floral needs to help the planning of your wedding run smoothly. Floral decorations in the church and reception hall as well as bouquets, boutonnieres and corsages are all beautifully done. Owner Marvin Floyd especially enjoys the creative freedom of working for a client who leaves the arrangements up to him.

Wine & Roses
919-D N. Howe St., Southport
(910) 457-4428

With 37 years in the florist business, 16 of those years owning Wine & Roses, Steve and Cheryl Dosher have a wealth of experience. In addition to floral decorations for the church and reception hall and the traditional flowers for the members of the wedding party, Wine & Roses offers a variety of invitations from which to choose. They can refer you to services such as photography, video operators and wedding-cake bakers as well.

TOPSAIL ISLAND AND VICINITY

The Flower Basket of Hampstead
14361 U.S. Hwy. 17, Hampstead
(910) 270-4141, (877) 607-7615

A full-service florist, The Flower Basket of Hampstead offers everything from lush houseplants to beautiful mixed bouquets. They maintain an extensive inventory of fresh-cut flowers and offer complete wedding floral services.

Surf City Florist
106 N. Topsail Dr., Surf City
(910) 328-3238

Scheduled or last minute, Surf City Florist is ready to provide beautiful, fresh flowers for your wedding. They offer full wedding

services, including rental of candelabras and other special equipment.

Bridal Shops and Formal Wear

Whether you opt for a highly formal church wedding or something more casual, the Wilmington area offers an abundance of stores from which to choose your wedding finery. Here are a few that specialize.

WILMINGTON

Bridal Boutique
800 Shipyard Blvd., Ste. 13, Wilmington
(910) 794-7070

For the latest in wedding gowns (sizes 4 to 30), bridesmaids' dresses and formal wear, visit the Bridal Boutique. Their professional bridal staff offer consulting and directing as well as a complete line of formal wear and accessories.

Cape Fear Formal Wear
218 N. Third St., Wilmington
(910) 762-8206
Westfield Shoppingtown Independence,
Wilmington
(910) 452-1106

Family owned and managed, Cape Fear Formal Wear has been serving the area for more than 40 years. These folks can dress all the men in your wedding party from head to toe. The only business of its kind in southern North Carolina that owns its merchandise, Cape Fear Formal Wear offers the area's largest selection of men's rentals and sales. Cape Fear Formal Wear will handle your special occasion with the utmost care and attention. Same-day service is available.

Dance & Romance
University landing Shopping Center, 415 S.
College Rd., Ste. 14, Wilmington
(910) 793-2090

Dance & Romance is the place to shop for shower or bachelorette party gifts, supplies and fun stuff. Along with massage oils, lotions, lubricants, movies and adult toys, you'll also find slenderizing corsets and fine lace lingerie in sizes petite to 4X. This unique shop also has jewelry and shoes with heels from two to eight inches in clear, white, silver or black to accent any outfit.

Elegant Brides
5424 Oleander Dr., Ste. 9, Wilmington
(910) 796-0602

Here you will find custom designs and alterations with prices to fit everyone's budget. A wide selection of accessories, invitations and references to other wedding services are sure to please.

Fountaine Bridals & Formals
5202 Carolina Beach Rd., Ste. 11, Wilmington
(910) 794-9959

Wilmington's oldest bridal shop, Fountaine Bridals & Formals has been dressing beautiful brides for over 25 years. Fountaine's is known for its large selection of fabulous gowns in many styles from size 2 to 28, as well as dresses for bridesmaids and mother-of-the-bride. Their experienced staff provides full bridal consulting. An exceptional line of bridal accessories includes shoes, jewelry, garters, veils and tiaras. Outfit every lady in your wedding party, including your flower girl. Alterations are done on the premises.

BRUNSWICK COUNTY BEACHES

Jeffrey's
120-9 Shallotte Crossing, Shallotte
(910) 755-5333

Jeffrey's is a men's wear shop carrying a full line of dress and casual wear as well as tuxedos. They have a full line of tuxedos, including Oscar de la Renta, After Six, Lord West, Andrew Fezza, Geoffrey Beene, Claiborne, Chaps Ralph Lauren and Perry Ellis. Dress shoes can also be purchased. Having a

Honeymoon registries online offer new alternatives to traditional wedding gifts, especially for couples who already "have everything." Create your own unique list of honeymoon gifts you'd like to receive, including lodging, airfare, romantic dinners and more. Shop around for registries that provide the best services for your honeymoon needs and charge reasonable fees.

large wedding? Jeffrey's offers a free groom's tux and a half-price ring bearer's suit with the rental of six to nine tuxedos. With the rental of ten or more, the ring bearer's suit is free.

Music

Music sets the mood of a wedding, adding to the beauty and enjoyment of the ceremony and reception. The Wilmington area abounds with musicians to please any ear. Here are a few varied choices for your special day.

Elena Davis, Harpist
(910) 616-4892

Classically trained and with more than 20 years of experience, Elena draws from her extensive repertoire to offer custom programs for your special day. From wedding standards and contemporary selections on the full-sized pedal harp, to Irish folk music on the smaller Irish folk harp, Elena's enchanting sounds will add to the magic of your ceremony and/or reception.

Key Productions
1027 Captain Adkins Dr., Southport
(910) 457-5243

Jim Minett has been providing music for more than 20 years. His professional music production company, a member of the Southport-Oak Island Chamber of Commerce, will customize music selections to suit your taste. Jim can provide live music, serve as a DJ/Master of Ceremonies using prerecorded music or perform a combination of both for your reception, ceremony, rehearsal dinner or other event. Key Productions presents your favorite music through incredible sounding, high quality Bose professional speakers. Karaoke is also available.

Maura Kropke, Violinist
117 Nun St., Wilmington
(910) 254-0758

Maura is a classically trained violinist available for indoor and outdoor weddings throughout the Wilmington area. She attended the School for Strings in New York City as well as Manhattan School of Music.

Elizabeth MacKay Field, Soprano
The Field Studio
3173 Wrightsville Ave., Wilmington
(910) 251-7797
www.fieldstudio.biz

This exceptional, classically trained vocalist is available to add elegance and beautiful music to your wedding ceremony. Elizabeth will work with the organist or music director at your church and will consult with you regarding music selection if you desire.

Port City Pipes and Drums
Pipe Major Andrew Simpson
5017 Hewlett's Run, Wilmington
(910) 232-5678, (910) 790-3580

Pipe Major Simpson played for the Queen of England and he will play for you! "Highland Cathedral" is a favorite, but he will play whatever you like. Expect upbeat, happy music for your reception.

Shoresound Productions
2049 Gilbert Rd. SE, Bolivia
(910) 253-7515

Tommy Robbins has been involved in providing musical entertainment in bands and as a DJ since 1970. In 1989 Shoresound Productions became a full-time venture for Tommy. Since then he and his wife, Teresa, have performed at more than 600 wedding receptions, providing professional entertainment with a personal touch. They have a large selection of music, including many of the top hits from the 1940s to the current hits of today. In addition to being a DJ, Tommy is a musician who books bands and music for all occasions. Tommy provides musical entertainment for all ages, including middle and high school dances, company parties, rehearsal parties, wedding ceremonies and receptions, anniversary parties and other events. Karaoke is available as well.

Westermark Voice Studio
Sara Graham Westermark, Soprano
620 Cobblestone Dr., Wilmington
(910) 233-1323
www.sarawestermark.com

Sara Graham Westermark is a classically trained soprano with a master's degree in Voice Performance from the University of Missouri-Columbia. She is an active singer in this region, appearing as a soloist with the Wilmington Symphony Orchestra, Southeastern Oratorio Society, Wilmington Oratorio Society, UNCW Concert Choir, UNCW Opera Scenes and other area organizations.

Gerry White
116 Bradley Creek Point Rd., Wilmington
(910) 256-9880

With more than 30 years in the entertainment field, Gerry delivers professional results utilizing state-of-the-art equipment. With his background as a TV and radio personality, Gerry offers a full program of activities along with winning songs on CDs that are sure to please all ages and tastes.

Wilmington Academy of Music
3830 Oleander Dr., Wilmington
(910) 392-1590

The Wilmington Academy of Music, long recognized as the area's premier music school, is an excellent source of wedding planners for music and musicians of the highest caliber. The academy offers a wide range of groups and ensembles made up of outstanding faculty members and other highly skilled, experienced area professionals. Music is carefully designed for your wedding ceremony or reception to complement the setting and create the mood you desire. The Academy of Music also offers a free consultation with an experienced music designer who will assist you in choosing the most appropriate music to ensure that your wedding will be totally unique and unforgettable.

Photography

You shouldn't have any trouble finding a reputable photographer in this area. There are hundreds of people out there who want to take your picture, and they have the artistry and craftsmanship to make you proud. Here are a few suggestions.

Boswell Photography II
1014 W. Dolphin St., Oak Island
(910) 278-7957

Mike Boswell has been a professional photographer for 27 years. Though his studio is traditional, using classical poses and settings, he intersperses these with candid photos and photojournalism shots for the wedding album. He views his work as recording family history and works with his customers to make that record reflect their part in the history. Mike works with black and white

Clothing provided by Lundie's Photography.

and/or color film and does restoration of old photos as well.

Calabash Photography Studio
9962 Beach Dr., Calabash
(910) 579-2093

The folks at Calabash Photography Studio take black and white and color photos in traditional, candid and photojournalism poses and offer you packages that include the wedding album. They will travel from the church to the reception hall in order to cover the whole event. They take wedding photos on the beach. A special service available is the posting of your wedding photos on their website, which allows your relatives and friends who live at a distance to share in the joy.

Matt McGraw Photography
417 Mosswood Ct., Wilmington
(910) 686-8583

Matt's experience in photojournalism and full-service portrait photography allows him to capture the essence of emotion in a single moment. He listens, inquires and adapts to the surroundings of the wedding party, recording the wedding celebration as it happens and telling a story that will last a lifetime. Referrals for videography are available upon request.

George Mitchell Photographic Services
(910) 326-4425

George Mitchell offers extensive experience in capturing your special day on film. He provides professional services for all types of events, from weddings and portraits to commercial and advertising shots. Images are supplied as prints and/or on CD. Whether you are interested in color or black and white, indoor scenes or outdoor, one shot or a complete package, he can create a treasure for you to enjoy for years to come.

Oceanview Photography
6209 Oleander Dr., Ste. 300, Wilmington
(910) 297-1320

Beach portrait photography has been Denis Lemay's expertise for the past 30 years, making him a natural as a beach wedding photographer. He will work locally or travel the Carolina coast. While beach weddings make up a large percentage of this business, Oceanview is also known for on-location photography of families, large groups and events. Photography at local plantations is also a specialty of this New York Institute–certified, award-winning photographer.

Al Patterson Photography
7092 Old Oak Rd. NW, Ash
(910) 287-7107

Award-winning photographer Al Patterson has been taking photographs for more than 30 years. You can find his work on the Visitor's Guide of the Brunswick County telephone directory and inside the Brunswick County Chamber of Commerce brochure. He has wedding packages available on location or in the studio. Digital video recording is available as well. Al and his wife, Sue, provide complete wedding services, including accommodations, cakes and catering, florists, entertainment, limo services, tuxedo rentals, party rentals and wedding locations. Al says, "You bring the bride in her dress, the groom in his boxers, and we furnish the rest."

Arrow Ross Photography
711-A N. Fifth St., Wilmington
(910) 762-2243

Photographing people is Arrow's specialty, and weddings offer an opportunity to capture the spirit of the moment in a telling photograph. Using his skills as a photojournalist, Arrow is able to anticipate and capture real moments that hold memories for a lifetime.

Tom Sapp Photography
3703 Tumbril Ln., Wilmington
(910) 794-9819
www.tomsapp.com

Tom Sapp has a long list of professional awards and achievements, including Creative Photographer of the year for 2003 awarded by the Connecticut Professional Photographers Association and a Fuji Masterpiece Award for his expert digital ability. He combines his creative genius and photojournalistic skills to offer you contemporary poses, classical poses and candid images of your wedding. Tom endeavors to put his subjects into situations where they can display their own personalities. His goal is to capture meaningful memories that are so realistic you feel them.

Harry Taylor Photography
Wilmington
(910) 792-0098

Harry Taylor offers quality artistic documentary wedding photography so you can preserve the memories and moments of your special day.

Videography

While photos are wonderful and portable, there's nothing like having a video of your wedding day. Filled with moments and memories you'll treasure forever, a thoughtfully created, artfully edited videotape is your very own masterpiece in motion. Here are some local videographers you can contact.

Blanchard Productions, Inc.
4922 Northeaster Dr., Wilmington
(910) 392-4211

If you want it done right, Michael Blanchard's upscale videography is for you. Using broadcast-quality digital equipment, he can assure superior results. His professional background includes news and documentary films aired internationally. Mike will provide

DVDs of your wedding reception, if you desire.

Mari Kittredge Video Productions
4930 Pine St., Wilmington
(910) 452-7239

Mari redefines the wedding video with her artistic approach. Unobtrusive and sensitive, she'll skillfully capture loving exchanges between family members while recording your special day. The resulting video will be creatively edited into a naturally flowing story.

Liam Video & Graphics
Wilmington
(910) 200-5777

Liam Video & Graphics offers clear, vivid and creative footage of your special day. With documentary-style editing, your final product will be both candid and comprehensive in its coverage. The goal of Liam Video & Graphics is to capture the essence of the wedding, and the journey that led up to it, in a medium that can be enjoyed for many years to come, forever preserved in VHS or DVD format. Choose from basic packages offering coverage only of the ceremony, or from more personalized, in-depth packages, including such items as customized music, still images, bridal preparation segments, photo montage and other specialized features. Liam Video & Graphics is happy to work with you to find what suits you best.

Lifetime Video Productions
110 Tara Dr., Wilmington
(910) 392-8163, (910) 538-7704

Peter Bruno believes in giving his wedding clients the service they desire, both during and after the wedding celebration. With more than 20 years of experience, Peter knows how to be unobtrusive in capturing the spirit of the moment. He has the equipment for full DVD coverage and can even video your photo album and set it to music.

Transportation

Want a fancy vehicle to get you to the church on time? Try one of these services. Also check the list of limousine companies in our Getting Here, Getting Around chapter.

Azalea Limousine Service
244 Princess St., Wilmington
(910) 452-5888

Azalea Limousine Service provides quality local transportation for weddings and other special events. They offer you your choice of a 20-passenger shuttle bus, two 2005 Lincoln Town Car limousines and a 15-passenger limousine bus, as well as a Lincoln Town Car sedan and mini-vans.

Horse-Drawn Wedding Carriage
Historic Downtown Wilmington
(910) 251-8889

Return to the antebellum era in a special French evening coach, the wedding carriage. Dressed in full tux and top hat, carriage man John Pucci or his son James will festoon both horses and coach with silver hearts and silk flowers, so you truly feel like a princess with your prince charming. Wedding ceremonies have actually been performed on the horse-drawn carriage while meandering alongside the Cape Fear River. Please make reservations as early as possible — four to five months ahead is advised. Call for price quotes.

Platinum Limousine
(910) 232-7475, (888) 464-9800

This company services Wilmington, Raleigh, Myrtle Beach and Jacksonville. You have your choice of a stretch Lincoln Naviga-

tor SUV, which holds 16 people, or a Lincoln Town Car stretch limo for 10 passengers. Ask about their wedding packages.

Rental Equipment

L & L Tent & Party Rentals
3703 Wrightsville Ave., Wilmington
(910) 791-4141

L & L will lighten your load by delivering, setting up and breaking down all your wedding supplies and equipment, including china, silver, flatware, small and large tents, lights, heaters or fans, dance floors, stages, sound equipment and much more.

Party Suppliers & Rentals
4013 Oleander Dr., Wilmington
(910) 791-0024, (800) 344-8368

For indoors or out, Party Suppliers & Rentals can provide all of your wedding rental needs. Don't let bad weather spoil your day. They offer a variety of tents, with or without side walls and French doors. In addition, they have Portofino lights, picket fencing, grills, flooring and staging, tables, chairs, china, linens and silver or polished aluminum serving pieces. You can also choose from their wide selection of candelabra. For more ideas, visit their showroom or website.

Publications

Keep an eye out for special sections in Wilmington's daily paper, the Star-News. An advertising supplement for Weddings comes out in January and other relevant features appear throughout the year. Here are some area publications devoted solely to weddings.

Cape Fear Wedding
5621 Athens Ln., Wilmington
(910) 392-5228

If you're looking for a complete wedding-planning sourcebook, this publication is it. Cape Fear Wedding is a handbook where you can make notes and keep track of your wedding details. Featuring timetables, objective articles, advice and checklists, Cape Fear Wedding is available free at bridal and formal wear shops, jewelers, florists, Belk, Hecht's and Dillard's department stores, plus many other locations in our area, or it can be ordered by mail for a small mailing charge.

Carolina Wedding Guide
Burgaw
(910) 259-8323

Published quarterly, Carolina Wedding Guide is the oldest of our local bridal publications. Filled with useful tips, articles, checklists, photos, ads and advice, this complete wedding planner is available free at more than 125 locations in Brunswick, New Hanover and Pender counties. Look for copies at florists, bridal shops, photography studios, attractions and restaurants, or call to have one mailed to you.

The Perfect Wedding Planner
1319-CC Military Cutoff Rd.,
Ste. 198, Wilmington
(910) 793-4044

Appropriately named, The Perfect Wedding Planner is published three times a year — in February, June and October. A magazine printed in full color on glossy paper, it contains a variety of wedding-related articles, checklists, ads and other material for wedding planning. This handy publication is free and is widely circulated in the three-county area.

Wedding Shows

Always fun and exciting for everyone involved in a wedding, bridal expos and fashion shows are held regularly in Wilmington. Belk and Dillard's at Westfield Shoppingtown Independence have in-house bridal shows, and several other shows, sponsored by consultants and wedding publications, are tremendously popular. Watch for announcements early in January.

Annual Bridal Mall
St. Thomas Preservation Hall, Wilmington
(910) 686-2690, (800) 254-1701

On a Sunday afternoon in February, Tonya Boulware and the professionals from A Carolina Wedding, a full-service event-planning company specializing in weddings, present a Bridal Mall to benefit St. Thomas Preservation Hall. For a $5 donation, you can visit this historical venue, which is customarily "dressed" inside and out for a wedding, including a tent set for a garden wedding complete with music, round tables, linens and all the rest. Available at the event are florists, representatives from wedding and reception

locations, photographers, hair and makeup artists, videographers and other wedding professionals.

Bride and Groom Expo
Schwartz Center, Cape Fear Community
College, Wilmington
(910) 259-8323

Mike Raab's Carolina Wedding Guide hosts the largest wedding event in coastal North Carolina each January. In addition to more than 80 exhibits and displays by most of the area's wedding-related businesses, the show features music, fashions, door prizes and more. Every future bride attending receives a video that includes wedding fashion shows videotaped at participating bridal shops, suggestions for your wedding location, plus vendors' commercials. Each bride-to-be also receives a Carolina Wedding Guide Sampler CD with musical selections by area musicians who advertise in the publication.

Southern Cape Fear Bridal Showcase
Southport Community Building,
223 E. Bay St., Southport
(910) 457-6964

The Southport-Oak Island Chamber of Commerce in conjunction with the City of Southport Tourism Division hosts this bridal showcase in the Southport Community Building, one of the loveliest locations available for a wedding. Representatives from caterers, reception venues, entertainment consultants, florists, photographers, jewelers, and more are on hand to assist with all your wedding plans.

Wedding Planners

Overwhelmed by all there is to do? Here are some professionals who are happy to help you, whether you want them to plan the whole event or just help you with some of the details. Many florists also assist with planning and directing both weddings and receptions.

A Carolina Wedding
6301 Single Tree Ct., Wilmington
(910) 686-2690

At A Carolina Wedding you can design the job description, then let these experienced professionals plan and coordinate packages tailored to fit your needs. Services are also available on an hourly basis. These planners become not only part of your staff, but your support system as well. A Carolina Wedding has planned events as small as 50 guests to productions involving 600 guests. Brides from as far as Chicago, California and even Hawaii have entrusted their special day to the talents of these professionals.

Eventz!
Wilmington
(910) 686-1891

One couple said that Eventz! coordinator Judy Bradley became their best friend during their wedding. She will help you choose the site, caterer, decorations, linens and anything else down to the smallest detail.

Ocean Isle Inn
37 W. First St., Ocean Isle Beach
(910) 579-0750, (800) 352-598

Your wedding day is one of the best days of your life, so why not consider a dream wedding on the beach or in an oceanfront garden at the Ocean Isle Inn (see our Wedding Locations section). You are invited to put yourself in the capable hands of the on-site event director who will save you the worry and take care of all the details so that you can be relaxed on this, your big day. Assistance is available in arranging for the caterer, photographer, florist, minister or any special needs you may have to make your wedding a perfect affair to remember.

A sunrise walk on the beach is the perfect way to start the day.

photo: Peter Doran

SALONS AND DAY SPAS

Beauty is big business on North Carolina's southern coast. Whether you want to look gorgeous in your swimsuit and sandals, wow 'em at a beach party, turn heads at the theater or just treat yourself to a total makeover, there are hundreds of professionals eager to assist you in accomplishing your goal. Besides feeling good about your appearance, you'll enjoy being pampered and fussed over.

Choose from a menu of dreamy services at one of the fine day spas. Get a new do at a popular salon. Beat the blahs with a manicure and pedicure. Refresh your skin with a facial or microdermabrasion. Keep your suntan all year. Learn makeup techniques. Get rid of unsightly blemishes or spider veins. Just do it!

Whatever your pleasure, here are some of our favorite local businesses where you can be pampered.

Salons

We hope this section will make it a little easier for you to find the local services you're looking for to help you groom those tresses, paint those nails, get some color and beautify yourself in all sorts of ways. The salon selection in southeastern North Carolina is truly impressive, so much so that we're not even going to attempt listing all there are, or even all the categories there are. Instead, we offer some tips for finding your own special places and we'll tell you about a few of our favorites.

For starters, flip through the yellow pages and coupon sections of local phone books. There you'll find listings for everything from beauty and tanning salons to day spas and tattoo studios. Of course, personal recommendations are the best way to find out about a potential haven of image enhancement. Many chains feature bargain-priced haircuts, and nail salons are abundant. Located in downtown Wilmington, Cape Fear Community College's Cosmetology Department, (910) 362-7352, offers a wide range of services at very reasonable prices.

WILMINGTON

La Mirage
5003 Wrightsville Ave., Wilmington
(910) 395-4333

Four licensed, long-time independent operators and a massage therapist occupy this cozy, home-like, full-service hair salon. These friendly, pleasant professionals also offer manicures, pedicures and body waxing. The shop is open Monday through Friday, but hours vary according to the operator. You may call the main shop number or call Joan, (910) 470-9278; Jeannette, (910) 264-5630; Maryann, (910) 392-2862; Phyllis, (910) 470-1778; Eleanor, (910) 392-3553. Walk-ins are welcome.

The Mane Event
University Landing, 419 S. College Rd., Ste. 38, Wilmington
(910) 395-4939

Owner/stylist Krista Rose and the independent operators at the Mane Event are talented, skilled hair professionals. Here you can be assured of high-quality service, a pleasing result and a thoroughly satisfying experience. Offering permanents, color, cuts, styling and careful attention to hair health as well as facial waxing, The Mane Event is popular with men and women of all ages. They specialize in creating beautiful looks for women on special occasions such as proms, weddings, anniversaries and pageants.

CAROLINA BEACH

Cut'N Up @ Tan Ya Hide
1140 N. Lake Park Blvd., Carolina Beach
(910) 458-8267

Offering a complete selection of services to meet your individual beauty needs, the experienced Cut'N Up @ Tan Ya Hide staff prides itself on keeping up with the latest in coloring and cutting trends. On the list of services you'll find perms, cuts, coloring, high and low lighting, waxing, manicures, pedicures, artificial nail enhancement (including the latest in gel applications). How about a relaxing massage with their licensed massage therapist, or look your bronzed best after a few sessions in their tanning beds. Getting married? A bridal package will assure that you'll be as pretty as a picture.

Saks Hair Salon
604-A N. Lake Park Blvd., Carolina Beach
(910) 458-6410

Since 1988, Saks Hair Salon has been a favorite with locals who enjoy friendly, personal attention in a relaxed shop where everybody knows everybody. Definitely a family hair salon, Saks specializes in haircuts for women, men and children. Their color services are also outstanding. Complete hair and nail services, waxing and special occasion packages are available. Hours are Tuesday through Saturday. Walk-ins are welcome.

BRUNSWICK COUNTY BEACHES

Watertown Hair
109 N. Howe St., Southport
(910) 457-4734

The "Steel Magnolias" welcome you to this elegant shop with smiles and greetings. They are professionals without a doubt, providing cuts, perms, straightening and their specialty, color. The nail tech will pamper you with acrylic or natural manicures, whichever you choose, as well as pedicures and foot therapy. Shopping for accessories? You will find hand-picked jewelry, handbags and lovely colored and scented candles just begging to go home with you.

Spa Rituals Hair Salon
1645 Seaside Rd., Sunset Beach
(910) 575-5435

The employees in this shop spoil their customers — make them princesses for a day by providing facials, manicures, pedicures, tanning and more. A complete line of beauty products is available as well. Looking for the perfect wedding updo? Call Spa Rituals for a free consultation. Choose from the services available and customize your package for the whole wedding party.

TOPSAIL ISLAND

A Beautiful New You
322 N. New River Dr., Surf City
(910) 328-2525

A Beautiful New You offers all the services for a complete makeover. Hairstyling by experienced specialists, spa manicures and pedicures, massage, tanning and waxing are just the beginning. Seaweed, clay and exfoliation body treatments and facials are also available.

Tanning

Body Rayz Tanning
5202 Carolina Beach Rd., Wilmington
(910) 392-5000

Exceptionally clean and well maintained, Body Rayz offers a number of tanning options, among them 20-minute custom beds with facials, high-intensity luxury beds, a VHR stand-up booth, and a high-intensity 10-minute leg tanner. These folks are experts in the tanning business and will assure you an informed, comfortable experience. Body Rayz is open seven days a week. They accept appointments, but walk-ins are also welcome.

Tropical Tans
5003 Wrightsville Ave., Wilmington
(910) 392-3311
402 Carl St., Ste. 101, Wilmington
(910) 790-0093

Visit one of Tropical Tans Tanning Centers where the friendly, certified staff, clean, relaxed atmosphere and many amenities make your tanning experience pleasurable. Tropical Tans offers both 30-minute and 15-minute beds, plus a standup booth, and a matrix high-pressure bed. Try their Mystic Bed sunless 38-second tanning spray booth, considered the best spray system in the world. They're open seven days a week and offer a wide variety of pricing and packages.

Skin Care and Cosmetics

Caring for you skin becomes especially important in this climate. The sun's rays can do serious damage if you don't use protection appropriate for your skin type and exposure level. Local urgent care centers and

Relaxation is...

ki

Spa ❀ Salon

Wilmington's Premier
Day Spa

Unlocking the energy of your
mind, body & spirit

Voted "Best Spa" 2005 by Star News
"Voted Best Massage"
by encore magazine readers

Massage•Facials•Nails
•Couples Massage Suite
•Microdermabrasion
•Aromatherapy Blending Bar

*Gift certificates, gift baskets
and large retail area*

The Forum | 509-0410

www.kispasalon.com

Start your week off

... refreshed

Visit us Mon - Wed and mention this ad
to receive $10.00 off one-hour massage,
one-hour pedicure or one-hour facial

doctors see a lot of wicked sunburns every summer. Wind, salt spray and sand blasts can be damaging as well. Every drugstore, supermarket, beach shop, sundry and convenience mart carries sunscreen products, though your largest high-end selections will be found in area department stores or salons.

Now that you've got a perfect tan, your hair is awesome and your nails look like a magazine ad, it's time to get a cosmetic makeover. We've got our contingent of Mary Kay, Merle Norman and Avon representatives, to find one ask around or just go back to the Yellow Pages. For a freebie, stop by any of the cosmetic counters at a local department store such as Belk, Dillard's or Hecht's. Many hair salons and most day spas can do make-up applications, also. For more extensive or medical services you may want to check out a professional skin care program.

Ocean of Youth
1404 Commonwealth Dr., Wilmington
(910) 256-9899

Ocean of Youth offers an extensive menu of personalized, medically and dermatologically based skin and facial programs in a relaxed, professional environment. You can feel confident your treatment program will be approved by a board-certified surgeon from Wilmington Plastic Surgery Specialists, supervised by a registered nurse and applied by a dedicated staff of licensed aestheticians and cosmetologists. Ocean of Youth offers you "everything you need to save your skin." Here you'll find the latest therapies such as peels, microdermabrasion, microsclerotherapy, BOTOX and more. Among the many available cosmetic lines and skin care products are Kinerase, Neova, and SkinCeuticals.

Relaxation Massage
Deep Tissue
Pregnancy Massage
(All Trimesters)
Trigger Point
Reflexology

CLOUD 9

Massage Therapy
Christopher Gates, LMBT 4135
910-616-4291

Day Spas

The southern coastal area has many types of day spa facilities. In some cases, a traditional hair salon has simply added services such as massages, aromatherapy, facials and wraps to call itself a "spa." However, true day spas are of two kinds. Standard day spas offer body treatments and lifestyle services.

Medical spas offer traditional spa services as well as services that must be provided by a licensed medical practitioner, which could be a doctor, nurse, acupuncturist, chiropractor, therapist or other professional.

Just because it's called a day spa, you're not required to spend an entire day there, but you can if you so choose. Basic menu offerings ordinarily include body treatments, facials, cosmetic, nail and/or hair services. Depending on your desires (and budget), you can find local day spas as homey as a bed and breakfast or as elaborate as a million-dollar oasis with lists of services to match.

WILMINGTON

Balanced Body Massage Therapy & Yoga
5101 Dunlea Ct. #104, Wilmington
(910) 619-9619

Annie Ashenfelter developed Balanced Body Massage Therapy & Yoga to offer complementary therapies emphasizing preventive healthcare through lifestyle changes and ongoing maintenance programs. She is a Licensed Massage and Bodywork Therapist (NC 4541) and a Certified Yoga Teacher as well as a Reiki Practitioner. She offers relaxation massage, deep tissue massage, orthopedic massage for soft tissue injury recovery, and Reiki. She also teaches private and small group yoga classes in several styles. Annie combines elements of massage, yoga and Reiki in order to create personalized sessions addressing the specific needs of each individual. She is a caring therapist who devotes her time and energy to nurturing every person she treats. She is available seven days a week by appointment.

Cloud 9 Massage Therapy
(910) 616-4291

Eager to experience the luxurious therapy of a personal massage but don't want to bother with a spa? Call Cloud Nine Massage Therapy's Christopher Gates, and he'll bring the spa to you. Or, for those who enjoy the experience of being pampered in a state-of-the-art spa facility, Cloud Nine has two locations that provide Swedish, Deep Tissue, Trigger Point, Sports Massage and Reflexology treatments. For expecting moms, Cloud Nine offers pregnancy massage to ease the physical discomfort associated with pregnancy. Choose your own method of relief

You Deserve The Best!
an Oasis for the Mind, Body & Soul
• Therapeutic Massage • Facials
• Manicures • Pedicures • BodyWraps
• Progressive Anti-Aging Treatments
Full-Service Salon
European Products

Lumina Station
1904 Eastwood Rd.
Suite 101
Wilmington, NC 28403
910-256-5020

HARBOUR CLUB
DAY SPA and SALON
www.harbourclubdayspa.com

from this licensed massage and bodywork therapist. Credit cards are welcome.

Day Spa of Wrightsville
Crosspoint Plaza, 7110-C Wrightsville Ave., Wilmington
(910) 256-6640

Inviting you to enjoy "The Ultimate Adventure in Indulgence," Day Spa of Wrightsville is a place were you can have a total-body experience. Choose one of their delightful special packages or simply select from an enormous list of a la carte services — everything from body polish, wraps and waxing to elastin facials, hand and foot care. Serving both men and women, this spa is truly customer focused, striving to make your visit a memorable one. Why not try an aromatherapy, deep tissue or stone massage?

Harbour Club Day Spa and Salon
Lumina Station, 1904 Eastwood Rd., Ste. 101, Wilmington
(910) 256-5020
www.harbourclubdayspa.com

A spa where guests can relax and rejuvenate in a haven of tranquility, Harbour Club's team of highly trained professionals is dedicated to providing personalized beauty and body treatment programs. On its long list of outstanding services are such specialties as Haute Couture Body Wellness and Advanced Facial Treatments. Also available are facials, therapeutic massages, depilatory services, manicures and pedicures.

Full sevice day spa

Featuring:
INCH LOSS BODY WRAPS
PERMANENT COSMETICS

At Centre Court
(Across from Target)
910-794-8041
www.wilmingtondayspa.com

Harbour Club offers a complete service package for the bride and her wedding party. Their coordinator can also arrange delivery of catered food and beverages on the day of the booking. To soothe and polish the bride and groom before their big day, they can choose from an array of facial and body treatments, hair, skin and nail options.

Head to Toe Day Spa
1970 Eastwood Rd., Wilmington
(910) 256-3370

Serenity and service walk hand in hand at this quality spa where guests enjoy a full range of salon, beauty and therapeutic spa services. The skin care menu includes facials, chemical peels, microdermabrasion, Vitamin C Renewal Complex Infusion, makeup application and brow/lash tinting. Among the hair-care services offered are design, color, straightening, perms, men's, women's and children's cuts and styling. Manicures, pedicures, body treatments, massages and waxing are also available.

Ki Spa and Salon
1125 Military Cutoff Rd., Wilmington
(910) 509-0410
www.kispasalon.com

At Ki Spa, the philosophy is simple and timeless. They combine natural products, pure aromatherapy and healing techniques to promote total body renewal. Ki, the ancient Japanese word for energy, is incorporated into all spa treatments. Ki Spa offers a tran-

quil environment that's ideal for specialty and couples massage, body treatments, facials, peels, microdermabrasion, permanent hair removal, waxing, manicures (natural nails) and pedicures. For weddings, relax and rejuvenate your spirit with a package designed especially for you, your bridal party and your guests. Ki Spa "unlocks the energy of your mind, body and spirit."

Ocean of Youth
1404 Commonwealth Dr., Wilmington
(910) 256-9899

Ocean of Youth offers an extensive menu of personalized, medically and dermatologically based skin and facial programs in a relaxed, professional environment. You can feel confident your treatment program will be done by licensed aestheticians and nurses. Ocean of Youth can provide you with "everything you need to save your skin." Here you'll find the latest therapies, such as Botox, medically based peels, particle-free microdermabrasions, pamper facials and massage therapy. They also have a fully equipped wet room for body treatments, manicures and pedicures.

Porters Neck Yoga & Spa
8044 Market St., Ste. A, Wilmington
(910) 686-6440
www.portersneckyogaspa.com

A full-service day spa, complete with hair and nail salon plus a yoga studio, Porters Neck Yoga & Spa is the perfect place to spend a morning or afternoon full of beauty, relaxation and bliss. The many spa services include a variety of massage therapies, couples massage, customized aromatherapy, reflexology, restorative facials, body scrubs and treatments, all designed to put you in a state of blissful contentment. Looking for the perfect gift? Porters Neck Yoga & Spa has gift certificates and packages available as well. Hours are Monday through Friday 9 AM to 7 PM, Saturday 9 AM to 5 PM and Sunday 11 AM to 1 PM (yoga only).

Prima Day Spa
At Centre Court, Wilmington
(910) 794-8041
www.wilmingtondayspa.com

Make a day of pampering yourself. Relax. Refresh. Recharge. In an environment of soft light, gentle music and pleasing aromas, expert massage therapists will help you transcend your earthly worries for a well-deserved respite. Perhaps you'd like a facial; choose from an impressive list that even includes photorejuvenation and microderm-abrasions. Have a "Baby Soft Salt Glow" treatment or a Mineral Inchloss Body Wrap. Go home with an awesome spray tan applied by expert technicians. Permanent cosmetics application by a specially trained artist is popular with women of all ages, especially in coastal communities where humidity, swimming and romping in the surf cause ordinary brow, eye and lip makeup to run or just wash off altogether. You can get a manicure, pedicure and hair services, too. Cellulite therapy, wet and dry heat therapies, and waxing are also available.

Porters Neck
Yoga & Spa

YOGA
FACIALS
MASSAGE
ORGANIC BODY TREATS
HAIR STUDIO
NAILS
AROMATHERAPY

910.686.6440
WWW.PORTERSNECKYOGASPA.COM

BRUNSWICK COUNTY BEACHES

E Spa & Salon
**Lowes Foods Shopping Ctr., 4961 Long Beach Rd., Unit 4, Southport
(910) 457-0009**

Step inside the door to E and let the serenity begin. The light, airy atmosphere with lush green palms and ferns and soothing music is bound to calm you. Here you can experience a Swedish, neuromuscular or deep tissue massage — even a pregnancy massage. An aesthetician will do a skin analysis, a rejuvenating facial and develop a regimen of skin care for you. Aromatherapy manicures and pedicures will complete the relaxation process. Gel and acrylic nails are available. Top it all off with a new hair color, perm or style for the new you. Treat your bridal party to a package of services that will have you all floating down the aisle.

Serenity by the Sea Day Spa
**4805-B Southport-Supply Rd. SE, Southport
(910) 457-0502, (910) 454-0704**

Services available at this full-service spa include haircuts, permanents, highlights, facials, tanning, waxing, eyebrow and eyelash tinting, basic and spa manicures, basic and spa pedicures, tanning beds, massages and a variety of body wraps. You can build your own package or choose from one of theirs. "My Treat" is a two-hour package that provides a half-hour massage, refreshing facial and a manicure. "A Little Luxury" (three hours) includes a one-hour massage, a one-hour facial and a manicure. And for the men, "The Gentleman" serves up a one-hour massage, foot therapy and a sports facial. Totally You Day Spa specializes in weddings and proms. Be sure to check out the Designer Boutique for special gifts or to treat yourself.

Kozo Hair Designs & Spa
**349 Village Rd., Shallotte
(910) 754-9477**

Kozo offers shampooing, haircuts, color, perms, straightening, hair treatments, facials, peels, make-up, waxing, manicures, pedicures, sculptured nails, massages and more. They do specialty hair designs for weddings and proms as well as a Deluxe Bridal Package and a Bridal Value Package. Why not treat yourself and your attendants before the wedding?

TOPSAIL ISLAND

A Beautiful New You Day Spa
**322 N. New River Dr., Surf City
(910) 328-2525**

A Beautiful New You offers all the services for a complete makeover. Hairstyling by experienced specialists, spa manicures and pedicures, massage, tanning and waxing are just the beginning. Seaweed, clay and exfoliation body treatments and facials are also available.

⒳ANNUAL EVENTS

E nrich your stay along North Carolina's southern coast by attending some of the many unique and festive special events listed in this chapter. Choose from rich cultural celebrations, civic events, fund-raisers or festivities surrounding the area's abundant natural resources. You'll find more things to do than you can ever fit into your calendar. If you're a newcomer to the area, there's no better way to get acquainted with your community than volunteering to help at a local event.

We've compiled a list of some popular annual happenings in a month-by-month format, however you'll want to check out other sources often. For events in the Greater Wilmington area, stop in or call the Cape Fear Coast Convention & Visitors Bureau, 24 North Third Street, Wilmington, (910) 341-4030 or (800) 222-4757. Visit your local chamber of commerce (see our Area Overview chapter for a list of chambers of commerce), read local publications (see our Media chapter) and keep an eye out for brochures or announcement posters around town. We list other annual events, such as fishing and golf tournaments, sailing regattas and athletic events, in the Golf, Sports, Fitness and Parks, and Watersports chapters.

January

Anniversary of the Capture of Fort Fisher
Fort Fisher State Historic Site, Kure Beach
(910) 458-5538

The fall of Fort Fisher on January 15, 1865, by Federal forces is commemorated each year in mid-January with an impressive living history reenactment program. In addition to tours, displays and demonstrations, cannon are fired throughout the day. Bring your ear plugs and dress warmly. Admission is free, though donations are appreciated.

Greater Wilmington Antique Show
Coast Line Convention Center, 501 Nutt St., Wilmington
(910) 686-3029

If you love antiques, this show's for you! Sponsored by North Carolina Junior Sorosis, the event hosts 30 dealers from North Carolina and throughout the Southeast who will tempt you with quality antiques, including glass, silver, china, jewelry, Oriental rugs and more. Hallmarks of this show are the high-quality items for sale, with only a limited number of reproductions permitted. Admission is $5. Held the last weekend in January, hours are Friday and Saturday 10 AM to 7 PM and Sunday 10 AM to 6 PM. Proceeds contribute to a full scholarship to UNC-Wilmington and area charitable organizations.

Martin Luther King Jr. Day March and Commemoration
Assorted Venues, Wilmington
(910) 763-4138

Martin Luther King Jr. Day has special resonance to Wilmingtonians because (among other reasons) Dr. King was scheduled to speak here the day he was assassinated. Wilmington honors his memory on the third Monday of January with a commemorative parade from Fifth and Castle Streets to Williston Middle School, 401 South 10th Street, beginning at 11 AM. A cookout sponsored by the Wilmington Sportsman's Club follows at 11th and Castle streets. In the morning, the NAACP hosts a breakfast. Additional programs are held throughout the day, with food, entertainment and speeches. Every Sunday prior to Monday's march, an ecumenical service sponsored by the ministerial round table is held at a rotating location.

Martin Luther King Jr. Celebration
Assorted Venues, Southport
(910) 457-5144

Southport typically celebrates Martin Luther King Day on the Sunday and Monday before the holiday. On Sunday, the annual

Memorial March begins at 2 PM in the parking lot of the I. L. A. Union HALL located on the corner of 10th and Lord Streets. A program focusing on the on-going project, "Do Something", follows. On Monday at 8 AM, a round-table breakfast will be held at the N.C. Baptist Assembly Conference Center honoring the legacy of King. This breakfast includes speakers, and attendees participate in discussions. The annual Walter Welsh Award, recognizing the recipient's work in promoting racial harmony, tolerance and understanding is presented at the breakfast.

Martin Luther King Jr. Celebration
Sunset Beach
(910) 287-4673

This celebration takes place the Monday before the holiday at noon in the Pleasant View Missionary Baptist Church. The program features a speaker, favorite songs and hymns of Dr. King and quotes presented by area youth.

Model Railroad Show
American Legion Post 10 Hall, 702 Pine Grove Dr., Wilmington
(910) 270-2696

Sponsored by the Cape Fear Model Railroad Club, this annual weekend event is held in late January. It's a must-see for both novice and experienced model-train enthusiasts. You'll be treated to awesome displays of operating model-train layouts in three different scales (sizes), a table of goodies for sale and free clinics in model-train display techniques. Admission is $4 for adults, $2 for children; kids younger than 5 get in free.

February

Fort Anderson Civil War Encampment
Brunswick Town State Historic Site, St. Phillips Rd., Winnabow
(910) 371-6613

This encampment of the 36th and 40th N.C. Civil War Regiments, a living history event, is interesting, entertaining and educational (but don't tell the kids!). There are programs focused on the Civil War, tours of Ft. Anderson (located at Brunswick Town State Historic Site, see our Attractions chapter) by uniformed personnel from the units bivouacked at the site. You'll also see

and hear small arms demonstrations, artillery demonstrations, uniform talks and lectures by Dr. Chris Fonville, historian and professor at UNCW. Also expect a re-enactment as well as raffles and a bake sale. Admission is free. Call for more information.

North Carolina Jazz Festival
Wilmington Hilton Riverside, 301 N. Water St., Wilmington
(910) 763-8585

The performers roster of the North Carolina Jazz Festival over the years reads like a Who's Who in Dixieland and mainstream jazz: Milt Hinton, Ken Peplowski, Art Hodes, Frank Tate, Bob Wilber, Kenny Davern and Bob Rosengarden. A preview performance takes place Thursday night on the main stage at UNCW's Kenan Auditorium; for tickets to this performance only, call (910) 962-3500 or (800) 732-3643.

A cabaret setting in the Wilmington Hilton's ballroom enhances the mood for Friday and Saturday evening eight-set performances. The Patron's Brunch, held Saturday noon at the Hilton, features a pro-am jam session for patrons who play instruments. Truly an extraordinary opportunity, these amateurs get to sit in with the professional musicians who'll be appearing during the first weekend each February. This event is so popular, tickets may sell out a year in advance.

Sweetheart Dinner Dance
Silver Coast Winery 6680 Barbeque Rd., Ocean Isle Beach
(910) 287-2800

Take your Valentine to the vineyard for Silver Coast Winery's annual Sweetheart Dance. Experience fantastic food while enjoying music, entertainment, dancing, and a bottle of Silver Coast's award winning wine.

Wilmington Garden Show
Coast Line Convention Center, 501 Nutt St., Wilmington
(910) 452-6393 ext. 211

Get an early jump on the long North Carolina growing season by viewing what's new in landscape design and know-how. Exhibits, vendors, lectures and demonstrations by speakers from throughout North Carolina present innovative products, designs and techniques for improving the surroundings of your home or business. Door prizes are awarded, and the show offers plenty of gift items that gardeners and landscapers would enjoy. The two-day show takes place the second weekend of February and is sponsored by the New Hanover County Cooperative Extension Arboretum Foundation Inc. By the way, the Arboretum is itself a wonderful place to visit any time of the year (see our Attractions chapter).

March

The Associated Artists of Southport
Spring Art Show
Franklin Square Gallery, 130 E. West St., Southport
(910) 457-5450

The Spring Art Show hangs in Franklin Square Gallery for the month of March. It's a great chance to see the two and three-dimensional artwork of the many talented artists of Southport and the surrounding area and to compare the awards given by the judge to your own thoughts about the art. Admission to the gallery is free, and artwork is for sale. Check out the website for more information.

Bid For Literacy Mardi Gras Auction
Coast Line Convention Center, 501 Nutt St., Wilmington
(910) 251-0911

In southeastern North Carolina, Mardi Gras arrives on the first weekend in March. The largest of two major fundraisers for the Cape Fear Literacy Council, this lavish annual event has become a popular evening for Wilmington's auction enthusiasts and 2006 marks the event's 20th anniversary. Decorated and built around a Mardi Gras theme, the evening begins with a lavish array of New Orleans style hors d'ouvres donated by Wilson's restaurant, donated beer and wine, live entertainment and a silent auction.

The vocal auction is the centerpiece of the evening, with all items donated from area merchants, professionals, local artists, the film community, restaurants and corporate sponsors. Past items won by lucky bidders have included cars, cruises to tropical islands, weekend getaway packages, celebrity items (a guitar signed by Reba McEntire comes to mind), signed movie scripts and film memorabilia, signed local art and much more!

Tickets are $30 per person and tables for ten can be reserved in advance for $300. Make your reservations through the Cape Fear Literacy Council, (910) 251-0911, or purchase tickets at the door. The fun begins with hors d'oeuvres and the silent auction at 6 PM; the vocal auction follows at 7 PM.

Coastal Living Show
Cape Fear C.C. Schwartz Center, 411 N. Front St., Wilmington
(910) 686-5904

An annual tradition for more than 25 years, this show features more than 100 exhibitors with everything for the home and garden — stonework, cabinets, fix-up, clean-up, jewelry, clothing, stained glass, spas, books, demonstrations and seminars. Sponsored by the Wilmington Woman's Club, it's held at the C.F.C.C. Schwartz Center. Admission is charged.

Kid's Art Day
Franklin Square Park, E. West St., Southport
(910) 457-5450, (910) 253-2672, (800) 222-4790

This event is held on the second Saturday in March from 10 AM to 2 PM beneath Southport's venerable live oak trees in Franklin Square Park. There are hands-on activities for children, music and stage entertainment, a clown or two, face-painting and a fun day for all. The event is sponsored by the Associated Artists of Southport, Brunswick County Parks and Recreation, Southport Parks and Recreation and Partnership for Children. Admission is free.

New Hanover County
Residents' Appreciation Day
Assorted venues, Wilmington and New Hanover County
(910) 341-4030

This popular annual event is a great opportunity for area residents to rediscover and savor New Hanover County attractions, including those in Wilmington, Wrightsville Beach, Carolina Beach and Kure Beach locations. Best of all, this Sunday event is free for residents. Contact the Cape Fear Coast Convention and Visitors Bureau at the number listed above for a list of participating attractions. Remember to carry proof of county residency for admission.

April

projects. And the event is fish-friendly, too; all the bopples are retrieved.

A Day at the Docks
Jordan Blvd., Holden Beach
(910) 842-4820

Ever hear of a Bopple Race? Care for a free ride on a charter fishing boat? Combine these with live entertainment, crafts, free Coast Guard boat inspections, a sunset boat parade and a blessing of the boats, and you've got Holden Beach's way of welcoming the return of spring. Something of a floating festival, the event offers various entertainments at ports of call along the island; thus, the free boat rides. All the food on sale is prepared by local restaurateurs as a showcase of local fare.

Sponsored by the Greater Holden Beach Merchants Association, the festivities take place on the first weekend in April, and admission is free. (By the way, a bopple is an apple boat that is assigned a number and three randomly selected crew. The bopples are dropped from the bridge into the Intracoastal Waterway, and the one that passes the finishing line first earns its crew cash prizes.) All proceeds are channeled into community volunteer groups and community

Airlie Gardens Concert Series
300 Airlie Rd., Wilmington
(910) 798-7700

From April through October, Airlie Gardens hosts a popular concert series the first and third Friday evening of each month. For just $8 per person (children 5 and younger get in free) or reduced rates or free for members depending on membership level, you can enjoy two hours of jazz (first Fridays) or folk music (third Fridays) while relaxing in these lovely Southern gardens. Bring a picnic, a blanket and your favorite person, but leave your pets at home, please. Alcohol is permitted and wine is available for purchase. Concerts begin at 6 PM under the awesome Airlie Oak.

Annual Bluegrass Festival
Silver Coast Winery, 6680 Barbeque Rd.,
Ocean Isle Beach
(910) 287-2800

The Annual Bluegrass Festival includes great music and barbecue among the vines at Silver Coast Winery. Gates are open from 11 AM to 6 PM. Look for bluegrass music, hog calling and even a corn-eating

The Battleship North Carolina now has a permanent berth on the Cape Fear River in Wilmington.

photo: Peter Doran

competition. For down-home fun, bring the family and spent the day!

Bald Head Island Regatta
Bald Head Island Marina, Bald Head Island
(910) 457-SAIL

Scheduled for the convenience of those interested in Key West Race Week, Miami Race Week, Charleston Race Week and Southern Bay Race Week, this regatta includes nine anticipated classes including: H20, B235, J24, J60, J105, B36.7, C&C 115, CF38, and J120. Offshore and protected inland racing is offered. Food and recreational activities are available on shore for non-race support staff. Ask about free dockage, launching and boat and trailer storage.

Dreams Center for Arts Education's Creative Spaces Open Studio Tour
515 Ann St., Wilmington
(910) 772-1501
www.dreamswilmington.org

Dreams Center for Arts Education helps fund its non-profit arts education programs for children through this self-guided tour of area artist's studios. A two-day event with over 35 participants, this peek at the inner spaces of glass blowers, painters, sculptors, photographers, weavers, potters and other creative types provides insight in to the artistic process. Both ACME Art Company and Independent Art Company participate and Dreams also features work created by the program's participants.

Museum of Coastal Carolina Family Day
21 E. Second St., Ocean Isle Beach
(910) 579-1016

Live dance music, storytelling, face painting, a shark-tooth hunt, crafts, fish printing and nature's footprints are some of the entertainment and activities geared to the whole family. Share this family day from 10 AM until 2 PM.

North Carolina Azalea Festival
Various locations, Wilmington
Office at 5725 Oleander Dr., Wilmington
(910) 794-4650

No matter what the weather, spring isn't official until the North Carolina Azalea Festival in early April, signaling the opening of the season in Wilmington and the southern coast of North Carolina. This lavish annual Thursday-through-Sunday celebration, one of the largest in the region, attracts more than 300,000 visitors from all over the United States and Canada. This annual rite features scores of musical and theatrical performances by local and national talent, celebrity guests, the Clyde Beatty-Cole Bros. Circus, breathtaking garden and home tours throughout historic Wilmington and area beaches, and, naturally, a wonderland of blooming azaleas.

The Azalea Festival garden tour, an annual fund-raising event for the Cape Fear Garden Club, is conducted Friday through Sunday. Proceeds from this tour are returned to the community through horticultural grants and UNC-Wilmington scholarships. Home tours are conducted on Saturday and Sunday. An admission fee is charged for both tours and proceeds benefit both the Azalea Festival and the Garden Club. Contact the North Carolina Azalea Festival office for admission information and a current list of featured homes and gardens.

Don't miss Saturday morning's three-hour grand parade downtown, which kicks off a weekend of free outdoor entertainment. A lively street fair along the Cape Fear River waterfront is held on Saturday and Sunday. This beloved Wilmington tradition features food vendors, several entertainment venues, art and craft booths, interactive exhibits, a children's area and thousands of friendly people.

Pleasure Island Chowder Cook-Off
Carolina Beach Lake Park, Carolina Beach
(910) 200-3288

Taste chowder entries prepared by some of the area's finest restaurants and vote for your favorite at the annual Chowder Cook-Off held mid-April in Carolina Beach. Live entertainment includes bands performing beach, rock and blues music. Children's activities are available, too. All that and more make this a fun (and filling) afternoon. Hours are 11:30 AM to 6 PM. The Cook-Off is presented by the non-profit Pleasure Island Merchants Association. Proceeds are used to fund local events and contribute to the Carolina Beach Fire Department, the Federal Point Help Center and Katie B. Hines Senior Center. Admission is $5 for adults, and children younger than 12 are admitted free. Take advantage of advanced sale tickets at reduced rates. No coolers or pets are allowed.

Poplar Grove Herb & Garden Fair
Poplar Grove Historic Plantation, 10200 U.S. Hwy. 17 N., Wilmington
(910) 686-9518, Ext. 26

Does spring fever have you itching to get into the garden? If so, join other garden and herb enthusiasts at Poplar Grove Historic Plantation. This annual spring event features a full day of interesting and informative workshops and speakers on the subject of herbs. (Pre-registration and pre-payment are recommended.) Another highlight of the fair is a garden and plant sale featuring live herbs and herbal products, perennials, shrubs, gardening accessories and more. For reservations or information on the class schedule and fees, call the number listed above.

Women Anglers in Training Weekend (WAIT)
Oak Island Recreation Department, 3003 E. Oak Island Dr., Oak Island
(910) 278-4747

This workshop sponsored by Oak Island Parks and Recreation and NC Sportsman Magazine offers a stress-free environment where women, from beginners to advanced, can ask questions and try their hands at a variety of angling activities. Introduction to surf, pier and bottom fishing, tying lures, casting, net casting, trolling, using bait and maneuvering boats are included in the class. The second day is a day of fishing either from a pier or by boat.

May

Airlie Arts Festival
300 Airlie Rd., Wilmington
(910) 798-7700

Occurring the first weekend in May, the festival is three days of art, music and food in the lush Airlie Gardens. Celebrating the arts through nationally known juried artists and musical performances, this festival is not to be missed.

Annual Spring Concert
Brunswick Concert Band
Hatch Auditorium, Caswell Beach
(910) 371-2062

Two formal Spring concerts are given by the Brunswick Concert Band (see the Music section of The Arts chapter). One concert is held in the Baptist Assembly at the easternmost tip of Oak Island and the other in Odell Williamson Auditorium at Brunswick Community College. The blend of ages of the individuals who make up this enthusiastic group and the blend of music, from jazz to show tunes to country to patriotic, always provides listening pleasure to the audience.

Battleship North Carolina Memorial Day Observance
Battleship North Carolina, U.S. Hwy. 421 N., Wilmington
(910) 251-5797

Memorial Day is observed aboard the monumental Battleship North Carolina with music, guest speakers and other special events. A tradition since 1968, the ceremony features a high-ranking military guest speaker, all-service color guard, a gun salute by Marines, taps and a memorial wreath dropped into the water. The ceremony begins at 5:45 PM and is free to the public. See our Attractions chapter for information about touring the ship during regular hours.

Greek Festival
St. Nicholas Greek Orthodox Church, 608 S. College Rd., Wilmington
(910) 256-5180

The Greek Festival is a wonderful opportunity (and for some people the only opportunity) to sample homemade moussaka, baklava and other Greek delicacies. Live Greek music, cultural presentations, cooking demonstrations, souvenirs, a tour of the church and a Greek-style marketplace round out this gala weekend-long celebration. Admission is $2 for adults. Children younger than 12 get in free. Fees are charged for food. The festival opens daily at noon.

Island of Lights Spring Fashion Show
Carolina Beach
(910) 458-7116, (910) 458-5507

Ladies love this annual luncheon event that features spring and summer outfits, beachwear, accessories and jewelry modeled by local gals. The event is a fundraiser for the Island of Lights organization, which sponsors many free activities, such as holiday fireworks displays. Linda's Fashions presents the show. The show occurs in mid-May at the Courtyard by Marriott at Carolina Beach. Call for details.

Kiwanis Sun Fest
Surf City
(910) 329-4446

This mid-May weekend-long fest celebrates the start of the summer season with entertainment, arts and crafts, exhibits, a food court, children's activities and amusement rides. This new event is sponsored by the Kiwanis Club of Topsail Island in cooperation with the Chamber of Commerce and Town of Surf City.

Leukemia Cup Regatta
South Harbour Village Marina, Southport
(910) 799-0075

This weekend event begins with the first of three races on Saturday with a Relentless for a Cure Silent Auction and dinner that evening. Sunday brings two more races and an awards celebration and barbeque. Both sail and power boats compete in the races with categories including: Harbor 20, J24, PHRF Non-Spinnaker and PHRF Spinnaker. Proceeds benefit the Leukemia and Lymphoma Society.

Port of Wilmington Maritime Day Festival
State Port at Wilmington
(910) 763-1621

Attending the annual Port of Wilmington Maritime Festival in late May is an entertaining and educational way to learn about the importance of maritime commerce on the Cape Fear River. The event also serves as an opportunity for the community to honor past and present members of our nation's Merchant Marine. Highlights of the day's activities include a dockside Maritime Day Memorial Ceremony, port and vessel tours. Maritime businesses as well as historical and environmental agencies have exhibits also. Because the Port of Wilmington has played such a vital role in the region's history and remains tremendously important to the area economy, residents and visitors alike find this a truly fascinating experience. Hours are 11 AM to 5 PM. Enter through the gate at 2202 Burnett Boulevard.

Relay for Life of Brunswick County
West Brunswick High School, Shallotte

This event raises funds for the American Cancer Society as well as celebrating survivorship and empowering individuals to fight back against the disease. During the event teams walk or run laps to raise funds for cancer research. awareness, education and patient and family care. In addition there is live entertainment and a "womanless beauty pageant." Sign up online at www.acsevents.org

June

Carolina Beach Music Festival
Carolina Beach
(910) 200-3288

Listen up all you shaggers and beach music aficionados, this is your chance to dance barefoot on the strand or just sway to the beat while standing in the surf. Held the first Saturday in June, the Beach Music Festival is billed as "the biggest beach dance party on the North Carolina Coast." Access is via the Carolina Beach Boardwalk from 11:30 AM to 5 PM. Sorry, no carry-in alcohol or pets are permitted. Beverages, including beer, and food vendors are available.

Pender County Blueberry Festival
Historic Downtown Burgaw
(910) 259-1278

If it's June, it's time for blueberries! Join the fun on the historic square in downtown Burgaw the last Saturday of June. There is a blueberry cook-off, parade, arts and crafts, food vendors and live entertainment.

Pleasure Island Summer Concerts
Fort Fisher Military Recreation Site
(910) 458-8434

The Pleasure Island Chamber of Commerce hosts four free Summer Concerts at the Fort Fisher Military Recreation site located on the Cape Fear River. They are always on the third Friday in June, July and August (weather permitting). Just bring your chair or a blanket and enjoy some great music from 6 to 8 PM. Food and beverages will be for sale. But please, no coolers and no pets. Call for more information.

Wilmington Nautical Festival
Along Water St., Downtown Wilmington
(910) 341-4030

Embracing its nautical heritage, Wilmington added this festival in 2003 to highlight one of the city's most attractive historical elements. The festival also recognizes the

U.S. Coast Guard's contributions to the city, a partnership that began in 1796. Attractions include tours of visiting tall ships, local art exhibits depicting nautical scenes, an entertainment stage, craft vendors, outdoor movie screenings, a boat show and a lighted, evening flotilla featuring recreational vessels. The event usually occurs in June or July.

July

Baskets of Summer
Poplar Grove Historic Plantation,
10200 U.S. Hwy. 17 N., Wilmington
(910) 686-9518, Ext. 26

Poplar Grove Historic Plantation holds a one-day, fun-filled basketry event for all skill levels. Instructing the classes are teachers from all around the Cape Fear region. They offer morning, afternoon and all-day classes from which to choose. Participants may select up to four basket choices in order of preference: two in the morning and two in the afternoon. For more information or to sign up for classes, call the number above.

Battleship Blast
On the riverfront, Downtown Wilmington
(910) 251-5797

People turn out by the tens of thousands on July Fourth for Wilmington's best fireworks of the year, a spectacular pyrotechnical display launched from Battleship Park. Primary viewing for the fireworks is from the downtown Wilmington riverfront. This breathtaking show, which starts at 9:05 PM, is free. Please note: The entire Battleship complex on Eagles Island closes at 6 PM that day and all cars must depart by 6:30 PM. You'll want to come early for the entertainment downtown (see prior listing).

Cape Fear Blues Festival
Assorted venues, Wilmington
(910) 350-8822

Presented by The Blues Society of the Lower Cape Fear, this popular summer music festival offers local, regional and national blues musicians an opportunity to show their stuff to enthusiastic audiences. It's held in Wilmington during the last weekend in July. Events during this blues-filled weekend begin with Thursday night's kick-off party, featuring food, drink and live blues followed by Friday night's not-to-be-missed Cape Fear Blues Cruise on Wilmington's riverboat, the Henrietta III, and a free Blues Musicians' Workshop on Saturday at noon.

Across the Cape Fear River from downtown Wilmington, join the fun at Battleship Park, located next to the Battleship North Carolina, for the festival's Saturday afternoon concert and the free All-Day Blues Jam at noon on Sunday. Hosting other artists, downtown restaurants and lounges participate as well, usually beginning late afternoon and evening. Advance tickets and all-inclusive Cape Fear Blues passes to all festival events are available. Due to frequent sellouts, early bookings for the Blues Cruise are highly recommended.

Fourth of July Fireworks
Holly Ridge Municipality Park,
Sound Rd., Holly Ridge
(910) 329-7081

The Holly Ridge Municipality Park is a wonderful setting for the annual fireworks display. Children can enjoy the playground equipment while waiting for the fireworks, and the spacious grounds allow room to spread a blanket for an old-fashioned picnic supper. Bring your own picnic or purchase hot dogs and drinks at the concession stand (a fund-raiser for Holly Ridge Parks Department). Entertainment precedes the fireworks, which start at approximately 9:15 PM. The location is only a short distance from Topsail Island and convenient for vacationers. Admission is free.

Fourth of July Riverfront Celebration
Along Water St., Downtown Wilmington
(910) 341-7855

Celebrate our nation's independence with food, entertainment and a street fair on the riverfront in historic downtown Wilmington. Featured entertainment performs on the main stage along Water Street. Festivities run from 5 to 10 PM, with a not-to-be-missed fireworks display scheduled at 9:05 PM (see next listing).

Island Fireworks
Surf City Town Park, Roland Ave., Surf City
(910) 328-4131

Get the jump on your July Fourth celebration with a summer concert and fireworks display at the new Surf City Town Park on the

Intracoastal Waterway. Be sure to bring your blankets and lawn chairs. Fireworks begin at dark following the concert.

July National Juried Art Competition and Exhibition
Franklin Square Gallery, 130 E. West St., Southport
(910) 457-5450

Franklin Square Gallery hosts the annual July National Juried Art Competition and Exhibition, which celebrates its 26th year in 2006. Artists from all over the USA submit slides of two dimensional or three dimensional artwork, from which only the best work is chosen by the professional judges. If you love art, this is an exhibition not to be missed. Admission to the gallery is free, and artwork is for sale.

North Carolina 4th of July Festival
Downtown Southport and Oak Island
(910) 457-5578
www.nc4thofjuly.com

People come from all over the state of North Carolina (and other states as well) to participate in this old-fashioned, small-town, family celebration. The population swells and traffic is heavy, but most folks are happy to wait a bit in order to be involved in the event. There is a parade, of course, with bands and clowns and horses. There are also firemen's games, which are quite wet, plus arts and crafts vendors and food vendors. And then there are fireworks over the water. But, most importantly, there is the naturalization ceremony, in which people of varying nationalities become citizens of the USA.

Pleasure Island Fireworks
Carolina Beach
(910) 200-3288

Do you love fireworks but can't get there on the Fourth? The Pleasure Island Merchants Association gives you a second chance to enjoy them. Come on out to the beach on the

When you're going to a special event or activity, prepare for unexpected expenses, such as parking fees, tips and "donations" by having extra cash with you. Small bills and correct change are always appreciated.

Saturday before the holiday for a fantastic display beginning at 9:30 PM. Location to be announced.

August

Annual Endless Summer Beach Blast
Various Locations, Wilmington Jaycees
(910) 359-1940

At the end of August the Jaycees host this huge event with thousands attending. All of the talent is booked through General Entertainment, which represents General Johnson and Chairmen of the Board. A non-profit organization, the Wilmington Jaycees support a number of charitable programs and organizations. For specifics and sponsorship opportunities, contact Susan Crowell at the number above.

Boiling Spring Lakes Raft Race
9 Boiling Spring Rd. Boiling Spring Lakes
(910) 845-2762

This annual race, held on the Big Lake in Boiling Spring Lakes, is fun for participants as well as spectators. The 4 X 8 self-propelled rafts must be homemade. Neither commercially manufactured hulls nor inner tubes are allowed. Put your imagination to work and come on out to join the fun!

Castles and Scoops Contest
Holiday Inn Sunspree Resort, Wrightsville Beach
(910) 254-3534

Held annually in August, the Castles and Scoops Contest is a day full of family fun in the sun. Local businesses, families, student and civic groups and area architects are among the competitors building awesome sand sculptures for awards in five different categories, including Public Favorite. The "scoops" of the contest refers to the ice cream sundaes built by the contestants while the judges make their decisions. Proceeds from this event benefit the Wilmington Children's Museum.

Dreams Center for Arts Education, Cabaret Fundraiser
515 Ann St., Wilmington
(910) 772-1501
www.dreamswilmington.org

Each year the Dreams Center for Arts Education holds its Cabaret Fundraiser to support their mission of providing free arts education and opportunities for Wilmington's most marginalized youth. Cabaret features a fabulous silent auction of visual art by local artists, as well as live performances by some of Wilmington's most talented performing artists. But, it's the kids that steal the show, displaying the skills they've learned from their teachers at Dreams. The event occurs in late August at UNCW's Warwick Center and tickets are $50.

Sneads Ferry Shrimp Festival
Community Building Field, Park Ln., Sneads Ferry
(910) 329-4446

This is the longest-running festival in the Topsail area and has been going on for more than a quarter of a century. The festival celebrates the heritage of the shrimping industry in the Sneads Ferry area. Always on the second weekend in August, it is a real crowd pleaser. A parade begins on Saturday at 10 AM at the corner of Old Folkstone and Peru roads, winding through the community and ending at Fulchers Landing Road. The festival begins after the parade on Saturday and ends with an evening concert. Sunday, the grounds are open from 11 AM until 5 PM.

The famous Shrimparoo dinner, consisting of mouth-watering local fried shrimp, french fries, cole slaw and hush puppies, is served in the community building. Be ready to wait in line during the lunch hour. Other festival events include carnival rides, arts and crafts, food vendors, military displays and daytime entertainment. Admission fee is $3, and there is also a charge for the Shrimparoo dinner and the carnival rides.

Wilmington African-American Heritage Festival
Robert Strange Park, Wilmington
(910) 762-5502

On an August weekend each year, Wilmington recognizes and celebrates the black community during the African-American Heritage Festival. Centered around an overall theme, the event honors those individuals whose lives impacted history in one way or another. Storytelling, food, music and dance highlight the festival, which features performing arts from various black cultures. The park

is located on Eighth Street, between Ann and Castle streets.

Wooden Boat Race
Southport Yacht Basin, Southport

The Wooden Boat Race was designed a number of years back by Russ Ferris to separate the sailors from the boys. Each year he is invited back to start the race with his claw hammer. The entertainment rivals that provided by the Three Stooges, as sails and people end up in the water, boats drag anchor lines and dinghies run aground, into pilings and into each other. Don't miss the fun!

September

Hampstead Spot Festival
U.S. Hwy. 17, next to Topsail High School, Hampstead
(910) 270-9642

Just a short drive down U.S. Highway 17, the Hampstead Spot Festival is an opportunity to enjoy a dinner of spot, one of the area's best-tasting fish, along with generous helpings of cole slaw and hush puppies. This festival opens on Friday night and ends on Sunday evening. Dinner is served on Saturday and Sunday only, and is not available for the Friday night opening. Other events for the whole family include amusement rides, a variety show, and arts and crafts. Admission to the festival is free, but there is a charge for amusement rides. A golf tournament in conjunction with the festival is held on Saturday. To find out more about this tournament, call the Greater Hampstead Chamber of Commerce at the number listed above.

Intercultural Festival
Brunswick Community College Main Campus
U.S. Hwy. 17 N., Supply
(910) 755-7306

The annual Intercultural Festival fills the air with the sound of music and laughter. Musical groups, dance troupes, clowns, arts, crafts and food booths all contribute to the festive atmosphere. Activities geared to little ones keep the children happy and occupied while you get to know your Brunswick County neighbors.

No Octane Regatta
The Adventure Company, 807-A Howe St.,
Southport
(910) 454-0607

A 3.9 mile kayak race/poker chase (kayak/canoe and bicycle event) and wooden boat show, the No Octane Regatta begins at 7:30 AM and includes refreshments and an event T-shirt.

North Carolina Big Sweep
Topsail Island Beaches and
Inland Waterways
(910) 328-0863

North Carolina Big Sweep, held October 1st, is an opportunity for visitors and residents alike to join in the cleaning of the beaches and inland waterways, keeping them safe for marine life and birds as well as improving the beauty of these natural resources. A free kickoff breakfast is held at the Moose Lodge, on N.C. Highway 50 between Surf City and Holly Ridge at 8 AM. Instructions, supplies and assignments are given at that time. For more information contact Inez Bradt, Pender County Big Sweep chairperson, at the number above, or call the Topsail Chamber of Commerce at (910) 329-4446.

Oak Island Art Guild
Labor Day Arts & Crafts Fair
Middleton Park, E. Oak Island Dr.,
Oak Island
(910) 278-7560

This annual Labor Day weekend festival is a celebration of local and regional artists and craftspeople who display and sell their goods, all within sight of the ocean (or nearly so). Proceeds from the festival are used toward grants for local high school students. The daylong fair is held from 10 AM to 5 PM and is free. Food is available at concession stands.

Purple Feet Festival
Silver Coast Winery, 6680 Barbeque Rd.,
Ocean Isle Beach
(910) 287-2800

"Oh Lucy...you have some 'splaining to do!" Each year the reigning "Lucy" crowns a new one. So dye that hair red and get out your stomping clothes. Enjoy music, great food, contests, arts and crafts and a lot of I Love Lucy look-alikes.

October

Annual Seafood, Blues & Jazz Festival
Fort Fisher Military Recreation Area
(910) 458-8434

Always the second weekend in October, when the weather's warm, the sun's shining and the ocean breezes are fluttering, bring your lawn chairs and family to the Pleasure Island Seafood, Blues and Jazz Festival. This popular event is held on the Fort Fisher Military Recreation Site, right on the Cape Fear River. Music lovers revel in two days of non-stop jazz and blues on three stages, performed by nationally and regionally recognized musicians.

Seafood lovers enjoy scrumptious seafood from some of the area's best restaurants. Featured attractions are the renowned Green Beret Sports Parachute Team and Michael's Famous Oyster Shucking Contest. There's plenty of shopping at booths hosted by crafters and local shop owners, a fine-arts plaza and a wine tasting. For the kids, there is a special Kidz Zone with inflatable amusements, magicians, jugglers and much more. Please, no coolers and no pets. Call the Chamber of Commerce at (910) 458-8434 for more information. Hours are Saturday 11 AM to 11 PM and Sunday 11 AM to 6 PM. Call for ticket information.

Autumn with Topsail
Assembly Building Grounds, Flake Ave. and
Channel Blvd., Topsail Beach
(910) 329-4446

This fall festival is hosted by the Topsail Island Historical and Cultural Arts Council and is a fund-raiser for the historic Assembly Building, now used as a community center. Held in mid-October, the festival opens with a Kiwanis Pancake Breakfast at 7 AM on both Saturday and Sunday mornings. A juried arts show, Taste of Topsail, beer and wine garden, horse-drawn trolley rides, children's activities and daytime entertainment are offered on both Saturday and Sunday. The Missiles and More Museum, housed in the Assembly Building, is open throughout the festival. On Saturday, activities begin at 10 AM with entertainment starting at 11 AM. On Sunday, activities begin at 11 AM and entertainment at 1 PM. A Saturday night concert at 7 PM features a professional band playing beach music. Admission is free.

Brunswick County Idol Show
Odell Williamson Auditorium, Supply
Brunswick County Parks and Recreation
(910) 253-2672, (800) 222-4790

Open auditions for the Brunswick County Idol Show are free and open to all Brunswick County residents 16 years of age and older. Judges are talent scouts and music professionals, and cash prizes and contracts with the Concerts on the Coast concert series are awarded. Finalists present a show at the Odell Williamson Auditorium where the winners are announced at the end of the show. Come and be amazed at the talent in Brunswick County!

Cape Fear Fair & Expo
Wilmington International Airport
(910) 313-1234

For 10 days beginning the last Thursday in October, the Cape Fear Fair & Expo comes to town. Ever popular for family-style fun, the fair seems to get bigger every year. A midway offers approximately 40 rides, food and games. You'll enjoy the livestock exhibits and competition, an agricultural tent, animal shows and live entertainment. Admission, which includes parking, exhibits, entertainment and all rides, is $11 ($8 advance purchase). Children younger than 2 get in free, and some days are set aside as freebies for seniors. Hours are from 5 to 11 PM daily, with the exception of Saturdays, when hours are from noon to midnight.

Halloween Festival
Poplar Grove Historic Plantation,
10200 U.S. Hwy. 17 N., Wilmington
(910) 686-9518, Ext. 26

The Halloween Festival is a popular, spooky event for the brave and faint-hearted alike. Planners guarantee that you will get totally scared from the haunted barn and haunted hayride that goes deep into the dark, dark woods. If this isn't your taste, there is a not-so-scary hayride and haunted barn along with carnival games and rides. A costume contest is offered for children of all ages (including adults).

Halloween History-Mystery Tour
Bellamy Mansion Museum, 503 Market St.,
Wilmington
(910) 251-3700

The gorgeous Bellamy Mansion takes on an eerie aspect just for Halloween and is the first stop on this popular Halloween tour on the weekend closest to trick-or-treating. The self-guided walking tour begins at the mansion and continues throughout historic downtown Wilmington from dusk (about 4 PM) until 8:30 PM. Experience the Port City's haunted and mysterious past as you visit historic homes and other venues, including a haunted cemetery. Costumed storytellers at various sites along the tour offer insights into Wilmington's rich and spooky past. Wear comfortable shoes and bring a flashlight. Call for current ticket prices.

North Carolina Festival By the Sea
Holden Beach
(910) 754-6644, (800) 426-6644

Thousands of people are discovering this festival centered on a traditional Halloween carnival for the island's children. On the last Saturday in October there's a parade on the causeway and a huge outdoor festival beneath the bridge, with live music, food and more than 160 craft booths. Contests on the beach (no fee) include kite flying, sand sculpture and a horseshoe toss. The fleet of feet may participate in the 1K, 5K or 10K races (for a nominal fee). Saturday night features an old-fashioned street dance with live music. Plan to carpool and arrive early. (Parking laws are relaxed for the festival.) Admission to the festival is free, and all proceeds benefit Holden Beach's volunteer groups and community projects.

North Carolina Oyster Festival
Ocean Isle Beach
(910) 754-6644, (800) 426-6644

If you can find a better oyster-shucking competition, go there, but the N.C. Oyster Shucking Championship at this Oyster Festival is hard to beat. A champion oyster shucker is selected to compete in the national oyster-shucking competition with hopes of going to the international competition in Ireland. Folks love it so much there's even an amateur division. Featuring mountains of the South Brunswick Islands' favorite food, in season at this time, the festival also offers continuous live music, arts and crafts vendors, entertainment for the kids, a 5K, 10K and fun run, an oyster stew cook-off and more. It's held the third weekend in October. Admission is $3, free for children younger than 12.

Oktoberfest
Silver Coast Winery
6680 Barbeque Rd., Ocean Isle Beach
(910) 287-2800

Lace up your lederhosen and let loose your yodel. It's Oktoberfest in wine country. Listen to German music, dance the polka, try out your yodeling skills and eat the best German food around.

Riverfest
Various locations, downtown Wilmington
(910) 452-6862

Riverfest is a wonderful family celebration of the area's rich heritage. It features river events, an enormous street fair with food and crafts, music, stage shows, live arts performances, music, fireworks and more. Special events include the annual Great Waiter's Wine Race, boat rides, military exhibits and a handmade self-powered Riverfest Raft Regatta. For landlubbers, there's the Annual Run the River 8K Race (Sunday at 8 AM) and a Classic Car Show. A Kidz Zone set up in the Cotton Exchange parking lot (Saturday and Sunday) offers face painting, interactive games, arts and crafts activities, entertainment, rides, displays, a petting zoo and more. The events are free. Riverfest is traditionally held the first weekend of October.

Sometime in October Film Festival and Screenplay Competition
Wilmington
(910) 200-2439

Mid-October is an exciting time for area filmmakers and screenplay writers who've submitted entries in this annual competitive event. Generally, several hundred entries of both films and scripts are submitted. The festival takes place at three locations: Hollywood East Cinema Grill, Firebelly Lounge and a new site selected each year. Hosted by The Cape Fear Independent Film Network, a nonprofit organization dedicated to education and promotion of the arts, the film festival is an opportunity for showcasing selected

works. The organization likes to focus on first-time filmmakers and those from the Carolinas, especially this area. Call for information on submission and festival details.

Stede Bonnet Regatta
Yacht Basin Provision Company, Southport
(910) 457-0654

This fun regatta has some unusual rules: all participants are required to be turned out in buccaneer costumes and act like pirates while the regatta is in progress (though there is no law against continuing during the celebratory time after the race is complete!). It is recommended that spectators arrive in time for the captain's meeting as this is a start-by-assignment regatta designed to bring the entire fleet home at the same time.

November

Annual Holly Ridge Holly Festival
Holly Ridge Municipality Park, Holly Ridge
(910) 328-7081

Get in the holiday spirit with the annual Holly Festival and parade on the first Saturday in November. The parade, to welcome Santa Claus to town, begins at 10 AM on U.S. Highway 17 at the north end of town then turns onto N.C. Highway 50 at the traffic light and proceeds to Hines Street and the park. Activities in the park include entertainment, amusement rides, arts and crafts, and food concessions.

Cucalorus Film Festival
Various locations, Wilmington
(910) 343-5995

Film buffs and aspiring filmmakers shouldn't miss this five-day cinematic festival filled with outstanding feature films, shorts, videos and live music. This annual non-competitive event draws entries from all over the globe — more than 600 in 2003. The best entries from each category are shown during weekend festivities so popular that local film-industry insiders — actors, filmmakers, musicians and artists — make it a point to attend every year. In 2002 MovieMaker magazine dubbed Cucalorus "the best kept secret on the indie fest circuit." Entries are accepted all year long; call for details.

Admission options range from the cost of a single feature film to a Festival Pass that in-

12th annual
cucalorus
film festival

pure.film.buzz

nov 8-11
www 2006
cucalorus
org

cludes all screenings and live entertainment. Oh, in case you're wondering, a cucalorus is a filmmaker's device used on a movie set to create a dappled light effect.

Festa Italia
Silver Coast Winery
6680 Barbeque Rd., Ocean Isle Beach
(910) 287-2800

Bocce anyone? Celebrate everything Italian — food wine, music and games — at Silver Coast Winery. Bring your favorite Italian or be Italian for a day. Carolina Italian American Organization (CIAO) will be on hand to help with the festivities.

Festival of Trees
Wilmington Hilton Riverside,
301 N. Water St., Wilmington
(910) 772-5444

The Festival of Trees, a benefit for Lower Cape Fear Hospice & LifeCareCenter, is a dazzling display of more than 100 beautifully decorated Christmas trees with a different theme each year. Visit the Holiday Room, featuring seasonal decorations, wreaths, ornaments, a gingerbread village and gift

baskets. Holiday crafts and gift items fill the holiday boutique with such things as wreaths, American Girl clothes, jellies, candy, dips, candles, jewelry, hand-painted furniture and ornaments, all for sale. Featured is the Hospice Memorial tree adorned with white doves representing Lower Cape Fear Hospice & LifeCareCenter patients who died during the year. Pay admission at the door; group rates are available.

North Carolina Holiday Flotilla at
Wrightsville Beach
Banks Channel, Wrightsville Beach
(910) 341-4030, (800) 222-4757

This floating parade of brightly lit and wildly decorated watercraft of all shapes and sizes is one of the true highlights of the holiday season. It's free and typically takes place at 6 PM on the last weekend of November. A fireworks display following the flotilla signals the start of this uniquely coastal celebration. A holiday fair, an arts and crafts show, a children's art show, rides, food and performing artists add to the festive atmosphere from 10 AM to 4 PM

Smith Island Art League Thanksgiving Show
Bald Head Association Center,
Bald Head Island
(910) 457-6229

Original artwork can be purchased by the public at this two-day Art League Thanksgiving Show. The league is comprised of Bald Head Island residents and property owners, and full-time employees (over 18 years of age) of the island. Artists and art enthusiasts are welcome.

Topsail Island Holiday
Boat Flotilla at Topsail Beach
Assembly Building, Topsail Beach
(910) 329-4446

Kick off the holiday season on Topsail Island with the annual parade of lighted boats traveling down the Intracoastal Waterway. Luminaries light the path to the Assembly Building in Topsail Beach, where spectators watch the flotilla and enjoy light refreshments. Holiday lighting by island residents and businesses adds to the festivities.

December

Airlie Gardens' Enchanted Airlie:
A Holiday Light Show
300 Airlie Rd., Wilmington
(910) 798-7700

Capture the holiday magic at Airlie Gardens by visiting the Holiday Light Show. This elaborate show of landscape lighting and colorful lighted displays runs nightly from Thanksgiving weekend through Christmas. Musical entertainment is included, and refreshments are available for purchase. Call for times and admission fee.

Candle Tea
Covenant Moravian Church,
4126 S. College Rd., Wilmington
(910) 799-9256

On the first Saturday in December, come to this warm, friendly church any time between 10 AM to 2 PM to enjoy a tour of the church, a brief explanation of Moravian history, spiced tea or sweet Moravian coffee with cookies, and demonstrations of traditional Moravian crafts. See the putz (Nativity scene), which has a special sound and light show, then go to the crafts area where you'll see traditionally garbed men and women

making Moravian stars, beeswax candles, Advent wreaths and Moravian cookies. These items plus crafts and carvings are available for you to take home.

Christmas By-The-Sea Festival
Oak Island, Southport and Boiling Spring
Lakes locations
(910) 457-6964, (800) 457-6964

A colorful holiday parade on Oak Island begins a nearly month-long celebration in the Southport-Oak Island area. Home tours, band and choral concerts, and two lighted boat parades are some of the events. Contact the Southport-Oak Island Chamber of Commerce at the numbers listed above for a schedule.

Island of Lights Festival
Various locations,
Carolina Beach and Kure Beach
(910) 458-7116, (910) 458-5507

The Island of Lights Festival on Pleasure Island features a number of weekend events, most of them free, beginning with Light Up The Lake on the Friday evening following Thanksgiving. A fabulous Christmas Parade begins at 7:30 PM the next Friday night; that Saturday evening, the popular Holiday Flotilla, featuring boats of all sizes in full seasonal regalia, runs from Snow's Cut to Carolina Beach boat basin and back. The Island of Lights Tour of Homes, held the following Saturday, features refreshments and Southern hospitality on a self-guided tour of some Carolina and Kure Beach's elegant homes. For more information on these events or ticket prices for the Tour of Homes, contact the number listed above.

Island of Lights
New Year's Eve Countdown Party
Kure Beach
(910) 458-7116, (910) 458-5507

End the year at this family-style, alcohol-free beach party in the heart of Kure Beach. Enjoy a street dance with live beach music, munch popcorn and drink hot chocolate while snuggling under a blanket on the sand, and watch the descent of an enormous beach ball at midnight. Top it off with an impressive fireworks display, and you've got yourself a true beach-style New Year's Eve to remember. Fun for the whole family, it is free and begins at 10 PM

Kwanzaa Celebration
Various locations, Wilmington

The Kwanzaa Celebration is a seven-day celebration of African-American roots, culture and tradition; it is held from the day after Christmas through January 1. A variety of events are featured throughout the week of Kwanzaa, culminating in a Kwanzaa Karnival that includes theatrical performances, crafts for children and a community feast on the last day. Foremost during the week is the daily lighting of a candle to symbolize one of the seven principles. Drumming, storytelling and other activities focus on African traditions and values. Watch the newspapers for details.

New Year's Eve Riverboat Cruise
Corner of Water and Dock Sts., Wilmington
(910) 343-1611, (800) 676-0162

Ring in 2006 aboard the Henrietta III on a New Year's Eve riverboat cruise down the Cape Fear River in Wilmington. Festivities include party favors, hors d'oeurves, a DJ and a traditional champagne toast at midnight. The cruise runs from 9 PM to 12:30 AM with boarding scheduled for 8:30 PM on Water Street, at the foot of Dock Street. Tickets are $65 per person and pre-paid reservations are required. Call the phone numbers above for more information or reservations.

Old Wilmington by Candlelight
Various locations, Wilmington
(910) 762-0492

This is one of the most popular and atmospheric of the holiday home tours. Each year, about 20 of Wilmington's most historic homes, churches and businesses are opened to guests for two days on the first weekend in December. Stroll into Christmases past and see how yesterday's lifestyles have been adapted to our time. The tour is self-guided. Times are Saturday from 4 to 8 PM and Sunday from 2 to 6 PM. Call for ticket information and a list of homes on the tour.

Poplar Grove Christmas Open House
Poplar Grove Historic Plantation,
10200 U.S. Hwy. 17 N., Wilmington
(910) 686-9518, Ext. 26

Few places evoke the Southern charm of bygone days as well as Poplar Grove Historic Plantation, especially at holiday time. Visitors easily step back in time to a Victorian Christmas. Traditional craftspeople demonstrate life's everyday necessities in decorated rooms of the 1850 manor house. Other highlights include a Christmas tree with all the trimmings and seasonal arts and crafts. Admission is free to this early December event. The plantation staff views the annual Open House as a Christmas gift to the community for its year-round support.

Sneads Ferry Winterfest
Community Building, Peru Rd.,
Sneads Ferry
(910) 329-4446

Get an early start on the holidays with the friendly folks in Sneads Ferry. Winterfest is held on the second weekend in December and begins on Friday night with a tree lighting at 7 PM. Christmas trees decorated by area clubs add to the festive decorations. Children are invited to a pancake breakfast with Santa on Saturday morning between 7 and 11 AM. There is an arts and crafts show on Saturday between the hours of 9 AM and 4 PM and Sunday between the hours of noon and 4 PM. Entertainment is held throughout the festival beginning on Friday night and ending on Sunday afternoon. The entertainment schedule is posted in local newspapers. All programs are free, but there is a charge for the pancake breakfast.

World's Largest Living Christmas Tree
Hilton Park, near the intersection of Castle Hayne Rd. and J.E.L. Wade Dr., Wilmington
(910) 341-7855

The lighting of the World's Largest Living Christmas Tree, an enormous live oak, has been a Wilmington tradition since 1928. On a Friday evening in early December, the town turns out with Santa, the mayor, a brass band and a chorus, and the festivities begin at 5:35 PM. At 6:15 PM, the tree is lit to the sounds of music and voices raised in song, and everyone joins in. The tree remains lit nightly from 5:30 to 10 PM until New Year's Day.

⊛ DAYTRIPS

ocals and visitors alike agree that Wilmington and North Carolina's southeastern coastal areas have a lot to offer, with more than enough attractions, restaurants, entertainment and fun activities to satisfy just about anyone. However, those with a wandering eye always want to see if the grass is greener somewhere else....

While we're definitely biased, we have to confess that traveling south to Myrtle Beach, South Carolina, heading north to the Central Coast of North Carolina or driving west as far as Interstate 95 can provide interesting adventures. These areas offer visitors three entirely different perspectives on life in the South. Even the hushpuppies and barbecue taste different. In this chapter, we've given you a snapshot of each area and what's there so you can choose a destination to fit your mood

MYRTLE BEACH, SOUTH CAROLINA

For a change of pace and scenery, plus some terrific food and an enormous variety of things to do, Myrtle Beach, South Carolina, is the place to go. Those of us who live and love the Wilmington area tend to see our neighbor to the south as a bit too busy and a bit too commercial. Nevertheless, we love to go there once in awhile because there's just so much going on.

The Myrtle Beach Area Chamber of Commerce reports that approximately 13 million visitors head to the Myrtle Beach area every

Late spring and early fall are the best times to take jaunts up and down the coast. Tourist traffic has diminished significantly, but most attractions and shops are open and eager to see your smiling faces.

year, many of them from North Carolina. Year-round visitors and snowbirds are attracted to the area's abundance of lodging, dining and shopping opportunities, world-class golf courses, impressive array of live entertainment venues and profusion of attractions. The Grand Strand's subtropical climate averages a pleasant 64 degrees with about 215 sunny days per year in which to soak up some rays on the magnificent beaches.

If you travel through North Myrtle Beach on U. S. Hwy 17 Bypass, a trip to where the action is will take approximately 1 1/4 hours from downtown Wilmington, about 69 miles. However, with the opening of the new S.C. Highway 31 expressway (just off S.C. Highway 9), you can access points of interest all along the Grand Strand without sitting in traffic waiting to get there. A trip to the Myrtle Beach Airport (via U.S. Highway 501, East) takes about 1 1/2 hours, or stay on S.C. 31 until it ends at S.C. Highway 544, take Highway 544 East to U.S. 17 Bypass, then south to Brookgreen Gardens and Murrells Inlet.

For the daytripper, Myrtle Beach is the Strand's entertainment nerve center. The focus of downtown Myrtle Beach is Ocean Boulevard, a hotbed of activity. Before entering Myrtle Beach proper, the length of U.S. 17 (here called Kings Highway) is known as Restaurant Row, where dining establishments stand shoulder to shoulder. Another rapidly growing Myrtle Beach entertainment hub is U.S. 17 Bypass between 21st and 29th Avenues North, with the huge Broadway At The Beach shopping and entertainment complex as its center (see the following Entertainment section).

There are more than 1,700 full-service restaurants along the Grand Strand, which includes Horry County and parts of Georgetown County. Along with fresh-catch seafood and all the usual regional specialties, you'll find other samples of Southern fare such as chicken bog (chicken, seasoned rice and sausage), she-crab soup, alligator stew, crawfish, Calabash-style seafood and the ever-present Southern staple — hushpuppies. Numerous upscale, fine-dining establishments have been added to the mix over the years. All-you-can-eat buffets are ubiquitous, so bring a hearty appetite.

Tourist Information

The **Myrtle Beach Area Chamber of Commerce** operates four information centers where you can pick up or order scads of information about the area: Myrtle Beach Office, 1200 N. Oak Street, Myrtle Beach, (843) 626-7444; South Strand Office, 3401 U.S. 17 S. (Business), Murrells Inlet, (843) 651-1010; the Ashby Ward Myrtle Beach/Grand Strand Welcome Center, 1800 U.S. 501 W., Aynor, (843) 626-7293; and Myrtle Beach International Airport, 1100 Jetport Road, Myrtle Beach, (843) 626-7444. To contact the chamber for information or to request brochures, call (800) 356-3016. For groups or meetings, call (800) 488-8998.

Another helpful resource is the **North Myrtle Beach Chamber of Commerce**, 270 U.S. 17 N., North Myrtle Beach, (843) 281-2662 or (877) 332-2662. There you can find out where to go for beach music and shag dancing besides getting the inside scoop on local restaurants. Separate from Myrtle Beach, the City of North Myrtle Beach has its own treasure trove of attractions, marinas, golf and a variety of accommodations.

The **South Carolina State Welcome Center** is on U.S. 17 right at the state line, near Little River, (843) 249-1111. This is a convenient place for daytrippers from the Wilmington and Brunswick County areas to gather a wealth of brochures about the Grand Strand or other South Carolina destinations, including nearby Georgetown, Charleston and Columbia, the state capital. Many of the publications contain discount coupons that are good at dozens of Grand Strand locations. Staff members are on hand to answer questions, make suggestions and offer assistance in making hotel/motel reservations. It's open seven days a week except for Thanksgiving, Christmas and New Year's days. Summer hours are March through October 9 AM to 5:30 PM. Winter hours are November through February 9 AM to 5 PM.

Of course, an excellent resource is the Insiders' Guide® to Myrtle Beach and the Grand Strand, which can be purchased in local bookstores or online at http://www.insiders.com/myrtle-beach

Shopping

Shopping is among the Grand Strand's most popular activities. The area is replete with shops and boutiques of every description and specialty, but it's the discount shops and factory outlet stores that are most renowned among die-hard shoppers.

Barefoot Landing, 4898 U.S. Highway 17 N. in North Myrtle Beach, (843) 272-8349 or (800) 272-2320, is one of the most popular shopping magnets in the area. The complex, which is open year round (although hours vary seasonally), emulates a charming seaport village atmosphere, surrounding a 27-acre freshwater lake and bordering the Intracoastal Waterway. With over 100 specialty shops and outlet stores plus 16 restaurants (most are waterfront), you can keep busy all day. Kids and adults will enjoy a break from the rigors of shopping by riding the Barefoot Carousel, (843) 272-8349, an authentic representation of an old Barnum & Bailey carousel with 41 animals cast from original molds.

After you've shopped 'til you dropped and eaten your fill, take advantage of convenient attractions that are within walking distance: the **Alabama Theatre**, (843) 272-1111 or (800) 342-2262, founded by the musical group of the same name; the **House of Blues**, (843) 272-3000, a Bayou-style bistro; **Great American Riverboat Company**, sightseeing on the Intracoastal Waterway (843) 650-6600 or (800) 685-6601; and **Alligator Adventure**, (843) 361-0789, a zoo of regional and exotic reptiles, amphibians and birds (hours vary seasonally).

Still in a mood to shop? More than 100 discount outlets and specialty shops await you at the **Tanger Outlet Center** (formerly Myrtle Beach Factory Stores) on U.S. 501 W., (843) 236-5100 ext. 107. Among the most popular shopping complexes, this one includes "Off Fifth," a Saks Fifth Avenue outlet, Banana Republic, Crabtree & Evelyn, Bass, Lenox, Nike, Reebok, Jones New York, Brooks Brothers and many more name-brand stores.

Growing rapidly is the newer **Tanger Outlet Center** on U.S. 17 North at Veteran's Highway (S.C. 22), (843) 449-0491. Tanger has more than 75 brand name stores including apparel, hosiery and intimates, home furnishings, footwear and accessories plus a food court and customer service lounge. The complex is close to Colonial Mall and Barefoot Landing, so you can have non-stop shopping.

For those of you who remember — or have heard about — the Highway 501 **Waccamaw Factory Shoppes,** (843) 236-8200, (800) 444-8258, be advised that many of the stores are currently closed. This once-huge, sprawling bargain paradise is in transition with only QVC and a handful of other shops open.

A huge new enclosed mall on a 170-acre site at the intersection of U.S. 17 Bypass and U.S. 501 at Harrelson Boulevard (on the south side near Myrtle Beach International Airport) will fulfill your shopping dreams. The **Coastal Grand-Myrtle Beach**, (843) 839-9100, is a 1.5-million-square-foot shopper's paradise. The mall offers five anchor department stores including Belk, Dillard's and Sears, and roughly 120 other stores, featuring national and regional retailers. Here you'll find everything from Victoria's Secret and Glamour Nails to the Gap, Bed, Bath & Beyond, Express, Starbucks, American Eagle Outfitters and Zales Jewelers. The mall features a selection of international and specialty food vendors plus a number of popular free-standing restaurants. A Cinemark movie complex features stadium seating in each of its 14 theaters.

Other shopping destinations include **Broadway at the Beach**, 1325 Celebrity Circle, (843) 444-3200; **Colonial Mall**, 10177 N. Kings Hwy.,(843) 272-4040; and, the **Myrtle Beach Flea Market**, 3820 South Kings Highway (843) 477-1550.

Attractions

The Grand Strand draws visitors by the thousands to an awesome range of attractions, including themed water parks, amusement rides, museums (both educational and just plain fun), arcades, go-cart tracks, sightseeing cruises and so much more. The listings in this section are a very small sampling of what's available so make plans to stop by

or phone the visitor centers listed in Tourist Information above.

You won't want to miss the array of shops along Ocean Boulevard. Places like the Gay Dolphin Gift Cove and the ubiquitous Wings, Eagles and Pacific Discount beach accessories stores make the stopping worthwhile, not to mention a plethora of small shops filled with fun beachy stuff.

For more than 50 years, the **Myrtle Beach Pavilion Amusement Park** on the oceanfront at Ocean Boulevard and Ninth Avenue N., (843) 913-5200, (800) 819-2282, has been the symbolic heart of Myrtle Beach. Summer 2006 marks its farewell season. After that, it will close forever. Those who have fond childhood memories of summers screaming down the slope of the wooden roller coaster will mourn its passing. Still, for one last season, you can enjoy this 11-acre playground and its 40 fun-filled rides, the arcade, skill games, shops, haunted house and snack concessions. **The Attic**, Myrtle Beach's only non-alcoholic, under-21 night club, located on the property, will continue to operate

The **NASCAR SpeedPark**, U.S. Hwy.17 Bypass at 21st Avenue N., (843) 918-8725, features action-packed excitement year-round for the whole family, with seven custom stock-car tracks, race simulators and racing games, plus the interactive games found in the SpeedDome.

Family Kingdom Amusement Park & Water Park, 300 S. Ocean Boulevard, (843) 626-3447, is the home of the legendary all-wooden roller coaster, the Swamp Fox, along with an interactive laser dark ride called The Pistolero and the 110-foot Slingshot. Among the park's 33 other rides and attractions is a section called Kiddie Land with 18 rides for very young children. This is the Grand Strand's only oceanfront water park.

Be sure to visit **Ripley's Aquarium**, (843) 916-0888, which is located at the edge of Broadway at the Beach. Fascinating sea life exhibits and enlightening programs are an integral part of this award-winning attraction. Sharks, jellyfish, stingrays and exotic fish are among the many creatures on display. The "Titanic" exhibit is well worth seeing.

Combine the excitement of a Las Vegas casino with the flair of a Southern riverboat to understand the appeal of the **Southern**

Elegance Casino Cruise, 4491 Waterfront Avenue in Little River. The 175-foot Southern Elegance is docked along the historic waterfront in Little River (about three miles north of North Myrtle Beach off U.S.17) and offers cruises daily. All three decks are devoted to casino entertainment. Las Vegas–style live dealer table games are offered on one deck, video poker and more than 200 slot machines are located on all decks. The Southern Elegance also features an observation deck, food and beverage service, an elevator and a full-service lounge that is available for private parties. For more information or cruise schedules, contact the Southern Elegance Casino Cruise office at (843) 249-9811 or (877) 250-LUCK (5825), in Wilmington call (910) 798-0250. Free shuttle service to and from the ship is provided.

The **Hurricane Fleet Deep Fishing Center**, (910) 579-3660, (800) 373-2004, offers a variety of cruise opportunities designed to show off the charms of the Myrtle Beach area from the waterway. These tours originate from Hurricane Fleet Marina, The Waterfront at Calabash in Calabash, North Carolina. One of the most popular excursions, the Dolphin Adventure Cruise, takes passengers from inland waterways to the ocean, where they can get a close-up glimpse of fishing vessels, shrimpers at work, or dolphins at play. Cost for this cruise is $21 per person ages 12 or older, and $18 per person for those younger than 12. Group rates are available. Call ahead for reservations or to inquire about schedules and deep-sea fishing cruises. All of the boats are U.S. Coast Guard approved. Fishing gear — bait, tackle, rods and reels — are supplied on all fishing cruises.

Entertainment

Nightlife and Myrtle Beach are practically synonymous. Live music, dancing, dinner attractions and stage shows form the core of one of the most active seaside scenes anywhere, and there are plenty of open-air bars along the boardwalk in which to relax over a drink with the sound of the surf as the backdrop.

All the fun after dark is not reserved only for adults. A nonalcoholic nightspot, **The Attic**, a club at the Myrtle Beach Pavilion, (843) 913-5200, caters to people younger than 21

who enjoy dancing, music and socializing. The Attic is open seasonally. Call for hours.

The preeminent dinner attractions and live theaters in the area are quite touristy, and tickets may be a bit pricey, but the shows are consistently well-done and family-friendly. Reservations are recommended for all of them. The first of its kind in the area, **The Carolina Opry** at the north junction of U.S. 17 Bypass and U.S. 17 Business, (843) 913-4000 or (800) 843-6779, is one of the state's top tourist attractions. Shows offer a mix of comedy and music — standard country hits, bluegrass, gospel and medleys drawn from popular oldies — plus a special Christmas spectacular.

Legends in Concert, 301 U.S. 17 Business S. in Surfside Beach, (843) 238-7827 or (800) 960-7469, and Tribute! The Concert, 701 Main Street in North Myrtle Beach, (843) 913-4444, (800) 313-6685, are Vegas-style musical extravaganzas featuring impersonations of famous performers of yesterday and today such as Frank Sinatra, Rod Stewart, Marilyn Monroe, Elvis and Ray Charles.

In the 1970s, a then-unknown group named Alabama played for tips in Myrtle Beach, earning a loyal following. Having since achieved superstardom, Alabama opened the 2,000-seat **Alabama Theatre**, 4750 U.S. 17 S., (843) 272-1111 or (800) 342-2262, at Barefoot Landing in North Myrtle Beach. The theatre features **One - the Show**, a one-of-a-kind entertainment experience combining music, comedy and Las Vegas–style glitz. On most weekends throughout the year, Alabama Theatre features touring celebrity performers such as Kenny Rogers, the Oak Ridge Boys, Eddie Miles, Billy Ray Cyrus, the Coasters, Drifters and The Platters.

One of the area's two dinner attractions, **Dolly Parton's Dixie Stampede Dinner & Show**, 8901-B U.S. 17 N. Business, (843) 497-9700 or (800) 433-4401, is a theatrical icon of Southern culture, complete with music, horsemanship and a colorful depiction of the conflict between the North and South. The 90-minute show, held in a huge 35,000-square-foot arena, is complemented by an impressive four-course dinner. Shows are staged nightly at 6 PM (6 and 8 PM during the summer and on weekends in December).

Travel back in time at the **Medieval Times Dinner & Tournament**, 2904 Fantasy

Way, for a hearty medieval feast. While you eat, chivalrous knights engaged in authentic jousting matches and hand-to-hand combat try to win your favor and the hand of a chosen Queen of Love and Beauty. The "castle," air-conditioned and wheelchair accessible, is located at the Fantasy Harbour-Waccamaw entertainment complex near Waccamaw Factory Shoppes on U.S. 501. For reservations, call (843) 236-8080 or (888) 935-6878.

One of the grandest entertainment complexes anywhere in the region is **Broadway at the Beach** on U.S. 17 Bypass at 21st Avenue N. Open year-round, this 350-acre attraction includes no fewer than 10 nightclubs in Celebrity Square, a lively nightlife venue. The grand Palace Theatre, (843) 448-9224, (800) 905-4228, seats more than 2600 and is home to Spirit of the Dance, a popular Irish dance show. It also hosts several different productions throughout the year. There are 20 restaurants (including Jimmy Buffet's Margaritaville and a pyramidal Hard Rock Cafe), a 23-acre lake featuring water-taxi tours and pedal boats, kiddie rides in Carousel Park and three hotels, plus enough specialty shops and boutiques to satisfy the most die-hard shoppers. For more information, call the offices at (843) 444-3200 or (800) 386-4662.

Here you'll also find Myrtle Beach's largest movie complex, the 16-screen Carmike **Broadway Cinema**, (843) 445-1600, plus **Ripley's Aquarium**, (843) 916-0888, the six-story movie screen housed at **IMAX Discovery Theater**, (843) 448-4629, and **Gondola Adventures**, a romantic tour in the tradition of old Venice, (843) 278-8148.

Adventure in Science, History & Nature, featuring "The H.L. Hunley Experience," (843) 913-7899, is an interactive, historically accurate exhibit devoted to the Civil War–era submarine the H.L. Hunley. It is housed in the new 4,200-square-foot Adventure in Science, History & Nature building. **MagiQuest**, (843) 913-9460, is an exciting, interactive family attraction utilizing patented technology to create a magical experience. After selecting a personal wand, participants are quickly trained as "Magi," allowing them to set off lightning bolts, control music, open treasure chests and perform heroic deeds.

Golf

The Grand Strand area boasts approximately 120 regulation courses, some designed by top names in the game, including Palmer, Fazio, Dye, Norman, Love and Nicklaus. Add in the mild year-round sub-tropical temperatures, a wide variety of accommodations and attractive golf packages, and the area's self-proclaimed title as the "Golf Capital of the World" is well-justified.

There are also plenty of driving ranges, par 3 courses and pro shops scattered up and down the Strand. Greens fees are lowest from November through February, and golf packages are accordingly most affordable during that time. When you tire of serious golf or just want to have fun with your family or friends, try some of the nearly 50 miniature golf courses — many are quite creative.

The **Myrtle Beach Area Convention and Visitors Bureau**, (843) 626-7444 or (800) 356-3016, can provide details on golf packages, or you can call **Myrtle Beach Golf Holiday**, (800) 845-4653, for a free color Golf Vacation Planner. Another good source for information is Myrtle Beach's golf magazine, On The Green, and accompanying DVD, available at chamber of commerce offices and visitors centers.

One of the longest-running annual Myrtle Beach golf highlights is the PGA Tour Superstore World Amateur Handicap Championship presented by DuPont, celebrating its 23rd year in 2006. Dubbed "The World's Largest Single Site Golf Tournament," this popular competition is played on 75 of the area's courses over the four-day event in late August/early September. It is the largest tournament of its kind with an incredible 4,000 players journeying from all over the United States and even from many foreign countries to compete. For more information on this and other area competitive golf events, call (800) 833-8798.

MURRELLS INLET, SOUTH CAROLINA

Growing in popularity, with a personality quite different from its big sister to the north,

Murrells Inlet is well worth the extra 10- or 20- minute drive. A true old fishing village, the Inlet is known for its delectable seafood; in fact it's called the "Seafood Capital of South Carolina." Fresh grouper, flounder, shrimp, clams, oysters and crabs are prepared by chefs at more than 30 restaurants along the creek.

Here you can walk among the wetlands, cruise the creek and tour the salt marsh. Rich in history, folklore and tales of pirate treasure, Murrells Inlet will captivate you. If you didn't stop to pick up tourist information before now, you can find it at the **Myrtle Beach Area Chamber of Commerce, South Strand Office**, 3401 U.S. 17 S. (Business), Murrells Inlet, (843) 651-1010. For starters, be sure to check out these places.

Brookgreen Gardens, U.S. Highway 17 S., 1931 Brookgreen Gardens Drive, Murrells Inlet, (843) 235-6000 or (800) 849-1931, demands a visit. Brookgreen, which is listed on the National Register of Historic Places, is located on a 300-acre section of a 9,100-acre coastal South Carolina wildlife preserve. Brookgreen boasts the first and largest permanent outdoor installation of American figurative sculpture. It features more than 550 works by hundreds of top-name sculptors and continues to expand in scope. Guided tours, lectures and occasional workshops and concerts are offered at this combination arboretum, aviary and outdoor museum. Brookgreen Gardens is 18 miles south of Myrtle Beach, off U.S. 17 at the south end of Murrells Inlet.

The gardens are open daily from 9:30 AM to 5 PM, but are closed Christmas Day. From the end of March through April, Brookgreen is open until 8 PM. The gardens are at their peak during this time and offer an unforgettable display of color. Admission is $12 for adults ages 19 to 64; $10 for seniors 65 and older, $10 for children ages 13 through 18, and free for children 12 or younger. The admission ticket is good for seven consecutive days. Admissions are sold until 30 minutes before closing time. Free wheelchairs and strollers are available on a first-come, first-served basis. Lunch is served at the Pavilion Restaurant 11:30 AM to 2:30 PM. Light refreshments including coffee, cappuccino, wine, beer, desserts, scones and muffins are available at The Old Kitchen from 10 AM to 4 PM. Or, bring your own picnic as tables are provided, but don't feed the alligators.

Huntington Beach State Park, directly across from Brookgreen Gardens on U.S. Highway 17 S. (16148 Ocean Highway), three miles south of Murrells Inlet, (843) 237-4440, has a pristine beach, freshwater lagoon, maritime forest, nature trail and boardwalk out in the salt marsh. It offers opportunities to observe the coast's diverse natural environment, watch tall wading birds, pelicans and raptors, glimpse alligators and commune with the wildlife. You can swim in the ocean and go crabbing, surf fishing or picnicking and camping (127 campsites). Huntington Beach State Park is the site of the historic Atalaya castle. The former winter home and studio of noted American sculptress Anna Hyatt Huntington and her husband Archer Milton Huntington, Atalaya is also listed as a National Historic Landmark. Park hours November through March are daily 6 AM to 6 PM; April through October, hours are 6 AM to 10 PM. Admission is $5 for adults age 16 and older; $3 for children ages 6 through 15 and free for children younger than age 6; South Carolina seniors age 65 and older pay $3.25. Pets are allowed in most outdoor areas, however they must be under physical restraint or on a leash not longer than six feet.

Head boats are available for 5-hour, 9-hour, 11-hour and 25-hour trips at **Capt. Dick's Marina**, 4123 U.S. 17 Business (Kings Highway South) on the waterfront in Murrells Inlet, (843) 651-3676 or (866) 557-FISH (3474). Capt. Dick's offers private charters as well as inlet fishing and shark fishing. Cruises include ocean sightseeing cruises and the Saltwater Marsh Explorer Adventure. Parasailing is available as well as Jet Ski, pontoon and boat rentals. Reservations are recommended. It's open March through November. Spring and fall hours are 9 AM to 5 PM; Memorial Day to Labor Day hours are 5 AM to 10 PM.

One of the most popular dining establishments is **Drunken Jack's** on U.S. 17 Business on the waterfront in Murrells Inlet, (843) 651-2044. The restaurant features seafood "right off the boat," prepared to perfection grilled, blackened, sautéed or Southern-fried and served with their famous hush puppies and honey butter. It's open daily for dinner from 4:30 to 10 PM. December and January hours vary and are usually weekends only, so call for times.

NORTH CAROLINA'S CENTRAL COAST

Within a two-hour drive north by northeast up the Ocean Highway (U.S. Highway 17) from Wilmington are a multitude of daytrip possibilities. The Central Coast area (Bogue Banks, Morehead City and quaint Beaufort), also known as the Crystal Coast, and nearby historic New Bern, as well as the waters that surround and connect them, promise delightful opportunities.

The Crystal Coast area shares much in common with the Cape Fear Coast. Both boast beautiful waters, miles of oceanside communities, great restaurants and, of course, deep historical roots. However, they are different enough to make visiting each of them a unique experience.

Boaters visiting this area will be charmed by its amenities. Most marinas are just a short stroll from shopping, dining, historic sites and services. A fast powerboat can reach the area from Wilmington in several hours. Although some people make this a daytrip on the water, you'll have more time to enjoy the local attractions if you drive.

By car, simply head up U.S. Highway 17 until it intersects N.C. Highway 24 in Jacksonville. Go east on N.C. 24 toward Beaufort. It is a trip of less than 100 miles from Wilmington, and there are many views of North Carolina's waters and coastal communities along the way.

An interesting shortcut passes through the U.S. Marine base at Camp Lejeune. If you care to try it, veer off U.S. 17 onto N.C. Highway 172 at Folkstone, heading toward Sneads Ferry. People who have never been on a military base will find this an unusual environment, with tank-crossing signs and trucks filled with Marines training in artillery practice. Be prepared to stop for questioning by a sentry at the gate. After crossing the base, go east on N.C. Highway 24. From time to time the base portion of N.C. 172 may be closed because of troop movements or maneuvers taking place; if so, simply return the way you came and turn right on N.C. 210 to rejoin U.S. 17.

To take a self-guided tour of Camp Lejeune, obtain a visitor's pass and tour book at the base Visitor Center, located at the main gate on N.C. 24 in Jacksonville; call for information (910) 451-7426. This is a great way to become familiar with the base, its history and environment. The tour consists of 25 points of interest marked by large, white, numbered signs that coincide with site numbers in the tour book. The tour takes you from pre-Colonial America to the cutting edge of technology.

Crystal Coast tourist information, maps and brochures are available at the **Crystal Coast Visitors Center**, 3409 Arendell Street, Morehead City, (252) 726-8148 or (800) 786-6962. Another useful resource is the Insiders' Guide® to North Carolina's Central Coast & New Bern; www.insiders.com/crystalcoast.

Swansboro

Swansboro, a historic coastal town that dates back to around 1730, is a pleasant stopover after about an hour and a half of car travel from Wilmington. Situated on the White Oak River and the Intracoastal Waterway, this lovely little town is surrounded by water on three sides.

Swansboro has a particularly charming downtown historic area lined with antiques shops, boutiques, art galleries and restaurants. Look for signs leading to the district just off N.C. 24. The area is concentrated within three blocks on the shores of the White Oak River. Parking is free, the merchants are friendly, and there are several quaint and interesting shops, including **Russell's Old Tyme Shoppe**, (910) 326-3790; **Noah's Ark**, (910) 326-5679; **Silver Thimble Gift Shoppe**, (910) 326-8558; **Gray Dolphin Boutique**, (910) 326-4958; **The Brass Binnacle**, (910) 326-2448; and **Through the Looking Glass**, (910) 326-3128.

The historic district is a great stopover for lunch or dinner. **Captain Charlie's Seafood Paradise,** 106 Front Street, (910) 326-4303, is a memorable place to enjoy some of North Carolina's best fried seafood. It serves dinner only. For breakfast or lunch, check out **Yana's Ye Olde Drug Store**, 119 Front Street, (910) 326-5501, where you can enjoy omelets, pancakes, old-fashioned milk shakes, made-to-order burgers and homemade onion rings in a '50s atmosphere. **Gourmet Cafe**, 99 Church Street, (910) 326-7114, has an extensive wine list and offers tasty lunch and dinner options. Lunch choices include salads, build-your-own sandwiches and homemade desserts. Dinner specialties include seafood, beef and veal. **Church Street Coffee and Deli**, 105 Church Street, (910) 326-7572, offers gourmet meats. It's open for coffee in the morning and lunch.

Bogue Banks

Back on N.C. 24, travel another 10 minutes to the intersection with N.C. Highway 58. A right turn is the western entrance to Bogue Banks, a barrier island separated from the mainland by Bogue Sound. You can choose to continue straight on N.C. Highway 24 or cross the bridge to take a parallel route on the barrier island. The bridge is worth the detour because its high arc gives motorists a dramatic view of the Intracoastal Waterway.

The beach communities along approximately 30 miles of the island are widely varied in tone. **Emerald Isle, Indian Beach** and **Salter Path** offer an astonishing diversity of neighborhoods, ranging from expensive beach homes and condominiums to fishing trailers. There are also a few attractions for the kids, including miniature golf, waterslides and bumper boats.

Pine Knoll Shores is an exclusive residential area of windswept live oaks and kudzu with attractive single-family homes and condominiums as well as hotels and the occasional restaurant. This beach is also home to the **North Carolina Aquarium at Pine Knoll Shores**, which has just reopened after an extensive expansion and remodeling. Educational programs and field trips are offered year-round. For information, call the Aquarium's off-site office at (866) 294-3477.

At the eastern end of the island is **Atlantic Beach**, a smorgasbord of beach amenities fishing piers, shopping opportunities, boat rentals, fast food places, full-service restaurants and motels.

Just beyond Atlantic Beach on the eastern tip of Bogue Banks is **Fort Macon State Park**, (252) 726-3775, an old Civil War fort and 385-acre state park. The old fort has been totally restored to the Civil War period and is open for tours, either guided or on your own. Take a picnic and make a day of it.

Visitors have access to picnic tables, outdoor grills, shelters, restrooms and drinking water in addition to the nature trails, abundant plant life and beachfront.

Morehead City

Cross over the bridge at the eastern end of Bogue Banks and enter Morehead City, home to the North Carolina State Port Authority — something else Wilmington and the Crystal Coast have in common — and a multitude of restaurants specializing in fresh seafood. The undisputed traditional leader of dining in Morehead City is the **Sanitary Fish Market & Restaurant**, 501 Evans Street, (252) 247-3111. The restaurant seats 600 diners and serves fresh broiled or fried seafood, homemade chowders and Tar Heel hushpuppies that truly melt in your mouth.

Capt. Bill's Waterfront Restaurant, 701 Evans Street, (252) 726-2166, is open for lunch and dinner and serves fresh-catch seafood with traditional hushpuppies, cole slaw, chowders and fresh pies. Finz Grill of Morehead, 105 S. Seventh Street, (252) 726-5502, occupies the former headquarters of the Morehead Gulf Oil Company. Open for lunch and dinner, it features fresh local seafood as the specialty of the house. Dine outside on nice days and enjoy the view from a second-story deck.

Downtown Morehead City is the home of the FishWalk, a series of wonderfully life-like, colorful art sculptures depicting various indigenous fish and other types of sea life. Each piece is a cement block covered on four sides with glazed stoneware plates, creating a textured mural. Located along the waterfront, Arendell Street and side streets, the FishWalk will eventually include 25 pieces.

The History Place, 1008 Arendell Street, (252) 247-7533, interprets the history of the Cape Lookout region from Native Americans through modern development. Admission is free, however groups are charged $2 per person for guide services. A tea room and gift shop are on site.

Morehead City offers a wide variety of shopping opportunities but none are more charming than the waterfront area facing Bogue Sound. Stroll along Evans Street and enjoy some of the shops that tempt you. **Dee Gee's Gifts and Books**, (252) 726-3314, is a waterfront tradition that offers a large selection of books, including local and regional titles. Also check out the selection of gifts, cards and nautical charts. **Windward Gallery**, (252) 726-6393, offers oils, pastels and acrylics by local artists, and **Arts & Things**, (252) 240-1979 has a fine array of art supplies and works by local and international artists.

Beaufort

Just a few miles from Morehead City is the magical town of Beaufort. Beaufort is so gorgeous it seems more like a postcard than a real place. This little laid-back coastal community nestles up to international waters and is a gateway from the Atlantic Ocean to America's waterways. Taylor's Creek, the body of water in front of the town's quaint commercial district, is filled with sailcraft and powerboats from all over the world. Just up Taylor's Creek you can catch sight of a menhaden fishing fleet. Beyond that is Core Sound and a view of Harkers Island, home to some of this country's earliest shipbuilders.

Beaufort boasts a very unusual view: wild horses on **Carrot Island** across from the waterfront. The horses are stocky, furry steeds that pretty much care for themselves on their little windswept island. In a world where horses are rarely seen running free, this is a stirring sight. If you want a closer look, ask about boat tours that depart from the Beaufort docks. The island chain across from the Beaufort Waterfront is the Rachel Carson Estuarine Research Reserve. Free guided tours are offered each month from April to August. Inquire at the North Carolina Maritime Museum about tour times. One catch: You have to provide your own water transportation to get to the island. If you use the ferry service, expect to pay up to $8 ($4 for kids) for a round-trip journey, but remember the island tour is free.

A fascinating history lesson awaits you when you visit the **Old Burying Ground**, where there are more than 200 markers predating the Civil War. Stories are told about a British officer buried standing up and the girl who died at sea and was preserved in a rum barrel until her father could get her home. Admission is free, but guided tours are available at $5 for adults and $3 for children.

The sheer beauty of the scenery at the Beaufort waterfront is enough to lull a visitor into sitting in a pleasant trance for a long time, but there is also the allure of nearby shops and attractions. Within an easy walk are stores, many appealing restaurants and the **North Carolina Maritime Museum**, 315 Front Street, (252) 728-7317, an 18,000-square-foot building that pays tribute to North Carolina's coastal heritage, natural resources and maritime history. The museum boasts the **Harvey W. Smith Watercraft Center** just across the street, a facility where students and craftsmen build wooden boats in traditional North Carolina design and welcome visitors to take a peek at boats-in-progress. As you stroll downtown, don't miss the **Beaufort Historic Site**, (252) 728-5225 or (800) 575-7483, enclosed by white picket fences in the 100 block of Turner Street. These authentically restored buildings and the costumed guides offer a fascinating glimpse of coastal Carolina living in the 18th and 19th centuries. Site tour and visitor information, special exhibits and historic artifacts are available on the grounds at the **Safrit Historical Visitor Center**, 130 Turner Street.

Shoppers will enjoy a variety of stores along the waterfront. **The Rocking Chair Book Store**, 400 Front Street, (252) 728-2671, has a fine selection of books for children and adults. **Scuttlebutt Nautical Books and Bounty**, 433 Front Street, (252) 728-7765, sells a large selection of books about the sea and boating. NOAA charts, cruising guides and chart books make this a must-stop for passing boaters. **Lavaughn's Pottery**, 517 Front Street, (252) 728-5353, is a show-stopper for shoppers interested in an extensive line of ceramics crafted by regional and local artists. **Boathouse By Jarrett Bay**, 507 Front Street, (252) 728-6363, is a good shop to buy gifts for boaters and home decor, and it's the only place to find must-have Jarrett Bay apparel. **The General Store**, 515 Front Street, (252) 728-7707, has hand-dipped ice cream for your summer daytripping pleasure. Highlighting North Carolina artists and craftsmen, **Handscapes Gallery** in Somerset Square on Front Street, (252) 728-6805, offers pottery, jewelry, paintings, glass creations and metalwork.

While shopping, don't miss **The Old Beaufort Shop**, 130 Turner Street, (252) 728-

5225, housed in the Safrit Historical Visitor Center . This unique shop is operated by the Beaufort Historical Association and offers one-of-a-kind items made by BHA volunteers, such as original photography, handmade dolls, books on local history and herb cuttings.

Diners will be overwhelmed with restaurant possibilities. **The Beaufort Grocery Co.**, 117 Queen Street, (252) 728-3899, a lunch and dinner restaurant, offers fine dining and a full delicatessen. Breads and desserts are baked daily. The **Front Street Grill at Stillwater** on the Beaufort waterfront at 300 Front Street, (252) 728-3118, has a reputation as an interesting restaurant that uses unusual spices in fresh presentations of seafood, chicken, pasta and homemade soups. Keep in mind they close for the winter months.

Spouter Inn, 218 Front Street, (252) 728-5190, is a charming spot where diners can enjoy a memorable clam chowder, creative seafood specialties and a great view thanks to its waterfront location. **Clawson's 1905 Restaurant & Pub**, 429 Front Street, (252) 728-2133, long a dining fixture on the Beaufort waterfront, serves wonderful all-American fare. Its coffee bar, known as Fishtowne Java, serves high-octane caffeine drinks.

New Bern

They say, "North Carolina Begins Here," in the city of New Bern, which lies along North Carolina's largest river, the Neuse. The Neuse River is one of the state's premier sailing areas because of the width and depth of the water. You'd have to try really hard to run aground in a sailboat on the Neuse. Car travelers will appreciate the lovely view of the river and will certainly enjoy the many opportunities to shop, dine and stay overnight in historic New Bern, which was settled by the Swiss and Germans in 1710. Reach it by car from Beaufort by taking U.S. 70 W. into New Bern. If traveling from Wilmington, take U.S. 17 N.

You may be interested to know that New Bern is the place where Pepsi Cola was invented. This uniquely historic town was the site of the first incorporated school in North Carolina, the permanent State Capitol Building, the first meeting of the North Carolina Legislature, the state's first bank, the first

public school for African-Americans, the state's first press and many more firsts.

At the heart of New Bern's past and present is **Tryon Palace Historic Sites & Gardens**, 610 Pollock Street, (252) 514-4900 or (800) 767-1560. William Tryon chose New Bern as the first permanent capitol of the Colony of North Carolina in 1767. He built the Palace as a home befitting his stature as Colonial Governor and a suitably imposing seat of government for the British Colony. Architecture critics of the day called it the finest public building in the American colonies. When American patriots drove out the British in 1775, they made the Palace the first capitol of the new state. A few years after the capitol was moved to Raleigh in 1795, the Palace burned. The reconstructed Palace opened to the public in 1959 as North Carolina's first great public history museum. Admission to Tryon Palace also gives you admittance to the Stanley House, Dixon House, Hay House and the New Bern Academy Museum. All are open year-round with tours, crafts demonstrations and costumed interpreters.

The **New Bern Historical Society**, 513 Broad Street, (252) 638-8558, offers tours of the 1790 Attmore-Oliver House, which features a fascinating collection of 18th- and 19th-century furnishings, New Bern artifacts and Civil War relics. Entrance to the building is located at 510 Pollock Street. Discover three centuries of history in a 1-hour narrated Trolley Tour of historic downtown New Bern. For information call (252) 637-7316 or (800) 849-7316. The **New Bern Civic Theatre**, 414 Pollock Street, (252) 633-0567, presents a wide variety of live attractions year round. The Craven Arts Council and Gallery, 317 Middle Street, (252) 638-2577, showcases an eclectic variety of artistic endeavors.

The **New Bern Fireman's Museum**, 408 Hancock Street, (252) 636-4087, features an impressive collection of early firefighting equipment and rare photographs. Children of all ages will delight in **A Day at the Farm**, 183 Woodrow McCoy Road, (252) 514-9494, a historic New Bern dairy farm that features live animals, duck ponds, milking equipment, antiques, hay rides and more. For other attractions and expert touring advice, drop by the **New Bern/Craven County Convention & Visitors Information Center** at 203 S. Front Street or call (252) 637-9400 or (800) 437-

5767. Ask for the New Bern Historic Homes Tour, the African-American Tour, The Church and Cemeteries Tour or the Civil War Heritage Tour information.

Once you've toured to your satisfaction, it's time to eat. For a small town, New Bern has an abundance of outstanding restaurants across the full spectrum of prices and cuisine. **The Chelsea**, 335 Middle Street, (252) 637-5469, offers varied, unique dining experiences in a restored 1912 pharmacy. Downstairs seating captures a turn-of-the-century drugstore atmosphere, while the second floor is casual Victorian in flavor. Open for lunch and dinner, the eclectic menu features a wide range of international and regional cuisine.

Fred and Claire's Restaurant, 247 Craven Street, (252) 638-5426, is a great choice for dining in New Bern's historic district. Everything is made fresh daily, and the menu offers lunch options of specialty sandwiches, daily specials, quiche, soups and salads. Dinner choices range from omelets to fresh seafood. **Latitude 35**, located in the Sheraton New Bern Hotel & Marina, 100 Middle Street, (252) 638-3585, has a great seafood buffet on Fridays. **Captain Ratty's**, 202 Middle Street, (252) 633-2088, features an exceptionally large variety of grilled, steamed or broiled seafood.

If shopping is your reason to travel, New Bern has antiques stores and unique gift shops galore. **Elegant Days**, 236 Middle Street, (252) 636-3689 is a "treasure trove of old things." **Jane Suggs Antiques**, 228 Middle Street, (252) 637-6985, carries period furniture and reproductions, silver, porcelain and glassware. Don't let the office supplies and furniture fool you, **Branch's,** 309 Pollock Street, (252) 638-5171, offers a range of fine

Remember to take along your Insiders' Guide when you're wandering about and check it for new things to do — it's a great resource. Books are available for the Central Coast and Myrtle Beach as well. You can purchase them in local bookstores or by going online to www.insiders.com and clicking on the area of your choice.

giftware, furniture, accessories, birdfeeders, lawn ornaments and more. For the kids there's **Snapdragon Toys**, 214 Middle Street, (252) 514-6770, a shop of toys that range from educational to just plain fun. **Carolina Creations**, 317-A Pollock Street, (252) 633-4369, showcases the works of local artists, contemporary crafts, glass, wood and metal sculpture. **Mitchell's Hardware**, 215 Craven Street, (252) 638-4261, is a 101-year-old working hardware store that resembles an old-fashioned dry goods emporium with something for everyone.

New Bern is such a pleasant and interesting spot, it invites the visitor back again and again. There are beautiful hotels and inns in the historic downtown area on the water, including the **Sheraton New Bern Hotel & Marina**, (252) 638-3585 or (800) 326-3745; the **Comfort Suites Riverfront Park**, (252) 636-0022 or (800) 228-5150; the **Bridgepoint Hotel & Marina**, 101 Howell Road, (252) 636-3637 or (877) 283-7713; the **New Bern House Bed and Breakfast**, 709 Broad Street, (252) 636-2250, which features mystery tour weekends in a restored colonial revival home; **Harmony House**, (252) 636-3810; **Meadows Inn**, (252) 634-1776 or (800) 551-1776; **The Aerie,** (252) 636-5553 or (800) 849-5553; **Howard House Victorian Bed & Breakfast**, (252) 514-6709 or (800) 705-5261; and **Hanna House**, (252) 635-3209 or (866) 830-4371. These hotels and inns are particularly convenient to all the attractions and restaurants mentioned in this brief overview.

Points West

When you're looking for something to do on a beautiful summer or autumn day, take a ride "out west" on U.S. Highway 74/76 and make a few stops along the way. Passing through tobacco and cotton country, this main route between Wilmington and Interstate 95 has a lot to offer if you just take a side road here and there. We've highlighted some cool places for you to visit, all within a reasonable day's drive. Enjoy!

LAKE WACCAMAW

From downtown Wilmington, it's about 45 minutes to your first stop, **Lake Waccamaw**, which is located 10 miles east of Whiteville, and 38 miles west of Wilmington. From U.S. 74/76 turn south at Chauncey Town

Road (you'll see a green directional sign for the Lake Waccamaw Depot Museum), then go straight for about a mile into this lovely town.

Housed in the 1904 former Atlantic Coast Line depot is the **Lake Waccamaw Depot Museum**, 201 Flemington Drive. You can't miss the big red caboose beside the building! In the 1850s, the railroad made its way into Lake Waccamaw, connecting this rural town with the outside world. The railroad made way for industry and visitors to the beautiful waters of the lake. The museum houses exhibits that interpret the area's fascinating history, including a 300-year-old canoe, marine fossils, personal articles of early European settlers, photographs and present-day items from the Waccamaw Siouan Indians. The hours are Wednesday, Thursday and Friday from 10 AM to 3 PM and Sundays from 1 to 3 PM. Admission is free. The museum is handicapped accessible. For more information call (910) 646-1992.

Lake Waccamaw State Park is on Bella Coola Road off SR 1947, six miles south of the town. This is a great park for hiking, picnicking, primitive group camping, swimming, fishing and boating; educational and interpretive programs are offered, too. Park hours are: November through February 8 AM to 6 PM; March and October 8 AM to 7 PM; April, May and September 8 AM to 8 PM; June through August 8 AM to 9 PM; closed Christmas Day. The park office is open 8 AM to 5 PM daily, (910) 646-4748.

Lake Waccamaw is estimated to be about 250,000 years old. This unique, tea-colored, freshwater lake measures roughly 5 by 7 miles, with an average depth of 11 feet. It is the largest of the natural Carolina Bay Lakes, one of the great geological mysteries of the eastern United States. Lake Waccamaw covers almost 9,000 acres and has 14 miles of shoreline. Here you'll find species of animals found nowhere else on earth, rare plants and endangered species. Nearby, you can catch a glimpse of a botanical wonder — the Green Swamp.

WHITEVILLE

In Whiteville, Columbus County's bustling county seat, you'll definitely want to visit the **North Carolina Museum of Forestry** at 415 S. Madison Street, (910) 914-4185. Housed in a 17,226-square-foot former bank building, the museum even has a drive-through window! Exhibits feature curiosities of the forest, including 65-million-year-old petrified wood, 800-year-old cypress tree cookies, giant wood specimens, interactive displays, large murals and a Tool Room. Enjoy the North Carolina Tree Trail on the Museum grounds. Hours are Monday through Friday 9 AM to 5 PM, Saturday 1 to 4 PM and Sunday 2 to 5 PM. Admission is free and the facility is handicapped accessible.

CHADBOURN

Another popular railroad museum is located in Chadbourn, easily accessed from U.S. 76 south on N.C. Highway 410. The **Chadbourn Depot Museum**, at Colony and Railroad streets, was originally a passenger railroad depot. Built in 1910, the railroad was used for many years by travelers going north, south, east and west. Today, the museum tells the history of railroading. Also offered are historical displays and information about North Carolina's strawberry industry, which originated in Chadbourn. Every year on the first weekend in May, the town draws thousands of people to its annual N.C. Strawberry Festival, and the museum offers train rides (reservations required). Open to the public at no charge, museum hours are Tuesday 10 AM to 5 PM, Friday 10 AM to 4 PM and Sunday 2 to 5 PM. For information, call (910) 654-4590.

FAIR BLUFF

Railroad buffs can travel a bit farther down U.S. 76 to N.C. Highway 904, where they can check out the **Fair Bluff Depot Museum**, 339 Railroad Street. The depot was built in 1897 as an Atlantic Coast Line passenger and freight depot. This is the home of the Greater Fair Bluff Historical Society, which was founded in 1990 for the purpose of collecting and preserving records of the Fair Bluff area. On display are many artifacts from the early 1800s to the 1940s, railroad memorabilia and an electric train that travels through a replica of 1930s Fair Bluff. Here is a great place to research local family genealogies, too. Admission is free. Hours are Tuesday 10 AM to 4 PM and Sunday 2 to 4 PM and at other times by special arrangement. For information call (910) 649-7707or (910) 649-7415.

ORRUM

If you feel the urge to "get away from it all" for a day, the **Lumber River State Park** is a great place to do it, particularly if you're into paddle sports, as the river invites adventure and exploration. How about a quiet walk along the river or a picnic under Spanish-moss covered oaks? Come all you nature lovers and feast your eyes. Discover rare plants, watch wildlife, breathe fresh air and just enjoy being here. They say the fishing is great, too.

The Lumber River flows through south-central North Carolina into South Carolina. The State Park itself comprises 7,936 acres of land and 115 miles of river, of which 81 miles are designated as national wild and scenic. The remaining 34 miles are regarded as state natural and scenic.

Recreational activities are primarily at the Princess Ann Area near Orrum. There you'll find a visitor contact station within the park office, a small boat ramp, canoe camping, trails, a picnic area and a picnic shelter. This is a fairly small, remote kind of park and is definitely not commercial. You'll need to bring your own food, drinks (no alcohol) and comfort items. Additional primitive canoe camping is available at the Piney Island area. Three small sites and a large group site are located along an easy overnight section of the Lumber River.

The Lumber River State Park headquarters is located in Robeson County, 12 miles east of Fairmont off N.C. 130. From I-95, exit onto U.S. 74 east, from Wilmington take U.S. 74 west to S.R. 2225 (approximately mile marker 373). Turn south onto S.R. 2225 and travel to S.R. 2246, where you'll travel east for two miles to the park entrance. Hours are November through February 8 AM to 6 PM; March and October 8 AM to 7 PM; April, May and September 8 AM to 8 PM; June through August 8 AM to 9 PM. For information call (910) 628-9844.

SOUTH OF THE BORDER

You have to see it to believe it . . . South of the Border at I-95 Exit 1 at U.S. 301-501 is in Dillon, South Carolina. Self-proclaimed to be "world famous," Pedro's province lures travelers with clever signs for hundreds of miles along this busy highway. Anyone with an ounce of curiosity turns off to see what South of the Border is all about. Whoever Pedro's marketing agent is, he or she must be one of the most creative on this planet. You'll find Pedro's Campground, Pedroland mini theme park, Pedro's 22-story Sombrero Tower with glass elevator, Fort Pedro & Rocket City, El Drug Store, Mexico Shops, Club Cancun and eateries with names like The Hot Tamale and Ice Cream Fiesta. Oh yes, you can sleep here, too, at Pedro's South of the Border Motel, which includes 20 honeymoon suites.

LUMBERTON AREA

One of our favorite places to go is the **Southeastern North Carolina Farmers Market** on N.C. 74, 1 mile east of I-95. Open Monday through Saturday 8 AM to 6 PM and Sunday 1 to 6 PM, this is the place to find awesome fresh produce, country hams, plants, quilts, dolls, pottery, gift baskets and crafts. It's operated by the North Carolina Department of Agriculture & Consumer Services, and you can get information on special events or what's available seasonally at www.ncdamarkets.org or by calling (910) 618-5699.

Exploration Station is well worth the trip if you've got young children (ages 6 months to about 5 years). This is a super place for children to explore and learn through creative role-playing and interactive experiences. The center provides lots of fun activities and gives kids the opportunity to milk a cow, play in the castle, pretend to be a fireman, shop in a grocery store and examine real X-rays in a make-believe hospital. Newly added is a Weather Station where kids can try their hands at forecasting the weather. Exploration Station is at 104 North Chestnut Street, Lumberton. Hours are Tuesday, Wednesday and Friday 10 AM to 5 PM, Thursday 10 AM to 8 PM and Saturday 10 AM to 4 PM; closed Sunday and Monday. Adults must accompany children. Call for information, (910) 738-1114.

Take a self-guided walking tour of Lumberton for a new kind of adventure. Stop by the **Lumberton Area Chamber of Commerce**, 800 N. Chestnut Street, (910) 739-4750, to pick up a brochure and maps. Learn about Lumberton's fascinating history, and view all the interesting buildings, churches and significant structures. Stop along the way to visit places like the African-American Cultural Center.

The **Robeson County Museum**, 101 S. Elm Street, is housed in a former railway express station built in 1908. The museum has a rotating historic display and artifacts that recount Robeson County life from the earliest inhabitants to more recent past. Admission is free. Hours are Monday and Tuesday 9 AM to 1 PM, Tuesday and Thursday 1 to 5 PM, Saturday 10 AM to 2 PM. Phone for information, (910) 738-7979.

Step into another cultural dimension as you tour the **Museum of the Native American Resource Center**, featuring artifacts, arts and crafts from tribal Lumbee Indian life. Major displays include an authentic log canoe and a log cabin. A variety of half-hour films are available for viewing (by appointment only) and a gift shop is on the premises. Admission is free. Hours are 8 AM to 5 PM Monday through Friday. The center is located on the University of North Carolina at Pembroke campus in the Old Main Building facing N.C. 711. Phone for information, (910) 521-6282.

ELIZABETHTOWN AND WHITE LAKE

Adjacent to the Bladen Lakes State Forest, the 2,208-acre **Jones Lake State Park** is popular for hiking, picnicking, swimming, boating (10 horsepower or less), fishing and camping. The park includes two natural lakes. Jones Lake, which comprises 224 acres, has a shoreline of 2.2 miles. The lake is quite shallow — less than 9 feet. The 315-acre Salters Lake is undeveloped, and permission to use it must be obtained from park staff.

The park is located 4 miles north of Elizabethtown on N.C. 242. From Wilmington, drive west on U.S. 74/76. Turn right onto N.C. 87 and travel north toward Elizabethtown.

Turn right onto N.C. 87 Business. At the second light, turn right onto U.S. 701. Go north for one mile, take a left onto N.C. 53 then take an immediate right onto N.C. 242. Go north for two miles.

Fees are charged for swimming, campsites, canoe and paddleboat rentals. More than 50 tables, some with grills, are available at the picnic grounds. A new Visitors Center with museum and educational programs opened in spring 2005. Park hours are November through February 8 AM to 6 PM; March and October 8 AM to 7 PM; April, May and September 8 AM to 8 PM; June through August 8 AM to 9 PM. It's closed Christmas Day. Park office hours are 8 AM to 5 PM weekdays; it's closed state holidays. Call (910) 588-4550 for information.

Tory Hole Park, located on the banks of the Cape Fear River in Elizabethtown, is the site of a famous Revolutionary War battle. The area has picnic sites, a fitness trail, amphitheater and a playground. For information call (910) 862-2066. To reserve a picnic table under the gazebo, call (910) 862-3979.

The town of White Lake, located seven miles from Elizabethtown, has the 1,120-acre spring-fed **White Lake** as its centerpiece. With crystal clear water, a white sandy bottom and safe swimming conditions, the lake is ideal for a variety of watersports. Perfect for family vacations, the town hosts thousands of tourists each summer. Here you'll find campgrounds, RV parks, cottages and motel accommodations as well as many permanent homesites. Arcades, amusement parks, restaurants, gift shops, golf, and other activities are available nearby. Rentals are plentiful, including personal watercraft. Call (910) 862-4368.

SUN, SAND AND SEA

nsiders and returning visitors understand the appeal of North Carolina's southern coastal region. Warm, semitropical weather, sandy beaches, friendly people and Carolina-blue skies, combined with the lure of the sea, make this area paradise. Bathing suits, shorts, golf shirts and sandals are a must for coastal Carolina living. Is it any wonder that visitors from all over the world return year after year or choose to retire here?

Take leisurely walks along the shore. Romp in the gentle waves of the ocean or cruise the area's waterways. Relish the sun's warmth and the sway of ocean breezes. Stand barefoot in the sand and witness truly magnificent sunrises and awesome sunsets. All of these activities lift the spirit and create memories for a lifetime. However, there are some important precautions to take while enjoying the area's bounty, and we let you know about them in this chapter. The beauty and pleasures of North Carolina's southern coast are some of the best available. Enjoy your visit and return often. Many of the Insiders you'll meet here started out as visitors too.

The Sun

On the southern coast of North Carolina the skies are gorgeous, but beware the sun's rays and intense heat. Dermatologists and health officials caution against prolonged exposure to direct sunlight. By all means, enjoy your days on the beach but keep in mind some tips to make your vacation safe and pleasurable, especially if you're determined to return home with a tan instead of a painful and peeling sunburn.

SUN PROTECTION
No matter what your skin type, age or previous tanning experience, always wear sunscreen with the appropriate SPF (sun protection factor) when exposed to the sun. Select one with the best protection you can

find and slather it on all exposed skin. Reapply after coming out of the water. Make a habit of putting on sunscreen.

Skin protection is especially vital on the open beach for several reasons. Sand, water and concrete surfaces can reflect 85 percent of the sun's rays. The intensity of the sun has increased in recent years so even if you've never been sensitive to the sun before, it's wise to take steps to protect your skin from burning or sun damage. Don't be fooled by a cloudy day. Ninety percent of the sun's burning rays penetrate the clouds.

Children are especially vulnerable to the sun's damaging rays and require special protection. Nearly half of the damage to skin occurs in childhood and early adolescence. Dermatologists recommend using sunscreen with an SPF-15 or higher for children. Waterproof sunscreens will eliminate constant reapplications as children play in and out of the water. Protect infants with a hat, lightweight clothing, an umbrella and sunblock. Remember that while an umbrella shades the child from direct sunlight, the reflective rays of the sun are still present, making sunblock a necessity.

Hats, especially the wide-brimmed variety, are not only a fashion statement in coastal Carolina, but also a great covering for sensitive facial skin while providing shade against the sun's glare. Also a must for comfort in the summer's heat is lightweight, light-colored clothing. The natural fibers of cotton and linen are preferable because of their ability to "breathe" more than synthetic fabrics. In the heat and humidity of a summer's day here, you'll appreciate the difference.

Daylight hours between 11 AM and 3 PM are usually the hottest part of the day and pose the greatest risk for skin damage from the sun. Cover up or spend those hours doing indoor activities. The area abounds in things to do and see for every interest and every member of the family. Check out what's available in other chapters in this book.

Occasionally during the summer months, weather reports will broadcast a heat index warning for the area. This indicates that the sun's heat and the atmosphere's humidity have pushed temperatures to feel hotter than the thermometer reads. These conditions are very dangerous, especially to the elderly, small children and pets. Try to limit your outdoor exposure, especially at midday, and drink lots of fluids — particularly water. Take indoor breaks often, in air conditioning if possible, and avoid exertion.

The Sand

Ah, the beach! There's nothing like taking a walk on a sandy beach, barefoot and gazing out into the ocean. The benefits include gentle exercise and stress relief, not to mention the fact that sand is a natural pumice for the soles of your feet. Did you arrive with weary, calloused feet? Chances are good that they'll be a lot smoother when you leave.

Keep your eyes open for strange, mushy-looking dead critters on the beach and be sure not to step on or touch them. Definitely don't let the kids play with them! They may well be jellyfish or the infamous Portuguese Man of War; these can still inflict painful, dangerous stings even when they're dead. If per chance, you or someone you're with does get stung, either by one that is alive or dead, symptoms can range from mild to severe; the treatment for each type of jellyfish is different. Lifeguards are knowledgeable and will assist you in such circumstances; if none is available, however, seek proper medical attention immediately.

Access to area beaches is free because North Carolinians are rigid in their belief that the shores belong to the people. Look for the orange and blue signs at frequent intervals along beach roads — they point out easements between homes where you can freely cross over to the beach. Stick to these paths, and don't walk across private property to get to the beach.

You are free to walk the length of all area beaches, including those on private islands such as Bald Head and Figure Eight (although you'll need a private boat or, in the case of Bald Head Island, a passenger ferry to get there). Oceanfront landowners' property lines stop at the high-water mark.

BEACH TREASURES

Stay alert for hidden treasures in the sand when beachcombing. After storms and especially after hurricanes, seekers of shells and shark's teeth are wise to get out early to treasure hunt as the frenzied sea will have tossed abundant loot upon the shore. When searching for shark's teeth, look for a characteristic glint along the water's edge or in wet, course sand. These interesting artifacts are ebony in color and varied in shape. Don't limit yourself to just one beach. Travel along the coast and visit Topsail and Brunswick county beaches as well because each offers a different variety of shells. To bring out the colors of shark's teeth, try painting them with clear nail polish or get special spray from the local craft stores.

Are you spending the day on Brunswick County beaches? Frequent finds there are whole sand dollars, but make sure you don't take live ones. The all-white skeletal sand dollars are the ones you want. The brown, furry ones may still be alive and should be returned to the water. In addition, if you're lucky or very observant, you may find arrowheads from ancient Native American tribes. Considering the colorful pirate history in the area, who knows what else you might find in your search?

A DAY AT THE BEACH

Beach hospitality includes public restrooms, showers and rinse-off spots located conveniently along most beaches. Restaurants that offer everything from hot dogs and barbecue to fresh seafood and even vegetarian dining are an easy walk from the beach in many communities.

Preparations for a day at the beach should include a blanket or old quilt, towels, a cooler packed with soft drinks, water, iced tea or Gatorade, and beach apparel for the whole family. A beach umbrella gives some much appreciated shade when old Sol is really hot. No matter what you do, grains of sand are going to creep into everything, but a blanket will at least give you protection from the warm sand. Make sure everyone has a hat, sunglasses and sturdy foot covering. Asphalt, concrete and sand above the high-water mark get very hot, making it difficult and painful to walk to and from the parking areas.

Remember to bring something for preventing and treating insect bites as well. Sometimes the sand fleas and mosquitoes can be nasty. Away from the beach, no-see-ums come out late in the afternoon. You can't see the little rascals unless they're in a pack, but they'll think you're a delicious evening snack.

Some laws worth noting: Don't take glass containers on the beach; don't let your dog run loose until you check local ordinances (and in all cases clean up your pet's "business" so you or other people don't step in it); don't let your parking meter expire; don't take alcohol to the beach; and don't litter. Take an ashtray with you if you plan to smoke because, as inconsequential as a butt or two may seem, millions of them cause environmental problems. Filters are not biodegradable and can harm sea life. Trash cans are placed on most beaches, please use them.

The most important rule of all: Protect the sand dunes by not disturbing the sea oats or other precious vegetation. Dunes buffer beachfront property and minimize erosion from tropical storms and hurricanes. Dunes also provide sanctuary for fragile turtle nests and a variety of shore birds. Damaging the dunes or disturbing turtle nests and beach vegetation will incur stiff fines, not to mention the wrath of environmentally conscious residents. Crossovers are provided for you to walk from the street or beachfront property. Use them rather than trudging across the dune line.

Taking your dog to the beach? Dogs have special needs in the sun, sand and sea. Sand and pavement can get very hot in the sun and can actually burn the pads of dog's feet. Carry your dog across hot pavement and sand, or find another route. Also, be sure to provide your dog with plenty of fresh water so it won't be tempted to drink salt water, which can lead to diarrhea, vomiting and dehydration. And don't forget to hose your dog off after he swims in the ocean. Salt water can damage his coat.

Speaking of sea turtle nesting, this is an awesome ritual that has captivated locals and tourists all along the North Carolina coast, but especially from Topsail Island to Ocean Isle Beach. Although five species of these gentle giants have been seen, almost all the nesting effort is made by the most common sea turtle in the region, the loggerhead, which weighs from 170 to 500 pounds. Every year in May, loggerheads find their way here from places as far away as the Azores and Canary Islands.

A network of turtle projects with hundreds of volunteers monitor sections of the beaches, identify the nest sites and stand guard over them near the end of the approximately 60 days incubation. When the two-inch-long baby turtles emerge from a nest and head down the beach to the sea, excited "nest parents" are there to clear a path and make sure no predator will eat them before they reach the water. At hatching time, lights all along the beach are dimmed or extinguished so as not to confuse these intrepid creatures. It's quite an event to behold. Be sure to read the closeup "Go Wild All Night - Join a Turtle Watch!" in our Attractions chapter. For more information or to volunteer, call Nancy Fahey at the Wrightsville Beach Sea Turtle Project, (910) 791-4541.

Nighttime on the beach can be magical, and a quiet stroll in the moonlight is nearly irresistible. In the fall, your walk might kick up a strange phosphorescent phenomenon as you move across the water's edge. A night swim may tempt you as well, but be careful. Currents can push you away from your wading-in spot, and the darkness can disorient you. Remember that the law requires that swimming attire be worn while frolicking in the waves.

BEACH ACCESS AND PARKING

Beach accesses are available and clearly marked. Some offer public parking, others have metered spaces. Please use these accesses, not someone's front yard, to reach the beach. Property owners will appreciate your consideration.

Parking is free on the street in the off-season (from November through February). All other times, be sure to bring a pocketful of quarters for parking meters at both Wrightsville Beach and Carolina Beach. The metered spaces are usually good for several hours, so you don't have to race back and forth to stay legal. At the Wrightsville Beach pay stations, you can eliminate the quarters and pay for a block of time with bills or a credit card. Do take seriously restaurant and business lots that have signs warning against unauthorized parking. In some cases, towing is strictly enforced.

On **Wrightsville Beach**, public access with restrooms, metered parking and a shower are across S. Lumina Avenue from the Oceanic Restaurant and Crystal Pier near Nathan Avenue. Restrooms and a shower are at the foot of Salisbury Street near Johnny Mercer's Pier. To the north, metered parking is also available adjacent to the Holiday Inn Sunspree Resort and on either side of the Duneridge Resort, about 1 mile north of Salisbury Street. One of the Duneridge lots has restrooms. On summer weekends, unless you're parking a bicycle, arrive before 10 AM or after 2 PM to find a space.

In **Carolina Beach**, **Kure Beach** and **Fort Fisher**, clearly marked public beach access points with limited parking are situated at regular intervals; spaces in Carolina Beach are metered. Public restrooms and showers are available at Kure Beach Pier and Fort Fisher State Park; in Carolina Beach they are located at the Boardwalk, on Hamlet Avenue, Sandpiper Lane and Alabama Avenue; restrooms are the only facility at Carolina Beach Lake.

Carolina Beach also has pay parking lots requiring dollar bills all year long. Parking spaces in Carolina Beach's public pay lots are plentiful most of the time. Several large lots are located on Canal Drive near the Boardwalk and marina where the cruise and head boats are docked; others are on Hamlet, Atlanta Avenue and Lake Park Boulevard, U.S. 421 South and Sandpiper Lane.

Bald Head Island has three beach environments with three distinct personalities. East Beach was recently recognized on Dr. Beach's list of top beaches in the country. The 14 miles of South Beach are accessible by numerous beach accesses. West Beach is a favorite local fishing spot. The beaches of Bald Head Island are home to sea turtle nesting as well as recreation for residents and visitors. Beachgoers are expected to respect nature. To that end, pets must be leashed dusk to dawn during the turtle nesting

season, though they are free to roam under their owner's supervision at other times. Water scooters are prohibited within 100 yards of shore, but bicycles are allowed on the beaches.

On Caswell Beach Road along eastern Oak Island, about a half-mile east of the Oak Island Lighthouse at **Caswell Beach**, one public beach access consists of a large gravel parking lot with no facilities. The area is open 5 AM to 11 PM, and camping, alcohol, firearms, fires and cars on the strand are prohibited; however bicycles are permitted on the beach. Dogs are required to be on leashes on the strand, except between dawn and 9 AM, when they are allowed on the beach without a leash as long as they are under owner control. Dogs may not be on the dunes at any time. Any person walking a dog must have suitable accommodation for removal of dog waste. A second beach access has been added directly across the street from the lighthouse. Parking, however, is limited to one hour.

With 65 beach accesses and more than 900 parking spaces (some at the beach access and some nearby), the **Town of Oak Island** beach is one of the most accessible beaches to owners, renters and the public alike. The Cabana at the foot of 46th Street East has handicapped access, as have most of the beach accesses. Bicycles are permitted on the beach. Surfing is prohibited within 350 feet of the piers, a bonfire permit is required for open fires, water scooters are prohibited in swimming areas, and dogs must be leashed at all times.

Of the 22 public beach accesses on 11-mile-long **Holden Beach**, most have parking available either at the access or on nearby streets. Handicapped access is available at two of them. A few provide only neighborhood access with no parking. There is beach access and parking available in the pier area as well. Parking along Ocean Boulevard is prohibited. A Regional Beach Access facility with showers, restrooms and parking, open 6 AM to 11 PM, is located nearly under the bridge off Jordan Boulevard, Limited parking and covered tables are available there. Bicycles are permitted on the beach in the Town of Oak Island. Surfing is prohibited near the pier. Campfires, driving on the beach and the operation of Jet Skis or personal watercraft within 500 feet of the shoreline are prohibited as well.

Ocean Isle Beach boasts 26 public beach accesses, 18 of them indicated by CAMA signs, four handicapped accessible and 12 with parking. There is also parking available at both piers, but be aware that no overnight parking is allowed in town-owned parking areas. Ordinances against littering, glass containers and open fires are enforced, as are the prohibition of bicycles on the strand from April 30 until October 1. Surfing is prohibited within 1,000 feet of the pier. Dogs are not permitted on the beach strand between the hours of 9 AM and 6 PM from June 1 until August 31 and must be leashed at all times.

There is a beach access at the end of every street in **Sunset Beach**, each marked by a CAMA beach access regulation sign. Three of these accesses are handicapped accessible. Next to the 45-car parking lot off Main street you will find a gazebo (handicapped accessible) with a walkway and portable toilets. Sunset Boulevard, which offers 75 parking spaces and a landscaped walkway, runs south to Main Street and the ocean. The pier is convenient to the beach and pier facilities but requires $5 per day for parking. Surfing is permitted in designated areas, and bicycles are permitted on the beach. Pets are prohibited from Memorial Day through Labor Day and must be leashed at all other times.

BEACH DRIVING

Although most beaches in our region prohibit vehicles, there are two areas where beach drivers (especially those who fish) can indulge themselves. But driving out on the sand is a double-edged sword: vehicles that access these beautiful areas also erode and damage them. Beach drivers are urged to observe regulations closely, drive responsibly and use common sense.

Unless you have a four-wheel drive vehicle with suitable tires, don't try driving on the beach, even if the sand seems packed hard. You'd be surprised how easy (and embarrassing) it is to get stuck with a "regular" car, or even a 4WD lacking sufficient clearance or wide tires.

The **Fort Fisher State Recreation Area**, an undeveloped 4-mile beach strand and tidal marsh, located 5 miles south of Carolina Beach, off U.S. 421, permits four-wheel-drive

vehicles beyond the public bathing areas. A $10 per day vehicle access fee is charged; an annual permit which allows unlimited visits is $40. The recreation area allows vehicles to drive on this stretch of beach only during normal park operating hours.

Vehicle beach access permits are available for sale at the park's visitors center from 8 AM to 4:30 PM payable by cash, money orders or personal checks with proper identification. Annual permits are in the form of windshield stickers; day-use permits are to be hung from rear-view mirrors. These permits are not transferable to other vehicles. Violation of park rules may result in revocation of the vehicle beach access permit without refund. The beach vehicle access road is closed and locked 30 minutes prior to the park's scheduled closing, and all vehicles are required to exit the four-wheel drive access area at this time.

Passage onto the beach is through marked crossovers only, and vehicles must follow designated routes, avoiding dunes, vegetation and marked nesting areas. The sand here is loose and deep. Sharp drop-offs are common. At high tide, the strand becomes very narrow and may even prevent you from turning around; also, the marshy areas tend to flood. Plan accordingly. Please, please, respect this beautiful natural area and all of its precious wildlife, birds and sea creatures.

There is no admission fee to the other Fort Fisher park facilities, including parking, visitors center, restroom facilities, trails and beach areas that are accessible to foot traffic. Fort Fisher State Park's operating hours are: December through February 8 AM to 6 PM; March 8 AM to 7 PM; April and May 8 AM to 8 PM; June through August 6 AM to 9 PM; September 1-to 14, 6 AM to 8 PM; September 15 through November, 24-hour access. The park office is closed on all state holidays.

On the north side of **Carolina Beach**, there's an area affectionately known to locals as "the north end," where four-wheel-drive vehicles may be driven on the beach. However, this is not Daytona-style beach driving. Here, the speed limit is 15 miles per hour and vehicles without four-wheel drive and proper tires will become stuck in the loose sand.

Popular for many years with fishermen in particular, along with swimmers and camp-

Soaring pelicans are a common sight over local waters.

photo: Peter Doran

ers, the area, now called Freeman Park, is now under the control of and policed by the Town of Carolina Beach. Portable restrooms are available and fencing is in place to protect private property, turtle nesting areas and dunes. The admission fee is $10 per day; an annual pass is $40.

The Sea

The ocean and waterways of North Carolina's beautiful southern coast satisfy a wide range of interests. Whether your passion is swimming, boating, surfing, fishing or simply watching waves, the sea offers endless possibilities for exploration, education and contemplation.

Binoculars are great for spotting ships at sea, watching the playful dolphins and whales, and keeping an eye on pelicans as they dive under water for fish. As ships enter Wilmington, be sure to wave to the sailors on deck because inbound ships have probably been at sea for months and the guys seem eager for a friendly greeting.

If you have time, consider taking the ferry across the wide mouth of the Cape Fear River from Fort Fisher at the south tip of Pleasure Island to the charming village of Southport (or vice versa). Take some bread to feed the seagulls during the trip; these brazen beggars will actually eat from your hands, but be sure to count your fingers afterward!

SWIMMING

If swimming is your watersport or relaxation of choice, you've come to the right place. The ocean offers numerous possibilities for everyone from the wader to the long-distance swimmer. For your safety in late spring and summer, lifeguards are posted at many of the beaches in the area. If you see someone running into the water with an orange or red float in hand, it's probably a

If you spot a shark while you're in the water, get out immediately if possible. Keep in mind that sharks will come into shallow water, so you don't have to be out far to see one. In exiting the water, try to keep sight of the shark at all times so you can determine if the shark's movements are smooth and leisurely or erratic and agitated. If the latter, move swiftly to shore, a rock, or even a floating kelp canopy. Loudly call for help.

lifeguard. You can be called closer to shore if the lifeguard thinks you're getting too far out for your own safety. These trained professionals are looking out for your best interests.

Rip currents and undertows are unseen dangers lurking beneath the waves — dangers that Insiders respect. If you are swimming and are suddenly pulled in a frightening way by the currents, the most important thing to remember is to stay calm. Panic leads to exertion, which leads to dangerous fatigue. If you find yourself in a rip current, relax and let it carry you on its natural course toward the sea. Within a few minutes, it will dissipate. Then you can swim parallel to the shoreline to get out of the rip current area and back to shore. Do not try to swim straight back into shore against the rip current; you'll only tire yourself out.

A few don'ts: Don't swim in inlets because you may not be seen by a speeding boat; don't swim alone; and don't swim in the Cape Fear River at and below Wilmington unless you can tolerate the company of alligators and big ships. Although the river is not particularly wide, it is deep — up to 42 feet — and has fast currents that have to be experienced to be believed. If it looks like the river is flowing upstream (northward), it is, during high tide.

SURFING

Wrightsville Beach, Carolina Beach and Topsail Island are popular places for surfing, but there are some regulations, and you should know about designated surfing zones, which shift each day in Wrightsville Beach. You must wear a leash and will be immediately chastised if you are not attached to your board. Lifeguards are fastidious about enforcing this rule. (See our Watersports chapter for more complete information on surfing.)

TIDES AND WEATHER

The tides are such an important factor in coastal communities that their comings and goings are part of the daily weather forecast. Be aware of them if you splash out to sandbars or islands at low tide. Changing tides could make the trip back to shore a daunting swim.

Storms and threatening weather are taken seriously on the coast. Get out of the water and off the beach when these often-spectacular weather events take place. Lightning on the beach means business, and you should seek immediate shelter inside a building or in your car. Small-craft advisories are to be heeded without fail.

If a hurricane watch is announced, it's a good idea to make plans to leave the area. Should the watch upgrade to a hurricane warning, area beaches are often evacuated. Emergency management professionals have their hands full in these events so avoid adding to the confusion by sight-seeing on the beach. On the positive side, storms often will be simple summer showers that pass quickly. Take your cue from the lifeguards as to when it's safe to return to the water.

BOATING

Ready to go boating? If you trailer your own boat, there are ample public boat ramps throughout the entire area (see our Fishing chapter). If you choose to leave your boat at the water, the area's marinas offer a variety of services, including dry-dockage, wet slips and storage (see our Marinas and the Intracoastal Waterway chapter). Boating possibilities include the Cape Fear River and its adjacent branches, the Atlantic Ocean, the Intracoastal Waterway (ICW) and area lakes.

Fuel and other amenities are available on the southern coastline, generally on the ICW. If you don't have a boat of your own, you can take advantage of one of the charter services for sailing craft and, of course, tour and deep-sea fishing boats that cater to all cruising needs (see our Watersports and Fishing chapters for listings).

Boaters should understand the rules of the water when operating their own boats or chartering someone else's. Many waterways, especially the ICW at Wrightsville Beach and Carolina Beach, can become heavily congested. Educate yourself on boating safety and navigation rules before going out on the waterways (see our Watersports chapter for information about safety, resources, regulations and other topics of importance to boaters).

Sand dunes help protect barrier islands, so please use designated public access walkovers to get to the beach.

photo: Peter Doran

⊛ WATERSPORTS

Whether you're passionate about watersports or just an enthusiastic novice, North Carolina's southern coast is the perfect place to hone your skills. With its combination of mild weather, warm water temperatures, good water quality and clean, uncrowded beaches, the region's overall subtropical climate allows watersports enthusiasts to indulge their particular passions from early spring through late fall. Add the Intracoastal Waterway, sounds, tidal marshes, rivers and their tributaries to a generous Atlantic coastline, and the opportunities for fun in the water are limited only by your sense of adventure.

Please make note of local ordinances. For example, swimming and surfing are forbidden within 100 feet of most fishing piers. Disturbing or walking on protected dunes is strictly prohibited and carries a fine. Dogs are not allowed on most beaches, especially during the warm weather months. Some communities permit you to walk your dog on the beach in the off-season, but the animal must be leashed and you are responsible for cleaning up after it. Fort Fisher State Recreation Area on Pleasure Island permits leashed dogs year round, except in the swimming areas.

This chapter is divided into sections dealing with the area's most popular watersports, where to do them, helpful resources, related businesses and places to find equipment for sale or for rent. Other chapters of this book that address water-related topics include the Sun, Sand and Sea, Fishing and Marinas chapters.

Boating

At times, boating in the lower Cape Fear involves competition with oceangoing vessels, shallow water or the treacherous shoals that earned the Carolina coast the moniker "Graveyard of the Atlantic." In contrast, the upper Cape Fear River, its northeast branch

and the winding creeks of the coastal plain offer a genuine taste of the old Southeast to those with small boats, kayaks or canoes. Tannins leached from the cypress trees keep these waters the color of coffee. Many creeks are overhung by trees, moss and, in summer, the occasional snake. Early spring and late autumn are particularly good times to go, since there are fewer bugs. See our Fishing chapter for boat ramp locations.

SAFETY AND RESOURCES

Perhaps the most important thing about boating is preparation. File a float plan; it can be as official or informal as your circumstances require. The point is that you should tell someone where you're going and when you expect to return. You are required to have one life jacket for each person on your boat, and the Coast Guard is within its rights to stop you and see that you have proper equipment. Adults may use their own judgment about wearing a life jacket, but children (and pets) should wear one at all times. Life jackets may not be comfortable or glamorous, but they save lives.

The U.S. Coast Guard Auxiliary conducts free vessel safety checks. The exams are not required for boat registration. For information, call the Marine Safety Office at (910) 772-2200. You will be referred to the examining flotilla officer nearest you. Various flotillas of the local Coast Guard Auxiliary offer Safe Boating courses five times a year (autumn, winter, spring and twice in summer). Locations include the Wrightsville Beach Recreation Center (at Wrightsville Beach Park) and Cape Fear Community College in downtown Wilmington and the Hampstead campus. These courses are strongly recommended for everyone who operates a motor boat. The fee averages $35 and includes all materials. Also inquire about the America's Boating Class, available on CD/ROM, and the Basic Coastal Navigation course. For information call The Coast Guard at (910) 256-4224 or (910) 256-

The Only Kayak Shop at Wrightsville Beach

SALES & RENTALS   TOURS & INSTRUCTION

SALT MARSH

KAYAK COMPANY

Adventures for the entire family
No experience necessary!

Daily Tours
Eco, Birding &
Parent-Child
Tandem Tours

Open 7 Days a Week
9AM-6PM
(Off-Season: 10am-5pm, Wed-Sun)

Rental facility located on Banks Channel
across the street from the Blockade Runner Hotel.

222 Old Causeway Drive
1·910·509·2989

www.saltmarshkayak.com
1·866·65·KAYAK

2615; for the Wilmington area Coast Guard Auxiliary, call Jim Belluche at (910) 458-9598. The U.S. Coast Guard website, www.uscg.mil, has excellent information on boating along with links to the Coast Guard Auxiliary and the Power Squadron.

Local chapters of the nonprofit U.S. Power Squadrons (USPS), America's largest private boating association, also offer the USPS Boating Course on a regular basis in Wilmington, Southport and Shallotte. The course is free, but there is a fee to cover the cost of the manuals, materials and expenses. The cost varies depending on the squadron location; you need not be a USPS member to participate. For information on the USPS classes closest to you, call (888) FOR-USPS (367-8777). The website is www.usps.org

Carry sufficient non-alcoholic liquids, not only for the humans aboard, but also for any pets you choose to take along. Carry an emergency kit that contains flares, a fire extinguisher, first aid supplies and various repair items. Make sure that the vessel is well-maintained with the following in good working order: safety equipment, protected and sealed electrical systems, and the inboard or outboard propulsion system. If you're going to be out after dark, turn on your running lights. The ICW is also a highway for commerce, and you want to be sure that barges know you're out there.

Understand how to use your ship-to-shore radio and practice in advance of an emergency. To report emergencies to the

Coast Guard, all initial radio calls should be made on channel 16/158.8 MHz. The Wrightsville Beach Coast Guard station's emergency telephone number is (910) 256-3469. Local boating and watersports enthusiasts also report that cellular phone reception is remarkably clear near the shoreline.

Boats under sail always have the right of way over powercraft. If power is your chosen method of boating, be aware of the instability your wake can create for sailboats or small boats. If you find yourself in the shipping lanes, give big ships a wide berth. Yielding the right-of-way is often necessary because big ships require at least a mile to stop.

Emergencies happen on the water. The Coast Guard is particular about what constitutes an emergency, and it will not immediately come to your rescue in all situations. Generally, only life- or environment-threatening situations will get its attention. Running aground in the waterway is rarely considered an emergency. A sailboat with a fixed keel is virtually guaranteed to go aground at some point, and it isn't always possible to get loose without a sturdy towboat.

If you've got a predicament, SeaTow, the largest professional marine assistance provider in the world, will respond 24 hours a day, every day of the year. To receive unlimited free towing plus other benefits, including jump starts, fuel drops, prop disentanglements and navigational assistance, become a member for $119/year. Call for information, (910) 452-3798.

WATERSPORTS

The area's waters are full of shoals, so keep an eye on your depth-sounder. If you don't have one and charts suggest shallow waters, steer clear of questionable areas. The ICW is susceptible to shoaling near inlets, and you can't rely on charts for accuracy because changes occur frequently. The markers entering the Cape Fear River from the ocean were renumbered in 1997, so be alert to the fact that these changes may not appear on older NOAA charts.

A very good source of boating information and courses is the BoatU.S. Foundation, (800) 336-2628. The North Carolina Coastal Boating Guide is another excellent resource, compiled by the N.C. Department of Transportation. To obtain a free copy, call (877) 368-4968 or log on to their website at www.ncdot.org/public/publications

BOAT REGISTRATION

North Carolina requires that motorized craft of any size (including water-jet craft) and sailboats 14 feet and longer at the waterline be registered. The cost is $25 for three years. Renewal forms are mailed about two months prior to expiration. Titles are optional ($20). More information on boating regulations may be obtained from the N.C. **Wildlife Resources Commission Boat Registration Section**, 1751 Varsity Drive, NCSU Centennial Campus, Raleigh, NC 27606-2576; (800) 628-3773. An extensive list of vessel agents authorized to process North Carolina registration is online at www.ncwildlife.org. The following area businesses and offices can provide necessary forms and information:

Canady's Sport Center, 3220 Wrightsville Avenue, Wilmington, (910) 791-6280

Division of Marine Fisheries Regional Office, 127 Cardinal Drive, Wilmington, (910) 796-7215

N.C. Department of Motor Vehicles License Plates Office, 14687 U.S. Highway 17 S., Hampstead, (910) 270-9010

Shallotte Marine Supplies, Main Street, Shallotte, (910) 754-6962

MOTORBOAT RENTALS

If you would like to rent a power boat, note that advance reservations are essential in summer. Most proprietors require a deposit, a valid driver's license or major credit card, plus a signed waiver of liability.

**Dockside Watersports
Southwest Corner,
Carolina Beach Municipal Docks
Carl Winner Blvd., Carolina Beach
(910) 458-0220**

Dockside Watersports rents a 23-foot pontoon boat and 19-foot center-console outboards. Rentals are available any day of the week all year long by reservation. Four-hour rentals begin at around $179. Reserve in advance. Major credit cards are accepted.

**Entropy Rentals
Wrightsville Beach
(910) 395-2401**

On the Intracoastal Waterway at Wrightsville Beach, Entropy rents its own line of Sea Mark 17 through 21-foot power boats. Fully equipped center-console vessels are available by the half-day, full day or week. For a nominal fee, Entropy also rents water skis and equipment. The 12-hour day rate is less than $300 and major credit cards are accepted. Call for off-season rates. Entropy is open year-round and serves the Wrightsville Beach area and the lower Cape Fear coast. Call ahead for reservations and location information.

**Nauti Times
Wrightsville Beach
(910) 452-7676**

Nauti Times rents several power boats you can use for fishing or touring. They also operate a 32-foot Express Cruiser for private charters, sightseeing or dive cruises. They are open March through November. Call for reservations and directions to their location.

**Paradise Landing
318 Fulchers Rd., Sneads Ferry
(910) 327-2114, (910) 327 2133**

Make waves in a canoe, pontoon boat, 24-foot Cobia or john boat. Charter a six-passenger fishing boat and captain for your party or join other fishermen aboard the 65-foot head boat departing daily from Paradise Landing. All of these options are available for your day on the water. Reservations are recommended.

**Pleasure Island Rentals
2 N. Lake Park Blvd., Carolina Beach
(910) 458-4747**

Pleasure Island Rentals has a 17-foot Grady White for rent. This boat is kept at

Oceana but rented out of the Lake Park Boulevard location. Pleasure Island Rentals is open daily Memorial Day to Labor Day. After hours and during the off-season, call the number above for equipment rental.

PEDAL-POWERED BOAT RENTALS

You'll find pedal-powered paddle boats available for rent seasonally on the 150-acre **Greenfield Lake** on U. S. Hwy 421 S. in Wilmington. Operated by Cape Fear River Watch Inc., the concession is located near the park's Third Street and Willard Avenue entrance. Hours are 11 AM to 6 PM from May through September. Off-season opening times apply from October through April as weather permits. For information and rates, call (910) 762-5606 or (910) 341-7868.

Wheel Fun Rentals, (910) 458-4545, operates a paddle boat concession at the Lake in Carolina Beach. A small kiosk and floating dock are located on the western side near the parking lot. During the summer season, boat rentals are available seven days from 9 AM to dusk. Off-season schedules vary, but you might even find them operating on a lovely warm winter weekend.

Paddle Sports

This region's paddling season is generally nine months long — March through November — but some experienced paddlers will argue that, due to the mild climate and warm waters, paddle sports can be enjoyed year-round. Along the coast and on inland rivers, the best time is from August to May, when boat traffic is down, temperatures are less humid, insects and snakes aren't a nuisance and the chances of seeing a wider variety of wildlife are increased.

Unlike boating, kayaking and canoeing have few rules and regulations. The one rule that applies is a requirement for one life jacket per passenger aboard a kayak or canoe. Currently, no legislation exists to force the issue, but professional kayaking guides strongly recommend wearing a life jacket as a safety precaution.

The great thing about paddling is that you can go almost anywhere. A particularly great place to paddle locally is Wrightsville Beach's 14.1-mile kayak and canoe trail. The trail is marked with buoys as it meanders through picturesque marshes and channels. It begins and ends at Wynn Plaza, located at the intersection of Waynick Boulevard and Causeway Drive. For information, contact Wrightsville Beach Parks & Recreation, (910) 256-7925.

KAYAKING

Local guides report that the popularity of kayaking along North Carolina's southern coast has doubled in the last several years. Not surprising when you consider the bounty of regional waterways and seemingly endless things to see and areas to explore. Tropical sea life, exotic vegetation, a variety of waterfowl, historic landmarks accessible by water, barrier islands and pristine wildlife sanctuaries are just a few of the treasures you'll find. Unique opportunities for guided tours or solo exploration are plentiful due to the abundance of water. Explore the coastline, the Intracoastal Waterway, sounds, channels and salt marshes as well as the inland rivers and their tributaries.

Several enterprises, including Salt Marsh Kayak Company, Island Style Adventure Company and Southport's The Adventure Company (see listings below), emphasize ecological responsibility and education and bring paddlers into intimate contact with wildlife and a primal silence. All kayaking trips listed in this section are guided by experienced paddlers who bring a love of the sport and dedication to safety on each excursion.

CANOEING

Touring the lower Cape Fear River in a canoe isn't recommended for beginners because the river is a commercial shipping channel. However, for the experienced canoeist, the lower Cape Fear holds some wonderful surprises. Paddlers who frequent these waters have been known to gather wild rice bequeathed by the vanished rice plantations of the past. The Black River, a protected tributary of the Cape Fear River noted for its old-growth stands of bald cypress, is an excellent scenic canoeing choice, as are several of both rivers' tributaries. A canoe also provides excellent transportation for exploring the tidal marshes and barrier islands all along our coast.

In 1997 the Town of Oak Island dedicated some 24 miles of canoe "trails" known as the Long Beach Canoe Trail System. Four trails make up the system: Lockwood Folly (4.2 miles), Montgomery Slough (7 miles), Howells Point (6.5 miles) and Davis Creek (6 miles). Conditions range from calm, protected waters to rough, exposed waters near inlets, and all are remarkably scenic, quiet and full of wildlife. An additional two floating dock access points on Oak Island are: one at NE 58th Street accessing the Intracoastal Waterway and one at SE 31st Street accessing the Davis Canal. For information visit or call the Oak Island Recreation Department, 3003 E. Oak Island Drive, (910) 278-5518.

KAYAK AND CANOE RENTALS
Wilmington

Cape Fear Kayaks & Outfitters
435 Eastwood Rd., Wilmington
(910) 798-9922, (888) 794-4867

This well-equipped canoe and kayak center offers kayak sales, rentals, tours, trips, instruction, repairs and rental deliveries to Wrightsville Beach and the surrounding area. They also sell canoes, such as Wilderness Systems, Riot, Mad River and Old Town, and offer canoe rentals, guided fresh- and saltwater trips and overnight camping trips. All rentals include canoe or kayak, paddles, personal flotation devices and a soft roof rack if needed. Extra paddles, safety equipment and other accessories are available for rent.

Cape Fear Kayaks & Outfitters is open year round, Monday through Saturday 10 AM to 6 PM and Sunday from noon to 5 PM. The store is convenient to the protected waters on the sound side of Wrightsville Beach. Call or stop by to check on rates, reservations and monthly rental specials.

Great Outdoor Provision Co.
Hanover Center, 3501 Oleander Dr.,
Wilmington
(910) 343-1648

Open seven days a week, this store sells a variety of canoes and kayaks as well as pad-

dling accessories, maps, guidebooks, backpacking and fly-fishing gear and outdoor clothes. Instructional clinics are available, and the staff at Great Outdoor Provision Co. will be happy to arrange demonstrations of the watercraft or equipment.

Greenfield Park
U.S. Hwy. 421 S., Wilmington
(910) 762-5606 or (910) 341-7868

Canoes can be rented seasonally on Wilmington's 150-acre Greenfield Lake. Operated by Cape Fear River Watch Inc., the concession is located near the park's Third Street and Willard Avenue entrance. May through September, hours are 11 AM to 6 PM. During the off-season from October through April, canoes may be rented as weather permits. Group outings and eco-tours are available by appointment. Call for information and rates.

Wrightsville Beach

Island Style Adventure Company
96 Salisbury St., Wrightsville Beach
(910) 509-9726

Owners Matt Farrell and Dan Shivone love kayaking, and their enthusiasm is infectious. By combining their considerable expertise with a touch of creativity, the two have taken this popular sport to another level. Island Style Adventure Company specializes in kayak tours through unique salt-marsh trails. How about trying kayak Frisbee golf? Maybe you'd like to go on a full moon kayak tour or an overnight adventure on Masonboro Island. Experienced, knowledgeable guides provide friendly, professional and personal service.

The company's rental facility is situated at the edge of a No Wake zone in an area where nearby waters are calm and protected. It's open April through October, seven days a week from 8 AM to 7 PM. Parking is free, rental rates are low, and there's an outdoor shower for your convenience.

Salt Marsh Kayak Company
222 Old Causeway Dr., Wrightsville Beach
(910) 509-2989,
(866) 65KAYAK (655-2925)
www.saltmarshkayak.com

The only full-service paddle shop on Wrightsville Beach, Salt Marsh Kayak Company offers kayak sales, rentals, tours and instruction. The company's extensive rental fleet includes recreational sit-on-top and

Canoeing and kayaking are perfect ways to navigate shallow salt marshes, where you'll find many types of fish and birds, such as herons, oystercatchers, egrets and ibis, along with turtles, oyster beds and (usually) tranquility.

decked boats, as well as high-performance touring kayaks. Rent a kayak and paddle on your own from their waterfront location opposite the Blockade Runner Hotel or take a guided nature tour with one of their many experienced guides. Bird watching and eco tours are available by appointment. Basic to advanced level kayaking instruction with ACA-certified instructors is also available.

Carolina Beach

Pleasure Island Rentals
2 N. Lake Park Blvd., Carolina Beach
(910) 458-4747

Located in the heart of Carolina Beach, this watersports equipment rental company goes by the slogan, "We rent FUN stuff." Single kayak rentals range from $20 for four hours to $35 for 24 hours and $90 for a week. Tandems run $30 (four hours), $45 (24 hours) and $110 (one week). All rentals include free pick-up and delivery, paddles and life jackets. Pleasure Island Rentals is open daily Memorial Day to Labor Day. After hours and during the off-season, call the number above for equipment rental.

Wheel Fun Rentals
107 Carolina Beach Ave. N. at the
Boardwalk, Carolina Beach
(910) 458-4545

Among many fun things for rent, this shop has kayaks. Just steps from the ocean, Wheel Fun Rentals can have you paddling the surf in minutes. Stop in and get outfitted. It's open seasonally; in-season hours are seven days a week from 9 AM to 10 PM, weather permitting.

Bald Head Island

Island Passage
Bald Head Island Marina
(910) 457-4944

An interesting area to explore by canoe or kayak is Bald Head Creek and salt marsh, the state's largest single expanse of salt marsh, on Bald Head Island. Island Passage provides half-day canoe and kayak rentals and guided kayak tours. Keep in mind that the creek is a tidal waterway so excursions and rentals are tide-dependent and should be planned accordingly. Call for rental rates and the daily schedule. Reservations are suggested.

Southport

The Adventure Company
807-A Howe St., Southport
(910) 454-0607

The Adventure Company specializes in kayak tours, lessons, rentals and coastal environmental education programs as well as kayak and gear sales. Tours are scheduled weekly and can be customized. Kayak rentals include paddles and life jackets. Single kayaks rent for $30 (four hours), $45 (full day) and $140 (five days). Tandems are available for $40 (four hours), $55 (full day) and $175 (five days). Local kayak tours are $45, and group and family discounts are available. In business for six years, owner Emma Thomas, a certified kayak and canoe instructor, has been kayaking for 20 years. Also available through The Adventure Company are bicycle tours of historic Southport and adventure travel to the Bahamas, Florida, Baja, Honduras and Costa Rica. Additional information can be found at the website or call for details, a schedule or reservations.

Holden Beach

Beach Fun Rentals
132 Ocean Blvd. W., Holden Beach
(910) 842-9600, (888) 355-4446

Beach Fun Rentals is the only full-service vacation equipment rental company on Holden Beach. Kayaks remain their top rental item. Single kayaks, including the Frenzy, Rapido, Yak Board, Yahoo, Scrambler and Scrambler XT, rent for $35 for a 24-hour time period. Tandem kayaks such as Malibu II rent for $55 per day. Weekly rentals are available, and they run $150 (single) and $190 (tandem). Surfboards, boogie boards, skim boards, bicycles, grills and more are also available. Beach Fun Rental is open daily from 9 AM to 5 PM from March 15 through November 1. (If the weather stays mild, they have been known to stay open a little later in the season.)

Boomer's Rentals
Causeway Plaza, 3468 Holden Beach Rd.,
Holden Beach
(910) 842-1400, (800) 287-1990

On the causeway in Holden Beach, this general beach rental store offers rentals on single or tandem kayaks as well as boogie boards ($20 a week) and surfboards ($40 a week). Single kayaks rent for $35 per day (24 hours) and $125 for a week. Tandems are available for $50 for 24 hours and $160 for a week.

Sunset Beach

Julie's Rentals
2 Main St., Sunset Beach
(910) 579-1211, (888) 579-1211

Julie's is a complete beach-rental shop that rents kayaks (singles and tandems) as well as many other recreational items. Rates for singles are $35 per day and $125 for a week. Tandem kayaks are $50 per day and $160 for a week. Julie's Rentals offers a delivery and pick-up service for $20 ($10 each trip) or you can pick up your rental from the store. Other rental items include bicycles, umbrellas and beach chairs as well as wagons to take your items to the beach.

Topsail Island Area

Herring's Outdoor Sports
701 N. New River Dr., Surf City
(910) 328-3291

Paddle the peaceful and interesting Intracoastal Waterway or challenge the waves of the Atlantic Ocean. Whatever your choice, Herring's has the right kayak available for rent or purchase. There are single and double passenger models and the popular sit-on-top styles. You can rent by the hour, half-day, full day or week. The kayaking experts at Herring's will outfit you with all you need for your adventure. Classes and guided tours are also available. Call for prices and information.

Holland's Shelter Creek
8315 N.C. Hwy. 53 E., Burgaw
(910) 259-5743

Here's your chance to enjoy a peaceful time exploring the North Cape Fear River. Canoes and kayaks are available for everyone from the solitary fisherman to families to groups. Boats can be rented by the day.

Personal Watercraft

If you have your own water buggy, there are access points on Wrightsville Beach that are suitable for beach trailers. One of the easiest is at the foot of Causeway Drive (straight ahead from the fixed bridge), but parking is rarely available there in the high season. Another is the paved access to the left of the Oceanic Restaurant on South Lumina Avenue, provided there are no volleyball tournaments that day. Again, parking is likely to be problematic.

On Topsail Island access points are fewer, largely due to dune erosion. Your best bet would be the crossover near the center of Surf City. Smooth riding is also available in the Northeast Cape Fear River, accessible from the several public boat ramps listed in our Fishing chapter, but these waters are frequently busy with other boaters, anglers and swimmers in summer. Exercise courtesy and extreme caution.

All the rental craft available in our area launch into the Intracoastal Waterway. Be sure to respect the limitations set by individual rental services, who must operate within the parameters of their permits. Wrightsville Beach, in cooperation with the local flotilla of the U.S. Coast Guard Auxiliary, offers personal watercraft safety courses at a cost of about $35 in spring, summer, fall and winter. Call Donna Sauer, (910) 270-9830, for more information.

REGULATIONS

If you own your own personal watercraft (PWC), be aware that North Carolina requires that it be registered (see the Boat Registration section later in this chapter). Although it is the responsibility of both the boat owner and the operator (including renter) to keep abreast of current regulations, here are some state-wide rules:

• Operators must be 16 years of age. Children ages 12 through 15 may operate personal watercraft if they are riding with a person who is at least 18 years of age, or if the youth has successfully passed a boater's safety education course approved by the state, the Coast Guard Auxiliary or the National Association of State Boating Law Administrators. Two forms of identification must be carried with the 12 to 15-year-olds — a photo ID and the safety course certificate; this is a state of North Carolina regulation. See www.ncwildlife.com and click on Boating/Waterways for complete information. (NOTE: the minimum age in New Hanover County is 13.)

• No one can operate a PWC on state waters between sunset and sunrise.

• A PWC must have a rearview mirror or an observer besides the operator on board to legally tow someone on skis or a similar device.

•All PWC riders, passengers and those being towed must wear approved personal flotation devices (PFDs).

Bear in mind that local ordinances may also be in force regarding the operation of PWCs. For example, the use of personal watercraft in certain New Hanover County waters is restricted to safeguard people, property and the environment. When operating in the Intracoastal Waterway from Carolina Beach Inlet north to Mason Inlet or within the sounds and channels behind Masonboro Island and Wrightsville Beach, watercraft speed is strictly limited to 5 mph within 50 feet of the marsh or shore, an angler, a person in the water, an anchored vessel, a posted waterbird sanctuary, piers or docks.

These restrictions have led many jetcraft operators to move into the waterways north of New Hanover County, where there are currently no county rules, but, please use common sense. Refrain from operating at speeds over 5 mph when in shallow water, especially at low tide, otherwise you will probably contribute to the destruction of oyster beds, plant life and other marsh wildlife. Be especially wary of watercraft larger than your own and of water-skiers, since jet craft are more maneuverable. Finally, respect the privacy of waterfront property.

PERSONAL WATERCRAFT RENTALS

Paradise Landing
318 Fulchers Rd., Sneads Ferry
(910) 327-2114, (910) 327 2133

Explore the New River on a Waverunner rented from Paradise Landing. Other rental choices are 18- or 24-foot pontoon boats, ski boats, kayaks and canoes. Reservations are recommended. Call for prices.

Performance Watercraft
7225 Wrightsville Ave., Wilmington
(910) 799-WAVE (799-9283)

Performance rents jet craft (sit-down models) for Wrightsville Beach–area waterways from April through October, weather permitting. They also offer pleasure and scuba charters. Reservations are not required but are strongly recommended during the

peak season. Rates are $45 for a half-hour or $75 for one hour. Safety equipment, basic instruction by a certified instructor, tax and fuel are included in the rental fee. A credit card is required to place a deposit. Patrons must be 25 years old to rent and 16 years old to operate the craft. Instruction clinics are also available for corporate and family groups.

Pleasure Island Rentals
2 N. Lake Park Blvd., Carolina Beach
(910) 458-4747

Available for rent are single, double and three-person Jet Skis. Pleasure Island Rentals is open daily Memorial Day to Labor Day. After hours and during the off-season, call the number above for equipment rental.

Rowing

Rowing along the Cape Fear River is a time-honored tradition, dating back to the early 19th century when river pilots guided large, ocean-going vessels safely through the river's waters to safe harbor in Wilmington. These sturdy, yet speedy, boats were manned with four to six rowers and a coxswain. Rowing competitions between river pilots in the port cities along the southern coast — Wilmington, Charleston and Savannah among them — and crews from visiting ships were common.

After the Civil War rowing regattas along Wilmington's riverfront became a weekly event during the warm summer months. Rowing for sport eventually diminished with the advent of motorboat racing until a group of enthusiasts revived the sport in 1989, forming the Cape Fear River Rowing Club (see listing below).

Today the Cape Fear and Northeast Cape Fear rivers provide both recreational and competitive rowers an opportunity to enjoy the sport. The enthusiast interested in a casual, scenic route can travel from historic Wilmington's riverfront and the Battleship North Carolina to the State Port of Wilmington and then beyond to areas surrounded by long-abandoned rice fields and inhabited by abundant wildlife, such as deer, osprey and alligators. A rower with competition in mind will appreciate the long portions of flat water in the rivers.

Cape Fear River Rowing Club
Downtown Wilmington Waterfront

Founded in 1989 by a group of enthusiasts, this rowing club's goal is to promote and increase interest in the sport in the Wilmington area. Anyone interested in rowing is welcome to join, and the club offers lessons for beginners and support and advice as a novice rower advances in skill. Members have access to a range of rowing crafts, from stable recreational boats to racing shells that challenge the seasoned scullers. Their current boathouse is located at Point Harbor Marina, 1500 Point Harbor Road, on the west bank of the Northeast Cape Fear River, just across the Isabel Homes bridge from downtown. Three rowing clubs use the facility, the CFR-RC, the UNC-Wilmington crew and the Cape Fear Academy crew, utilizing a mix of boats from single and double, to fours and eights. CFRRC sponsors group activities including an annual trip, drill exercises and group rows. Members also compete in a variety of regattas along the East Coast, including the local Wilmington regatta, Head of the Cape Fear, in early October. For more information about the club, contact one of these members: Larry Gilman, (910) 262-7911; Morris Elsen, (910) 362-7301; David Butts, (910) 794-3160, or write to Cape Fear River Rowing Club, P.O. Box 1586, Wilmington, NC 28402.

Sailing

Anchorage in Banks Channel at Wrightsville Beach is free. The limit is 30 days every 180 days. Find complete information on area anchorage and marina services in our chapter on Marinas and the Intracoastal Waterway.

Wrightsville Beach Ocean Racing Association
P.O. Box 113, Wrightsville Beach

The Wrightsville Beach Ocean Racing Association (WBORA) was founded in 1967 to promote local keelboat ocean racing and cruising. Like most sailors, WBORA folks love a relaxing daysail, but racing stretches your sailing skills, pumps the adrenalin, and tests your mettle against the forces of the sea. Competition is friendly, and sailors can find casual or more serious competition within the fleet. Crew spots are often available, check the website www.wbora.org

The WBORA spinnaker fleet typically races standard buoy courses, while the non-spinnaker (cruising) fleet typically sails a modified triangle course using government markers. While WBORA hosts a standard point race series for members during the summer season, several invitational races are open to non members for folks who'd like to give racing a try.

WBORA also coordinates cruises to out-of-town regattas or just for fun. WBORA has coordinated cruises to Southport, Beaufort, Mile Hammock Bay, Long Bay and downtown Wilmington. Cruises to regattas offer an event to attend when you arrive. For more information about WBORA, call Doug Day, WBORA Commodore, at 431-6862.

SAILING INSTRUCTION, SALES AND RENTALS

Cape Fear Yacht Works
111 Bryan Rd., Wilmington
(910) 395-0189

Looking for the ideal racer or cruiser? Meet with designer Bruce Marek, tour the shop and talk to expert craftsmen. Explore your options and let Cape Fear Yacht Works custom build your dream sailing vessel. Here's where you can create a boat most exactly suited to your wants and needs or refurbish your existing yacht by making changes as simple as interior fabrics to changes in the keel and rig. All CFYW boats are built by hand to ORC Category 1 Compliance Standards.

Cape Fear Kayaks & Outfitters
435 Eastwood Rd., Wilmington
(910) 798-9922, (888) 794-4867

Cape Fear Kayaks & Outfitters offers four different kinds of trimarans: the Windrider 10, 16, 17 and the Rave. They also have the Vanguard line, including Sunfish and Lasers.

Priority Sailing
606 W West St., Southport
(910) 454-4479

David and Carolyn Pryor provide individual, couple or group instruction for youths and adults aboard the 52-foot cutter, Carolina Gale, on weekdays or weekends. Using standards set by the U.S. Sailing Association, their vast experience sailing and racing, their Senior Navigator status through the U. S. Power

Squadrons and their long-time involvement with the Southport Sail and Power Squadron, they will plan an instructional program with you. Certification levels achievable through these classes include: Basic Keelboat, Bareboat Cruising and Coastal Passagemaking. Certificates are issued to those who meet U.S. Sailing benchmarks.

The Carolina Gale is exciting to sail. Why not participate in a Learn-to-Cruise Adventure on the Cape Fear River and Long Bay any time of year? If you have completed the Basic Keelboat Course, try Captained Charters to Charleston or Georgetown, South Carolina, or to Cape Lookout or Beaufort, North Carolina. Team training for business groups is available as well. To quote the Pryors: "You will learn to sail the seven Cs: captain, crew, charting, compass, currents, communication and courage."

If your interest is in sight-seeing cruises, such as a Full Moon Cruise or a Sunset Cruise, or a wedding or family reunion, Priority Sailing is a great place to arrange it. (See our Attractions chapter.) Because Priority Sailing is affiliated with the non-profit organization Priority Human Services, your sailing adventure helps to promote child, youth and family development.

Salt Marsh Kayak Company
222 Old Causeway Dr., Wrightsville Beach
(910) 509-2989,
(866) 65KAYAK (655-2925)
www.saltmarshkayak.com

Salt Marsh Kayak Company rents small sailboats and teaches sailing at a facility across from the Blockade Runner Resort Hotel on Wrightsville Beach. The rental facility is open seven days a week during the spring, summer and fall, and kayak rentals, lessons and tours are also available. For more information contact Salt Marsh Kayak Company.

Southport Sail and Power Squadron
(910) 454-4479

David Pryor, who has been sailing since he was a child, recognized the need for a local chapter of the U.S. Power Squadrons when he moved to Southport from Michigan. In January 2002, the Southport Sail and Power Squadron was chartered. The Squadron teaches Boat Smart, Chart Smart, GPS, Introduction to Sailing, Skipper Saver and Instructor Development courses free of

charge (except for the cost of materials) to anyone who is interested. Members of the organization have the opportunity to take numerous additional courses related to boating, including Sail, Piloting, Weather, Seamanship, Cruise Planning, Celestial Navigation, Marine Electronics and Engine Maintenance. The Southport Squadron has more than 100 members, and there are quite a bit of expertise and education resources available within the membership. Some members are licensed by the U.S. Coast Guard to take passengers for hire as well as to offer custom cruises and private instruction in both sailing and power boating to the general public. The squadron provides monthly programs or activities. It renders free safety inspections to the general public.

SAILING AND BOATING SUPPLIES, ACCESSORIES AND REPAIR

There are many area businesses that provide service for marine supplies and repairs. One of the biggest and most well-stocked is **Boater's World Discount Marine Center** in University Commons Shopping Center on S. College Road in Wilmington, (910) 452-3000. For additional listings, see the Yellow Pages of local phone books and our Marinas chapter.

Masonboro Boat Yard & Marina, Inc.
609 Trails End Rd., Wilmington
(910) 791-1893

Located at ICW mile 288 on Whiskey Creek (5 miles south of Wrightsville Beach), Masonboro Boat Yard and Marina is a private facility that offers dockage (for sale or rent) up to 55 feet, and dry rack storage to 25 feet. A three-story clubhouse includes four private showers, laundry facilities, a club room and a glorious unobstructed view of the water and unspoiled Masonboro Island. You're guaranteed to find some interesting conversation among the residents.

Wilmington Marine Center
3410 River Rd., Wilmington
(910) 395-5055
www.wilmingtonmarine.com

This is an exceptional marine center where you'll find various marine-oriented businesses including a yacht service company with 75-ton travelift and railway haulout capacity to 400 tons. There are a chart and ship supply company, fabricators and welders, boat builders, dock manufacturers and diesel mechanics. The facility is located at marker 59 on the Cape Fear River between Snows Cut and historic downtown Wilmington.

Blackbarry Marine
4701 Long Beach Rd., Southport
(910) 457-0667

When Barry Adkins was a young man and working in a shop, he was really into his work and was always the grimiest one at the end of the day. His co-workers began calling him Black Barry and it stuck. When he opened his marine repair shop ten years ago, he had difficulty coming up with a name that someone else had not already thought of, so he decided on his nickname, knowing no one else would have that! Blackbarry Marine carries G-3 aluminum john boats ranging in size from 10 to 20 feet and packaged with Yamaha outboard engines. With at least 50 in stock, they are bound to have just what you are looking for. They carry the Triumph line of boats with either Yamaha or Honda outboards as well. The newest line of boats is the Cape Horn. These offshore boats are from 17 to 31 feet and offer incredibly dry and soft rides. The parts department can outfit your boat from stem to stern with everything from anchors to zincs; and the service department can take care of all repairs and services to your boats, motors and trailers.

Shallotte Marine Supplies Inc.
4607 Main St., Shallotte
(910) 754-6962

Serving the southern Brunswick County area since 1968, Shallotte Marine Supplies' motto is "service is our policy." They offer complete boat and motor repair by factory-trained mechanics, motorboat sales, marine

hardware and accessories. Boat storage by the month or the year is available, and Shallotte Marine specializes in saltwater rigging.

Scuba Diving and Snorkeling

Diving the southern coastal waters offers rewarding experiences to collectors, nature-watchers and wreck divers, despite there being no true coral reefs in these latitudes. A surprising variety of tropical fish species inhabit these waters, including blue angel fish, damsel fish and moray eels as well as several varieties of sea fans, some as large as 3 feet in height. Spiny oysters, deer cowries, helmet shells, trumpet tritons and queen conchs can be found here. Among the easiest places to find tropical aquatic life is 23 Mile Rock, part of a 12-mile-long ledge running roughly perpendicular to the coast. Another 15 miles out, the Lobster Ledge, a low-lying formation 120 feet deep, is a collectors' target. There are several smaller ledges close to shore in shallower water better suited for less-experienced divers.

Visibility at offshore sites averages 60 feet and often approaches 100 feet, but inshore visibility is seldom better than 20 feet. The coastal waters can be dived all year long, since their temperatures range from the upper 50s in winter and low 80s in summer. However, many local charters typically end their diving season in early fall. Some charters organize destination trips after that.

Good snorkeling in the region is a matter of knowing when and where to go. Near-shore bottoms are mostly packed sand devoid of the rugged features that make for good viewing and collecting, but a good guide can lead you to rewarding areas. When the wind is right and the tide is rising, places such as the Wrightsville Beach jetty offer good viewing and visibility. The many creeks and estuaries support an abundance of life, and the shorter visibility, averaging 15 to 20 feet, is no obstacle in water so shallow.

The waters around piers in Banks Channel at Wrightsville Beach are fair but often murky, and currents are strong. Only experienced snorkelers should attempt these waters or those in local inlets, which are treacherous, and then only at stopped tides. It is neither safe nor legal to swim beneath

> *When romping in the ocean, if a large wave is coming and you don't have enough time to get away from it, try to dive into the base of the wave just before it breaks, keeping your body as low as possible until it passes over you. If the water is too shallow, just crouch and keep a low body profile.*

oceanside fishing piers. When in doubt, contact a local dive shop for information.

This region of the Graveyard of the Atlantic offers unparalleled opportunities for wreck divers. From Tubbs Inlet (near Sunset Beach) to New River Inlet (North Topsail Beach), 20 of the dozens of known shipwrecks resting here are accessible and safe. Most are Confederate blockade runners, one is a tanker torpedoed by the Nazi sub U-158, and several were sunk as part of North Carolina's artificial reef program (see the Fishing chapter for more on artificial reefs). These and higher-risk wrecks can be located with the assistance of dive shops.

Wreck diving is an advanced skill best undertaken by professionals. Research prior to a dive is essential in terms of the target, techniques and potential dangers, which in this region include live ammunition and explosives that may be found on World War II wrecks. If you observe anything suspicious while you're diving, leave it alone! Under state law, all wrecks and underwater artifacts within three miles of shore that remain unclaimed for more than 10 years are declared state property.

Charter boats can be arranged for dive trips through all the dive shops listed here, but there are others. Also check the Fishing chapter for fishing charter boats that accommodate dive trips. Many charter boats are primarily fishing boats, so if you need custom diving craft, be sure to inquire. Most dive shops can lead you to a certification class if they don't offer one themselves. Also, proof of diver's certification is required by shops or dive masters when renting equipment, booking charters or purchasing air fills.

Aquatic Safaris & Divers Emporium
5751-4 Oleander Dr., Wilmington
(910) 392-4386

This PADI training facility is one of Wilmington's largest full-service charter services and dive shops, offering air fills, including Nitrox, and a full range of equipment for sale and rental. Dive charters are available and range from $40 to $110 per person, depending on the trip's distance. Snorkeling equipment is for sale only. The shop is certified by major manufacturers to perform repairs on most life-support equipment and most other equipment as well. It's open seven days a week all year.

Cape Fear Descenders Dive Club
(910) 845-2330

This Southport-based dive club was started as a small group of diving enthusiasts in January 1996. Monthly meetings are held year-round in Southport on the second Tuesday of each month at 7 PM. Call for the location of the meeting. Group dives, guest speakers, parties, continuing education classes, advance dive classes and a newsletter are all perks of membership. Annual dues, pro-rated after July 1, are $20 for individuals and $30 for the family. For more information, see their website.

Scuba Tech
Wilmington
(910) 329-1666, (800) NITROX1 (648-7691)

This is a SDI-TDI and PADI five-star facility and one of the largest sport diving and snorkeling facilities in the region. Services include rentals, repair, sales, air (standard and NITROX) and instruction in diving and snorkeling. Local charters and customized dive travels to warmer climes during the winter are available. The staff is fully certified. It's open Monday, and Thursday through Saturday 9 AM to 6 PM. They are closed Tuesday, Wednesday and Sunday.

Scuba South Diving Company
222 S. River Dr., Southport
(910) 457-5201

Among the most respected diving experts in the Southport area is Wayne Strickland, who specializes in dive charters to some of the less-frequented targets off the Cape plus such well-known sites as the City of Houston, a passenger freighter that sank in 1878 and which Strickland salvaged for the North Carolina Maritime Museum at Southport (artifacts are on display). Strickland will arrange dives to any site along the southern coast. Trips are aboard his custom 52-foot Scuba South II. Scuba South sells and rents a full store of equipment, including wet and dry suits, and provides air fills. Nitrox is available.

Surfing

California surfers who come to the southern coast of North Carolina agree: The surf may be less spectacular than on the West Coast, but the water is warmer and the season is longer. Conditions were considered good enough for the U.S. Amateur Surfing Championships Mid-Atlantic Regionals that were held at Wrightsville Beach in 1997. The East Coast Wahine Championships were held in Kure Beach in 2001 and 2002 and in Wrightsville Beach in 2003, 2004 and 2005.

In recent years, many surfers from this area have been achieving awards and recognition worldwide. With surfing now part of the pantheon of Olympic events, local surfing has naturally gained further status. Surf shops throughout the region can provide information on surfing competitions.

The beaches running north to south, from Topsail Island down to Fort Fisher, experience consistently better surf than the Brunswick beaches, with their east-west orientation. However, the Brunswick beaches are fine for bodyboarding. A favored surfing spot is Masonboro Island's north end near the jetty. However, it's not an easy place to reach, since Masonboro Inlet is an active boat channel with dangerous currents. Crossing over from the soundside (the Intracoastal Waterway) and hiking to the beach is a good idea.

The northernmost point of the Wrightsville Beach, off Shell Island Resort, is the preferred long-board break because it has a consistent lined-up sand-point style wave. More aggressive waves are at the middle of the island, near Columbia Street, an area favored by the more progressive, younger surfers. Wrightsville Beach has stringent rules governing surfing. Surfing within 500 feet of any commercial fishing piers or the Masonboro Inlet jetty is prohibited year round. Leash laws are in effect all the time. Between 11 AM and 4 PM during the summer (Memorial Day to Labor Day), surfing is restricted to two 600-foot surf zones; one zone is on the southern end and one on the northern end. Swimming is prohibited in the surf zones, which are rotated along the entire beachfront and are marked with signs and flags. Surfing zone restrictions will not be in effect when red flags are posted. Any lifeguard can tell you where the zone currently stands, or call Wrightsville Beach Parks and Recreation, (910) 256-7925, for zone location. Zones do not apply during the off season. For Wrightsville Beach surfing information, tide table, daily surf report and rotating zones, go to www.townofwrightsvillebeach.com/surfing. htm. The "Local" section of the Star-News also carries a tide schedule and surf forecast each day.

SURFING LESSONS

Wrightsville Beach Parks and Recreation Department
1 Bob Sawyer Dr., Wrightsville Beach
(910) 256-7925

Beginner surfing lessons are conducted weekly from June through the end of August. The three-day class is for advanced ocean swimmers age 10 to adult and is limited to six students per session. The course covers surfing etiquette, paddling, wave-catching, maneuvers and basic surfing principles. Fees are charged for courses and you must provide your own surfboard. Call for more information and a schedule.

SURFING GEAR AND SUPPLIES

Many shops in our area offer a complete selection of surf gear, apparel and accessories, including wet suits and videos. You can buy a new or used board, rent one by the day or week and get yours repaired. Shops can lead you to local people who build customized boards too. Most area shops are open seven days a week in season. Call ahead in the off-season.

Aussie Island Surf Shop, Landfall Shopping Center, 1319 Military Cutoff Road, Wilmington, (910) 256-5454

Bert's Surf Shop, 5740 Oleander Drive, Wilmington, (910) 392-4501 and 800 N. Lake Park Boulevard, Carolina Beach, (910) 458-9047

The **Cove Surf Shop**, 604 N. Lake Park Boulevard, Carolina Beach, (910) 458-4671.

Hot Wax Surf Shop, 4510 Hoggard Drive, Wilmington, (910) 791-9283

Sweetwater Surf Shop, 10 N. Lumina Avenue, Wrightsville Beach, (910) 256-3821

Surf City Surf Shop, 530 Causeway Drive, Wrightsville Beach , (910) 256-2265, www.surfcity1.com

Boomer's Rentals, Causeway Plaza, 3468 Holden Beach Road, Holden Beach, (910) 842-1400, (800) 287-1990

Holden Beach Surf & Scuba, 3172-4 Holden Beach Road SW, Holden Beach, (910) 842-6899

Local Call Surf Shop, 8417 E. Oak Island Drive, Oak Island, (910) 278-3306

North Shore Surf Shop, 12 E. First Street, Ocean Isle Beach, (910) 579-6223

Bert's Surf Shop, N. New River Drive (N.C. Hwy. 210), Surf City, (910) 328-1010

Spinnaker Surf Shop, 111 N. Shore Dr., Surf City, (910) 328-2311.

In addition to many of the above shops, the following businesses rent surfboards by the hour, day or week

Pleasure Island Rentals, 2 N. Lake Park Boulevard, Carolina Beach, (910) 458-4747

Wheel Fun Rentals, 107 Carolina Beach Avenue N at the Boardwalk, Carolina Beach, (910) 458-4545

Beach Fun Rentals, 132 Ocean Boulevard W, Holden Beach, (910) 842-9600, (888) 355-4446

Swimming

The southern coast is blessed with clean, relatively clear, refreshing waters and a long outdoor season. The ocean water temperature becomes comfortable usually no later than the middle of spring, generally hovering in the 75- to 85-degree range by summer. Most area beaches consist of fine, clean sand. Together with the shores of the Outer Banks and beaches farther north, the southern coast gives evidence that North Carolina does indeed have the finest beaches in the east.

Except for the threat of rip currents, the surf is generally moderate. Several beach communities employ lifeguards during the summer, but the beaches are not staffed otherwise. Swimming in a few areas is hazardous, such as at the extreme east end of Ocean Isle Beach and along the Fort Fisher Historic Site, because of either strong currents or underwater debris. All hazardous areas are well-marked. See our chapter on Sun, Sand and Sea for more on beach swimming. Check the facilities listed below if pool swimming is more to your liking.

**City of Wilmington Recreation Division
302 Willard St., Wilmington
(910) 341-7855, (910) 341-4602**

The City of Wilmington maintains three public swimming pools: Shipp Pool at Southside Park (beside Legion Stadium), 2221 Carolina Beach Road, (910) 341-7863; Jack-son Pool at Northside Park, 750 Bess Street, (910) 341-7865; and Murphy Pool at Robert Strange Park, 410 S. Eighth Street, (910) 341-7866. All locations are handicapped accessible and equipped with bathhouses. During the summer season, beginning Saturday of Memorial Day weekend, the pools are open Monday through Saturday afternoons (hours are limited and vary at each pool). From mid-August until Labor Day, they are open only on Saturdays. Admission fees are 50¢ for children and $1 for adults.

During the summer, the Cape Fear Chapter of the American Red Cross conducts swimming lessons Monday through Friday at the Shipp Pool (Southside Park) from 9 AM to noon. For more information, contact the American Red Cross, (910) 762-2683.

**Wilmington Family YMCA
2710 Market St., Wilmington
(910) 251-9622
www.wilmingtonfamilyymca.org**

The YMCA boasts two indoor pools to accommodate its many members year round. Water fitness, swim lessons, swim team, triathlon clubs and life-guarding classes are among its many offerings. Membership is required to enjoy general use of these facilities, which are open seven days a week. Some classes are open to the community with discounted fees for members. Call the YMCA for current individual or family rates.

**YWCA of the Lower Cape Fear
2815 S. College Rd., Wilmington
(910) 799-6820**

The YWCA has excellent facilities, water aerobics, lap swimming, a swim team, swimming instruction by highly qualified staff and rentals for birthday parties. Instruction in lifesaving is one of its specialties. The pool is outside and is open for summer from mid-May to September. September through May, the pool's bubbled roof is installed, allowing year-round swimming. YWCA membership is required to enjoy the facilities.

Tours

In this land of waterways, ocean and rivers, tours of various sorts abound. Depending on your interests and boating preference, you can choose from the formal *Henrietta III* Riverboat or casual Capt. *J.N. Maffitt*, both located on the riverfront in downtown Wilmington, (910) 343-1611, to guided adventure tours offered by most of the local kayak companies. Some fishing charters double as tour boats, too, especially out of Wrightsville Beach, Southport and Carolina Beach Marina, where Winner Fishing & Cruise Boats, (910) 458-3474, operates a variety of popular waterway cruises.

Sea Tours, Inc.
308 S. Lake Park Blvd., Carolina Beach
(910) 617-5030

Specializing in local maritime history and wildlife tours, Captain David Lawn fills a void in our local water exploration offerings. For those of us who aren't into paddle sports, Sea Tours, Inc. provides opportunities to explore near-shore shipwrecks, backwater areas, rivers and other fascinating coastal vistas in a custom-built ZODIAC, a rigid inflatable craft powered by a 115 hp outboard motor. Boat and captain are also available for ferry service, photography trips and lighthouse tours. Perhaps you're looking at coastal property to buy — why not see how it looks from the water? Call David to arrange your special adventure.

The Naturalist Company
1605 Hawthorne Rd., Wilmington
(910) 763-9418

Trained biologist and ornithologist Joseph Abate offers exceptional ecological tours of the area's tidal creeks, state park wetlands and the Intracoastal Waterway with a focus on local birds and birding. Bradley Creek and Masonboro Island are favorite tour destinations. For $40 you can enjoy a two-hour guided tour by kayak or catamaran where you'll learn about the history and habitats of local birds, environmental issues, and view native plant life.

Water-Skiing

The protected waters of the lower Cape Fear River, from Carolina Beach south, are the most popular for water-skiing in the greater Wilmington area. These waters are convenient to public boat ramps in Carolina Beach, including those at the marina at Carolina Beach State Park and at Federal Point. Throughout most of the region, the wider channels of the Intracoastal Waterway and

adjoining sounds offer water-skiing opportunities, but be alert to other boat traffic.

The relatively hushed surf along the Brunswick Islands is well-suited to skiing, yielding about 22 miles of shoreline from Ocean Isle Beach to Sunset Beach. Big Lake, in the community of Boiling Springs Lakes, 8 miles northwest of Southport on N.C. 87, is a long, narrow body of water that's excellent for water-skiing. There is a free public boat ramp off Alton Lennon Drive. Check with the rental services listed in the Motorboat Rentals section above if you need to rent a towing craft. Many, if not most, services and some boating supply shops also rent skis and equipment.

Windsurfing and Kiteboarding

One of the best and most popular windsurfing areas is the Basin, the partially protected body of water off Federal Point at the southern end of Pleasure Island (Carolina and Kure beaches). Accessible from a public boat ramp down the road from the ferry terminal, the Basin is enclosed by the Rocks, a 3.3-mile breakwater that extends to Zeke's Island and beyond. Motts Channel and Banks Channel on the sound side of Wrightsville Beach are popular spots, but you'll have to contend with the boat traffic. Advanced windsurfers prefer the oceanside of the jetty at the south end of Wrightsville Beach, where action is fairly guaranteed.

Around Topsail Island, the choices are the Intracoastal Waterway and the ocean. The inlets north and south of the island are not well-suited to uninterrupted runs. Along Oak Island and the South Brunswick Islands, the ocean is your best bet, although limited stretches of the ICW are OK for beginners (near the Ocean Isle Beach bridge when it's not busy, for example). Shallotte Inlet and River are narrow but worth a shot.

Kiteboarding is one of the hottest, up-and-coming watersports. Kiteboarding is similar to wakeboarding, using a large kite to pull you instead of a boat. It requires less wind than windsurfing, the gear packs up much smaller than windsurfing gear, and you don't need a boat to do it. Riders can jump 10 to 40 feet in the air while performing amazing tricks. Since they need less wind to have fun,

side effects may include:

**chronic grinning,
hallucinations of flying,
and elevated levels of
adrenaline**

**treatment
approach:**

GOKITESURF.COM

PROFESSIONAL KITESURF
LESSON CENTER

PASA CERTIFIED INSTRUCTORS
JET SKI SUPPORTED LESSONS
EQUIPMENT PROVIDED

910.509.9989
(TOLL FREE) 888.509.9989
INSIDE BLOWING IN THE WIND
222 CAUSEWAY DRIVE
WRIGHTSVILLE BEACH
NORTH CAROLINA 28480

go kitesurf

BLOWING IN THE WIND
KITESURF GEAR,
ADVICE & SERVICE

kiteboarders get more good days in the Cape Fear area than windsurfers do.

The sport uses the principles of sailing in that you tack against the wind and can travel upwind or downwind. The boards are specially designed for the sport, and the kites can re-launch you if you crash in the water. Different sized kites are available for different wind conditions and different weight riders. You can kiteboard in flat water and waves. The most popular spots to kiteboard around here are the south end of Wrightsville Beach, the Fort Fisher Basin and the north end of Carolina Beach. Riders go where the wind conditions suit them. Kiteboarding is a thrilling sport, but like any extreme sport, it can be dangerous. You are strongly urged to seek expert advice or take lessons.

**Blowing In The Wind
222 Causeway Dr., Wrightsville Beach
(910) 509-9989, (888) 509-9989
www.blowinginthewind.com
www.gokitesurf.com**

Whether you're looking to get into kiteboarding or are already proficient, this is the shop for you. Blowing in the Wind is the Cape Fear area's expert on kites and kiteboarding. They offer the latest gear from top manufacturers and have lots of accessories. From beginner packages to high-performance gear, this place has it. Jet-Ski assisted lessons taught by professional instructors are available. Want to know where the locals ride? Blowing in the Wind can tell you where to go for different wind directions. Blowing in the Wind has two locations, Wrightsville Beach and downtown Wilmington at the Cotton Exchange, 312 Nutt Street, (910) 763-1730. All kiteboarding products and lessons are offered through the Wrightsville Beach location.

FISHING

North Carolina's long strand of barrier islands lie between the ocean and shallow waters, which form estuaries, brackish swamps and mud flats that are nurseries for shrimp, crabs, finfish and shellfish. As one of the top 10 seafood-producing states, North Carolina has more than 4,000 miles of shoreline and 2.5 million acres of marine and estuarine waters. Approximately 5,000 full-time commercial fishermen and 1.7 million recreational anglers enjoy the state's marine resources.

The southern coast of North Carolina is an angler's paradise. As long as the weather cooperates, an angler can enjoy fishing 12 months of the year. With ocean temperatures ranging from the 70s in the Gulf Stream to the 50s near shore in the winter months, king mackerel, sea bass and tuna can be caught in the ocean, while striped bass can be caught in the rivers. During the spring, summer and fall months, sheepshead, spot, tarpon, red drum, Spanish mackerel, bluefish, whiting, trout, flounder, amberjack, striped bass, croaker, white marlin, blue marlin, sailfish, shark, wahoo and dolphin are available.

The North Carolina Recreational Coastal Waters Guide for Sports Fishermen, listing length minimums and creel limits for various species, is online at www.ncdmf.net/index. html. Many other sources for information on fishing can be linked from this site; or you can call (252) 726-7021 or (800) 682-2632 (NC only). At www.ncfisheries.net/fishfind/ fishfin2.htm is information identifying and describing all North Carolina fish by common name, with data and color illustrations of the species. Extensive data on the fishing licenses required, especially the new N.C. Saltwater Fishing License, which goes into effect in 2007, can be linked from the DMF site, or you can call (252) 726-7021 or (800) 682-2632 and ask for the license office.

Since the early 1970s, the Division of Marine Fisheries has helped create artificial reefs that provide habitat for sea life. These reefs consist of old ships, railroad cars, bridge rubble, concrete and FADs (fish-attracting devices). Using the motto "We sink 'em – you fish 'em," reef architects have built 39 ocean sites and seven estuarine sites. Judging by the number of sheepshead and mackerel landed on an average day, the program seems to be paying off. Charts are available to lead you to these sites. GPS coordinates are available at www.ncfisheries.net/reefs/gp-sreef.pdf.

Fishing is quite good in the Cape Fear River, with available species including largemouth bass, sunfish, catfish, herring and American and hickory shad. Spring is the peak season for largemouths, which usually range between 1.5 to 3 pounds. Bass can be located near the mouths of the larger tributary creeks, such as Turnbull, Hammonds, Sturgeon, Livingston and the upper reaches of Town Creek.

Bluegill are plentiful in the Cape Fear River and are available during the spring spawning season near locks and dams. Bluegills average one-half and three-fourths of a pound, while redear sunfish run about a pound.

Catfish fishing is excellent in the Cape Fear River, which also hosts the three largest members of the freshwater catfish family — the channel, blue and flathead, available from Lillington to the Black River. Catfish are considered non-game fish and they have no size or creel restrictions. They can be taken by a variety of fishing methods. April, May, September and October are the best months.

American and hickory shad can be found in the lower Cape Fear River below Wilmington and can be taken by recreational fishermen below each of the three locks and dams above Wilmington. Information on inland water limits and licenses is available at www.ncwildlife.org or by calling (919) 707-0391 or (888) 248-6834.

The North Carolina Regulations Digest, containing regulations for inland fishing, hunting and trapping, is available from North Carolina Wildlife Resources Commission, 1722 Mail Service Center, Raleigh, NC 27699-1722. The entire digest is also online at the aforementioned web site.

Note that fishing from most bridges in the area is restricted or prohibited because the bridges often traverse boat channels. Be sure to check the signs on bridges before casting. Small-boat owners have many fishing opportunities around the mouths of creeks and inlets, especially during incoming tides when the boat and the bait can drift in with the bait fish. Small boats should use caution at ocean inlets during outgoing tides because the currents can be strong.

If you're traveling without tackle, rental gear is fairly abundant. Among places to check are these shops in addition to some of the fishing piers listed below. Rod and Reel Shop at 3401 Holden Beach Road SW (on the mainland side of the bridge in Holden Beach), (910) 842-2034. Rod and Reel also repairs tackle. Another renting location for both onshore and offshore tackle is Seagull Bait & Tackle at 608 S. Lake Park Boulevard in Carolina Beach, (910) 458-7135. Tackle shops abound along the coast, but be sure to call ahead to determine if they rent equipment.

Fishing Licenses

In 2007 a new N.C. Saltwater Fishing License is planned to go into effect. It will be required for saltwater rod and reel fishing, and you must observe size and bag limits. Contact the North Carolina Division of Marine Fisheries for saltwater regulations or for more information. Familiarize yourself with regulations, which are posted at most piers and marinas. Freshwater licenses are issued by the North Carolina Wildlife Resources Commission. Call (888) 248-6834 for credit card purchases or purchase from one of the locations listed below. Nonresident fishing licenses for 12 months cost $30. Three-day licenses cost $15, a license for one day is $10, and trout fishing is an additional $10. For residents, the annual 12-month fee is $15 with an additional $5 for a comprehensive license that includes trout fishing. A one-day license

(not including trout waters) is $5. Licenses may be combined with a hunting license and can be obtained at slightly higher rates. As regulations and fees are complex and subject to change, you're advised to check the website for complete information http://www.ncwildlife.org/

WILMINGTON

Canady's Sport Center, 3220 Wrightsville Avenue, Wilmington, (910) 791-6280

Dick's Sporting Goods, 816 S. College Road, Wilmington, (910) 793-1904

Division of Marine Fisheries, North Carolina D.E.N.R., 127 Cardinal Drive, Wilmington, (910) 796-7215

Kmart, 815 S. College Road, Wilmington, (910) 799-5360

Wal-Mart, Monkey Junction, Wilmington, (910) 452-0944

Wal-Mart, 5226 Sigmon Road, Wilmington, (910) 392-4034

BRUNSWICK COUNTY BEACHES

Doodle's Convenience Store, 132 Country Club Drive, Oak Island, (910) 278-9991

Stewart's True Value Hardware, 8848 River Road, SE, Southport, (910) 457-5544

Wal-Mart, 1675 N. Howe Street, Southport, (910) 454-9909

Calabash True Value Hardware, 10050 Beach Drive, SW, Calabash, (910) 579-3513

Coastal Hardware & Supply Center, 594 Seaside Road, Sunset Beach, (910) 579-6006

Holden Beach True Value Hardware, 3008 Holden Beach Road, Holden Beach, (910) 842-5440

Island Tackle and Gifts, 6855 Beach Drive, Ocean Isle Beach, (910) 579-6116

Wal-Mart, 4540 Main Street, Shallotte, (910) 754-2880

Fishing Reports

The most up-to-date sources of fishing information are charter captains, fishing piers and tackle shops. Frequent detailed reports appear in the Star-News print editions in the Sports section.

Fishing Piers

Each pier in the area has its own personality. Some have become bent and bowed after years of battering by the ocean and hurricanes, and some have been rebuilt time and again. Most are festooned with odd novelties and memorabilia and proudly display photographs of trophies reeled up from the sea. On busy days, expect to be rubbing elbows with other pier-fishers between Kure and Topsail. Almost all piers charge a fee for fishing permits good for a 24-hour period. Fishing generally costs about $5 to $6 per day, and king fishing costs about twice as much. Most piers offer seasonal fishing permits, tackle shops, snack bars, wet cleaning tables and restrooms. People who want to walk out on the pier without fishing are usually permitted free of charge, but you may have to pay a small fee.

WILMINGTON

River Road Park
6300 River Rd., Wilmington
(910) 798-7198

River Road Park, south of the State Port about 8 miles from downtown Wilmington near the end of Cathay Road, features a handicapped-accessible fishing pier on the Cape Fear River. The park features playground equipment, bathroom facilities and a shelter that can be rented for social occasions. The park is open from 8 AM to dusk.

WRIGHTSVILLE BEACH

Johnnie Mercer's Pier
Foot of E. Salisbury St., Wrightsville Beach
(910) 256-2743

This magnificent structure is the first concrete pier in North Carolina able to sustain 200 mph winds. The windows are able to withstand storm gales up to 150 mph. The light poles consist of spun concrete, and even the trash receptacles are made of stone. Twenty-five feet above sea level, Johnnie Mercer's Pier maintains a year-round presence. The arcade and restaurant offer a sunrise breakfast, lunch and dinner with indoor/outdoor seating. General fishing is $8 per rod, and the service is first class.

CAROLINA BEACH

Carolina Beach Fishing Pier
1800 Carolina Beach Ave. N.,
Carolina Beach
(910) 458-5518

The 700-foot Carolina Beach Fishing Pier is owned and operated by the Phelps family. The pier features a snack bar, grill, upstairs lounge with ABC permits, game area and a tackle shop, which offers new equipment, rentals and bait. There is a cleaning sink on the pier. The charge for general fishing with one or two rods is $7. King mackerel three-rod fishing is $12. Free parking is available for fishing.

KURE BEACH

Kure Beach Pier
Ave. K, Kure Beach
(910) 458-5524

Facilities include a snack room with cold sandwiches, drinks and other goodies, a complete tackle shop, a souvenir store and an arcade with four pool tables. Permits are good from midnight to midnight. This pier is handicapped accessible. Permit for a single-rod and reel per person is $5, and a king mackerel permit allowing three rods is $12. No rentals are available. No alcoholic beverages are permitted.

A great local publication, Fisherman's Post, "the saltwater fisherman's guide to NC's southern coast," contains a wealth of information, news, tide tables, events, articles and ads of interest to saltwater anglers. It is available free in places where fishermen hang out and also by subscription. They print 22 issues a year, including weekly issues Memorial Day to Labor day. Phone (910) 452-6378.

BRUNSWICK COUNTY BEACHES

City Pier
Waterfront Park, Bay St., Southport

This small, handicapped-accessible pier near the mouth of the Cape Fear River is a municipal facility, and usage is free. It is located adjacent to Waterfront Park, where amenities include a water fountain, park benches, a gazebo, swings and usually an ice cream truck during the season.

Ocean Crest Pier
1411 E. Beach Dr., Oak Island
(910) 278-6674, (910) 278-3333

This 1,000-foot pier near 14th Place East, voted most popular fishing pier in North Carolina in 2005 by Fisherman's Post, has a full line tackle shop where special orders are available. You will also find gifts for friends at home or as souvenirs for yourself. Handicapped anglers fish for free, and the owners provide a community live bait tank and a shelter at the T-shaped far end that is reserved for king fishers. Season permits are available for bottom fishing and king fishing. A full-service restaurant and a motel adjoin the pier. Pier Manager Dave Cooper claims it is the premier king mackerel fishing pier.

Yaupon Pier
Foot of Womble St., Oak Island
(910) 278-9400

Yaupon is not only the highest pier in the state (27 feet above the high-tide line), but it also boasts the state record for the largest fish caught from a pier to date — read it and weep — a 1,150-pound tiger shark caught on rod and reel. Yaupon Pier is a family pier, handicapped-accessible, and sight-seers are welcome to stroll the pier for free. Fishing lures and monofilament are available for sale and rods can be rented. Stop for a meal or snack at the attached restaurant.

Holden Beach Pier
441 Ocean Blvd. W., Holden Beach
(910) 842-6483

Holden Beach Pier sells daily, seasonal, three-day and seven-day fishing permits and live bait. A grill and snack counter adjoin a beach gift shop. Holden Beach Pier charges spectators a fee of 50¢ for walking the pier. Handicapped access is available to the pier.

The owners prohibit the use of nets and the consumption of alcoholic beverages.

Ocean Isle Pier
Foot of Causeway Dr., Ocean Isle Beach
(910) 579-3095

The large game room and small grill at this pier are quite popular in summer. Available are ice cream, drinks, ice, supplies, fishing bait, tackle and rods, season passes, and rod and equipment rentals. Fishing fees are $6 per rod. Adult spectators are charged $1, and the fee is 50¢ for children under the age of 16.

Sunset Beach Pier
Foot of Sunset Blvd., Sunset Beach
(910) 579-6630

The 900-foot pier has a special area for king fishermen. Amenities at Sunset Beach Pier include a double sink at the cleaning table, a snack bar with grill serving breakfast and hot sandwiches, a game room and ATM in the air-conditioned pier house. Bait is for sale at the pier, and rod rentals are available. Not only is the pier handicapped accessible but scooter chairs are provided free of charge to handicapped persons.

TOPSAIL ISLAND

Jolly Roger Pier
803 Ocean Blvd., Topsail Beach
(910) 328-4616

The Jolly Roger is a pier complex with a motel, convenience store and bait and tackle shop with small restaurant facilities. This 850-foot ocean pier, at the southern end of the island, is open from March through November.

Seaview Pier
New River Inlet Rd., North Topsail Beach
(910) 328-3172

Located on the north end of the island, Seaview is the island's newest pier and is 1,000 feet long. You catch 'em, you clean 'em and they'll cook 'em at the pier's restaurant, or you can just order off the menu. The pier shop has bait and tackle, snack foods and ice. It's open March through November.

Surf City Ocean Pier
112 S. Shore Dr., Surf City
(910) 328-3521

This 937 feet long pier is in the center of downtown Surf City. Rod rentals, bait and tackle are all available. The newly expanded grill is open daily during the summer season (sometimes 24 hours a day when the fish are biting) with reduced hours in the fall and spring. They offer fried chicken, hamburgers, hot dogs or if you've had a good day fishing, they will cook your catch. Spectators are welcome to stroll the pier for a $1 charge for a 24-hour pass. Alcohol is not allowed on this pier which is open from mid-March until sometime in December.

Surf Fishing

The best time for surf fishing is during high tide with an outgoing tide. There's still a tranquil, serene spot to be found in the ever-popular Wrightsville Beach area. Behind the jetty at Masonboro Inlet, on the south end of the island, you'll find an almost hidden oasis perfect for surf fishing.

For anglers looking to get away from it all, the Fort Fisher State Recreation Area is an undeveloped 4-mile stretch of beach and tidal marsh approximately 5 miles south of Carolina Beach that is accessible by four-wheel-drive vehicle only. The entrance to the area is off U.S. Highway 421 before the North Carolina Aquarium (bear left at the fork) and to the right of the beach parking lot. There is also a public beach here with changing rooms, restrooms and shower, a snack bar (open seasonally only) and a ranger contact station. Phone (910) 458-5798 for information about hours, fees and permits; daily fee is $10, an annual fee is $40. Otherwise, there are no services, so bring everything you'll need and pack out everything you bring. (Also see the "Off-Roading" section in our Sports, Fitness and Parks chapter).

Another good spot, near the Carolina Beach Inlet at the north end of Canal Drive on Pleasure Island, is also accessible by four-wheel-drive only. A lesser-known and more restricted fishing spot on Pleasure Island lies off Dow Road. For 3 miles south of Spartanburg Avenue, foot paths enter the woods from the roadside (you may notice vehicles parked there). Foot traffic only is permitted since this is an environmentally sensitive area owned by the federal government. Trails lead to the Cape Fear River, but the northernmost trails lead to a secluded inlet known as the Dredge Pond, where bait fish are often stirred

into a frenzy by the unseen feeders. It's also a good place to picnic and relax if the mosquitoes aren't too voracious, but keep an eye open for the resident alligator. He's never gone after a human (that we know about) but don't give him any chance at you.

If you're looking for something a bit more adventurous, try fishing The Rocks, a 3.3-mile breaker extending from Federal Point, south of the Fort Fisher Ferry terminal. The enclosed water around Zeke's Island is called the Basin, and fishing on both sides of the barrier is excellent. However, The Rocks can be very dangerous, especially at high tide when they're slippery, wet and partly under water, so be sure to enter and leave the area during low tide.

Although surf fishing is popular on all the beaches of Oak Island, a great spot can be found at The Point, at the west end of Oak Island bordering Lockwood Folly Inlet. The Town of Oak Island has built a parking lot adjacent to the beach access. You can see the eastern end of Holden Beach and the Holden Beach bridge, but you can't get there from here!

Fly-Fishing and Light Tackle

Saltwater fly-fishing is quickly gaining in popularity, probably because it's a type of fishing that requires great skill and a fantastic love of the sport. Neophytes and aficionados of saltwater fly-fishing should take note of the following resources in the Wilmington area and in many tackle shops throughout the region.

Gottafly Guide Service
Bridge Tender Marina next to
Wrightsville Beach drawbridge
(910) 350-0890

Spend the day light tackle or fly fishing with Captain Lee Parsons on his 23-foot Boston Whaler Outrage. There's Atlantic bonito in April, then sailfish, Spanish or king mackerel from June through September, or try wreck fishing for big amberjack in August and September. You might prefer world-class fishing for false albacore at Cape Lookout in October and November. If you like inshore fishing, Lee can take you out on the 18-foot Polarcraft tunnel boat chasing stripers on the

The best in
light tackle fishing
at Wrightsville Beach.
Sightseeing or
After Dinner Cruises

Bring the kids & join me for a
great day on the water!

Capt. Lee Parsons
Safe & comfortable
23' Boston Whaler

910-350-0890 • gottaflylee@ec.rr.com

Roanoke River in May or flounder gigging from June through September. Night fishing for ladyfish or poling flats for our state fish, red drum, is exciting. Rather not fish? Try an after-dinner cruise around the beach or walk undeveloped islands. Be sure to bring your camera to record the gorgeous coastal birds along the marshes.

East Coast Sports
Village Mall, Roland Ave. Cswy., Surf City
(910) 328-1887

The friendly, professional staff at East Coast Sports is ready to help you select the best bait and tackle for inshore or offshore fishing. All major brands are offered in their large selection. If you need a charter, let Capt. Chris Medlin arrange one for you. East Coast also has a full line of sports clothing, including Columbia, Sperry, Topsiders and many other name brands. East Coast is open year round.

Boat Ramps

The North Carolina Wildlife Resources Commission maintains free ramps for pleasure boaters and anglers. Parking is generally scarce in the summer months at the busier locations such as Wrightsville Beach (which now has mostly metered parking, so be prepared and carry many quarters). The ramps are identified by black-and-white, diamond-shaped Wildlife signs. For information on public boat access, call (919) 707-0150.

Detailed information with directions for ramps throughout the area, including access areas for the disabled, are at www.ncwildlife.org/fs_index_05_boating.htm.

WILMINGTON

Dram Tree Park on the corner of Castle and Surry streets off Front Street in downtown Wilmington is almost beneath the Cape Fear Memorial Bridge and gives access to the Cape Fear River.

CASTLE HAYNE

Access to the Northeast Cape Fear River is by a ramp on Orange Street off N.C. Highway 117 bridge, a half-mile north of the intersection with State Route 1002.

SUTTON LAKE

From U.S. 17, take U.S. 421 north 3.2 miles. Turn left on Sutton Lake Road and go 1.5 miles to the road's end.

PENDER COUNTY

The Northeast Cape Fear River and its tributary creeks are accessible by three public ramps. A ramp that allows access to the west bank of the river from I-40 can be reached by taking N.C. Highway 53 east about 1.7 miles, then County Road 1512 to its end. A public ramp on the east bank is off County Road 1520 about 7.7 miles north of N.C. Highway 210. The intersection of N.C. 210 and Secondary Road 1520 lies about 3 miles east of I-40 (Exit 408). Holland's Shelter Creek Campground and Restaurant,

(910) 259-5743, is 7.5 miles east of I-40 down N.C. 53. Canoe rentals are available and the restaurant offers a memorable glimpse of local style. The private ramp gives access to Holly Shelter Creek. (For more on Holland's Shelter Creek, see our chapters on Camping and Restaurants).

THE BEACHES

Wrightsville Beach, at the east end of U.S. Highway 74/76 drawbridge, has a public ramp accessible from either side of the main road. This access to the Intracoastal Water-way is very busy in summer months, espe-cially on weekends, and parking is limited.

On **Pleasure Island**, there are four ramps east of U.S. 421 at Snow's Cut. Coming south, make a hairpin right turn at the south end of Snow's Cut bridge onto Bridge Barrier Road. Turn right at Spencer Farlow Road and follow it less than a half-mile to the Wildlife sign. The dirt parking lot is down a short road on your left. If you're coming north from Carolina Beach, exit U.S. 421 at Lewis Road just before the bridge and take an immediate left onto Access Road. Spencer Farlow Road is less than a half-mile ahead. Another ramp is at the end of U.S. 421, south of the Fort Fisher ferry terminal and gives access to the Basin off Federal Point.

Also on Pleasure Island, Carolina Beach State Park, off Dow Road, (910) 458-8206, has four ramps, a marina, ample parking and provides access to Snows Cut and the Cape Fear River. The ramp directly beneath the N.C. 210 high span in North Topsail Beach is generally uncrowded. It is accessible from the last turnout from the northbound side of N.C. 210 before the bridge. Access is to New River Inlet.

For information concerning salt-water fishing, contact N.C. Division of Marine Fisheries (252) 726-7021, (800) 682-2632; www.ncfisheries.net For information on freshwater fishing, contact N.C. Wildlife Resources Commission, Inland Fisheries Division, (919) 707-0220, or go to their website www.ncwildlife.org/fs_index_03_fishing.htm

BRUNSWICK COUNTY BEACHES

At the foot of County Road 1101, acces-sible from N.C. Highway 133 on the mainland side of Oak Island, the public ramp gives direct access to the Intracoastal Waterway (ICW). At Sunset Harbor, east of Lockwood Folly River, a public boat ramp gives access to Lockwood Folly River and Inlet and the ICW. From N.C. 211, take County Road 1112 about 6 miles south and turn right at Lock-wood Folly Road. Follow to its end. At the Wildlife Boat Ramp on Fish Factory Road, there is access to the ICW.

At the Oak Island Parks and Recreation Center, 3003 Oak Island Drive, Oak Island, access is into the Davis Canal.

Boat ramps at 55th Street NE and 57th Place W offer access on the Intracoastal Waterway.

At Holden Beach, public boat ramps are under the N.C. Highway 130 bridge on the is-land side. Freshwater anglers may launch into the east bank of the Waccamaw River at the N.C. Highway 904 bridge at Pineway, about 5 miles north of the South Carolina border or the Boiling Spring Lakes Boat Ramp & Dock on Alton Lennon Drive.

TOPSAIL ISLAND

The Town of Surf City has public boat ramps at their new Soundside Park, 517 Roland Avenue (just over the swing bridge) offering access to the Intracoastal Waterway.

In North Topsail Beach, boat ramps are located under the high-rise bridge on Shrimp Lady Lane. Ramps are free, and there is plenty of parking.

Head Boats and Charters

If you're looking to fish with a group of people, you've come to the right place. From Topsail's Treasure Coast to Calabash, there are fishing vessels aplenty. Choose the large head boats (a.k.a. party boats) accommo-dating dozens of people or the "six-pack" charters accommodating up to six passen-gers. Head boats average $40 to $100 per person for full-day excursions, and walk-ons are always welcome. The boats are equipped with full galleys and air-conditioned lounges. Handicapped accessibility to most large head

CLOSE-UP North Carolina Fishing: What's Hot and When!

January: Trout, sea bass, some grouper, some snapper, bluefish, oysters, clams

February: Trout, sea bass, some grouper, some snapper, bluefish, oysters, clams

March: Grouper, sea trout, sea bass, bluefish, croaker, oysters, some snapper, some clams

April: Bluefish, channel bass, grouper, snapper, croaker, sea trout, sea mullet, some king mackerel, some oysters, some clams

May: King mackerel, bluefish, grouper, some flounder, cobia, tuna, some sharks, crabs, soft crabs, some sea mullet, dolphin

June: Blue marlin, white marlin, dolphin, wahoo, cobia, king mackerel, bluefish, tuna, summer flounder, snapper, grouper, some Spanish mackerel, crabs, soft crabs, sharks

July: Dolphin, wahoo, tuna, blue marlin, white marlin, snapper, grouper, summer flounder, bluefish, Spanish mackerel, crab, some soft crabs, some sea mullet, sharks, king mackerel, barracuda

August: Dolphin, wahoo, tuna, grouper, snapper, Spanish mackerel, bluefish, some speckled trout, some spots, some sea mullet, sharks, crabs, king mackerel, barracuda, flounder

September: Grouper, snapper, Spanish mackerel, king mackerel, spots, sharks, bluefish, some speckled trout, sea mullet, some channel bass, tuna, dolphin, wahoo, flounder

October: King mackerel, bluefish, snapper grouper, channel bass, spots, speckled trout, some flounder, sharks, some oysters, tuna dolphin amberjack, wahoo

November: King mackerel, bluefish, speckled trout, flounder, snapper, grouper, clams, some sharks, some sea mullet, drum

December: Bluefish, flounder, speckled trout, oysters, clams, sea trout, some snapper, some sea bass, some grouper

Courtesy of N.C. Department of Environment, Health & Natural Resources, Division of Marine Fisheries, (252) 726-7021 or (800) 682-2632 http://www.enr.state.nc.us/

boats tends to be good, but varies from boat to boat and with weather conditions.

Charters offer a variety of trips, half-day or full-day, inshore or offshore, and sometimes overnight. Most are available for tournaments and diving trips, but it's a good idea to reserve early. If you can't find enough friends to chip in to cover the cost, ask about split charters. Many captains book them. Most charter captains prefer reservations but will accept walk-ons when possible. Charters range anywhere from around $300 for half-day excursions and $650 to $1,200 for an entire day of fishing in the Gulf Stream, which from here can be 40 to 70 miles offshore,

depending on currents and the marina from which you embark.

Certain provisions are common to all charters and include first mate, onboard coolers and ice, all the bait and tackle you'll need for kings, tuna, dolphin, wahoo, billfish and more. With advanced notice, many captains will arrange food packages, and some may even arrange hotel packages. Optional electric reels may be available. Although most six-pack charters are unable to bring wheelchairs aboard, crews are often very accommodating of handicapped passengers, sometimes leaving the wheelchair ashore and providing secure seating on deck, right where the action is. Call the vessel of your choice in advance for details. Remember that no one can guarantee sea conditions. If your captain decides to turn back before you've landed a smoker, rest assured he knows what he's doing. Captains reserve the right to cancel trips if conditions are unsafe for the vessel or passengers.

Carolina Beach is the Gulf Stream fishing hub between Bald Head and Topsail islands. A large number of vessels run out of the Carolina Beach Municipal Docks at Carl Winner Street and Canal Drive. Paid parking is available on the marina's west, south and east sides. There is no central booking office for the charter boats, but since you should know something about what you're chartering in advance, your best bet is to simply walk the docks and eye each one. Signs and brochures there will give you all the booking information you'll need. Ticket booths for the head boats are located at the south end of the marina. Also, check the phone book's Yellow Pages under fishing guides, charters and parties.

Charters in southern Brunswick County are concentrated at the Southport Marina, Blue Water Point Marina on the western end of Oak Island, at Holden Beach and Ocean Isle Beach. There are no charters running directly out of Wilmington. Look instead for charters and head boats running from Wrightsville Beach and Carolina Beach.

Listed below are marinas and boats that booking fishing charters. The types of vessels

If you're contemplating a charter fishing adventure, take time to walk around the area where the boats are docked. Chat with different captains to see how comfortable you are with them. You're going to be out on the water in tight quarters with someone for several hours or a whole day, so pick a captain you like. Ask questions. Is he/she licensed? What are the boat's facilities (is there a "head" or just a bucket)? How far off shore does he go? What is the policy for bad weather? What about drinking alcohol on board?

available at each location, six-packs or head boats, are indicated.

WRIGHTSVILLE BEACH

Fortune Hunter Charters, Wrightsville Beach, Custom charters, (910) 619-4665

gottafly, inc., Wrightsville Beach, Fly fishing, light tackle charters, (910) 350-0890

OnMyWay Charters, Wrightsville Beach, Custom, charters, (910) 798-6093

Rod-Man Charters, Wrightsville Beach, Inshore, near shore custom charters and tours for 1 to 4 people, (910) 799-6120, (910) 520-7661

Wrightsville Fishing Charters, Six-packs, (910) 617-4160, Wilmington

Cape Fear Charters, Inshore custom charters for 1 to 4 anglers, (910) 620-1683, Carolina Beach

Bird Dog Charters, Carolina Beach, Six-packs, (910) 452-9395

Blue Marlin Charters, Carolina Beach, Six-packs, (910) 458-6136, (866) 420-6136

Captain John's Fishing Charters, Carolina Beach, Custom charters, (910) 458-9111

Class Action Charters, Carolina Beach, Custom charters for 1 to 6 anglers; offshore/inshore, (910) 458-3348

Fish Witch Charters, Carolina Beach, Six-packs, (910) 458-5855

Hooker Fishing Charters, Carolina Beach, Six-packs, (910) 313-2828, (800) 946-1616

Hot Ticket Fishing Charters, Carolina Beach, Six-packs, (910) 791-0443

Large Time Charters, Carolina Beach, Six-packs, (910) 458-3362, (800) 582-5524

Lookout Charters, Carolina Beach, Inshore, offshore, 1 to 6 anglers, (910) 458-1307, (910) 619-0928

Musicman Charters, Inc., Carolina Beach, Six-packs, (910) 796-8889, (800) 294-5482

Reel Pleasure Charters, Carolina Beach, Six-packs, (910) 458-6424

Winner Gulf Stream Fishing & Cruise Boats, Carolina Beach, Head boats, (910) 458-FISH (3474)

BALD HEAD ISLAND

Impulsive Charters, Six-packs, (910) 457-5331

Deep Sea Fishing
aboard the
Vonda Kay
www.fishtopsail.com

FULL & HALF DAY TRIPS
MOONLIGHT CRUISES

Information & Reservations

(910) 545-FISH (3474)

SOUTHPORT/OAK ISLAND

BlueWater Princess, Oak Island, Head-boat fishing/cruises, Custom charters, up to 6 anglers, offshore, (910) 278-1230, (888) 634-9005

Boss Lady Charter Boat Services, Oak Island, Six-packs, (910) 278-3433

Fugitive Charter Boat, Oak Island, Six-packs, (910) 278-3796, (910) 523-0845

Get Reel Charters Gulf Stream Fishing, Oak Island, Six-packs, (910) 294-2005, (910) 294-2004

Liquid Asset Sport Fishing Charter Boat, Oak Island, Four-packs, (910) 278-4199

Salty Dog Charter Boat, Southport, Six-packs, (910) 278-9834

Southport Fishing Center, Southport Head Boat, Two, Three, Four and Six-packs, (910) 454-4000

Yeah Right Sportfishing Charters, Southport, Six-packs, (910) 845-2004, (336) 239-5429

HOLDEN BEACH/OCEAN ISLE BEACH/CALABASH

Holden Beach Charters, Holden Beach, Six-packs, (910) 842-9055

Sea Bear Fishing Charters, Ocean Isle Beach, Four-packs, (910) 575-4736, (828) 403-1204

Sea Hawk III, Holden Beach, Six-packs, (910) 754-6169, (910) 231-8909

Swag Charters, Holden Beach, Six-packs, (910) 842-9055 (910) 842-4930

Hurricane Fleet Deep Sea Fishing Center, Calabash, Head Boats, Six-packs, Ten-packs, Twenty-Packs, (843) 249-3571, (800) 373-2004

Red Snapper Charter Boat, Calabash, Six-packs, (910) 579-2050

White Dove Charters, Calabash, Six-packs, (843) 392-1124 (910) 579-4220

Captain Brandt's Fishing Charters, Ocean Isle Beach, Six-packs, (910) 575-3474

Voyager Fishing Charters, Ocean Isle Beach, Six-packs, (910) 575-5978, (843) 626-4900

TOPSAIL ISLAND

Vonda Kay Head Boat, 720 Channel Blvd. Topsail Beach, Head Boats, (910) 545-FISH, (910) 545-3474, www.fishtopsail.com

Paradise Landing, Sneads Ferry (north of Topsail Island), Six-packs and Head Boats, (910) 327-2114

Wooden shrimp boats, though a dying breed, can still be seen dancing on the sea in southern coastal North Carolina.

photo: Peter Doran

Saltwater Fishing Tournaments

Tournament fishing has been luring ever-larger schools of anglers, and no wonder. Top prizes can be $200,000 or more, and proceeds often benefit worthwhile charities. Many contests recognize tag-and-release as part of the Governor's Cup Billfishing Conservation series. The area has literally hundreds of competitive fishing events. Some of the popular tournaments are listed below, however you should watch the newspapers, check current listings at tackle shops, marinas, piers and visitors centers as well.

MAY

Annual Cape Fear Disabled Sportsmen Fishing Tournament, Kure Beach Fishing Pier, Kure Beach, (910) 458-5524 or Dawson at (910) 458-1202

The Spring Flounder and Trout Classic Fishing Tournament, Ocean Isle Fishing Center, Ocean Isle Beach, (910) 575-3474

The Far Out Shoot Out Fishing Tournament, Ocean Isle Fishing Center, Ocean Isle Beach, (910) 575-3474

JUNE

Annual Carolina Beach Parks & Recreation Youth Pier Fishing Tournament, Kure Beach Fishing Pier, Kure Beach, (910) 458-5524 or (910) 458-2977

Annual Flounder Tournament, Shallotte Point, (910) 579-3757.

Bald Head Island Fishing Rodeo, Bald Head Island Marina, (910) 457-3779, (800) 234-1666

U.S. Open Pier Fishing Tournament, Ocean Crest Pier, Oak Island, (910) 457-6964

Greater Wilmington Hydra Sports King Mackerel Tournament, Wilmington, (910) 452-9940

JULY

Cape Fear Blue Marlin Tournament, Wrightsville Beach Marina, Wrightsville Beach, (910) 256-6666

East Coast Got-Em-On Classic King Mackerel Tournament, Carolina Beach Yacht Basin, Carolina Beach, call Ty Cobb at (910) 512-0542

Captain Eddie Haneman Sailfish Tournament, Bridge Tender Marina, Wrightsville Beach, call Tripp at (910) 256-6550

King of the Cape Classic King Mackerel Tournament, The Shrimp House 2 Restaurant, Southport, (910) 278-4575

Long Bay Artificial Reef Association Club Challenge, Oak Island VFW and South Harbor Marina, Southport, (910) 278-4137

Long Bay Lady Anglers King Mackerel Tournament, South Harbour Marina, Southport, (910) 278-4137

AUGUST

Annual Sneads Ferry Rotary Club King Mackerel Tournament, (held in conjunction with the Sneads Ferry Shrimp Festival), Sneads Ferry, (910) 329-4446

Ladies King Mackerel Tournament, South Harbor Marina, Southport, (910) 278-4137.

Topsail Offshore Fishing Club King Mackerel Tournament, Topsail Beach, (910) 329-4446

The South Brunswick Islands King Classic King Mackerel Tournament, Holden Beach Marina, Holden Beach, (800) 546-4622

SEPTEMBER

Wildlife Bait & Tackle Flounder Tournament, Southport, (910) 457-9903

Wrightsville Beach King Mackerel Tournament, Wrightsville Beach Marina, Wrightsville Beach, (910) 256-6666

OCTOBER

Seagull Fall Tournament, Seagull Bait & Tackle, Carolina Beach, (910) 458-7135

U.S. Open King Mackerel Tournament, Southport Marina, Southport, (910) 457-5787,(800) 457-6964

NOVEMBER

Thanksgiving Flounder & Trout Classic, Ocean Isle Fishing Center, Ocean Isle Beach, (910) 575-3474

MARINAS AND THE
⚠ INTRACOASTAL
WATERWAY

Southeastern North Carolina's Cape Fear Coast is, in short, a boater's paradise. The entire length of the four-county coastal region is fronted by the Atlantic Intracoastal Waterway (AIWW, or simply the Intracoastal Waterway, ICW), a series of barrier islands, numerous sounds and a variety of rivers and streams, all connecting with the Atlantic Ocean.

Authorized by Congress in the Rivers & Harbors act of 1938, the AIWW was originally developed for commercial water traffic. Over the years, it evolved into a route that is now used more by pleasure craft than by commercial vessels. The total waterway is about 3,000 miles in length and ranges from Boston to Key West on the Atlantic coast, and from Apalachee Bay in northwest Florida to Brownsville, Texas, on the Rio Grande River.

The toll-free waterway is maintained by the Army Corps of Engineers to a minimum depth of 12 feet for most of its length, although 7 and 9 foot minimum depths will be found in some areas. Because of shoaling, depths as little as 5 or 6 feet can also be encountered. Check current information before setting sail either with the Army Corps of Engineers or at the Atlantic Intracoastal Waterway Association online at www.atlintracoastal.org.

The Cape Fear segment of the AIWW is a bonanza for nature and wildlife lovers because so much of it traverses the sounds and marshes between the barrier islands and the mainland. Some of these areas are protected and accessible only by boat. In addition, because of the mild climate in the southern coastal region coupled with the warming effect of the Gulf Stream, boating enthusiasts can enjoy a nearly yearlong season on the waterway.

In addition to numerous private and residential community boating facilities, there are well over 40 marinas and boatyards in operation, providing a full spectrum of services and supplies for the boating public. Detailed information about facilities, along with a wealth of other boating information and a searchable database, is available online at www.NCWaterways.com. A valuable resource for the boater is the North Carolina Coastal Boating Guide, which can be ordered there online or by calling (877) 368-4968. Another valuable source of information about the towns and facilities along the Southeastern coast can be found online at www.icw-net.com. Follow the links to the various coastal communities. Further information and photos of many of the marinas can be found by clicking Marinas North Carolina at www.cruisingguide.com.

Marinas

A number of marinas and boatyards dot the four-county Cape Fear Coast. The vast majority of these are located along or adjacent to the Intracoastal Waterway, or on rivers and streams connecting to the waterway. The following list, although not complete, is representative of facilities available for boaters and ranges from north to south. Facilities that are for the exclusive use of a private community or its guests are not listed.

In a few instances, the address shown reflects a mailing address rather than a physical location. For maps and detailed, candid information on all these marinas, pick up a copy of native North Carolinian Claiborne

The ICW is shallow in some areas, occasionally with very narrow cuts. Almost constant shifting of sand and mud bars are associated with storms, especially hurricanes. A good depth alarm is helpful. So is the knack for reading the water. Most groundings are only temporary inconveniences — careful attention to steering is usually all that's needed to stay out of trouble.

Young's Cruising Guide to Coastal North Carolina. Most of the marinas are listed and pinpointed on the North Carolina Coastal Boating Guide map available on the South-port-Fort Fisher Ferry, at local boating stores and by calling (877) 368-4968.

PENDER COUNTY

Harbour Village Marina
101 Harbour Village Dr., Hampstead
(910) 270-4017

Just off U.S. Highway 17 north of Wilmington, turn into Belvedere Plantation and follow the road and signs to the marina. From the water, this marina is to the north of flashing day marker #96 and south of red marker #94. The marina has all the amenities a boater could want, including a boaters' lounging area, showers, laundry facilities and many area restaurants that will deliver. Contact Harbor Master John J. King.

Scott's Hill Marina
2570 Scott's Hill Loop Rd., Wilmington
(910) 686-0896

Located north of Ogden, Scott's Hill Marina offers 62 wetslips that accommodate boats up to 38 feet. Transients are welcome, although no fuel or restaurant is available. However, you'll find a boat ramp, restrooms, marine supplies and a repair facility.

NEW HANOVER COUNTY

Inlet Watch Yacht Club
801 Paoli Ct., Wilmington
(910) 392-7106
www.inletwatch.com

Just north of Snow's Cut, this exceptionally clean, well-maintained marina offers a ship's store, parts and a full assortment of repair services. Inlet Watch is a private yacht club with 123 wet slips up to 45 feet and 420 dry storage units up to 30 feet. Slips can be rented on a six-month or yearly basis, or can be purchased as an investment. Direct ocean access and first-rate service coupled with a picturesque setting and quiet, relaxing environment make Inlet Watch Yacht Club one of the area's best marine facilities. Enjoy the Club's pool and tennis court, have a picnic on the point, then watch the moon rise over the sea while sipping a cool drink in your deck chair.

Inlet Watch Yacht Club

- *Full Service Marina / Ships Store*
- *Wet & Dry Slips for Sale or Lease*
- *Swimming Pool, Tennis Court, Bath House, Club House, Picnic Area*
- *Direct Ocean Access, Located on the ICW at Mile Marker 294*
- *Wet slip sizes are 25', 35' & 45'*
- *Dry slip sizes are 20', 22', 25' & 30'*

801 Paoli Court
Wilmington, NC 28409
910-392-7106
www.inletwatch.com

To get there by land from Wilmington, take S. College Road and head toward Carolina Beach. Drive through Monkey Junction, continuing straight on U.S. 421 heading south. Inlet Watch Yacht Club is on the left just before crossing the bridge over Snow's Cut into Carolina Beach.

Masonboro Boat Yard, Incorporated
609 Trails End Rd., Wilmington
(910) 791-1893

Drive through the neighborhood to where the land meets the ICW to find this private facility offering slips to rent or purchase. A three-story clubhouse includes four private showers, laundry facilities, a club room and a glorious unobstructed view of the water and unspoiled Masonboro Island. You're guaranteed to find some interesting conversation among the residents.

To get there by land, take Piner Road from Monkey Junction (junction of U.S. 421 and N.C. 132) for about a mile east to where the road forks. Veer left onto Masonboro Loop Road and go about two miles to Trails End Road on your right just south of the bridge over Whiskey Creek. Turn right at the

Because the Cape Fear Coast is a popular boating area, marinas may be quite busy during summer months. You're wise to radio or call well in advance of your need for dockage, repairs or fuel.

blue sign to Masonboro Boat Yard. By water, the marina is located near mile marker 288 on the Intracoastal Waterway at Whiskey Creek between Wrightsville Beach and Carolina Beach.

Pearsall On-The-River Marina
479 Blossom's Ferry Rd., Castle Hayne
(910) 675-3094

Above Wilmington, up the Northeast Cape Fear River, you'll find a small marina with four wet slips that will accommodate boats up to 30 feet. Transients are accepted when slips are available.

Pages Creek Marinas

Near mile marker 280 on the Intracoastal Waterway at Pages Creek are two marine facilities offering a variety of services. Both facilities can be reached by going north out of Wilmington on Market Street (U.S. Highway 17) and turning right onto Middle Sound Loop Road at the traffic light in Ogden.

Canaday's Yacht Basin, 7624 Mason Landing Road, Wilmington, (910) 686-9116. Features include supplies, restrooms, 72 wet slips and gas.

Johnson Marine Services, 2029 Turner Nursery Road (near Pages Creek), Wilmington, (910) 686-7565. Features include ramp, repairs, supplies, restrooms and 60 wet slips.

WRIGHTSVILLE BEACH

Boaters love Wrightsville Beach's many accommodating marinas, terrific seafood restaurants and relaxed ambiance. Whatever your marine needs, they can be met here. Facilities are available for everything from repairs to fishing gear. However, if you require groceries or want to do major shopping, you'll have to go to the mainland.

To get to Wrightsville Beach by land, take U.S. 74 and/or U.S. 76 straight to the ocean. If you're coming from downtown Wilmington, take Oleander Drive, Wrightsville Avenue or Market Street to Eastwood Road and head east.

By sea, Wrightsville Beach is approximately at mile marker 283. For the exact location, check your marine charts.

Several marinas are located on Airlie Road, just before the drawbridge leading to Wrightsville Beach. Others are across the bridge on Harbour Island. For those with

trailerable craft, there's a free Wildlife Access Ramp just to the north of the drawbridge on Harbour Island.

Atlantic Marine
101 Keel St., Wrightsville Beach
(910) 256-9911

Located on Harbour Island at Motts Channel and open seven days a week, this marina offers repair services and is oriented to serving locals with its dry-docked, small-craft facilities. Gasoline is the only service for transients.

Bradley Creek Marina
6338 Oleander Dr., Wilmington
(910) 350-0029

Just south of the Bradley Creek bridge on Oleander Drive and on the western shore of the ICW, this private membership marine facility serves the local community, but no transients. Wet slips can accommodate watercraft up to 65 feet, and dry storage is available for up to 28 feet. Slips are leased by the year, or they may be purchased. Fuel is available nearby. Bradley Creek Marina is close to Masonboro Inlet which allows access to the Atlantic Ocean.

Bridge Tender Marina and Restaurant
1418 Airlie Rd., Wilmington
(910) 256-6550

On Airlie Road at the Wrightsville Beach drawbridge is a marina with a bonus: a great local seafood and steak restaurant. The marina offers all amenities, including gas and diesel fuel. All docks are new as of 2005. One word of caution, however, the current is very swift here, so mind your slippage on entering and be ready with a boathook to fend off any craft docked nearby.

Dockside Restaurant & Marina
1308 Airlie Rd., Wilmington
(910) 256-3579, VHF Channel 16

Dockside Restaurant & Marina is located just south of the Wrightsville Beach drawbridge at about mile marker 283 on the ICW. You'll find more than 170 feet of transient dockage, fuel, 30 and 50 amp power, as well as an excellent, casual seafood restaurant. This marina is a great location for an overnight stay. Call ahead for dockage reservations.

Seapath Yacht Club
330 Causeway Dr., Wrightsville Beach
(910) 256-3747

On Motts Channel, just off the ICW, this well-appointed facility has some transient dockage with power, water, fuel, waste pump-out, wireless Internet and cable TV connections. A store provides many essential supplies. Seapath is very close to Banks Channel and is the nearest approach to the Atlantic Ocean. You can't miss Seapath because it adjoins a high-rise condominium building that clearly marks the spot for miles.

Wrightsville Beach Marina
6 Marina St., Wrightsville Beach
(910) 256-6666, VHF Channel 16

On the eastern shore of the ICW, just south of the Wrightsville Beach drawbridge, lies a luxurious place to dock for the night. Wrightsville Beach Marina offers power, water, telephone service, cable TV and Internet connections, fuel and mechanical repairs. A swimming pool is even available for transients. The Bluewater Grill overlooks the docks, welcoming famished boaters to enjoy prime rib and seafood.

CAROLINA BEACH

Below Masonboro Sound is a stretch with no marinas. The shoreline becomes residential in character, and there is not another port until you get close to Carolina Beach.

Carolina Beach Municipal Marina
300 Canal Dr., Carolina Beach
(910) 458-2540

Mooring is tight at this city marina located off the ICW at the southern end of the channel in Carolina Beach. The marina is dedicated to fishing charter and party boats. Transient slips are not available, but there is a designated anchorage area in the northeast corner of Myrtle Grove Sound. Contact the Harbor Master at this number for information.

Carolina Beach State Park Marina
Carolina Beach State Park, Carolina Beach
(910) 458-7770

At the west end of Snow's Cut, which connects the Cape Fear River with the ICW, is Carolina Beach State Park. On land, just go over the Snow's Cut Bridge on U.S. 421 S., take the first right at the second traffic light, which is Dow Road, then after about

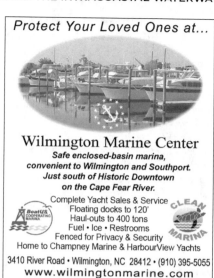

Protect Your Loved Ones at...

Wilmington Marine Center
Safe enclosed-basin marina,
convenient to Wilmington and Southport.
Just south of Historic Downtown
on the Cape Fear River.

Complete Yacht Sales & Service
Floating docks to 120'
Haul-outs to 400 tons
Fuel • Ice • Restrooms
Fenced for Privacy & Security
Home to Champney Marine & HarbourView Yachts

3410 River Road • Wilmington, NC 28412 • (910) 395-5055
www.wilmingtonmarine.com

0.2 mile, take another right onto State Park Road. The park marina offers a ramp, fuel, a modified ship's store and ample overnight dockage. If you're weary of being on a boat, you can pitch a tent and roast marshmallows over a campfire in the park, or you can take advantage of some of the park's five great trails. The Fly Trap Trail is one of the favorites. Along the trail you can look at the hungry plants known as Venus's fly traps, but don't touch! These plants bite. The Sugarloaf Trail follows along the Cape Fear River, providing beautiful water views as you explore nature.

WILMINGTON

Coming from Carolina Beach by boat, it's a 15-mile ride from Snows Cut across the Cape Fear River into Southport and the more protected Intracoastal Waterway. This is a major shipping lane to the State Port at Wilmington, as well as the route for the Southport-Fort Fisher Ferry, so do keep a watchful eye. Before crossing over, take a side trip and enter the Cape Fear River at Snows Cut, unless you have a sailboat with mast taller than 65 feet. The Cape Fear Memorial Bridge is a bascule bridge with a clearance of 65 feet. Head north up the river for one of the most memorable trips on your cruise. You'll find increasingly improved opportunities to dock, and you can take advantage of visiting Wilmington's Historic District. "Those who miss the many attractions of this seagoing community will be less for the omission," wrote Claiborne Young in his Cruising Guide to Coastal North Carolina.

After stopping to enjoy the city's downtown, head up the Northeast Cape Fear River. You'll pass under the Isabelle Holmes Bridge, which opens at 10 AM and 2 PM and on demand from 6 PM to 6 AM (the bridge tender monitors channels 13 and 18A), and you'll soon find yourself in spectacular scenery. Continue upriver and you'll see the ruins of antebellum rice plantations from 200 years ago, with endless creeks to explore. You can cruise for miles in complete tranquility with breathtaking scenery and not see a single other boat.

Bennett Brothers Yachts
Cape Fear Marina
1701 J. E. L. Wade Dr., Wilmington
(910) 772-9277

Just beyond the Third Street Bridge on the Northeast Cape Fear River, is Bennett Brothers Yachts, a good place to stop if you need repairs or a location to tie up. Celebrating 18 years as a family business, Bennett Brothers Yachts is a full-service boatyard, custom builder and yacht brokerage. With a 70-ton Marine Travel Lift, they can haul out just about anything. Twenty-five skilled craftsmen do everything from dinghy repair to cockpit extensions. Their location at the Cape Fear Marina offers 77 slips, each with power, water, telephone, pump and cable TV connection. The dock house has clean bathrooms, showers and laundry facilities and Internet access. The slips are for sale or lease and can accommodate yachts up to 200 feet with very deep draft. The marina is built on a site discovered in 1663 by William Hilton, who chose the spot for its superb protection from foul weather.

Watermark Marina of Wilmington
4114 River Rd. at Independence Blvd.,
Wilmington
(910) 794-5259

Located on the Cape Fear River, about 7 miles north of Snow's Cut and 5 miles south of downtown Wilmington, Watermark Marina offers 24-hour access, a ship's store, fuel, pump-out station, and showers inside and out. Slips are for lease only and overnight transient dockage is not available. However, boaters may tie up for fuel or to use the ship's store. Club members have access to

a club house, wet bar, showers, kitchen and swimming pool. The club is gated with land access available only to members.

Wilmington Marine Center
3410 River Rd., Wilmington
(910) 395-5055
www.wilmingtonmarine.com

Wilmington Marine Center, located at marker 59 on the Cape Fear River between Snows Cut and historic downtown Wilmington, is a 102-slip marina situated inside a safe, enclosed, all-weather basin. At this marine center you'll find a yacht service company with mobile and railway haul-out capacity to 400 tons, a chart and ship supply company, fabricators and welders, boat builders, dock manufacturers, diesel mechanics, and three yacht brokerages and sales companies that handle power boats from 20 to 80 feet.

The marina has floating docks with 110/220V electricity for yachts ranging from 20 to 120 feet, sells diesel and unleaded gasoline seven days a week, and has shipshape bath facilities on site. Numerous restaurants, museums, historic sites and entertainment venues are nearby. Friendly, professional service is the hallmark of this storm-safe marina; beautiful sunsets are an added bonus. Wilmington Marine Center is a member of the BOAT U.S. Cooperating Marina network.

WILMINGTON'S DOWNTOWN WATERFRONT

Cruising the downtown Wilmington waterfront offers a wonderful alternative to the hectic pace of the Intracoastal Waterway. Step off your boat onto one of the docks along the Riverwalk and wander into some of the appealing shops or dine in one of downtown's great restaurants. You'll be within walking distance of museums, historic residences, visitor information centers and theaters.

City of Wilmington Municipal Docks
Downtown Wilmington Riverfront
(910) 520-6875

At the City of Wilmington Municipal Docks, you will find dockage on the Cape Fear River alongside Historic Downtown Wilmington, including some adjacent to the Hilton Wilmington Riverside Hotel. Dockage is available by reservation only. Facilities include 850 feet of floating dock space and

11 floating slips. Power (30 and 50 amp) and water are available, and boaters can take advantage of amenities offered through the Hilton Riverside Hotel and the Best Western Coastline Inn. The fee for docking is $1 per foot/per day or $1.25/per foot per day with power and water hookups. Limited long-term and day dockage at $5 for six hours is also available. The dock master monitors channel 16 on VHF.

BRUNSWICK COUNTY BEACHES
Bald Head Island

Bald Head Island Marina
Bald Head Island
(910) 457-7380

Bald Head Island Marina offers slips, high-speed diesel pumps, free pump out at the fuel dock as well as restaurants and a gracious welcome to this lovely island. The marina is not reachable by road, the only way you're going to get there is by boat. Odds are you're not going to take the ferry if the marina is your destination for boating. You'll just boat right in and be delighted you did. This marina primarily serves a private, residential community where many of the homes are also vacation rentals, but it has the welcome

mat out for visitors. Stop by for a rest in a beautiful setting. You'll find fuel and the opportunity for a walking adventure on this historic island or a drive in a rented golf cart to the Maritime Market for provisions.

Southport-Oak Island

South Harbor Village Transient Dock
Fish Factory Rd., Southport
(910) 454-7486

At 1,000 feet in length, this is the longest transient dock in North Carolina. It's a floating dock in 15 feet of water at low tide and sits at a perfect parallel to the channel, making it an easy-in, easy-out dock. Amenities include 30, 50 and 100 amp power, cable TV, water, gas, diesel, a pump-out station, a courtesy phone, Internet access, laundry, showers, a full-service restaurant, a deli and an 18-hole golf course on site. A swimming pool and tennis courts are available as well as taxi service. As of this writing, in addition to the transient dock, there are 141 slips with an additional eight slips under construction to be completed in the spring of 2006. The facility is located at Mile Marker 311, Green Channel Marker 9, one mile south of the Cape Fear River inlet. Ask about the Fractional Sailing Program available here.

Picturesque marinas reflect the variety of boating enthusiasts in the southern coastal region.

photo: Peter Doran

Southport Marina Inc.
W. West Pl., Southport
(910) 457-5261

This immaculate marina is on the Southport waterfront just south of downtown. By land, take U.S. 17 from Wilmington and a left onto N.C. Highway 133 to Southport. At the intersection of N.C. Highway 211, take a left and go as far as you can without going into the water. Then take a right and drive a few blocks until the marina comes into view on the left. This marina's extensive docks welcome the cruising boater with fuel, 100 amp power, transient slips, repair service, a clubhouse, a laundry facility, a bath house and supplies as well as covered slips. Recent renovations provide more power and a more modern facility. It is one of only about a dozen North Carolina marinas with pump-outs. This marina is owned by the federal government and leased to operators who are planning expansion in the near future.

Blue Water Point Marina Resort
57th Pl. and W. Beach Dr., Oak Island
(910) 278-1230, (888) 634-9005

Blue Water Point offers slip rentals, boat rentals, gas and diesel fuel, bait, tackle and ice. Deep-sea fishing is available on two charter boats: a 60-foot head boat which carries up to 59 passengers and a 34-foot sport-fisher six-pack. Both boats have the latest electronics and equipment to fulfill your fishing needs. The marina is at Intracoastal Waterway marker 33. The owners are obviously pleased to see to boating visitors and are very accommodating. (See our Hotels and Motels chapter.)

Ocean Isle Beach

Pelican Pointe Marina
2000 Sommersett Rd., Ocean Isle Beach
(910) 579-6440

This full-service marina at marker 98 on the ICW offers gas and diesel fuel, extensive dry indoor boat storage for boats up to 32 feet, and a staff of certified mechanics. A 9-ton boat forklift is available. Pelican Pointe has a ship's store complete with boat parts and supplies, beer, ice and fishing tackle. It also offers boat rentals.

TOPSAIL ISLAND

Beach House Marina
111 N. New River Dr., Surf City
(910) 328-2628

This new marina has 192 dry storage spaces available monthly or yearly. There are also some permanent water slips and limited docking on a daily or weekend basis for transient boaters. Diesel fuel, gasoline and ice are available on site, while boating supplies can be purchased across the street. The marina is located in downtown Surf City, close to restaurants, shopping and the beach.

 CLOSE-UP

MARAD Ships and the Sunny Point Terminal

Crossing the bridge over the Cape Fear River near downtown Wilmington, you may notice two large, mysterious-looking gray ships berthed on the west side of the river to the south. These are the Cape Lobos and the Cape Lambert, part of the Maritime Administration's (MARAD) 72-ship Ready Reserve Force (RRF), an arm of the U.S. Department of Transportation.

Owned by MARAD, the ships of the RRF augment the 125-vessel Navy Military Sealift Command and come under its control when activated. While berthed in Wilmington, the two ships are maintained by a retention crew of 10 civilian merchant mariners responsible for operating, inspecting and maintaining the vessels' machinery on a scheduled basis. If the ships are activated, the crew complement is increased to 31 merchant mariners each, and must be able to proceed to a load port within 240 hours.

Built in Canada in 1973, the ships were named Federal Lakes and Federal Seaway, and were originally used to transport rolls of newsprint and coils of steel from Canada to Europe and return to Canada with about 2,000 small cars. The ships were purchased by the U.S. Government in 1988. As Roll On/Roll Off vessels, their mission is to transport wheeled and tracked vehicles such as flat-bed trailers, articulated front-end loaders, dump trucks, water tankers and Hummers for the Department of Defense.

Vehicles with a maximum weight of 30 tons can be driven aboard on either bow or stern ramps. Deck cargo area is 76,400 square feet, and there's a cargo hatch for loading armored vehicles. Displacing 30,375 tons, the ships are 682 feet long with a 75-foot beam. They have a max speed of 19 knots and are powered by two 18-cylinder diesel engines providing 8,500 HP each.

Both ships served in Operation Desert Storm in 1991. In 1994, Cape Lobos participated in a mission to Haiti, and both vessels last saw service in Operation Iraqi Freedom.

About 15 miles south of downtown, on the west bank of the river, is the Sunny Point Military Ocean Terminal ,operated by the 597th Transportation Group on 16,000 acres owned by the Army. As the largest ammunition port in the nation, Sunny Point is the Army's principal deep-water port on the East Coast and the key Atlantic Coast shipping location for the Department of Defense.

Providing world-wide transshipment of DOD ammunition, explosives and other dangerous cargo, Sunny Point is under the command of the 1303d Major Port Command. Supporting Fort Bragg and the 82nd Airborne Division, Sunny Point receives munitions, heavy equipment and bulk supplies for the division and its supporting units via rail and truck and reloads them aboard ships.

More than 90 percent of resupply munitions for Desert Storm, Desert Shield and Desert Sortie were transshipped from Sunny Point to support those operations, with 2.1 million tons of munitions loaded onto 186 vessels. With 80 percent of munitions arriving by train, the facility unloaded 27,000 rail cars during the operations. Sunny Point is the only Department of Defense terminal equipped to handle containerized ammunition.

The Sunny Port Terminal is the largest ammunition port in the nation.

photo: Terry Moore

SPORTS, FITNESS AND PARKS

Sports are very big on the southern coast. Whether you want to participate or just be a spectator, you'll find almost everything you want right here. In this chapter, we've included information about most of the area's sports and recreational activities. Look for Golf, Fishing and Watersports in separate chapters. A section on fitness centers and descriptions of area parks with their facilities follows the sports listings in this chapter. Related businesses and services are described along the way.

University athletics and professional team sports are popular, as are auto racing (especially NASCAR) and other motor sports. Because we mention only a few local teams in this chapter, you may want to explore what's available in the Raleigh-Durham-Chapel Hill area and the cities of Charlotte and Fayetteville. The area's major phone books provide a surprising amount of useful information, such as how to obtain tickets, driving directions and stadium/arena seating plans.

Look in Wilmington's daily paper, the Star-News "Sports" and "Today" pages plus weekly "Currents" and "Neighbors" sections to find announcements about sports clubs and events throughout the region. Increasingly, groups and organizations are publishing information about their activities on the Internet, so check for a website if you're unable to find what you need in this section. New Hanover County has an excellent online listing of local participation sports activities, clubs and programs which will give you a good starting place: www.nhcgov.com/PRK/PRKprograms.asp. Be sure to check the Summer Camps section in our Kidstuff chapter for summer sports camps.

Parents should note that registration fees for youth league sports are often discounted when registering more than one child in the same league. Frequently, seniors get discounts, too. Be sure to inquire.

Recreation Departments

Local and county parks and recreation departments organize a staggering selection of activities, including team sports for all ages. Check with them when looking into the sport of your choice. Addresses and phone numbers of the local offices are listed here.

Carolina Beach Parks and Recreation (office), 1121 N. Lake Park Boulevard, Carolina Beach, (910) 458-2976; Recreation Center (910) 458-2977

City of Wilmington Parks, Recreation and Downtown Services, 302 Willard Street, Wilmington, (910) 341-7855; Athletics (910) 343-3682 or (910) 343-3680; Parks (910) 341-7852

New Hanover County Parks Department, 230 Market Place Drive, Suite 120, Wilmington, (910) 798-7181

Wrightsville Beach Parks and Recreation, 1 Bob Sawyer Drive, Wrightsville Beach, (910) 256-7925

Oak Island Parks and Recreation, 3003 E. Oak Island Drive, Oak Island, (910) 278-5518

Southport Parks and Recreation, Stevens Park, 107 E. Nash Street, Southport, (910) 457-7945

Brunswick County Parks and Recreation, Parks & Recreation Building, Government Complex, Bolivia, (910) 253-2670, (800) 222-4790

Onslow County Parks and Recreation Department, 1244 Onslow Pines Road, Jacksonville, (910) 347-5332

Badminton

Wilmington Athletic Club
2026 S. 16th St., Wilmington
(910) 343-5950
www.wilmingtonathleticclub.com

The Wilmington Athletic Club (WAC) is becoming the place for a competitive game of badminton. This is not your backyard variety, so you'd better come ready for serious play. The badminton club meets every Friday night and Sunday afternoon.

Baseball and Youth Leagues

Somewhere in between youth baseball and semi-pro are the American Legion baseball programs. Area high schools are the feeder system for these high-level amateur teams, which accept outstanding players up to age 19. Fun to watch, these games are listed in the Star-News and other local media.

However, if your little Ty Cobb is just starting out, the region has several youth baseball leagues. The youth leagues offer divisions from T-ball for toddlers to baseball for teens through age 18, and some offer softball too. Registration generally takes place from early February through mid-March and fees vary. The playing season begins in April. Registrants need to present their birth certificates. Contact one of the organizations below for specifics.

The Optimist clubs sponsor many, many teams in our area. Their clubhouse numbers are listed here, but be advised, you'll seldom get an answer except during the evenings when meetings are held, so watch for flyers at schools, announcements in the newspapers and notices posted in the parks.

Cape Fear Optimist Club, (910) 762-7065 (1st, 2nd & 3rd Tuesdays after 7 PM)

New Hanover County Parks Department, (910) 798-7181

Supper Optimist Club, (910) 791-5272 (1st & 3rd Mondays after 7 PM)

Winter Park Optimist Club, (910) 791-7907

Wilmington Family YMCA (T-Ball only), (910) 251-9622. www.wilmingtonfamilyymca.org

Brunswick County Parks and Recreation, (910) 253-2670, (800) 222-4790

Onslow County Parks and Recreation, (910) 347-5332

SPECTATOR BASEBALL

Wilmington Sharks
U.S. Hwy. 421 (Carolina Beach Rd.),
Wilmington (910) 343-5621

One of 15 teams in the Coastal Plain League, the Wilmington Sharks debuted in 1997and now average 1,500 fans per game. This summer league features undergraduate college players competing in 15 cities in North Carolina, South Carolina and Virginia. The level of play is said to be comparable to that of single A minor league teams. The Sharks are officially sanctioned by the NCAA and Major League Baseball and draw players from top college programs like University of North Carolina at Wilmington (UNCW), North Carolina State University, University of North Carolina at Chapel Hill, East Carolina University and Clemson University.

The league's 56-game regular season is capped by a best-of-three championship playoff in mid-August. The Sharks play their 28 home games, beginning around Memorial Day, at Legion Stadium Sports Complex on Carolina Beach Road. Single-ticket prices range from $5 to $8. Season tickets cost $150 for box seats, $125 for reserved seats and $100 for general admission.

Basketball

Popular year round, but especially in the cooler months, basketball leagues are available for adults, boys and girls throughout our area. Watch the newspapers for information on registration. The following organizations have programs and most are open to the public. Call for specifics.

Carolina Beach Parks and Recreation, (910) 458-2977

City of Wilmington Parks, Recreation and Downtown Services, (910) 343-3682

Wilmington Family YMCA, (910) 251-9622, www.wilmingtonfamilyymca.org

Wilmington Athletic Club, (910) 343-5950, www.wilmingtonathleticclub.com

Wrightsville Beach Parks and Recreation, (910) 256-7925

Brunswick County Parks and Recreation, (910) 253-4357, (800) 222-4790

Onslow County Parks and Recreation, (910) 347-5332

Onslow County Parks and Recreation
1244 Onslow Pines Rd., Jacksonville
(910) 347-5332

Onslow County sponsors church basketball leagues playing December through March. Players must attend the church for whom they are playing. Fees are charged per team and per player. Call the above number for more information.

Bicycling

Touring most of North Carolina's southern coastal plain by bicycle can be a real pleasure. Roads tend to be lightly trafficked and flat, and most motorists have a fairly good awareness of cyclists. However, formal "bike paths" do not exist in this area. Instead, we have a system of well-marked "Share The Road" bike routes, some of which have paved bike lanes on both sides of the road that make trekking fairly easy (see the chapter on Getting Around for information about Bike Routes).

In Wilmington, bike registration is encouraged for your protection as it may help you recover your wheels in the event of theft. Most bikes recovered by the police are never claimed and are auctioned off at year's end. You can register your bikes at police headquarters downtown, 115 Red Cross Street, (910) 343-3600. Registration is free for city residents and $1 for non-residents.

New Hanover County sponsors a Bicycle Advisory Committee (BAC) with members representing law enforcement, transportation, planning, recreation, education, commerce and bicycle user groups. Interested persons may apply and are appointed by local governments for two-year terms. A strong supporter of bicycle advocacy, the committee works with local government groups in planning bicycle routes and developing multi-use trails. This is an active group that works hard to promote bicycle safety and transportation.

A bicycle is one of the best means of touring Bald Head Island —
and a visit to the "Old Baldy" lighthouse is a must.

photo: Peter Doran

As part of the nationwide Bicycle Awareness Month in May, the Committee supports Bike to Work Week and an annual 20-mile River to the Sea Ride. Open to experienced and recreational riders, the round-trip ride runs from the Coast Guard parking lot on Water Street in downtown Wilmington along secondary roads to Wrightsville Beach. For information, contact the New Hanover County Planning Department at (910) 341-3258 or visit the BAC website at www.bikewilmington.com.

Bicycle clubs can be an excellent way to meet other cyclists and learn about places to ride, upcoming events and current issues. In the Greater Wilmington area, check out the Cape Fear Cyclists. This group is touring-oriented, with rides that often are at a casual or moderate pace. For information, visit their website at www.capefearcyclists.org.

In Brunswick County, the Brunswick County Pedalers welcome interested bicycle enthusiasts to their meetings at 7 PM the third Wednesday of every month. The president has established a website at www.pedalers.southport.org where you can find dates and times of rides. Weekly rides are held each Sunday leaving at 8 AM from Southport Bicycles at 619-D N. Howe Street in Southport. Call Doug Macomb at (910) 454-8949 for more information.

Several excellent bicycle specialty shops in our area sell new and used bicycles and provide repair services. Some businesses, particularly in beach communities, offer rentals. Rates are typically around $20 to $30 per day.

Chain Reaction Cycling Center
228 Eastwood Rd., Wilmington
(910) 397-0096

Chain Reaction Cycling, in the Home Depot Shopping Center off Eastwood Road, carries a full range of mountain bikes and beach cruisers. It also sells new high-performance cycles, components, accessories and used bikes. Come here for repairs too. The store is open Monday through Saturday.

Two Wheeler Dealer
4408 Wrightsville Ave., Wilmington
(910) 799-6444

One of the largest bicycle shops around, Two Wheeler Dealer stocks a vast array of bicycles, including some vintage models and secondhand bikes, plus touring equipment, tricycles, bike trailers, infant seats — practically anything that rolls on spoked wheels. They also carry a wide variety of accessories. Professional repair work and fitting are done on the premises. Two Wheeler Dealer is also a place to find racing information and equipment and to connect with the local cycling clubs.

Wheel Fun Rentals
107 Carolina Beach Ave. N. at the
Boardwalk, Carolina Beach
(910) 458-4545

Whether you want to rent a mountain bike, tandem or cruiser, here's the place to be outfitted in Carolina Beach. But we guarantee as soon as you get inside the store, you'll start yearning to try out a Deuce Coupe, Chopper or surrey. Popular anytime, and equipped with lights, the four-wheeled covered surreys can seat up to six adults and two children. Owners Duke and Tracee Hagestrom promise you a fun ride, no matter what you choose. Call for more information or reservations.

Southport Bicycles
619-D N. Howe St., Southport
(910) 457-1878

If you are looking for a full-service bicycle shop, stop at Southport Bicycles. You will find bicycles for the whole family along with anything for the bicycle enthusiast, from clothing to safety gear to a complete line of parts and accessories. They service all brands as well. The experienced and friendly staff can help you find just the right bicycle for a challenging "century" or a cruise around the neighborhood. You will also find tricycles for the kids, adult three wheelers and recumbents. All new bicycles include one year of service and warranty, and used bicycles are available. Rentals are offered hourly, daily and weekly.

Boomer's Rentals
3468-4 Holden Beach Rd., Holden Beach
(910) 842-1400

For all your vacation rental accessories, go to Boomer's. On the mainland, at the foot of the bridge, this shop has everything you need from beach to household items, from bikes to cribs.

Julie's Rentals
2 Main St., Sunset Beach
(910) 579-1211

Julie's is a bicycle/beach-rental shop that offers beach cruisers, adult tricycles (which are excellent for the physically challenged) and Suncycle recumbent bikes. The shop is open year-round, although you may need to call ahead in the off-season.

Bowling

Most bowling centers in our area host not only leagues, but also private parties. Some have even added live music and dancing to their lounge entertainment, and all are family-oriented. Competitive prices average about $3 to $3.50 per game for adults on weekends. Prices on weekdays and for children 11 and younger may be lower, but not necessarily.

Cardinal Lanes has two locations: 3907 Shipyard Boulevard, Wilmington, (910) 799-3023, and 7026 Market Street, on the south side of Ogden, (910) 686-4223

Ten Pin Alley is at 127 S. College Road in Marketplace Mall, (910) 452-5455. They have special daytime rates for everybody until 5 PM: Monday through Thursday $1.75, Fridays $2.50 and weekends and holidays $3.50

Brunswick County Bowling Center, 630 Village Road, Shallotte, (910) 754-2695

Boxing

**City of Wilmington Boxing
and Physical Fitness Center
302 S. 10th St., Wilmington
(910) 341-7872**

Known for its outstanding boxing program, the center offers boxing training for both males and females ages 8 and older, including a non-competitive basic boxing course for non-athletes. Additionally, the center provides individuals and families opportunities to participate in traditional health-club activities. Equipped with free weights, weight machines, treadmills, cross trainers, stationary bicycles and stairclimbers, the center offers strength training, prescription exercise and cardiovascular workouts.

Classes in aerobics (including instructor training), modern aerobics/step, yoga and cardio kickboxing are taught by certified instructors. A program geared toward the physically challenged is offered. Call for details. Locker rooms and shower facilities are available. Memberships are among the best bargains in town, just $50 for city residents, and $80 for those living outside the city or outside New Hanover County. Hours are Monday through Friday 9 AM to 8 PM and Saturday 10 AM to 2 PM. The center is closed on Sunday.

**Brunswick County Parks & Recreation
Parks & Recreation Bldg.,
Government Complex, Bolivia
(910) 253-4357, (800) 222-4790**

Youth boxing is a year-round program for males and females ages 8 years and older and is held in the Leland area. Registration requires a birth certificate and two photos from the waist up. The membership dues are $35 a year and cover insurance. The club is sanctioned by USA Boxing under the State of North Carolina. The program is designed to help keep kids off the street and increase discipline inside and out of the ring.

Disc Golf

**New Hanover Disc Club
New Hanover County Parks Department
(910) 798-7181**

One of the world's fastest growing sports is disc golf, which combines the fun of Frisbee with the challenge and strategy of traditional golf. Instead of using clubs and balls, the game is played with specially designed discs that are somewhat smaller and heavier than regular flying discs and can travel very complicated paths. A disc golf course can have anywhere from nine to 27 holes (actually heavy wire baskets on posts), though most courses have 18. Course length is roughly one-third that of a traditional golf course.

Locally, disc golf can be played at Castle Hayne Park off Parmele Road at the end of Old Avenue. It's free and fun. Discs may be purchased at Play It Again Sports, 3530 S. College Road, (910) 791-1572, and Buddha's Belly, 4405 Wrightsville Avenue, (910) 792-0085. They cost between $8 and $15. Call the New Hanover County Parks Department for more information.

COMING SOON

DEMAREST VILLAGE SWIM CLUB

THE MIDDLE SOUND PENINSULA ON THE INTRACOASTAL WATERWAY

Fitness Center   **Daycare Center**   **Swim Team/Olympic Pool**   **Club Dining**

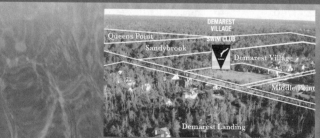

Visit www.DemarestCompany.com for early registration

Fitness Centers

Many fine fitness centers along the coast offer state-of-the-art apparatus and certified instructors. Aerobics classes have become standard, as has the use of bikes, treadmills, free weights, stair-climbers and other equipment. Membership costs usually include a onetime registration fee plus a monthly fee for a required term, but some local centers cater to the short-term visitor by offering daily, weekly and monthly rates. Additional benefits at some clubs are referral rewards, travel passes that allow members to visit affiliated clubs around the country and suspension of membership for medical reasons or extended absences.

The larger, more sophisticated clubs offer a variety of amenities that may include a well-stocked pro shop, food bar or cafe serving healthy snacks and drinks, locker room facilities, nutritional supplement sales, tanning beds, spas, massages, child care and even laundry and dry-cleaning pickup/delivery.

Body Dimensions
5241 Main St., Shallotte
(910) 754-3808

Emphasizing the natural approach to lifelong fitness, the folks at Body Dimensions offer a full line of free weights, some aerobics classes, treadmills, stair climbers and Badger/Magnum strength systems. Visitors to the area benefit from daily, weekly, monthly and other short-term rates, and no contracts are required. The center is open every day except Sunday and is in the South Park Plaza along U.S. 17 Business (Main Street).

Brunswick County Parks and Recreation
Parks & Recreation Bldg.,
Government Complex, Bolivia
(910) 253-2670, (800) 222-4790

For $20 per month or $5 per class, you may participate in various aerobics classes twice each week at several Brunswick County locations. Total Body Conditioning classes are held at Lockwood Folly Community Building in Supply and at Body Dimensions Gym in Shallotte. Total Body Conditioning classes run from January to May and September to November, and registration is available on location. Water aerobics is offered twice weekly, June through September, at The Winds Inn and Suites, and pre-registration is required. Call for specific information and a class schedule.

Carolina Beach Parks and Recreation
1121 N. Lake Park Blvd., Carolina Beach
(910) 458-2977

Essentially a do-it-yourself fitness facility, the Recreation Center has a weight-training room and a cardiovascular room with limited equipment and instruction. The hours are Monday through Friday from 8 AM to 9 PM, Saturday from 10 AM to 5 PM, and Sunday from 1 to 5 PM. Also available are a racquetball court and basketball gym, along with locker and shower facilities. Resident and non-resident memberships are available; guest fee is $5 per day. The Recreation Center offers a number of different classes, including yoga, step aerobics and Kung Fu, to name a few. Call to receive a fitness schedule.

City of Wilmington Boxing
and Physical Fitness Center
302 N. S. 10th St., Wilmington
(910) 341-7872

The Boxing and Physical Fitness Center provides individuals and families opportunities to participate in traditional health-club activities. Equipped with free weights, weight machines, treadmills, stationary bicycles, cross trainers and stair climbers, the center offers strength training, prescription exercise and cardiovascular workouts.

Classes in modern aerobics/step (including instructor training), yoga, basic boxing and cardio kickboxing are taught by certified instructors. A program geared toward the physically challenged is offered. Call for details. Locker rooms and shower facilities are available. Memberships are among the best bargains in town, just $50 for city residents and $80 for those living outside the city or outside of New Hanover County. Hours are Monday through Friday 9 AM to 8 PM and Saturday 10 AM to 2 PM. The center is closed on Sunday.

Cory Everson's
Aerobics & Fitness for Women
4620 Oleander Dr., Wilmington
(910) 791-0030

Focusing exclusively on women's health, Cory Everson's offers a wide range of fitness

Maryhelen
Cycling Instructor

Amy
Personal Trainer

Susan
Aerobics Instructor

Colleen
Yoga Instructor

Get the results you want, from experts who care!

wilmington
ATHLETIC ◆ CLUB

2026 S. 16th St. Wilmington • 343-5950

Directly across from the New Hanover Regional Medical Center
www.WilmingtonAthleticClub.com

aerobics classes
after school care
aquatic classes
badminton
basketball
cardio center
strength equipment
day spa
free weights
wellness program
indoor cycling
juice / smoothie bar

personal training
pilates studio
pro shop
racquetball
running clubs
saunas & steam
senior fitness
squash
yoga / mat pilates
youth camps
volleyball
weight loss plans

activities. Their aerobics program includes sculpting, yoga and fitness evaluations, and they also have spin classes. The club maintains a staff of certified personal trainers who can provide long-term personal training, though there's an additional charge. Also available are two Sun Dash System tanning beds. The center is clean, nicely laid out and features state-of-the-art equipment, including Cybex and Nautilus equipment designed especially for women. Cory's has special rates for guests, corporate groups, seniors (65 and older), students and families. It's located at the southeast corner of Oleander Drive and College Road.

The Crest Seaside Fitness Club
6766 Wrightsville Ave., Wrightsville Beach
(910) 509-3044

14653 N. U.S. Hwy. 17, Hampstead
(910) 270-3049

An inclusive club where you'll always feel welcome, The Crest, which is open seven days a week, offers the latest in cardio equipment, exercise machines and fitness expertise with seven certified personal trainers. Pilates, yoga and kickboxing are among the group classes. Besides a good workout, you can get a relaxing massage. Their Phuza Juice Smoothie Bar, tanning salon (Wrightsville Beach location only) and Vitamin and Sports Supplement Store are open to the public.

Curves
"30 Minute Fitness and Weight Loss Centers"

8211 Market St., Wilmington
(910) 686-6424

5725 Oleander Dr., Ste. A-1, Wilmington
(910) 791-1115

2307 N. College Rd., Wilmington
(910) 313-1021

5941-F Carolina Beach Rd., Wilmington
(910) 313-2466

1018 N. Lake Park Blvd., Carolina Beach
(910) 458-8808

4381 Port Loop Rd., SE, Southport
(910) 454-8365

4830-B Main St., Shallotte
(910) 754-8607

1018 Grandiflora Dr., Leland
(910) 371-0074

1424 S. J.K. Powell Blvd., Whiteville
(910) 642-9900

10195 Beach Dr., Calabash
(910) 575-0572

1617 U.S. Hwy. 17 N., Hampstead
(910) 270-8686

13775 N.C. Hwy. 50, Ste. 103, Surf City
(910) 329-1221

1072 Old Folkstone Rd., Sneads Ferry
(910) 327-3911

Get a complete workout in just 30 minutes utilizing the Quick Fit system found only at Curves For Women. Fast, fun and proven effective, the Curves method combines strength training and cardiovascular fitness in an innovative way that's easy to master and totally self-controlled. Curves provides an exercise environment designed for women, plus nutritional guidance and weight-management counseling. The Quick Fit system incorporates hydraulic resistance equipment, alternating with low wooden, padded exercise platforms and peppy music; a cue tape directs participants to change stations every 30 seconds and check their heart rate every eight minutes. In contrast to other strength-training equipment, the Quick Fit system doesn't use weight stacks, which greatly diminishes soreness and injury. Curves membership has options that include travel passes allowing vacationers to keep up with their fitness programs. Curves For Women's newest location is in Sneads Ferry and recently moved to a brand new, 3,000-square-foot facility.

Forever Fit Fitness Center
214 Sneads Ferry Rd., Sneads Ferry
(910) 327-2293

Focusing on a balanced regimen for fitness, Forever Fit offers strength training, a full line of cardio equipment, group training in step, circuit and dance, a personal trainer on staff and AFAA–certified instructors. Water aerobics classes are offered in June, July and August. Visitors are welcome and can pay daily and weekly rates; individual memberships begin as low as $40 per month. Forever Fit is convenient to the northern Topsail Island area.

Gold's Gym
7979 Market St., (Porters Neck), Wilmington (910) 686-1766
Longleaf Mall, 4310 Shipyard Blvd., Wilmington (910) 350-8289
5026 Market St., Wilmington (910) 392-3999
5051 Main St., Shallotte (910) 754-2270

Meticulously equipped and maintained, Gold's Gym offers three locations in Wilmington. Gold's is a full-service fitness center known for its attentive staff and its array of equipment. Gold's is noted for personally designed exercise programs and one-on-one training by certified trainers. All locations offer the newest circuit, cardiovascular and hammer-strength equipment available. They

have free child care, locker rooms with showers, and dry saunas. The center at 5026 Market Street is open 24 hours during the week.

Gold's pro-shops offer sports clothing, smoothie bars and a large selection of supplements and power bars. Group exercise classes vary at each club, ranging from yoga and Pilates to Power Punch, Body Pump, Body Flow, step and senior classes. Call the Hotline for daily updates on all classes, (910) 792-9000. The Longleaf Mall location has Wilmington's only climbing tread wall, while 5026 Market Street offers a Women Only area, group classes including Body Pump, Body Step, Body Flow and Spinning. Porter's Neck and Longleaf Mall locations both have heated workout pools with group classes and a Guppies program for kids. Members of Gold's Gym are entitled to unlimited use of 10 locations in the Carolinas and 650-plus other locations worldwide.

Oak Island Recreation Department
3003 E. Oak Island Dr., Oak Island
(910) 278-5518

The Oak Island Recreation Center features a complete weight room facility, including a Smith machine, cable crossover, lat pull down, leg extension, bench press, decline bench press, pec dec, free weights, dumb bells and body bars. The fitness facility offers a variety of cardio equipment, including Concept II Rowing Machines, a Lifecycle, a recumbent cycle, NuSteps, StarTrac treadmills, StarTrac elliptical trainers and a StarTrac stepper. Fitness classes and activities include mature aerobics, TOPS, aerobics, table tennis and yoga.

Second Wind Fitness Center
98 Quarter Horse Ln., Hampstead
(910) 270-4044

Perfect for the workout buff or the beginner, Second Wind has treadmills, stationary bikes, a complete line of circuit machines and free weights. Second Wind Fitness Center also has the area's only full-sized heated pool. Surf and turf aerobics are offered on the 1,680-square-foot suspended aerobic floor and in the pool. Personal trainers and certified fitness professionals are on hand to help you design a workout program that fits your needs. The Jungle Room day care is available for the kids while you work out. Second Wind also has a dry heat sauna, tanning beds and

A YMCA MEMBERSHIP
CAN DO WONDERS
FOR YOUR HEART.

Want to become a stronger person? Join the Y. Through programs like exercise classes, youth sports, and family events, you can get closer to those you love in a healthy, caring environment. Besides being a great way to lay the foundations for a healthy lifestyle, a Y membership cultivates strength, instills core values and brings balance to many lives. Think of it as an investment in the well-being of self, family and community. In doing so, your heart will be strengthened in ways you've never imagined.

Call 910-251-9622 for more information about YMCA memberships.

YMCA
We build strong kids,
strong families, strong communities.

Wilmington Family YMCA 2710 Market St. 28403
www.wilmingtonfamilyymca.org

a refreshing juice bar. Swimming lessons are also offered. Day passes and memberships are offered, and they are open seven days a week.

Wilmington Athletic Club
2026 S. 16th St., Wilmington
(910) 343-5950
www.wilmingtonathleticclub.com

The region's largest, most complete fitness facility, the Wilmington Athletic Club (WAC), is not only a spectacular place to work out, play, indulge yourself and improve your health status, it's a tremendous bargain. Locally owned and operated, this outstanding facility has just about everything you could want or need, from state-of-the-art Pilates and cardiovascular training equipment to a complete day spa. The club's refurbished two-floor interior is entirely air conditioned, clean and attractive. From the locker rooms to the aerobics and yoga studio, this place is first class.

A long list of activities can be accommodated, including volleyball, basketball, racquetball, squash, badminton, swimming and running. The inviting, competition-size outdoor pool is heated for year-round swim lessons, aqua aerobics classes and fun. How about trying a "road trip" using the latest indoor cycling bikes? Or maybe you'd like to tone those muscles in the expanded weight room furnished with highly advanced Cybex Eagle machines.

Personal training, VO2 max assessments, weight management, sport-specific training, senior fitness programs, social events, youth camps and massage therapy are just a few of the special features that make the Wilmington Athletic Club an all-around place for the entire family. Activity-oriented child care is available while mom or dad work out, and a terrific after-school care program is available to keep kids busy and constructively occupied.

The Wilmington Athletic Club, open seven days a week to members and their guests, is affiliated with the International Health, Racquet and Sports Club Association (IHRSA) and offers reciprocity privileges through the "Passport Program." Members may use affiliated facilities around the world for free or at a discounted rate.

Wilmington Family YMCA
2710 Market St., Wilmington
(910) 251-9622
www.wilmingtonfamilyymca.org

Offering a wide variety of fitness and educational activities, the Wilmington Family YMCA features ample facilities, such as a large gymnasium, two indoor pools, a hot tub, four racquetball courts, a free-weight room, Cybex equipment and even sunbathing decks. Athletic fields, including a track, are also available. Aerobics (including land and water exercise), arthritis classes, yoga, Pilates and cycling are just a few of the Y's vast offerings. League sports for youth and adults are organized seasonally.

Wrightsville Beach Parks and Recreation
1 Bob Sawyer Dr., Wrightsville Beach
(910) 256-7925

Wrightsville Beach Parks and Recreation offers low impact (age 50 and older) and tone and stretch (all ages) aerobics classes on a regular basis. Call for class times and fees ($1.50 to $3). Pilates classes are offered Monday, Wednesday and Friday from 10 to 11 AM and Tuesday and Thursday from 7:30 to 8:15 AM. Call for current fees.

YWCA of Wilmington
2815 S. College Rd., Wilmington
(910) 799-6820

Indoor Health & Wellness activities include aerobics, karate, yoga, Pilates and Tai Chi classes. Many arts programs are available, such as dance in many styles, improvisational acting, calligraphy, painting and cake decorating. Especially for the kids are tumbling, dance, karate and golf. A full aquatics program offers everything from basic swim lessons to lifeguard classes, water aerobics and a swim team. The YWCA offers preschool and kindergarten, full-service day care and after-school programs.

Flying

The local shortage of sizable hills, and therefore reliable updrafts, limits local aviation to powered flight. However, quite good weather conditions, large runways and pilots who fly in a radar-controlled area make Wilmington a great place to learn how to fly a plane. Why not check out the **Be A Pilot Program**, a non-profit organization that offers introductory flights for only $49. Call (888) 232-7456 for information.

Among the surprises of a bird's-eye view of the area is sighting the so-called "Carolina bays," enormous elliptical depressions in the earth first discovered from the air (see Lake Waccamaw State Park in our Camping chapter).

Besides flying lessons, local companies offer plane rentals, introductory flights and flight instruction (see our Getting Here, Getting Around chapter.)

Air Wilmington
1831 Hewlett Dr., Wilmington
(910) 763-0146, (910) 763-4691

Air Wilmington can arrange for flight instruction with a private instructor and charters for companies or groups. They can also arrange for accommodations and meal delivery. A courtesy car is available with a one-hour time limit.

ISO Aero Service Inc. of Wilmington
1410 N. Kerr Ave., Wilmington
(910) 763-8898, (800) 526-0285

ISO offers rentals, flight-training instruction for all ratings, aircraft maintenance and participates in the Be A Pilot Program. ISO has an executive aviation/FBO facility at Wilmington International Airport next to U.S. Customs.

Football

League football beyond the scholastic realm is offered primarily by two organizing bodies, the Pop Warner program and Brunswick County Parks and Recreation. Look into registration in May or June as most teams commence practice early in August.

Coastal Pop Warner
(910) 798-2141

Pop Warner organizes tackle football and cheerleading teams for boys and girls age 7 through 14 in Pee Wee, Junior Pee Wee, Midget and Mighty Mights divisions. Flag football for 5- and 6-year-olds is offered, too. More than 1,800 youngsters in New Hanover, Pender and Brunswick counties participate in the Pop Warner program each year. Games are played at Ogden Park (see the Parks section at the end of this chapter).

Wrightsville Beach Parks and Recreation
1 Bob Sawyer Dr., Wrightsville Beach
(910) 256-7925

A flag football 7-on-7 adult league, sponsored by Wrightsville Beach Parks & Recreation, is offered in both spring and fall. The cost is $365 per team.

Brunswick County Parks and Recreation
Parks & Recreation Bldg.,
Government complex, Bolivia
(910) 253-4357, (800) 222-4790

The American Youth Football League is for 10 to 12 year olds. The five county teams are: Leland, Southport, Shallotte (2) and Town Creek. A child must be less than 140 pounds in shorts to participate. Games begin in September and last until the end of November and are played on Saturday nights at North Brunswick High School, South Brunswick High School and West Brunswick High School. Registration fee is $35 per child.

Horseback Riding

Although English (hunt and saddle seat) style is favored in this region, Western is available. Most stables and riding academies offer boarding and instruction; some offer rentals and trail rides. Blacksmiths and tack shops are scarce, but the horse business in this area is thriving and bringing joy to a lot of horse lovers. New Hanover County Parks Department's programs and activities site is a good place to find contacts and information about area shows and clubs: www.nhcgov.com/PRK/PRKprograms.asp.

For serious equestrians, breeders, trainers and anyone interested in purchasing, selling, showing, boarding or watching horses, the Agricultural Review is a must-have resource. Published monthly by the North Carolina Department of Agriculture and Consumer Services, this fascinating paper features state-wide horse events in each issue. There's a classified section that includes horses and supplies for sale (or wanted). Subscriptions are free; call (919) 733-4216.

Canterbury Stables
6021 Wrightsville Ave., Wilmington
(910) 791-6502

Situated on 14.5 acres of land, Canterbury Stables is owned and operated by Linda Shelhart, who was inducted into the United

Professional Horsemen Association of the Carolinas Hall of Fame in September 2001. Shelhart trains and shows Saddlebred horses and teaches English Equitation. Canterbury specializes in private and group riding instruction, boarding, training and showing, but no rentals.

Circle K Stable
612 Vallie Ln., Wilmington
(910) 793-5550

Just south of Monkey Junction off Carolina Beach Road, Circle K offers classes in basic English style (hunt seat), horse training and boarding. They have two show rings, one lighted, but no trails. The stable's primary focus is showing Arabians. A small on-site tack shop has feed, hay and some equipment for sale. Horses are available for instruction but not for rent. They also offer birthday parties on site and after-school programs for children.

Dolorosa Arabians
131 Via Dolorosa, Rocky Point
(910) 602-3808

Owners Jan and DeCarol Williamson have been involved in the Arabian horse industry since 1978. Situated on more than 140 acres, Dolorosa Arabians boasts 150-plus stalls, two barns with tack rooms, a lounge, an office, and a grooming and wash rack area. There is a spacious 80-by-220-foot covered arena, a 50-foot covered round ring with a six-horse hot walker located nearby, a 32-stall show barn with a 50-foot covered round ring, a half-mile track, an outdoor arena and turnouts. An exceptional, highly experienced staff, together with spacious, state-of-the-art breeding facilities, a laboratory and large foaling stalls equipped with cameras, are evidence of Dolorosa's excellence. With extensive experience in all divisions of the Arabian show horse (English, Western, Halter, Driving, Hunter and Show Hack), the training and conditioning staff enjoy working with the amateur and junior rider divisions and can instill confidence in riders of all ages.

Desperado Horse Farm
7214 N.C. Hwy. 210., Rocky Point
(910) 675-0487

This horse farm offers everything from horse rentals to day or night beach rides for the horse enthusiast. Open seven days a week during daylight hours (except Sunday when they open at 2 PM), Desperado can host a special event for your church or business, provide a pony for that special birthday party, or offer trail rides, lessons, boarding or training. Reservations are required for special events and preferred for other activities. This farm is easily accessible from Wilmington on I-40, Exit 408, right on U.S. Highway 210 to Running Deer.

Hanover Stables
5901 Bizzel Ave., Castle Hayne
(910) 675-8923

Offering 13 acres with 15 segregated pastures, two lighted outdoor arenas and numerous trails, Hanover Stables provides boarding service and has a full-time, on-site manager. A great service for vacationers to the area is short-term boarding. Leave your horses here while you sightsee, then take them out to Topsail Island for a beach ride.

Hanover offers professional instruction in both Western and English (hunt seat) styles of riding, including dressage. Hanover Stables also offers instruction and participation in Western games such as barrel racing, pole bending and barrel crawl.

Exceptionally family oriented, Hanover Stables holds camps, birthday parties, hayrides, cookouts and trail rides on a regular basis. They have a show team and travel to many area shows. Believing that horsemanship teaches youngsters responsibility and respect for both animals and the environment, the owners and stable personnel strive to set good examples. Hanover Stables is an approved North Carolina Equine Rescue League site. Horses are available for sale, but not for hire.

Peachtree Equestrian Center
810 Hickman Rd., Calabash
(910) 287-4790

With 127 acres nearly adjacent to the South Carolina state line, Peachtree Stables is convenient to the entire southeastern corner of Brunswick County and northeastern South Carolina. The trails traverse 70 acres, much of it shady. Peachtree offers hourly trail rides, full boarding facilities, training, two outdoor riding rings and an indoor riding arena. Group and private instruction for ages 6 and older are offered in English and Western styles. Horses are available for lease and for sale.

Sea Horse Sports
5751 Oleander Dr., Wilmington
(910) 791-0900

Sea Horse Sports specializes in English riding apparel and equipment, including saddlery, boots and grooming supplies. The store also features a consignment area for buying and selling gently used tack and apparel. Located about .75 mile from the intersection of College Road and Oleander Drive, in Philips Plaza, the shop's hours are Monday through Saturday 10 AM to 6 PM.

Triple J Stables
120 Lake Haven Dr., Sneads Ferry
(910) 327-0577

Triple J Stables is a new attraction in the Topsail Area and offers trail rides and riding lessons. Guided trail rides are by appointment and should be reserved at least one day in advance. The stables are open seven days a week. Summer day camp is also available.

Hunting

Among North Carolina's oldest traditions are hunting, trapping and fishing. Regulations governing these activities are designed to preserve and promote these resources so that they are abundantly available for present and future outdoor enthusiasts.

There are several game lands in the region where hunters may pursue big and small game, including dove, deer, rabbit, wild turkey and black bear. Game lands include state and federal land as well as land leased from individuals and companies. Most game lands are accessible from public roads, while some have only water access. Green diamond-shaped signs identify game lands.

The 50,120-acre **Holly Shelter Game Land** in Pender County is the largest local game land. It is a varied wetland of pocosins (peat-bottomed lowlands) and pine savannahs threaded by winding creeks and existing in some noncontiguous parcels. It's north of Wilmington, roughly between U.S. Highway 17 west to the northeast Cape Fear River and between N.C. highways 210 and 53.

The **Green Swamp Game Land**, a 14,851-acre expanse lying in nearly one contiguous block bordered by N.C. Highway 211 in Brunswick County, is among the most isolated areas remaining in southeastern North Carolina.

Foot travel only is permitted here, and it's an easy place get lost. The Nature Conservancy owns this land, and much of it, as the name suggests, is low-lying wetland and pocosin.

Lying within New Hanover County, the **Sutton Lake Game Land** is a 3,322-acre land leased from CP&L. It is bordered by N.C. Highway 421 and the Cape Fear River.

Roan Island is a 2,757-acre island situated in Pender County at the confluence of the Cape Fear River and the Black River, a National Scenic River that is still in relatively pristine condition. The island lies in the flood plain and has the oldest stand of bald cypress trees in the eastern United States. Partly covered by water, it supports wild turkey and black bear as well as various smaller game, including some rare and endangered species such as the short-nose sturgeon. Access to Roan Island is only by boat.

Hunting licenses are issued by the North Carolina Wildlife Resources Commission, License Section. They can be purchased specifically for big game or small game and are also available combined with fishing licenses. A wide variety of licenses is available for both residents and non-residents. Short-term, annual and lifetime licenses can be purchased for hunting, fishing, trapping and combinations thereof.

For more information, contact North Carolina Wildlife Resources Commission, Division of Wildlife Management, NCSU Centennial Campus, 1751 Varsity Drive, Raleigh, NC 27606-2576, (919) 707-0010. Maps and information are available on the website www.ncwildlife.org.

The North Carolina Inland Fishing, Hunting and Trapping Regulations Digest offers up-to-date details about game lands, seasons, fees and regulations. It's free and is available licenses are sold. The entire Digest is online at www.ncwildlife.org.

Hunting licenses may be purchased online or by phone at (888) 248-6834. Call the License Section of the North Carolina Wildlife Resources Commission at (919) 707-0391 for more information. Licenses may also be purchased at the following locations:

Kmart, 815 S. College Road, Wilmington, (910) 799-5360

Wal-Mart Super Center, 5226 Sigmon Road, Wilmington, (910) 392-4034

Wal-Mart, 5135 Carolina Beach Road at Monkey Junction, Wilmington, (910) 452-0944

Wal-Mart Super Center, 1675 Howe Street, Southport, (910) 454-9909

Holden Beach True Value, 3008 Holden Beach Road, Holden Beach, (910) 842-5440

Island Tackle & Gifts, 6855-3 Beach Drive SW, Ocean Isle Beach, (910) 579-6116

Wal-Mart Super Center, 4540 Main Street, Shallotte, (910) 754-2880

Canady's Sport Center
3220 Wrightsville Ave., Wilmington
(910) 791-6281

Canady's is among the best one-stop retail stores for hunters. Staffers are knowledgeable in rifle and bow hunting. Clothing, field gear and a good selection of binoculars are stocked as well as rifles, shotguns, bows, arrows, knives, boots and just about anything else a hunter needs. Canady's is open Monday through Friday 8:30 AM to 6 PM and Saturday 9 AM to 5 PM.

Dick's Sporting Goods
816 S.College Rd., Wilmington
(910) 793-1904

All of Dick's Hunting Department staff are knowledgeable, active hunters and fishermen. The store carries rifle and bow hunting equipment plus knives, binoculars, clothing and other hunting supplies. The store is open Monday through Saturday 9 AM to 9:30 PM and Sunday 11 AM to 7 PM.

In-line and Roller Skating

Adults and kids alike enjoy this immensely popular activity and can be seen skating on the nearly 5-mile-long bike path or in the lighted skating facility, the Greenfield Grind Skate Park, at Greenfield Lake (see Skateboarding in this chapter).

Inline skating is banned in Wilmington's downtown central business area and Historic District. Recreational and commuter skaters on city streets and sidewalks can be fined. So where do you go to skate? UNCW offers long stretches of wide, paved walks, including

smooth, curvy stretches surrounding the lake at the university commons.

One of the best places to skate is the Loop at Wrightsville Beach. Consisting of paved walks totaling approximately 2.45 miles, the Loop runs along Wrightsville Beach Park, Causeway Drive, Lumina Avenue and Salisbury Street. There are plenty of places to stop for a cool refreshment or a dip in the ocean along the way. The Loop is busy during peak times with walkers, runners and strollers packing the pathway, so an early morning skate is just the ticket.

Bald Head Island is a true skate haven, where the only other traffic on the smoothly paved byways is golf carts and bicycles.

Jelly Beans Family Skating Center
5216 Oleander Dr., Wilmington
(910) 791-6000

Jelly Beans hosts its own inline hockey league for ages 14 and younger. Players must provide their own equipment, which may be purchased on site. A team jersey will be provided. Jelly Beans offers instruction, practice and game time. Sessions are held in winter, spring and fall. A summer camp is also offered. The registration fee for each 10-week session is $100 per player with discounts for families with more than one child. Hours vary, so please call ahead.

Oak Island Recreation Department
3003 E. Oak Island Dr., Oak Island
(910) 278-4747

The Recreation Department of the Town of Oak Island offers an In-Line Winter Hockey League for youths 6 to 18 years of age. Protective gear and skates are required. Registration is held at the recreation center. All games and practices are held at Middleton Park.

Kite Flying

Kite flying is a great individual, group or family pastime and the steady beach winds are ideal for it. There are simple, easy-to-fly kites that go up and stay up, exciting stunt kites that do loops and dives, and even power kites to give you a good workout. For thrill seekers, kiteboarding is the latest rage. Kiteboarding uses a large powerful kite to pull you on a board in the water. Other ideas for kites? Use a kite for marking your spot on the beach or your beach house. Tie a good stable kite to your beach chair or deck railing and it will fly all day long.

Nowadays, kites are made of durable nylons with fiberglass or carbon frames, which helps them hold up to the beach winds, and they'll last for years. Popular spots for kite flying are the north and south ends of Wrightsville Beach, north end of Carolina Beach and Fort Fisher State Recreation Area. In fact, most of our beaches are terrific places to fly kites, just make sure you're in a clear area if flying a stunt kite.

Blowing In The Wind
The Cotton Exchange,
312 Nutt St., Wilmington
(910) 763-1730, (888) 691-8034
222 Causeway Dr., Wrightsville Beach
(910) 509-9989, (888) 509-9989
www.blowinginthewind.com
www.gokitesurf.com

Blowing in the Wind has plenty of kite-flying fun for everyone. As the area's largest full-service kite shop, with locations in downtown Wilmington and Wrightsville Beach, they carry a huge selection of colorful kites for all ages and skill levels, from easy-to-fly single line kites, delta kites and box kites, to controllable stunt kites and big show kites. Looking for a thrill? Try one of their Jet-Ski assisted kiteboarding lessons (read all about this exciting sport in the Watersports chapter). Blowing in the Wind in Wrightsville Beach is the area's only supplier of kiteboarding products and lessons. Come check out the dazzling array of kites and explore their wide selection of windsocks, wind chimes, puzzles and wooden toys for kids.

Lacrosse

This rugged and almost legendary game has been gaining momentum recently in the greater Wilmington area. New Hanover County is one of the few counties in North Carolina that offers lacrosse at most public middle and high schools. UNC-Wilmington has both men's and women's lacrosse club teams open to students, faculty and staff. Play is on the campus recreation fields in fall and spring; for information call the UNCW Coordinator of Sports Clubs at (910) 962-7758.

Cape Fear Academy Lacrosse Camp
3900 S. College Rd., Wilmington
(910) 791-0287

This highly successful summer day camp is for boys in grades 3 through 8 in two age divisions; it runs for one week in June. Three-hour sessions are directed by the academy's lacrosse coaching staff. Instruction emphasizes fundamentals of basic stick work, rules and team play. Each camper is "drafted" onto a team for a final round-robin tournament.

Cape Fear Lacrosse Club
(910) 686-1962

Beau McCaffray is the contact person for the Cape Fear Lacrosse Club. Men and women age 18 and older who are lacrosse enthusiasts may join the club at any time, and dues are $50 per year. All are welcome. Experience is preferred, but not necessary. Play is on weekends at Wrightsville Beach Park in fall and spring. Players need to have their own equipment.

Wilmington Family YMCA
2710 Market St., Wilmington
(910) 251-9622
www.wilmingtonfamilyymca.org

Youth outdoor lacrosse is offered at the YMCA February through April and September through November. Coed youth grades 3 to 5 play in mixed leagues and youth grades 6 to 9 play boys or girls lacrosse in separate leagues; all play games on Sunday afternoons at the YMCA. Individuals 14 years of age and older play each Saturday night January to February. Individual leagues are offered for men's and women's lacrosse. All games are held in the YMCA gym.

Marksmanship and Riflery

Jim's Pawn and Guns
4212 Oleander Dr., Wilmington
(910) 799-7314

The largest gun shop in Wilmington, Jim's carries a huge selection of firearms. Here you can find new and used guns, gun safes, plus an array of accessories and ammunition. The sales staff is extremely knowledgeable and friendly. Jim's is a fully licensed federal firearm dealer.

Ye Olde Gun Club & Shooting Range
N.C. Hwy. 211, Southport
(910) 278-3763, (910) 523-0203

This large and secluded shooting range offers safety classes and concealment certification along with a covered area and practice ranges that include black powder, archery and trap shooting ranges, 25 to 500 yard rifle ranges, and 7 to 25 yard pistol ranges. Call for directions, times of operation and other information.

Martial Arts

Whether it's the sword technique of iaido, the open-hand style of karate or the throws and take-downs of ju-jitsu that interest you, or it's self-defense, confidence, physical fitness and competition you desire, it's all available in our region. Martial arts schools are proliferating, with many offering family rates and classes.

Champion Karate & Kickboxing Center
147 S. College Rd., Wilmington
(910) 792-1131

Owner/instructor John Maynard was personally trained by Chuck Norris, and his studio is part of Norris's United Fighting Arts organization. Champion offers instruction in karate, kickboxing, ground defense, ju-jitsu and personal fitness for men, women and children. In October 2003 this facility was the site where the fourth Annual Joe Lewis Fighting Systems Black Belt Research Conference was held.

Choe's Hap Ki Do
7419-C Market St., Wilmington
(910) 686-2678

Hap Ki Do, a Korean martial art, was originally introduced to the Korean royal court in 372 A.D. and has been in Grandmaster JiMong Choe's family for many generations. Grandmaster JiMong Choe has more than 55 years of martial arts experience; he is a 9th degree black belt in Hap Ki Do and an 8th degree black belt in Tae Kwon Do. His expertise extends to more than 20 weapons.

Hap Ki Do is a versatile martial art, emphasizing circular movements and leverage as opposed to physical strength and brute force. For this reason, Hap Ki Do is suitable for every one of all ages. In addition to self defense, some of Hap Ki Do's benefits are self discipline, self confidence, increased

A feat of engineering, this bridge carries you over the Cape Fear River between Wilmington and Brunswick County.

photo: Happi, student of DREAMS Center for Arts Education

concentration and mental strength, weight loss, muscle tone and a youthful appearance. Participants learn about philosophy and culture in a family-oriented setting.

Shaolin Kempo Martial Arts
3512 S. Carolina Beach Rd., Wilmington
(910) 793-1161

Stressing physical fitness, flexibility, confidence, coordination and balance, this school uses a well-rounded system with kempo, ju-jitsu, kung-fu and weapons. Quality not quantity is the main concern here. Classes are small to enhance the learning process. The low monthly fee is $55. You'll not be asked to sign a contract or pay miscellaneous fees. Head instructor Brian Watkins is a Shihan 5th Degree Black Belt who has experience in this system since 1982; his wife Christine is an experienced instructor, too. They invite individuals ages 8 and older to become part of their family in learning. Both day and evening classes are available.

Wilmington Family YMCA
2710 Market St., Wilmington
(910) 251-9622
www.wilmingtonfamilyymca.org

The Family Y offers karate, Tae Kwon Do and self-defense classes.

YWCA of the Lower Cape Fear
2815 S. College Rd., Wilmington
(910) 799-6820

Kids can learn basic karate techniques and self defense from a professional instructor at the YWCA. The Y also has a Black Belt Club for all Yellow Belts and above who are striving to reach Black Belt status. Call for class times and fees.

Racquetball

In addition to these listings, check the Fitness Centers section in this chapter to locate those that have racquetball courts.

Carolina Beach Parks and Recreation
1121 N. Lake Park Blvd., Carolina Beach
(910) 458-7416

For those wishing to play racquetball, this center has one court and will furnish racquets, balls and goggles. The hours are Monday through Friday from 8 AM to 9 PM,

Saturday from 10 AM to 5 PM, and Sunday from 1 to 5 PM.

Wilmington Athletic Club
2026 S. 16th St., Wilmington
(910) 343-5950
www.wilmingtonathleticclub.com

The Wilmington Athletic Club is southeast North Carolina's premier location for racquetball. The club has six championship courts. Daily challenge courts ensure you'll find a great game any day of the week. The club also offers instruction, challenge ladders and some of the top competitive events in the region. See the entry for Wilmington Athletic Club in our Fitness section for more information about this outstanding facility.

Wilmington Family YMCA
2710 Market St., Wilmington
(910) 251-9622
www.wilmingtonfamilyymca.org

Four racquetball courts are available at the Wilmington Family YMCA, and reservations are recommended. We have challenge courts and racquetball games. Use of the facility is free with a Y membership, or guests can purchase a $10 day pass.

Rugby

Cape Fear Rugby Club
Flytrap Downs,
21st and Chestnut Sts., Wilmington
(910) 383-0067

The Cape Fear Rugby Club has about 100 members and is the five-time Division II state champion. Members play and practice at the club-owned pitch (field) located at Flytrap Downs in Wilmington. Whenever their ships are in our port, British sailors like to play traditional rugby games with the Cape Fear Rugby Club. The club is always interested in recruiting new players and social members.

Each July, the club holds its annual Cape Fear Sevens Rugby Tournament at Ogden Park field, off Gordon Road. Considered one of the finest showcases of Sevens Rugby in the United States, the event attracts about 70 teams with 700 to 900 players from all over the world. July 2006 will feature the United States versus France.

Running and Walking

Sure, you can run or walk just about anywhere in creation. One good place to do that includes downtown Wilmington, where you can jog over the bridges and do the hills or briskly traverse the Riverwalk from end to end, all the while enjoying beautiful historic surroundings. You may want to check out some of the following prime locations or participate in one of the area's several annual racing events. Our Triathlons section later in this chapter lists several challenging events.

Brunswick County Parks and Recreation Walking Club
Parks & Recreation Building,
Government Plaza, Bolivia
(910) 253-2670, (800) 222-4790

The Walking Program was created as a self-motivation tool for individuals who walk on a regular basis. In order to keep a daily record of miles walked, logbooks are distributed for a fee of $5 each. If you walk more than 200 miles by December 31 you receive a T-shirt. If you walk more than 1,000 miles you receive a T-shirt and a plaque. For more information or to receive a log book, call Brunswick County Parks and Recreation.

Carolina Beach Lake Park
Atlanta Ave. and U.S. Hwy. 421,
Carolina Beach

A .75-mile wide concrete trail circling this picturesque lake is ideal for walkers and joggers who are looking for a convenient, safe place to exercise all year long. It's very popular with dogs as well, so pet walkers will appreciate having clean-up bags and trash containers conveniently located along the way.

Greenfield Park
U.S. Hwy. 421 (Carolina Beach Rd.),
Wilmington

Among the most beautiful places in Wilmington to jog or walk is the 5-mile loop around Greenfield Lake, south of downtown. The scenic paved path bears mile markers and follows the undulating lake shore across two wooden foot bridges (slippery when wet).

Halyburton Park
4099 S. 17th St., Wilmington

Located in the southwest district of Wilmington, the 58-acre Halyburton Park is the most recent major addition to the city's park system. The park has a handicap-accessible, 1.5 mile walking/bike trail that traverses some lovely natural areas.

"The Loop" at Wrightsville Beach

This scenic sidewalk circuit is an approximately 2.45-mile course that is very popular among locals. It encompasses a portion of the perimeter of Wrightsville Beach Park along Causeway Drive, plus Lumina Avenue and Salisbury Street. Bring the pooch. There's a free Dog Bar (serving only water) beside Bryant Real Estate at the corner of N. Lumina and Salisbury plus two additional doggy fountains along the route. Benches and drinking water are available for people, too. Pet owners are required to clean up after their pets.

Southport Parks and Recreation
201 E. Moore St., Southport
(910) 457-7923

The Walking Challenge is a program that asks Southport residents to simply get out and walk. It abides by the honor system and allows walkers to participate at their own pace and on their own schedule. Participants log their miles on a calendar and at the end of the year the calendars are turned in and the miles are tallied — and awards are given to those who have walked the most miles. The program is free to Southport residents but carries a $5 fee for non-residents.

Walking is the number one participation sport worldwide. It's easy to do and requires no special skills, equipment or clothing. All you need is a good pair of walking shoes. Except for some physically challenged individuals, everyone can enjoy the many benefits of a regular walking program, including enhanced stamina, reduced tension, improved muscle tone, weight control and lowered blood pressure. Try it. You'll like it.

Wilmington Roadrunners Club
c/o Wilmington Family YMCA,
2710 Market St., Wilmington
(910) 251-9622

The Wilmington Roadrunners Club, headquartered at the Family YMCA, sponsors races, picnics, fun runs and evening runs, and provides information on technique and safety. Entire families are welcome. Membership in the Roadrunners Club includes newsletter and magazine subscriptions, discounts on gear, and other perks. This is the place to learn what's going on in the running world, especially the events being held in the Cape Fear area. Call, watch the YMCA bulletin board or visit www.wilmingtonroadrunners. org.

Wilmington Athletic Club
2026 S. 16th St., Wilmington
(910) 343-5950
www.wilmingtonathleticclub.com

The Wilmington Athletic Club (WAC) is adjacent to beautiful Greenfield Lake Park, where you can have a scenic 5-mile walk or run to give you an invigorating workout. Return to the club for a relaxing massage, steam and shower. Raining? No problem. The club is equipped with the latest in treadmills and cross trainers.

Oak Island Recreation Department
3003 E. Oak Island Dr., Oak Island
(910) 278-5518

Beach Walkers meet three times per week to enjoy a stroll along Oak Island's beautiful strand while improving physical fitness. Each member keeps a record of their mileage and reports it at the end of the month as part of an incentive program.

RACES

Races of different sorts are popular in our area, thanks to the gentle terrain and mild weather. Just a few of the regulars are listed here, but if you keep an eye on the Star-News "Sports," "Today," "Neighbors" and "Currents" sections, you'll likely find more. Some places in Wilmington to pick up event brochures and flyers are:

Boseman's Sporting Goods, 5050 New Centre Drive, Wilmington, (910) 799-5990

Dick's Sporting Goods, 816 S. College Road, Wilmington, (910) 793-1904

Great Outdoor Provision Company, 3501 Oleander Drive, Wilmington, (910) 343-1648

Omega Sports, 3501 Oleander Drive, Wilmington, (910) 762-7212

Play It Again Sports, 3530 S. College Road, Wilmington, (910) 791-1572

Wilmington Family YMCA, 2710 Market Street, Wilmington, (910) 251-9622

New Hanover County

Battleship North Carolina
Half Marathon and 5K
c/o YMCA of Wilmington, 2710 Market St., Wilmington
(910) 251-9622, ext. 224
www.wilmingtonfamilyymca.org

The Battleship Race Half Marathon (13.1 miles) and 5K (3.1 miles) is a challenging race that starts at the Battleship North Carolina. The half-marathon goes over two bridges, then through Historic Downtown Wilmington, tours beautiful Greenfield Lake, crosses the Memorial bridge to finish back at the Battleship. The 5K is an out-and-back course crossing one bridge and returning to the Battleship. This event is presented annually in mid-November by Ed and Gray Fore in cooperation with the Battleship North Carolina staff, Wilmington Family YMCA and members of the Wilmington Roadrunners Club. It is the largest half-marathon in the state. Funds benefit the Battleship Restoration Fund and the Wilmington Family YMCA.

Seaside Shuffle 5K
c/o Wilmington Family YMCA,
2710 Market St., Wilmington
(910) 251-9622
www.wilmingtonfamilyymca.org

Organized by the Wilmington Roadrunners Club, this event is held in Wrightsville Beach the third weekend in November. The Seaside Shuffle is based at the Blockade Runner Resort Hotel. Men and women

Be a good spectator. Have respect for participants, fans, coaches and those whose job it is to referee or judge activities you enjoy watching. Don't spoil an event for yourself or others by being obnoxious, violent, overly boisterous, rude or destructive.

compete separately in a 5K road race over a USATF certified course. This is billed as a "race for runners" and includes a post-race awards ceremony and party on the hotel's beautiful oceanfront patio.

Wilmington Dog Jog
Greenfield Park, Wilmington
(910) 341-4602

On a Saturday in October, Wilmington Parks and Recreation hosts the highly popular Wilmington Dog Jog to benefit the New Hanover Humane Society. The Wilmington Dog Jog is a 5K Run (3.1 miles) and a 1.5 mile Fun Walk, which encourages people of all ages to run, walk or jog with their dogs. The run begins at 9 AM, and the Fun Walk begins at 10 AM at Greenfield Park in the main arrival area at Third and Willard Streets. This unique event is always an overwhelming success in our community, with more than 400 dogs participating.

The Wilmington YMCA Tri-Span Run
c/o Wilmington Family YMCA, 2710 Market St., Wilmington
(910) 251-9622
www.wilmingtonfamilyymca.org

Sponsored by the Wilmington Family YMCA and several area businesses, the Tri-Span 10K and 5K takes place around the first of July. The 10K course crosses all three bridges along the Wilmington waterfront, and the 5K goes through historic downtown Wilmington. Money raised goes to the YMCA Children's Sustaining Fund for after-school programs and scholarship memberships to the YMCA. Call Gray Fore at the YMCA for detailed information.

Brunswick County

Bald Head Island Maritime Classic Road Race
Bald Head Island Management
(910) 457-3701, (800) 234-1666, ext. 3701

The Maritime Classic takes place the first Saturday in November and features a 10K and 5K footrace along some of the most scenic byways in the region, ranging through dense maritime forest, open meadow and through a manicured golf and beach community. Pre-registration includes the ferry ride from Southport.

Freedom Run
Southport-Oak Island Area
Chamber of Commerce
4841 Long Beach Re., SE, Southport
(910) 457-6964, (800) 457-6964
www.nc4thofjuly.com

The annual 5K Freedom Run in Southport is an integral part of the NC 4th of July Festival activities. The early morning race, which has attracted runners from as far away as Arizona, begins at Waterfront Park, heads west on Bay Street, then winds through the Yacht Basin on to Brunswick, W. West, Atlantic, Leonard, Fodale, Moore and Rhett Streets and finishes right where it started. Refreshments and live music await all participants.

Oak Island Lighthouse 10K/5K Run/Walk
Southport-Oak Island
Area Chamber of Commerce
4841 Long Beach Rd., SE, Southport
(910) 457-6964, (800) 457-6964
www.oakislandlighthouse10k.com

The route of this popular run/walk begins at the Brunswick County Airport, crosses the Oak Island Bridge, turns through tree-lined streets, follows the beachfront and ends just past the Oak Island Lighthouse at the N.C. Baptist Assembly. Framed prints by Ricky Evans are awarded to the three top runners overall and the three top runners in each age group. Come join the competition!

North Carolina Oyster Festival Road Race
Brunswick County Chamber of Commerce
(800) 426-6644

The Oyster Festival Road Race is part of Ocean Isle Beach's North Carolina Oyster Festival, held the third weekend in October. Held on Saturday morning, this fun event is open to all ages. Three races include 10K, 5K and a 1-mile Fun Run. The race begins and ends at the pier. Call the chamber office for more information or to register. The pre-registration deadline is mid-October.

Sea Trail 5 Mile Run
Brunswick Family Assistance Agency
(910) 754-4766

This race begins and ends at the Jones-Byrd Pavilion in Sea Trail Plantation. It is a 5-mile loop course on mostly paved roads in Sea Trail and Sunset Beach. Awards are given to the top three finishers in each age group and to the top three overall male and female finishers.

Skateboarding

Most public areas are off-limits to skateboarders and in-line skaters. That means no boarding on streets, sidewalks, parking lots, boardwalks or other tempting places. Skateboarding is permitted on the UNCW campus, where responsible boarders who respect property may ride freely. Bald Head Island allows boarding on roadways, and Carolina Beach permits it on the walkway around Carolina Beach Lake. Also, the area has several well-designed, safe skate parks where boarding is very much alive and well. Surf shops are the best places to find everything you'll need for skateboarding and in-line skating, including parts and accessories, as well as skate wear, designer eyewear and shoes. (See the Watersports chapter for a list of surf shops.)

Greenfield Grind Skate Park
Greenfield Park, U.S. Hwy. 421, Wilmington
(910) 362-8222

The City of Wilmington's lighted outdoor skate park is open to both in-line skaters and skateboarders. All use the same area, which features a banked street course, hips, rails, bowls and ledges. In the spring, the park hosts the Grind Games, where participants of all levels go head to head in several skilled categories including street, pool and best trick. Watch the paper for notices or call the park for information about this popular event.

Entry fee is $2 for non-members; members are admitted free. Annual membership rate for New Hanover County residents is $50. All others must pay $75. A helmet, pads and waiver are required, and skaters must be at least 7 years old. Skaters 12 and younger must have parental supervision. Skate park hours are Tuesday through Saturday noon to 10 PM and Sunday 1 to 8 PM; it's closed on Mondays.

Oak Island Skate Park
49th St. SE, Oak Island
(910) 278-4747

Even if you are a mere spectator sitting in the bleachers, you will enjoy watching the creativity and athletic ability displayed at this skate park designed by the youth of Oak Island. The 140-foot by 60-foot skate park contains combinations of quarter pipes, half pipes, banks, a street spine, a fly box, a spine

and a pyramid — none of which exceeds 4 feet in height. Users are required to wear protective equipment including helmet, knee and elbow pads, and wrist guards. Skateboards, inline skates and roller skates are acceptable, but they must have rubber wheels and be in good working condition. Regular sessions and sessions grouped according to age and/or skill level are scheduled. Call the recreation center for times and fees.

The Skate Barn
155 Pansy Ln., Hampstead
(910) 270-3497

This is the area's indoor skateboarding facility of note. The Skate Barn features a 6-foot ramp, 3-foot and 5-foot-deep bowls and a full street course as well as an accessories shop, snacks, video games and a Foosball table. Release forms must be signed to use the facility (parents or guardians must sign for children younger than 18). To get there, take U.S. 17 to Hampstead, turn west onto Peanut Road, then right onto unpaved Pansy Lane. The Skate Barn is open Monday through Friday noon to 10 PM. On Saturdays 11 AM to 1 PM is for beginners only and 1 to 10 PM is for everyone else. Sunday it's open from 1 to 6 PM. Call for off-season hours. Check out the new Double-Wide Skate and Surf Shop behind the Skate Barn for name-brand surf and skate gear and boards.

Soccer

Soccer fever continues to sweep this area. Youth and adult leagues are growing in popularity, and the fields are constantly busy on weekends. Perhaps the best news for parents and players is that the investment necessary to play soccer is fairly low, generally limited to a one-time registration fee in the neighborhood of $65 to $70 and shin guards that can cost less than $20. Wilmington is home to the United Soccer League's professional team, the Wilmington Hammerheads.

Wilmington Hammerheads
420 Raleigh St., Wilmington
(910) 796-0076

The United Soccer League Second Division Wilmington Hammerheads Professional Soccer Team call Legion Sports Complex on Carolina Beach Road their home. In addition to hosting other professional soccer teams for exciting matches, the team conducts affordable, specialized clinics and camps. Individual instruction for players and coaches is available. Clinics run year round and include spring break and summer sessions. With an average of 1,000 kids registering, it pays to sign up early. Visit the website for information about programs and match tickets.

Cape Fear Soccer Association
6726 Netherlands Dr. #700, Wilmington
(910) 392-0306

With more than 220 teams and 3,400 players participating in several divisions, Cape Fear Soccer Association (CFSA) is the leading soccer organization in southeastern North Carolina and the second largest in the state. Every player has the opportunity to play soccer at his or her own level of competition. Emphasis is placed on the development of soccer skills, participation, sportsmanship and enjoyment of the game.

Youngsters ages 4 to 8 play non-competitively, while scores and standings are kept for teams of older children. Boys and girls play separately from U5 through U18. Teams are divided into Recreational, Challenge and Classic youth leagues. The Challenge league comprises teams from New Hanover and Columbus counties playing in three age groups. Classic league teams are the most competitive. They compete against other North Carolina teams and play in tournaments in other states. Recreational teams are formed based on neighborhoods. Challenge and Classic teams are chosen through tryouts. The association supplies a jersey, shorts and socks, while the player supplies shoes, shin guards and a ball. Registration takes place in May for the fall session, in December for the spring season.

Adults ages 19 to 50-plus participate in recreational and competitive amateur adult leagues. The most competitive is the A-Premier, which is open to male and female players who have had experience on high school, college and/or professional levels. Additionally, CFSA offers the A-Open for male and female players who desire to play in a less competitive setting, and A-Over 30, open to male and female players of all skill levels. The adult league division of CFSA is a member of the North Carolina Amateur Soccer Association. CFSA provides referees, player passes and facilities for matches.

The Recreational B Co-ed division invites players of all skill levels to play in a low-impact setting. Male players must be older than 35, females must be older than 18. The Recreational C division is for players (at least 18 years of age) who desire to play in a no-impact setting with a pickup style atmosphere; it's also for players with little to no experience playing soccer. Registration begins in December, and the season begins in February.

CFSA hosts three youth and two adult tournaments each year, with teams from throughout the state and region competing. The Hanover Cup, held in the spring, is the association's year-end tournament for U9 through U18. In summer 2005 and 2006, CFSA will host the Veterans Cup, a national adult tournament that draws teams from across America.

A special-needs soccer league is open to anyone who is physically or mentally challenged. Soccer is a sport that can be enjoyed by all participants, regardless of developmental level. The building of self esteem and confidence that result from being part of a team sport is especially beneficial to challenged individuals. They practice once a week and play on Sundays. Call for more information or visit the website www.capefearsoccer.com.

Soccer Stop
5725 Oleander Dr., Ste. B-5, Wilmington
(910) 792-1500

This is the only dedicated shop of its kind in the area. Soccer apparel, accessories, player gear and even some field equipment can all be found here. Discounts apply for registered local league players. The store is in the Oleander Oaks strip mall across from Bert's Surf Shop and is open Monday through Friday 11 AM to 7 PM, Saturday 10 AM to 5 PM and Sunday 1 to 5 PM.

Wilmington Family YMCA
2710 Market St., Wilmington
(910) 251-9622
www.wilmingtonfamilyymca.org

Youth coed soccer is offered in the spring and summer. Organized games are played March to May and September to November. This program is offered to youth 3 to 11 years of age. Games and practices are held at the YMCA. Age groups 5 to 11 play games on Saturday. Microns ages 3 and 4 have 30-minute sessions one day per week for 8 weeks during the spring and fall seasons.

Oak Island Recreation Department
3003 E. Oak Island Dr., Oak Island
(910) 278-4747

Teams in this adult soccer league can be co-ed. All teams are guaranteed ten matches with a single elimination tournament. Games will be played on the Oak Island Soccer field at Middleton Park.

Onslow County Parks and Recreation
1244 Onslow Pines Rd., Jacksonville
(910) 347-5332

Onslow County Parks and Recreation hosts a league for adults age 30 and older that plays from February to May, and an adult women's soccer league (ages 18 and up) that plays from August to October. Games are seven-on-seven. Teams can register for $225 and $7 per player, unlimited roster. Games are played at Hubert Bypass Park in the town of Hubert, convenient to the northern reaches of this guide's coverage.

Softball

Ballplayers of all ages have many opportunities to join leagues or indulge in games for fun in local parks. Except in winter, fields are often heavily scheduled for league play, especially in the evenings and on weekends. Pickup games must defer to league teams. Churches and community recreation departments frequently have solid programs as well. These Optimist clubs sponsor many, many teams in our area. Their clubhouse numbers are listed here, but be advised, you'll seldom get an answer except during the evenings when meetings are held, so watch for flyers at school, announcements in the newspapers and notices posted in the parks.

Cape Fear Optimist Club, (910) 762-7065 (1st, 2nd and 3rd Tuesdays after 7 PM)

Supper Optimist Club, (910) 791-5272 (1st and 3rd Mondays after 7 PM)

Winter Park Optimist Club, (910) 791-7907

City of Wilmington Parks, Recreation and Downtown Services
302 Willard St., Wilmington
(910) 343-3682

The Recreation Division hosts 80 adult men's, women's and coed leagues, including a league for seniors, during the spring, summer and fall. Team registration for the summer/fall season is in August. Registration for

Row, row, row your boat and explore the waterways of the southern coastal region.

photo: Peter Doran

the spring/summer season is in March. Play is at Empie Park and Trask Middle School. Fees range from $200 to $540 per team. Call for information and registration forms.

New Hanover County Parks Department
230 Market Place Dr., Ste. 120, Room 103, Wilmington
(910) 798-7198

Softball leagues and other groups desiring to use diamonds in the county parks need to reserve them through the Parks Department office. Also, this department maintains a list of organizations offering adult and youth softball. Call them for contact information.

Wilmington Senior Softball Association
7231 Lounsberry Ct., Wilmington
(910) 791-0852

Well-established for years in the North, senior softball made its Wilmington debut with one team in 1995. Now the local association boasts nine teams in two divisions: the Atlantic Division, ages 53 to 62 and the Coastal Division, ages 63 and older. In total, about 130 men ages 50 to 78 participate. Spring training commences the first Tuesday in March. The season of seven-inning games runs from the first Tuesday in April through October.

Doubleheaders are played on Tuesdays and Thursdays in Empie Park located at Park Avenue and Independence Boulevard in Wilmington, Ogden Park on Market Street in Ogden, and Veterans Park off Carolina Beach Road in Wilmington. Warm-ups start at 8:15 AM and play begins at 9 AM. All the teams are sponsored by local businesses. Registration for the season (60 games) is $70. Worthy of note: In 2001 and 2005, three division teams won their respective division state championships. For information, contact League Commissioner Phil Rose at (910) 791-0852.

Wrightsville Beach
Summer Co-ed Softball League
1 Bob Sawyer Dr., Wrightsville Beach
(910) 256-7925

Wrightsville Beach Parks and Recreation organizes league play for teams of all skill levels. Registration for the summer league opens in March and games start in April. Registration for the fall league opens in August with play beginning in September. The cost is $395 per team.

Carolina Beach Parks and Recreation
1121 N. Lake Park Blvd., Carolina Beach
(910) 458-2977

In spring and fall, the Carolina Beach Parks and Recreation Department sponsors a men's softball league. Registration is $425 per team. Softballs are provided. Play is at Mike Chappell Park on Dow Road.

Elegant gazebos and lush plants are a lovely combination found in area parks and gardens.

photo: Peter Doran

Brunswick County Parks and Recreation
Parks & Recreation Bldg., Government
Complex, Bolivia
(910) 253-2670, (800) 222-4790

Brunswick County sponsors a men's league, a women's league, a co-ed league and a girls' league. Registration for a men's or a women's league is in July and play is August through November. The team fee is $450. Co-ed adult leagues play at Lockwood Folly. Teams are required to have a team name and a contact person. Registration is in the middle of May and play is June through August. The team fee is $450. The league for 13 to 15 year old girls follows Dixie Softball rules and regulations. Teams are located in Shallotte, Waccamaw, Lockwood Folly, Southport and Leland. The registration fee is $25. All-Star teams are chosen at the end of season to play in the state tournament.

Oak Island Recreation Department
3003 E. Oak Island Dr., Oak Island
(910) 278-4747

Dixie Youth Softball, a league for girls, is divided into appropriate age groups of 6 to 8 and 9 to 12 year olds. Teams play against other county teams, and practices (no more than two a week) are held the softball field in Middleton Park. Games are held primarily on weeknights.

Onslow County Parks and Recreation
1244 Onslow Pines Rd., Jacksonville
(910) 347-5332

Onslow County sponsors adult softball leagues from late July to late September. Fees are charged per team and per player. Call the above number for more information.

Softball - Girls' Fast Pitch

Tremendously popular in the South, fast-pitch softball teams for girls up to 18 years old abound, and most of them travel extensively. To find teams, however, may be a bit of a challenge. Watch the local newspapers for notices, inquire at a school or search online. A good place to start is online at www.eteamz.com/fastpitchK-O.html. Here are some we found that recruit area players.

Carolina Rockers, Two teams for 16 and younger, one team for 18 and younger, Fayetteville, Contact Glen Rogers, (910) 424-1940 or (919) 868-4563

Carolina Cougers, 12 and younger, 16 and younger, 18 and younger Burgaw, Contact Tom Roper, (910) 259-9777

Coastal Bigstix, 10 and younger, 12 and younger, 14 and younger, Wilmington, Contact Lyle Johnston, (910) 392-6183

Squash

Wilmington Athletic Club
2026 S. 16th St., Wilmington
(910) 343-5950
www.wilmingtonathleticclub.com

The only place to play squash in Wilmington is the Wilmington Athletic Club. Need a game? WAC game finder can locate an opponent of any level for you. Instruction is also available.

Tennis

Practically every large park and many smaller neighborhood parks have public tennis courts (see the Parks section at the end of this chapter). The **Legion Sports Complex** on Carolina Beach Road has four newly refinished, lighted courts that are open until 11 PM seven days a week, no reservation required. For information call (910) 341-7855. In addition, often you can find courts at area golf clubs. Watch the local papers for tournament information and use the New Hanover County Parks online listing for tennis events: www.nhcgov.com/PRK/PRKprograms.asp.

City of Wilmington Parks,
Recreation and Downtown Services
302 Willard St., Wilmington
(910) 343-3682

Mr. PeeWee tennis for ages 4 through 8 takes place April through November. Junior and adult clinics also run from April through November. Play is at Empie Park. Call for more information and registration forms.

Greater Wilmington Tennis Association
8825 Sawmill Creek Ln.
(910) 686-5457

Over the past few years, tennis has grown by leaps and bounds in the Cape Fear area. To help support and promote the sport, the Greater Wilmington Tennis Association (GWTA) was formed.

The GWTA is a non-profit, all volunteer, organization for all tennis activities in the area, with more than 3,500 active players of all ages and skill levels. In affiliation with the North Carolina chapter of the United States Tennis Association (USTA), the GWTA sponsors USTA sanctioned tournaments and events for both adults and juniors. The group also sponsors local clinics, leagues, social events, "fun" tournaments, the Wilmington Tennis Ladder and the Wilmington Junior Tennis Ladder.

Adult league teams range in level from 2.5 to 5.0 and include men's and women's singles, doubles, mixed doubles, combo league (mixed levels of play) and Super Seniors ages 60 and 70 years young.

One of the organization's main projects is to make tennis available to youth through after-school programs and to make tennis part of the schools' physical education curricula. Through grants, special events and other funding, the GWTA has donated more than $20,000 in tennis equipment to schools and youth organizations.

Any USTA member or Wilmington Tennis Ladder (WTL) participant residing in New Hanover, Brunswick or Pender counties is automatically a member of the GWTA. Check out their website or call them for more information or to sign up for a league or a ladder.

Tennis With Love
4303 Oleander Dr., Wilmington
(910) 791-3128

If your racquet needs repair or you need a new tennis outfit, stop by Tennis With Love in the Landmark Plaza across from Cape Fear Ford. This shop specializes in restring-

ing tennis and racquetball frames and carries court clothing, shoes and accessories. They're open Monday through Saturday from 10 AM to 6 PM.

Wrightsville Beach Parks and Recreation
1 Bob Sawyer Dr., Wrightsville Beach
(910) 256-7925

Wrightsville Beach Parks and Recreation offers private, semi-private and group tennis lessons for adults and youth (age groups 6 to 8, 9 to 12 and 13 to 16). Group lessons meet on Mondays and Wednesdays. Other lessons are by appointment. Call for fees and hours or to schedule a lesson. A Ladies Singles Tennis Ladder begins in early June. Fees to join the ladder are $10 for Wrightsville Beach Residents and $15 for non-residents.

Brunswick County Parks and Recreation
Parks & Recreation Bldg.,
Government Complex, Bolivia
(910) 253-2670, (800) 222-4790

The Brunswick County Tennis Association, in coordination with Brunswick County Parks and Recreation and the North Carolina Tennis Association, offers summer tennis lessons. The lessons are open to children between the ages of 8 to 12 years of age and are held at Shallotte, Lockwood Folly, Smithville and Town Creek Parks on Tuesdays in June and July from 10:30 AM until noon. A parent or guardian may register an applicant at the Parks and Recreation Building in Bolivia. A copy of the applicant's birth certificate is needed, and the registration fee is $5.

Oak Island Recreation Department
3003 E. Oak Island Dr., Oak Island
(910) 278-4747

The Recreation Department at Oak Island offers four levels of tennis. Pee Wee Tennis, for ages 3 to 6 is designed to introduce the game to youngsters in a fun and rewarding way. Future Stars for ages 6 to 12 is designed for students to learn the fundamental strokes and techniques for a solid basic foundation. Junior Championship, with its emphasis on movement, court sense, strategy and advancement to varsity levels of play is available for intermediate and advanced players ages 9 to 17. Adult Lessons are available for adults who are just starting out and want to develop a solid foundation for their tennis game and for those who wish

Include a basic First Aid Kit in your car, boat, bike bag and fishing gear. Besides adhesive bandages, antiseptic wipes, antibiotic ointment and gauze pads, be sure to carry small scissors, tweezers, cloth for a sling, plastic sandwich baggies, an elastic bandage, pain reliever and some of those great instant ice packs, too.

to improve their swing, serve and position on the court.

Triathlons

Triathlons are very popular in this area. For further opportunities, also check the section on Running and Walking in this chapter.

Azalea Festival Triathlon
Set-Up, Inc., Wilmington
(910) 458-0299

This triathlon, sanctioned by USA Triathlon, coincides with Wilmington's most famous annual festival, usually occurring on the first or second weekend in April. The event consists of a 275-meter pool swim, a 20K bike race and a 5K run. Except for some of the bike leg, the entire triathlon takes place on the UNCW campus in Wilmington in early April. Contestants are divided into the nationally standard age and gender brackets. Registration begins January 1.

Greenfield Adventure Sprint
City of Wilmington Parks,
Recreation and Downtown Services
302 Willard St., Wilmington
(910) 794-6001

If you want a different challenge, try this 23-mile adventure. A co-ed two-person team event, the course consists of canoeing 3 miles on Greenfield Lake, Mountain Biking (on/off road) for 12 miles, and trail running for 4 miles, capped off with 4 miles of "mystery events." In keeping with the adventure spirit, the race is run rain or shine. For other events, call the Adventure Pathways office at (910) 794-6003

Kure Beach Double Sprint Triathlon
Set-Up, Inc., Wilmington
(910) 458-0299

Here's an event tailored for overachievers. After you get through the 375-meter ocean swim, the 1.5K run and the 10K bike leg, guess what? You get to do the entire thing all over again — in reverse — bike, run and swim. The overall distance is less than half that of an Olympic triathlon, but considering that this USA Triathlon–sanctioned race is in the heat of late June, the challenge is formidable. Contestants are divided into the nationally

standard age and gender brackets. Registration begins January 1.

Surf & Turf Triathlon
Surf City Baptist Church parking lot, New River Dr. and Wilmington Ave., Surf City
(910) 329-4446

This sprint triathlon for novice and serious competitive tri-athletes is held on the last Saturday in April as part of the North Carolina Triathlon Series, managed by Set-up Inc. The triathlon is a fund-raiser for the Chamber of Commerce and is sanctioned by the U.S. Triathlon Association. Advance registration for USTA members, non-members and relay teams can be made via Set-up Inc. and costs less than on-site registration. On-site registration (space in triathlon is limited to 400 athletes) and packet pick up are at the Surf City Fire Department next to the Transition Area in the parking lot of the Surf City Baptist Church.

Wilmington Family YMCA Triathlon
c/o Wilmington Family YMCA,
2710 Market St., Wilmington
(910) 251-9622
www.wilmingtonfamilyymca.org

Sponsored by the Wilmington Family YMCA, this is a sprint triathlon that takes place in September in Wrightsville Beach. Participants swim Banks Channel (a 1.5K swim), bicycle 20K and run 5K. The race starts in front of the Blockade Runner Resort and finishes at the park. More than 1,100 people participate in this annual event, which is organized by Set-Up, Inc.

Triathlon Club - Wilmington Family YMCA
c/o Wilmington Family YMCA,
2710 Market St., Wilmington
(910) 251-9622
www.wilmingtonfamilyymca.org

The YMCA Triathlon Club provides training and coaching for all levels. We offer a broad range of practices that meet your individual schedule. Our qualified coaches will assist you in all the different phases of a triathlon. We have over 120 members and we continue to grow! We also have a Kids Triathlon Club that starts in June and helps prepare the kids for the Kids Triathlon, taking place in August. The club and race are for ages 5-13. We arrange different milestones for all the different age groups to help them complete the race. Call extension 253 at the number listed.

Ultimate

Like any beach community worth its salt, Wilmington takes disc sports seriously. Ultimate is particularly popular in the Port City. Ultimate, which places heavy emphasis on sportsmanship and fair play, is a seven-versus-seven team sport that combines throwing skill, speed and endurance. Players pass a flying disc (Frisbee) to one another until it is caught in the end zone for a goal. Having no referees, players call fouls and settle disputes themselves. Ultimate is one of the fastest growing team sports in the world.

The UNCW women's team (Seaweed) won two National Collegiate Championships (1992 and 1996) and placed second in 2000. The UNCW men's team (Seamen) won a National Championship in 1993. They advanced to the College Nationals as the Atlantic Coast Regional Champion in 2001and 2002; in 2002, the men finished sixth in the Nationals.

Wilmington's three current Ultimate club teams are: The Wahine (women), the Warriors (men) and HOSS (men's masters, over age 33).

Wilmington Ultimate Frisbee Federation (WUFF)
(910) 794-1045

More than 100 players participate in Ultimate pick-up games that are open to anyone, and about 200 play in the WUFF Summer League, which is coed, for all ages and skill levels. Games are held at Castle Hayne Park off Parmalee Road at the end of Old Avenue, from June 1 to August 1.

In February, WUFF sponsors the WUFF Co-ed National Championships at Ogden Park; this is definitely the single most competitive co-ed event of the year in Ultimate Frisbee. Call Mike Gerics for information about the league, local teams and tournaments.

Volleyball

If you're not accustomed to playing in sand, you're in for a real workout, and if you survive, your improved agility and jumping may manifest themselves dramatically on a hard court. As you might expect, competition is fairly stiff, and local players generally take their games seriously. Sand volleyball courts are common in area parks and beaches, and anyone can use them, so enjoy!

Capt'n Bill's Backyard Grill
4240 Market St., Wilmington
(910) 762-0111

The only sand courts within the Wilmington city limits can be found at this popular volleyball-restaurant complex behind the North 17 Shopping Center. Year round, you can join a pickup game on one of eight courts or register your team in one of Capt'n Bill's leagues, which are for all skill levels. Operated by the husband and wife team of John and Erin Musser, Capt'n Bill's has a friendly staff, hot food, cold drinks, three bars, outside and inside seating and 15 TV sets.

City of Wilmington Parks,
Recreation and Downtown Services
302 Willard St., Wilmington
(910) 343-3682

The City of Wilmington offers fall and spring co-ed indoor volleyball for adults. Six-person teams may register for the fall league in August and for the spring league in February. Call for information and forms.

Wilmington Athletic Club
2026 S. 16th St., Wilmington
(910) 343-5950
www.wilmingtonathleticclub.com

The region's largest, most complete fitness facility, Wilmington Athletic Club (WAC), offers great volleyball on its "Court of Champions." Call about pick-up games or seasonal league play.

Wrestling

Port City Pirates
c/o Wilmington Family YMCA, Wilmington
(910) 251-9622

Under the direction of Coach Dan Willis, the Port City Pirates offer a quality wrestling program that helps build a youngster's self-esteem, confidence and ability. Sanctioned by and competing in the AAU, the Pirates travel to tournaments statewide and will host three tournaments in 2006. The Pirates compete and practice at the Wilmington Family

• Drop-ins Welcome
• Anusara Yoga
• Gentle Yoga
• Qi Gong
• Meditation
• Pilates
• Thai Yoga
• Private Sessions
• Massage Therapy
• Teacher Training
• Workshops

sea S side
Y O G A

5725 Oleander Dr. B-10
(Oleander Oaks Center)
910-792-9303
www.seasideyoga.com

YMCA, and welcome wrestlers in grades Pre-K through 8th (boys and girls). Grades 2nd and younger practice Wednesdays from 6 to 7:15 PM. Grades third and older practice Mondays 6 to 7:30 PM and Thursdays 7:15 to 8:45 PM. The cost for the season, which runs from November 21st to March 11th, is $55 for YMCA members and $70 for non-members. Registration includes a T-shirt and shorts. Call the YMCA or Coach Willis (910) 332-7311 for more information and a registration form.

Yoga, Pilates and Tai Chi

In addition to the listings below, some fitness centers also offer classes. To find individual instructors or places that focus on these increasingly popular skills, look for business cards and ads in local publications. Frequently, chiropractic offices, coffee shops and health food stores have yoga, Pilates and Tai Chi information available.

Balanced Body Massage Therapy & Yoga
5101 Dunlea Ct. #104, Wilmington
(910) 619-9619

Annie Ashenfelter is a Certified Yoga Teacher who has trained at The Kripalu Center in Lenox, Massachusetts, and with Baron Baptiste at his Power Yoga studios in Boston. She teaches private and small group yoga classes in several styles and welcomes students of all ages and experience levels. Annie is also a Licensed Massage and Bodywork Therapist (NC 4541). Included in her classes are safe assisted stretching and positional release techniques. She is available seven days a week by appointment.

Island Yoga
Live Oak Center, 2011 Elk Rd.,
Suite 6, Supply
(910) 842-2100

Melissa Parker Lee, owner and instructor at Island Yoga, was certified in Yoga and Pilates by Seaside Yoga of Wilmington with Advanced Teacher Training at Asheville Yoga Center. She was Pilates equipment trained by Inbalance Pilates Studio. Her other credits include Personal Trainer (AFPA) and RYT (200) Yoga Alliance, CYTA, Phoenix Rising Yoga Level I. A variety of classes and class times are offered Monday through Saturday including: Introduction of Yoga, Gentle Yoga, Power Yoga, Pilates and Yoga-ilates (a combination of Yoga and Pilates). Drop-ins are welcome. Specific workshops and seminars are offered as well.

New Hanover County Department of Aging Senior Center
2222 S. College Rd., Wilmington
(910) 452-6400

Today's seniors like to try new things and more than ever, they're physically, mentally and spiritually active. So, among the senior center's many offerings, yoga, Tai Chi and Pilates are on the schedule regularly. Call or

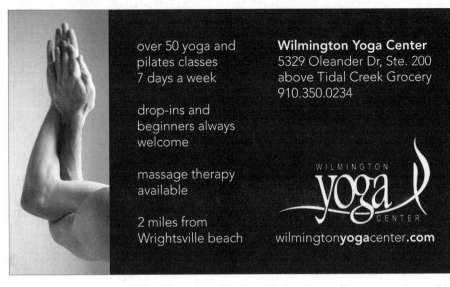

over 50 yoga and
pilates classes
7 days a week

drop-ins and
beginners always
welcome

massage therapy
available

2 miles from
Wrightsville beach

Wilmington Yoga Center
5329 Oleander Dr, Ste. 200
above Tidal Creek Grocery
910.350.0234

wilmington**yoga**center**.com**

stop by for a copy of the Tides and Times newsletter to find out when classes are held.

Porters Neck Yoga & Spa
8044 Market St., Ste. A, Wilmington
(910) 686-6440
www.portersneckyogaspa.com

A full-service day spa, complete with hair salon and yoga studio, Porters Neck Yoga & Spa offers classes and individual instruction in yoga and Pilates. Their schedule includes more than 25 classes with a variety of yoga styles, including Basic Yoga, Hot Yoga, Ashtanga and restorative. Porters Neck Yoga & Spa also has yoga cards, gift certificates and gift packages. Hours are Monday through Friday 9 AM to 7 PM, Saturday 9 AM to 5 PM and Sunday 10 to 11:30 AM (yoga only). For information and current schedule, call or visit the website.

Seaside Yoga and Boutique
5725 Oleander Dr., Ste. B-10, Wilmington
(910) 792-9303
www.seasideyoga.com

Seaside Yoga and Boutique welcomes you to try their complete schedule of non-competitive classes. They are open 7 days a week with a variety of styles and levels, with special emphasis on therapeutic healing and restorative techniques. Thai yoga, Qi Gong, Pilates and Guided Meditation classes are also available, as well as private one-on-one sessions and Massage Therapy by appointment. Seaside Yoga also offers a registered

Yoga Alliance Teacher Training program. Their recently added boutique features a full line of yoga active wear and accessories. Drop in students are always welcomed. Visit their website for the current schedule, workshops and upcoming events.

Wilmington Athletic Club
2026 S. 16th St., Wilmington
(910) 343-5950
www.wilmingtonathleticclub.com

The Wilmington Athletic Club (WAC) features a spacious yoga studio. Classes are held daily in various concentrations of yoga and are taught by top instructors. Pilates and Tai Chi are also available.

Wilmington Yoga Center
5329 Oleander Dr., Ste. 200, Wilmington
(910) 350-0234
www.wilmingtonyogacenter.com

Director Kristin Cooper, RYT, Yoga Alliance Certified, invites you to the Wilmington Yoga Center for a multi-disciplinary approach to yoga. With more than 50 classes weekly and experienced, Yoga Alliance–certified teachers, you will find a class that is safe and that fits your needs. The Wilmington Yoga Center is a registered training school for yoga teachers and offers a variety of workshops and yoga retreats. The center offers classes throughout the day and evening for all levels; beginners and drop-ins are welcome. In addition, private classes are available for one-on-one instruction. Call for information or visit the website for schedule, directions, photos and more.

Wilmington Family YMCA
2710 Market St., Wilmington
(910) 251-9622
www.wilmingtonfamilyymca.org

Come relax while taking one of our Yoga and Pilates classes. They improve flexibility, posture, balance, as well as strengthen muscles and unite spirit, mind and body. All classes are adaptable levels. We have classes daily and are free to YMCA members.

Wrightsville Beach Parks and Recreation
1 Bob Sawyer Dr., Wrightsville Beach
(910) 256-7925

Wrightsville Beach Parks and Recreation offers year-round classes emphasizing flexibility, alignment, conditioning and stress-reduction techniques. Gentle Yoga meets on Wednesday from 6:30 to 7:30 PM. Continuing Yoga is an advanced class that meets on Tuesday from 6:30 to 8 PM. Drop-ins are welcome. Call for current fees and a schedule.

YWCA of the Lower Cape Fear
2815 S. College Rd., Wilmington

Among the YWCA's Health & Wellness offerings, you'll find a Yoga/Pilates Combination class designed to create a routine of exercises to strengthen muscles surrounding and supporting the body's core. This Mind, Body & Spirit Workout offers restorative, low-impact exercises for all ages and fitness levels. Call for scheduled times and fees.

Parks

The southern costal region is rich in parks ranging from inviting walkways along the river in downtown Wilmington to the Fort Fisher State Recreation Area with seven miles of beach, wildlife reserves and a visitor center. You can find neighborhood parks, beautiful gardens, hiking trails, playgrounds, athletic fields and family-friendly county facilities. Here are some places for you to explore.

NEW HANOVER COUNTY

The New Hanover County Parks Department maintains 25 parks, three trails and two gardens. Facilities vary and may include gazebos, tennis courts, athletic areas such as soccer or baseball/softball fields, playground

equipment, a disc golf course, an equestrian ring or picnic tables. In some cases, a fee is required. For information on specific parks or to make facility reservations, call (910) 798-7181.

Hugh MacRae Park
S. College Rd. and Oleander Dr.,
Wilmington

One of the oldest and best-known parks in the county, 98-acre Hugh McRae Park is well-known for its outdoor concerts and Annual Chili Cook-Off. The tranquil pond, alluring garden and picturesque gazebo are very popular for weddings, especially in spring when the azaleas are in bloom and the weather is balmy. Facilities include a playground, ball fields, lighted tennis courts, an equestrian ring, picnic shelters and restrooms.

Ogden Park
7069 Market St., Ogden

This 125-acre county park, located on North Market Street, offers four baseball fields, lighted soccer/football fields, lighted tennis courts, picnic areas, restrooms, playgrounds, walking/jogging trails and a concession building. The entrance is on the west (southbound) side of Market Street, about 0.2 miles north of the intersection of Military Cutoff Road, a few minutes north of Wilmington city limits. Look for the entrance beside Mt. Ararat AME Church at Planter's Walk.

Snow's Cut Park
River Rd., near Snow's Cut Bridge

Divided into two sections along River Road, one directly beneath the bridge and the other some 100 yards west, this county park offers shady picnic grounds, sheltered tables, a gazebo and pedestrian access to Snow's Cut. It is very near Carolina Beach Family Campground. Call (910) 798-7181 to reserve the shelter.

Castle Hayne Park
Off Parmale Rd., at the end of Old Ave.,
Castle Hayne

Up in the far north-central part of New Hanover County, this 50-acre park is home to several sporting teams. Castle Hayne is a great family park. You'll find lighted tennis courts, soccer/football fields, playground equipment, picnic shelters, a ball field, restrooms and the area's first disc golf course.

Veterans Park
Carolina Beach Rd

Veterans Park is a unique development of educational, recreational and cultural facilities in the southern portion of New Hanover County. This 212-acre complex is home to Ashley High School, Murray Middle School, the 1,000-seat Minnie Evans Performing Arts Center and an array of athletic facilities, playgrounds and walking trails.

WILMINGTON

The 13 city-wide parks and 56 neighborhood parks, 14 green spaces and 23 landscaped areas maintained by the City of Wilmington add up to 495 acres of parkland, and they all differ widely. From the historic Riverwalk of downtown's Riverfront Park and the athletic fields of Empie Park to the sculpted benches of Carolina Courtyard and sunken cypress stands of Greenfield Lake, there is always a park nearby with the kind of recreation or quiet you desire. Of city parks, we list a cross-section of the larger ones. Inquiries about particular facilities at Wilmington parks should be directed to the parks office, (910) 341-7852.

Empie Park
Park Ave. at Independence Blvd., Wilmington

Empie's amenities include athletic fields, picnic shelters, a children's playground, lighted tennis courts, basketball courts, restrooms, open space and a senior activity area with shuffleboard, Bocce and horseshoes. Bike racks are available and there's a concession stand. Due to popular demand, tennis courts here should be reserved in advance by calling the Wilmington Athletics office at (910) 343-3682.

Greenfield Park
U.S. Hwy. 421 (Carolina Beach Rd.), Wilmington

Greenfield Lake and its surrounding gardens are the centerpiece of Wilmington's park system and a scenic wonder that changes character from season to season. Among the city's oldest parks, it was at one time a working plantation and, later, carnival grounds. The lake attracts a wide variety of birds and contains alligators. When the azaleas bloom in early spring, the area explodes in a dazzling profusion of color. Stands of flowering magnolia, dogwood, long leaf pine and live oak, many hung with Spanish moss, line the shady Lake Shore Drive. On the north side of the 158-acre park are tennis courts, playgrounds, picnic areas, a skate park, a concession stand and docks where canoes and paddleboats are available for rent. A free public boat ramp is on W. Lake Shore Drive immediately east of U.S. 421. The benches at mid-span on Lions Bridge are a wonderful spot to relax on a breezy day. Open-air performances are presented in summer at the amphitheater off W. Lake Shore Drive, adjacent to the Rotary Wheel. For additional information, call the Parks Division (910) 341-7852.

Halyburton Park
South 17th St. Ext., Wilmington

Located in the southwest district of Wilmington, the 58-acre Halyburton Park is the most recent major addition to the city's park system. Here, in the midst of suburban sprawl, is a hidden treasure of gently rolling sandhills, wet pine flatwoods and limesink depressions know as Carolina Bay Ponds, one of which holds water year round. Halyburton Park offers an abundance of diverse undisturbed plant collections as well. While the park emphasizes the property's natural areas, light recreational facilities are also available. A community building serves as a public gathering place, volunteer center, educational facility and an event area for public rentals. The park has a handicapped-accessible 1.5 mile walking/bike trail, a picnic shelter and a playground.

Legion Sports Complex
U.S. Hwy. 421 (Carolina Beach Rd.), Wilmington

Beside Greenfield Lake, approximately 1.75 miles south of the Cape Fear Memorial Bridge, is Legion Stadium, home to New Hanover High School sports teams. Also calling the complex home are the Wilmington Hammerheads, a member of the Professional D-3 United Soccer League, and the Wilmington Sharks, a collegiate Coastal Plain League baseball team. The site also has lighted athletic fields, lighted tennis courts and a swimming pool as well as plenty of parking.

Riverfront Park
Water St., Wilmington

For many locals, this park epitomizes Wilmington life. Once congested with the wharves of the state's busiest port, the River-walk is now a place for quiet strolls, sightseeing, shopping, live outdoor music and dining. The sternwheeler Henrietta III docks here. You'll also find a visitors information booth. Historic sailing ships visiting town often dock here and usually offer tours.

Robert Strange Park
Eighth and Nun Sts., Wilmington

The heart of this park is its swimming pool. Other facilities include a recreation center, restrooms, a playground, picnic shelters, softball fields and lighted tennis and basketball courts.

WRIGHTSVILLE BEACH

Wrightsville Beach Park
Causeway Dr., Wrightsville Beach

This sprawling recreation and athletic facility is impossible to miss when traveling Causeway Drive. It spans 13 acres and includes four tennis courts, a basketball court, a softball field, a football/soccer field, sand volleyball courts and playground equipment. The 2.45-mile sidewalk Loop, bordering much of the park and traversing both of the island's bridges, is popular among walkers and joggers. Parking and restrooms are available.

CAROLINA BEACH
AND KURE BEACH

Carolina Beach State Park
1010 State Park Rd., Carolina Beach
(910) 458-8206

This is one of the most biologically diverse parks in North Carolina and a contender for the most beautiful park in the area. Maritime forest, sandhill terrain, waterfront and sand ridges support carnivorous plants and centuries-old live oaks. Six miles of easy trails wind throughout the park. The marina offers boat ramps ($5) and 42 boat slips off the Cape Fear River. Excellent overnight camping facilities are available. The park is on Pleasure Island, 1 mile north of Carolina Beach and less than a half-mile from U.S. 421, off Dow Road. Day use is free.

Carolina Beach Lake Park
Atlanta Ave. and U.S. Hwy. 421,
Carolina Beach

Primarily a picnic site, this 11-acre park has four small gazebos, sheltered picnic tables and a playground. A .75-mile concrete trail circling the lake is ideal for walkers, skaters, bikers and joggers who are looking for a convenient, safe place to exercise. A small amphitheater is the site of local holiday events and concerts. An especially popular feature is the pedal-boat concession operated by Wheel Fun Rentals.

McDonald Park
Wilson Ave., Carolina Beach

This quarter-acre community park is tucked away in a neighborhood setting. A great place for taking the toddlers to play and picnic, the park has slides and swing sets and tables.

Mike Chappell Park
Dow Rd., Carolina Beach

Two lighted ball fields and a football/soccer field make up the largest area of this 10-acre park, which also offers picnic tables, two tennis courts, two lighted sand volleyball courts and a playground. The park is bounded by Sumter Avenue and Clarendon Boulevard.

Fort Fisher State Recreation Area
U.S. Hwy. 421 S., Kure Beach
(910) 458-5798

Miles of white sandy beach, salt marshes, tidal creeks, mudflats and wildlife habitats make the Fort Fisher State Recreation Area a true treasure among the state's park offerings. Located on the southern tip of Pleasure Island, with the Atlantic Ocean on the east and the Cape Fear River on the west, this well-maintained park offers visitors a wide variety of pleasurable activities. Swimming, sunbathing, strolling and shelling are among the favorites for beachgoers. Fishing, hiking and birding rank high with many folks, along with boating or canoeing through shallow bays and channels. Loggerhead turtles and other endangered species make nests in the park's protected areas. Park staff offer interpretive and environmental education programs as well as surf-fishing clinics. Call for availability. If you're interested in driving your four-wheel-drive vehicle out onto the beach strand, please read the Sun, Sand and Sea chapter's section on Beach Driving for fees and regulations.

Facilities include a Visitors Center, concession stand (10 AM to 6 PM, Memorial Day through Labor Day), restrooms and outside showers. Park hours are: November through February 8 AM to 6 PM; March 8 AM to 7 PM; April, May and September 1 to 14, 8 AM to 8 PM; September 15 to November, 24-hour access; June through August 6 AM to 9 PM.

The Cove at Fort Fisher State Historic Site
U.S. Hwy. 421 S., Kure Beach

The Cove is a beautiful getaway about 6 miles south of Carolina Beach. Bordering the beach and a rocky sea wall, a grove of wind-swept live oaks provides shade for the picnic tables and grills. Come to fish and sunbathe but don't swim. Dangerous currents and underwater hazards make swimming extremely hazardous. Parking is available south of the area near the Fort Fisher Memorial and at the Fort Fisher State Historic Site museum across the road.

Joe Eakes Park
K Ave. at Seventh St., Kure Beach

This small park, a short walk from the beach, offers a playground, two tennis courts, a picnic area and volleyball and basketball courts.

Gurney Hood Barking Lot
K Ave. at Seventh St., Kure Beach

Adjacent to Joe Eakes Park, the Gurney Hood Barking Lot is a fenced pooch-play area. Sandy soil, trees, play equipment, Frisbees, balls and other doggie amenities make this a fun place for your pet. Water is available, a couple of benches are provided, and clean-up bags and trash containers are supplied so you can be a responsible pet handler. An especially good feature is a fenced entry area for holding your dog until you're ready to go into the main play area. Latches on both gates prevent your pup from accidentally getting loose outside the Barking Lot.

BRUNSWICK COUNTY

The following parks are maintained by the Brunswick County Parks and Recreation Department. All have excellent facilities, including tennis courts, ball fields, football/

soccer fields, basketball courts, playgrounds and picnic shelters. Most of them also feature shuffleboard courts and horseshoe pits, plus community buildings for use by groups for such occasions as reunions, exercise classes and other events. For specific information about any of these parks or to reserve picnic shelters and community buildings, call (910) 253-2670. Tennis players at Ocean Isle Beach also may note the town's public courts on Third Street across from the Museum of Coastal Carolina.

Brunswick River Park
574 River Rd., Leland
(910) 253-2670

This 11-acre park includes restrooms and a boat ramp.

Leland Community Park
1490 Village Rd. NE, Leland
(910) 371-9606

This is an 11-acre community park, situated behind the Leland Post Office. Facilities include two baseball fields, a community building, a concession stand with restrooms, a playground and three picnic shelters.

Lockwood Folly District Park
430 Green Swamp Rd., Supply
(910) 754-8414

The 20-acre park is a mile north of the town of Supply. Its community building, however, is at Holden Beach. The park offers three baseball/softball fields, a football/soccer field, a concession stand with restrooms and a separate restroom facility, a basketball court, two tennis courts, three picnic shelters and a playground.

Northwest District Park
1937 Andrew Jackson Hwy. NE, Leland
(910) 371-9222

This 35-acre park lies 15 minutes west of Wilmington, on the south side of U.S. 17. You will find three baseball/softball fields, one football/soccer field, a concession stand with restrooms, two basketball courts, four tennis courts, four picnic shelters and a playground.

Shallotte District Park
5550 Main St., Shallotte
(910) 754-7710

To find this 64-acre park from U.S. 17, follow signs for U.S. 17 Business. Amenities include four baseball/softball fields, a concession stand with restrooms, a basketball court, two tennis courts, three picnic shelters, a playground and four soccer fields.

Smithville District Park
8340 River Rd. SE, Southport
(910) 457-9105

Smithville District Park covers 23 acres and includes two baseball/softball fields, one regular football/soccer field and five mini football/soccer fields, a concession stand with restrooms, a basketball court, two tennis courts and two picnic shelters.

Town Creek District Park
6420 Ocean Hwy. E, Winnabow
(910) 253-4610

You can't miss this park on the east side of U.S. 17, about 15 or 20 minutes southwest of Wilmington. Contained in 35 acres, it offers four baseball/softball/soccer fields, a concession stand with restrooms, a basketball court, two tennis courts, two picnic shelters, a playground and a community building as well as shuffleboard and horseshoes.

Waccamaw Park
5855 Waccamaw School Rd. NW, Ash
(910) 287-3658

Though this park comprises 35 acres, 20 remain undeveloped at this writing. The remaining 10 acres provide two baseball/softball fields, a football/soccer field, a concession stand with restrooms, a basketball court, two tennis courts, a beach-style volleyball court, two picnic shelters, a playground and a community building.

E. F. Middleton Park
E. Oak Island Dr. at S.E. 47th St., Oak Island

The primary city park in Long Beach, Middleton Park offers a large playground with sand pits, swings and climbing bars, plus two

tennis courts, basketball courts, a baseball field and picnic tables with some shade. The park is across the street from Town Hall and the emergency medical station.

Ev-Henwood Nature Preserve
6150 Rock Creek Rd., Town Creek
(910) 253-6066, (910) 962-3107

This nature preserve, owned and administered by UNCW, comprises 174 acres of lush woodland with educational displays and ten miles of hiking trails. One of these trails meanders along the banks of the beautiful Town Creek. Among the many natural points of interest is an old tar kiln of the type once ubiquitous throughout the region. Suitable for families, the preserve is open during daylight hours seven days a week. Picnic tables and a restroom are available, and there's an onsite caretaker. Don't forget the camera and lunch. Admission is free.

TOPSAIL ISLAND

Soundside Park
N.C. Hwys. 50/210, East of Surf City swing bridge

This 19-acre park located on Topsail Sound is a real gem. A wooden boardwalk winds around the park's shoreline, and fishing piers invite anglers to drop a line. The park has boat ramps, covered picnic shelters with grills, a play area and restrooms.

Stump Sound Park
N.C. Hwy. 172, Sneads Ferry

Softball fields, basketball courts, tennis courts, a children's playground and picnic shelters are available at this Onslow County Park. It opens daily at 10 AM and closes at dusk. The park is between U.S. 17 and N.C. 210, less than 1 mile from the Four Corners traffic light.

GOLF

olfers appreciate the southern coast's relaxed, laid-back feeling. Great weather, beautiful views all around, majestic long leaf pines, stately live oaks, and flat to gently rolling land are just a few of the reasons golf is a very popular sport here. Most of the local courses offer prices that encourage multiple rounds per day, too. PGA and fund-raising organizations find area courses ideal for hosting their tournaments and events.

More new golf courses sprout up along the southern coast than anywhere else in North Carolina. Brunswick County alone boasts 36 courses, many located in residential golf communities. The area features challenging course designs bearing the signatures of Arnold Palmer, Rees Jones, Tom Fazio, Pete Dye, Jack Nicklaus, Dan Maples, Donald Ross, Hale Irwin, Fred Couples, Tim Cate, George Cobb and Willard Byrd, among others.

Most local courses are semiprivate, which means they're open to the public and club memberships are available. Membership, of course, offers various benefits and privileges, such as lower fees or preferred tee times. Greens fees vary according to season and location. At semiprivate courses, fees range widely, from about $20 to $100 and more, but average between $30 and $40 for 18 holes. Fees are highest at the more exclusive clubs and during the peak seasons (March 1st to mid-May and mid-September to early November). Look for special packages during non-peak times, such as three rounds at drastically reduced prices for either morning or afternoon. Discounts for seniors, corporations and groups are commonplace.

Overall, the region's courses offer an excellent balance between price and playing conditions. Many courses also offer practice ranges and club rental. Teaching pros are plentiful and eager to help you polish your game. You'll find a proliferation of golf publications at visitors centers, hotels and other touristy locations. Check out The Insiders' Guide® to Golf in the Carolinas at http://www.insiders.com/carolina-golf/

In this chapter we describe some of the area's better courses, judged by overall beauty, location and variety of challenge. We've also included independent driving ranges plus retail shops that offer equipment and repairs; information on golf packages and services; and some local annual tournaments. Complete listings of courses can be found at chambers of commerce (see our Area Overviews chapter for a listings).

Courses

WILMINGTON

Beau Rivage Resort & Golf Club
649 Rivage Promenade, Wilmington
(910) 392-9022, (800) 628-7080

Elevations up to 72 feet and scads of bunkers (including two waste bunkers) place this course among the more dramatically landscaped in New Hanover County. It is a semiprivate par 72 course in which water hazards come into play on eight holes. Hole 4 (206 yards, par 3) is notable for its island tee box for women and a carry that is entirely over water. The course's greens, made of a genetically engineered form of bermudagrass called ultra dwarf TifEagle, are well maintained and quite pleasing to golfers. Beau Rivage offers a fully stocked golf shop, PGA instruction and club rental. Memberships are available.

A bar and grill serving breakfast and lunch provides an attractive setting for post-round analysis. A 32-suite hotel adjoins the clubhouse. Formal banquet facilities accommodating up to 250 guests are popular for weddings, corporate retreats and family reunions.

"Sharpen Your Short Game"
at INLAND GREENS GC
• Open Everyday at 8am
• Juniors and Families Welcome
• Rental Clubs Available
• Play All Day for One Low Price

18 Hole, Regulation Par 3 Golf Course
Call 910.452.9900
5945 Inland Greens Dr. Wilmington, NC
www.inlandgreens.com

The Cape Golf & Racquet Club
535 The Cape Blvd., Wilmington
(910) 799-3110

A mile north of Carolina Beach, this semiprivate, meticulously landscaped, par 72 championship course sits amid 24 lakes, ponds and marshland. The Bermudagrass fairways equal 6800 yards. The grounds include a driving range plus putting and chipping greens as well as a fully stocked pro shop, locker rooms with showers, a cocktail lounge, a full-service restaurant, banquet facilities and a snack bar. Club members also have access to The Cape's swimming pool and tennis courts. Greens fees range from inexpensive to moderate.

Country Club of Landfall
800 Sun Runner Pl., Wilmington
(910) 256-8411

Golfing on Landfall's two superlative courses, designed by Jack Nicklaus and Pete Dye and situated along the Intracoastal Waterway, is for members (and their guests) of Country Club of Landfall. The rewards for golfing members include challenges unparalleled on the majority of courses. The par 72 Nicklaus course has added another nine holes, giving it a total of 27. Overall, the Nicklaus course is perhaps the less forgiving of the two. It looks easier on paper than it really is, thanks largely to the many carries over marshes and water. The 6th hole, for instance, is a tough par 3 playing 190 yards from the back, with little more than marsh all

the way to the ocean. Hole 8's island green is backed with a bunker with a 5-foot forward lip. Another island green is the signature hole on the Dye course. Completely waterbound, hole 2 slopes away from the sand trap that collars half its perimeter. The Dye course is a par 72. Plenty of uneven lies, marshes and pot bunkers demand that players push the envelope of their game to the utmost.

Members also have access to Landfall's elaborate sports center, which has 14 tennis courts (with grass, clay and hard surfaces) and an Olympic-size pool. In addition, members enjoy a fitness center, aerobics room and spa services, as well as a casual grille, formal dining rooms and lots of exciting social activities.

Echo Farms Golf & Country Club
4114 Echo Farms Blvd., Wilmington
(910) 791-9318

Some of the best features of Echo Farms are its stands of moss-draped hardwood and some of the finest Tif-Eagle greens, installed in 2004 along with new drainage, in the area. Rolling hills and bunkers make for a challenging game. A former dairy farm (the original farmhouse near the 17th hole is still occupied), it's now a par 72 challenge. Lakes come into play on nine holes. A driving range, practice greens, grill, bar and snack lounge are open to all. Echo Farms has developed a fine teaching facility, offering clinics and private lessons. The course is 5 miles south

Magnolia Greens
GOLF PLANTATION

WILMINGTON'S PREMIER GOLF COURSE

Rated ★★★★★ by Golf Digest

Public Welcome

Tee Times
910.383.0999 or 800.677.7534

5 Miles South of Wilmington on Hwy 17

www.magnoliagreens.com

of downtown Wilmington off Carolina Beach Road (N.C. Highway 421).

Inland Greens
5945 Inland Greens Dr., Wilmington
(910) 452-9900
www.inlandgreens.com

Sharpen your short game on this public 18-hole, par 3 course. For all ages and skill levels, holes average just more than 100 yards, and the greens are in good condition. It's strictly a walking course, but pull-carts are available for rent. Almost midway between Wrightsville Beach and downtown Wilmington, the course is hidden off Cardinal Drive between Eastwood Road and Market Street.

Magnolia Greens Golf Plantation
U.S. Hwy. 17, Leland
(910) 383-0999
www.magnolia-greens.com

This magnificent, 27-hole golf plantation with "always perfect" bent grass greens is located just 5 miles south of Wilmington, North Carolina. Magnolia Greens hosted the PGA Tour Qualifying in 1998 and 1999. Rated as a top five golf destination on the Carolina Coast by NC Magazines Executive Leaders Poll and was recently awarded a four and one half star rating by Golf Digest . This signature golf course provides five sets of tees for various skill levels, making it challenging yet fair for all golfers. Magnolia Greens provides a complete practice facility and golf instruction. One of the Carolina coast's

best golf experiences which includes a fully stocked pro shop, great food at the bar and grill, food and beverage service on the course, and friendly starters and rangers. Magnolia Greens is open to daily public play and offers stay-and-play golf packages.

Porters Neck Plantation and Country Club
8403 Vintage Club Dr., Wilmington
(910) 686-1177

Porters Neck is an aficionado's course, aesthetically perfect and strategically challenging. Designed by Tom Fazio, this is a championship course (par 72) that emphasizes careful club selection. Impeccably maintained fairways undulate in sometimes deceptive fashion. Enormous waste bunkers and lakes abound, some of which span from tee to green (holes 11, 13, 14). Distinctive waste mounds planted with native grasses add to the course's character. Each hole presents conditions to make the most accurate golfer uncomfortable, yet leave no player unfulfilled. About 6 miles from Wilmington, this course winds through a private residential development adjacent to the Intracoastal Waterway. Public play is invited, but limited. A full-service pro shop and PGA-trained staff are available. The entrance gate is a little over a mile in from the property limit on Porters Neck Road.

Wilmington Golf Course
311 S. Wallace Ave., Wilmington
(910) 791-0558

This 1925 Donald Ross course received a face-lift in 1998, which brought it back to its original architectural design. Many sand traps and bunkers were added, making it a more challenging course. In 2001–02, this course was named the seventh best of 100 Public & Resort Courses in North Carolina by Golfweek magazine, placing it among such respected courses as Pinehurst No. 8 (ranked fifth) and Pinehurst No. 7 (ranked eighth). In its July-August issue, Travel and Leisure Magazine voted this venerable course the No. 1 Donald Ross Course worldwide.

Enter this par 71 facility from either Oleander Drive or Pine Grove Drive, a seven-minute drive from downtown. Compared to other local courses, the Muni, as it's called, has a relative dearth of water hazards, but the stream crossing the fairways of holes 2 (495 yards, par 5) and 12 (519 yards, par 5) is in just the wrong place for many golfers. The clubhouse and pro shop are open every day from 7 AM until sundown. The building will be renovated in 2005 to include upgraded locker and restroom facilities and a restaurant.

Greens fees are about the cheapest you'll find, especially for city residents, and nine-hole rounds are available. This historic course is a "must-play" hidden gem within the city. Groups are limited to foursomes, and no singles or twosomes are permitted before 1:30 PM. The course is home to the annual Wilmington City Golf Championship, which features local amateurs.

WALLACE

River Landing Country Club
116 Paddle Wheel Dr., Wallace
(910) 285-6693, (800) 959-3096

Home to five U.S. Open Qualifiers, the 2001 Mid-Amateur Championship and the 2005 North Carolina Open, River Landing was rated one of the best courses in the state by North Carolina Magazine. The 36-hole layout combines artful landscape design and horticultural diversity with a variety of challenges from its five sets of tees. The Clyde Johnston–designed course features bentgrass greens and bermudagrass fairways and roughs. It totals more than 7000 yards from the back, with mixed elevations and carries over a variety of water hazards, including creeks, ponds and a river. The 6th, 8th, 16th and 17th holes hug the banks of the northeast Cape Fear River, while the 9th features par-resistant ravines. The signature 18th is a 402-yard, par 4 with a multi-tiered green; it's a dogleg left sloping downhill that dares you to avoid the ball-hungry bunker on the right. The elegant brick bridge there is one of many aesthetic delights. Also featured are a driving range, putting greens and snack bar. River Landing is a tranquil, private course (play is open to club members and their guests) in a golf community about 35 minutes north of Wilmington. The management welcomes corporate outings, group functions and fundraisers. To get there from Wilmington, drive north on I-40 to Exit 385, N.C. Highway 41 East. Paddle Wheel Drive is a quarter-mile ahead on the right.

BRUNSWICK COUNTY
Bald Head Island

Bald Head Island Club
Bald Head Island
(910) 457-7300, (866) 657-7311

If your idea of heaven is an island golf course that can be reached only by boat or ferry, where cars are banned in favor of golf carts and the course extends across an expanse of dunes overlooking the Atlantic Ocean, the Bald Head Island Club is bound to fulfill your fantasy. Much of this George Cobb–designed course follows the natural terrain carved by wind and water, like the first courses in Scotland. Exposed greens on its ocean side contrast sharply with interior holes, where palms, maritime forests and the natural wildlife habitats surround the holes, which are separated from fairways with virtually no playable rough. Awarded 4.5 stars from Golf Digest's Places to Play and extremely demanding, due as much to the ocean wind as to the late George Cobb's brilliant design, this 18-hole, par 72 championship course is among the scenic gems on the East Coast. Four sets of tees yield course lengths up to 7040 yards. The club currently hosts its own pro-am tournament, to which spectators are welcome. Tee times are required, and there is rarely an occasion when a preferred tee time is not available. A driving range and snack bar are available as well. A Day Golf Package, available by calling the golf shop, includes ferry, transfers, cart and greens fee for 18 holes.

Bolivia

Carolina National Golf Club at Winding River Plantation
1643 Goley Hewett Rd. SE, Bolivia
(910) 755-5200

Carolina National Golf Club is a Fred Couples signature golf facility. It features 27 challenging holes arranged in three nines — Egret, Heron and Ibis — named after the wildlife that inhabits this Audubon Certified Sanctuary Golf Course. Set along the Lockwood Folly River and carved out of low country marshlands, the course offers an endless variety of playing experiences and stunning natural beauty that will enchant every visitor.

Through its innovative design and multiple tee placements, the course will thrill players of every skill level. In addition, Carolina National Golf Club features a 14,000-square-foot putting and chipping green and 320-yard driving range, which provide a great warm-up for the challenges to come. In the clubhouse you will find the pro shop and the Plantation Grille. It's a great place to relax with a drink or a meal after your round of golf. Carolina National Golf Club is located 2.5 miles east of Highway 17 along NC Highway 211 in Winding River Plantation.

Southport/Oak Island

St. James Plantation - The Founders Golf Club
N.C. Hwy. 211, Southport
(910) 253-3008, (800) 247-4806

Designer P. B. Dye called this his most challenging course yet. Its many carries over water hazards have been described as heroic, while its multilevel fairways, bulkheads and variety of grasses are stamped with the Dye hallmark. The final three holes play into and over a series of marshes and lakes for a spectacular finish. Five sets of tees present a variety of plays. Most greens are elevated. The Founders Club and its companion course, the Members Club (see next entry), are 4 miles outside Southport and offer fine views of the Intracoastal Waterway. A complete practice facility and lessons are available. A restaurant and lounge are close by.

St. James Plantation - The Members Club
N.C. Hwy. 211, Southport
(910) 253-9500, (800) 474-9277

Opened in 1996, this Hale Irwin–designed par 72 course utilizes the natural lay of the land to good effect, forgoing flashy, amusement-park landscaping. The course has been called user-friendly, although its proximity to the Intracoastal Waterway means winds can be deeply trying. Watch out for the 15th hole, a par 5 with lateral water hazards squeezing the fairway into a bottleneck about 200 yards down and more water in front of the green — potentially an express ticket to bogeyland. Recently, Tim Cate designed nine holes that were added to this course. The entire facility has all the amenities of the most exclusive clubs, such as practice greens and sand traps, a driving range and on-site professionals. There is a Jimmy Ballard golf

school at The Members Club for all ages. The Members Club invites nonmembers to be "members for a day."

St. James Plantation - The Players
N.C. Hwy. 211, Southport
(910) 457-0049, (800) 281-6626

Designed by Tim Cate, this 18-hole golf course is friendly and difficult. Watch out for the 6th hole, regarded as the most challenging. The course is very aesthetically pleasing, with wild flowers and heather grass in bloom all around. The course is in excellent condition year round. At this writing construction is in progress on the clubhouse, which is expected to be completed by spring of 2005. Private lessons and a fully stocked golf shop are on the premises. There is also a restaurant, lounge and a practice range close by. The Players is open to the public.

Oak Island Golf & Country Club
928 Caswell Beach Rd., Caswell Beach
(910) 278-5275, (800) 278-5275

One of Brunswick County's vintage courses, this George Cobb creation is home to the Southport-Oak Island Masters Putting Tournament. It is a forgiving course (6304-yard, par 72) that can be enjoyed by players of varying skills. Its wide bermudagrass fairways are relatively short, lined with live oaks and tall pines and not overly fortified with water hazards. But that ocean wind! The clubhouse is less than 200 yards from the Atlantic, and sea breezes can frustrate even the best players. Hole 9 may send you to Duffers Pub and Grill early. Even so, the Tif-Eagle greens, driving range, putting green and swimming pool make this course quite popular.

Holden Beach

Lockwood Folly Country Club
19 Clubhouse Dr., Holden Beach
(910) 842-5666, (877) 562-9663

Lockwood Folly is a Willard Byrd–designed "Hidden Gem." The par 72, 18-hole course is carved in a magnificent setting from a 100-year-old private hunting preserve, bordering the Intracoastal Waterway and the Lockwood Folly River, with an ocean view. Lockwood Folly received a Golf Digest Four Star Award for "Places to Play" in 2000, 2002 and 2004; a Best Golf Course Community 2002; Most Picturesque Course 2002 (finalist); and Friendliest Golf Course Staff 2002 (finalist) by the Myrtle Beach Golf Magazine golfer voter poll. The course sports excellent greens and Bermuda fairways and is always well maintained. For your convenience, you will find a well-stocked pro shop, cafe, practice range and turn room. Thirty minutes south of Wilmington, Lockwood Folly is semi-private and open to the public.

Ocean Isle Beach

Brick Landing Plantation
1882 Goose Creek Rd., Ocean Isle Beach
(910) 754-5545, (800) 438-3006

With 41 sand traps and water hazards on 17 out of 18 holes, this handsome waterfront course was rated by Florida Golf Week magazine as among the top 50 distinctive golf courses in the Southeast. The Brick's fairways wind among freshwater lakes and through salt marshes, offering striking visual contrasts and championship challenges. The 18th hole finishes dramatically along the Intracoastal Waterway. The course is 6586 yards and a par 71. Amenities include a snack bar, lunch and cocktail lounge, and practice facilities. Instruction is available, as are tennis and family vacation packages and memberships.

Sunset Beach

Oyster Bay Golf Links
N.C. Hwy. 179, Sunset Beach
(910) 579-3528, (800) 697-8372

The two signature holes at Oyster Bay Golf Links are sure to push you to excel. The par 3 17th is one of two island greens and the par 4 13th has water on the right, which then becomes sand. This is an exceedingly challenging and imaginative public course (par 70), featuring stark elevations, deadly lakes and even a few trees smack in the middle of some fairways. Oyster Bay is one of the area's five Legends courses. It was voted Resort Course of the Year (1983) and among the top 50 public courses in the country (1990) by Golf Digest. The notorious 3rd hole (460 yards, par 4) presents one of the course's toughest greens. Each cart is equipped with club and ball cleaner, a cooler and ice. Beverage carts roam the course. The management enforces a dress code, and fees tend toward the medium-to-high.

Sea Trail Golf Resort & Conference Center
211 Clubhouse Rd., Sunset Beach
(800) 624-6601

Sea Trail Golf Resort & Conference Center offers three golf courses and a choice of two clubhouses at which to celebrate your round. Each clubhouse has a full-service golf shop. The Jones/Byrd Clubhouse is home to Magnolias Restaurant & Lounge, serving breakfast, lunch and dinner as well as live entertainment in the lounge on weekends. On the grounds as well are putting greens, a lighted driving range and a PGA–sanctioned Golf Learning Center. 70,000 square feet of meeting space make it a super place to combine those business meetings with a round of golf. In fact, Sea Trail Golf Resort and Conference Center is the only N.C. resort to have been added to the prestigious list of America's Best Resort Courses of Distinction in Golfweek.

Maples Course – One of Dan Maples finest courses, this par 72 course sits among ancient live oak trees and Carolina pines. Five of the holes wind beside the Calabash Creek, where nature displays the beauty of southeast coastal wildlife. The course has A1/A4 bentgrass greens and is peppered with waste bunkers, one of which extends the full length of the fairway, adding to the challenge. This course is rated in the top 5 of the coastal region as "Best Conditioned Course" by NC Magazine; "America's Best residential Course of Distinction" by Golf Week; and "One of the Top 50 courses in the Myrtle Beach area by Golf Digest.

Jones Course – This par 72 course opened in 1990 and being a straightforward course with typical Rees Jones bounding it's a great course for all skill levels. Its wide emerald fairways with large mounds are surrounded by water. In fact, water hazards can be found on 11 holes. The large expanse bunkers make it an interesting and challenging course. Golf Carolina rates this course one of "100 Must-Play Courses of the Carolinas; Golf Digest rates it as "One of the Top 50 Courses in the Myrtle Beach Area";

For best results while changing your golf swing, try combining it with a flexibility program to be sure your muscles can handle your new action.

and Golfweek Magazine named it "2005 Best Resort Course."

Byrd Course – Another par 72 course, this Willard Byrd course, in a beautiful setting, is built around several very large man-made lakes. Strategically placed tee shots and exacting play is necessary, with every hole requiring a different approach. The 18th hole is situated between two ponds and finishes at the Jones-Byrd Clubhouse. The Byrd Course is listed as "One of the Top 50 Courses in the Myrtle Beach Area" and is given 4 stars by Golf Digest.

Calabash

Carolina Shores Golf & Country Club
99 Carolina Shores Dr., Calabash
(910) 579-2181, (800) 579-8292

Located near the shores of the historic fishing village of Calabash, Carolina Shores achieved early recognition for its unique design and was rated "#1 on the Grand Strand" by Golf Course Rankings of America. One of the two courses on the new Shore Golf Tour, Carolina Shores features rolling tree-lined fairways and well-protected Bermuda greens. This is a shot-maker's dream with watery challenges and strategically placed bunkers rewarding a player for skill rather than brute strength. Under new ownership, Carolina Shores has completely renovated its golf course and clubhouse featuring a beautiful new restaurant with 11 TVs, making it one of the finest 19th holes anywhere.

The Pearl Golf Links
N.C. Hwy. 179, Calabash
(910) 579-8132

Winding through a 900-acre low-country pine forest on the banks of the Calabash River, the Pearl Golf Links is known as the jewel of the Carolinas. These two, par 72 Dan Maples–designed courses are unique in character and will challenge you at every turn. After your round, sit and relax in the newly renovated clubhouse sipping your favorite

i

Driving range practice sessions are a great way to improve your golf game, but be careful to avoid injury. Take breaks, walk around and stretch; never putt for more than 15 minutes without taking a stretch break.

beverage while enjoying one of the many big screen TVs. It's open year round.

Shallotte

Brierwood Golf Club
27 Brierwood Rd., Shallotte
(910) 754-4660, (888) 274-3796

Brierwood was the first golf community built along the South Brunswick Islands. About 7 miles north of Ocean Isle Beach, it is a player-friendly, par 72, championship course distinguished by plenty of freshwater obstacles and surrounded by residential properties. Fourteen holes present water hazards, including part of a 3-acre lake that traverses the 10th fairway. The clubhouse includes a pro shop and the Blue Heron Bar & Grill, with its superb outdoor balcony seating above a lake. The entrance to this semiprivate course with well-manicured, traditional greens is just off N.C. Highway 179 at the Shallotte town limit.

Rivers Edge Golf Club & Plantation
1960 Arnold Palmer Dr., Shallotte
(910) 754-2224, (800) 789-0535

At Rivers Edge Golf Club & Plantation, ideally located in the heart of southeastern North Carolina, miles of pristine beaches, invigorating waterways and Carolina sunsets are waiting for you. Come experience the coastal lifestyle you've always dreamed of while indulging in the luxury of 18 holes of Arnold Palmer signature golf, miles of walking and biking trails, and an array of amenities off the course, including 27 acres of freshwater lake and a full-service clubhouse. Remarkable views of the course and Shallotte River, a private resident's club and more make Rivers Edge a complete community. Explore the new waterfront, golf front and nature homesite opportunities. Call to learn more.

TOPSAIL ISLAND AREA

Belvedere Plantation
Golf & Country Club
2368 Country Club Dr., Hampstead
(910) 270-2703

Belvedere is a narrow, par 72, 18-hole course with small greens and water hazards. The length is 6059 yards with a slope of 125. Hole 3 stands out for its carry over water to an elevated green. Greens fees range from $25 to $45, depending on the season and time of day. Fees include range balls and state-of-the-art golf carts equipped with a GPS system and a 10" computer screen. Yardage, water hazards and all the other information a golfer needs can be displayed on the computer screen with a push of a button. Players can also use the system to order food or check on the latest sports scores. Reservations are available and can be made far in advance. Belvedere has a small pro shop, clubhouse and driving range on the premises. It offers PGA professional lessons and three- to four-day golf schools with accommodations provided. Tennis courts and a restaurant are also available on site.

Castle Bay Golf and Country Club
2516 Hoover Rd., Hampstead
(910) 270-1978

Castle Bay offers authentic Scottish-style links with a rolling terrain and natural indigenous grasses. This par 72 course has lengths ranging from 5466 to 6713. Open to the public year round, seven days a week from sunup to sundown, Castle Bay is about 2 miles off U.S. 17 on Hoover Road in Hampstead. You can't miss the castle-type gates at the entrance. Standard rates are $48 Friday through Sunday and $40 Monday through Thursday. Reservations can be made in advance. There is a practice complex, pro shop and snack bar on the premises.

North Shore Country Club
N.C. Hwy. 210, Sneads Ferry
(910) 327-2410, (800) 828-5035

North Shore is among the best-conditioned courses in the Topsail Island area, with a four-star rating from Golf Digest. This course has 6866 yards, a 73.1 rating and a slope of 135, with water coming into play on 10 of the 18 holes. Thick bermudagrass fairways and well-bunkered bentgrass greens place a premium on accurate shots. This course is quite popular with Raleigh and Tri-angle-area golfers, who come down to spend a day or two on the coast. The course is built on both sides of N.C. Highway 210, and an underground tunnel connects the two sides of the course. North Shore is lined with homes and tall pine trees. Golfers can sometimes be surprised and amused with alligator sightings in the course waterways.

The ninth hole is memorable for its required 250-yard tee shot — anything less

is in the drink. Greens fees, including a cart, range from $40 to $60, and reservations can be made up to a year in advance with a credit card. A reservation of less than two days in advance doesn't require a credit card. Driving range, putting green, professional lessons, club repairs and custom fitting are available. A clubhouse, bar and snack bar are on the premises, with a Holiday Inn Express next door.

Olde Point Golf and Country Club
U.S. Hwy. 17 N., Hampstead
(910) 270-2403

Olde Point is a mature, traditional course, opened in 1975 and designed by Jerry Turner. Featuring tree-lined fairways, scenic ponds and lakes, this 18-hole, par 72 course is 6253 yards with a slope of 120. Greens fees range from $30 to $50 depending on the season and time of day. Fees include a cart. A reserved starting time is required. The 11th hole is a long, narrow, 589-yard par 5 with a gradual dogleg right that slopes laterally downward to the right into the woods and consistently defies players' depth perception. It has been recognized by amateurs and professionals alike as one of the toughest in the area. Olde Point offers a pro shop, clubhouse, driving range, restaurant and snack bar.

Paradise Point Golf Course at Camp Lejeune
Building 2015, Camp Lejeune
(910) 451-2273

The golf courses of Camp Lejeune have recently been opened to the public. These two military courses were built on flat terrain and are considered easy to walk. The 36-hole Gold Course was renovated during the summer of 1996 with new green resurfacing, fairway grass, bunkers, five new ponds and only a few trees that can alter your shots. Ed Ault redesigned several holes on the Gold Course in 1979. The Scarlet Course has narrow fairways and well-bunkered greens. Again, renovations were made in 2003/2004. Additionally, numerous plaques have been placed around the course identifying various historical sites on or near Paradise Point. As an example, when the #12 hole was being rebuilt 100 yards west of it's original location, a suspected gravesite was found. Archeologists searched the area and discovered an American Indian burial ground. This area has been enclosed by a white fence and has been designated and registered as a historical site. Green fees range from $24 to $26.

Rock Creek Golf & Country Club
308 Country Club Blvd., Jacksonville
(910) 324-5151

Rock Creek is convenient to Jacksonville, Topsail Island, Wilmington, Emerald Isle and even New Bern. This 18-hole, 7102 yard, Jerry Turner & Assoc.–designed par 72 features numerous water dangers and pine tree–lined fairways with lush Bermuda carpeting. Onslow County's first planned recreational community, the facility truly caters to its golf-crazy residents. After a hot round of summer golf, the bar and Mitchell's Steakhouse await your arrival. The pro shop is open at 7 AM for all the early birds, and lessons and clinics are available for every level of golfer. PGA Pro Rick Morton calls Rock Creek his home, and you'll be tempted to do the same.

Topsail Greens Golf Club
500 Topsail Greens Dr., Hampstead
(910) 270-2883

Topsail Greens is an 18-hole, 6200-yard, par 71 course featuring player-friendly, tight fairways, sand bunkers and several holes with water hazards. The 17th hole, a 159-yard with a par 3, is an island green playable only by a small bridge. The greens, similar to those designed by Donald Ross, are cleverly contoured in a way that allows a misplayed shot to roll off the putting surface. Greens fees range from $20 to $40 depending on the time of day and season. Fees include a cart. Reservations are accepted. A pro shop, snack bar, putting green and chipping green are on the premises.

Driving Ranges

WILMINGTON

Carolina Golf Services, Inc.
5814 Oleander Dr., Wilmington
(910) 791-7155

Have a great time playing 25 championship courses using the only golf simulator in our area, and while you're at it, improve your game with the help of Carolina Golf Services owner, PGA pro Thom Harrison. This innovative indoor driving range and fitting studio opened in October 2003; Harrison formerly owned and operated Tee It Up Golf & Learning Center. Here's the place to go for serious golf instruction, including digital video analysis and ball flight trajectory tracking. Frequency matched custom golf clubs and appropriate golf balls ensure your personal best equipment according to your style and skill level. It's open daily except holidays.

Valley Golf Center & Driving Range
4416 S. College Rd., Wilmington
(910) 395-2750

Convenient to Carolina Beach and Wilmington, this large range has 40 lighted tee stations, mats and a grass hitting area as well as sand bunker areas. A covered hitting area allows practice during inclement weather. The fully stocked pro shop offers repairs, accessories and instruction with PGA staff professionals. The center, which is just north of Monkey Junction, is open every day from 9 AM to 10 PM (9 PM in winter).

Sully's Range
5026 Oleander Dr., Wilmington
(910) 392-1988
6987 Market St., Wilmington
(910) 392-1988

Sully's has two locations in the Wilmington area to provide you with all the tee practice you might need. The Oleander location features all grass tees. Call about their programs for children, which include summer camp and after-school instruction. Sully's also offers clinics for women, including tee instruction and a round of golf following the workshop. Hours are 9 AM to 9 PM Monday through Saturday at the Oleander location and 9 AM until dusk Monday through Saturday at the Market Street range. Both ranges are open 10:30 AM until 8 PM on Sundays.

BRUNSWICK COUNTY BEACHES

Holden Beach Driving Range
N.C. Hwy. 130, Holden Beach
(910) 842-3717

This lighted practice facility offers lessons by Class-A PGA professionals, a small pro shop and, as any good resort-area attraction should, batting cages next door. A unique feature is that when unattended by staff, the range operates on the honor system. Payment instructions are posted beside the ball baskets.

Pro Tee Practice Range
N.C. Hwy. 179, Ocean Isle Beach
(910) 754-4700

Two 18-station grass tee areas flank a mat area with rubber tees, all fully lighted. The pro shop stocks basic accessories, refreshments and snacks, and the management performs minor equipment repairs. Other amenities include two batting cages and a newly renovated mini golf course. Play golf at the locals' rate of $25 to $30. Pro Tee is a half-mile west of the Brick Landing Plantation Golf Course, is open daily and operates on the honor system.

Equipment and Repairs

The Golf Shop at Dick's Sporting Goods
816 S. College Rd., Wilmington
(910) 793-1904

One of 160 stores nationwide, Dick's has a 10,000-square-foot golf shop with a tremendous selection of golf equipment, clothing, shoes, accessories and gift items. A well-trained staff and golf pro are available to assist customers at all times. An indoor driving range is available to test those new clubs. The store is open seven days a week.

Nevada Bob's
4107-E Oleander Dr., Wilmington
(910) 799-4212

Nevada Bob's is a chain store that boasts a broad selection of new equipment and accessories and a knowledgeable staff. It has the air of a connoisseur's shop, right down to the indoor netted tee station on which to test clubs. There is also an artificial indoor putting green. Nevada Bob's is in the Anderson Square shopping center on the westbound side of Oleander. The store is open seven days a week.

Pro Golf of Wilmington
323-C Eastwood Rd., Wilmington
(910) 794-8223

Whether you're a novice or professional, Pro Golf has the right equipment for you. This complete 4,200-square-foot golf store is one of more than 140 stores worldwide. A friendly, experienced, knowledgeable staff can fit you with the right clubs for your ability, style and level of play. Besides a full line of equip-

ment, Pro Golf has accessories, gift items and clothing for ladies, men and juniors. It's open Monday through Saturday 10 AM to 7 PM.

Tee Smith Custom Golf Clubs
323-C Eastwood Rd., Wilmington
(910) 395-4008

Located within the Pro Golf store, Tee Smith has been customizing and repairing clubs commercially since 1975 and has the approval of pro shops throughout the area. Simple repairs often have a one-day turnaround. The shop is open Monday through Saturday year round.

Golf Etc.
4956-19 Long Beach Rd., Southport
(910) 457-1950

Owner Alan Mattison is especially excited about the computerized swing analysis and True Temper Shaft Lab© available in Golf Etc. — something you won't find for many miles around. You will find a full line of pro equipment, custom club building, re-shafting and repairs available as well. In fact, everything needed for a golfing lifestyle can be purchased at Golf Etc., from golf balls and bags to indoor putting greens, to clothing and shoes, to teapots and mugs, to videos and software, books and more. Don't hesitate to shop during the broadcast of your favorite golf tournament, it's bound to be tuned in on one of the TVs in the store.

Lori's Golf Shoppe
9966 Beach Dr., SW, Calabash
(910) 575-0871, (800) 606-0871

Ladies! If you play golf (or want to) and have been searching for a place to fulfill all your golfing needs, search no more. The owner of this golf shop caters to women. Lori DiSimone has a background in golf that includes college competition, assistant golf pro, professional competition and instruc-

What you eat and drink before and during a round can significantly impact performance. Avoid eating a big meal in the two hours before tee time; drink at least a pint of water each hour you're on the course; avoid caffeinated and alcoholic beverages; and eat two snacks as you play.

tion. You will find women's golf apparel, golf bags, shoes, accessories and women's golf equipment including custom-made clubs. Lori provides individual lessons and group clinics, and the shop organizes golf leagues and outings as well.

Packages and Services

The **American Lung Association Golf Privilege Card** offers discounts for one year on more than 700 rounds of golf at 300 courses throughout North Carolina, South Carolina and Virginia. All courses offer a reduced rate and some have unlimited play. The card (which is really a 48-page book) costs $40; buy three and get one free. Some restrictions apply. To order contact the American Lung Association of North Carolina, (800) 849-5949, or order on the website www.lungnc.org

Most travel agencies, many local hotels and vacation rental companies will assist in arranging golf packages. **Coastal Golfaway**, on Wrightsville Avenue, (910) 799-0336 or (800) 368-0045, books customized packages in all price ranges, from Wilmington to Pawley's Island, South Carolina, including Myrtle Beach and the Brunswick Islands/Calabash area.

The **Greater Topsail Area Chamber of Commerce** has established a Golf Association with local area golf courses, restaurants, accommodations and activities. Information can be requested through the chamber at (910) 329-4446

Annual Tournaments

Exciting and challenging courses in beautiful settings plus wonderful weather set the stage for competitive golf events throughout the area. Tournaments are popular as fund-raising activities, and a number of local organizations sponsor annual events. Many local courses host their own tournaments as well. Local chambers of commerce can provide information (see our Area Overviews chapter for a listing). Major tournaments are announced in the Star-News "Today," "Currents" or "Sports" sections; some weekly publications, such as Encore, carry details, too.

Wilmington Golf Course, 311 S. Wallace Avenue, Wilmington, (910) 791-0558, sponsors an annual **Men's Amateur Championship** and a **Women's Amateur Championship** in September. These tournaments are open to golfers age 18 or older who have an established U.S.G.A. handicap. The fee for this two-day event is $55 for women and $60 for men, which includes lunch the first day.

Tournaments, which are held nearly year round in the Southport/Oak Island/South Brunswick Islands, include the following.

In May the Brunswick County Chamber of Commerce, (910) 754-6644, (800) 426-6644, hosts the **Brunswick County Chamber Golf Tournament**; the **Master's Putting Tournament** is held at the Oak Island Golf Club, (910) 457- 6964, (800) 457-6964; and the Southport-Oak Island Chamber of Commerce, (910) 457-6964, (800) 457-6964, hosts the **Southport-Oak Island Area Golf Classic**.

In June the **Brunswick Literacy Council Golf Tournament**, (910) 754-7323, and the **Southport Rotary Club Golf Tournament**, (910) 253-0470 are held.

In August the county women's golf clubs, (910) 754-5726), hold the **Women's Golf Club County Championship**, which benefits Hope Harbor Home. The **National Shriners Touchstone Energy Golf Tournament** is held in Southport, (910) 579-8160, and **Coastal Federal Bank** raises funds for Brunswick County Habitat for Humanity with its tournament.

In October Brick Landing Plantation's **Annual Rally for a Cure**, (910) 754-5545, (800) 438-3006, benefits the Susan G. Komen Breast Cancer Foundation.

In November there are the Calabash VFW Post 7288 **Annual Charity Golf Tournament**, (910) 579-3577; the **Annual L & L Montessori School Scholarship Golf Tournament,** (910) 454-7344, and the **Annual Southport Christian School Golf Tournament**, (910) 457-5060.

In December **Calabash Elks Annual Spirit of Christmas Golf Tournament** is held at Meadowlands Golf Club, (910) 287-7529, (888) 287-7529, to benefit veterans and families of active-duty military personnel as well as children participating in the Elks annual Christmas party.

Associations

Golf associations are primarily connected to local courses. For example, Porters Neck Country Club (PNCC) has a Men's Golf and Ladies Golf Association that are open to members only. However, Topsail Greens Golf Club men's and women's golf associations are open to both members and non-members. Wilmington Golf Course is a municipal course, which doesn't have members, therefore, anyone can join the Men's or Women's Golf Associations. So, you need to check the courses that interest you regarding associations.

Wilmington Single Golfers
Wilmington
(910) 799-8366

A chapter of the American Singles Golf Association, which has more than 4,000 members, the Wilmington organization includes unmarried men and women ages 30 and up from Pender, New Hanover and Brunswick counties. The group holds two events each month, year round — a business/social meeting the second Thursday of the month at Wilson's at 6:30 and a golf outing usually the weekend following the meeting. Golf outings take place on some of the best courses available in the area. Four multi-chapter events of three to four days are held at the time of these holidays: New Year's, Valentine's Day, Memorial Day and Labor Day. Membership is $70, which includes national and chapter dues and newsletters.

REAL ESTATE AND NEIGHBORHOODS

R eal estate is big business in the southern coastal region, due in large part the desirable nature of the Carolina coast. The climate, the amenities of North Carolina's largest coastal city, beaches, a thriving university, extensive shopping and dining options, first-rate medical services, attractions, historical sites, varied recreational opportunities and beautiful coastal scenery conspire to lure newcomers and maintain a lifelong hold on residents.

Since the entire region from Topsail Island to Sunset Beach hugs the shore, land is limited to an approximately 180-degree angle. Naturally, the closer a property is to the water, the higher the price. Nevertheless, housing remains remarkably affordable throughout the southern coastal region compared to some more affluent parts of the country. There is also tremendous diversity in terms of neighborhoods, housing styles, scenery and price. The highest level, from $500,000 to beyond $3 million, consists of properties for buyers interested in waterfront and luxury homes. At the other end of the scale, there are smaller, new homes ranging from $80,000 to $130,000, just right for first-time homeowners and retirees seeking affordable housing.

Because new neighborhoods are continually sprouting in the area, we aren't even going to try describing all that are available. What follows is information about established neighborhoods, average prices (these may fluctuate according to the market) and other general facts. For specific information, contact an area real estate agent (a partial list of agencies is included in this chapter) or visit sales offices in a community that appeals to you.

Note: The real estate prices given in this chapter are intended to serve as a general guideline to area property values. Due to the constant state of flux in the market, prices can change considerably in a very short time.

NEIGHBORHOODS

Wilmington

DOWNTOWN WILMINGTON

It is often said that downtown Wilmington is a separate place from the rest of the city and New Hanover County. The tone is absolutely different from any other neighborhood in the region. If you appreciate being at the crossroads of the community, downtown is the place for you. If you are looking for history and charm as well as an energetic and culturally/socially inspirational atmosphere, downtown Wilmington is definitely the place to be. It's lively, warm and relentlessly interesting.

Many of the homes date from the mid- to late 1800s and the first quarter of the 20th century. There are stunning examples of Victorian, Italianate, Renaissance, Neoclassical and Revivalist architecture. Homes in the area, small cottages and large mansions alike, feature high ceilings, hardwood floors, fascinating detail, front porches and all of the interesting characteristics one would expect of vintage homes.

The population is as eclectic as the architecture. This vibrant downtown community attracts an interesting mix of lifelong Wilmingtonians and newcomers. What the entire neighborhood seems to have in common is a mutual appreciation for the particular amenities of downtown: easy accessibility to cultural arts opportunities, fine dining, friendly shopping, city and county government centers, a beautiful riverfront for strolling, and a strong sense of community identity.

Relatively few homes come on the market in the more established center of the neighborhood, and the ones that do aren't available for long unless they are very large and, therefore, quite expensive. As one local real estate agent put it, there is a range of

Over time some come to discover what a special place this is...

...others just know by instinct

View all home and homesites for sale in The Brunswick Islands, from Bald Head Island to Sunset Beach and everywhere inbetween.

www.BrunswickCountyHomes.com

Martha Lee Realty

Providing Real Estate
Showcase Tours Daily

Waterfront Specialist
Toll Free: 866-696-6232

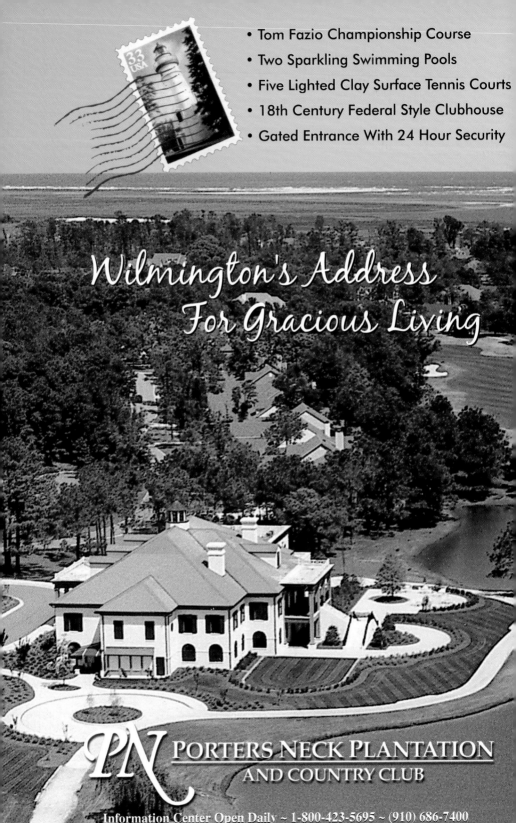

- Tom Fazio Championship Course
- Two Sparkling Swimming Pools
- Five Lighted Clay Surface Tennis Courts
- 18th Century Federal Style Clubhouse
- Gated Entrance With 24 Hour Security

Wilmington's Address
For Gracious Living

PN PORTERS NECK PLANTATION
AND COUNTRY CLUB

Information Center Open Daily ~ 1-800-423-5695 ~ (910) 686-7400
8204 Fazio Drive ~ Wilmington, North Carolina 28411 ~ www.porters-neck.com

A Full-Service Office. A Landfall Location.
A Price Your Business Can Thrive On.

ull-service monthly office rentals including:

Elegantly Furnished Office Suites

Use of Four Expertly Appointed Conference Rooms

Grand Entrance, Reception and Waiting Areas

Full Service Reception and Office Support options

Corporate ID Packages
that could include:

• Professional Reception

• Virtual Mail Address

• Monthly Conference Room Time

Ready to take your business to the next level?
As the owner of Landfall Executive Suites, I'm proud of the comprehensive services we offer. Contact me directly to learn more about our Standard Office Package or to customize a package just for you.

Eric Goldfarb – OWNER

© 2006 LANDFALL EXECUTIVE SUITES

LANDFALL EXECUTIVE SUITES
FIRST CLASS OFFICES FOR GROWING BUSINESSES

213 Culbreth Drive (off Military Cutoff Road) Wilmington, NC 28405   (910) 256-1900   www.landfall.biz

natural elegance.
creating your picture of perfection.

TUSCANY
TILE & DESIGN

3801 Market Street
Wilmington, NC 28403
910.792.0102

7751 N. Kings Hwy
Myrtle Beach, SC
843.839.3301

custom tile & marble and granite countertops ❧ tuscanytile.net

BiRD

Decorative Hardware & Bath

5702 Oleander Drive
Wilmington, NC
910-793-6293
www.birddecorativehardware.com

DACOR FILLS YOUR KITCHEN

Is your kitchen filled with savory aromas, familiar sounds, and fond memories?
Dacor invites you to fill your kitchen with exceptional performance and
refined style. Introducing the complete **Dacor Epicure** kitchen -
appliances designed to feed your needs and enhance your life.

dacor®
The life of the kitchen™
800.793.0093 | www.dacor.com

MAJOR APPLIANCES • HARDWARE FOR BATH, CABINETS & DOORS

Atlantic Since 1948
APPLIANCE & HARDWARE

914 South Kerr Ave.
Wilmington, NC 28403
910-791-2222
www.atlanticappliance.net

CONNECTING THE BEST OF WILMINGTON'S HISTORY, SPIRIT AND LIFESTYLE

IN ONE HOMETOWN NETWORK!

SALES • VACATIONS • LONG-TERM RENTALS

Wilmington Office
1601 S. College Rd.
Wilmington, NC 28403
(910) 395-4100
1-800-747-1968

Historic Downtown Office
106 N. Water St. Suite 112
Wilmington, NC 28401
(910) 772-1622
1-800-882-1622

Carolina Beach Office
1029 N. Lake Park Blvd.
Carolina Beach, NC 28428
(910) 458-8881
1-800-830-2118

Brunswick Office
1109 New Pointe Blvd., Suite 4
Leland, NC 28451
910-371-9937
877-370-9937

Network® Real Estate **Call For A Free Relocation Package.**

www.networkwilmington.com

everything in the way of housing and prices downtown, from larger homes in the district to small cottages with prices ranging from $120,000 to more than $1 million, depending on the location and condition. Condominiums, often housed in renovated buildings, can range from the low $100,000s and up.

Within the Historic District proper, many homes have been restored, but there are still handyman bargains to be had, especially in the areas outside of the district in the Historic Overlay. It takes a person with vision to redo some of the deteriorated architectural gems in these neighborhoods. The level of downtown neighborhood restoration is most stable at the river and diminishes as you head east toward the ocean at about Eighth Street.

The residential neighborhoods to the north of Market Street are generating high interest at this time and are seeing quality restoration efforts. The North Fourth Street Business District Project, a renewal effort supported in part by the City of Wilmington, business owners and residents along this corridor, promises to open new options to people who want to live downtown. To the south, the natural boundary of the neighborhood is the Cape Fear Memorial Bridge. Quality restorative development has taken place on South Second, Queen and Castle streets.

Although every type of housing style is available, the general downtown real estate market consists of single-family homes. There are also a growing number of condominiums and a few duplex developments. Some op-portunities to have a rental apartment within one's own home are available.

Rental prices in the downtown area range from $800 to $1,200 a month for one-bedroom rentals. If the notion of living over a storefront or in an urban, loft-type space has appeal, ask a Realtor to show you buildings in the downtown commercial district.

Some solidly rediscovered older neighborhoods beyond downtown are the **Mansion District** and nearby **Carolina Heights** and **Carolina Place**. Both flank Market Street beyond 15th Street. These neighborhoods date from the 1920s, and architectural styles vary. In the Mansion District you can certainly purchase a mansion-style home ranging from $400,000 to $1,000,000, but there are also appealing cottages. Many of the larger homes started out as handyman bargains or fixer-uppers and were returned to their former elegance.

Carolina Heights and Carolina Place begin at around 17th Street and continue to 23rd Street. Carolina Heights is almost exclusively single-family homes with a price range from $160,000 to $300,000. In Carolina Place, the home buyer will find more diversity in architecture and price. Homes start in the $115,000 range and go up into the high $160,000s. It is regarded as the new frontier for not only residential investors, but also homeowners, largely thanks to its relatively new status as an Historic Registry District. It also is comfortably close to venerable Forest Hills.

Makes take out feel like fine dining.

Classic cool by Hinkley

HINKLEY
LIGHTING
design·illuminate·enjoy

AVAILABLE AT

BUTLER'S
ELECTRIC
SUPPLY

STOP BY OUR STORE AT
2013 CASTLE STREET, WILMINGTON N.C. 28403
Ph. (910) 762-3345 Fax. (910) 251-1044
WWW.BUTLERSELECTRICSUPPLY.COM

SUBURBS

Forest Hills is, without dispute, a fine address. This large and very stable neighborhood was once a suburb of downtown. Today it is a conveniently located neighborhood of older homes that date from as early as the 1920s. Well-maintained lawns, large setbacks, quietness, alleys for backyard access and trash pickup, and gorgeous live oaks are the hallmarks of this neighborhood. There are ambling canopied lanes and lots of Southern-style shade. Diversity in square footage and architectural style allows for diversity in price, ranging from $230,000 to $350,000 and up. An attractive feature of this neighborhood is its proximity to shopping and services. It is minutes from the largest mall in the region.

Pine Valley, near South College Road around Longleaf Mall, is about three decades old as a development and still enjoying active home sales. It has attracted many Wilmingtonians to its quiet, pine tree–dotted blocks. A nearby golf course and clubhouse are easily accessible to people who want to live in a stable neighborhood that isn't necessarily exclusive in terms of price. Homes range from the $160,000s to $400,000.

Just off River Road, is **River Pointe**, another high-quality, traditional neighborhood community by the Davy Group (see also Harbour Point in the Carolina Beach section of Neighborhoods). With 45 townhomes situated along the Cape Fear River, each boasting quality construction, a swimming pool with a lovely river view, plenty of boating and beaches nearby, a location that's a one-minute drive from Ashley High School and Murray Middle School, and convenient proximity to Monkey Junction shopping centers, River Pointe promises to become one of Wilmington's most sought-after new neighborhoods. There are two designs to choose from, the Cape Fear and the Cape Hatteras; both plans include a wide front porch and back deck, with all of the charm of traditional, Southern architecture.

Sunset South is a new neighborhood located off Carolina Beach Road adjacent to historic Sunset Park. Close to beaches, restaurants, shopping and golf courses, this community features sidewalks, beautiful landscaping and benches, tree-lined streets, a community park, underground utilities and designer street lighting. These attractive, brand-new, two- or three-bedroom homes start in the affordable $95,000 price range and include kitchen appliances, adequate cabinets and a separate pantry. The homes also come with a one-year builder's warranty and a 10-year structural warranty. There are also several customizing options, allowing you to create a home that is uniquely your own.

INTRACOASTAL WATERWAY COMMUNITIES - MAINLAND

On the mainland side of the Intracoastal Waterway (ICW) is the planned community of **Landfall,** 1816 Mews Drive, Wilmington, (910) 256-6111. This gated community of-

FREE!!!

Welcome & Referral Service for Newcomers

We'll bring you:
Gift Package, Map, & Information
from some of the best business and
professional people in Wilmington!

Special family & retiree packets available.

Nancy Wilcox, owner
910-793-0950
nkwilcox@ec.rr.com

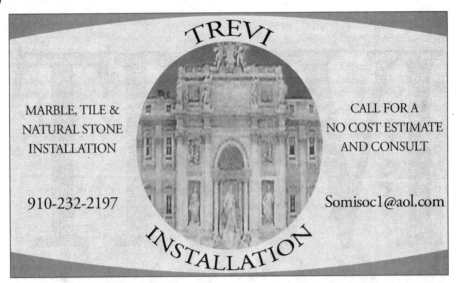

TREVI

MARBLE, TILE &
NATURAL STONE
INSTALLATION

910-232-2197

CALL FOR A
NO COST ESTIMATE
AND CONSULT

Somisoc1@aol.com

INSTALLATION

fers a pristine environment of immaculate lawns, beautiful homes, three clubhouses, two private golf courses (27 holes designed by Jack Nicklaus and 18 holes designed by Pete Dye), a tennis facility designed by tennis legend Cliff Drysdale, an eight-lane Olympic-size swimming pool and more. Single-family homes range from $400,000 to more than $4 million; home sites range from $200,000 to more than $1 million. Landfall currently has 1,300 homes. The Landfall Clubhouse, a large banquet/dining/special occasions facility of 31,000 square feet, is also on the premises.

NORTH OF WILMINGTON

Demarest Landing, located on the high bluffs of Howe Creek, is a waterfront Middle Sound neighborhood. This exceptional community of 46 home sites is accessible to every convenience of suburban living, including area schools. Amenities of this well-planned community were designed to appeal to kids of all ages and include tennis, volleyball, basketball, a swimming pool, a waterfront pier and stocked boathouse, a clubhouse, 1.5 miles of sidewalks, a post office, two fountains, parks and rear service lanes for residents' garages. Endorsed by the Governor's Taskforce for Smart Growth as the "cutting edge" in Traditional Neighborhood Design, Demarest Landing is a community of great neighbors with a child-friendly atmosphere. Half-acre home sites start at $120,000. Established homes range from $500,000 to $1.5 million. For more information about Demarest Land-

ing, visit the Demarest Company's website at www.demarestcompany.com

Inspired by and built across from Demarest Landing, **Demarest Village** is a new Middle Sound neighborhood offering a diverse collection of residential choices that include single-family homes, townhomes and row houses. Residences in this exceptional community have unique and historic architectural features and are woven among tree-lined streets. Sidewalks surround and connect homes to the neighborhood's eight acres of open space, parks and a swim club. Home sites begin at $80,000, and residences begin at $320,000. For information about Demarest Village, contact Paula Ferebee at Intracoastal Realty, (910) 540-8787. You may also contact Demarest Company, (910) 686-4482, or visit on the web at www.demarest-company.com.

Porters Neck Plantation, 8204 Fazio Drive, (910) 686-7400 or (800) 423-5695, is north of Wilmington and Wrightsville Beach just off U.S. Highway 17. The setting — 650 acres of pristine, lush coastal land adjacent to the Intracoastal Waterway — is fitting for this community of extraordinary homes. The Tom Fazio–designed golf course is a key feature of the very attractive neighborhood that appeals to active people. There is a sports complex, complete with a lap pool, clay tennis courts and a fitness center. Traditional single-family homes are available in a variety of sizes and proximity to the golf course, which will determine the price, ranging from

$280,000 to $450,000. Patio homes start at $230,000 for 1,800 square feet.

Figure Eight Island is a private island of upscale homes and homesites ranging from $475,000 to over $1 million; single-family home prices range from the $800,000s to nearly $4 million. There is a yacht club and private harbor for members. This lovely island has no commercial development; shopping is available in nearby Ogden and Hampstead. Call your real estate agent for information.

River Landing, 110 River Village Place, Wallace, (910) 285-4171 or (888) 285-4171, is just over the Duplin-Pender counties line off Interstate 40, about 35 minutes from Wilmington. It is a private, residential golf community consisting of primary residences and second homes with a wide variety of recreational facilities. Club memberships include a 27-hole championship golf course designed by Clyde Johnston, a swim and tennis center, private guest cottages, fishing and boating and walking/jogging/nature trails. The new River Club is a perfect place for a family picnic, community group or enjoying a canoe or kayak. Home sites throughout the 1,400-acre community range from the mid-$50,000 mark and up, and home prices start at $225,000 to $1,000,000

SOUTH OF WILMINGTON

The area to the south of Wilmington is currently the fastest growing part of New Hanover county. Along College Road south of Market Street to Shipyard Boulevard, dense

Joe & Dave sell
Wilmington & The Beach
New Homes • Resales • Luxury

FREE School Reports
www.JoePascal.com
(910) 313-0027

⭐ **5 Star Real Estate**

commercial growth has been taking place for years. However, with significantly increased residential development farther to the south down to Pleasure Island, commercial development has been following at a rapid pace. This is especially true in the **Monkey Junction/Myrtle Grove** area at the junction of Carolina Beach Road (U.S. Highway 421) and College Road (N.C. Highway 132), where there is a Lowe's hardware store and a Wal-Mart Super Center, along with numerous other businesses and restaurants.

South of Monkey Junction along Carolina Beach Road, quite a few residential areas have been developed, ranging from moder-

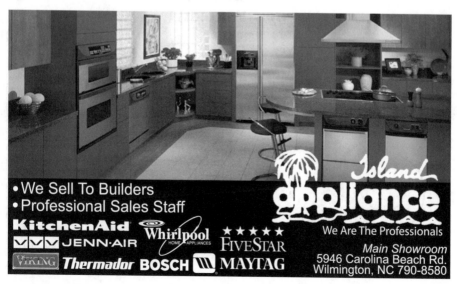

• We Sell To Builders
• Professional Sales Staff

KitchenAid **Whirlpool** ★★★★★ **FiveStar**
JENN-AIR **FiveStar**
Viking **Thermador** **BOSCH** **MAYTAG**

Island **appliance**
We Are The Professionals
Main Showroom
5946 Carolina Beach Rd.
Wilmington, NC 790-8580

If You Thought A Mattress Couldn't Do Miracles, Think Again

Doctor Approved & Recommended

Miracle Mattress™ automatically adjusts and molds to:

- Every body size
- Every body height
- Every body weight
- Every body shape
- Every body contour
- EVERY BODY

If you want...
Pain relief!
No partner disturbance!
Increased energy!
More restful sleep!
Best support ever!
Best Warranty!

Doctor Approved & Recommended

furniture galleries

27 Years of Quality Sales & Service!

Hours: Monday–Friday 8:30am–5:30pm
Saturday 9am–5:30pm Closed Sunday

3514 South College Road Wilmington • 799-4010

Professional Profile - Real Estate

Glenda Newell, GRI
Coldwell Banker Sea Coast Realty - Landfall Office
1400 Commonwealth Drive, Suite 102
Wilmington, NC 28403
910.616.3282 • www.GlendaNewell.com
www.WilmingtonCoastalHomes.com

With the resources of Coldwell Banker Sea Coast Realty behind her, and her in-depth knowledge of the area market, Glenda Newell will provide you with not just the knowledge, but the know how to make your real estate experience as simple, easy, and as pleasant as possible.

Glenda's goals are one with her clients, her values the highest, and her desire to serve always first. Choose the agent whose professionalism and experience ensures success.

ately priced to upscale gated communities, interspersed with commercial establishments. The four-lane, divided highway allows easy access to any of these businesses, communities and Pleasure Island.

Just north of the Snow's Cut Bridge on River Road is the growing development of **Cypress Island.** Developed by Cypress Green Inc., (910) 790-8010, (888) 395-4770, this neighborhood consists of 1,400- to 2,000-square-foot single-family homes and 1,200- to 1,800-square-foot townhomes. Homes and lots are offered as a package deal starting at $208,500 to $300,000 for single-family homes and $145,900 and up for townhomes. The community has a 14-acre nature preserve with a nature trail, three stocked fishing lakes, a clubhouse, a pool and tennis courts. It has a 9-hole, par 3 golf course.

Wrightsville Beach and Vicinity

Wrightsville Beach is highly residentially developed. For the most part, houses are close together, and a person who craves the mythical remote island life is not going to find it here. Development has been largely controlled, thanks to vigilance on the part of local residents and the high cost of land, so the relative density of development is palatable. In 1998 the community put building ordinances into effect that limit the size of

new houses based on square footage relative to lot size.

This is a pretty beach town with a year-round population of slightly less than 3,000 residents. It's clean, there is little in the way of garishness, and the local constable does a fine job keeping order in the face of huge crowds of visitors. A person who appreciates small-town living in a beach atmosphere with the convenience of a nearby city will adore this place. There are 5 miles of clean beach on which to jog or simply stroll. On just about any day of the year, you'll see surfers waiting for the big one to roll in.

The Wrightsville Beach real estate market is stable. If a property comes onto the market, it will often sell quickly. Many of the existing homes stay in families generation after generation. Quite a few of these properties are used only as summer homes. When homes do go on the market, the price tag is large. Expect to pay between $600,000 and $3 million for any single-family home, and don't be surprised by much higher prices for oceanfront property. Those homes begin at about $1,000,000.

Since the available land is all but exhausted in terms of development on the island and high-rises are limited to 96 feet, most of the opportunities for purchase are either replacement of older houses with new ones or, more likely, in condominiums. You could easily spend $350,000 to $1.3 million for a two-bedroom condominium on Wrightsville Beach, with those on the lower end of the

The Right Location for Your Business.

As the owner of Landfall Executive Suites, I'm proud of the full service office packages we provide. Contact me directly to learn more about our Standard Office Package or to customize a package just for you.

Eric Goldfarb – OWNER

See our full page ad in the Commerce and Industry section.

1213 Culbreth Drive (off Military Cutoff Rd.) Wilmington, NC 28405
(910) 256-1900 www.landfall.biz

© 2006 LANDFALL EXECUTIVE SUITES

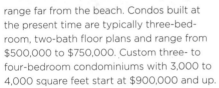

LANDFALL EXECUTIVE SUITES
FIRST CLASS OFFICES FOR GROWING BUSINESSES

range far from the beach. Condos built at the present time are typically three-bedroom, two-bath floor plans and range from $500,000 to $750,000. Custom three- to four-bedroom condominiums with 3,000 to 4,000 square feet start at $900,000 and up.

There are however, a few residential developments springing up near Wrightsville Beach, and these developments offer patio and single-family homes in an affordable price range.

One of the newest developments near Wrightsville Beach is **The Village at Mayfaire**, a 31-acre, 208-unit residential development on Military Cutoff Road. Developed by the Charlotte-based State Street Companies, this community offers a fresh, engaging and luxurious condominium experience. Here, homeowners find private estate comforts beautifully composed within a strikingly handsome architectural style. Each building in The Village at Mayfaire comprises six graciously appointed floor plans. Two- and three-bedroom floor plans range in size from 1,260 to 2,490 square feet and include large outdoor terraces, a private garage and assigned courtyard parking.

With prices starting at the $300s, The Village at Mayfaire offers coastal living for a fraction of what homeowners pay for a comparable condominium at Wrightsville Beach, located 2.5 miles from the property. Amenities include a 5,525-square-foot clubhouse, 24-hour cardio center and weight-lifting area, 25-seat movie theatre and multi-media room,

billiards room, conference and gaming room, junior Olympic size pool with 75-foot lap lanes, expansive 18,000-square-foot sunning deck, outdoor heated spa, gas barbecue grill area, lighted tennis courts and residents' picnic pavilion.

Perhaps The Village at Mayfaire's most distinctive amenity is the half-mile link to The Mayfaire Town Center. This inviting "new urbanism" community brings a vital and enchanting living, shopping and working environment, the first of its kind, to the Wilmington area. Here, residents can walk, browse and shop all day among national and local restaurants and merchants along a traditional "main street," with storefronts facing bustling sidewalks and public squares. For more information about The Village at Mayfaire, contact the sales center at (910) 509-9771 or toll free at (877) 971-9771.

Carolina Beach and Kure Beach

Cross over the bridge on U.S. 421 at Snow's Cut, a U.S. Army Corps of Engineers project that connects the ICW with the Cape Fear River and the Atlantic Ocean, and you come directly into Carolina Beach. This island community represents some very interesting prospects for home ownership in the Cape Fear region.

The beach communities of Carolina Beach on the north and Kure Beach to the

The most productive real estate agents in the Greater Wilmington area!

Wrightsville Beach • Topsail Island • Carolina Beach
Historic Downtown Wilmington • Mayfaire • Leland
Six Convenient Locations, One Number to Call...

(910) 256-8171 or (800) 883-9584
"No One in the World Sells More Real Estate than RE/MAX!"

south are located on the land area known as Pleasure Island. Home to about 10,000 year-round residents, these friendly, family-oriented communities are often mistaken by visitors as one long island beach town referred to as Carolina Beach. This is an understandable error due to the similarities of the towns. Both have clean, wide beaches, an abundance of fishing opportunities, several nice restaurants and a growing sense of community pride that makes living here a charming prospect.

Although Carolina Beach has been a community since 1857, the whole of Pleasure Island has been experiencing substantial residential growth during recent years as an affordable place to locate by or near the ocean. The assortment of ownership opportunities range from condominiums to cottages to upscale homes. There are several high-rises, many multi-story condominium buildings on the northern end, an abundance of small residences and — particularly toward the central and southern parts of the island — quite a few larger homes.

Currently, the island is experiencing considerable commercial growth, and revitalization is underway. A new shopping center has a Food Lion as its anchor store. Two major chain hotels have recently been opened in the area, increasing the number of visitors to downtown Carolina Beach and the Boardwalk.

Single-family homes along Carolina Beach and Kure Beach range between $175,000 to $500,000 and up, with townhomes and condominiums priced in the mid-$60,000s to the $400,000s. Not surprisingly, oceanfront properties in both markets fall into the upper range of price quotes, $400,000 to $700,000 and up. The farther south you go on this island, the more fascinating the scenery becomes. In Fort Fisher, beautiful live oak foliage has been sculpted over the centuries by the sea breezes. At the southernmost tip of this strip of land, the Cape Fear River converges with the Atlantic Ocean near Bald Head Island.

Farther south on Pleasure Island in the village of Kure Beach, you'll find **Seawatch**, a residential development with homes on 101 sites ranging from oceanfront to wooded. Single-family, cottage-style homes are from 1,400 to 3,200 square feet in size and are grouped around a community pool, cabana, playground and tennis courts. A private, oceanfront beachwalk features a cabana with showers, restrooms and a covered deck.

Among Pleasure Island's notable residential developments is **Harbour Point**, a traditional waterfront neighborhood and yacht club located on the Intracoastal Waterway at the juncture of Snow's Cut in Carolina Beach. Its 90 townhomes feature tin roofs, white picket fences, pastel exteriors, romantic porches and classic styling. It's a Charleston-like community with a relaxed ambiance and quiet sophistication. This neighborhood is a truly unique blend of Southern architecture that combines functionality and spaciousness with just plain charm. A 98-slip marina that can accommodate boats up to 100 feet, a waterfront pool and a clubhouse make this picture complete.

Brunswick County Beaches

BALD HEAD ISLAND

It takes 20 minutes to cross from the ferry landing at Indigo Plantation to Bald Head Island, a beautiful bit of land where there are no high-rises, no shopping malls, no crowds and no cars. Everyone travels by electric golf cart or bicycle. You'll find a clubhouse with a pool, a George Cobb–designed golf course, tennis courts, a marina and limited shopping. Opportunities for fine and casual dining range from the elegant Bald Head Island Club to the deli at the Maritime Market. There is a resort atmosphere and the year-round residential population count is quite low, about 220. It is largely a vacation spot where most of the homes are available for weekly rental.

Home sites range from $350,000 to more than $2.5 million. Home sales begin in the mid-$700,000s and climb upward to well above $3 million. Condos and stand-alone town homes start in the mid-$500,000s, while four-week timeshares can be purchased anywhere from $100,000 to $250,000. Single-family homes, villas and townhouses dot the island and are connected by paved golf cart paths.

SOUTHPORT/OAK ISLAND

The charming fishing village of Southport attracts not only retirees, but also families and folks who have decided to get out of the rat race. Southport's geographical location on the Cape Fear River near the Atlantic Ocean provides some lovely coastal scenery. Bald Head Island lies just off Southport to the east. Oak Island serves as a barrier to the ocean on the south side.

Southport's quaint, historic homes date from the late 1800s and offer mostly restored, single-family residences. Houses on the waterfront are larger, and a 2,500-square-foot home may run upward from $1.2 million. Newer homes may cost more. Along River Drive, one can spend more than $900,000. Naturally, the farther back from the water, the lower the price. A nice finished house in Southport will average around $600,000 for 1,500 square feet. Subdivision areas are growing rapidly in and near Southport. These include **Indigo Plantation**, **Arbor Creek**, **The Landing at Southport**, **Winding River**, **Carolina Place** and **Marsh Creek**. These neighborhoods offer a broad range of surprisingly affordable new homes in attractive settings with some very pleasant amenities.

Located between Southport and the Oak Island beaches on the Intracoastal Waterway, you will find secluded **South Harbour Village**. A planned unit development, it is divided into six unique neighborhoods: patio homes in Glen Cove and Westport; Village Green Garden Homes and Golf Course Villas in Glen Cove; gated waterfront estate lots and Marina Club condos in Barnes Bluff. Included in the community are an 18-hole executive golf course, a clubhouse, a swimming pool, a full-service marina (see our Marinas chapter), several tennis courts, access to a boat ramp, three restaurants, retail shops and a nine-room waterfront inn. Also on the grounds is a non-denominational chapel, a Baptist church and a Montessori school. Homesites range from $125,000 to $950,000 depending on size and location. Base prices for single-family homes range from $200,000 to $500,000 with garden homes and golf villas from $150,000 to $250,000. Marina condominiums are priced from $355,000. Custom homes are priced upon request. The newest neighborhood, South Harbour Station, offers two- and three-bedroom condos with garages and elevators starting in the mid-$100,000s.

Oak Island has two beach communities: **Caswell Beach** and the **Town of Oak Island**. Both of these communities have resort rentals, but they are overwhelmingly occupied by permanent residents. And why not? Many people who have been vacationing here for the fishing, swimming, watersports and the natural beauty of the area end up retiring to this family-oriented island. Caswell Beach is home to the Oak Island Lighthouse, which has the second brightest light in the world. Magnificent views of both the Atlantic Ocean and the Intracoastal Waterway can be had from the second floor of homes on the east end of the island. Prices for single-family homes range from $200,000 to more than $1.5 million. At the center of the island, you can expect to pay from $200,000 to $450,000 for a home. The Town of Oak Island, the biggest geographical area on the island, has ocean-side properties from $375,000 to $1.7 million and Intracoastal Waterway properties from $500,000 to $1.3 million.

HOLDEN BEACH

The next island down the coast is Holden Beach. A remarkable bridge that rises 65 feet above the Intracoastal Waterway provides a stunning view of the ocean and a sweeping entry to the island. Some say it's a surprise attraction in itself.

Holden Beach is known for its laid back atmosphere of family gatherings, fresh seafood, fishing, walking the beach, beautiful sunrises for early morning coffee and sunsets for the end of a memorable day.

Holden Beach has seen an appreciation of real estate over the past few years. An oceanfront, single-family home may cost from $750,000 to more than $2.8 million. Second-row homes, canal homes and dune homes can range from $450,000 to $1.5 million. Condominiums and town homes range from $325,000 to $650,000.

OCEAN ISLE BEACH

Ocean Isle Beach is an 8-mile-long, quarter-mile-wide island that lies at the center of South Brunswick's three barrier islands. The sandy beaches face directly south, providing sunshine all day. Beach residents are ac-

customed to seeing the sun rise and set over the ocean. The island has a stable year-round population of about 450 residents, ensuring a sense of community. Ocean Isle Beach is an appealing residential environment of largely single-family homes that start at over a million dollars on the oceanfront and Intracoastal Waterway and range from $500,000 to a million dollars in the middle of the island.

SUNSET BEACH

This beach may have thousands of visitors in the summer, but it is home to only about 1,800 year-round residents. It is overwhelmingly occupied by single-family dwellings, but there is a trend toward large duplexes on the oceanfront. This is because the island homes are on septic systems, and the oceanfront lots are the only ones that can accommodate two systems on one lot. Lots may range from $550,000 up depending on location. Four finger canals, regularly dredged, escalate the cost of interior lots. Duplexes of 2,000 square feet can cost $650,000. Single-family homes may range from $425,000 to more than $1 million.

CALABASH

The town of Calabash is a fishing village with its share of world-famous restaurants that specialize in Calabash-style seafood. Calabash attracts a wide range of families and individuals who appreciate the easy pace of the area and proximity to the Myrtle Beach and Wilmington entertainment and cultural activities.

Devaun Park is a 142-acre waterfront neighborhood built in the Traditional Neighborhood Design concept for smart growth, an increasingly popular style of neighborhood planning. Devaun Park has been endorsed by the N.C. Governor's Taskforce For Smart Growth. Situated on the high bluffs of the Calabash River, Devaun Park offers a varied collection of residential choices that include single-family homes, townhomes, row houses and more. When completed, the planned 483 residences will be surrounded by 8 miles of sidewalks that connect to 12 extraordinary parks and six exceptional neighborhoods. Recreational areas, a health club and a Town Square are additional amenities. For information, contact the office at Devaun Park Pavilion, (910) 575-6500.

A peaceful waterway view is typical of the area.

photo: Peter Doran

Topsail Island

Many of the properties on Topsail Island are second homes or investment properties. However, the number of year-round residents continues to grow as more small subdivisions are built on the sound and Intracoastal Waterway and nestled in the maritime forests. The majority of these homes are occupied by retirees who enjoy the relaxed beach lifestyle. Properties most in demand are the large homes on the oceanfront and other waterfront locations. The trend continues to be toward rising prices, and property purchased today will be viewed as a bargain tomorrow. You can expect to pay an average of $650,000 to $1.5 million for a single-family oceanfront home. Land is limited on this barrier island, and many retirees and new families relocating to the area often choose to live on the mainland, which is still close enough to the beach to feel like they are on a lifelong vacation.

Creeks Edge, a premiere water-oriented community, is located in the quaint fishing village of Sneads Ferry. This upscale planned community offers large waterfront, water-view and interior lots. Heavily wooded, the community features hardwood trees and

plenty of natural high elevations. In fact, the waterfront lots have elevations up to ten feet above the waterline. Located just five minutes from North Shore County Club, a golf course rated 3 stars by Golf Digest magazine and equally close to Topsail Island and the magnificent Atlantic Ocean, this four-star community also has direct access to the Intracoastal Waterway. Adding to its old South charm and ambiance is a lovely outdoor gazebo in its common area for family gatherings and entertainment. For information call Bud Rivenbark at (910) 327-7711 or (800) 497-5463.

REAL ESTATE AGENCIES

Any one of an abundance of area real estate agencies will be happy to assist you in your search for a new home. The agencies included here represent a fraction of the reputable companies working along the southern coast of North Carolina. Although we've grouped the agencies geographically, many of them sell properties in other communities, and some have offices in several locations throughout the area. Regardless of the office location, choose a Realtor who is knowledge-

BACHMAN REALTY

"The Buyer's Broker"
Waterfront Specialist
Figure 8 Island, Wrightsville Beach & Landfall

(910) 470-4099 • (800) 470-4099
sales: *www.waterfrontnc.net*
rentals: *www.figure8rentals.com*

Bunnie Bachman
GRI,CRS,ABR
Owner/Broker

able about the areas you're interested in and with whom you feel comfortable working.

Wilmington

5 Star Real Estate
4607 Franklin Ave. Ste. 110, Wilmington
(910) 313-0027, (888) 333-0083
www.joepascal.com

This innovative Wilmington real estate broker offers both buyers and sellers a creative marketing edge. 5 Star assists buyers to find their perfect home while at the same time helping sellers to locate hard-to-find buyers. Utilizing innovative financing strategies and advanced computer technology, 5 Star offers a complete and comprehensive real estate package. Serving the Cape Fear region including Wilmington, Leland, Brunswick County, Carolina Beach, Kure Beach, Wrightsville Beach and Landfall, 5 Star specializes in waterfront properties. Executive realtors Joe Pascal and David Girardot promise to make the real estate transaction experience positive and hassle-free.

Bachman Realty
2411 Middle Sound Loop Rd., Wilmington
(910) 686-4099, (800) 470-4099
www.waterfrontnc.net
www.figure8rentals.com

Whether you're an avid golfer or simply want the comfort of luxury beach house, Bunnie Bachman can help you find your slice of paradise. A Figure 8 Island real estate

agent for the past 25 years, Bachman has a unique perspective on the area and a comprehensive knowledge of what's necessary in purchasing a home on this private, secluded island. With connections in the Landfall, Porter's Neck, Turtle Hall, Masonboro Harbour, Oyster Bay and Tangle Oaks areas, Bachman connects discriminating buyers with the kind of properties that most people only dream of. Bachman's knowledge of water rights, property values and neighborhood regulations allow her clients to make educated choices regarding their purchases. Whether you're looking for an investment property, second home or primary residence, Bunnie Bachman knows where to find the ideal location for you.

Bryant Real Estate
501 N. College Rd., Wilmington
(910) 799-2700, (888) 364-1307
www.bryantrealestate.com

Offering vacation rental homes, condos and townhomes with locations from the ocean to the sound, Bryant Real Estate has been providing quality sales, rental and property management service in the Wilmington, Carolina Beach, Kure Beach and Wrightsville Beach areas for more than 50 years. For year-round rentals, call (910) 799-2700. Daily, weekly and monthly rates are available in Wrightsville Beach, Carolina Beach and Kure Beach. Bryant also has offices in Wrightsville Beach and Carolina Beach.

SOLD

We can help you every step of the way!
Use our knowledge and experience
to guide you through *Buying* and
Selling Real Estate, as well as:

☑ Relocation
☑ Property Association Mngmt
☑ Real Estate Education
☑ Rentals
☑ Mortgage Services
☑ Investment Property
☑ Maintenance Division
☑ the list goes on...

SWEYER & ASSOCIATES

(910) 256-0021 • (800) 848-0021

www.Century21Sweyer.com
When it comes to Real Estate...You can trust the Experts!
©2006 CENTURY 21 Real Estate Corporation. An Equal Opportunity Company. Equal Housing Opportunity. Each CENTURY 21 Office is independently owned and operated.

Century 21 Sweyer & Associates
1630 Military Cutoff Rd., Wilmington
(910) 256-0021, (800) 848-0021
www.century21sweyer.com

The staff at Century 21 Sweyer & Associates boasts a sales force of more than 160 sales associates, each trained in making sure your real estate purchase or sale goes smoothly. David and Polly Sweyer have been in the local real estate business since 1987. The #1 Century 21 office in the eastern Carolinas, Century 21 Sweyer & Associates offers residential sales, long-term rental management for tenants and property owners, community association management, mortgage services and residential maintenance. Century 21 Sweyer & Associates office features training services for new agents, relocation assistance for clients new to the area, and a top-notch in-house marketing department that can aid you in selling your property. They also have offices in Topsail Island, Hampstead, Monkey Junction, and Carolina Beach.

During an interview with a prospective real estate agent, ask such questions as:
How long have you been in business in this area?
Do you work full-time in the real estate market?
Are you G.R.I., C.R.S., or A.B.R.?
(These are the highest real estate degrees.)

Coastal Communities Residential
and Commercial Real Estate
4555 Fountain Dr., Wilmington
(910) 395-4770, (888) 395-4770
www.coastalcommunitiesrealty.com

Specializing in residential, commercial and recreational properties, Coastal Communities has an extensive listing of fine homes and estates as well as mid-range properties. This agency also offers real estate services from Wilmington to Calabash, which results in high visibility and maximum exposure. Two small offices, each staffed with highly experienced professionals, provide quality individualized service and personal attention. Coastal Communities also has an office in Wilmington.

Coldwell Banker Sea Coast Realty
5710 Oleander Dr., Ste. 200, Wilmington
(910) 799-3435, (800) 522-9624
8211 Market St., Unit CC, Wilmington
(910) 686-6855, (800) 435-7211
1430 Commonwealth Dr.,
Ste. 102, Wilmington
(910) 256-1155, (800) 497-7325

Coldwell Banker Sea Coast Realty is one of the dominant real estate companies in the area, with more than $818 million in closed sales and 4,394 transactions in 2004. The company was named the 11th fastest growing real estate company in the United States by Real Trends, Inc. Having more than 200 professional Realtors with proven results, the company handles all types of residential properties, resort/vacation properties,

442

Martie Rice
Your Coastal Connection

You Deserve the BEST...

I Guarantee It.

My Specialty is Working FOR You!

910-256-6764
800-533-1840, #1947

Intracoastal
REALTY CORPORATION

www.MartieRice.com

homesites/land/acreage, as well as commercial properties and relocation services. The company represents an impressive list of new home communities in Wilmington and across New Hanover, Pender and Brunswick counties. For additional information, contact any one of Coldwell Banker Sea Coast's area offices; the others are in Carolina Beach, Surf City and Southport.

Demarest Company
(910) 686-4482
www.demarestcompany.com

The Demarest Company represents the communities of Demarest Landing, Demarest Village, Demarest Village Swim Club and Day Care Facilities as well as other prestigious planned communities in the southern coastal area. The Demarest communities are the area's first neighborhoods to offer traditional home designs reminiscent of historic Wilmington, all integrated with beautiful parks and tree-lined streets.

EXIT Homeplace Realty
3825 Market St., Ste.6, Wilmington
(910) 762-1951

EXIT Realty is a locally owned and operated, full-service real estate company, with agents and offices in Wilmington, Hampstead, Topsail Island/Surf City, Jacksonville and Brunswick County. Established in 1997, Homeplace Realty became the first EXIT office in North Carolina in 2001. Founded by Martin J. Evans, owner/broker, EXIT Home-

place's single goal is to be the foundation of service to customers in their real estate transactions.

Intracoastal Realty Corporation
Lumina Station, 1900 Eastwood Rd.,
Ste. 38, Wilmington
(910) 256-4503, (800) 533-1840
www.intracoastalrentals.com

This market leader has been in business in the area since 1974. An exclusive affiliate of Christie's Great Estates, it is a resort and residential property specialist. This company has listings throughout the region, including historic downtown Wilmington, Wrightsville Beach and Landfall. It is a member of the RELO relocation service. The agency's New Home division represents several new home communities in the area, offering homes that range from the mid-$100,000 range up to $700,000 and higher. Intracoastal offers a vacation and long-term rental office in Wrightsville Beach at 605 Causeway Drive; for weekly vacation rentals call (910) 256-3780, (800) 346-2463; for long-term rentals call (910) 509-9700, (800) 826-4428.They also have offices in Carolina Beach and on Topsail Island.

LampPost Realty
1209 Market St., Ste. A, Wilmington
(910) 763-1118, (800) 760-LAMP
www.lamppostrealty.com

Whether you're looking to buy a starter home, sell your million dollar property or anything in between, LampPost Realty

Buy any property with LampPost Realty® today...
receive a check tomorrow.

Yes.
It's that simple.

LampPost Realty®
Reinventing Real Estate.

Residential Real Estate • Commercial Real Estate
Waterfront Property • Luxury Homes • Investment Property
910-763-1118 • 800-760-LAMP toll free
www.LampPostRealty.com • info@LampPostRealty.com

will provide a level of service that exceeds your expectations and leaves more money in your pocket. LampPost Realty offers a Buyer Rebate based upon a percentage of the purchase price on any property listed with LampPost Realty or any other MLS broker. For sellers, LampPost goes beyond traditional real estate services, with Seller Benefits designed to sell properties quickly and profitably. LampPost Realty charges sellers less and provides them with more. With LampPost Realty's Commercial Division, you can buy or sell commercial real estate and still enjoy all the same advantages as their residential clients.

Landfall Realty
1816 Mews Dr., Wilmington
(910) 256-6111, (800) 227-8208

Landfall Realty deals exclusively with the fine properties in Landfall, a private gated neighborhood of single-family custom homes, villas, patio homes, townhomes, condominiums and home sites. The community boasts numerous amenities, including two championship golf courses — a Jack Nicklaus 27-hole course and the Pete Dye 18-hole

course - -and the Landfall Sports Center, designed by tennis legend Cliff Drysdale. Two well-appointed clubhouses overlook Landfall's golf courses: the luxurious Landfall Clubhouse near the Nicklaus course and the Dye Clubhouse on Landfall's Pete Dye course.

Network Real Estate
1601 S. College Rd., Wilmington
(910) 395-4100, (800) 747-1968
106 North Water St., Wilmington
(910) 772-1622, (877) 882-1622
www.networkwilmington.com

Locally owned and operated by lifelong residents Bob and Marilyn McKoy, Network Real Estate has been providing top-notch real estate services in the greater Wilmington area for the past 24 years. Specializing in residential and single family homes, Network will connect you with its trained staff of more than 60 agents who provide a comprehensive look at all properties available and invite you to utilize the "internet office" that their well-equipped website provides. In addition, commercial and land properties are another avenue that Network includes in its vast array

The Beals Team
910-352-2000
Sandy and Dick Beals
Wilmington#1Experts ™

Your Complete Guide
To Wilmington is:

www.WilmingtonRealEstate4u.com
www.BealsTeam.com

Search **All Homes** For Sale in
Wilmington and the surrounding
Areas On Our Website at:

www.WilmingtonRealEstate4u.com
Toll Free 24 Hour Info Hotline
1-888-391-0882

Email "The Beals Team" at:
dickandsandy@bealsteam.com

Three Offices To Serve You:
Wilmington, Southport & Topsail
RealtyExecutivesofWilmington.com

of services. Network also has offices in Carolina Beach and Brunswick County.

Port City Properties
17 S. Second St., Wilmington
(910) 251-0615

Established in 1995, Port City Properties represents residential and commercial properties throughout New Hanover, Brunswick and Pender counties. This full-service realty company covers a full geographical and price spectrum, specializing in historic downtown Wilmington and all area beach communities.

Porters Neck Plantation
8204 Fazio Dr., Wilmington
(910) 686-7400, (800) 423-5695

Porters Neck offers an extraordinary setting, with 650 acres of pristine, lush coastal land adjacent to the Intracoastal Waterway and a Tom Fazio–designed golf course. The sports complex, complete with a lap pool, clay tennis courts and a fitness center, also draws active individuals to this community. Traditional single-family homes and patio homes are available in a variety of sizes. Porters Neck is north of Wilmington and

Wrightsville Beach just off U.S. Highway 17. Contact the office for more information.

Prudential Carolina Real Estate
Relocation Services: 1437 Military Cutoff Rd., Ste. 201, Wilmington
(910) 239-5799, (888) 220-4665
Sales Offices: Forum at Landfall, 1131-B Military Cutoff Rd., Wilmington
(910) 256-0032, (800) 521-8132
www.PruCarolina.com

This company is one of the largest real estate agencies servicing the Cape Fear area. Residential sales include single-family homes, townhomes, condominiums, and lots. Prudential Carolina Real Estate has six sales offices including Topsail Island, Forum at Landfall, Wrightsville Beach, Carolina Beach, Southport and Ocean Isle Beach. Prudential offers corporate relocation services provided by certified relocation specialists, a Fine Homes program for exceptional properties and a rental partner in Southern Retreats for investors. Visit the website above for more information on their agents, services and available properties.

Professional Profile - Real Estate

Joe Capellini - REMAX Coastal Properties
Realtor/Broker, Seniors Real Estate Specialist,
Fine Homes Specialist
2018 Eastwood Road • Wilmington, NC 28403
(910) 619-0164, (800) 883-9584
www.come2wilmington.com
email: joe@come2wilmington.com

Customer Service is the cornerstone of my professional
career, first as a CPA and now as a Realtor. I feel a great
responsibility to my clients. As your Realtor, my job is to
protect you and your interests. I will help you negotiate the
best deal possible. I will guide you through each step of the transaction right up to closing.
My knowledge and expertise will actually save you money. Whether you're a newcomer to
Wilmington or are moving within town, you can rely on me.

Realty Executives of Wilmington
6766 Wrightsville Ave. Ste. H, Wilmington
(910) 256-4686, (910) 352-2000,
(877)-379-2589
www.realtyexecutivesofwilmington.com

Dedicated to providing their clients with
a level of service beyond their expectations,
Sandy and Dick Beals believe that buying or
selling a home is an important life transition
and they work hard to ensure that it's worry
free. With an experienced team of professionals, Realty Executives of Wilmington
guarantees privacy and respect while delivering results. The conveniently located office is
fully equipped and has an integrated network
of computer and communications systems
to facilitate access to all the Multiple Listing
Services, public record searches and other
tools that agents need in order to better
serve clients. Since its inception in Phoenix,
Arizona, more than 35 years ago, Realty
Executives has become one of the fastest
growing franchises internationally; this is the
first office in the Wilmington area.

Realty World - Cape Fear
1113-A Military Cutoff Rd., Wilmington
(910) 256-3528, (866) 405-4147
www.haroldchappell.com

With access to more than 1,500 homes,
condos and apartments in the Wilmington
area, Harold Chappell and the agents at Realty World-Cape Fear have their finger on the
pulse of the surrounding real estate market.
Whether you're looking for short-term relocation information or thinking about making a

real estate investment, you'll find what you're
looking for with Realty World-Cape Fear. And
if you're interested in selling your property,
the agency's vast knowledge of Wilmington's
diverse neighborhoods and current price
trends will insure that you get the best value
in your sale. A top producer that ranks in the
top 1 percent of realtors locally and nationally,
Harold Chappell and his associates will find
the ideal place for your needs.

RE/MAX Coastal Properties
2018 Eastwood Rd., Wilmington
(910) 256-8171, (800) 833-9584
112 A Market St., Wilmington
(910) 792-1523, (800) 833-9584
www.wilmingtonhomesonline.com

With more than 5,500 offices in over
50 countries, RE/MAX is a market leader in
real estate sales worldwide. Averaging three
times the production and more advanced
industry education than other agents,
RE/MAX associates are leaders in quality
customer service. Customer satisfaction is
reflected in their rate of repeat and referral
business. Affiliation with the global RE/MAX
network provides associates with multiple
competitive advantages in serving real estate
needs. From national television advertising to
personal advertising controlled by associates,
RE/MAX enjoys brand-name recognition
worldwide. Belonging to a real estate network with vast market presence and market
share, RE/MAX associates have a lot to offer.
RE/MAX also has an office in Surf City on
Topsail Island.

REALTY WORLD®
CAPE FEAR

With Sales of over $26 Million completed in 2005, Harold Chappell is one of the area's leading producers.

Specializing in coastal and waterfront properties, he understands what it takes to make your dream home a reality.

Call and start today.

Office: 910.256.3528 • Toll Free: 866.405.4147
Fax: 910.256.5889 • Mobile: 910.512.1948
beachchapp@haroldchappell.com
www.haroldchappell.com

Tregembo & Associates Realty
5813 Carolina Beach Rd., Wilmington
(910) 799-9234
www.tregemborealty.com

Sherry Tregembo is a lifelong resident of Wilmington and that experience helps her and her team of agents be "a small company that's big on service." Dedicated to providing comprehensive services to homeowners looking to sell their property, Tregembo's team is also skilled in finding the ideal home or vacation property for prospective buyers. Covering the Wilmington area along with all local beach locations, the company also serves Pender and Brunswick counties. If you're looking for a real estate company that can provide services tailored to your specific needs, Tregembo is it.

Wells Realty
4607 Franklin Ave., Ste. 217, Wilmington
(910) 350-0550, (877) 843-0287

At Wells Realty, you'll find a real estate agent who will focus on your needs, answer all of your questions, and guide you step-by-step through this important investment.

Owner Sofia DeFelice Wells is an ABR, GRI, licensed broker who has been helping buyers find the right house at a fair price since 1979. That's the kind of experience and expertise you need on your side in order to make an informed, smart decision. Whether you're looking to buy or sell, when you work with Wells Realty, you'll have an agent that will be there for you from the first showing to the final closing.

Wallace

River Landing
110 River Village Pl., Wallace
(910) 285-4171, (888) 285-4171

Home to five U.S. Open events, River Landing is an exceptional golfing community. Just 35 minutes from Wilmington off I-40, this is a private neighborhood of primary residences and second homes with a variety of recreational facilities. Club memberships include a 36-hole championship golf course designed by Clyde Johnston, a fitness center with an indoor Junior Olympic pool and an

Prudential
Carolina Real Estate

you'll love our views on real estate.

PruCarolina.com

HOMES | LAND | LIFESTYLES

carolina beach   ocean isle beach   southport   topsail island   wilmington   wrightsville beach
910.458.9672   910.575.3113   910.454.8451   910.329.4466   910.256.0032   910.256.9299

outdoor pool, a tennis center, private guest cottages, fishing and boating and walking/jogging/nature trails. Home prices start in the mid-$200,000 range. Contact the office at the number above for more information.

Wrightsville Beach

Bryant Real Estate
1001 N. Lumina Ave., Wrightsville Beach
(910) 256-3764, (800) 322-3764
www.bryantre.com

Offering vacation rental homes, condos and townhomes with locations from the ocean to the sound, Bryant Real Estate has been providing quality sales, rental and property management service in the Wilmington, Carolina Beach, Kure Beach and Wrightsville Beach area for more than 50 years. For year-round rentals call (910) 799-2700. Daily, weekly and monthly rates are available in Wrightsville Beach, Carolina Beach and Kure Beach. Bryant also has offices in Wilmington and Carolina Beach.

Intracoastal Realty Corporation
534 Causeway Dr., Wrightsville Beach
(910) 256-4503, (800) 533-1840

This market leader has been in business in the area since 1974. An exclusive affiliate of Christie's Great Estates, it is a resort and residential property specialist. This company has listings throughout the region, including historic downtown Wilmington, Wrightsville Beach and Landfall. It is a member of the RELO relocation service. The agency's New Home division represents several new home communities in the area, offering homes that range from the mid-$100,000 range up to $700,000 and higher. Intracoastal offers a vacation and long-term rental office in Wrightsville Beach at 605 Causeway Drive; for weekly vacation rentals call (910) 256-3780 or (800) 346-2463; for long-term rentals call (910) 509-9700 or (800) 826-4428. Intracoastal Realty also has offices in Wilmington, Carolina Beach and on Topsail Island.

Prudential Carolina Real Estate
527 Causeway Dr., Wrightsville Beach
(910) 256-9299, (800) 562-9299
www.PruCarolina.com

This company is one of the largest real estate agencies servicing the Cape Fear area. Residential sales include single-family homes, townhomes, condominiums, and lots. Prudential Carolina Real Estate has six sales offices including Topsail Island, Forum at Landfall, Wrightsville Beach, Carolina Beach, Southport and Ocean Isle Beach. Prudential offers corporate relocation services provided by certified relocation specialists, a Fine Homes program for exceptional properties and a rental partner in Southern Retreats for investors. Visit the website above for more information on their agents, services and available properties.

Sales
910-458-5878

Toll Free Sales
877-428-5878

Rentals
910-458-4975

Toll Free Rentals
800-289-0028

9 South Lake Park Blvd. | A-3 | Carolina Beach NC | 28428

www.AtlanticShoresRealty.com

Wrightsville Realty Group
2004 Eastwood Rd., Ste. 101, Wilmington
(910) 256-3626

An exclusive buyer's agency designed to assist the discriminating buyer, Wrightsville Realty Group specializes in homes along the Intracoastal Waterway, gated communities, beachfront and historic Wilmington properties. A full-service agency, Wrightsville Realty Group says it will leave no stone unturned in finding the ideal property for its clients. And, with detailed knowledge of properties in Wrightsville Beach, Landfall, Porters Neck, Figure Eight Island, Topsail Island, Bald Head Island and Carolina/Kure beaches, they offer a great selection. At Wrightsville Realty, they know purchasing real estate is an important investment.

Figure Eight Island

Bachman Realty
2411 Middle Sound Loop Rd., Wilmington
(910) 686-4099, (800) 470-4099
www.waterfrontnc.net
www.figure8rentals.com

While the Carolina Beach and Wrightsville Beach areas are awash with tourists each summer, you can still stroll the morning sand without seeing another soul at Figure Eight. This exclusive barrier island is extremely desirable. With 25 years of real estate experience Bunnie Bachman knows the ins-and-outs of the local market better than anyone. From cozy sound side getaways to

oceanfront manors, Bachman has her finger on Figure Eight's pulse. Looking to buy that summer retreat you've always dreamt of? Perhaps you'd prefer an investment property that will recoup its mortgage on summer rentals. Why share the beach with the masses when you can let Bunnie Bachman find your own private beach retreat?

Figure Eight Realty
15 Bridge Rd., Wilmington
(910) 686-4400, (800) 279-6085

This agency, which is located on Figure Eight Island, focuses on the island's neighborhood of luxury, single-family homes. Oceanfront, marshfront and soundfront properties are available. Figure Eight Realty also offers vacation rentals on the island.

Carolina Beach and Kure Beach

Atlantic Shores Real Estate
9 S. Lake Park Blvd., Ste. A-3
Carolina Beach
Sales (910) 458-5878, (877) 428-5878;
Rentals (910) 458-4975, (800) 289-0028
www.AtlanticShoresRealty.com

Located in the heart of Carolina Beach, Atlantic Shores Real Estate is an independent, full-service company that represents both buyers and sellers in residential, commercial and investment transactions within Carolina Beach, Kure Beach, Fort Fisher,

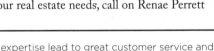

Professional Profile - Real Estate

Renae Perrett - RE/MAX Coastal Properties
718 N. Lake Park Blvd. • Carolina Beach NC 28428
Office: 910.458.3985 Fax: 910.458.3255
Mobile: 910.232.5065 Toll Free: 800.883.9584
www.RenaePerrett.com

Realtor Renae Perrett has never regretted answering
the call of the Carolina Coast – and there's nothing she
enjoys more than helping others make the most of their
dream investment here.

Renae understands just how much buying or selling
your beach or waterfront property means to you, and her enthusiasm for the area and
strong work ethic offer an unbeatable combination for a successful transaction. For a
professional you can trust to handle all of your real estate needs, call on Renae Perrett
and Coast Into Success. Call her today!

Wrightsville Beach and all of Wilmington. Atlantic Shores is also a member of the National Association of Realtors®.

The professionals at Atlantic Shores Real Estate place emphasis on delivering personal service to each and every client and providing the professional guidance necessary to make an informed decision based on your specific needs. Known for their knowledge, dedication and integrity, Atlantic Shores Real Estate has everything you're looking for in a real estate agency and much more.

Blue Water Realty
1000 S. Lake Park Blvd., Carolina Beach
(910) 458-3001, (866) 458-3001
www.bluewaterrealtyinc.com

Centrally located between Carolina and Kure beaches and specializing in magnificent oceanfront properties on Pleasure Island, Blue Water Realty is the agency to call when you're looking for your own piece of paradise. True to its name, Blue Water Realty offers a wide selection of waterfront properties and serves the New Hanover, Brunswick and Pender county areas. Are you longing to own a place on the beach with a spectacular view? Let Blue Water Realty help you make that dream a reality. Their experience and

expertise lead to great customer service and client satisfaction.

Bowman Realty
106 K Ave., Kure Beach
(910) 458-5211

Celebrating its 10th year on this popular island, with its ever-changing real estate market, Bowman Realty specializes in the beach properties of Kure Beach and Carolina Beach. As local Realtors, living where they work, Bowman provides you with the right choices in your real estate property. Whether buying for investment, second home or primary residence, Bowman can make it a smooth and pleasant experience. It's located in downtown Kure Beach, across form the Kure Beach Pier at 106 K Avenue.

Bryant Real Estate
Snow's Cut Crossing, 1401 N. Lake Park Blvd., Carolina Beach
(910) 458-5658 (800) 994-5222
www.bryantrealestate.com

Offering vacation rental homes, condos and townhomes with locations from the ocean to the sound, Bryant Real Estate has been providing quality sales, rentals and property management services in the Wilmington, Carolina Beach, Kure Beach and Wrightsville Beach areas for more than 50 years. For year-round rentals, call (910) 799-2700. Daily, weekly and monthly rates are available in Wrightsville Beach, Carolina Beach and Kure Beach. Bryant also has offices in Wilmington and Wrightsville Beach.

i *Most coastal North Carolina homes lack a basement, so make sure your potential new home has adequate storage space.*

Bullard Realty, Inc.
1404 S. Lake Park Blvd., Carolina Beach
(910) 458-4028, (800) 327-5863

Established in 1989, Bullard Realty Inc. is a full-service real estate company specializing in sales and rentals on Carolina and Kure Beaches. Owner Beth Bullard and her staff can represent buyers and sellers in Wilmington, as well as the beaches. As members of the Wilmington Association of Realtors and the Multiple Listing Service, Bullard Realty can meet all of your real estate needs. Bullard Realty offers the personalized service of a small company with the professionalism and technology of a larger agency. See the Weekly and Long-term Vacation Rentals chapter for rental information.

Century 21 Sweyer & Associates
5215 Junction Cir., Ste. 102,
Wilmington
(910) 332-0336, (800) 474-3090
www.century21sweyer.com

The staff at Century 21 Sweyer and Associates boasts a sales force of over 110 agents, each trained in making sure your real estate purchase or sale goes smoothly. David and Polly Sweyer have been in the local real estate business since 1987 and their business has expanded throughout southeast North Carolina in that time. The #1 Century 21 office in the eastern Carolinas, Sweyer and Associates offers residential sales, long-term rental management for tenants and property owners, community association management, mortgage services and residential maintenance. This Century 21 office features training services for new agents, relocation assistance for clients new to the area and a top-notch marketing department that can aid you in selling your property. It's the personal touch that Sweyer and Associates' agents provide that fuels their reputation as one of the Southeast's top real estate agencies.

Coldwell Banker Sea Coast Realty
1001 N. Lake Park Blvd., Carolina Beach
(910) 458-4401, (800) 847-5771

Coldwell Banker Sea Coast Realty is one of the dominant real estate companies in the area, with more than $818 million in closed sales and 4,394 transactions in 2004. The company was named the 11th fastest growing real estate company in the United States by Real Trends, Inc. Having more than 200 professional Realtors with proven results, the company handles all types of residential properties, resort/vacation properties, homesites/land/acreage, as well as commercial properties and relocation services. The company represents an impressive list of new home communities in Wilmington and across New Hanover, Pender and Brunswick counties. Coldwell Banker Sea Coast has five other area offices, three in Wilmington, one in Southport and one in Surf City.

Intracoastal Realty Corporation
1206 N. Lake Park Blvd., Carolina Beach
(910) 256-4503, (800) 533-1840

This market leader has been in business in the area since 1974. An exclusive affiliate of Christie's Great Estates, it is a resort and residential property specialist. This company has listings throughout the region, including historic downtown Wilmington, Wrightsville Beach and Landfall. It is a member of the RELO relocation service. The agency's New Home division represents several new home communities in the area, offering homes that range from the mid-$100,000 range up to $700,000 and higher. Intracoastal also offers a vacation and long-term rental office in Wrightsville Beach at 605 Causeway Drive; for weekly vacation rentals call (910) 256-3780 or (800) 346-2463; for long-term rentals call (910) 509-9700 or (800) 826-4428.They also have offices in Wilmington, Wrightsville Beach and on Topsail Island.

Latitude 34° Realtors
104 Winner Ave., Carolina Beach
(910) 458-7212
www.Latitude34Realtors.com

Owner/Broker Tammy Hanson believes that your real estate transaction does not have to be a stress-inducing process. With 11 years of experience in the Wilmington area, Tammy and her team have developed a knack for finding properties that are perfectly suited for the needs of their clients. Latitude 34 is a small office that offers all the amenities of a larger business but with much more personal service. Their professional staff believes that communication between agent and client is key, and they strive to make sure that their customers are satisfied. An avid animal lover, Tammy donates a percentage of every commission to the animal protection group of her client's choice. For the best the

Carolina Beach market has to offer, set your course for Latitude 34.

Network Real Estate
1029 N. Lake Park Blvd., Carolina Beach
(910) 458-8881, (800) 830-2118
www.networkwilmington.com

Owners Bob and Marilyn McKoy recognize the popularity that the Carolina Beach, Kure Beach and Fort Fisher areas have gained each season. You'll be happy you chose a connected real estate company like Network to guide you through your potential property purchase. The company's more than 60 agents have access to each MLS listing in this booming market and they will make every effort to accommodate your needs and desires in either a second vacation home, a primary residence or your dream retirement location. Network also has two offices in Wilmington and one in Brunswick County.

Prudential Carolina Real Estate
1025B N. Lake Park Blvd., Carolina Beach
(910) 458-9672, (888) 313-9738
www.PruCarolina.com

This company is one of the largest real estate agencies servicing the Cape Fear area. Residential sales include single-family homes, townhomes, condominiums, and lots. Prudential Carolina Real Estate has six sales offices including Topsail Island, Forum at Landfall, Wrightsville Beach, Carolina Beach, Southport and Ocean Isle Beach. Prudential offers corporate relocation services provided by certified relocation specialists, a Fine Homes program for exceptional properties and a rental partner in Southern Retreats for investors. Visit the website above for more information on their agents, services and available properties.

Tregembo Realty
5811 Carolina Beach Rd., Wilmington
(910) 799-9234

Sherry Tregembo is a lifelong resident of Wilmington and that experience helps her and her team of agents "a small company that's big on service." Dedicated to providing comprehensive services to homeowners looking to sell their property, Tregembo's team is also skilled in finding the ideal home or vacation property for prospective buyers. Covering the Wilmington area along with all local beach locations, in particular the

Carolina Beach waterfront, the company also serves Pender and Brunswick counties. If you're looking for a real estate company that can provide services tailored to your specific needs, Tregembo's the place.

Walker Realty - Island Beach Rentals
501 N. Lake Park Blvd., Carolina Beach
(910) 458-3388

With the Carolina and Kure Beach areas more popular than ever for those seeking a serene and relaxed environment, why not let the team at Island Beach Rentals set you up in the perfect home? Featuring a wide variety of condos, town homes and beach houses, you'll be able to find the ideal spot just minutes from the beach. With fantastic dining only a short trip from every location, Carolina and Kure beaches have become a popular alternative to the Wrightsville Beach madness. Looking for reasonable homes with all the amenities a beach community offers? You'll have it all if you let Island Beach Rentals work for you.

Bald Head Island

Bald Head Island Limited
5079 Southport-Supply Rd., Southport
(910) 457-7400, (800) 888-3707
www.baldheadisland.com

Bald Head Island Limited sells single-family homes, cottages, condominiums, townhouses and home sites on Bald Head Island as well as Indigo Plantation & Marina in Southport. Properties are located along the Cape Fear River, the Atlantic Ocean, the Intracoastal Waterway, Bald Head Island creeks and marshes, the 18-hole George Cobb–designed golf course and the pristine Maritime Forest on the island.

Bald Head Island Real Estate Sales, Inc.
1111 Howe St., Southport
(910) 457-6463, (800) 350-7021

This brokerage firm, the largest independent agency for Bald Head Island not associated with a developer, handles real estate on Bald Head Island. The island is a paradise that includes 14 miles of beaches, maritime forest and a 10,000-acre salt marsh. Bald Head Island Real Estate Sales, Inc. represents buyers as well as sellers.

www.latitude34realtors.com

Consider a change in latitude!

Latitude 34'
REALTORS

910-458-7212 Office
877-457-7212 Toll Free

104 Winner Avenue, Suite 1
Carolina Beach, NC

A percentage of our personal commission is donated to
the non-profit animal protection group of the client's choice

Cape Fear Realty
303 N. Howe St., Southport
(910) 457-1702, (800) 680-8322

Cape Fear Realty invites you to discover real estate opportunities on Bald Head Island, Middle Island Plantation, Southport, the Intracoastal Waterway, the Cape Fear River, St. James Plantation and the Brunswick Islands. As a full-service real estate company, Cape Fear Realty specializes in home re-sales, island home sites and new-home construction. The agency is a member of the Multiple Listing Service and, therefore, can assist you in the role of buyer's agent.

the Jack Cox group
58 Dowitcher Tr., Bald Head Island
(910) 457-4732, (888) 603-1956

This family-owned and independent real estate agency opened on Bald Head Island six years ago. Their motto is: "We've got the solution to your North Carolina real estate needs." The agency specializes in property on exclusive Bald Head Island as well as in Southport, Oak Island, Caswell Beach and St. James Plantation. They offer residential sales of single-family homes, condominiums and cottages. Land is available, as is commercial property.

Martha Lee Realty
2669 Holden Beach Rd., Holden Beach
(910) 846-2402, (866) 696-6232
www.brunswickcountyhomes.com

Martha Lee Realty, with 32 years of experience, is in the unique position of represent-

ing all of Brunswick County. This includes Bald Head Island, Southport, Oak Island, St. James, Sunset Harbor, Lockwood Folly, Holden Beach, Ocean Isle Beach, Sunset Beach, Shallotte, Calabash and Carolina Shores as well as acreage in the interior. Martha Lee Realty specializes in waterfront property, new communities, commercial property and large tracts of land. Real Estate showcase tours are offered daily.

Old Baldy Associates
1105 N, Howe St., Southport
(910) 457-5551

Involved in sales for more than 27 years, Old Baldy Associates specializes in resale and rental of Bald Head Island and Middle Island Plantation property. Homesites are available overlooking the ocean and high dunes, the golf course, the maritime forest and saltwater creeks. In Middle Island Plantation, a residential-only community at the eastern end of Bald Head Island, all homesites are more than a half-acre, and amenities include a keyed beach walk, Bald Head Island Club member-

When contemplating the *purchase of beach property, ask about availability of homeowner's, wind and hail, flood and tenant insurance. You may be surprised to find that these are difficult to obtain in some locales.*

ship, a swimming pool, a tennis court and a floating dock system for boats up to 25 feet.

Brunwick County Beaches

SOUTHPORT/OAK ISLAND

Cape Fear Realty
303 N. Howe St., Southport
(910) 455-9112, (800) 281-5360

Cape Fear Realty invites you to discover real estate opportunities on Bald Head Island, Middle Island Plantation, Southport, the Intracoastal Waterway, the Cape Fear River, St. James Plantation and the Brunswick Islands. A full-service real estate company, Cape Fear Realty specializes in home re-sales, island home sites and new-home construction. The agency is a member of the Multiple Listing Service and, therefore, can assist you in the role of buyer's agent.

Century 21 Dorothy Essey
and Associates Inc.
6102 E. Oak Island Dr., Oak Island
(910) 278-3361, (877) 410-2121
113 S. Howe St., Southport
(910) 457-4577, (877) 410-2121

This real estate company services all of Brunswick County, including Southport and Oak Island as well as Boiling Spring Lakes, Bald Head Island, Caswell Beach and the South Brunswick beaches. It offers general brokerage and services for single-family homes, condominiums, duplexes, lots and commercial properties. The company has a new-home specialist on staff.

Coastal Development & Realty
8118 E. Oak Island Dr., Oak Island
(910) 278-6111, (888) 278-2611

A progressive, full-service real estate firm with offices on Oak Island and Holden Beach, Coastal Development & Realty has been representing coastal Brunswick County since 1984. Professionals without a doubt, they can assist you with buying, selling, construction or home design, lots, land and commercial buildings. Their tasteful and attractive Coastal Home Designs are known for easy maintenance and durability and are custom-ized to your specifications. If you like, you can search their listings online or complete the

Dream Home Finder application and let them do the searching for you. Whatever process you choose, you will find a commitment to complete customer satisfaction.

Coldwell Banker Sea Coast Realty
4633 Long Beach Rd. SE, Southport
(910) 457-6713, (910) 278-3311,
(800) 346-7671

Coldwell Banker Sea Coast Realty is a full-service real estate company. This Real Estate Information Center is dedicated to providing real estate services and products to home buyers and sellers in Brunswick County. More than 30 highly trained sales associates offer their clients the programs, systems and best marketing tools available to achieve customer satisfaction. Coldwell Banker Sea Coast also has offices in Wilming-ton, Carolina Beach and on Topsail Island.

Corporate at the Beach
4983 Glen Cove Dr., Southport
(910) 262-3311, (910) 798-1060
www.myoakisland.com

Pat Maloney, owner of Corporate at the Beach, specializes in finding homes in resort areas for corporate use. Each home is well designed and spacious enough to accom-modate large groups. Located in or near beach communities, these homes offer a relaxing atmosphere for off-site company meetings, trainings or special events. A week at your company's resort facility would also make a terrific productivity incentive for staff members. Some of the properties lend themselves to weekly resort rentals, particu-larly in June, July and August. That allows you to earn income on your purchase if you schedule the corporate use for September through May. Professional property manage-ment companies are available to handle rent-als and maintain your investment in your absence. The Brunswick County Airport is nearby and can accommodate fairly sizeable jets. The Myrtle Beach and Wilmington Inter-national Airports are available for commercial flights.

the Jack Cox group
5001 O'Quinn Blvd., Ste. H, Southport
(910) 457-6884, (888) 603-1956

From their waterfront offices at South Harbour Village just outside of Southport, the Jack Cox group handles real estate sales for a large geographic area. In addition to handling sales on Bald Head Island, agents in this office can help you solve your real estate needs in much of Brunswick County, including Southport, Oak Island and Shallotte. They deal extensively in both residential and commercial properties.

Walter Hill & Associates
6101 E. Oak Island Dr., Oak Island
(910) 278-5469, (800) 603-5469

This company serves Southport, Oak Island's two beach communities and Brunswick County through the sale of residential and commercial properties near the water and on the mainland.

Martha Lee Realty
2669 Holden Beach Rd., Holden Beach
(910) 846-2402, (866) 696-6232
www.brunswickcountyhomes.com

Martha Lee Realty, with 32 years of experience, is in the unique position of representing all of Brunswick County. This includes Bald Head Island, Southport, Oak Island, St. James, Sunset Harbor, Lockwood Folly, Holden Beach, Ocean Isle Beach, Sunset Beach, Shallotte, Calabash and Carolina Shores as well as acreage in the interior. Martha Lee Realty specializes in waterfront property, new communities, commercial property and large

tracts of land. Real estate showcase tours are offered daily.

Oak Island Real Estate Company, Inc.
8601 E. Oak Island Dr., Oak Island
(910) 278-1116, (866) 462-5158
4857 Long Beach Rd., Southport
(910) 457-1141

Enthusiasm is the hallmark of the folks at Oak Island Real Estate Company. They can't wait to share the area they love with you. Whether you are interested in Southport, Oak Island or Boiling Spring Lakes, oceanfront, waterway, waterfront, soundside, wooded area or second row, Oak Island Real Estate Company can help you locate your special vision. They can build to your specifications as well. Oak Island Real Estate Company is the exclusive agent for Ocean Walk and Ocean View Condominiums. At Ocean Walk you will find spectacular views and amenities specially geared to your convenience and comfort, including elevators.

Prudential Carolina Real Estate
4565 Long Beach Road, Southport
(910) 454-8451, (800) 204-0786
www.PruCarolina.com

This company is one of the largest real estate agencies servicing the Cape Fear area. Residential sales include single-family

The flight of a heron is poetry in motion.

photo: Peter Doran

homes, townhomes, condominiums, and lots. Prudential Carolina Real Estate has six sales offices including Topsail Island, Forum at Landfall, Wrightsville Beach, Carolina Beach, Southport and Ocean Isle Beach. Prudential offers corporate relocation services provided by certified relocation specialists, a Fine Homes program for exceptional properties and a rental partner in Southern Retreats for investors. Visit the website above for more information on their agents, services and available properties.

RE/MAX at the Beach
6237 E. Oak Island Dr., Oak Island
(910) 278-1950, (866) 350-SOLD

One of four office locations in Brunswick County, this Alan Holden company is a leader in southeastern North Carolina real estate, selling all kinds of properties.

Southport Realty
114 S. Howe St., Southport
(910) 457-7676, (866) 883-4783

The friendly professionals at Southport Realty invite you to "stroll Southport with a local." You can enjoy views of the Cape Fear River while sitting on their porch and discussing options. Whether you are interested in Southport, the beach communities, historic homes, waterfront property, land or even commercial property, the folks at Southport Realty are ready to serve you.

HOLDEN BEACH

Brunswickland Realty
123 Ocean Blvd. W., Holden Beach
(910) 842-1300, (800) 842-6949

Brunswickland, a leader in property sales, is a buyer/seller agency. In addition to offering homes for sale in all locations on Holden Beach, Brunswickland offers properties on the mainland. Included are homes and lots in Lockwood Folly Country Club, bounded by the Lockwood Folly River on the east and the Intracoastal Waterway on the south.

Coastal Communities Realty
3270 Holden Beach Rd., Holden Beach
(910) 842-3190, (877) 752-0151
www.coastalcommunitiesrealty.com

Specializing in residential, commercial and recreational properties, Coastal Communities has an extensive listing of fine homes

and estates as well as mid-range properties. This agency also offers real estate services from Wilmington to Calabash, which results in high visibility and maximum exposure. Three small offices, each staffed with highly experienced professionals, provide quality individualized service and personal attention. Coastal Communities also has an office in Wilmington.

Coastal Development and Realty
131 Ocean Blvd. W., Holden Beach
(910) 842-4939, (800) 262-7820

Coastal Development and Realty is a unique company with general brokerage offices located in Holden Beach and Oak Island. Established in 1985 and a leader in Brunswick County real estate, Coastal provides professional services in real estate sales, vacation rentals and custom-designed homes. SeaScape at Holden Plantation, SeaWatch at Sunset Harbor, Rivers Edge Golf Club and Ocean Ridge Plantation are affiliated specialized residential neighborhoods offering the marvelous Carolina lifestyle.

Hobbs Realty
114 Ocean Blvd. W., Holden Beach
(910) 842-2002, (800) 655-3367

A drive across beautiful Holden Beach Bridge, a turn to the left and a stop at the second office on the left will bring you to Hobbs Realty. Situated on the island of Holden Beach close to both Wilmington and Myrtle Beach, this family-owned and operated business with 28 years of building experience offers resort real estate sales, rentals and new construction from the ocean to the waterway and everywhere in between. The company has an in-house relocation service as well. Check out the website for both interior and exterior views of homes.

Lockwood Folly Realty
309 Clubhouse Dr., SW, Supply
(910) 842-5500, (800) 443-7891

Lockwood Folly Realty specializes in property in the 500-acre Lockwood Folly golf and water community. It is a gated, residential, family community situated midway between Myrtle Beach and Wilmington where the Lockwood Folly River meets the Intracoastal Waterway. Here you will find custom-built luxury homes, patio homes, townhouses and condominiums. You can choose from views of woodlands, the fairway of the Willard Byrd–designed golf course, lakes, ponds, the river or the waterway. Amenities include the property-owners clubhouse, a private pool with lap lanes and a hot tub, tennis courts, a picnic area on the waterway, and the Lockwood Cafe.

Martha Lee Realty
2869 Holden Beach Rd., Holden Beach
(910) 846-2402, (866) 696-6232
www.brunswickcountyhomes.com

Martha Lee Realty, with 32 years of experience, is in the unique position of representing all of Brunswick County. This includes Bald Head Island, Southport, Oak Island, St. James, Sunset Harbor, Lockwood Folly, Holden Beach, Ocean Isle Beach, Sunset Beach, Shallotte, Calabash and Carolina Shores as well as acreage in the interior. Martha Lee Realty specializes in waterfront property, new communities, commercial property and large tracts of land. Real estate showcase tours are offered daily.

RE/MAX at the Beach
128 Ocean Blvd. W., Holden Beach
(910) 842-8686, (800) 360-9770
10239 Beach Dr., Calabash(910)
575-2200, (800) 765-3203

With four RE/MAX at the Beach locations (Holden Beach, Sunset Beach, Calabash and Oak Island), all Alan Holden companies, they have the Brunswick County coast covered and are leaders in southeastern N.C. real estate, selling all kinds of properties.

OCEAN ISLE BEACH AND SUNSET BEACH

Century 21 Sunset Realty
502 N. Sunset Blvd., Sunset Beach
(910) 579-1000, (800) 451-2102

Century 21 Sunset Realty, founded in 1984, is a great choice in the South Brunswick Islands when it comes to a full-service real estate company. With two offices, it offers every type of real estate investment opportunity available in the area. Visit the mainland office or the beach location and discover the large list of inventory. You will also find agents equipped to help you with beach, waterway, golf course, vacant land or commercial properties.

Coldwell Banker-Sloane Realty Inc.
16 Causeway Dr., Ocean Isle Beach
(910) 579-1144, (800) 237-4609
790-2 Sunset Blvd., Sunset Beach
(910) 579-1808, (877) 369-5777

Owned by the first permanent family to live on Ocean Isle Beach and serving the region for nearly 50 years, Sloane Realty Inc. offers a wide range of new-home construction and residential re-sale options, including oceanfront living, deep-water canal homes, golf course communities and the adjacent mainland. Properties include single-family homes, condominiums and home sites. They also have offices in Calabash and Holden Beach.

Cooke Realtors
1 Causeway Dr., Ocean Isle Beach
(910) 579-3535, (800) 622-3224
www.cookerealty.com

This well-established island realty company offers complete real estate sales services for homes, condos, townhouses and home sites as well as 480 rental homes, cottages and condominiums. They offer properties on the oceanfront, second- and third-row, canalside, West End and Island Park, as well as off the island. Mainland sites include golf course and Intracoastal Waterway locations. Their professional construction division is waiting to assist you with your plans or theirs.

Corporate at the Beach
4983 Glen Cove Dr., Southport
(910) 262-3311, (910) 798-1060
www.myoakisland.com

Pat Maloney, owner of Corporate at the Beach, specializes in finding homes in resort areas for corporate use. Each home is well designed and spacious enough to accommodate large groups. Located in or near beach communities, these homes offer a relaxing atmosphere for off-site company meetings, trainings or special events. A week at your company's resort facility would also make a terrific productivity incentive for staff members. Some of the properties lend themselves to weekly resort rentals, particularly in June, July and August. That allows you to earn income on your purchase if you schedule the corporate use for September through May. Professional property management companies are available to handle rentals and maintain your investment in your absence. The Brunswick County Airport is

Specializing In All Brunswick Beaches & Islands, Boiling Spring Lakes, Southport and Shallotte.

Pat Maloney, REALTOR®, Broker, RRS
910-798-1060 • 910-262-3311
www.myoakisland.com
Pat@MyOakIsland.com

PAT MALONEY GROUP

CORPORATE AT THE BEACH, LLC

COLDWELL BANKER

SEA COAST REALTY
Each office is independently owned & operated

R. H. McClure Realty Inc.
24 Causeway Dr., Ocean Isle Beach
(910)579-3586, (800) 332-5476

R. H. McClure Realty, Inc. is a full-service realty brokerage that has been established on Ocean Isle Beach for more than 20 years. The firm specializes in residential re-sales, property management, long and short-term vacation rentals, and design and construction of new homes. Ralph McClure has been the premier builder on Ocean Isle Beach for many years. Their inventory of homes and home sites include oceanfront, deep-water canal, mid-island, condos, golf course communities and mainland properties. Friendly and knowledgeable agents will provide the individual attention and personal service you deserve.

Ocean Isle Beach Realty, Inc.
15 Causeway Dr., Ocean Isle Beach
(910) 575-7770, (800) 374-7361
www.oibrealty.com

This well-established real estate company has been an Ocean Isle Beach tradition since 1953, offering residential sales and vacation rentals for single-family homes, condominiums and cottages. Island locations for the dream vacation or a home of your own include waterway, canal, oceanfront and interior. OIB Realty is the exclusive agent for the luxurious Islander Resort, located on the west end of the island. The Islander Resort is a master-planned development featuring four-bedroom, four-bath villas in well-appointed buildings with elevators. The development also features The Isles Restaurant and Beach Club located on the oceanfront with spectacular views.

nearby and can accommodate fairly sizeable jets. The Myrtle Beach and Wilmington International Airports are available for commercial flights.

Island Realty, Inc.
109-2 Causeway Dr., Ocean Isle Beach
(910) 579-3599, (800) 589-3599

Island Realty is a family-owned company that specializes in sales and rentals of residential property on Ocean Isle Beach and the local mainland areas. They have a select group of private homes in areas from oceanfront to deep-water canal and many condominiums and villas to choose from. Their motto is: "We offer you ... Service ... the way it used to be!" The Island Realty professionals want to help you live your dream.

Martha Lee Realty
2669 Holden Beach Rd., Holden Beach
(910) 846-2402, (866) 696-6232
www.brunswickcountyhomes.com

Martha Lee Realty, with 32 years of experience, is in the unique position of representing all of Brunswick County. This includes Bald Head Island, Southport, Oak Island, St. James, Sunset Harbor, Lockwood Folly, Holden Beach, Ocean Isle Beach, Sunset Beach, Shallotte, Calabash and Carolina Shores as well as acreage in the interior. Martha Lee Realty specializes in waterfront property, new communities, commercial property and large tracts of land. Real estate showcase tours are offered daily.

Prudential Carolina Real Estate
120-1 Causeway Dr., Ocean Isle Beach
(910) 575-3113, (800) 988-1313
www.PruCarolina.com

This company is one of the largest real estate agencies servicing the Cape Fear area. Residential sales include single-family homes, townhomes, condominiums, and lots. Prudential Carolina Real Estate has six sales offices including Topsail Island, Forum at Landfall, Wrightsville Beach, Carolina Beach, Southport and Ocean Isle Beach. Prudential offers corporate relocation services provided by certified relocation specialists, a Fine Homes program for exceptional properties and a rental partner in Southern Retreats for investors. Visit the website above for more information on their agents, services and available properties.

RE/MAX at the Beach
6900 Ocean Hwy. W. (US 17), Sunset Beach
(910) 575-SELL, (888) 414-SELL
10239 Beach Dr., Calabash
(910) 575-2200, (800) 765-3203

With four RE/MAX at the Beach locations (Holden Beach, Sunset Beach, Calabash and Oak Island), all Alan Holden Companies, they have the Brunswick County coast covered and are leaders in southeastern N.C. real estate, selling all kinds of properties.

Sand Dollar Realty Inc.
102 Causeway Dr., Ocean Isle Beach
(910) 579-7038, (800) 457-7263

In business since 1985, this real estate company is a full-service brokerage and sells properties on Ocean Isle Beach and along the coast of Brunswick County. Conveniently located on the causeway, Sand Dollar Realty takes pride in the fact that all of its agents are professional brokers and long-term residents of the area. It's also licensed in North Carolina and neighboring South Carolina.

Simmons Realty Inc.
641 Shoreline Dr. W, Sunset Beach
(910) 579-0192, (888) 683-0550

This small real estate company has been working in sales on Sunset Beach since 1990, but broker Beth Simmons is a lifelong native of the area. The company offers general real estate services on the Brunswick Islands and the adjacent mainland. It handles general brokerage to include commercial, residential and development.

Sunset Properties
419 S. Sunset Blvd., Sunset Beach
(910) 579-9900, (800) 446-0218

On the island and family-owned since 1988, this company regularly handles properties only on Sunset Beach. With the purchase of the Odom Company in the fall of 2004, Sunset Properties now handles more than 430 homes. Single-family homes dominate this quiet residential island that attracts second-home investors, retirees and people who simply appreciate living away from it all.

Williamson Realty, Inc.
119 Causeway Dr. SW, Ocean Isle Beach
(910) 579-2373, (800) 727-9222

Serving the Ocean Isle Beach area since 1975, Williamson Realty, Inc. specializes in the

The ocean is beautiful and calm; the ocean is wild and strong.

photo: Peter Doran

REAL ESTATE, INC.

P.O. Box 2367
522 N. New River Dr.
Surf City, NC 28445

**Sales * Rentals
Property Management**

Serving The Topsail, Onslow
and Pender areas for over 20 years.

1-800-745-4480
(910) 328-SOLD(7653) fax: (910) 328-1933
www.topsailbeaches.com
jeanbrownrealestate@msn.com

sale of beach properties, including condominiums, rental cottages, permanent homes and residential construction. The friendly staff has the experience and expertise to help you find the home of your dreams on Ocean Isle Beach.

Topsail Island and Vicinity

SURF CITY

A Beach Place Realty
**106 N. Topsail Dr., Surf City
(910) 328-2522, (877) 884-2522**

Laura Bageant's full-service real estate company handles vacation rentals, residential and commercial properties on Topsail Island and the surrounding mainland areas. A member of the Topsail Island Multiple Listing Service, A Beach Place Realty is proud to offer virtual tours of all their properties so you can see what you're renting or buying. This professionally staffed office offers personal service to help you find your perfect beach property. A Beach Place also has an office in Hampstead.

Access Realty
**513 Roland Ave., Surf City
(910) 328-4888, (800) 867-7245
www.accessthebeach.com**

Access Realty provides friendly, personalized service for buyers and sellers on Topsail

Island and the adjacent mainland. This full-service brokerage company handles residential, new construction and commercial sales.

Bryson & Associates
**809 Roland Ave., Surf City
(910) 328-2468, (800) 326-0747**

High-end, oceanfront, single-family homes are Bryson & Associates specialty. Committed to quality customer service, Bryson and Associates are also homeowner association managers.

Century 21 Action, Inc.
**518 Roland Ave., Surf City
(910) 328-2511, (800) 255-2233
www.century21topsail.com**

An established business since 1969, Century 21 Action professionally markets real estate in the entire greater Topsail Island area from offices in Surf City and Sneads Ferry. With more than 20 agents and two offices, there is always someone ready to assist with a sale or purchase anywhere on Topsail Island or on the mainland from north of Hampstead to Holly Ridge and Sneads Ferry. This company also has a large and well-managed vacation and long-term rental division. Century 21 Action, we'll get you there.

Century 21 Sweyer & Associates
**13775 Ocean Hwy. 50, Surf City
(910) 329-0105, (888) 329-0105**

David and Polly Sweyer have been in the local real estate business since 1987 and their business continues to expand throughout southeastern North Carolina. In the last ten years their Hampstead office experienced such tremendous growth they opened an additional office in Surf City to better serve their clients. This office specializes in residential, commercial and investment properties, as well as new homes and land development. With manager Jackie James and a staff of 12 sales associates to assist you, you're guaranteed to find just the right island or mainland property.

Jean Brown Real Estate, Inc
522 N. New River Dr., Surf City
(910) 328-1640, (800) 745-4480
www.topsailbeaches.com

Jean Brown Real Estate, Inc. has been a top-producing island real estate firm for many years. Sales agents offer a wide range of experience in both residential and commercial real estate. This office consistently maintains one of the most diverse listing inventories of properties for sale and is a member of both the Topsail Island and Wilmington MLS Services.

Coldwell Banker Sea Coast Realty
206 N. Topsail Dr., Unit B, Surf City
(910) 328-2625, (866) 385-2624
326 New River Dr., Surf City
(910) 328-5626, (877) 786-7787

With two offices on Topsail Island, a mainland office in Sneads Ferry and more than 30 professional real estate agents on staff, Coldwell Banker Sea Coast Realty is one of the largest real estate firms serving the island. They also offer offices in Carolina Beach, Wilmington and Southport. Coldwell Banker Sea Coast offers single-family oceanfront homes, condominiums and townhouses, soundfront hideaways, mainland property and commercial real estate.

EXIT Homeplace Realty
1775 N.C. Hwy. 210 E, Surf City
(910) 329-0900, (877) 879-3948

EXIT Realty is a locally owned and operated, full-service real estate company, with agents and offices in Wilmington, Hampstead, Topsail Island/Surf City, Jacksonville and Brunswick County. EXIT Homeplace's prides itself on its customer service in all real estate transactions.

ACCESS Realty

Your Key to Coastal Living

1-800-TOPSAIL
2 Locations to Serve You!

513A Roland Ave. (beside post office)
*13480 Hwy 50/210
Surf City, NC 28445
910-328-4888

*opening this summer in the
Surf City Gateway Plaza

Harbor Real Estate
307A Roland Ave., Surf City
(910) 328-3060

This island real estate agency offers residential and commercial sales between Jacksonville and Wilmington. Harbor promises to do their best to help you find a particular type home in the area you select.

Intracoastal Realty
302 N. New River Dr., Surf City
(910) 328-0719, (800 753-2975

The professionals at Intracoastal Realty can help you with all of your real estate needs. From commercial real estate and condominiums to single or multi-family homes, Intracoastal does it all. Members of Topsail Island and Wilmington MLS, Intracoastal Realty serves Topsail Island and surrounding properties from Southport to Sneads Ferry.

Island Real Estate by Cathy Medlin
The Fishing Village, Roland Ave., Surf City
(910) 328-2323, (800) 622-6886
www.topsailvacation.com

Cathy Medlin has been selling properties on Topsail Island and the mainland in Onslow and Pender counties since 1979. She was one of the founders of the Topsail Island Board of Realtors in 1992. This company sells beach, waterway and mainland homes and lots as well as commercial buildings and property. The company also handles 200 rental properties.

Reservations: 1-800-622-6886
info@topsailvacation.com
www.topsailvacation.com
P.O. Box 2690 Surf City, NC 28445
"The Fishing Village"

King Co Real Estate
202 S. Shore Dr., Surf City
(910) 328-0239, (800) 513-8957

An Onslow County native, Nathan King has been an area builder since 1983. His full-service real estate business consists of residential and commercial sales and new construction both on Topsail Island and the surrounding areas. He is also a licensed real estate appraiser.

Prudential Carolina Real Estate
13567 NC Hwy 50, Surf City
(910) 329-4466, (888) 870-6500
www.PruCarolina.com

This company is one of the largest real estate agencies servicing the Cape Fear area. Residential sales include single-family homes, townhomes, condominiums, and lots. Prudential Carolina Real Estate has six sales offices including Topsail Island, Forum at Landfall, Wrightsville Beach, Carolina Beach, Southport and Ocean Isle Beach. Prudential offers corporate relocation services provided by certified relocation specialists, a Fine Homes program for exceptional properties and a rental partner in Southern Retreats for investors. Visit the website above for more information on their agents, services and available properties.

Realty Executives of Wilmington
614 N. New River Dr., Ste A, Surf City
(877)-379-2589

Dedicated to providing their clients with a level of service beyond their expectations,

Sandy and Dick Beals believe that buying or selling a home is an important life transition and they work hard to ensure that it's worry free. With an experienced team of professionals, Realty Executives of Wilmington guarantees privacy and respect while delivering results. Their conveniently located Surf City office is fully equipped and has an integrated network of computer and communications systems to facilitate access to all the Multiple Listing Services, public record searches and other tools that agents need in order to better serve clients. Since its inception in Phoenix, Arizona, more than 35 years ago, Realty Executives has become one of the fastest growing franchises internationally.

RE/MAX Coastal Properties
208 A. N. New River Dr., Surf City
(910) 328-4300

Broker Michael Nelson offers full-service sales and listings of residential, land and commercial properties in Topsail Beach, Surf City, North Topsail Beach, Sneads Ferry and Hampstead. Whether you're dreaming of the quintessential beach house or searching for a mainland wooded lot, Michael is at your service. The office is open Monday through Saturday (closed Sundays). RE/MAX also has two offices in Wilmington.

Turner Real Estate
Surf City (IGA) Shopping Center, Surf City
(910) 328-1313, (800) 326-2926

Specializing in sales of everything from single-family homes and condominiums to commercial property and building lots, Turner Real Estate has been serving all of Topsail Island since 1988. Broker-in-charge Rick Turner offers personalized service, including forwarding business calls to his home after regular business hours.

Ward Realty
116 S. Topsail Dr., Surf City
(910) 328-3221, (800) 782-6216
www.wardrealty.com

The original developer of Topsail Island, Ward Realty has more than 50 years of dedicated service in sales, home construction and vacation rentals. Broker David Ward continues the family tradition of commitment to the buyer's interest. The rental and sales departments are strong assets which work hand-in-hand to provide a compatible, full-service real estate program.

TOPSAIL BEACH

Sea Path Realty
920 S. Anderson Blvd., Topsail Beach
(910) 328-4201

Located just south of the Topsail Beach business district in a round, yellow house, Sea Path Realty is easy to find. Their five agents can assist you with your residential real estate and beach rental needs. Sea Path Realty is a member of Multiple Listing Service (MLS). Office hours are 9 AM to 4 PM and they are closed on Wednesdays.

SNEADS FERRY

Century 21 Action, Inc.
200 N. Shore Village, Sneads Ferry
(910) 328-2511, (800) 255-2233

An established business since 1969, Century 21 Action professionally markets real estate in the entire greater Topsail Island area. With more than 20 agents and two offices (the other is in Surf City), there is always someone ready to assist with a sale or purchase anywhere on Topsail Island or on the mainland from north of Hampstead to Holly Ridge and Sneads Ferry. This company also has a large and well-managed vacation and long-term rental division.

Coldwell Banker Coastline Realty
Topsail Way Shopping Center, 965
Old Folkstone Rd., Ste. 108, Sneads Ferry
(910) 327-7711, (800) 497-5463
www.cbcoastline.com

This company, established in 1994 and owned and operated by Duplin County native Bud Rivenbark, works primarily with oceanfront condominiums and soundside properties on Topsail Island and in the Sneads Ferry area. Coastline Realty offers single-family homes, townhomes and lots. It is a member of the Coldwell Banker Relocation Network and is an MLS member. This company also handles commercial sales.

Coldwell Banker Sea Coast Realty
1350 N.C. Hwy. 210, Sneads Ferry
(910) 327-2441, (866) 327-2441

With two offices on Topsail Island, a mainland office in Sneads Ferry and more than 30 professional real estate agents on staff, Coldwell Banker Sea Coast Realty is one of the largest real estate firms serving the island. They also offer offices in Carolina

Creeks Edge

A Premier Water Oriented Community
www.creeksedge.net

Waterfront • Waterview • Interior Homesites

• Rolling Terrain • Paved Streets
• Underground Utilities • County Water
• Waterfront Gazebo • Street Lights
• Protective Covenants

COLDWELL BANKER
Coastline Realty 910-327-7711

*Located in the fishing village of Sneads Ferry.
45 Minutes to Wilmington and 20 minutes to Jacksonville.*

Beach, Wilmington and Southport. Coldwell Banker Sea Coast offers single-family oceanfront homes, condominiums and townhouses, soundfront hideaways, mainland property and commercial real estate.

Treasure Realty
Treasure Plaza, N.C. Hwys. 210 and 172,
Sneads Ferry
(910) 327-4444, (800)762-3961

Treasure Realty is proud to be the top-producing firm in North Topsail Beach and Sneads Ferry for the past 15 years. Waterfront property and condominiums are their specialties. With their many years of experience, Treasure Realty's professional sales

DDT—Outlet
3 Locations to serve you!
Wilmington • Hampstead • Sneads Ferry
Visit Our Newest Location at
7222 Market St., Wilmington, NC
(Formerly Pinehurst Pottery)

Complete Condo Packages

Custom Ordered Sofas

Large Selection of
Wicker Furniture
& All Weather Wicker

Everything you need for your home in one place!

We Carry a Complete Line of Mattresses

LARGEST
Collection of Coastal Furniture & Nautical Gifts & Accessories in North Carolina!

www.DDTOUTLET.com
Call Toll Free 1-877-954-6367
Local 910-329-0160

Ward Realty Corp.

SALES • RENTALS • CONSTRUCTION

"Original Developers of Topsail Island"

800-782-6216 • 910-328-3221
www.wardrealty.com
e-mail: info@wardrealty.com
116 S. Topsail Dr., Surf City, NC

staff is ready to serve as a buyer or seller's agent.

HAMPSTEAD

A Beach Place Realty
20184 Hwy. 17, Hampstead
(910) 270-1221, (888) 270-1221

Laura Bageant's full-service real estate company handles vacation rentals, residential and commercial properties on Topsail Island and the surrounding mainland areas. A member of the Topsail Island Multiple Listing Service, A Beach Place Realty is proud to offer virtual tours of all their properties so you can see what you're renting or buying. This professionally staffed office offers personal service to help you find your perfect beach property. A Beach Place also has an office in Surf City.

Castle Bay Country Club
410 Castle Bay Dr., Hampstead
(910) 270-1247

A dream come true for the golfing enthusiast, Castle Bay Country Club offers patio, town and custom-built homes, all with a golf course view. Built in the old English style, these brick homes can be purchased as built or personalized to fit your lifestyle. Home ownership comes with a country club membership that includes use of the pool as well as the tennis, volleyball and racquetball courts. There is also a fitness center on the premises. It's a great setting for retirees and families.

Century 21 Sweyer & Associates
14865 N.C. Hwy. 17 N, Hampstead
(910) 270-3606, (800) 476-3606

David and Polly Sweyer have been in the local real estate business since 1987 and their business has expanded throughout southeast North Carolina in that time. Sweyer and Associates offers residential sales, long-term rental management for tenants and property owners, community association management, mortgage services, and residential maintenance. This Century 21 office features training services for new agents, relocation assistance for clients new to the area and a top-notch marketing department that can aid you in selling your property. It's the personal touch that Sweyer and Associates' agents

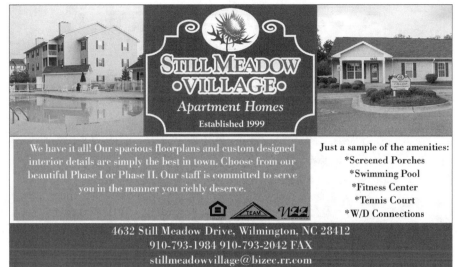

STILL MEADOW VILLAGE

Apartment Homes

Established 1999

We have it all! Our spacious floorplans and custom designed interior details are simply the best in town. Choose from our beautiful Phase I or Phase II. Our staff is committed to serve you in the manner you richly deserve.

Just a sample of the amenities:
*Screened Porches
*Swimming Pool
*Fitness Center
*Tennis Court
*W/D Connections

4632 Still Meadow Drive, Wilmington, NC 28412
910-793-1984 910-793-2042 FAX
stillmeadowvillage@bizec.rr.com

provide that fuels their reputation as one of the Southeast's top real estate agencies. They also have an office in Wilmington.

EXIT Homeplace Realty
15470 N.C. Hwy. 17, Hampstead
(910) 270-2221, (910) 270-8891

EXIT Realty is a locally owned and operated, full-service real estate company, with agents and offices in Wilmington, Hampstead, Topsail Island/Surf City, Jacksonville and Brunswick County. EXIT Homeplace's prides itself on its customer service in all real estate transactions.

Laney Real Estate
100 W. Fremont St., Burgaw
(910) 259-8502, (877) 507-9157

Laney Real Estate began serving the great Wilmington area in 1978, and current broker Vicki Foster brings a lifetime of experience as a Topsail resident to her role as agent. Specializing in residential sales, including homes, waterfront property and investment opportunities, Laney is also a member of the Wilmington and Topsail multiple listing services and has access to a fairly comprehensive set of property listings.

APARTMENTS

If you're not ready for the hassles of home ownership or you're saving up for that down payment, renting an apartment is an affordable way to handle your housing needs. Wilmington features a myriad of apartments ranging from low-income, affordable housing to lovely historic spaces downtown.

Prices for rentals range from around $500 to more than $1,000 depending on the location and extras. While newer apartment complexes generally offer more modern amenities, the downtown area features the coolest apartments in town. Be prepared to provide a deposit, a month's rent and references in addition to undergoing credit and background checks when renting an apartment. For some suggestions on apartments, see the following list. Or try a real estate agency that has a rentals department.

Wilmington

Brightmore of Wilmington
2298, 2320 and 2324 41st St., Wilmington
(910) 332-6899
www.brightmoreofwilmington.com

Brightmore offers seniors an opportunity to live their golden years in comfort with all amenities they could possibly require. The Brightmore complex features apartments with spacious common areas where meals are served and social activities occur. The Kempton, a separate locale within the complex, offers assisted living services while The Commons is a facility for those requiring more intensive personal care.

THE RESERVE
AT MAYFAIRE

- 9' Ceilings With Crown Molding
- Smooth Surface Ranges
- Maple Cabinetry & Stainless Steel Appliances in Select Units
- Washer/Dryer Included

- 26 Seat Movie Theatre
- Resort Style Pool
- 24 Hour State Of The Art Fitness Center
- Grilling Pavilion With Shuffle Board

Don't just change your address...change your lifestyle!

Call (910) 256-4019 the leasing office today

From Market St. take 74 East Go 1.5 miles and turn left onto Town Center Dr. We are on the right.

Carolina Apartments
420 Market St., Wilmington
(910) 763-4003

Ever wanted to live in one of the apartments featured in the film Blue Velvet? You could get your chance at this downtown mainstay. Featuring mostly two-bedroom units, the Carolina is a classic space with a spiral staircase and great views of the surrounding architecture. You'll have the downtown experience dialed in if you manage to snag a spot here, just a few minutes stroll from all the action.

Glenmeade Village
1518 Village Dr., Wilmington
(910) 762-8108, (910) 790-3560 fax

Located in a quiet, secluded setting, Glenmeade is a retirement community convenient to shopping, medical facilities, the senior center, the Cameron Art Museum, beaches and the riverfront. With its small vintage charm, indoor heated pool, greenhouse, tennis court and clubhouse along with sociable residents, the atmosphere is warm and friendly.

The Keys
17th St., Wilmington
(910) 350-1133

These luxurious apartments are located only 3 miles from New Hanover Medical Center and minutes from shopping, downtown and local beaches. Take advantage of the peaceful community and excellent amenities. You'll flip for the style, features and ambience of the Keys at 17th Street.

Lake Shore Commons
1402 Hospital Plaza Dr., Wilmington
(910) 251-0067

This retirement complex offers studios, one and two bedroom units, as well as separate cottage spaces. With three meals a day and housekeeping, plus utilities and transportation services included, this community is appealing for a number of reasons. Numerous activities and a multi-use facility keeps residents fit and on their toes.

New Centre Commons
119 Dapple Ct., Wilmington
(910) 799-4402

This facility features one and two bedroom units with plenty of parking and affordable rents. Located close to UNC-Wilmington and not too far from downtown, New Centre is a flexible spot for the person on the go. With tons of shopping and dining opportunities just seconds away, this spot is great for newcomers.

The Reserve At Mayfaire
1411 Parkview Cir., Wilmington
(910) 256-4019
www.thereserveatmayfaire.com

Located off Eastwood Road just a stone's throw from Wrightsville Beach, The Reserve at Mayfaire features top-of-the-line, brand-new apartments that are spacious and packed with amenities. Featuring one, two and three bedroom units, the Reserve's living spaces are beautifully appointed with touches like crown molding, track lighting, stainless steel appliances and washer/dryer systems. A community clubhouse with a gorgeous pool area and workout space is open to residents and their guests, and pets are welcome with a non-refundable pet deposit.

Seahawk Management Co.
504 N. Kerr Ave., Wilmington
(910) 512-5552

Seahawk Management takes great pride in maintaining a clean, safe living environment for all ages. Minutes away from both the UNC-Wilmington and Cape Fear Community College campuses, their affordable units are ideal for students and professionals alike. All apartments come with washer/dryer and on-site maintenance.

Still Meadow Village
4632 Still Meadow Dr., Wilmington
(910) 793-1984

Still Meadow Village offers new, fine apartment homes with spacious floor plans,

tons of storage space and numerous other amenities. Residents enjoy screened-in porches during spring evenings, and some units offer fireplaces for those chilly winter nights. With one to three bedroom configurations, there's an apartment for almost any renter requirements. Their friendly staff members are certified by the National Apartment Association.

Southport

Egret Crossing Apartments
4850 Tobago Dr. SE, Southport
(910) 454-0600

If apartment living suits your lifestyle, be sure to check out Egret Crossing. With efficiency, one-bedroom, large one-bedroom and two-bedroom apartments to choose from, Egret Crossing has something for everyone. Add to that its convenient location near Southport as well as the beach. An on-site swimming pool and the clubhouse with a fully equipped exercise room are desirable amenities. Units feature outdoor porches, ceiling fans, ranges, refrigerators, dishwashers, disposals, microwaves and more.

Hampstead

Hampstead Place Apartments
101 Leeward Ln., Hampstead
(910) 270-5383

Tucked into the tall pines along U.S. Highway 17, Hampstead Place Apartments is the area's only large rental complex. Renters may choose between a variety of studio and two-bedroom apartments. Some apartments have balconies, and all units have washer/dryer hook-ups. You'll find a nice pool, on-site laundry facilities and on-site management.

Retiree-friendly pretty well characterizes the four-county area known as the Cape Fear Coast. With Historic Wilmington and New Hanover County as its focal points, the southern coast of North Carolina has been attracting retirees to its sunny, warm shores in ever-increasing numbers for years.

Naturally, the mild, temperate climate of our area is a major attraction for retirees from the North, who are tired of frigid winters, snow, ice, potholes and gray skies. Winter, such as it is here, is moderated considerably by the warming effect of the Atlantic Ocean and the Gulf Stream.

The area is also experiencing an increasing popularity with retirees moving here from Florida. Known as "Halfbacks," these new residents are usually retirees from the North who moved to Florida, became disenchanted and decided to move halfway back up, where they can enjoy moderate seasonal changes without extremes.

For those interested in gardening, the southern coastal area is in USDA growing zone 8, averages 248 or more growing days per year and has an annual rainfall of 54 inches. The heaviest rainfall months are June, July and August, and more often than not, it rains at night and is sunny during the day — Camelot right here in Dixie. Several varieties of flowers bloom all winter, and numerous shrubs and trees retain their foliage all year. The average summer high temperature is 88 degrees, the average winter low is 36 degrees and the overall average for the year is 64 degrees.

Another aspect of the southern coast area attracting retirees is a considerably expanded health-care system that is increasingly focused on the needs of seniors. In addition, quite a few new retirement homes are opening, and there is a strong upswing in the development of retirement communities, many of them with golf courses, tennis courts and swimming pools and offering a wide variety of housing choices.

Although progressive and growth-oriented, this area still possesses elements of charm, graciousness and gentility from the old South, which, coupled with the cosmopolitan influence of retirees and new residents from all across the nation, results in a delightfully relaxed but upbeat ambiance. Also, partly due to the enormous number of activities available to them, retirees tend to feel more included living in the the southern coast communities than they would living in a large urban area.

Downtown Wilmington offers many activities for seniors, including horse-drawn carriage, trolley or walking tours of the Historical District, riverboat tours, unusual stores and boutiques, the Riverwalk and a number of antebellum homes open for visiting, to mention just a few (see our Attractions chapter). Any given evening will find both seniors and younger folk strolling about, shopping and dining outside, enjoying the good life.

Deciding Where To Live

Variety certainly is not lacking in home styles and homesites in the four-county southern coastal area. Nor is variety in cost. As might be expected, oceanfront property in older exclusive communities commands the highest price, partially because there is so little of it remaining. Generally speaking, the closer to the water, the more expensive the property. However, in the Cape Fear region, we are fortunate to have a surprisingly large amount of property on or near water of one sort or another, so the dream of living on the water is within the means of other than the very wealthy. In addition to the ocean, we have sounds, which are bodies of water between the mainland and the ocean-facing barrier islands, plus rivers, the Intracoastal

OF WILMINGTON

Wilmington's Preferred Continuum of Lifestyle Choices

Your Destination for the Ultimate
in Retirement Living

Brightmore

Independent Living Community

(910) 350-1980 or 1-800-556-6899

The Kempton at Brightmore

Assisted Living Community

(910) 332-6899 or 1-888-751-1544

The Commons at Brightmore

Personal Care Community

(910) 392-6899

*All Three Communities are centrally located midtown
on Forty-First Street between the
Cape Fear River and Wrightsville Beach.*

**2324 Forty-First Street
Wilmington, North Carolina 28403**

www.BrightmoreofWilmington.com

Waterway, lakes and canals. More reasonably priced housing, especially condominiums, is available on or near these waters. Often a group of homes or a condominium complex is built in conjunction with boat slips or a marina. (See our chapter on Real Estate for more in-depth information about locations and developments.)

Retirement Communities

Senior adult or retirement communities are those with congregate housing intended specifically for older occupants. These communities feature single homes and/or apartments providing several services, which may include meals in a central location, housekeeping services, a pool, transportation and social activities. They may or may not offer health-care services. We have listed only some of these communities. For further assistance, contact the chamber of commerce in the area you choose for relocation (see our Area Overview chapter for a list of chambers) or one of the government agencies listed at the end of this chapter.

Alterra Clare Bridge of Wilmington
3501 Converse Dr., Wilmington
(910) 790-8664

Alterra Clare Bridge is designed specifically for people with Alzheimer's disease or other memory impairments. Everything is geared to help individuals with memory problems to live the most independent and fulfilling life possible. Residents can choose from private or companion suites in a neighborhood environment. Floor plans offer helpful cues to help residents remember where they are at all times. Small living and dining rooms encourage a sense of community and help residents feel less confused as they so-

cialize with one another. The outdoor patios and courtyards are enclosed and secured. Even pets are allowed to help the residents feel more at home. Other amenities include 24-hour staff and licensed nurse, assistance with personal care and hygiene, laundry and linen service, mealtime and feeding assistance, housekeeping, medication management, and an audio-security system. Alterra Clare Bridge also offers life-enrichment activities, memory-support programs and outings to increase self-esteem and independence.

Brightmore of Wilmington
Continuum of Care Brightmore -
Independent Living
2324 41st St., Wilmington
(910) 350-1980, (800) 556-6899
www.brightmoreofwilmington.com

Brightmore welcomes active retirees who wish to combine independence with a small-town atmosphere. Studio, one-bedroom, one-bedroom deluxe, two-bedroom and two-bedroom deluxe apartments are available for a monthly rental fee. Each apartment home includes a full kitchen, all utilities (except phone service), 24-hour security and medical emergency call stations, weekly housekeeping and flat linen service, scheduled transportation, daily choice of meals, recreational/exercise programs, and an onsite beauty/barber shop.

The new Aquatic/Fitness Center features an exercise room and pool with a flume for resistance lap-style swimming and walking, and a seated whirlpool area. Brightmore is located midtown between the Cape Fear River and Wrightsville Beach. It is on the same campus with The Kempton (assisted living) and The Commons (personal care). Brightmore residents are priority listed for services at any of the other communities that make up the continuum of care. Call to learn more about the refundable priority deposit program.

The Kempton at Brightmore -
Assisted Living
2298 41st St., Wilmington
(910) 332-6899, (888) 751-1544
www.brightmoreofwilmington.com

For assisted living, The Kempton provides a supportive environment promoting an

i *Want to meet other retirees for fun and friendship? Aside from the usual volunteering, church and employment venues, take up a new activity altogether. Senior Centers offer many opportunities to get acquainted while keeping fit, trying different activities and having a good time. Check them out.*

independent lifestyle with the benefit of onsite, professionally managed services. It is designed for those individuals who may need assistance with certain everyday activities, but who do not require continued medical services.

Residents choose from a variety of studio and one-bedroom units. Each unit is equipped with a kitchenette and an emergency call system. All meals are provided along with housekeeping service, flat linen service and utilities (except phone service). Staffed 24 hours a day, The Kempton offers a full social calendar, scheduled transportation, an exercise room, Country Kitchen and an onsite beauty and barber shop. The Kempton is part of the continuum of care offered at Brightmore of Wilmington.

The Commons at Brightmore - Personal Care
2320 41st St., Wilmington
(910) 392-6899
www.brightmoreofwilmington.com

The Commons is a community where dignity, choice and individuality make the difference in personal care in all activities of daily living. Each of the spacious rooms is individually climate controlled and has ample closet space with a private bathroom and shower. Residents are encouraged to bring their own furnishings to reflect their own personal tastes. Each room is equipped with an emergency call-response system to which staff respond 24 hours a day.

The monthly rate includes three meals a day, assistance with personal care, housekeeping and laundry, administration of physician-directed medication, utilities and free transportation to the doctor. Cable television and private telephones are optional.

Residents may choose among optional services such as a barber and beauty shop and physical and speech therapy. Licensed practical nurses and assistants are on call 24 hours a day. Residents enjoy a full calendar of social events and activities. The Commons also offers a 32-bed memory care unit, Paraklay Way. The Commons at Brightmore is part of the continuum of care offered at Brightmore of Wilmington.

Coastal Plantation
U.S. Hwy. 17 N., Hampstead
(888) 716-9744

Just north of Wilmington, Coastal Plantation is a beautifully landscaped community of individually manufactured homes. Residents purchase the house and lease the land. These quality homes range in price from $65,000 to the low $100s, depending on size and options. The price includes quite a few amenities. Most homes have a utility shed, peripheral plantings, a cement driveway, all appliances, energy-efficient heating and cooling systems, a wooden deck and more. This is a community for individuals who are at least 55 years of age and appreciate independence within the context of a planned community. A clubhouse, a swimming pool, regular potluck suppers and activity groups provide social opportunities.

Glenmeade Village
1518 Village Dr., Wilmington
(910) 762-8108
www.glenmeadevillage.com

Conveniently located in a quiet, secluded setting, Glenmeade Village offers 104 apartment homes available in four floor plans. Choose from spacious one, two or three-bedroom units on one level, or a two-bedroom townhouse design. All of the tastefully decorated apartments are air-conditioned, energy efficient and fully carpeted, with mini-blinds throughout, and either a private patio or porch and storage room. Other features include ample closet space, large windows, washer/dryer (three-bedroom units only) and fully equipped kitchens.

The enclosed heated pool is open year round, with aqua fitness classes offered two days a week. An inviting clubhouse provides residents a comfortable place for socializing, having a cup of coffee, reading the paper or watching cable TV. It's open every day and is the site of frequent socials and card games. A tennis court, greenhouse and laundry room are also available. Twenty-four-hour emergency maintenance service is an added plus. Small pets are accepted.

This small community is within walking distance of New Hanover Regional Medical Center, physicians' offices and other medical facilities as well as shopping. Convenient to Wilmington's riverfront, Westfield Shoppingtown Mall, the Senior Center, golf courses and beaches, Glenmeade Village is just right for active, mature individuals age 55 or older.

Lake Shore Commons
1402 Hospital Plaza Dr., Wilmington
(910) 251-0067

For seniors seeking elegant, gracious retirement living in beautiful surroundings convenient to shopping, health-care providers and medical facilities, Lake Shore Commons, owned by Holiday Retirement Corporation, is the right place. One of Wilmington's best kept secrets, this outstanding retirement community offers attractive, spacious, unfurnished apartment homes with a variety of floor plans. Units are available in studio, one or two-bedroom styles at surprisingly affordable month-to-month rents; a lease or buy-in is never required.

Within the main building, each apartment has a kitchenette, carpeting and window treatments; most feature a balcony or porch. Free laundry facilities are located on each floor. Eight cottages are equipped with full kitchens and washer/dryer. Within the main building are many comfortable, well-appointed common areas, a huge fully equipped kitchen for resident use, exercise facilities, a pool table, two libraries and several multi-purpose rooms. The resident vegetable garden and dance floor keep everyone active,

as does the newly formed Red Hat Society Chapter, The Red Snappers.

Peace of mind is a priority here. Resident managers are on duty 24 hours every day for assistance. Included in the monthly rent are heating/air conditioning, electricity, water, cable TV, all maintenance and repairs, weekly housekeeping (including linens and towels) and three nutritious, chef-prepared meals daily with a choice of entrees. Transportation at no charge is available on a scheduled basis for residents who have appointments or shopping to do. Also part of the package are numerous organized activities, movies, tours and excursions. A unique Travel Club enables residents to free visits in other company-owned retirement communities.

Plantation Village
1200 Porters Neck Rd., Wilmington
(910) 686-7181, (800) 334-0240 in state,
(800) 334-0035 out of state

Plantation Village is a life-care retirement community on 56 acres within Porters Neck Plantation. The campus has a library, bank facilities, auditorium, gym, swimming pool, woodworking shop, crafts room and many more amenities. Plantation Village is a unique retirement community in that it receives people in good health age 62 and older and offers professional, long-term nursing care services from nearby Cornelia Nixon Davis Center and Champion Assisted Living. Before nursing care is needed, residents have access to a wellness center on the campus, a 24-hour nurse on call and the visit of a doctor each week.

The Woods at Holly Tree
4610 Holly Tree Rd., Wilmington
(910) 793-1300

The Woods at Holly Tree provides a caring environment in a secure and gracious surrounding. One all-inclusive monthly rent begins with several styles of apartments and ends with a large list of amenities including three chef-prepared meals a day served in a beautiful dining room, weekly housekeeping and flat linen service, all utilities (except telephone), cable TV, free laundry facilities, social and recreational activities. The Woods at Holly Tree is an affordable residence where attention to detail and personal consideration are paramount. No lease or buy-in fee is ever required. The Woods at Holly Tree has two sets of resident managers on site 24 hours a day.

For the convenience of residents, scheduled transportation is available. On the premises are a beauty/barber shop, an exercise/activity room, a billiards and game room, library, chapel and large-screen TV lounge as well as several cozy nooks for visiting or reading. A Travel Club enables residents to free visits in other company-owned retirement communities. The Woods at Holly Tree incorporates the latest technology in safety, style and beauty.

Carillon Assisted Living
1125 E. Leonard St., Southport
(910) 454-4001

For assisted living, Carillon is an excellent choice. Carillon has wraparound porches with Carolina rockers, parlors with fireplaces, sunrooms, patios, courtyards and dining on linens and china. Carillon has all the comforts of home and more — from lovely furnishings to light and airy private studios, semi-private studios and suites to the spa with whirlpool bath. The caring, dedicated professionals reinforce self-reliance, dignity and social well-being. At the same time, assistance with daily activities, home health and therapy services, daily exercise classes and walking programs, massage and whirlpool spa therapy are offered. Carillon has The Garden Place where residents with Alzheimer's live and participate in an activity-programmed environment focused on reducing anxiety, restoring socialization and enhancing life skills. Respite and rehabilitative care are available as well.

Senior Centers

The following senior centers offer a variety of exercise programs, meal services, health and wellness activities, and lots of fun things to do. Depending on the center, you can find everything from aerobics and line dancing to crafts and social events. They may offer Meals on Wheels and hot lunch programs. Some offer medical transportation, while others offer travel opportunities. All offer fellowship, support and friendships.

Katie B. Hines Senior Center, 308 Cape Fear Boulevard, Carolina Beach, (910) 458-6609

New Hanover County Department of Aging Senior Center, 2222 S. College Road, Wilmington, (910) 452-6400

Pender Adult Services Inc., 901 S. Walker Street, Burgaw, (910) 259-9119

Shallotte Senior Center, 5040 Main Street, Shallotte, (910) 754-8776

Southport Senior Center, 209 N. Atlantic Avenue, Southport, (910) 457-6461

Topsail Senior Center, 20959 U.S. Highway 17, Hampstead, (910) 270-0708

Employment Services

Senior AIDES Program
613 Shipyard Blvd., Ste. 100, Wilmington
(910) 798-3910

This excellent program offers job counseling and training for qualified people age 55 and older who are residents of New Hanover, Pender, Brunswick and Columbus counties; applicants must meet certain income-level requirements. With grant monies from the Federal Government administered by the Cape Fear Area United Way, the Senior AIDES program benefits individuals by providing them temporary part-time employment at local agencies in order to gain skills and work experience. The goal is to help these individuals move into permanent full-time or part-time positions.

Bridge players will be happy to know that they can play until the cows come home around here. The YWCA of the Lower Cape Fear (910) 799-9643 has an extensive bridge program, from lessons for beginners and those interested in learning to play duplicate bridge to clubs that meet at various times, six days a week. Our Senior Centers, country clubs and various community organizations also offer a variety bridge-playing opportunities. Watch the Wednesday "Neighbors" section of the Star-News for details and competitions.

Senior Volunteer Opportunities

Although our area offers a wide range of volunteering options (see our Volunteer Opportunities chapter), there are some jobs that can be handled best by people with a lifetime of experience. Following are several organizations that would appreciate your help.

Retired Senior Volunteer Program (RSVP)
2222 S. College Rd., Wilmington
(910) 452-6400

RSVP is a clearinghouse for seniors who want to volunteer in New Hanover County. They will match your interests, talents and skills with the needs of the community. RSVP volunteers provide many different kinds of community services, such as tutoring, neighborhood watch, building houses and helping organizations operate more efficiently. If you want to volunteer, but aren't sure where to start, RSVP is the place.

Service Corps of Retired Executives (SCORE)
4010 Oleander Dr., Wilmington
(910) 452-5395

A resource partner with the U.S. Small Business Administration, SCORE is dedicated to aiding in the information, growth and success of small businesses. SCORE counselors provide free, confidential counseling to help solve business problems. By volunteering your time, talent and expertise, you'll be assisting entrepreneurs who need your skills and insights. This is essentially a mentoring program. New members participate in a training program and orientation.

Maybe you're one of the many retirees who decide to start a small business here. Resources abound to help you from the ground up. We recommend Service Corps of Retired Executives (SCORE), 4010 Oleander Drive, Wilmington, (910) 452-5395 and the Coastal Entrepreneurial Council (CEC), 3904 Oleander Drive, Wilmington, (910) 452-9910.

Senior Corps

The Senior Corps is a national service program that puts the experience and talents of seniors ages 55 and older to work getting things done in the community. Several entities come under this umbrella, allowing for a variety of volunteer opportunities.

Seniors Health Insurance Information Program (SHIIP)
2222 S. College Rd., Wilmington
(910) 452-6400

An arm of RSVP, the SHIIP program utilizes volunteers who are trained by the North Carolina Department of Insurance to help people with Medicare problems and questions about supplemental (Medigap) or long-term care insurance; they also assist with medical claims paperwork and policy comparisons. Volunteers receive 24 hours of training and are schooled in counseling techniques.

Special Needs Registry
2222 S. College Rd., Wilmington
(910) 452-6400

This RSVP–sponsored program helps identify New Hanover County residents who have special needs and are potentially at greater risk during a disaster. RSVP volunteers personally telephone each person in the Special Needs Registry prior to a disaster and assist them with their disaster plans. Volunteers also help educate registrants on disaster preparedness.

Volunteer Income Tax Assistance Program (VITA)
2222 S. College Rd., Wilmington
(910) 452-6400

Extensively trained volunteers assist taxpayers with special needs, including persons with disabilities, non-English speaking persons and seniors. This free service, available from the beginning of February through April 15, is very popular and greatly appreciated. Locally, VITA is sponsored by RSVP.

Foster Grandparents Program
2222 S. College Rd., Wilmington
(910) 452-6400

Foster grandparents devote their volunteer services to children with special or exceptional needs. A one-on-one service, Foster Grandparents gives you the opportunity to enrich the life of a child by offering emotional support to child victims of abuse and neglect, tutoring children who lag behind in school subjects, or mentoring troubled teenagers. Foster grandparents must be age 60 or older, meet certain income eligibility guidelines and receive training. This requires a time commitment of about 20 hours per week. A modest tax-free stipend and reimbursement for some expenses is offered to offset the cost of volunteering.

Senior Net Computer Center
2222 S. College Rd., Wilmington
(910) 452-6400

This organization needs volunteers to provide basic and advanced computer training to older adults in New Hanover County. If you're computer literate and would like to assist with program coordination or instruction, be sure to get involved with this program.

Keep on Going

Senior Games and SilverArts Event
2222 S. College Rd., Wilmington
(910) 452-6400

Senior Games by the Sea, a year-round health-promotion program for mature adults (55 and up), is part of a state-wide network sanctioned by North Carolina Senior Games Inc. Each spring, Senior Games by the Sea holds the local athletic and SilverArts competition. Winners at the local level can participate in the State Finals held in Raleigh each fall. In five-year incremental age groups, seniors compete in more than 20 sports, such as archery, billiards, cycling, swimming, track and field, tennis, spin casting and horseshoes. In addition, senior artisans and performers have an opportunity to showcase their talents in the SilverArts competition. Categories include visual, literary, performing and heritage arts, everything from painting, woodwork, dance and music to sculpting and crafts.

University of North Carolina at Wilmington
Lifelong Learning
601 S. College Rd., Wilmington
(910) 962-4034

UNCW's Lifelong Learning program offers a tremendous selection of lectures, concerts, plays, institutes, educational courses and activities, many of them geared especially to the retired population. You could keep busy all year long by taking advantage of the extensive offerings. Choose from art, history, music, languages, women's courses, personal growth, travel and professional development programs. A variety of topics are also covered in the breakfast or lunch lecture series and the foreign policy discussions. Call for your free copy of the catalogue, Pathways.

Through UNCW's Adult Scholars Leadership Program, older adults learn about past and current problems in the region together with possible solutions. Some subjects covered in this excellent seven-week program include history, Southern culture, health and human services, media, government, arts and economic development. Adult Scholars are encouraged to use what they've learned to become more actively involved in enhancing the community through volunteer and entrepreneurial service. For information about this program, call (910) 962-7074.

In-Home and Adult Day Care

Coastal Adult Day Services
220 Avondale Ave., Ste. 103, Wilmington
(910) 799-8818

A welcoming, home-like setting and heaping measures of old-fashioned tender loving care combine to make Coastal Adult Day Services a truly unique place. The dedicated staff have created a relaxed environment for their clients, many of whom suffer from memory disorders. Caregivers and volunteers provide stimulation by encouraging conversation, socialization and physical activity. Therapies include art, dance, music, pets, reminiscent, puppetry, horticulture, field trips and other appropriate forms of recreation.

"Our family caring for your family" is their motto, and they live up to it. The center has convenient, flexible hours and a philosophy of going the extra mile for their clients. Family Focus Groups meet regularly to give family members and caregivers an opportunity to discuss therapies, treatments and home care. All work together to ensure that older adults can receive the assistance they need with activities of daily living and still retain positive feelings of dignity and self worth.

Comfort Keepers
3975-A Market St., Wilmington
(910) 342-9200

Comfort Keepers offers both personal care, as well as services designed for individuals or couples who are capable of handling their own physical needs, but may require assistance with functions of daily living. Available by the hour, day or week, Comfort Keepers will prepare meals, shop, help with grooming and dressing, do laundry, provide transportation, do light housekeeping, run errands and assist with mail. In addition, a licensed CNA is available for transferring and positioning, bathing, assistance with incontinence and other personal needs. From daily "check-in" phone calls to 24-hour care, Comfort Keepers can fill the bill when it comes to non-medical, in-home care.

Elderhaus
Elderhaus at The Lake - Alper Center
1950 Amphitheater Dr., Wilmington
(910) 343-8209

Offering adult day care, adult day health and weekend group respite programs, the Alper Center in Wilmington serves residents of New Hanover and Brunswick counties. Elderhaus provides qualified, professional, appropriate care, supervision and assistance for ambulatory or semi-ambulatory individuals 18 years of age or older, but primarily for seniors over the age of 60. A geriatrician is on site once a week to see participants requiring medical services.

A variety of program services are provided in a bright, cheerful, nurturing atmosphere. Exercise, discussion groups, educational activities, arts/crafts, games and recreational therapies are built into each day's schedule. In addition, field trips, community projects and special events keep participants stimulated and active. A nurse is on site who will administer medications, assist with personal care such as feeding, ambulation and toileting, and oversee individual health-care needs.

A variety of payment options are available. Of special note is the fact that veterans with service-related conditions may attend free once they are approved by the VA. The Alper Center is open at least one Sunday a month to permit caregivers time to attend church and/or enjoy dining out at midday.

Home Instead Senior Care
1804 Glen Meade Rd., Wilmington
(910) 342-0455

Offering a wide range of non-medical services for the elderly, Home Instead Senior Care can help your elderly loved one remain at home and comfortable when you can't be there to provide assistance or companionship. They provide everything from meal preparation and light housekeeping to conversation, errands, medication reminders, incidental transportation, shopping, pet care and many more services. Respite care is popular and gives families time to enjoy a vacation or a just a relaxing weekend away.

Each Home Instead bonded and insured CAREGiver completes a comprehensive, customized 14-month training program followed by testing. The company also offers its CAREGivers an advanced Alzheimer's curriculum. Their services are designed to fit the individual's needs, with emphasis on maintaining independence and respecting personal preferences. Rates are hourly with a minimum of three hours per visit; discounted rates are available for 12 and 24-hour service.

Government Agencies

Seniors can learn a lot about North Carolina's many valuable programs by calling the state CARE-LINE, (800) 662-7030, or by visiting the Division of Aging and Adult Services website: http://www.dhhs.state.nc.us/aging/. County departments of aging offer a variety of services, including congregate and/or home-delivered meals, transportation, minor home repairs, senior center operations, in-home aides, health promotion/disease prevention, and fan/heat relief.

The North Carolina Division of Aging and Adult Services has a wealth of information for retirees and those considering retiring in the state. From moving assistance, long term care and help with finances to employment, home and community services, this is a great resource. Call (919) 733-3983 or visit the website www.ncgov.com/asp/basic/citizen.asp

If you're age 60 or older, ask about getting a free Senior Tar Heel Card for discounts at local businesses. To receive a Senior Tar Heel Card, a person must typically present two appropriate identifications, such as a driver's license and a social security card. Honored throughout the state, this card extends the purchasing power of older adults, especially those living on low, fixed incomes. Participating businesses typically display the Senior Tar Heel Card emblem decal, but seniors are encouraged to ask if the store honors the card even if there is no posted emblem. For more information about the card or other assistance for seniors, contact one of the following agencies:

Brunswick Senior Resources, Inc., Brunswick County Government Complex, Bolivia, (910) 253-2199

Cape Fear Council of Governments, Area Agency on Aging, 1480 Harbour Drive, Wilmington, (910) 395-4553, (800) 218-6575

New Hanover County Department of Aging, 2222 S. College Road, Wilmington, (910) 452-6400

Pender Adult Services, 901 S. Walker Street, Burgaw, (910) 259-9119

SHIIP, Brunswick County Cooperative Extension, Government Center, 25 Referendum Dr., Bolivia, (910) 253-2610

Ⓗ HEALTH CARE

The southern coast's excellent health-care facilities and services — a result of rapid growth, increased development and a booming retirement population in North Carolina's southern coastal region — rival those in larger cities. However, that hasn't always been the case and, as recently as 20 years ago, residents sought advanced medical treatment in larger university medical centers or metropolitan hospitals. Now, in the 21st century, residents and visitors have access to more sophisticated health care and state-of-the-art technology and are no longer forced to travel inland for treatment of serious illness or injury.

In New Hanover County, more than 450 practicing physicians in a wide range of medical and surgical specialties now utilize some of the most technologically progressive facilities and equipment in the state through the New Hanover Health Network. This network, the primary source of health care in the Greater Wilmington area, comprises three formerly independent hospitals — New Hanover Regional Medical Center, Cape Fear Hospital and Pender Memorial Hospital — as well as two facilities located on the medical center's campus — Coastal Rehabilitation Hospital and The Oaks Behavorial Health Hospital. Affiliate agencies include New Hanover Regional Medical Center Emergency Medical Services, Pender Home Health, Lower Cape Fear Hospice & LifeCareCenter and the New Hanover Regional Medical Center Foundation. This far-reaching partnership enlarges and enhances the region's overall health-care capabilities through upgraded and expanded facilities, more options in a range of medical and surgical specialties and improved access to health care.

Although smaller in size, Brunswick County's two hospitals — Brunswick Community Hospital and Dosher Memorial Hospital — offer a wide range of services from general medicine and round-the-clock emergency room physicians to medical/surgical special-

ties and community health-care affiliates. When necessary, medical care beyond the scope of their services is referred to Wilmington's larger hospitals. Residents and vacationers along the Brunswick beaches will find these smaller hospitals more convenient and an excellent source when medical attention is needed.

Hospitals

WILMINGTON

Cape Fear Hospital
5301 Wrightsville Ave., Wilmington
(910) 452-8100
www.nhhn.org

Cape Fear Hospital is full-service community hospital with 141 licensed beds. It provides a range of services, including medical, surgical and ambulatory care, 24-hour emergency services, outpatient surgery, radiology (MRI, CT scan, Ultrasound), laboratory facilities and a specialized orthopedic center.

The Cape Fear Orthopedic Specialty Center features trained teams of nurses, technicians and orthopedic surgeons who are board-certified or eligible in orthopedic surgery. The center includes specialists in hand, foot, ankle and spine as well as arthroscopic surgeries, sports medicine and joint replacement. The Oleander Rehabilitation Center is conveniently located near Cape Fear Hospital for those patients who need further therapy after their procedures.

Total joint replacement patients can benefit from an innovative program called Joint Camp at Cape Fear Hospital. Similar to an athletic training program, Joint Camp takes a team approach to pre-surgical care and post-surgical rehabilitation. Joint Camp participants seem to recover quicker than their traditional joint replacement surgery counterparts.

Cape Fear Hospital, a member of New

WHEN VISITING WILMINGTON, QUICK, CONVENIENT MEDICAL CARE IS AS CLOSE AS OUR NEAREST OFFICE.

Medac provides a variety of affordable, professional, Urgent Care Medical Services for injury or illness:

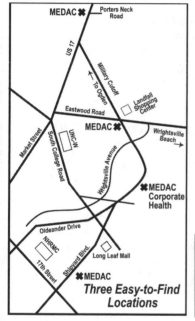

✚Minor Accidents and Injuries
✚Lacerations, Sprains, Fractures
✚Burns, Bites and Stings
✚EKG, X-ray and Lab Services
✚Sports and School Physicals
✚Drug and TB Screening
✚Flu and Pneumonia Shots
✚Referrals to Specialists
✚Worker's Comp
✚Occupational Health Services

Three Easy-to-Find Locations

3710 Shipyard Boulevard ✚ 910-791-0075
1442 Military Cutoff Road ✚ 910-256-6088
8115 Market Street ✚ 910-686-1972

OPEN 7-DAYS-A-WEEK...8-AM-8PM...WALK-INS WELCOME

MEDAC CORPORATE HEALTH SERVICES
5220 Oleander Drive, 2nd Floor ✚ 910-452-7000
MON-FRI...8AM-5PM...APPOINTMENTS PREFERRED

www.medachealth.com

The Heart Specialists

John A. Williams III, MD	Craig O. Siegel, MD
L. Ashley Stroud, MD	Alex R. Kirby, MD
John J. Gould, MD	Richard DiNardo, D.O.
Kevin M. Young, MD	Angela M. Park, MD, FACC
Shannon C. Semple, PA-C	Susan W. Clarke, FNPC
Sonya Williams, RN	Donna K. Fagan, PA-C

CONSULTATIVE, DIAGNOSTIC & INTERVENTIONAL CARDIOLOGY

1001 Newman Rd.	31 Office Park Dr.	3332 Bridges St., Suite 3B
New Bern, NC 28562	Jacksonville, NC 28546	Morehead City, NC 28557
252-635-6777	910-577-8881	252-808-0145

Hanover Health Network, is accredited by the Joint Commission on Accreditation of Healthcare Organizations.

New Hanover Regional Medical Center
2131 S. 17th St., Wilmington
(910) 343-7000
www.nhhn.org

New Hanover Regional Medical Center has long-standing roots in Southeastern North Carolina. The medical center has been offering quality care close to home for generations of families through all stages of life as well as to those who are here visiting.

The 628-bed regional referral center provides a full continuum of care from the littlest ones in the Level III Neonatal Intensive Care Unit and pediatric unit to those in need of adult health services and palliative care. Behavioral health and rehabilitation hospitals are also part of the full scope of care. The medical center has one of the state's few trauma centers certified at Level II or above. And, it operates New Hanover Regional EMS, which provides paramedic services, air and ground critical care transport and 24-hour nurse information services.

As a cardiac care leader in the state, New Hanover Regional's Coastal Heart Center has the area's only open-heart surgery program. The Heart Center houses a 16-bed Coronary Care Unit and a 14-bed Cardiovascular Intensive Care Unit as well as cardiac catheterization, electrophysiology and cardiovascular labs. The Coastal Heart Center is host to one of the state's largest cardiac rehabilitation programs and offers preventive cardiac risk reduction programs such as Intervent™ and Fit Family.

Zimmer Cancer Center, a 30,000-square-foot facility on the medical center's grounds, consolidates all cancer services into one location. The Cancer Center's program has been designated nationally as a teaching hospital with services that include chemotherapy, radiation therapy, gynecological oncologists specializing in cancer care for women, surgical and medical treatments, as well as participation in cancer research. A linear accelerator, used in conjunction with a CT scanner, allows technicians more accuracy in the treatment of tumors.

With a mission of providing family-cen-

Over 30 years of helping you care for the ones you love.

You always put your family first.
They're your number one priority.

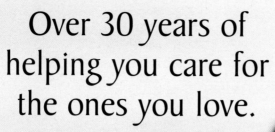

It's good to know there's
someone here to help you.

Wilmington Health Associates has been taking care of you,
your parents, your children and your friends for over thirty
years. With ten state-of-the-art facilities in Wilmington, Leland,
Carolina Beach and Porter's Neck, our staff and physicians are
ready to provide you and your family with the most
comprehensive medical care in the area.

Call our main office for a complete listing of physicians
and office locations or visit us on the web.

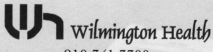

Wilmington Health

910.341.3300
www.wilmingtonhealth.com

A Full-Service Office. A Landfall Location. A Price Your Business Can Thrive On.

Full-service monthly office rentals including:
- Elegantly Furnished Office Suites
- Use of Four Expertly Appointed Conference Rooms
- Grand Entrance, Reception and Waiting Areas
- Full Service Reception and Office Support options

Corporate ID Packages that could include:
- Professional Reception
- Virtual Mail Address
- Monthly Conference Room Time

Ready to take your business to the next level? As the owner of Landfall Executive Suites, I'm proud of the comprehensive services we offer. Contact me directly to learn more about our Standard Office Package or to customize a package just for you.

Eric Goldfarb – OWNER

LANDFALL EXECUTIVE SUITES
FIRST CLASS OFFICES FOR GROWING BUSINESSES

1213 Culbreth Drive (off Military Cutoff Road) Wilmington, NC 28405   (910) 256-1900   www.landfall.

New Hanover Health Network

We're more than just a name.

- Ranked in the Top 5 percent nationally for Total Hip and Knee Replacement
- Ranked in the Top 10 percent nationally for Orthopedic Care
- Designated Teaching Hospital Cancer Program
- A Level IV Neonatal Intensive Care Unit
- Only open-heart surgery program in the region
- Designated as North Carolina's first Model EMS System
- Region's largest employer with more than 4,700 employees
- Comprehensive medical staff with more than 470 physicians
- An accredited Nursing Magnet hospital

New Hanover Health Network is proud to serve the people of Southeastern North Carolina. As the region's leading provider of quality health care, we make a difference every day in thousands of lives. Want to learn more about New Hanover Health Network and its extensive services? Visit our new website at

www.nhhn.org

Exceptional People   Making a Difference

tered care, Women's and Children's Services at New Hanover Regional delivers care for families in need. The Women's Unit serves women needing gynecological or other surgical procedures, while the Family Birthplace delivers 3,400 babies a year, including high-risk deliveries. The Family Birthplace specializes in obstetrical services that allow for a family-centered birthing experience. In Women's Health Specialties clinics, a team of perinatologists care for women with high-risk pregnancies, and a board-certified reproductive endocrinologist works with those who are having difficulty conceiving. The High Risk Antepartum Unit cares for women who require hospitalization during their pregnancy.

New Hanover Regional Medical Center has the only Pediatric Unit in a six-county region. The unit is specifically designed to meet both the medical and post-surgical needs of children. Medical equipment is hidden from view, and specially trained therapists help children cope with being in the hospital. The Neonatal Intensive Care Unit and the Neonatal Transitional Care Unit provide care for critically ill newborns. In the Transitional Unit, parents room with their preterm babies while learning skills, under the supervision of a nurse, to prepare them for caring for their babies at home.

New Hanover Regional also offers comprehensive imaging and outpatient diagnostic services at several locations to make it as convenient as possible for patients. The Forum Diagnostic Center on Military Cutoff offers CT scans, ultrasound, routine radiography, mammography, bone density scans and lab services. The Medical Mall, beside the hospital on 17th Street, recently added a PET/CT scanner so that cancer patients can have their procedures without having to drive hours away. At New Hanover Regional, patients who are claustrophobic can choose to have an MRI in the open magnet or use special goggles to watch a DVD to make it more relaxing.

The Coastal Rehabilitation Hospital is for patients with traumatic brain injury, spinal cord injury, neurological disorders, orthopedic conditions, stroke and other conditions that create a loss of mobility. It utilizes general rehabilitative programs, therapeutic equipment, a day hospital program, a thera-

peutic pool and Easy Street™, a nationally recognized program that simulates real life environments. The Independence Rehabilitation Center and the Oleander Rehabilitation Center offer outpatient services.

Also located on NHRMC's campus is the Oaks Behavioral Health Hospital. It offers inpatient and outpatient programs for adults with special units for women and dual-care unit for those who have problems with chemical addiction and psychiatric needs. The partial hospitalization program provides outpatient treatment and counseling services. Psychiatric evaluations are available 24 hours a day.

New Hanover Regional Medical Center is part of the New Hanover Health Network along with Cape Fear Hospital and Pender Memorial Hospital. The network enjoys prestigious Nursing Magnet status and is a prominent teaching site affiliated with the UNC-Chapel Hill School of Medicine.

As a public, not-for-profit network, NHHN offers care to everyone who needs it, regardless of his or her ability to pay. The hospitals in the network provide more than $30 million a year in indigent care, often to those who would not otherwise have access to health care.

New Hanover Health Network is one of the largest health networks in the state, with about 4,500 employees, 470 physicians and 900 volunteers. Its volunteer Board of Trustees is appointed by the New Hanover County Commissioners, with representation from Pender County. The network receives no local tax support.

BRUNSWICK COUNTY

Brunswick Community Hospital
1 Medical Center Dr., off U.S. Hwy. 17, Supply (910) 755-8121

Serving area residents since 1977, Brunswick Community Hospital, centrally located in Supply, is a 60-bed JCAHO–accredited acute care facility offering a wide range of medical and surgical services from cardiology to orthopedics. With a medical staff of more than 90 physicians and specialists, the hospital has a 24-hour, board-certified, physician-staffed emergency department, a full-service laboratory and blood bank, a maternity center, cardiopulmonary services including a chest pain emergency center, radiology services, physical therapy and intensive and critical care units. The hospital's comprehensive medical services include general/family medicine, internal medicine, obstetrics/gynecology, ophthalmology, pain management, urology, pediatrics, geriatrics, otolaryngology, gastroenterology, neurology, orthopaedics, podiatry, allergy medicine, physical therapy and cardiac rehabilitation. Community outreach programs include H2U at Brunswick, a program for people 50 years of age and older offering a wide variety of social, travel, educational, health and wellness opportunities. Addressing the needs of Brunswick County's rapidly growing population, Brunswick Community Hospital's recent renovations include an expanded emergency room and surgical department as well as expansion and new equipment in the imaging department. Brunswick Community Hospital offers a free Physician Referral Service, (910) 755-1416, or patients can visit the hospital's comprehensive website for a complete physician listing including doctors' credentials.

Dosher Memorial Hospital
924 N. Howe St., Southport
(910) 457-3800

Dosher Memorial Hospital is a nonprofit, public hospital with 36 acute care and 64 skilled nursing care beds. Established in 1930, this community hospital serves Brunswick County, attracting patients from Southport, Bald Head Island, Oak Island, St. James, Boiling Spring Lakes, Bolivia, Supply and surrounding areas.

Dosher Hospital's scope of services include emergency medicine; endoscopy/colonoscopy; outpatient surgery; acute (inpatient) and skilled nursing care; cardio-pulmonary and respiratory therapy; diagnostic imaging with nuclear medicine, MRI, CT scanning, osteoporosis screening with DEXA, mammography using SecondLook technology, and cardiac CT scoring; physical, occupational and speech therapies; comprehensive lab services; and a new cardiac rehabilitation program. Medical specialties include family practice, internal medicine, gynecology, pediatrics, orthopedics, general surgery, cardiology, otolaryngology and urology.

Dosher Memorial Hospital offers free flu shots to the high-risk population annually in November; a health expo in spring and fall;

a holiday tree lighting with Santa in early December and other events throughout the year. Information on the events can be found at the hospital's website.

The hospital provides a valuable publication to visitors and newcomers — Newcomers' Survival Guide — that advises people about health hazards and safety tips for this region (sunburn, dangerous aquatic life, avoiding alligators, hurricane information, rip currents, etc.). Call the Marketing and Public Relations Department at (910) 457-3900 for a copy of The Dosher Directory or the hospital's award-winning 75th Anniversary Magazine. Dosher Memorial Hospital is accredited by the Joint Commission on Accreditation of Healthcare Organizations.

PENDER COUNTY

Pender Memorial Hospital
507 Fremont St., Burgaw
(910) 259-5451

Celebrating more than 50 years of quality health-care services to the Pender County area, Pender Memorial Hospital is an 43-bed general acute medical facility that provides both inpatient and outpatient services to the community. In addition to general acute medical care, the hospital's second floor houses a 43-bed skilled nursing facility. Inpatient departments include a medical/surgical unit, an intensive care unit, emergency services, a surgical suite and a radiology department, along with laboratory, pharmacy, respiration therapy and rehabilitation services. Outpatient services include ambulatory surgery, laparoscopy, general and vascular surgery, orthopedics and podiatry. Diagnostic services include CT Scans, mammography, MRI and endoscopy. Rehabilitation therapists provide inpatient, outpatient and home health rehabilitation services.

Board-certified emergency physicians provide 24-hour emergency services to patients with acute medical and surgical needs. If more advanced care is needed, VitaLink or AirLink transport critically ill patients to New Hanover Regional Medical Center. Pender Memorial, a member of the New Hanover Health Network, is accredited by the Joint Commission on Accreditation of Healthcare Organizations.

HEALTHCARE

Immediate/ Urgent Care

For non-surgical medical services, Wilmington and surrounding communities offer an ample number of immediate-care centers, sometimes referred to as urgent-care centers. Vacationers or residents with relatively minor injuries, illnesses or conditions may prefer the convenience of visiting these centers over making an appointment to see a private doctor. Illnesses and injuries beyond the centers' capabilities are referred to area hospitals.

These are convenient places to get flu and tetanus shots or to have a limited variety of tests or physicals for school, sports or insurance purposes. Most centers have their own labs and X-ray services, and all are staffed by qualified, licensed physicians and nurses. Be advised that most of the centers operate on a first-come basis, so don't expect to be able to make an appointment. However, serious illnesses, injuries or conditions will receive first priority.

These medical service facilities are not open 24 hours a day. In many cases, they are not open seven days a week. A few medical or family practice centers offer walk-in appointments. If you need attention and choose any of these centers, you're advised to phone ahead. Listing here is for your convenience only and does not imply endorsement of any facility.

Visitors to Topsail Island are within a one-hour drive to hospitals and clinics in Wilmington; another public hospital within driving range is Onslow Memorial Hospital, (910) 577-2345, in Jacksonville.

For serious injuries and illnesses, the coastal region has ample emergency response services that can be reached by calling 911.

WILMINGTON

Carolina Family Medical Practice, 6927 Market Street (northeast area of Wilmington), (910) 799-1249

Doctor's Urgent Care Centre, 4815 Oleander Drive, Wilmington, (910) 452-1111

MEDAC Shipyard Boulevard Convenient Medical Care
3710 Shipyard Blvd.
(south side of Wilmington)
(910) 791-0075

MEDAC Military Cutoff Convenient Medical Care
1442 Military Cutoff Rd.
(northeast area of Wilmington)
(910) 256-6088

MEDAC Porters Neck Convenient Medical Care
8115 Market St. (north on U.S. Hwy. 17)
(910) 686-1972
www.medachealth.com

Those in need of immediate medical attention will be pleased to know that a facility like MEDAC is there to serve them at a moment's notice. With doctor's appointments difficult to come by and emergency room visits often prohibitively expensive, MEDAC allows patients to receive fast, affordable treatment for most minor ailments and injuries. Staffed by board-certified, local physicians with a solid grasp of urgent-care patients' needs, these centers continue to be a vital source of medical assistance for Wilmington residents.

Med Care of North Carolina, 5245 S. College Road (Monkey Junction area, south of Wilmington), (910) 392-7806

Northside Medical Center, 1925-A Oleander Drive (south central area of Wilmington), (910) 251-7715

Pee Dee Clinic, 1017 Ashes Drive, Suite 100 (east side of Wilmington), (910) 256-8087

Southeastern Healthcare, 2595 S. 17th Street (at Shipyard Boulevard, south central area of Wilmington), (910) 791-2788

The Downtown MedCenter, 119 Chestnut Street, (downtown Wilmington), (910) 762-5588

Urgent Care of Wilmington, 1135 Military Cutoff Road, Suite 103, (northeast area of Wilmington), (910) 256-6222

BRUNSWICK COUNTY

Dr. Gary Ross Express Care, 25 Union School Road, Suite 3, South Brunswick

Islands Medical Park, Ocean Isle Beach, (910) 579-9955, (910) 579-0800

Coastal Immediate Care Center, 4654 Long Beach Road, Southport, (910) 457-9564

IntraMed Family Practice & Urgent Care, 602 Thomasboro Road, SE, Calabash, (910) 579-1872

North Brunswick Family Practice, 117-H Village Road, Leland, (910) 371-0404

Oak Island Medical Center, 8715 E. Oak Island Dr., Oak Island, (910) 278-3316

Seaside Medical Center, 710 Sunset Boulevard N., Suite A, Sunset Beach, (910) 575-3923

Shallotte Urgent Care, 110-2 Shallotte Crossing Parkway, Shallotte, (910) 755-5440

Southeastern Healthcare, Chiropractic and Medical, 110-D Village Road, Leland, (910) 371-1000; 716 Ocean Highway West, Supply, (910) 754-9000, (910) 457-9007

TOPSAIL AREA

Beach Care, 204 N. New River Dr., Surf City, (910) 328-4729

Topsail Family Medicine & Urgent Care, 16747 U.S. Highway 17, Hampstead, (910) 270-0052

Medical Services

Wilmington Health Associates
1202 Medical Center Dr., Wilmington
(910) 341-3300

With more than 80 providers and 350 employees, Wilmington Health Associates (WHA) is one of the largest multi-specialty medical practices in southeastern North Carolina. State-of-the-art facilities and highly trained specialists provide patients with a full range of medical testing, laboratory, diagnosis and treatment options.

Comprehensive care for the entire family is provided by physicians and other health-care professionals who are dedicated and patient-focused. A variety of exceptional medical services are provided, including audiology, cardiac special testing, mammography, vascular studies and sleep studies. Hospitalists ensure that WHA patients receive

URGENT, PROFESSIONAL MEDICAL CARE

7-Days-a-Week 8AM-8PM
No Appointment is Ever Necessary

Three Convenient Locations:
3710 Shipyard Blvd. 791.0075
1442 Military Cutoff 256.6088
8115 Market St. 686-1972

Medac Corporate Health
5220 Oleander Drive 452.7000
8AM-5PM, M-F

timely, appropriate care and treatment while hospitalized at New Hanover Regional Medical Center.

In addition to its main site at 1202 Medical Center Drive, WHA satellite offices are located in Carolina Beach, Porters Neck, Leland and Northchase. Off-site clinics include Dermatology, Family Practice, Pediatrics, OB-GYN, ENT and the Sleep Disorder Center.

The Heart Center of Eastern Carolina
31 Office Park Dr., Jacksonville
(910) 577-8881

The Heart Center of Eastern Carolina is a full-service cardiology practice in Jacksonville, specializing in the diagnosis, treatment and prevention of cardiac and vascular diseases. All aspects of cardiac care are offered, including invasive and non-invasive cardiovascular treatments. Seven board-certified cardiologists have skill and experience in many prevention and treatment options, including diagnostic catheterization, balloon angioplasty, nuclear cardiology, peripheral vascular disease treatment, atherectomy, stent placement, pacemaker implant and follow-up, echocardiography, hypertension treatment and lipid management. The Heart Center also conducts clinical research trials. Patients are seen by appointment and referral. The practice also has offices in New Bern and Morehead City.

Pelicans soar close to the ebbing tide.

photo: Peter Doran

Substance Abuse

Numerous organizations and agencies in the area help people struggling with substance abuse. Make sure you inquire about the credentials of any therapist you engage. Licensure, accreditation, certification and academic degrees vary according to professional fields and levels of counseling service.

While it is always best to get a proper referral from a physician or licensed professional, you can contact with confidence one of the following organizations. Additional listings are in area phone books under headings such as "Alcohol & Drugs," "Alcoholism (or Drug Addiction) Information & Treatment Centers" or "Drug Abuse & Addiction."

Alcoholics Anonymous, Call the AA Referral Service and Treatment Program 24-hour National Help Line at (800) 711-6375 or locally at (910) 794-1840

Coastal Horizons Center Inc., 615 Shipyard Boulevard, Wilmington, (910) 343-0145

Southeastern Center for Mental Health, Developmental Disabilities, Alcohol and Substance Abuse Services, 2023 S. 17th Street, Wilmington, (910) 251-6440, (800) 293-6440

Wilmington Treatment Center, 2520 Troy Drive, Wilmington, (910) 762-2727 (in-patient facility); Local out-patient services are available at 1524 Harbour Drive, Wilmington, (910) 793-5662

Alternative and Complementary Health Care

Acupuncture Alternative
Oleander Oaks, 5725 Oleander Dr.,
Ste.E-2, Wilmington
(910) 392-0870

Owner/therapist Karen Vaughn describes Acupuncture Alternative's services as combined therapies to treat physical, mental, emotional and spiritual levels. She incorporates classical Chinese acupuncture, herbal therapy formulas, auricular therapy, Qi Gong and nutritional and lifestyle counseling. These elements are used to create a treatment plan as unique as the individual client. Sessions are by appointment only Monday through Saturday.

Balanced Body Massage Therapy & Yoga
5101 Dunlea Ct. #104., Wilmington
(910) 619-9619

Annie Ashenfelter developed Balanced Body Massage Therapy & Yoga to offer complementary therapies emphasizing preventive health care through lifestyle changes and ongoing maintenance programs. She is a Licensed Massage and Bodywork Therapist (NC 4541) and a certified yoga teacher as well as a Reiki practitioner. She offers relaxation massage, deep tissue massage, orthopedic massage for soft tissue injury recovery, and Reiki. She also teaches private and small group yoga classes in several styles. Annie combines elements of massage, yoga and Reiki in order to create personalized sessions addressing the specific needs of each individual. She is a caring therapist who devotes her time and energy to nurturing every person she treats. She is available seven days a week by appointment.

Cameron Clinic of Chinese Medicine
1928 S. 16th St., Wilmington
(910) 342-0999

After more than 20 years in nursing practice, Nan Cameron, a Registered Nurse, completed studies at the International Institute of Chinese Medicine in Santa Fe, New Mexico, followed by a clinical internship at hospitals in China. Using her extensive knowledge and experience with both Western and Chinese medicine, she integrates the two into her health-care services. All patients receive a complete consultation and evaluation at the time of their first visit. Therapeutic modalities include acupuncture, Chinese herbs, cupping, gua sha, moxabustion, as well as lifestyle and dietary counseling. Call for an appointment.

Cloud 9 Massage Therapy
(910) 616-4291

Eager to experience the luxurious therapy of a personal massage but don't want to bother with a spa? Call Cloud Nine Massage Therapy's Christopher Gates, and he'll bring the spa to you. Or, for those who enjoy the experience of being pampered in a state-of-the-art spa facility, Cloud Nine has two locations that provide Swedish, Deep Tissue, Trigger Point, Sports Massage and Reflexology treatments. For expecting moms, Cloud Nine offers pregnancy massage to ease the physical discomfort associated with pregnancy. Choose your own method of relief from this licensed massage and bodywork therapist. Credit cards are welcome.

McKay Acupuncture & Chinese Medicine
1047-C S. Kerr Ave., Wilmington
(910) 232-5802

Leon McKay, a North Carolina native, is a master's graduate of Santa Barbara College of Oriental Medicine of Santa Barbara, California. He also has studied with master herbalists and medical doctors and has received in-depth training that combines Western medicine and Chinese herbal medicine. Using his collective knowledge and skills, he treats a variety of discomforts, such as neck, back and knee pain, migraines, sinus trouble, anxiety, colds, fatigue, PMS, hepatitis C, insomnia, arthritis and high blood pressure. If you're looking for a holistic approach to health care and a professional practitioner who treats the entire person, Leon McKay invites you to call for a free consultation.

Sea of Health
Oleander Oaks, 5725-F Oleander Dr.,
Ste. 1, Wilmington
(910) 395-4545

Sea of Health offers personal fitness training, massage therapy and La Stone therapy. Owners Kristen Ashton and Molly Hall are highly experienced in the services they offer. Kristen, a certified personal fitness trainer, holds a BS degree in Exercise Science, and Molly is a licensed massage therapist and member of the American Massage Therapy Association. This center is open Monday through Friday from 9 AM to 5 PM. After 5 PM or Saturday is by appointment only.

Chiropractors

Chiropractors are available in astonishingly high numbers in the region. A national movement toward alternative health care and nontraditional medical treatment of pain as well as an approach to wellness have focused attention on chiropractic care. Some well-established chiropractic offices are listed here. Check the local phone books for more listings. The Insiders' Guide does not endorse any practitioner, but offers the following listings as an example of what is available.

WILMINGTON

Alternative Health Care Center, 4706 Oleander Drive, Wilmington, (910) 392-3770

Atlantic Coast Chiropractic, 6841-D Market Street, (910) 798-0101 and 3208 Oleander Drive, (910) 392-8896

Back In Motion Chiropractic, 6303 Oleander Drive, Suite 102-A, Wilmington, (910) 313-1322

James Clinic, 7491 Market Street, Wilmington, (910) 686-5433

Reese Family Chiropractic, 2003 Carolina Beach Road, Wilmington, (910) 763-3611

Sea Coast Chiropractic, 2451 S. College Road, Wilmington, (910) 392-3100

Dr. Glenn Weckel, 5215-B Market Street, Wilmington, (910) 392-3333; 1300-3 Bridge Barrier Road, Carolina Beach, (910) 458-0804

BRUNSWICK COUNTY

At The Beach Chiropractic Health Center, 6934 Beach Drive SW, Suite 2, Ocean Isle Beach, (910) 575-2225, (910) 575-7810

Tina S. Axelsson, D.C., 7290 Beach Drive SW, Suite 13, Ocean Isle Beach, (910) 579-4888

Cagle Chiropractic & Acupuncture, 121 Holden Beach Road, Holden Beach, (910) 754-7737

Chirohealth Family Chiropractic, 417 N. Howe Street, Unit A, Southport, (910) 454-8100

Coastal Breeze Chiropractic P.C., 6934-2 Beach Drive, Ocean Isle Beach, (910) 575-7809

Coastal Carolina Chiropractic, 712 Village Road, Suite 101, Shallotte, (910) 755-5400

Cypress Chiropractic PA, 814 N. Howe Street, Southport, (910) 457-1919

Family First Chiropractic, 4911 Bridgers Road, Shallotte, (910) 755-5483; 4870 Long

Beach Road SE, Suite 1, Southport, (910) 454-4041

Hammond Chiropractic, 717 N. Howe Street, Southport, (910) 457-9133

Holden Beach Family Chiropractic, 2345 Holden Beach Road, Supply, (910) 846-3300

Island Healing Chiropractic, 6402 E. Oak Island Drive, Oak Island, (910) 278-5877

Loomis Chiropractic & Acupuncture Center, 10195-1 Beach Drive SW, Calabash, (910) 579-8891

Lundy Chiropractic & Rehab, 4647-6 Main Street, Shallotte, (910) 754-2225

Sito Chiropractic, 4501 Main Street, Shallotte, (910) 754-5676

Southport Chiropractic, 1456 N. Howe Street, Southport, (910) 454-0909

TOPSAIL ISLAND AREA

Barnes Chiropractic, 14365 U.S. Highway 17, Hampstead, (910) 270-9990

Hampstead Family Chiropractic, 14548 U.S. Highway 17, Hampstead, (910) 270-9009

Massage Therapy

The region also has an abundance of practitioners of massage therapy for wellness, chronic pain, strain and injuries. Therapists offers various methods that range through Swedish, deep tissue, myofascial release, neuromuscular, craniosacral therapy, trigger point, foot reflexology, polarity, Shiatsu, acupressure, prenatal and sports. Some massage therapists work in their homes, others in offices or fitness clubs, and a few will be happy to come to your own home.

The City of Wilmington has an ordinance that requires licensed massage therapists to have a minimum of 500 hours of training at an accredited school. Therapists are also required to carry liability insurance, and North Carolina's General Assembly now recognizes massage therapy as a licensed profession throughout the state.

Miller-Motte Technical College, 5000 Market Street, Wilmington, (910) 254-0995, offers massage-student clinics that are open to the public.

Listed below is a sampling of the massage therapists available in Wilmington for your convenience. The Insiders' Guide does not endorse any practitioner. Check area phone books for more listings.

WILMINGTON

Balanced Body Massage Therapy & Yoga, 5101 Dunlea Ct. #104, Wilmington , (910) 619-9619

East Coast Acupuncture & Massage, 1213 Calbreath Drive, Suite 209, Wilmington, (910) 509-7207

Harbour Club Day Spa & Salon, Lumina Station, 1904 Eastwood Road, Wilmington, (910) 256-5020

Rachel Mann Massage Therapy, Oleander Oaks, 5725-E Oleander Drive, Suite 5, Wilmington, (910) 520-2238

Seaside Yoga and Boutique, 5725 Oleander Drive, Suite B-10, Wilmington, (910) 792-9303 www.seasideyoga.com

Still Waters Renewal Spa, Barbara Dols, L.M.B.T., 4514 Fountain Drive, Wilmington, (910) 792-0101

BRUNSWICK COUNTY

Holistic Essentials, 5081 Southport-Supply Road SE, Southport, (910) 454-9006

Jodi Kilde Massage Therapist, 109 Causeway Drive, Ocean Isle Beach, (910) 575-8054

Gail McGee, CMT, 109 Causeway Drive, Ocean Isle Beach, (910) 575-7838

Resort Massage & Spa Services, Village Activity Center, Sea Trail Resort & Golf Links, Sunset Beach, (910) 287-1193

Right Touch Therapy, 109-5 Causeway Drive, Ocean Isle Beach, (910) 575-3944

Sunset Wellness, 10152-5 Beach Drive SW, Calabash, (910) 575-0990

In-Home Care

NURSES, COMPANIONS & HELPERS

Because of the increasing demand for in-home care, the area has seen a rise in the number of private businesses and not-for-profit agencies offering in-home nursing care services such as certified nursing assistants (CNAs), LPNs, RNs, companions and other assistance. As needs change and agencies grow, additional services may be added, such as physical, occupational or speech therapy, medical social services, equipment and supplies. For your convenience, we've compiled a list. Some companies in our list are more comprehensive than others. The Insiders' Guide does not endorse any particular provider.

Cape Fear Home Care, 513 Market Street, Wilmington, (910) 343-1184

Choice Caregivers, 107 Ridgeway Drive, Wilmington, (910) 790-3376

Coastal Companion Care, 4841 Long Beach Rd., Southport, (910) 201-9970

Comfort Keepers, 3975-A Market Street, Wilmington, (910) 342-9200

Eldercare Convalescent Service, 5003 Randall Parkway, Wilmington, (910) 395-5003

Liberty Home Care, 1303-B Independence Boulevard, Wilmington, (910) 251-8111, (800) 999-9883; 1120 Ocean Highway W., Supply, (910) 754-8133; 204 South Walker Street, Burgaw, (910) 259-1150

Lower Cape Fear Hospice & LifeCare-Center, 725-A Wellington Avenue, Wilmington, (910) 772-5444 for administrative office; (800) 207-6908 for centralized patient referral; Hospice Care Center, 1406 Physicians Drive, Wilmington, (910) 762-9422

Pender Home Health, 507 E. Fremont Street, Burgaw, (910) 259-1224

Well Care Health Services Inc., 2715 Ashton Drive, Suite 200, Wilmington, (910) 452-1555; 118 Ocean Highway, Supply, (910) 754-9700

THERAPY

At Home Therapy
530 Causeway Dr., Ste. B-3,
Wrightsville Beach
(910) 509-2810

When your physician orders physical or occupational therapy, inquire about having it done in the comfort and privacy of your home. With a staff of highly qualified therapists, At Home Therapy offers a full range of services and specializes in geriatrics. Hours are Monday through Friday from 8 AM to 5 PM and by appointment.

Adult Day Care

When you're looking for appropriate in-home or adult day care for yourself or a loved one, check with one of these qualified, reputable organizations. Depending on the age, level of care and particular needs of the person to be enrolled, you can probably find what you need. These are not nursing care providers. Only Elderhaus' Alper Center offers minimal health-care services on site; the others can assist with some activities of daily living, however. Adult day care facilities listed here are detailed in the Retirement chapter.

Coastal Adult Day Care and Day Health
220 Avondale Ave., Ste. 103, Wilmington
(910) 799-8818

This facility offers a relaxed, homey atmosphere where older adults can spend the day. Assistance with activities of daily living is provided. Meals and snacks are provided. Coastal Adult Day Care offers a variety of therapeutic and recreational activities. It's primarily open weekdays, but flexible hours can be arranged, including some evening and weekend care.

Elderhaus
Elderhaus at The Lake - Alper Center,
1950 Amphitheater Dr., Wilmington
(910) 343-8209

In addition to its regular adult day-care program services, Alper Center offers limited health-care services provided by a professional nurse, and a geriatrician is on site once a week. Supervision, assistance and therapeutic recreation are provided for adults age 18 or older, but primarily for those older than 60, by qualified staff and volunteers. Weekend Group Respite, a program designed to give temporary relief for caregivers, is available for anyone who is older than the age of 60 or has a caregiver older than 60.

Elderhaus
Elderhaus at Porters Neck,
1013 Porters Neck Rd., Wilmington
(910) 686-3335

Weekday care is provided for adults older than 18, although most participants are older

than 60. Ambulatory and semi-ambulatory individuals receive caring supervision and socialization services. No nursing or health-care services are offered.

HealthMate Home Care, Inc.
3132 Wrightsville Ave., Wilmington
(910) 762-0050

A licensed home-care agency, Health-Mate provides nurses, medical social workers, personal-care attendants, companion and in-home aide services. Also, emergency monitoring, in-home respite care, secondary management and a medication dispensing system are available. The agency specializes in creating affordable solutions and support services for seniors. Senior Care case managers are available 24 hours a day.

Home Care Management Corporation
890 S. Kerr Ave., Ste. 200, Wilmington
(910) 796-6741

When you or a loved one need help with activities of daily living, housekeeping, meal preparation or other personal services, Home Care Management Corporation offers a variety of solutions. Also available to provide health care assistance are Certified Nursing Assistants and in-home aides — all of whom are supervised by Registered Nurses. Transportation is not provided. Referrals may be made by a physician, social worker or other human service provider. The client must be eligible for Medicaid, with a blue card.

Home Instead Senior Care
1804 Glen Meade Rd., Wilmington
(910) 342-0455

Offering a wide range of non-medical services for the elderly, Home Instead Senior Care can help your elderly loved one remain at home and comfortable when you can't be there to provide assistance or companionship. They provide everything from meal preparation and light housekeeping to conversation, errands, medication reminders, incidental transportation, shopping, pet care and many more services. (See the Retirement chapter.)

Tidal flats and big sky are a peaceful combination.

photo: Peter Doran

SCHOOLS AND CHILD CARE

The southern North Carolina coast is served by three public school systems. New Hanover County has the largest system, as it encompasses the largest city on the state's entire coastline. Brunswick County Schools and Pender County Schools serve largely the rural populations to the southwest and north of New Hanover County.

Additionally, the region offers a growing list of independent (private) schools, both secular and religion-based, that meet a broad range of educational requirements. Home schooling has become increasingly popular, so we have included some helpful information about state and local resources.

School-age children in New Hanover County should be immediately enrolled in a public or independent (private school) unless they are home-schooled. To enroll a child in the public schools, the parent or guardian must bring to the school a certified copy of the child's birth certificate along with the child's Social Security card, completed health assessment, immunization records and proof of residence. Children entering kindergarten must be 5 years old on or before October 16 of that year. Parents of students who were enrolled in a different school should bring the student's last report card and copies of standardized test reports to the new school.

Schools

PUBLIC SCHOOLS

**New Hanover County School System
6410 Carolina Beach Rd., Wilmington
(910) 763-5431**

The New Hanover County School System, the 10th-largest public school system in the state, serves the city of Wilmington and the county, including the beach communities of Figure Eight Island, Wrightsville Beach, Carolina Beach and Kure Beach. The system serves over 24,000 students from kindergarten through Grade 12 in 35 schools (three pre-kindergarten centers bring the total to 38).

Through the ABCs of Public Education, end-of-grade tests measure student achievement in reading and math for grades 3 through 8. High school students take end-of-course tests in 10 subjects. New Hanover County Schools had 14 Schools of Excellence, which means 90 percent or more of students at grade level met or exceeded growth; seven Schools of Distinction (80 percent or more of students at grade level, met or exceeded growth) and three Schools of Progress (60 percent or more of students at grade level, met or exceeded growth). Combined SAT scores were 1025, compared to 1010 for the state and 1028 nationally, which puts New Hanover County schools above the state scores.

In 2004/2005, 93.1 percent of the system's graduates planned to continue their education beyond high school. More than $6 million in scholarships and financial aid was awarded to 2005 graduates.

Twenty two students were selected for enrollment in the North Carolina Governor's School, and two were selected to attend the North Carolina School of Science and Math. Six hundred sixty-eight students were recognized by the state for superior academic achievement and were North Carolina's Scholars recipients.

The system has had the benefit of tremendous support from the business community and community volunteers. Volunteers in 2004/2005 numbered 7,000 and contributed more than 175,000 documented hours of service to the system. These individuals contributed in many different ways, including tutoring, working to lower the dropout rate and offering opportunities for students to gain exposure to the corporate realm beyond the classroom. The Greater Wilmington Chamber of Commerce Education Foundation, a community education support organization, provides an estimated $10,000 annually to fund mini-grants to support classroom teachers. Other businesses in the area have shown tremendous support for the school system, including a large grant initiative with the GE Foundation and significant volunteer support from GE staff.

The 2004/2005 budget for New Hanover County Schools was $179 million, with 58.8 percent coming from the state, 37.7 percent from local monies and 6.5 percent from the federal government. Per-pupil expenditure for 2003-04 was $7,171.

The system is organized as kindergarten through grade 5, grades 6 through 8, and grades 9 through 12, using the middle school concept instead of junior high schools.

The school year runs from August until early June, although year-round schooling is now available at Johnson Elementary, Codington Elementary and Eaton Elementary schools. The year-round program is voluntary for students and teachers. After considerable investigation, the Board of Education found that the advantages of year-round schooling include increased learning, a reduction in stress levels for both students and teachers, more time, greater opportunity for effective enrichment and remediation, and higher motivation.

While still in high school, students in New Hanover County schools may engage in advanced studies at the University of North Carolina at Wilmington or enroll in courses at Cape Fear Community College for part of the instructional day.

In 1993 the Gregory School of Science, Mathematics and Technology opened its doors to allow elementary school students to experience a high-tech program of study that integrates science and mathematics throughout the curriculum. This was the first magnet school in the system, and it has been enthusiastically received within the community.

Lakeside High School is an academic alternative/school-of-choice for students in grades 9 through 12 who qualify for admittance.

There are four senior high schools in New Hanover County, and the seven middle schools that feed into these according to district lines. The county student popula-

tion is approximately 27 percent minority enrollment, and lines are periodically shifted to ensure balanced racial populations at all schools.

More than 250 courses are available to high school students, including social studies, mathematics, computer science, English, foreign languages and the full range of sciences. Students can participate in Army, Navy and Air Force JROTC Honor units as well as a broad range of extracurricular activities and programs. There are many programs in vocational education, including marine sciences and oceanography. A cultural arts curriculum includes band, orchestra, chorus, drama, art and dance.

Middle schools offer a similar, though more limited, curriculum to that of the senior high schools. Elementary schools emphasize hands-on experience in all disciplines. Elementary school students participate in a curriculum based on the use of manipulatives and inquiry to build a foundation that will support the learning of concepts in the middle grades and high school. A comprehensive program has been designed for exceptional children at all grade levels.

Basketball and football figure largely in interscholastic athletic programs. What else would you expect from the sports-minded city that produced such athletes as Michael Jordan, Meadowlark Lemon and Roman Gabriel on its public school courts and fields? Volleyball, baseball, soccer, wrestling, golf, tennis, lacrosse and track are also offered.

Brunswick County School System
35 Referendum Dr., N.E., Bolivia
(910) 253-2900

The Brunswick County School System has a student population of approximately 11,600 and operates three high schools, four middle schools and eight elementary schools. It offers an alternative middle/high school, the Brunswick Learning Center, which provides education for students who have not been successful in the traditional program.

The school system has a five-year facility plan initiated to accommodate anticipated rapid growth of the population. An instructional program has been established that provides creativity and flexibility from Pre-K through grade 12. In addition to the basic K-12 instructional program, Brunswick County

Schools offer a comprehensive program of instructional services for the exceptional child, career technical education, remediation and an enhanced program for the gifted learner. The Brunswick County Academy will open in the fall of 2006 with numerous alternative program opportunities and provide expanded education opportunities for youth in partnership with Brunswick Community College.

The Center for Advanced Studies, a joint partnership with Brunswick Community College, encourages and offers more advanced courses in all areas of the curriculum, including vocational coursework and AP programs. Juniors and seniors can get credit toward trades occupations. In addition to helping students pursue vocational careers, the program also is intended to expose students to college life and make them aware of higher-education options. An Early College High School will open on the community college campus in the fall of 2006.

The trend in test scores exemplifies a school system of excellence. This comes from a strong partnership of school employees, families, and the community working together.

Pender County School System
925 Penderlea Hwy., Burgaw
(910) 259-2187

Pender County Schools are strategically located across the fifth largest county in the state. Fifteen schools serve approximately 7,200 students in seven elementary schools, four middle schools, three high schools, and one alternative learning center. With a con-

tinuing commitment to excellence, progressive leadership, dedicated professionals and community support, Pender County Schools have been rewarded with numerous academic achievements.

The school system has an A+ School of the Arts, one school on a year-round calendar, and after-school care/enrichment programs at each elementary school. Eighteen sports are available for high school students. Seven sports are available for middle school students.

Cape Fear Center for Inquiry
3131 B Randall Pkwy., Wilmington
(910) 362-0000

Cape Fear Center for Inquiry (CFCI) is a state-funded, public K–8 charter school. CFCI is an innovative "school of choice" that does not discriminate in its admission procedures nor charge for enrollment. CFCI is committed to promoting students' abilities to think and create in personally meaningful ways through an inquiry-based, integrated curriculum in a nurturing environment.

Experienced, licensed teachers strive to ensure that every child develops knowledge in the traditional content areas. Because CFCI considers the teacher/child relationship of paramount importance, class size is small (no more than 20 per class with K–3 being even smaller). Teachers for the elementary grades (K–5) stay with their classes for two school years. Emphasis is on individualized instruction utilizing each child's strengths.

Total school enrollment cannot exceed 336 pupils, and a waiting list exists for each grade. If more applications are received than CFCI can accommodate for the coming school year, a lottery is held, usually in March.

The school teaches the North Carolina Standard Course of Study, complies with the North Carolina ABC's Accountability Program requirements, and administers all required state tests.

If you choose to educate your child at home, you need to 1) notify the Department of Administration, Division of Non-Public Education of your intent to operate a school, include your school name, and name of chief administrator; and 2) tell the child's current school that you have notified DNPE and that you are withdrawing your child from the school. It is best to document your decision with a letter and give the date at which you will start home-schooling.

INDEPENDENT (PRIVATE) SCHOOLS

The Cape Fear region's private schools offer curricula and activities for children from preschool to high school. While tuition and expenses are the responsibility of the parent or guardian, most of these schools offer financial aid or easy-pay plans. In many cases,

CAPE FEAR ACADEMY

Community, Respect, Integrity, Excellence

*A college preparatory school
teaching skills to last a lifetime
from the classroom to the workplace*

Contact the Admissions office
at (910) 791-0287 for more information.

3900 South College Road
Wilmington, NC 28412
www.capefearacademy.org

*Cape Fear Academy is a college preparatory, independent school for grades PK-12,
which admits qualified students of any race, religion, ethnic origin, or other legally
protected status. A financial aid program is available.*

having more than one child in a particular school allows a discount on tuition for other children within the same family. All of the area's independent/private schools aren't included here, but the following list suggests some alternatives to public education.

Wilmington

**Cape Fear Academy
3900 S. College Rd., Wilmington
(910) 791-0287**

Cape Fear Academy is the dominant secular private school in the region. Established in 1967, this coeducational day school is open to students interested in a traditional, challenging, college-preparatory education. The program offers a developmentally appropriate curriculum within a stimulating learning environment.

The academy's mission statement, "To be a learning community sharing a commitment to respect, integrity and academic excellence," forms the framework for student life at the school as well as fostering a spirit of unity and high ideals. Close relationships with teachers are encouraged.

There are approximately 580 students in pre-kindergarten through grade 12. Pre-kindergarten and kindergarten students participate in half-day programs, with after-school care available. The Lower School comprises pre-kindergarten through grade 5. Instruction by professional faculty includes art, music, science, foreign language (Spanish), drama, computer science and physical education.

The Middle and Upper schools concentrate on college preparation in the classroom coupled with individual development through extracurricular activities. Students in grades 6 through 8 must satisfactorily complete courses in English, science, social studies, math, physical education, art, music, computer science and foreign language. During the Middle School years, importance is placed on building positive peer relationships, particularly through outdoor education opportunities that include rock climbing and ropes courses.

At grade 9, students begin to fulfill graduation requirements within a curriculum that offers Honors and Advanced Placement courses as well. Emphasis is placed on devel-

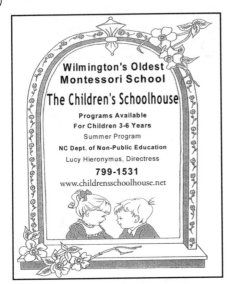

Wilmington's Oldest Montessori School

The Children's Schoolhouse

**Programs Available
For Children 3-6 Years**

Summer Program

NC Dept. of Non-Public Education

Lucy Hieronymus, Directress

799-1531

www.childrensschoolhouse.net

Charter Day School
7055 Beacon's Way., Leland
(910) 655-1214

Serving the counties of Brunswick, New Hanover, Bladen and Pender, Charter Day School offers a Direct Instruction curriculum that includes reading with phonics instruction as well as particular attention to penmanship, spelling, grammar and style. More than just the mechanics of education, CDS utilizes numerous classical sources in its mathematics, science, music and art classes. Students find themselves intellectually stimulated and well versed in the aesthetic and moral traditions of western civilization.

A North Carolina School of Distinction, CDS received its charter in 2000, enrolling 53 students in grades K–2. In 2005 CDS is designated an "Honor School of Excellence" by the State Board of Education and is among the top 25 K–8 schools in the state for exemplary academic growth. In 2005 they served 620 children in grades K–7.

Charter Day School is a public, tuition-free charter school open to all N.C. children. An independent Board of Trustees oversees the school's management by the Roger Bacon Academy. Each student is expected to embody the four classical qualities of prudence, justice, fortitude and temperance and to practice the virtues of faith, hope and charity. Members of the school community are accountable for ensuring their actions comply with these principles. As a result, CDS students develop the necessary skills to become valuable members of society and leaders in their community.

oping study skills, organization, note-taking and test preparation.

Community service is a key component of the Middle and Upper school programs. The Upper School student government organization has an entire branch devoted to community service. Group and individual activities are planned as students work to serve a minimum number of hours required for graduation.

Present facilities include three classroom buildings, a gymnasium and a student center. The Primary Building contains kindergarten and first-grade classrooms as well as a multi-purpose commons and a teaching kitchen. The Beane Wright Student Center includes a dining hall, music and art classrooms and a fitness/weight training area. An Upper School building, Cameron Hall, which includes drama and media/technology spaces, was completed in August 2000. Along with the Bruce B. Cameron gymnasium, there are three athletic fields, tennis courts and a Lower School playground.

One hundred percent of graduates attend four-year college programs, and approximately 75 percent of those students are accepted into their first-choice college or university. The average SAT score is around 1210, which is more than 200 points higher than local, state and national averages.

To arrange for a tour, call the Admissions Office at (910) 791-0287 ext. 1015.

The Children's Schoolhouse - Montessori
612 S. College Rd., Wilmington
(910) 799-1531

Wilmington's oldest Montessori School, The Children's Schoolhouse offers classes for youngsters ages 3 to 6 years old. A small, warm, home-like, nurturing environment fosters positive growth and development along with a solid educational programming. Located within St. Matthew's Lutheran Church, the school includes a state-recognized kindergarten curriculum, high-quality instruction and lots of fun, too.

Owner/Director Lucy Hieronymus oversees every facet of the school's operations as well as teaching kindergarten and working

Friends School of Wilmington

18 months – 8th grade

Montessori Preschool
and Elementary Program
(910) 791-8221

Middle School Program
(910) 792-1811

www.fsow.org

12 years of opening eyes, hearts and minds.

with her staff of well-trained, experienced professionals; each classroom has a certified Montessori Directress. Each child gets daily individualized instruction in math and reading mixed in with a wide variety of educational activities that include such things as botany, music, art, geography, earth science, history and zoology. Although everything the child does at the school is called "work," and reflects a level of responsibility, nothing appears further from it — these kids love it!

Days and hours of attendance vary according to the child's age, level of development and parents' preferences. Generally, younger children attend from 9 AM to 1 PM; kindergartners may choose to stay until 2:30. Children bring their own snacks and lunches.

Friends School of Wilmington
Middle School: 350 Peiffer Ave., Wilmington
(910) 792-1811
Elementary/Pre-school: 207 Pine Grove Dr.,
Wilmington
(910) 791-8221
www.fsow.org

Friends School of Wilmington is a warm, nurturing, educational community where faculty really get to know the students and their families so that they can all work together to benefit children. Celebrating its 10th year of opening eyes, hearts and minds, Friends School of Wilmington continues a 300-year Quaker educational tradition of fostering intellectual and spiritual integrity while affirming the value of each individual.

A nurturing environment, a well-rounded, compelling academic program, developmentally appropriate curriculum and intellectual integrity combine to give students a sound educational base upon which to build their own destinies. An excellent, dedicated faculty prepare challenging, relevant, hands-on learning activities, including frequent projects, field trips and personalized growth opportunities, creating a dynamic setting for learning.

By manifesting Quaker values of simplicity, community, social justice, diversity, equality, harmony and peace, Friends School of Wilmington guides students to incorporate these values into their lives, helps them to develop an awareness of the interdependence of life that extends to the world at large, and encourages them to develop habits of respect, trust, cooperation and responsibility. Permeating the entire approach to education is the school's basic philosophy that young people who are convinced of their own value, will, in turn, seek and speak to the good in others. Accordingly, individual differences are honored, cooperation is fostered, responsibility is expected, and personal standards of excellence are developed.

The school now has two campuses spanning ages 18 months through 8th grade. Preschool is an established Montessori program, and the elementary school builds on this developmental approach to learning. The teacher-pupil ratio is quite low (1:12). A very active Parent/Teacher Organization and

Growing in Excellence

Myrtle Grove Christian School

Affordable Tuition
Accredited by S.A.C.S. and I.C.A.A.

806 Piner Road Wilmington, NC 28409
910.392.2067 *www.mgcs.org*

a high rate of family involvement help build community and keep tuition low.

The pre/elementary school is located in a 6,000-square-foot building at 207 Pine Grove Drive next to Winter Park Elementary School's playground. Call (910) 791-8221 for admissions information. The middle school is located on a 5-acre campus at 350 Peiffer Avenue off Oleander Drive near Greenville Loop Road. Call (910) 792-1811 for admissions information.

Myrtle Grove Christian School
806 Piner Rd., Wilmington
(910) 392-2067

Biblical principles serve as a framework and spiritual foundation for all that is taught at Myrtle Grove Christian School. Academic excellence combined with strong moral values ensures a sound learning environment for nearly 400 students in preschool through ninth grade. A ministry of Myrtle Grove Evangelical Presbyterian Church, the school offers a Christ-centered education that aims at a well-balanced development of mind, spirit and body. The school strives to equip each student with the knowledge necessary to develop a strong Christian character in order to meet the challenges of life and to serve Christ in the world.

An important component of Myrtle Grove Christian School's approach to education is cooperation with home and church. Parents are expected to take an active role by helping

with school activities as well as assisting their child academically. Regular church attendance is encouraged.

Enrichment programs in the lower school include computer, art, music, library, Spanish and physical education. Upper school non-core classes are required in Bible, physical education and computer, while electives may be selected from dance, drama, art, praise band, school newspaper, and creative and life skills. Piano lessons (ages 5 and older) and concert band (fourth grade and higher) are available to students at an additional cost. A sports program that competes in tennis, basketball, soccer and cheerleading is offered to boys and girls grades 7 through 9 (sixth graders may try out for tennis).

Kindergarten through ninth grade students annually take the Stanford Achievement Test and consistently score in the top 20 to 25 percent in the nation in core subject areas. The school meets the accreditation standards of the Southern Association of Colleges and Schools (SACS) and the International Christian Accrediting Association (ICAA).

New Horizons Elementary School
3705 S. College Rd., Wilmington
(910) 392-5209

At New Horizons Elementary School, students in kindergarten through fifth grade learn in a highly creative, positive environment that provides ongoing opportunities for self development as well as academic growth. An unusual, home-like campus, small class size and a stimulating curriculum, coupled with a professional, friendly, and nurturing staff, make this school an excellent choice.

Founded in 1983 by a group of parents and three current faculty members to provide a quality educational alternative for area children, New Horizons Elementary School's educational program stresses reading, oral and written expression, mathematics, science and social studies. Instruction in critical thinking, problem solving and study skills is integrated throughout the various subject areas. The school's challenging, innovative curriculum is designed to help a child develop internal motivation, self-reliance and self-discipline. The curriculum includes P.E.

An Educational Oasis...
WILMINGTON CHRISTIAN ACADEMY
Your Refreshing School Alternative!

- Christian Philosophy
- Challenging Academics
- Qualified, Caring Faculty
- Biblical Teaching
- Conservative Values
- Grades K4-12

- Excellent Facilities
- Affordable Tuition
- Championship Athletics
- Fine Arts Instruction
- Serving Wilmington
  since 1969

1401 North College Road Wilmington, NC 28405
(910) 791-4248 www.wilmingtonchristian.com

daily and once-a-week Spanish class and choral music for all grades.

In keeping with the school's philosophy and mission, active parental involvement is a required component. This includes monitoring a child's homework, projects, independent reading, returned class work and evaluations. Parents are expected to serve on committees, attend school events, help with fund-raising, chaperone field trips and even assist with building maintenance.

Upon enrollment, each family becomes a voting member of New Horizons Elementary School, Inc., a non-profit organization. The governing body is a board of directors made up of parents and teachers. The professional staff oversees day-to-day operations as well as instructional, curricular and academic matters.

For more information, contact the school office between the hours of 8:30 AM and 12:30 PM on Mondays, Wednesdays and Thursdays.

St. Mary Catholic School
217 S. Fourth St., Wilmington
(910) 762-5491

Located downtown in the historic district, St. Mary Catholic School serves kindergarten through grade 8. The school's mission is to "ensure learning for all our students within the framework of Catholic Christian values, to help our students grow in a manner consistent with their needs, interests and abilities, and to prepare them to live in a changing world as self-directing, caring, responsible citizens."

Grades K through 5 are structured, self-contained classes. The curriculum includes math, science, social studies, computers, Spanish, music, art, physical education, religion, reading, language, (phonics in grades K through 2) and creative writing. Grades 6 through 8 have departmental teachers, and students rotate to different classrooms. Classes include religion, science, social studies, math, language arts, literature, writing, computers, Spanish, music, art and physical education. St. Mary Catholic School graduates are prepared to enroll in the honors courses offered by area high schools. The school's emphasis is on preparing students to be independent learners who maintain high academic achievements and standards throughout their high school and college years.

St. Mary Catholic School is historically notable as the first Catholic school in North Carolina. The school proudly carries on its 135-year history by providing Catholic education to the children of Wilmington.

Wilmington Christian Academy
1401 N. College Rd., Wilmington
(910) 791-4248

Situated on a large campus at the beginning of I-40, Wilmington Christian Academy is the largest private school in southeastern North Carolina. WCA was founded in 1969 as a ministry of Grace Baptist Church and serves kindergarten through 12th grade students. The school focuses on providing conservative Christian education and is committed to offering students an academically challenging course of study in an environment that is conducive to spiritual growth. The goal is to produce students who will glorify God with their lives while successfully competing in today's world.

Academics, athletics and the fine arts are combined to give students a well-rounded educational experience. The elementary curriculum strongly emphasizes the basic skills of reading and math augmented by studies in English, spelling, science, history, handwriting and health. Phonics-based reading instruction is given from kindergarten through grade 3. Hands-on learning projects and practice drills are combined to enhance math instruction. Students are also taught art, music, physical education and library skills. Private and group lessons are available in the instrumental music program. Subject integrated computer application training begins in kindergarten.

Students in grades 9 through 12 follow one of three academic tracks: general, college preparatory or honors. Honors and advanced courses in math and science, such as calculus and physics, are available. Computer training is integrated with the curriculum, giving graduates a working knowledge of word processing, spreadsheets, desktop publishing, Internet research, multi-media presentations and more. Students can also take advantage of formal group training in art, drama, music (choral and instrumental) and journalism. Private instrumental lessons are also available. Resource classes are available for students with mild learning disabilities.

The Academy's sports program includes soccer, basketball, baseball and golf for boys and volleyball, tennis, basketball, softball and cheerleading for girls.

Most students graduate with more than 26 high school credits. Graduates gain acceptance into major Christian colleges as well as public and private universities across the United States. Students also enjoy the benefits of excellent facilities, including a well-equipped 25-station computer lab, two science labs, a media center, a gymnasium, a full-service cafeteria and several athletic fields and playgrounds. WCA is a member of the North Carolina Christian School Association and the American Association of Christian Schools.

Wilmington Academy of Arts & Sciences Middle School
4126 S. College Rd., Wilmington
(910) 392-3139

Providing a high-quality, academically challenging curriculum and a learning environment free of behavioral disruptions, Wilmington Academy of Arts & Sciences (W.A.A.S.) offers students in grades 4 through 8 an exceptional educational opportunity. With class size limited to 18 and an experienced, professional faculty, the Academy strives to meet the needs of young adolescents preparing for a successful future. Teachers encourage students to reach well beyond the minimum standards, allowing them to thrive in a positive, dynamic environment.

A traditional core of subjects including language arts, literature, social studies, math and science are approached with integrated and interactive methods. Spanish, physical education, band and art are offered also. Tennis, student government, Science Olympiad, Odyssey of the Mind and MathCounts are available as extracurricular activities. Students use computers extensively and learn word processing, database management, spreadsheet design and interpretation, presentation software and Internet applications.

A parent-driven, nondenominational, not-for-profit corporation, W.A.A.S. depends on parent participation, requiring 35 volunteer hours per year from each enrolled family. Information and application materials can be received by calling the school or visiting the school website.

Wilmington Montessori School
4008 S. College Rd., Wilmington
(910) 612-5678

Wilmington Montessori School opened its doors in 2003 with a classic program of instruction for children ages three through 12 years. Here students work at their own pace and are able to choose appropriate work in an environment specially designed for them. In addition to its Primary Program for three through six-year-olds, WMS offers the area's only Montessori Elementary Program; two age groups, designated as Junior and Senior, discover the world beyond themselves and develop their intellect with the aid of an experienced professional staff.

A broad, inquiry-based, individualized curriculum developed by the Albanesi Educational Center incorporates all aspects of learning and is tailored to the developmental needs and abilities of each age. Included are the traditional subjects of math, language, science and social studies. WMS also offers studio art and art history, chess, foreign language, yoga, health and physical education. The school provides a well-rounded music education, including choir, an individual weekly piano lesson for each elementary-aged student, Orff instruments and recorder.

Students benefit by having a talented staff of experienced Montessori professionals who bring to the school a wealth of knowledge. With diverse backgrounds, these dedicated women have impressive credentials and great love for what they do, which shows in the progress they achieve with each child.

The school enjoys a beautiful, spacious setting that includes ample grassy areas, a nature trail, a fenced play yard, an outdoor learning center, and basketball and volleyball courts. A homelike feeling and positive atmosphere foster a wonderful environment for learning. A nondenominational, non-profit, 503 (c) (3) organization, the Wilmington Montessori School invites parents to join them in watching their children grow into healthy, happy individuals. For information about tours and admissions, call (910) 612-5678.

Brunswick County

L&L Montessori School
4150 Vanessa Dr., Southport
(910)454-7344

Montessori education is based upon the principles developed by Maria Montessori, the first woman physician to graduate in Italy. When you enter L&L Montessori School, you will see that the tables and chairs are child sized and the shelves are low so that materials are readily accessible to the students. You can see that the environment has been designed to reflect the children. The focus of the system is the development of materials, educational techniques and observations which support the natural development of children, and many of the

skills were designed to teach children how to become more independent. The students are taught one on one and move ahead at their own pace, fulfilling contracts made with the teacher. In addition to basics, students learn zoology, botany, geology, history and even Latin. Some work is done using computers, and art classes are held weekly.

Southport Christian School
8070 River Rd. SE, Southport
(910) 457-5060

Southport Christian School is an independent, interdenominational Christian school dedicated to the spiritual and academic growth of children. Parents and clergy concerned about quality education for their children founded the school in 1996 to provide an aggressive, solid academic foundation in a nurturing, loving environment. The school is housed in an addition to the Cape Fear Alliance Church and is a permitted use of the church itself for weekly Friday chapel service. During this time pastors, puppet and mime ministries, singers, missionaries and others give a program. Growth from 24 students (Pre-K to K–5) in the first year to 137 students in 2005 speaks well for the success of the endeavor. Each class has a maximum of 16 students. The school stresses a traditional education with phonics-based reading and incremental math and is a member of the Association of Christian Schools International. In addition to basic subjects, each student is exposed to art, music, physical education, sign language and Spanish. The Spanish class stresses culture as well as the language. P.E. and art classes are sometimes held outdoors in the woods surrounding the school where nature walks and exploration on the trails are included.

The Evelyn Smith Wray Village School
720 Whiteville Rd., NW, Shallotte
(910) 754-2072

The folks at The Evelyn Smith Wray Village School understand their role in helping your child to become responsible, informed, compassionate individuals. Their philosophy states: "...children learn best through active, hands-on, meaningful experience and individual attention in a positive learning environment." The curriculum is literature based and integrated. Phonics as well as whole language skills are taught. All teachers are certified by the State of North Carolina, and the North Carolina Standard Course of Study is the minimum taught to students. In addition to the basics, children are introduced to music, including classical musicians and various instruments; art, which introduces the style and works of artists such as Picasso and Monet and encourages the talent inherent in each child. As part of the physical education program all students participate in the Presidential Physical Fitness Program. Other classes include introduction to Spanish, computer classes and etiquette. As their motto — "It takes a village" — indicates, they are well aware of the role each person plays in a child's growth. In this vein parents are encouraged to volunteer at the school, guest speakers are invited to talk to the children and field trips are taken to such places as museums and libraries.

Special Education

Child Development Center, Inc.
3802 Princess Place Dr., Wilmington
(910) 343-4245

The Child Development Center is a developmental preschool serving both typically developing and special needs children from 1 to 5 years old. The center has a long history of working with children who have developmental delays and disabilities. All children are served in small classes with a highly qualified staff. The center is a United Way partner agency. Operating hours are 7:30 AM to 5:30 PM weekdays. Call for information on enrollment and openings.

Easter Seals UCP
Developmental Center, Inc.
500 Military Cutoff Rd., Wilmington
(910) 392-0080

Children from New Hanover and surrounding counties who have physical and/or other developmental delays can be referred by a parent, physician or community agency to this inclusive preschool. The Easter Seals UCP Developmental Center is a five-star licensed center and is accredited by NAEYC. The center serves children from birth to 5 years of age who have cerebral palsy, motor delays or other developmental concerns. They also accept students without special developmental needs because the agency believes it is beneficial to bring students with and without special needs together in a quality preschool program. Educators and therapists facilitate learning through play and promote development in areas such as gross and fine motor skills, speech and language, social, emotional, cognitive and independence skills. ESUCP also has an outreach program, ECHOES (Enhancing Childhood through Outreach & Educational Services) that serves children in New Hanover and the surrounding five counties. They support inclusion of children with, or at risk of, special needs through consultation and technical assistance in community child care or preschool settings.

Home Schooling

The State of North Carolina permits schooling outside both public and private schools for children whose parents/guardians prefer to administer their education. Under the auspices of the N.C. Division of Non-Public Education in Raleigh, home schooling requires, for children between ages 7 and 16, registration, participation in annual standardized achievement testing and maintenance of immunization records. The educational program must operate on a regular schedule, excluding reasonable holidays and vacations, during at least nine calendar months a year by a person with a high school diploma or equivalency certificate; attendance records are required.

State statute defines a home school as "a non-public school in which the child receives academic instruction from the parent, legal guardian or a member of the household in which the child resides." The law also permits (no more than) two households to combine as one home school and allows the children from both households to be taught together by members of either household.

Growing consistently in popularity, home-school enrollment in Brunswick, Pender and New Hanover counties has soared. Statewide, the number of home schools went from 1,385 in 1988–89 to 31,530 in 2004–05, with a total enrollment of 53,780 home-schooled students.

A family considering home instruction would begin by obtaining a Home School Information Packet from the N.C. Division of Non-Public Education, either by going to their website www.ncdnpe.org, or calling (919) 733-4276. Twenty-four-hour voicemail is available.

Support for home-schooling families is offered by North Carolinians for Home Education (NCHE). This organization was instrumental in formulating the bill that the state legislature approved. NCHE is the state's primary advocacy group today. An excellent resource, NCHE has a full-time staff in Raleigh and can be reached at (919) 790-1100. The web address is www.nche.com; links to support groups and other resources are available.

Several local support groups can be found in New Hanover, Pender and Brunswick counties; however, it's not always easy. First call Kathryn Iandoli, Region 11 Director for NCHE, who is also President for Christian Home Educators of Wilmington, (910) 452-9685. She can be quite helpful in directing you to other groups, most of which are centered in private homes; they tend to change leadership, and consequently phone numbers, often.

Child Care

A wide range of child-care facilities, preschools and programs is available in the greater Wilmington area. While we cannot list all of them here, we've provided a starting place. We encourage parents/guardians to visit facilities they are considering at least once and preferably several times prior to enrolling their youngsters.

After-school enrichment and youth development programs are offered by many day-care centers, schools, churches, the Wilmington Family YMCA and YWCA, the Wrightsville Beach Parks & Recreation Department, Girls Inc., Brigade Boys & Girls and other organizations. Check our chapters on Sports, Fitness and Parks and Kidstuff (Summer Camps, in particular). Again, a visit or two in advance is advisable.

Child Advocacy Commission
Child Care Resource and Referral Center
1401 S. 39th St., Wilmington
(910) 791-1057 ext. 18
The Child Advocacy Commission Child Care Resource and Referral (CCR&R)

maintains a detailed database of child-care resources in the area. As of November 2004, the Wilmington area had approximately 63 child-care centers and 119 family child-care homes listed in this database. A family child-care home can serve a maximum of five children ages infant to 13, but various stipulations may impact each situation. The CCR&R offers information and referrals at no cost, allowing parents to make informed decisions. The CCR&R provides helpful guidelines in determining which child-care situation is most appropriate for you and your family. They will provide a detailed list of questions to ask and things to look for.

The Division of Child Development licenses and regulates child-care facilities in North Carolina. Licensed child-care facilities are rated on a Star Rated License system. There are three components of the Star Rated License: Program, Education and Compliance Standards. A rating of "one star" identifies that the program meets North Carolina's minimum standards for a licensed child-care facility. Licenses with two to five stars represent higher levels of quality, with five stars signaling the highest level of quality care available. It is up to the child-care facility to apply for more than one star; it may apply for additional stars after the program has been open for at least six months. Each licensed facility must display its license.

The CCR&R encourages all parents to visit a prospective site several times in order to make the best choice possible. Complaints or concerns about a particular child-care facility should be directed to the Division of Child Development (DCD) at (800) 859-0829. A parent may also obtain a child-care facility's compliance history record by calling DCD.

The CCR&R also works to develop cooperative efforts with governmental and other community agencies to promote an awareness of children's issues. It sponsors community service activities, educational information and gives assistance to community agencies, civic groups and individuals. The CCR&R offers on-site training for child-care providers as well as parents. Check with the Child Advocacy Commission Child Care Resource and Referral Monday through Friday from 8:30 AM to 5 PM or visit the website for more information http://www.childadvocacy-wilm.org/

CLOSE-UP

South Brunswick High School's Aquaculture Program

High school students take an interest when learning is fun.

photo: Rebecca Pierre

Imagine yourself in a room surrounded by 18 display aquariums ranging in size from 55 to 200 gallons. Add to that six 500-gallon rearing tanks and four hatching troughs, and you will find yourself smack in the middle of the Aquaculture Lab at South Brunswick High School in Southport. In addition to the laboratory, there are four half-acre ponds, a reservoir and a classroom.

Instructor Byron Bey began the Aquaculture Program in 1987, raising fish in a ditch on school property. His creativity and excitement about the program along with hard work, the support of the school system, the enthusiasm of the students, a grant from the N.C. Fisheries Resource Grant Program and a great deal of community support have built the program to a level of excellence that sets a standard for the state and the nation. Testament to these facts are the awards the program has received, including being awarded Best in Show in the New Hanover County Fair for the past 15 years. The program also won the 2000 Governor's Program of Excellence in Education Award from N.C. Governor Mike Easley.

Mr. Bey was voted the South Brunswick High School Teacher of the Year in 2001 and in 2004 by his peers and the Brunswick County Association of Educators. In 2003, Mr. Bey was appointed N.C. Ambassador of Agriculture by Meg Phipps, N.C. Commissioner of Agriculture. And in 2004 he was nominated for the national Disney Hand Teacher Awards.

The South Brunswick High School Aquaculture Program participates in the Governor's Vocational Rehabilitation Program and the Governor's Job Ready Program as well. This program strives to provide work experience, jobs and scholarships for as many students as possible. Students volunteer at the US Open King Mackerel Tournament and, in 2003, in concert with Mr. Bey, at the Fort Fisher Aquarium where they also made a presentation.

Many skills are required for the day-to-day operation of the program. Using the Aquaculture Science textbook as a guide and having Mr. Bey as a leader, the students not only study the materials, but experience their practical applications as well. Mr. Bey says this hands-on approach is key to preparing the students for the next level. The chapters in the textbook read like a list of separate occupations, an indication of the many fields of study and the diverse occupations, from fish farming to research, which await graduates of the program:

In the third year of the program, students spend two days a week at Brunswick Community College studying college level aquaculture and the other three days at the high school doing hands-on tasks. This gives them the advantage of a smooth transition from the high school setting to a college and has sometimes been the impetus behind students furthering their education. In North Carolina, students can continue their education at Brunswick Community College and UNC Wilmington or NC State in Raleigh in fields such as Aquaculture, Mariculture or Fisheries Biology.

Ponds are essential to any aquaculture program. They allow the students live experience and training needed to survive in the field. Because the program is almost self-sustaining in that few fish are purchased and most are raised in the program, a lesson in the life cycle underlies the activities performed by the students. Eggs are gathered from the spawning pens in the ponds and transported to the hatching troughs. When they have hatched, they are moved to the rearing tanks where they are fed, tended and allowed to grow to adult size. From there they are transported back to the ponds and/or spawning pens and the cycle begins again. Sound simple? About as simple as life.

But Aquaculture does not stop here. In 2004, Tim Barefoot of Barefoot Fishing and Bonner Stiller, a local legislator approached Bob Wilkerson, high school principal, about the possibility of including a southern Flounder Hatchery in the program. Mr. Bey and the students did some informational research and found that Dr. Wade Watanabe of UNCW and Dr. Harry Daniels of NCSU are achieving the best results in southern flounder culture.

With the help of Representative Bonner Stiller, Tim Barefoot and a committee of NC CCA members, Mike Ward and Will Morgan, a site for the hatchery was located at South Brunswick High School after which Speaker of the House of Representatives, Richard Morgan, offered $18,000 for development of the southern flounder hatchery. Subsequently, the Brunswick County School Board voted unanimously to provide matching funds.

A training tour of UNCW's Southern Flounder Hatchery Facility lead by Dr. Wade Watanabe and staff in Wrightsville Beach was provided to students of the program. An advisory committee formed by Mr. Bey worked with the NC Marine Fisheries, UNCW and NCSU. Aquatic Eco-Systems from Apopka FL volunteered to help design and construct the hatchery which was completed in 2005. Royce Potter of Potter's Seafood in Southport provided adult flounder for the hatchery and Chris Woolridge at UNCW helped obtain eggs and fry. NC Marine Fisheries granted the only license ever granted for stock enhancement of 25,000 southern flounder in NC public waters. As a model program for other schools, the program will receive visits from far flung school systems beginning with a recent visit from Virginia Beach. The effect this hatchery will have on the promotion of ocean conservation will help pave the way for saltwater hatcheries in NC and beyond.

South Brunswick High School's Aquaculture lab.

photo: Rebecca Pierre

Below we have listed child-care facilities with four or five stars as indicated on the Child Advocacy Commission website and N.C. Department of Health and Human Services, Division of Child Development website in November 2003. The Insiders' Guide provides this information for your convenience only and does not endorse any facility.

WILMINGTON

A Child's World Daycare Home, 501 Manet Road, Wilmington, (910) 350-1332

Adventurous Beginnings, 202 Westchester Road, Wilmington, (910) 395-0751

AAI Industries Learning Center, 1206 N. 23rd Street, Wilmington, (910) 254-7384

Brighter Day Daycare Center, 1409 Church Street, Wilmington, (910) 343-9651

Cape Fear Community College Child Development Center, 415 N. Second Street, Wilmington, (910) 362-7336

Charlie's Daycare Home, 4817 Calder Court, Wilmington, (910) 791-5102

Chesterbrook Academy, 4102 Peachtree Road, Wilmington, (910) 392-4637

Child Development Center, 3802 Princess Place, Wilmington, (910) 343-4245

Childcare Network #128, 6640 Gordon Road, Wilmington, (910) 397-9090

Childcare Network #83 1553 41st Street, Wilmington, (910) 395-5400

Childcare Network #82, 4808 New Centre Drive, Wilmington, (910) 452-4444

Children's Learning Center, 71 Darlington Avenue, Wilmington, (910) 762-7735

Community Action Child Development Center, 527 Red Cross Street, Wilmington, (910) 763-0056

Creative Angels Childcare, 2404 Invergordon Court, Wilmington, (910) 799-1938

Creative World Preschool, 4202 Wilshire Boulevard, Wilmington, (910) 791-2080

Creative World II, 2411 Flint Drive, Wilmington, (910) 799-5195

East Coast Solutions Kelly House, 1507 Martin Street, Wilmington, (910) 251-8944

Grandma & Grandpa's Child Care, 705 S. Third Street, Wilmington, (910) 251-1015

Happy Kids Development Center, 6320 Carolina Beach Road, Wilmington, (910) 395-5286

Head Start of New Hanover County, 507 N. Sixth Street (Sixth and Red Cross Streets), Wilmington, (910) 762-1177

Helping Hands, 712 Autumn Leaves Ct., Wilmington, (910) 799-0995

Hoods Day Care Center, 419 Rutledge Drive, Wilmington, (910) 799-6266

Kid Cam Preschool, 5901 Wrightsville Avenue, Wilmington, (910) 799-6882

Little Feats Day Care, 214 Mohican Trail, Wilmington, (910) 392-5564

Little Sisters Day Care Home, 7213 Quail Wood Road, Wilmington, (910) 791-8614

Ms. Peaches Christian Day Care, 1403 Castle Street, Wilmington, (910) 763-1133

Nanatta's Day Care, 1006 N. Eighth Street, Wilmington, (910) 762-2490

Noah's Ark Children's Center, 1501 Beasley Road, Wilmington, (910) 395-0059

Ms. Susan's Child Care, 310 Windemere Road, Wilmington, (910) 791-8048

Park Avenue Preschool, 1306 Floral Parkway, Wilmington, (910) 791-6217

Pat's Toyland Child Care, 613 Fitzgerald Drive, Wilmington, (910) 395-0391

Peek-a-boo Childcare, 4820 Weybridge Lane, Wilmington, (910) 392-6975

Potter's House Child Development Center, 4918 Randall Parkway, Wilmington, (910) 793-6730

Precious Little Angels, 305 Godfrey Court, Wilmington, (910) 452-2401

Progressive Child Development Center, 4403 Northchase Parkway NE, Wilmington, (910) 313-0083

Rich's Child Care and Learning Center, 625 S. 4th Street, Wilmington, (910) 762-4066

Rich's Child Care and Learning Center #2, 812 D Castle Street, Wilmington, (910) 763-1891

Rich's Child Care & Learning Center #3, 3910 Market Street, Wilmington, (910) 341-7577

Rising Stars Child Care Center, 6743 Amsterdam Way, Wilmington, (910) 452-2231

Sprouts Day Provider for Infants and Toddlers, 805 Sago Bay Drive, Wilmington, (910) 792-9399

Sunny Days Child Care, 1216 Potomac Court, Wilmington, (910) 791-2833

Total Child Care Center, Inc., 4304 Henson Drive, Wilmington, (910) 799-3556

Twilight Child Care, 111 Green Meadows Drive, Wilmington, (910) 262-0917

UCP Developmental Center, 500 Military Cutoff Road, Wilmington, (910) 392-0080

Vic's Child Care, 406 Kingston Road, Wilmington, (910) 313-1597

UCP Developmental Center, 500 Military Cutoff Road, Wilmington, (910) 392-0080

Winter Park Baptist Preschool and Kindergarten, 4700 Wrightsville Avenue, Wilmington, (910) 799-2029

BRUNSWICK COUNTY

Babies Learning Center, 705 N. Lord Street, Southport, (910) 457-9262

Calabash Day Care, SR 1371 Thomasboro Road, Calabash, (910) 579-1104

Childcare Network #85, 802 E. Leonard Street, Southport, (910) 457-0555

For Kids Only & Brunswick Academy of Total Learning, 344 Mulberry Road, Shallotte, (910) 754-7777

For Kids Only Child Development Center, Inc. After School Program, 344 Mulberry Street, Shallotte, (910) 754-7777

Kids World, 713 Caswell Avenue, Southport, (910) 457-0187

Leland Family Literacy Center, 9272 Post Office Road, Leland, (910) 371-5760

Little Sandpiper's Learning Center, 972 Old Ocean Highway, Bolivia, (910) 754-3113

Longwood Head Start Center, 360 Mt. Zion Road, Longwood, (910) 287-3637

Piney Grove Head Start Center, SR 1445, 71 N. Piney Grove Road, Bolivia, (910) 253-8155

**SOLA – School of Learning and Art
216 Pine Grove Rd., Wilmington
(910) 798-1700**

SOLA offers something for creative children of all ages and abilities. Among the many wonderful programs are the following.

SOLA's Pre-School is a program for 3- to 5-year-olds, offering a curriculum balanced with school preparatory academics, fine arts and developmental skills. Morning Half Day is from 8:30 AM to 12:15 PM. Space is limited, so call for wait list information.

SOLA's After Pre-School Art Program is held from 1 to 3 PM or until 5 PM. Drop-ins are welcome on a daily or weekly basis. This class is for 3- to 5-year-olds not registered for SOLA's morning pre-school. Students will experience a very relaxed class, plenty of fun and exploration with pottery, paint, glue and more. Think of it as a very artsy midday pre-school.

SOLA's After-School program offers classes in drawing, painting, mixed media, pottery and music. Also available is a non-traditional after-school care program for young artists ages kindergarten through fifth grade from 2:30 to 6 PM.

SOLA's Home School program can take care of the art and music instruction for your curriculum. Classes are designed to meet all media and cultural exposure across grade levels in a child-friendly art studio. Students are thoroughly immersed in the creative process. Parents are welcome to stay and play, too!

SOLA's Summer Camp for boys and girls puts the fun in summer camp; it features week-long sessions with age-appropriate groups and activities. Choose either Half Day Camp from 8:30 AM to 12:30 PM or Full Day Camp from 8:30 AM to 4:30 PM. Kids enjoy both indoor and outdoor activities. Messy, fabulous arts and crafts are an integral part of every day. Students create pottery on the wheel and by hand, make their own T-shirts, experience paint and glue in ways they never have before while building a variety of theme-based projects. Campers play with new and old friends in a home-like workshop and backyard environment. Teachers at SOLA don't just babysit, they rock the house. Signing up is "easy as pie in the face!"

HIGHER EDUCATION AND RESEARCH

Southeastern North Carolina features some of the most outstanding universities and colleges in the state. Dating back to its beginnings, this area was famous not for its tourism, but its prosperous commercial industries. As a result, education and research have played a major role in helping the southern coast continue to grow and expand to meet the needs of local businesses.

Now, as North Carolina's southern coast finds itself thrown in the limelight of popularity, more people are deciding to move here permanently, including many new and exciting industries. Research companies such as PPD and AAI Pharma have made Wilmington their home, as have major corporations such as DuPont and General Electric Company. Higher education, therefore, is working hard to meet the demands of booming industry.

The University of North Carolina at Wilmington is focusing its academics to connect student learning across four broad themes: information technology, internationalization, natural environment and regional engagement, so students graduate with a sense of civic responsibility and leadership. Cape Fear Community College and Brunswick Community College have added new buildings to meet the needs of their expanding enrollment.

The research industry also is increasing in importance and size. Not surprisingly, the major emphases of the research performed in the area are in the fields of oceanography,

wetland and estuarine studies, marine biomedical and environmental physiology, and marine biotechnology and aquaculture.

Universities and Colleges

University of North Carolina at Wilmington
601 S. College Rd., Wilmington
(910) 962-3000

At UNCW, passionate and engaged teaching, learning and research matter. It is unique in its dedication to combining a small-college commitment to excellence in teaching with a research university's opportunities for student involvement in significant faculty scholarship. UNCW has the fourth highest freshman SAT average (1134), the third highest freshman retention rate (85.7 percent), and the third highest six-year graduation rate (61.2 percent) in the UNC system. For the eighth year, UNCW was seventh among the top public master's universities in the South by U.S. News & World Report, and Barron's Profiles of American Colleges lists UNCW at the "very competitive" level. Founded in 1947, UNCW's enrollment has grown to more than 11,600 students. A total of 73 undergraduate and 28 graduate programs are offered. The university is committed to service as both an obligation and opportunity to improve the quality of life of the institution and the quality of life in the region. It has a strong commitment to adult learners and offers short, non-credit university courses, seminars, lectures, travel excursions and other educational opportunities. With more than 1,900 faculty and staff and $160 million in campus construction in process, UNCW has a significant economic impact on the region.

At UNCW, passionate and engaged teaching, learning and research matter. UNCW is an active learning community that uniquely combines a small-college commitment to excellence in teaching with a re-

Adults can continue their education or just have fun by taking courses or attending programs offered by UNCW's Division for Public Service and Continuing Studies. Call for information and request a copy of Pathways, their Lifelong Learning Catalog, (910) 962-4034.

search university's opportunities for student involvement in significant faculty scholarship.

The university offers a culture that fosters creative, critical and reflective thinking; lifelong learning; communication and interaction; a celebration of diversity of people and ideas; commitment to improving the quality of life on and off campus; ecological diversity and sound environmental stewardship; and personal achievement and integrity.

Excellence in undergraduate teaching at the forefront of knowledge and technology has been a hallmark at UNCW, recognized and rewarded since its inception. At UNCW, students are afforded opportunities to learn through collaborative scholarly activities with world-class faculty at a level that rivals exclusive research institutions of a similar size.

The university is committed to service as both an obligation and an opportunity to improve the quality of life of the institution and the quality of life in the region.

UNCW, which is ranked as one of the top 10 public comprehensive universities in the South by U.S. News & World Report, enrolls approximately 11,300 students and offers 71 bachelor's degrees, 22 master's degrees and a Ph.D. in marine biology. The university is made up of the College of Arts and Sciences; the Cameron School of Business; the Watson School of Education, one of only three UNC institutions producing more than 300 teachers each year; the School of Nursing; and the Graduate School, whose 978 students are engaged in cutting-edge research and scholarship and fill a vital role in the undergraduate instructional mission of UNCW.

Situated on a 661-acre tract bordering South College Road, UNCW is in the midst of the largest construction effort in its history. A classroom building and resource center for the Watson School of Education opened in fall 2004, and a new student services center was opened in the renovated and expanded Westside Hall in 2005. Currently under construction, renovation or expansion is historic Hoggard Hall, a sports medicine facility; a cultural arts building; and the University Union. Work will soon begin on a computer information systems building and a 524-bed apartment-style complex.

UNCW offers four-year programs leading to the Bachelor of Arts, the Bachelor of Fine Arts, the Bachelor of Music, the Bachelor of

Science and the Bachelor of Social Work degrees. Graduate programs lead to the Master of Education, Master of Arts, Master of Science, Master of Fine Arts in Creative Writing, Master of Public Administration, Master of Social Work, Master of School Administration, Master of Business Administration, Master of Science in Accountancy and Master of Science in Nursing degrees. A Ph.D. in marine biology, the only such degree in the state and one of only three on the East Coast, is offered in addition to a cooperative Ph.D. in marine science with N.C. State University.

Also offered are 44 disciplinary and interdisciplinary minors as well as undergraduate certification in geographic information science and professional writing. Post-baccalaureate certification programs are offered in environmental studies, gerontology and Hispanic studies.

Pre-professional programs are offered in allied health, health-related careers, dentistry, law, medicine, optometry, pharmacy, physical therapy, podiatry, veterinary medicine and cooperative environmental science and environmental engineering programs with N.C. State University and one in engineering with North Carolina's three state-supported Colleges of Engineering.

UNCW's Randall Library contains more than 530,000 volumes, subscribes to more than 3,668 serial titles and employs state-of-the-art electronic informational resources. The library is a partial repository for U.S. government publications and has a current inventory of 623,000 items in hard copy and microtext. Randall Library is a full repository for North Carolina documents, which are available to all users, including non-students. Non-students may obtain checkout privileges for up to four items per visit. Those under age 65 with a N.C. driver license pay $15 a year; there is no charge for people over 65 with a valid N.C. driver license.

Other instructional and research resources at UNCW include the Center for Marine Science at Myrtle Grove, the Upperman African-American Cultural Center, campus-wide computing services with wireless Internet access and the Ev-Henwood Nature Preserve at Town Creek. Kenan Auditorium hosts theatrical, symphonic and instructional events year round.

As a part of its regional engagement, UNCW offers lifelong learning programs through the Division for Public Service and Continuing Studies. Because they respond to the interests and feedback from the region, lifelong learning activities encompass the interests and passions of youth, professionals and retirees.

The Adult Scholars Leadership Program and Leadership Wilmington, sponsored by UNCW and the Greater Wilmington Chamber Foundation, provide opportunities for participants to discuss regional issues with leaders in economic development, education, government and the business communities. The scholars program is geared to older adults and retirees who have recently relocated to the area. Leadership Wilmington attracts mid-level managers who seek to serve on regional boards and influence policy.

The Lifelong Learning Society presents opportunities for intellectual, cultural and social growth through quality programs consistent with the university's outreach mission. For those selecting intellectual stimulation along with social interactions, the Tabitha Hutaff McEachern Lifelong Learning Series features educational and entertaining programs with a catered meal.

Based at the Center for Marine Science at Myrtle Grove, MarineQuest is a popular youth program that offers marine and environmental education through the Summer Science-by-the-Sea Day Camp, Coast Trek and OceanLab. It also offers the Odyssey Program for adults.

The area's colleges and universities provide our community with a tremendous pool of human resources, talent, energy and ability. Whether you're looking for child-care helpers, part-time office staff, interns, computer support, maintenance assistance, lawn care or what-have-you, remember that college students almost always need extra money and often are more than willing to offer their services. A good place to start would be the Student Affairs or Student Development office at UNCW.

UNCW partners with the community in Celebrate Wilmington! to promote the arts in the region through programs like the Walk of Fame and Lifetime Achievement Award in the Arts.

The UNCW Executive Development Center at the New Hanover County Northeast Regional Library offers corporate and community groups a state-of-the-art facility for professional meetings, retreats and small conferences. The center is designed to accommodate groups of various sizes and needs and offers high-speed wireless Internet, video conferencing, an on-site technician, a convenient location and ample parking.

UNCW's athletes excel not only on the playing field but in the classroom as well. The university's student-athletes have consistently recorded the highest graduation rates among NCAA Division 1 public universities in North Carolina for the four-year class average. The first NCAA Division I national average Academic Progress Rate rankings, released in March 2005, placed UNCW second behind Duke University. In the CAA UNCW ranks second behind William & Mary.

In March 2005, the men's swimming and diving team won its third consecutive Colonial Athletic Association championship. On the baseball diamond, the Seahawks won their first outright CAA title in 2004 when the conference championship was staged at Brooks Field. The Seahawks placed a record six players on the All-Conference team and went deep into the NCAA Regionals for the second straight year, winding up with a 40-23 mark. In 2005 UNCW hosts the CAA baseball championship for the second straight year.

UNCW sponsors 19 varsity teams, including men's and women's programs in basketball, tennis, golf, track and field, cross country, swimming, diving and soccer. Other varsity programs include volleyball, softball and baseball. Athletic facilities include the 6,100-seat Trask Coliseum; an Olympic-sized natatorium with diving well; a 3,000-seat baseball stadium, Brooks Field; a 2,000-seat soccer stadium; the Harold Greene Track and Field Complex; and Boseman Softball Field. Construction was also recently completed on an 18,000-square-foot sports medicine building.

CFCC *Works!*

- Over 50 job-training programs!
- College transfer degree
- Continuing Education classes
- Small class sizes
- Affordable tuition
- Day and night classes

Call (910) 362-7000

COMMUNITY COLLEGE

411 N. FRONT ST., WILMINGTON, NC 28401 - www.cfcc.edu

UNCW's school year is divided into four sessions consisting of the standard fall and spring semesters plus two summer sessions. For general university information, call (910) 962-3000. For information on undergraduate admissions call (910) 962-3243; for graduate studies call (910) 962-3135. For information on Public Service Programs and Continuing Studies call (910) 962-3195. Contact Randall Library at (910) 962-3760.

Cape Fear Community College
411 N. Front St., Wilmington
(910) 362-7000
www.cfcc.edu

CFCC is one of the fastest growing community colleges in North Carolina, both in enrollment and in program offerings. Dedicated to providing workforce training through trade, technical and college transfer programs, full-time and part-time, Cape Fear Community College exerts a major educational presence in the area and serves more than 26,000 students yearly.

The main campus is located along the Cape Fear River in downtown Wilmington. A new North Campus located on a 140-acre site in northern Hanover County offers over a dozen programs and continuing education classes. A Pender County satellite center is located in Burgaw, about 21 miles north of Wilmington, (910) 259-4966. Classes are also held at area schools and community centers.

CFCC offers 60 technical and vocational fields, along with a very popular college transfer program. The college's two-year Associate in Applied Science (A.A.S.) Degrees include: accounting, architectural technology, associate degree nursing, automotive systems technology, business administration, chemical technology, computer engineering technology, criminal justice technology, dental hygiene, e-commerce, early childhood associate, electrical/electronics technology (instrumental concentration), environmental science technology, heavy equipment and transport technology (marine systems concentration), hotel and restaurant management, information systems, interior design, landscape gardening, machining technology, marine technology, mechanical engineering technology, mechanical engineering technology (drafting and design concentration), network administration and support occupational therapy assistant, office systems technology, paralegal technology and radiography.

One-year diploma programs include: air conditioning, heating and refrigeration technology, auto-body repair, boat building, carpentry, cosmetology, dental assisting, early childhood associate, electrical/electronics technology (marine systems concentration), film/video production, industrial maintenance technology, marine propulsion systems, masonry, medical transcription, pharmacy technology, practical nursing and welding technology.

Twenty-two Certificate Programs range from six weeks to two semesters. They include many of the same areas as the diploma and degree-granting programs, but training is less comprehensive and of shorter duration. Some others are truck driver training, manicuring/nail technology, real estate and real estate appraisal, customer service and licensed practical nurse refresher.

As part of its continuing education services, the Cape Fear Community College's Center for Business, Industry and Government offers low-cost computer classes and provides customized seminars, workshops and training programs for local companies and organizations. Through the Gateway Program, CFCC offers college classes to high school students so that they can earn college credit while still in high school. The college offers free courses in high-school equivalency (GED), English as a Second Language (ESL) and adult literacy. Many other special programs and seminars are free or very reasonably priced.

CFCC's Marine Technology program is the only one of its kind on the East Coast. The college maintains small and large oceangoing vessels for the program, which is enhanced by a deep-water pier on the Cape Fear River at the Wilmington campus. One of these vessels was integral to the recovery of artifacts from the wreck of what is believed to be Blackbeard's flagship, Queen Anne's Revenge.

The college has a growing number of intercollegiate sports teams in men's basketball, golf and women's volleyball.

Day and evening classes in semester-long cycles are available at all campuses, and financial aid is available for eligible applicants. Cape Fear Community College is one of 59 colleges in the North Carolina Community College System and is accredited by the Southern Association of Colleges and Schools. The public is always welcome to visit the campus to see all that CFCC has to offer.

Miller-Motte Technical College
5000 Market St., Wilmington
(910) 392-4660, (800) 784-2110

For three-quarters of a century Miller-Motte Technical College has been a reputable leader in private career education. When it was founded in 1916 by Judge Leon Motte, the school provided courtroom stenography training. Today, the college has adjusted its course offerings as changes in business and industry have mandated. Building on a 90-year foundation, the college is poised to educate the next generation of Americans by offering a varied, cutting-edge curriculum that includes training in Microsoft Certified Systems Administrator (MCSA), A+ computer repair, information processing, administrative office technology, cosmetology, esthetics, massage therapy, medical assisting, surgical technology, management, and accounting, These programs range from nine-month certification programs to two-year Associate of Applied Science (A.A.S.) degrees. Bachelor of Science Degrees are now offered in Allied Health Management and Business Administration.

Classes are available day, evening and online. Registration is ongoing throughout the year. Financial Assistance is available for those who qualify, and the college offers lifetime job placement services for its graduates.

To further enhance the skills of its graduates and in order to increase the quality of its curriculum, Miller-Motte has partnered with Microsoft in offering computer education. Miller-Motte is accredited by the Accrediting Council for Independent Colleges and Schools and approved by the University of North Carolina Board of Governors and the North Carolina Community College System. The Miller-Motte campus moved to 5000 Market Street in 2004 in order to accommodate its expanding programs and an increase in student enrollment. Plans are underway for additional expansion.

**Mount Olive College, Wilmington Campus
1426 Commonwealth Dr., Wilmington
(910) 256-0255, (800) 300-7478**

With locations in Mount Olive, Wilmington, Goldsboro, New Bern and Research Triangle Park, MOC has made earning a college degree more achievable than ever for adults who are at least 21 years of age. A private, liberal arts institution dedicated to the total development of its students in an environment nurtured by Christian values, the college was founded in 1951 and is sponsored by the Convention of Original Free Will Baptists.

Mount Olive College offers two Bachelor of Science degrees, one in Management and Organizational Development and the other in Criminal Justice Administration. The college has a School of Business and six academic departments, including Fine Arts, Language and Literature, Recreation and Leisure Studies, Religion, Science, Mathematics and Social Studies.

Students with 60 semester hours of college credit may complete their degrees in Management and Organizational Development or Criminal Justice Administration by attending one four-hour class per week for 55 to 59 weeks. Registration is ongoing throughout the year.

A series of curricula designed specifically for working adults is called the Heritage Program. The three-semester format provides students with the core courses needed for associate or baccalaureate programs. MOC has a tradition of student-focused, supportive programming and teaching styles. Courses are discussion-oriented, emphasizing critical thinking and research papers. Classes, which meet at night and on weekends, are limited to 20 students who proceed through the curriculum together as a group, called a cohort. Tuition includes all books and fees.

The North Carolina Independent Colleges and Universities publication lists Mount Olive College as the third most affordable private college in the state. Mount Olive College is accredited by the Commission on Colleges of the Southern Association of Colleges and Schools to award associate and baccalaureate degrees. Financial assistance is available to all qualified students.

Find your place in the sun in the southern coastal region.

photo: Peter Doran

CLOSE-UP A Hermit's Path

His life has been the subject of a book, a documentary, several articles and countless stories. Thousands of people visited him, some traveling great distances, even paying to have their photo taken with him. Those who have met him are still talking about their encounters more than 30 years later. Movie star? Famous athlete? No, just a man who longed for something we all crave at times — a simple life.

A marker tells the story of the Fort Fisher Hermit

photo: Gretchen Saule

The Fort Fisher hermit himself explained his popularity in an article published in the New Hanover Sun in 1968, "Everybody ought to be a hermit a few minutes to an hour or so every 24 hours, to study, meditate, and commune with their creator... millions of people want to do just what I'm doing, but since it is much easier thought of than done, they subconsciously elect me to represent them, that's why I'm successful..."

In 1956, 63-year-old Robert Harrill, the man now known as the Fort Fisher hermit, moved into an abandoned WWII army bunker in the marshland along Carolina Beach. He wanted to be closer to nature and further from society, an escape that may have been prompted by a painful past (he grew up in a violent, dysfunctional family and his eldest son committed suicide during the Depression). The tiny concrete bunker would be his home for the next 16 years. He furnished the bunker with scraps of wood and assorted debris brought in by the tide. The marshes supplied him with plenty of seafood, which he called a "millionaire's rations." Several stray cats and dogs along with raccoons, skunks and other wild creatures shared the rations and gave him companionship. He told anyone who asked that he was there to write a book about his family, entitled "A Tyrant in Every Home." Although a complete manuscript has never been found, letters to family and friends as well as notes for the book provide some insight into his personal history before he began life as a hermit.

During the turbulent '60s, word spread about the small, weatherworn old man who loved to talk and would share his philosophy and the day's catch with anyone who dropped some change in his frying pan. Before long his guest book contained thousands of signatures. The Fort Fisher hermit captivated visitors of all ages with his passionate harangues against the ills of society. He referred to these lectures as his School of Common Sense. Never shy about speaking his mind, the hermit had an opinion about everything. According to his common sense philosophy, "The folks on this old globe live too doggone fast. They should slow down and live... and learn to relax."

Despite what many would like to imagine, life on the beach wasn't always idyllic. Complications came in the form of mosquitoes, brutal heat, hurricanes, drunken teenagers, local authorities who considered him a vagrant, and developers who wanted to utilize the land surrounding the bunker. The Fort Fisher hermit had to struggle continuously to maintain his way of life. He was even kidnapped once by two men who robbed and beat him. Living in isolation made him vulnerable while his different approach to life sometimes made him the target of violence and cruelty. These hardships only gave the hermit more tales to tell, bolstering his determination to persevere.

People continue to be fascinated by the Fort Fisher hermit for many reasons, not the least of which is the individuality and self-sufficiency he has come to represent. Apparently, he was also quite a character. He often used wit and humor to get himself out of trouble. After falling asleep on the beach one sunny afternoon, and subsequently being charged with vagrancy, Mr. Harrill defended himself by informing the judge that perhaps he should lock up the tourists in the area, because they all appeared to be vagrants as well.

The abandoned bunker where the hermit lived.

photo: Gretchen Saule

More than 30 years after his death, the Fort Fisher hermit still touches the lives of people who've met him. Michael Edwards, the President of the Hermit Society and author of The Battle for Independence: The Story of the Fort Fisher Hermit, describes how the hermit's life has become a source of inspiration, "His life is a story made for movies – about adversity and human courage and strength through hardship, failure and disappointment. Robert felt people needed to take responsibility for their lives. He never gave up on himself – that's the story I want to tell adults and the elderly." The Hermit Society is made up of friends of Robert Harrill and those inspired by him, who get together to swap stories, plan celebrations in his honor and support one another in their individuality. Memories of the Fort Fisher hermit continue to reflect the epitaph on his headstone, "He Made People Think."

Although Robert Harrill died in 1972 (and there are some questions surrounding the cause of his death), the empty bunker remains. While enjoying Kure Beach, take some time out to follow a hermit's path. There's a hiking trail along the Fort Fisher area of Kure Beach that winds through the marshes and past the hermit's bunker. You can enter the trail from behind the Fort Fisher Recreation Center or the Aquarium. Or take the Fort Fisher Hermit Kayak tour (Kayak Carolina, 1337 Bridge Barrier Road, Carolina Beach, (910) 458-9111), and kayak through the waterways to an observation deck in the marsh. From there it's a short hike to the bunker, where you'll hear tales of the Fort Fisher hermit. With a little imagination, everyone can experience the life of a hermit for a couple hours.

Brunswick Community College
U.S. Hwy. 17 N., Supply
(910) 755-7300
705 N. Lord St., Southport
(910) 371-2400
Leland Industrial Park, Leland
(910) 457-6329, (800) 754-1050

Brunswick Community College has been serving Brunswick County since 1979 and currently enrolls more than 10,000 curriculum and continuing education students at its three locations. The college offers one and two-year certificates, diploma and associate's degree programs in addition to job skills training and workforce development.

BCC is meeting the future needs of Brunswick County through expansion and is currently constructing new facilities for Horticulture/Turfgrass and Early Childhood Education. Continuing Education Centers will be built in Supply, Southport and the South Brunswick Islands and a new Student Center is planned along with additions to the BCC Odell Williamson Auditorium and Leland Center.

Associate Degree Programs may allow students to transfer credits to a four-year college and include: aquaculture, associate degree nursing, electronics engineering, health information, horticulture, industrial systems, office systems, turfgrass management technologies, business administration, college transfer, computer programming, cosmetology, information systems, early childhood associate, early childhood associate/special education, and early childhood associate/teacher associate.

Diploma and Certificate Programs provide an opportunity for advanced training in less than two years. Programs include: air conditioning, heating and refrigeration, aquaculture, general occupational, health information, Internet, office systems, and turfgrass management technologies, cosmetology, business administration/electronic commerce, early childhood associate, information systems/network administration and support, and practical nursing.

BCC offers a variety of distance learning classes in both curriculum and personal enrichment areas. These courses are taught via Internet, telecourse and interactive video.

Community and continuing education courses provide an outlet for community members to learn news skills or participate in classes for fun. Learning opportunities include emergency services training, and computer skills classes and free basic skills training include English as a Second Language (ESL), adult high school and high school equivalency (GED). Individuals have access to more than 300 online courses through BCC. The college also houses the BCC Interagency program, an educational/ vocational/ developmental program for adults with developmental disabilities.

Through its New and Expanding Industry Program and its Small Business Center, BCC works closely with area business and industry to tailor skills training to their needs. The college assists industry in seeking, evaluating, training and retraining employees according to changing standards. BCC will custom-design courses to fit various needs and typically conducts industrial courses at the job site to upgrade employees to associate degree levels.

The BCC library provides college students, faculty, staff, and adult residents of the county with access to a variety of educational resources and services. Twenty thousand educational resources are available in the library collection and can be searched using the online catalog. Several computer workstations are available in the library for access to educational information online.

The Brunswick Educational Transition Center serves residents whose first language is not English. The center is a collaboration between BCC, Brunswick County Public Schools and the government of Mexico. This is the first center of its kind in the United States.

The BCC Odell Williamson Auditorium is a 1,500-seat facility that serves as the Center for the Arts in Southeastern North Carolina. The center provides artistic expression to the region in the form of music, theatre, concerts, and much more. (See our Arts chapter.)

The purpose of the BCC athletic program is to promote and encourage in such a way that results will be consistent and supportive with the total educational purpose of Brunswick Community College. In 2004–2005 the BCC Men's Basketball team won the NJCAA Region 10 Division 1 championship. The college also offers women's basketball, a cheerleading squad, and a mascot, Dunkin the Dolphin.

BCC is widely known as an educational value for the tuition dollar. Some classes are tuition free for N.C. residents 65 years old and older. The main campus in Supply is about 25 miles south of Wilmington.

Research Facilities

UNCW Center for Marine Science
5600 Marvin K. Moss Ln., Wilmington
(910) 962-2301

The Center for Marine Science at the University of North Carolina at Wilmington is dedicated to interdisciplinary approaches to questions in basic marine research. The mission of the center is to promote basic and applied research in the fields of oceanography, coastal and estuarine studies, marine biology, marine chemistry, marine geology, marine biotechnology and aquaculture. Faculty members conducting marine science research in the departments of biology and marine biology, chemistry and biochemistry, earth sciences, and physics and physical oceanography participate in this program.

Faculty also serve on regional, national and international research and policy advisory groups, thereby contributing to the development of agendas on marine research in the United States and the world. International interactions with labs in Europe, North and South America, Australia, New Zealand, Asia, Africa, Bermuda, the Bahamas and Caribbean, and all regions of the coastal United States augment extensive programs addressing North Carolina coastal issues. By integrating these advisory functions with research programs of the highest quality, CMS enhances the educational experience provided by UNCW for both undergraduate and graduate students in marine science.

Located on the Intracoastal Waterway (ICW), just six miles from the main campus, the Marine Science Center has a total of 75,000 square feet of net indoor space, which includes group meeting facilities for up to 150 individuals, fully equipped research laboratories, classrooms, marine science laboratories, a greenhouse with running seawater, a radioisotope lab, computer workrooms, cold rooms, walk-in freezers, temperature-controlled rooms, fireproof data storage vault and shower/locker rooms. Core facilities include harmful algal identification and toxicology; nutrient analysis; DNA sequencing; and NMR spectroscopy.

A 900-foot pier, which can accommodate several coastal research vessels, is in place on the Intracoastal Waterway. The location of the new center provides easy access to regional marine environments such as tidal marshes/mud flats/sand flats; tidal creeks; barrier islands and tidal inlets; the Atlantic Intracoastal Waterway; near-shore forests; and both highly developed and minimally developed estuarine environments. The center maintains 19 research vessels ranging in size from 16 to 70 feet and specialized equipment including a Superphantom Remotely Operated Vehicle (ROV), an ocean environmental sample (SBE-CTD), and an ADCP current profiler.

The center serves as host for the NOAA-sponsored National Undersea Research Center; an extension office for the North Carolina Sea Grant; the Marine Mammal Stranding Network; the North Carolina National Estuarine Research Reserve; and UNCW's Marine Quest Program, which is an extensive community outreach program for public schools and adult education.

North Carolina National Estuarine Research Reserve
UNCW Center for Marine Science, 5600 Marvin K. Moss Ln., Wilmington
(910) 962-2470

The U.S. Congress created the National Estuarine Research Reserve system in 1972 to preserve undisturbed estuarine systems for research into and education about the impact of human activity on barrier beaches, adjacent estuaries and ocean waters. The reserves are outdoor classrooms and laboratories for researchers, students, naturalists and others.

The headquarters of the North Carolina National Estuarine Research Reserve (NCNERR) is housed at the UNCW Center for Marine Science Center in cooperation with the N.C. Division of Coastal Management. The NCNERR program manages four estuarine reserve sites as natural laboratories and coordinates research and education activities.

Masonboro Island and Zeke's Island are two of the four components of NCNERR, the others being Rachel Carson Reserve near Beaufort and Currituck Banks in northeastern North Carolina. Nationally threatened loggerhead sea turtles nest at Zeke's Island, Rachel Carson and Masonboro Island. Brown pelicans and ospreys are common to all four points.

With more than 5,000 protected acres, Masonboro Island is the last and largest undisturbed barrier island remaining on the southern North Carolina coast and one of the most productive estuarine systems along the coast. The Zeke's Island component of the Reserve, immediately south of Fort Fisher, includes almost 2,000 acres and actually consists of three islands — Zeke's, North Island, No-Name Island — and the Basin, the body of water enclosed by the breakwater known locally as the Rocks.

NCNERR allows traditional activities to continue, such as fishing and hunting within regulations, on Zeke's and Masonboro Island. (For further information about these islands, see our chapters on Attractions; Camping; and Sports, Fitness and Parks.)

Another reserve that has received its share of scientific scrutiny is Permuda Island. This linear 50-acre island bears substantial archaeological significance in that large tracts consist essentially of extensive shell middens created by prehistoric inhabitants over a vast span of time. Such sites are rare in the ever-shifting, acidic soils of barrier islands. Despite decades of farming, the archaeological resources survived fairly intact. The island passed into state ownership in 1986.

Of further interest is the theory that Permuda Island represents an original barrier island later eclipsed by the growth of what today is called Topsail Island. A similar theory has been posited for North Island, mentioned above, and other privately owned islands along the Pender County coast such as Hutaff and Lee islands. (The only other islands behind the barriers are dredge material islands.) Permuda Island is accessible to the public only by boat. It remains in a natural state and is managed by the North Carolina Department of Environment and Natural Resources, NCNERR and the Department of Marine Fisheries.

**North Carolina State
Horticultural Crops Research Station
3800 Castle Hayne Rd., Castle Hayne
(910) 675-2314**

Another field of research important to the region is horticulture. The North Carolina Department of Agriculture and North Carolina State University run 18 horticultural research stations around the state. The station in Castle Hayne is the primary local research site. Its varied, ongoing programs concentrate on crops of local economic importance, such as blueberries, strawberries, grapes, ornamentals and cucurbits. Variety trials, breeding, insect and disease control, and herbicide tests are among the studies performed.

The station works in limited association with the New Hanover County Extension Service arboretum, especially regarding soil studies, but primarily serves local horticulturists by making useful publications available to them through the N.C. Cooperative Extension Service.

**LaQue Center
for Corrosion Technology, Inc.
702 Causeway Dr., Wrightsville Beach
(910) 256-2271**

LaQue (pronounced la kwee) Center for Corrosion Technology, Inc. is a corrosion testing, research and consulting services firm that has specialized in marine corrosion for more than 50 years and is internationally recognized as a pioneer and leader in the field. LaQue Center is capable of providing any and all corrosion and testing services related to marine material and machinery. Since 1935, this center has performed contract services in the areas of natural seawater testing, marine atmospheric corrosion, weathering and durability testing, cyclic corrosion cabinet testing, prototype equipment evaluations and performance, and electrochemical, mechanical and metallurgical testing. LaQue also conducts on-site corrosion monitoring, corrosion failure analyses, consulting and expert witnessing, corrosion classes and seminars, and has sponsored The Sea Horse Institute, a marine corrosion conference. The center's natural seawater facility at Wrightsville Beach and marine atmospheric test site at Kure Beach offer various testing options.

Mother Nature's artistry is ever-present.

photo: Peter Doran

VOLUNTEER OPPORTUNITIES

One of the most wonderful aspects of this coastal community is that people love living here. And when people appreciate their home towns, they want to share that joy. Maybe that's why this area is filled with so many tireless volunteers.

Dedicated volunteers are always in high demand, and your willingness to serve in any capacity will definitely be appreciated. As you'll read in this section, there's a need to suit just about anyone's interest. Involvement with good causes and organizations not only helps the community, it benefits each individual who supports them.

First Call for Help, an excellent 24-hour information and referral service agency, located at 615 Shipyard Boulevard in Wilmington, (910) 397-0497, can provide information about human service organizations throughout the region. The Community Services pages of the phone books contain listings of most area human service agencies as well. Look, too, in Wilmington's Sunday Star-News, Section D, which has a spread called "Community Connection"; there you'll find features about different organizations and volunteers plus an extensive list of agencies and churches needing volunteers in New Hanover, Brunswick and Pender counties.

In Brunswick County, **The Volunteer Center** is the place to contact if you are interested in volunteering but are not sure exactly what it is you want to do. Located at the Brunswick County Government Center, 25 Referendum Drive (Building N) in Bolivia, this organization has listings of nearly 100 agencies, public and private, that involve volunteers. They will match you with agencies that need volunteers in your line of interest and expertise. The Volunteer Center holds annual volunteer recognition events with the cooperation of private enterprise as well. The center has met required standards to be included in the Points of Light Foundation and Volunteer Center National Network. This network can be reached at (800) VOLUN-TEER. The local number for The Volunteer Center is (910) 253-2412.

The arts, health services, nutrition, historic preservation, environment, minority interests, business development, human relations, housing, schools and education, and special festivals make up a fraction of the volunteer possibilities in our area. The following is a condensed list of some organizations that would appreciate your involvement.

Human Services

American Red Cross, Cape Fear Chapter
1102 S. 16th St., Wilmington
(910) 762-2683

Volunteer positions include blood service aides, disaster team members, service-to-military caseworkers, health and safety class instructors and office aides. A maximum of four classes are offered each month to train volunteers for the disaster team or to become service-to-military caseworkers. This very active organization has a high community profile and is extremely responsive to people in need. It responds to emergencies both inside and beyond the region with shelter, food and funds. The simple act of giving blood is an easy way to volunteer, and this is a critical need because only 5 percent of the population donates blood. Give blood or volunteer at a blood drive and help save lives.

The Bargain Box
4213 Princess Place Dr., Wilmington
(910) 362-0603

The Bargain Box, a resale boutique, is an outreach ministry of Wilmington's Church of the Servant, Episcopal. They encourage the recycling of pre-owned goods and the creative utilization of pre-loved merchandise. A wide variety of affordable, quality merchandise is offered, including a complete assortment of clothing, furniture and household

"It's tiring and frightening. You get in a certain situation and don't know what to expect... Your heart is exploding inside of you. Do you stand here or do you run?"

Nearly 30,000 adults in the Wilmington area know what this man is talking about. For them, illiteracy is not about books and diplomas. It's driving without street signs. It's staying home instead of applying for a job. It's making excuses instead of reading to their children. It's living in fear of being exposed.

The Cape Fear Literacy Council is helping over 400 adults learn to read. We provide area adults with individual tutoring in reading, writing, math, and English language skills. But there is more we could do. Help us tell them they don't have to run anymore.

For more information about volunteering
call the Cape Fear Literacy Council at 251-0911
www.cfliteracy.org

items, collectibles and records, tapes and CDs, toys and games, jewelry and accessories. Income is re-distributed to existing ministries through a grant program. Vouchers are available from specified churches and social service agencies for people with emergency needs. There is also a bin full of free, usable clothing. Volunteers are needed to steam clothing, work the cash register, provide customer service, pick up furniture, deliver bags of clothes to migrant workers, organize the library, do garden and lawn work and perform handyman duties. Volunteer your time and talents, or help by shopping at The Bargain Box or bringing donations. Encourage your friends and family to do likewise. The Bargain Box is open Tuesday through Friday 11 AM to 6 PM and Saturday 10 AM to 5 PM. They are open on Monday from 10 AM to 4 PM for donations only.

Brunswick Family Assistance Agency
(910) 754-4766

This organization needs volunteers to help families in need of food, shelter, furniture and other necessities. It also needs help with the pantry, fund-raisers, food drives to stock the pantry, and distributing clothes. The agency is in the fund-raising stages of establishing a homeless shelter. It distributes more than 500 Christmas baskets across Brunswick County and has a food pantry that distributes more than 20,000 pounds of food each year.

Brunswick County Literacy Council Inc.
282 Ocean Hwy., Supply
(910) 754-7323, (800) 694-7323

The Brunswick County Literacy Council promotes literacy for people of all ages in Brunswick County, focusing primarily on adult and young adult learners. The council helps students with reading, writing, math, computers and English-speaking skills, in a one-on-one confidential setting, by pairing them with volunteers who are carefully trained and matched with each student. Tutoring is free of charge, as is the training for volunteer tutors. In addition, assistance is available with earning a GED, a driver's license and US Citizenship. The Literacy Council impacted the lives of approximately 2,035 individuals in 2004 through free tutoring workshops and special projects, such as Books for Babies, Holiday Book Share and National Children's Book Week. In concert with the Brunswick Family Assistance Agency, the council runs the Family Thrift Store at Twin Creek Plaza in Shallotte, plus contributes to the Holiday Basket program with Book Share, a collection of new or almost new books for youth. In addition to tutoring, volunteers are needed for interpreting, fundraising, publicity and other duties.

Cape Fear Area United Way
613 Shipyard Blvd., Wilmington
(910) 798-3900

The Cape Fear Area United Way funds 56 human care programs in Brunswick, New Hanover and Pender counties in southeastern North Carolina. These programs provide food and shelter for those in need, daycare and after-school care for local children, job training, family support, health services, domestic violence shelters and crisis intervention. The Cape Fear Area United Way also helps build a strong community through programs such as Project BUILD, a recruitment and training program for volunteers to serve on nonprofit boards; information and referral services through First Call For Help; and volunteer recruitment and training through the United Way Volunteer Center. The Cape Fear Area United Way needs donations of money, services and event sponsorships as well as individuals to serve on the board, volunteer for the fund-raising campaign, fund distribution teams and to serve on the communication committee.

Cape Fear Hospital
5301 Wrightsville Ave., Wilmington
(910) 452-8384, (910) 343-7704
www.nhhn.org

Cape Fear Hospital continues to recruit increasing numbers of volunteers to meet the growing needs of this busy facility. As the number of orthopedic surgeries increase, more volunteers are needed to staff the Surgical Waiting Room, especially during the third shift (5 to 7:30 PM). Emergency room facilitators and office assistants are needed as well. The Gift Garden and the main lobby reception desk are lovely places to volunteer and serve patients, visitors and staff. Volunteers are also being recruited for the laboratory. If you're interested, call (910) 452-8384 to find out about the next volunteer orientation.

Burberry • Dooney & Bourke • J. Crew

Bargain Box of Wilmington

A Different Kind of Thrift Store

- Affordable clothing for the entire family • Linens
- Antiques & collectibles
- Vintage room • Housewares
- Designer clothes
- New & like-new items
- Lots of gift ideas

A not-for-profit outreach ministry of Church of the Servant

4213 Princess Place Drive •
910.362.0603
Wilmington, NC 28405
Tuesday - Friday 11AM - 6PM
Saturday 10AM - 5PM
Donations accepted Monday-Saturday

Ann Taylor • Ralph Lauren • Banana Republic • Fubu • Christian Dior

Tommy Hilfiger • Gucci • Bill Blass • Abercrombie & Fitch • Nautica

Coach • Ferragamo • DKNY/DonnaKaran

Cape Fear Literacy Council
1012 S. 17th St., Wilmington
(910) 251-0911

The Cape Fear Literacy Council works to help adults of all ages improve their literacy skills in reading, writing, math and English language. Adults at all skill levels are welcome. There is a computer literacy lab on site. In addition to the Adult Literacy program, CFLC has a significant English for Speakers of Other Languages (ESOL) program, training instructors and tutors to work with students with limited or no English skills. More than 300 tutors are needed each year to provide one-on-one tutoring or help in small group classes. Over 400 adults work to improve their literacy and/or English skills. CFLC holds monthly orientation and tutor training workshops. The September Spelling Bee for Literacy fundraiser ties into September's National Literacy Month. The festive Bid for Literacy Mardi Gras auction, held the first Saturday in March, is the agency's major fund-raiser for the year. In October 2005, CFLC unofficially set a new Guinness World Record for "longest reading aloud marathon by a team" (pending confirmation from Guinness World Records).

Cape Fear River Watch, Inc.
617 Surry St., Wilmington
(910) 762-5606

Cape Fear River Watch, Inc. is committed to the improvement and protection of the water quality of the Lower Cape Fear River Basin through education, advocacy and action. Volunteers are needed to assist with many programs, including outdoor education and recreation, clean-ups, outreach, wetlands restoration, fund-raising and administrative tasks. To raise funds for its work, this organization manages the paddleboat/canoe concession at Greenfield Lake. Eco-tours are available at the lake upon request.

Cape Fear Volunteer Center
3201 Jared Ct., Wilmington
(910) 799-9321

The goal of the Cape Fear Volunteer Center is to recruit, train and mobilize volunteers in the Wilmington Community. The organization also looks to strengthen existing volunteer services within other entities such as churches and civic groups. Aiding numerous non-profit organizations such as the Red Cross, Habitat for Humanity and the Cape Fear Literacy Council, the volunteer center is a great resource for those looking to give something back to their community.

Coastal Horizons Center
615 Shipyard Blvd., Wilmington
Crisis Intervention Line (800) 672-2903
First Call For Help (910) 397-0497
Rape Crisis Center (910) 392-7460
Substance Abuse Services (910) 343-0145
Open House: Emergency Youth Shelter
(910) 392-7408
All services available 24 hours

This private, nonprofit agency serving the tri-county area is for individuals who need assistance recovering from chemical dependency/substance abuse, sexual assault and other crisis situations. There is also an emergency care shelter for youths ages 8 through 17. Other programs include HIV/AIDS Outreach, pregnancy testing, criminal justice alternatives and food vouchers. Volunteers are needed to work with children at the shelter, respond to calls to assist victims at their home or in the hospital, and to answer the crisis line. A 48-hour training program is required. The training program is offered twice a year in January and September.

Domestic Violence Shelter and Services Inc.
2901 Market St., Wilmington
(910) 343-0703

This agency shelters women and children who have suffered domestic violence. Volunteers are needed for the Vintage Values resale shops, office work, transportation, children's programs, court advocacy, fund-raising, outreach/education and direct services. Volunteers can assist with emergencies on an on-call basis. More than 1,500 women and children are assisted yearly by the shelter. Volunteers are always needed at the stores to serve customers and sort donations. You can also help by donating gently used clothing and re-sellable merchandise. The Vintage Values stores have locations at 413 S. College Road and 5226 S. College Road. All proceeds from the Vintage Values stores go to the Domestic Violence Shelter and Services.

Elderhaus, Inc.
1950 Amphitheater Dr., Wilmington
(910) 343-8209

Elderhaus provides structured and stimulating daycare activities for adults, primarily the elderly, and weekend daytime respite for caregivers. Elderhaus serves persons with a variety of needs, including those with Alzheimer's disease and dementia. Elderhaus also serves veterans. Volunteers are needed as program aides, activity assistants, meal servers and van assistants. Volunteer board members oversee fund-raising, public relations, educational activities and more. Elderhaus has a 7,000-square-foot center to serve the area's increasing need for these services and a second facility on the grounds of Davis Health Care Center in the Porters Neck area. Elderhaus serves New Hanover, Pender and Brunswick counties.

Good Shepherd House
811 Martin St., Wilmington
(910) 763-4424

This day shelter for homeless people needs volunteers to work at the front desk greeting guests, answering the phone and distributing toiletry items for the shower. Volunteers are also needed to sort clothing, distribute fresh clothing and drive the van to take clients to work or on errands. People interested in working in the kitchen are needed to set up for lunch, serve meals and clean up. Volunteers are also needed for Second Helpings, a food re-distribution program. A new overnight shelter opened in November of 2005 and last year the program redistributed 700,000 pounds of food to 21 different social service agencies. People can stop by between 8 AM and 3 PM to donate food and clothing.

Hope Harbor Home
(910) 754-5726, (910) 754-5856 24-Hour
Crisis Line

Volunteers are needed at this domestic violence shelter to work on the speakers bureau and in the office, to provide childcare, help organize and implement fund-raising activities, assist clients in preparing paperwork, and to provide moral support during court proceedings. Volunteers are needed as well for transportation and to help distribute and sort donated clothing at the Hope Chest

Thrift Stores in Holden Beach, Leland, Bolivia and Oak Island.

LINC, Inc.
1202 Castle St., Wilmington
(910) 762-4635

Leading Into New Communities (LINC) is a non-profit organization assisting individuals in realizing their goals by creating bridges between them and valuable resources.

LINC provides shelter and services to men and women who have been released from local and/ federal prisons and on occasion young adults who have been released form detention centers. Additionally, LINC provides services to children who are at risk due to parental incarceration. They also host a program called LITE (LINC Initiative To Educate), an after-school mentoring program held at New Hanover County Schools. LINC furthermore supports children with school attendance issues and helps them get back on track in their schoolwork.

Volunteers are utilized in various parts of the program and inquiries can be made by calling the number listed above.

Lower Cape Fear Hospice & LifeCareCenter
725A Wellington Ave., Wilmington
(910) 772-5444

Hospice serves the needs of clients and their families when terminal illness occurs. Volunteers are needed to visit terminally ill clients, do office work and help with fund-raising events. An 18-hour volunteer training course is required and is offered free of charge three to four times a year. The Annual Festival of Trees is a major fund-raiser for Hospice. Hospice also offers a 12-bed inpatient facility for end of life care, which is especially helpful when caregivers desire a respite. If interested, call the Volunteer Department at (910) 791-4860.

New Hanover Regional Medical Center
2131 S. 17th St., Wilmington
(910) 343-7784

The Medical Center has many areas of volunteer involvement, and opportunities for new services are constantly evaluated. An average of 750 active volunteers give their time and skills each year in direct patient care services. If you feel you have four or more hours per week to give to a service of your choice, call the above number.

Providence Home of the Family Emergency Teen Shelter, Inc.
5310 Dosher Cutoff SE, Southport
(910) 457-0440

In November 1997 Providence Home opened its doors as the result of efforts of area churches, civic organizations, volunteers, grant money, donations and fund-raisers in the renovated Dosher House, former home of Dr. Dosher. A temporary residential facility with a maximum length of stay of 90 days, it serves at-risk children between the ages of 10 and 17. The home offers a nurturing atmosphere with safety, food, clothing and shelter to youth in need of a short-term safe haven. In addition to volunteer needs in Sheltered Treasures and the thrift store, which raises funds for the home, Providence Home needs volunteers to work on fund-raising projects, such as the annual golf tournament. Donations of household supplies, toiletries, art supplies and gift certificates are always helpful. If you have a special talent such as art, playing an instrument or making crafts, the administration would be happy to hear from you.

Salvation Army
820 N. Second St., Wilmington
(910) 762-7354

The Salvation Army provides shelter for the homeless and assistance for people in difficult circumstances. It needs volunteers in fund-raising activities and public relations efforts. Volunteers may serve on the Advisory Board and Ladies Auxiliary and in the shelter, which serves men, women and children. Volunteers may also work at the thrift store, the Woodlot Project, Christmas fund-raisers, the toy and food distribution center, the annual Coats for the Coatless drive and on disaster relief teams.

The shelter provides emergency housing to more than 20,000 individuals each year and has a Soup Line serving meals seven days a week between 5:30 and 6 PM for the public. This food program serves nutritious meals to more than 60,000 people each year in Bladen, Brunswick, Columbus, Pender and New Hanover counties.

Sheltered Treasures
5030 Southport-Supply Rd. SE, Southport
(910) 457-1078
4924 Main St., Shallotte
(910) 755-5491
1637 Seaside Rd., Sunset Beach
(910) 575-3506
10045 Beach Dr., Calabash
(910) 575-7332

Sheltered Treasures accepts clothing, housewares and other donations. The sale of these items benefits Brunswick County youth who stay at the Providence Home Family Emergency Teen Shelter in Southport. Volunteers are needed to sort and price goods, set up displays and provide customer service at the sites in Sunset Beach, Calabash, Shallotte and Southport.

Children's Services

Public Schools

School systems offer a variety of volunteer opportunities that are essentially the same from system to system: helping in the classroom, tutoring, serving as a mentor for at-risk students, working in dropout-prevention programs, helping minority students achieve success, getting involved with the PTA/PTO. If you want to volunteer your time to the public schools, contact the Community Schools/Public Information Office in each system: New Hanover County School System, Wilmington, (910) 763-5431; Brunswick County School System, Central Office, Southport, (910) 253-2900; Pender County School System, Burgaw, (910) 259-2187.

Boy Scouts of America, Cape Fear Council
110 Longstreet Dr., Wilmington
(910) 395-1100

This organization requires a tremendous number of volunteers to assist the many Boy Scouts in the Cape Fear area. The Boy Scouts need board and committee members as well as a host of leaders, coaches and advisors. Volunteers are needed for the Sports Club Program, which combines traditional Scout activities with a basketball league for inner-city boys from ten housing developments. They meet Saturday mornings to play basketball and participate in Boy Scout meetings. If you're interested in volunteering

"When I open the door to Dreams, I never even think about going back because anything is possible" -- words from a 13-year-old student

drawing by Ethan McGee

About Us

The Dreams Center for Arts Education, a non-profit organization dedicated to providing high-quality free-of-charge arts education to our area's most marginalized youth, seeks volunteers to act as classroom assistants and cultural mentors.

The Miracle of Dreams

Dreams serves over 500 young artists a week in over twenty outreach sites throughout New Hanover County. We offer classes in all artistic disciplines, including dance, drama, painting, pottery, weaving, graphic design, photography, and creative writing.

DREAMS
center for arts education

For More Information, please contact:
Dreams Center for Arts Education, PO Box 363 Wilmington, NC 28402
910-772-1501 • www.dreamswilmington.org • dreamscenter@ec.rr.com

for the Sports Club Program call (910) 395-1100 ext. 26

Community Boys and Girls Club
901 Nixon St., Wilmington
(910) 762-1252

The Community Boys and Girls Club is a youth development organization dedicated to promoting the health, social, educational, vocational and character development of girls and boys ages 6 to 17. Some of the club's outstanding alumni who achieved professional stardom in the NBA are Michael Jordan, Clarence Kea, Chuckie Brown, Kenny Gadison and Harlem Globetrotter legend Meadowlark Lemon. NFL athletes who participated in this program are Clyde and Jimmy Simmons. For more than 65 years the program has provided leadership and guidance to area youngsters. The club is in constant need of financial as well as volunteer support.

Dreams Center for Arts Education
515 Ann St., Wilmington
(910) 772-1501
www.dreamswilmington.org

Dreams seeks volunteers all year long to act as cultural mentors, teaching assistants and office help. Volunteers must be 18 years or older. Volunteers should be enthusiastic and eager to work with children. Experience in the arts is helpful but not necessary. One great aspect of volunteering is getting to experience the classes in the same way that the children do, and learning something yourself in the process.

Family Services of the Lower Cape Fear
1506 B Dock St., Wilmington
(910) 794-2100

This organization offers family counseling, after-school enrichment, consumer credit counseling and the Big Buddy program for the lower Cape Fear area. Volunteers are needed as office helpers, fund-raisers, board members, public relations representatives and, most of all, to be Big Buddies. The Big Buddy program provides reliable, trusted friends to boys and girls in need of positive role models and requires a minimum commitment of four hours per week for one year. Please call (910) 791-8510 to request an application. The after-school enrichment program needs tutors and support persons to work one-on-one with the children and help with

homework or activities. People with special skills or life experiences are also needed to speak to area children. Chaperones for field trips and mentors for at-risk children are welcomed too.

Guardian ad Litem
316 Princess St., Ste. 122, Wilmington
(910) 341-1515

The Guardian ad Litem (GAL) program matches trained volunteers with children who have been indicated in abuse or/and neglect cases. Volunteers, paired with attorney advocates, make recommendations regarding the best interest of the children in order to ensure a safe, nurturing and permanent home. Volunteers collaborate with community agencies and provide written reports to the court regarding the children's needs and status. Thirty hours of pre-service training are required. This program serves more than 525 children in New Hanover and Pender counties. The GAL program has an ongoing waiting list with an average of 100 children in need of volunteer advocates.

Girls Inc. of Wilmington
1502 Castle St., Wilmington
(910) 763-6674

Girls Inc. is an after-school and summer program primarily for girls ages 4 through 18. It offers programs in career and life planning, health and sexuality, leadership and community action, sports, culture, heritage, self-reliance and life skills. Volunteers are needed as tutors, group leaders and fund-raisers. Girls Inc. also needs people to assist with homework, sports, cooking, field trips and adolescent pregnancy prevention programs.

Girl Scout Council of Coastal Carolina
Wilmington
(800) 558-9297

The Girl Scouts need volunteers to serve in many positions. Adults serve as troop leaders, outdoor activities facilitators, trip chaperones, consultants, organizers, trainers, product sales coordinators (we're talking cookies here) and communicators. People with special skills and talents are also needed to share their wisdom. This council serves girls ages 5 to 18 in Brunswick, Columbus, New Hanover and Pender counties and offers leadership development through fun and rewarding programs.

Junior Achievement
of the Cape Fear Region
Wilmington
(910) 762-3690

Junior Achievement's programs inspire kids to learn the economics of life and gain the keys to success in a free enterprise system. Volunteers are needed to provide role models and facilitate activity-based programs that help students develop their own business sense. Through the generous sponsorship of local corporations, Junior Achievement of the Cape Fear is able to provide its programs to area schools and give its volunteers all of the training, materials and support they'll need for a rewarding class-room experience. A volunteer teaching com-mitment would involve one hour per week for five to six weeks. All volunteers are welcome, regardless of background or level of experi-ence. Besides teaching, volunteers are also needed to help with fundraising, public rela-tions and administrative work.

Project Linus
(910) 201-1608

Brunswick County volunteers involved in Project Linus make blankets, which are distributed to babies, children and teens who are ill or have been traumatized and are being helped in shelters, in hospitals and in foster care. The blankets are also carried by EMT personnel and Sheriff's units to comfort children in emergency situations. Blankets can be crocheted, knitted, quilted or fleece and can be made in your home and/or at the monthly meetings the first Tuesday of each month. In 2005 the members made more than 1,600 blankets. Donations of materials such as yarn and fabric are welcome as well.

Wilmington Family YMCA
2710 Market St., Wilmington
(910) 251-9622

If you're a real hands-on volunteer, this is certainly the place for you! Be a youth sports coach, nursery attendant, Special Olympics volunteer or a person who helps maintain the facility. The Y has a great aquatics program that offers activities for all individuals and needs volunteers for its Special Popula-tions program for those with disabilities. The YMCA is always looking for volunteers with a wide variety of skills and interests, so give

them a call and let them know what you can do.

YWCA
2815 S. College Rd., Wilmington
(910) 799-6820

The YWCA needs volunteer assis-tance with youth, clerical and maintenance programs at three locations in the Cape Fear area. If you'd like to tutor after school, facilitate a racial dialogue group or help with a special event, call the YWCA, which serves women and their families with fitness, health, personal development, job training, coun-seling and childcare programs. The YWCA functions as an advocate for women's rights, diversity and the elimination of racism.

Yahweh Center Children's Village
5000 Lamb's Path Way, Castle Hayne
(910) 675-3533

The Yahweh Center Children's Village provides a comprehensive continuum of residential treatment, child placing/adoption and outpatient therapy for abused and/or ne-glected children ages 5 to 12. A family coun-selor is located onsite to provide outpatient therapy for children and their families. With four buildings already occupied and more to go, the Yahweh Center Children's Village con-tinues to expand its services. Volunteers are needed to help with gardening, landscaping, tutoring, office work, teaching arts and crafts, special projects and fund-raising events. There are also group volunteer opportunities, especially around the holidays. Those who work directly with children must go through a specialized training.

The Arts

Some of the organizations listed in The Arts chapter also appreciate volunteers.

Louise Wells Cameron Art Museum
3201 S. 17th St., Wilmington
(910) 395-5999

This extraordinarily fine museum of visual arts needs volunteers to work in many capacities. Things are always happening at this lively center, and volunteers are needed to serve as docents and in membership, information desk, publicity, fund-raising, the gift shop and much more. The museum constantly has new projects underway, such as a cookbook, art trips to other cities, a film series, art sales, exhibitions, educational and outreach programs and special events. If you love the visual arts, this is a wonderful place to offer your volunteer services.

Historic Preservation and Community Development

Brunswick County Habitat for Humanity
4819 Port Loop Rd., Southport
(910) 454-0007

As of December 2005, Brunswick County Habitat for Humanity is in the process of completing its 14th house. The homes are built and no interest loans extended to families in need who meet minimum income requirements. "Sweat Equity" in the form of helping to build their own home — or the home of someone else — is part of the bargain as well. Committees needing volunteer participation include: volunteer coordination and church relations, fund-raising, communications, family selection, family support, site selection, construction and resale store.

Cape Fear Habitat for Humanity
1208 S. Third St., Wilmington
(910) 762-4744

Founded in 1987, Cape Fear Habitat for Humanity has served New Hanover, northeastern Brunswick and Pender counties by creating affordable homes for qualified families to purchase. To date, nearly 70 homes have been built, making home ownership a reality for many families who might not have been able to own their home otherwise. Volunteers are part of the essence of this group and aid the overall organization by creating fundraising events, working in the HomeStore or with the Family Selection Committee or simply by providing on site labor. If you're older than 16 and want to help improve your community, Habitat is a great place to begin.

Friends of the Oak Island Lighthouse
1100 Caswell Beach Rd., Caswell Beach
(910) 278-5471

Friends of the Oak Island Lighthouse was formed to preserve the lighthouse, which,

along with five acres of beachfront property, was gifted to the Town of Caswell Beach by the federal government. Volunteers with expertise in education, fund-raising, gardening, landscaping, retailing, special events and more are needed to assist with the preservation and with promotion and maintenance of these properties. For more information check out their website.

Historic Wilmington Foundation
Wilmington
(910) 762-2511

Volunteers interested in preserving the architectural heritage of the region are invited to work in these areas: public relations, membership, office work, events, education, preservation action and urban properties. There is a yearly gala, the primary fund-raiser, that relies on lots of volunteers for logistics, publicity, entertainment, food and everything else required to throw a major party and auction. The organization sponsors Home Tours during the Azalea Festival in April and a Repair Affair in spring. Maybe you'd like to help out at the Wilmington Architectural Salvage, 20 Brunswick Street, on Saturdays from 9 AM to 1 PM — that's where they sell historic architectural elements.

Lower Cape Fear Historical Society
126 S. Third St., Wilmington
(910) 762-0492

Volunteers are needed for publicity, fund-raising, membership drives and planning at this venerable organization, which seeks to accurately preserve the history of the area. Volunteers also work as docents and archivists in the society's home, the Latimer House. The society sponsors the annual Olde Wilmington by Candlelight Tour of Homes.

North Carolina Maritime Museum at Southport
116 N. Howe St., Southport
(910) 457-0003

The North Carolina Maritime Museum at Southport displays fascinating artifacts related to the maritime history of the Cape Fear Area (see our Attractions chapter). Volunteers are needed for building exhibits, tours and summer programs.

Smith Island Museum of History
101 Lighthouse Wynd, Bald Head Island
(910) 457-7481

Run by the Old Baldy Foundation, the Smith Island Museum is a replica of the historic light-keepers cottage. The $3 fee for touring the lighthouse is collected here, and the building houses artifacts and small items for sale. Volunteers are needed to staff the museum, to help with fund-raising and to give lectures and educational programs.

Southport Visitors Center
113 W. Moore St., Southport
(910) 457-7927, (800) 388-9635

The Southport Visitors Center is a great place to stop and rest in the rockers on the porch. Inside is a fascinating wall display of the history of the area, and included in the decor are historical artifacts. There are also films shown here. The center has ongoing recruitment for volunteers to work seasonal hours. These volunteers answer questions, provide visitors with brochures and maps of the self-guided walking tour, and sometimes sit in the rockers and shoot the breeze with folks eager to hear the old stories about the town of Southport.

Wilmington Downtown, Inc.
225 Water St., Wilmington
(910) 763-7349

Wilmington Downtown, Inc. concentrates on revitalization of the Central Business District in downtown Wilmington. Thirty-six volunteers representing a cross-section of the community serve on the Board of Directors, which is led by executive director Susi Hamilton. Thirteen are designated by other orga-

nizations, seven are elected based on their profession, and 16 serve as at-large members. This body expedites quality development of the commercial district by offering a wide range of services and detailed information to potential downtown businesses.

Animal Welfare

Karen Beasley Sea Turtle Rescue
and Rehabilitation Center
822 Carolina Blvd., Topsail Beach
(910) 328-3377

Dedicated to the care and release of sick and injured sea turtles, this rehabilitation canter is staffed entirely by volunteers. Volunteers feed and care for sea turtles in the hospital and survey the beach daily during the summer nesting season.

Operation Topcat
North Topsail Beach
(910) 328-4769

Topcat provides free spaying and neutering for Topsail Island stray and feral cats. Since 1995, their bi-weekly clinic has treated more than 1,000 cats and has placed over 220 cats into loving homes.

Topsail Humane Society
Hampstead
(910) 270-2660

Eastern Pender County's new no-kill shelter places pets in loving adoptive homes. Volunteers are always needed to walk, feed and play with the animals. The shelter is open seven days a week from 8 to 10 AM and 4 to 6 PM.

MEDIA

A wealth of print and broadcast media sources keep Wilmington and the surrounding coastal communities well-informed on topics of national, international and local importance. The region's large and well-established business, arts, education and film communities create a talented pool of writers, performers and media professionals. In terms of staying power, the area's dominant newspapers, magazines, radio and television stations are stable sources of information. In the print medium, visitors will also notice an abundance of tourist-oriented publications in street racks. We haven't listed all of them here, but they are generally handy guides to the area's attractions. Some of these periodicals have been around for years, while others seem to drift in one day and out the next. There's a robust business in publications on real estate; in fact, these magazines and booklets are so pervasive you can hardly go anywhere without encountering them.

Choices for radio listening are eclectic, ranging across talk, country music, religious, urban contemporary, Top 40 and the diverse offerings of the city's own National Public Radio affiliate.

Television is a somewhat limited medium without cable or satellite services, in which case a whole spectrum of channels becomes available. Public Television, broadcast from Jacksonville by way of Chapel Hill, has a strong signal.

The media resources listed in this chapter have settled into their own niches on what seems to be a permanent basis as a result of their thoroughness of coverage, accuracy, reliability and professionalism. In an ever-changing and expanding industry, these information/entertainment outlets have proven themselves over time.

Newspapers and Journals

Brunswick Beacon
208 Smith Ave., Shallotte
(910) 754-6890

A weekly community newspaper published on Thursdays, the Beacon has won dozens of awards during the past decade for advertising and editorial content. It covers and is distributed to all of Brunswick County, with particular emphasis on the southwestern portion of the coast. The Beacon is available through subscription, retail outlets and news racks throughout Brunswick County.

Greater Diversity News
272 N. Front St., Ste. 406, Wilmington
(910) 762-1337, (800) 462-0738

Greater Diversity News is a statewide, African-American–focused publication based in Wilmington, with additional distribution in Fayetteville. Published weekly on Thursday, it is a subscription-based periodical with limited news rack distribution.

Greater Wilmington Business Journal
130 N. Front St., Ste. 105, Wilmington
(910) 343-8600

Greater Wilmington Business Journal is the region's best source for local business news and information covering New Hanover, Brunswick, Pender and Columbus counties. Regular features of each issue include an in-depth industry spotlight, a business profile, a guest editorial, business achievement news, a calendar of events and a wealth of informative business-related articles. This monthly publication is available through subscription; newsstand sales are exclusively at Port City Java locations in New Hanover, Pender and Brunswick counties.

MEDIA

The Island Gazette
1003 Bennet Ln., Ste. F, Carolina Beach
(910) 458-8156

Published weekly on Wednesdays since 1978, The Island Gazette is a well-established source of local news, sports, features and real estate in southern New Hanover County, with an emphasis on Carolina Beach and Pleasure Island. Copies are available in news racks throughout the coverage area or by subscription.

Lumina News
Wrightsville's Weekly Newspaper
7220-C Wrightsville Ave.,
Wrightsville Beach
(910) 256-6569

Published every Thursday, Lumina News reports the weekly activities of Wrightsville Beach and its surrounding waterfront communities. From local government news and school events to sports and fishing, each issue is information-packed. Available by subscription and at more than 400 locations in and around Wrightsville Beach, Lumina News is free.

Mundo Latino
1902 Carolina Beach Rd., Wilmington
(910) 362-1330

Mundo Latino is distributed throughout eastern North Carolina and serves as a major communication link for the state's significant Latino population. Mundo Latino News is distributed every second and fourth week, and in it you will mainly find local, national and world news as well as sports, editorials, entertainment, fashion, decoration, music, cinema, gossip and much more.

Star-News
1003 S. 17th St., Wilmington
(910) 343-2000
www.starnewsonline.com

The Star-News, is the only major daily paper along the southern coastal region of North Carolina. Owned by The New York Times, the Star-News covers national, international, state and local news. Regular features cover regional politics, community events, arts, sports, weather, real estate, the local film industry, business news and more. Supplements to the daily paper include Neighbors, published every Wednesday for New Hanover and Brunswick counties; Real Estate Showcase; Currents, a weekly entertainment guide

published on Friday; and periodic special sections on a range of topics from health care to wedding planning to hurricane preparedness. Their annual Fact Book for New Hanover County, published in August, contains a wealth of intriguing facts, figures and community data. In addition, the Star-News now publishes Wilmington Magazine, a high quality glossy publication that covers the area in an in-depth manner. Subscribers have the option to receive all editions or just the Sunday edition. Home delivery is available, and the paper can be found in news racks and stores throughout Wilmington and North Carolina's southern coast.

The State Port Pilot
114 E. Moore St., Southport
(910) 457-4568

Covering eastern Brunswick County in the Southport-Oak Island sphere, including Bald Head Island, Boiling Spring Lakes, St. James and Caswell Beach, this award-winning newspaper features regional and community news, special event coverage, local sports, weather, feature articles and more. The Pilot is available by subscription or in news racks throughout its coverage area every Wednesday.

Topsail Advertiser
206-A S. Topsail Dr., Surf City
(910) 328-3033

The Topsail Advertiser is a weekly community newspaper that covers news, sports and special events in the Topsail area. The Advertiser is free and is available at most area shops.

The Topsail Voice
Hampstead
(910) 270-2944

Publishing since 1991, The Topail Voice covers community and school news, local sports and special events in Pender County. The Topsail Voice is available via home delivery and can be found in news racks throughout the area.

The Wilmington Journal
412 S. Seventh St., Wilmington
(910) 762-5502

Founded in 1927 as The Cape Fear Journal, this weekly began as the offspring of R. S. Jervay Printers and describes itself

MEDIA

The perfect accent for your home.

Wilmington: The Magazine for Fine Cape Fear Living is a publication designed to showcase the best of our city and the Cape Fear Coast. Enjoy reading a magazine that focuses on the unique and sophisticated lifestyle found only here, with an emphasis on local dining and culture, all told with richly detailed writing and compelling photography.

Wilmington
THE MAGAZINE FOR FINE CAPE FEAR LIVING

To subscribe to Wilmington Magazine, call 343.2080. To advertise, call 343-2342 as the voice and mirror of the African-American community in New Hanover, Brunswick, Pender, Onslow, Columbus, Jones and Craven counties. The name changed to The Wilmington Journal in the 1940s. It is available each Thursday at news racks throughout the city or by subscription.

Magazines

The Beat
Wilmington's Music Magazine
Burgaw
(910) 259-8323

Dedicated to reporting music news of Wilmington and the southeastern North Carolina coastal region, The Beat is free. This is the absolute best place to find out when, where, who and what's going on musically. Look for it in cafés, bars, lounges and anywhere music lovers hang out. Because of its handy size, you can carry it with you as you go out for a fun evening visiting all the swinging places and listening to our great local musicians.

Brunswick Alive!
Shallotte
(910) 754-3030

Brunswick Alive! is a monthly informative and entertaining magazine covering the beaches and all of Brunswick County. It contains features, articles and departments about people and events in the area including current happenings and profiles. Regular features include tide tables, an events calendar, fishing, racing and computer columns. Mailed to businesses in Brunswick County, this free magazine can be picked up at Brunswick County retailers.

Encore Magazine
210 Old Dairy Rd., Ste. A-2, Wilmington
(910) 791-0688

Publisher Wade Wilson describes this as a "general what's happening" magazine for the Wilmington area. Arts, entertainment, local sports and essays/fiction make up this free weekly, which has published each Tuesday since 1984.

Certainly the most widely distributed free entertainment periodical in the region, Encore's many highlights include festival and holiday roundups, movie and theater reviews,

a dining guide, attractions, nightlife and Chuck Shepherd's syndicated "News of the Weird" column. Perhaps the most outstanding feature is a detailed calendar of weekly events.

The magazine is available at news racks practically everywhere in the Wilmington area. Encore cosponsors an annual fiction contest in cooperation with the Lower Cape Fear Historical Society. In addition to the magazine, Encore also publishes Alternatives, a free summer and fall guide for school-age kids looking for interesting things to do. The company also publishes the Wilmington Regional Film Commission's Production Guide.

Focus on the Coast
Focus on Communication, Inc.
6406 Shinnwood Rd., Wilmington
(910) 799-1638

Focus on the Coast focuses on where to eat, where to shop and where to play at the coast. This up-scale, full-color, digest-size magazine is a connection to the arts, entertainment, dining and culture and contains features, columns, reviews and previews on people and places in the Cape Fear region. You can pick up a complimentary copy in more than 400 area locations or by subscription.

Health Matters
Focus on Communication, Inc.
6406 Shinnwood Rd., Wilmington
(910) 799-1638

Health Matters is the area's best medical resource for both the medical community and the general public. It includes a helpful directory of physicians, dentists, health-care providers as well as health-related information about the latest technology and treatments available in the Cape Fear Region.

The Pelican Post
Oak Island Press, P.O. Box 1073, Oak Island
(910) 452-2773

Serving the Southport-Oak Island area since 1993, this small regional magazine is crammed with information and interesting tidbits for visitors and locals. Regular features include a calendar of events, a listing of area attractions, a chart for daily high and low tides, the Southport-Fort Fisher Ferry schedule, an area map, plus recipes, a dining guide and more. The covers feature works of art

FOCUS ON THE COAST

Your guide to Culture, Dining, Entertainment, & Shopping

www.focusonthecoast.com • focuscom@bellsouth.net

Your new doctor is just a click away

www.HealthMattersOnline.com

YOUR RESOURCE GUIDE FOR HEALTHCARE PROVIDERS
IN NEW HANOVER, BRUNSWICK & PENDER COUNTIES.

WWW.HEALTHMATTERSONLINE.COM • 910-799-1638

by local artists and local authors contribute interesting stories about the area as well. The Pelican Post is distributed free throughout the Cape Fear region monthly from April through November, with a holiday issue for December/January and a winter issue for February/March. It is also available by subscription — 10 issues for $12 per year.

Reel Carolina: Journal of Film and Video
1903 Galahad Ct., Wilmington
(910) 233-2926

This monthly magazine is unquestionably your best local source of information about moviemaking in the Carolinas. Production Notes, EUE Screen Gems Studios Clips and News & Notes are regular columns packed with information about what's going on in the area. To get the scoop on film-related websites, classes, workshops, groups and meetings, turn to Lagniappe, which also has a section on film festival news. Other features include business profiles, reports from regional production facilities, celebrity interviews and film production feature articles plus a wide range of industry-related ads. Reel Carolina is available by subscription or free in racks across both Carolinas.

wilma!
Wilmington's magazine for women
130 N. Front St., Ste. 105, Wilmington
(910) 343-8600

The new girl in town, wilma! is for and about women of all ages. With an easy style and airy format, here's a magazine you'll read cover-to-cover, clip, save and share. Content of each issue centers around an overall theme, such as traditions, passions or back to school. Regular features include fashion, home decor, humor, book reviews, art, health, legal, financial and relationship issues. wilma! is published monthly and distributed free throughout the greater Wilmington area.

Wrightsville Beach Magazine
the magazine for the people of the beach
(910) 256-4568

Available monthly, Wrightsville Beach Magazine is full of informative and entertaining features, articles and departments covering life, people and events in and around the beach. Subjects range from current happenings to history and profiles. Regular departments include fishing, tide tables and photo contest winners. Pick up a copy of this free magazine at more than 400 locations in Wrightsville Beach and the surrounding area or by subscription.

Television Stations

WECT-TV 6, NBC
322 Shipyard Blvd., Wilmington
(910) 791-8070
www.wect.com

NBC-affiliated TV 6 is one of the major television stations in southeastern North

A shorebird seeks a meal at the water's edge.

photo: Peter Doran

Carolina. It offers full news coverage and exceptional meteorological programming.

WSFX-26, Fox
322 Shipyard Blvd., Wilmington
(910) 791-8070

This station's strength is its Fox affiliation, featuring Fox news and entertainment programming. WSFX also carries local news.

WILM-TV 10, CBS
3333-G Wrightsville Ave., Wilmington
(910) 798-0000

WILM-TV is Wilmington's CBS affiliate and broadcasts on channel 10 (channel 12 for Time-Warner Cable viewers and channel 16 for Charter Cable viewers). Regional news and major local events broadcast through the CBS Raleigh affiliate, WRAL-TV, until a Wilmington news bureau is established.

UNC-TV 39, PBS
Research Triangle Park
(800) 906-5050

Quality national and local public television programming is the hallmark of UNC-TV. Fans of the BBC enjoy delightful offerings in drama, news and comedy. The station's yearly pledge drive is enthusiastically supported by southeastern North Carolinians. UNC-TV has made a transition to digital television,

which allows viewers to receive four channels instead of one. The other three channels are UNC-KD a full-time children's channel, UNC-NC dedicated to local happenings in NC, and UNC-ED an educational channel of high school and college courses.

WWAY-TV 3, ABC
615 N. Front St., Wilmington
(910) 762-8581

ABC–affiliated WWAY NewsChannel 3 is another of Wilmington's major television stations broadcasting throughout the southeastern coastal region. WWAY offers full national and regional news and complete meteorological forecasts.

Cable

Cable television and high-speed Internet access services are available throughout southeastern North Carolina's coastal region from two primary sources. **Time Warner Cable**, (910) 763-4638 or (800) 222-8921, covers Wilmington and much of Brunswick County, including Oak Island, Holden and Ocean Isle beaches. **Charter Communications**, (866) 472-2200, provides service to Pleasure Island (Carolina Beach and Kure Beach), the southern end of New Hanover

County and parts of Pender County, including Topsail Island.

Alternative cable providers available in Brunswick County are **Atlantic Telephone**, covering Sunset Beach, (910) 754-4311 or (888) 367-2862, which offers DSL Internet access, and **Tele-Media Cable Communications Inc.**, (800) 533-7048, which does not offer Internet service at this time.

Radio Stations

Adult Alternative
WPPG 105.3 FM

WUIN 106.7 FM

Adult Contemporary and Top 40

WAZO 98.3 FM

WGNI 102.7 FM (classic and current)

Christian
WDVV 89.7 FM

WWIL 90.5 FM (contemporary Christian)

WMYT 1180 AM (Spanish Christian)

WLSG 1340 AM (Southern gospel)

WVCB 1410 AM

WWIL 1490 AM (urban gospel)

Country
WWQQ 101.3 FM (contemporary)

WCCA 106.3 FM (classic country)

National Public Radio
WHQR 91.3 FM (classical, jazz, blues, news, Radio Latino, National Public Radio (NPR) and Public Radio International)

www.whqr.org

News, Talk, Sports
WAAV 980 AM

WMFD 630 AM (ESPN radio)

WLTT 103.7 FM

Rock, Classic Jazz and Oldies
WFXZ 93.7FM

WKOO 98.7 (classic rock/oldies)

WKXB 99.9 FM (classic rock)

WWTB 103.9

WRQR 104.5 FM (classic/contemp. rock)

WXQR 105.5 FM (rock)

WSFM 107.5 FM (surf)

Urban Contemporary
WMNX 97.3 FM (hip hop)

WKXS 94.1 FM

COMMERCE AND INDUSTRY

The amenities of coastal living and a moderate year-round climate continually attract new residents to southeastern North Carolina. According to the Bureau of Census for 2000, the coastal counties of New Hanover, Brunswick and Pender grew nearly 35 percent overall, surpassing the state's 21.4 percent growth rate. Brunswick County alone earned distinction as the fifth fastest growing county in North Carolina. Growth for the Wilmington metropolitan statistical area (MSA), which includes parts of these counties, was 36.9 % — 14th highest in the nation.

In the last decade of the 20th century, the Lower Cape Fear region's economy remained, like the weather, moderate and relatively stable. This stability, according to local business and economic leaders, helped the area to be somewhat less affected by state and national economic trends. Despite both good and bad economic periods in its history, the Greater Wilmington area hasn't experienced the excessive highs during more prosperous eras nor the drastic lows during recessions as other demographically similar regions.

During the early years of the 21st century, the trend in economic growth has continued. Overall economic growth for the three-county region rose 9.7 percent over 2004 to $8.5 billion, and was projected to rise 7 percent in 2005 and another 7 percent in 2006 to $9.7 billion according to William W. Hall Jr., Director of the Center for Business & Economics Services at UNCW.

For the twelve months ending May 2005, retail sales were strong in the three Cape Fear coastal counties; Brunswick County was up 11.5 percent with sales reaching $1.2 billion, Pender County was up a whopping 22.9 percent to $360.2 million and New Hanover County was up 11.2 percent to $3.9 billion.

Despite a growing trend toward year-round tourism in southeastern North Carolina,

the rise and fall of economic activity throughout the year, especially during the summer months, is a fact of life for coastal counties. Employment trends have been difficult to predict during recent years because of rapid population growth, new companies entering the marketplace and other factors. However, on a historical basis, both the labor force and the number of people employed peak during June through August and bottom out during the December to January period.

Geography is an inevitable factor that sets Wilmington apart from the overall North Carolina economy, and it is driving trends that are positioning Wilmington to take advantage of a new and prosperous era at the beginning of the 21st century. Its maritime environment creates opportunities for business based on what is naturally available — the sea, the river, the many beautiful views — in addition to manufacturing and commerce. Examples include tourism, the influx of retirees drawn to the coastal amenities and the rise in championship golf courses in the area, especially in Brunswick County.

There have been, of course, significant times in history when Wilmington relied heavily on its natural resources for both manufacturing and agriculture. Early 18th-century settlers used the area's lush pine forests to foster a lumber industry that continues today. The manufacture of lumber-related by-products, such as tar, turpentine and pitch, was the dominant business in the 19th century, but this type of manufacturing has since declined.

Rice and cotton were an early source of income for the area; the downtown wharves were once the site of the largest cotton exporting operation in the world. After the War Between the States, the economy shifted away from cotton and rice plantations because the free labor supply was no longer available to work the labor-intensive plantations. Railroads provided jobs for 4,000 families in the first part of the 20th century, as Wilmington became a major rail center. The Atlantic Coast Line, the evolution of the Wilmington and Weldon Railroad, was a technological marvel and the pride of the Wilmington economy at the time. Many an opulent downtown home was built thanks to railroad dollars.

Trains moved the area's products efficiently into the inland market, and there was popular speculation that the rails would move the economy into prosperity. Then in 1955, the railroad announced the closing of its corporate office and subsequently sent a significant segment of Wilmington's workforce south to Jacksonville, Florida. This was a severe economic loss that forced Wilmingtonians to ponder their destiny. Not only were good-paying jobs lost with the railroad, but service businesses all over the area lost customers.

Although manufacturing continues to be an economic force in the region, statistics compiled by the University of North Carolina at Wilmington's Cameron School of Business indicate that the bulk of today's employment opportunities are in the services sector. This is a broad category that includes such diverse occupations as physicians, government workers, real estate brokers, educators, service-oriented business, hotel staff and restaurant employees.

The Port

The North Carolina State Ports Authority was created by the state legislature in 1945. Its mission was to promote a better atmosphere for the development of North Carolina industry by establishing two deep-water ports, thus breaking the state's dependence on ports in Virginia and South Carolina. The terminals, one in Morehead City and one in Wilmington, were equipped to handle ocean-going vessels and opened in 1952. They are the backbone of the North Carolina shipping industry.

The Wilmington facility annually receives more than 375 ships and barges loaded with diverse cargoes from Europe, South America, the Far East and beyond. Cargo tonnage through the Port of Wilmington for fiscal year 2005 was over 3 million tons, up from the 2004 figure of 2.3 million tons. Warehousing at the port includes more than a million

square-feet of covered storage, all with road and rail access. The entire Wilmington Terminal is designated Foreign Trade Zone 66.

Countries that do significant business through the North Carolina Port at Wilmington include Germany, Korea, Italy, China, Columbia, Taiwan, Sweden, Brazil, Hong Kong and the United Kingdom. Leading imports are forest products, chemicals, cement, general merchandise and metal products. The largest export in 2005 was wood pulp at 576,684 tons, and the largest import was forest products at 514,244 tons. Italy was the largest shipping destination from the port, while Germany was the largest shipper to the port.

In 2004 the Cape Fear River from its mouth to the State Port was deepened from 38 feet to 42 feet to accommodate increasingly larger ships. This project, begun in 2000, was crucial to the future of the port in terms of servicing current customers and attracting new business. The balance of the project — deepening the river's shipping channel past downtown to the industrial area to the north — is expected to be completed by 2008 with a total cost for the entire project at $440 million. Completion of the project is expected to allow container traffic growth of 15% annually to more than 187,000 containers in 2009, while shipment of bulk materials is anticipated to grow by 5% per year. Each year in May, the Port holds the Maritime Day Festival, which is an opportunity for the public to visit at no charge. Enjoy guided bus tours, exhibits, military equipment, visiting vessels, demonstrations, music and live entertainment. Food vendors and fun children's activities are also available. Watch the Star-News for announcements, contact the Public Affairs office at (910) 343-6491, (800) 334-0682 or visit the website at www. ncports.com.

Tourism

Tourism remains one of the most important industries in North Carolina's southern coastal region. With an appealing variety of attractions — beaches and waterways, breathtaking gardens, a rich arts environment, well-established cultural events, beautiful historic homes and landmarks — in moderate year-round temperatures, this industry provides a strong economic center. This translated into nearly $700 million in revenue for the region in 2004, according to tourism statistics from the North Carolina Department of Commerce. Tourism is one of the state's largest industries, and North Carolina ranks eighth in person-trip volume by state behind California, Florida, Texas, Pennsylvania, New York, Illinois and Ohio.

In the year 2004, domestic travelers spent approximately $328 million in New Hanover County, maintaining its rank as number eight among North Carolina's 100 counties in tourism expenditures. Brunswick County's tourism dollars followed closely, totaling over $313 million, while Pender County brought in over $57 million. The economic impact is significant in terms of jobs and and payroll dollars in the three-county area. The NCDOC report for New Hanover, Brunswick and Pender counties directly attributes a total of 10,680 jobs and more than $168 million in payroll as a result of tourism.

Summer is no longer the sole tourism season. Visitors Bureau officials recognize that Wilmington and the surrounding communities have moved from a three-month to a nearly year-round tourism season with the majority of visitors arriving from March through November. With that in mind, the Cape Fear Coast Convention and Visitors Bureau has several locations starting with the main office at 24 N. Third Street, (910) 341-4030, and the River Booth, located along the Cape Fear riverfront near the corner of Water and Market streets. Other centers include one in the town hall at 1121 North Lake Park Boulevard in Carolina Beach and at 305 West Salisbury Street in Wrightsville Beach. Tourism is expected to grow even more significantly when the planned downtown convention center, hotel and marina complex on Wilmington's north side are completed.

Accommodations are plentiful in the Greater Wilmington area and coastal Brunswick County. Historic downtown Wilmington and picturesque Southport offer a bounty of bed and breakfast inns. With such an abundance of accommodations at their disposal, visitors are only limited in choice by their budget or their imagination. Still, it is often difficult to find lodgings on short notice during the summer, and advance reservations for these months are highly recommended, especially for weekends.

With more than 50 championship golf courses and a long mid-March through mid-November playing season, golf is another major draw to the region. Restaurants number in the hundreds and continue to proliferate at an astounding rate, with the best of them enjoying capacity dining on weekends. Special attractions and activities such as horse-and-carriage rides in the historic district, boat tours, sailing charters, a downtown Wilmington walking tour, the free trolley, Riverwalk and educational tours in the historic district continue to respond to high demand.

Trade

With the area's booming growth has come more and new shopping. The past few years have seen the opening of such national and regional chains as The Home Depot, Office Max, Barnes & Noble, Wal-Mart Super Centers, Target, Hecht's' and Kohl's — stores Wilmingtonians never thought they would see 15 years ago. The city's retail corridor is pushing north, with extremely heavy development in the vicinity of Landfall, near Wrightsville Beach, including four large upscale shopping complexes — Landfall Shopping Center, The Forum, Lumina Station and the newest, Mayfaire Towncenter. On every corner, there seems to be a new shopping plaza going up, and retail stores stocking everything from beachwear and souvenirs to designer clothing and high-ticket household furnishings are everywhere.

In the last few years retail and service industry businesses have made inroads in the southern corridor from Wilmington's city limits to Carolina Beach as well. Of particular note is the recently completed Lowe's Home Improvement Superstore, the first phase of a large shopping complex in the Myrtle Grove area at the end of South College Road. This complex features Wilmington's second Wal-Mart Superstore and a Lowe's plus other strip centers offering several places to eat and a variety of shopping opportunities.

While lacking the density of retail development seen in Wilmington and New Hanover County, the number of retail stores and shopping centers are increasing in Brunswick County as the trend toward year-round residents and visitors continues. The Southport-Oak Island area and Shallotte to the south both have acquired large Wal-Mart Superstores and Lowe's Home Improvement Centers, not to mention boutiques and stores of every description. In the past two years, Shallotte has continued to grow as a retail hub for southern Brunswick County with a new shopping center and the addition of more regional and national retailers — Belk, Home Depot and Office Depot.

The Film Industry

The Wilmington Regional Film Commission, located on the EUE/Screen Gems Studios lot, 1223 N. 23rd Street, Wilmington, (910) 343-3456, facilitates on-location filmmaking in the Cape Fear region. With the largest film studio facility outside of Los Angeles, Wilmington consistently ranks as one of the top filmmaking locations in the nation.

Since the industry's beginning in 1983, filmmaking activities in the Port City include more than 300 feature film, television movie-of-the-week and mini-series productions. Seven television series — Matlock, The Young Indiana Jones Chronicles, The Road Home, American Gothic, Dawson's Creek, One Tree Hill and Surface — have filmed here, and numerous music videos, television commercials and still photography shoots have utilized the amenities found in the area. Film makers have access to a broad base of local talent and professional film crews along with the facilities at Screen Gems Studios and, of course, fabulous natural scenery.

Feature films and television movies made in the Wilmington area include Lolita, Billy Bathgate, Divine Secrets of the Ya-Ya Sisterhood, Domestic Disturbance, The Hudsucker Proxy, I Know What You Did Last Summer, Betsy's Wedding, The Runaway, 28 Days, Black Knight, Muppets From Space, Rambling Rose, Year of the Dragon, Elmo In Grouchland, The Jackal, Maximum Overdrive, Silver Bullet, Blue Velvet, Firestarter, Sleeping With the Enemy and Weekend at Bernie's.

Commercials filmed here include local, regional and national companies such as Sun-Com, Nautica, American Express, National Geographic, Mattel, Smithfield Farms, the New York Ballet, J. Crew, Kodak, Harley Davidson, Rolling Stone magazine, McDonald's, RJ Reynolds, Wachovia Bank and more.

EUE/Screen Gems Studios offers a multitude of amenities to film and television production companies under the guidance of president Frank Capra Jr. The studio's lot features nine sound stages, post-production services, more than 20,000 square feet of production office space, a 40-seat screening room, editing suites, sound transfer services, lighting and grip equipment rental, set construction shops and much more. In addition to the studios, production companies discover a wealth of experienced film crew professionals here. WRFC director Johnny Griffin estimates that number at 650 in the Greater Wilmington region.

Senior Services

A major industry is beginning to arise around the retirement population, thanks largely to our maritime location, which makes the climate unusually mild for our latitude. Although there is a brief, mild winter, March through November weather is relatively warm, an important factor for northern retirees who have grown weary of Florida's almost single season. Warm spring breezes, hot summers and occasional freezing temperatures create a more interesting yearly cycle for retirees who yearn for a little diversity. See our Retirement chapter for more about senior services.

On the state level, 12 percent of North Carolina's population is in the age 65 and older category, while about 13 percent of New Hanover County residents are over age 65. The percentage of residents older than 65 is projected to grow in the future as the flow of retirees continues to increase. In response and expectation, planned retirement communities, senior services, recreational opportunities aimed at retirees, and other enterprises will represent a major component of the local economy. As retirees flow into the area from more prosperous economies in the north and west, they bring their nest eggs with them, thereby giving a considerable boost to our economy. An added benefit is their contribution of skills and knowledge to area volunteer organizations.

Health Care

Health care is big business in the region. More than 450 physicians and five hospitals employ large numbers of medical personnel. One of the largest employers is New Hanover Regional Medical Center, with 4,500 employees.

Local health-care services are extensive, and many are comparable with the best state-of-the-art medical facilities and services in the nation. An example is the Zimmer Cancer Center at the New Hanover Regional Medical Center, providing complete cancer care in one facility.

The rapidly expanding seniors health-care market is a national phenomenon, but it is particularly pronounced in coastal/resort communities. In addition to extensive medical services, New Hanover, Brunswick and Pender counties offer a large — and constantly growing — number of domiciliary care facilities. See our Health Care chapter for more information about area hospitals and medical services in the three-county area.

Real Estate

Several factors contribute to the overall good health of the region's new-home construction and existing home sales. Among them are a 41-year record low in interest rates, the good quality of life found here, the overall economic climate and a positive home-price appreciation. The real estate sales business in general is phenomenal. In New Hanover County, home sales for July 2005 were up 3 percent over July 2004 and building permits for new construction were up 12 percent. In Brunswick County, housing sales were up a whopping 52 percent for July 2005 over July 2004. See our Real Estate chapter for more about the local market.

Industry

The largest industrial companies in the area include Corning Glass Works (the Wilmington location is the largest manufacturer of optical fibers in the world); General Electric (aircraft engine parts, nuclear fuel components); Progress Energy; International Paper; KoSa (chemicals), Victaulic Company of America (pipe fittings), Rampage Sport

Fishing Yachts; Louisiana Pacific (wood products); Terex American Crane; VisionAir (software); Verizon (wireless phone service); Oracle Packaging; Archer Daniels Midland; Chloride Systems (lighting); Del Laboratories; L.L. Building Products; PPD (pharmaceutical research); aaiPharma (pharmaceutical products); Caterpillar, Inc. (hydrostatic transmission); and Interroll (conveyor components).

For a complete industrial directory, contact the Wilmington Industrial Development, Inc., at 1739 Hewlett Drive, (910) 763-8414. In Brunswick County, contact the Brunswick County Economic Development Commission office, 25 Courthouse Drive, Bolivia, (910) 253-4429, for information on the county's five industrial parks or a listing of local manufacturers.

The University

With an economic impact of more than $400 million on the Southeastern North Carolina Coast, including New Hanover, Pender, Brunswick and Columbus counties, is it any wonder that the University of North Carolina at Wilmington is a major economic force in the area? The Greater Wilmington Chamber of Commerce lists the university as one of the Top 25 Employers in the region with 1,627 employees. Serving a student body of over 11,600 as of the fall 2005 semester, the university is among the fastest-growing and most technologically advanced in the 16-campus University of North Carolina system. UNCW is ranked seventh in the 2005 U.S. News & World Report listing of top public undergraduate universities in the South.

Organized into the College of Arts and Sciences (including a marine biology program ranked fifth best in the nation), the Cameron School of Business Administration, the Donald R. Watson School of Education, the School of Nursing and the Graduate School, the university offers 71 undergraduate programs and 24 graduate programs. See our Higher Education and Research chapter for more about education in our area.

Employment Agencies

As the greater Wilmington area has a fair number or employment/staffing agencies, we're listing only a representative sample

The Right Location for Your Business.

As the owner of Landfall Executive Suites, I'm proud of the full service office packages we provide. Contact me directly to learn more about our Standard Office Package or to customize a package just for you.

Eric Goldfarb – OWNER

See our full page ad in the Commerce and Industry section.

1213 Culbreth Drive (off Military Cutoff Rd.) Wilmington, NC 28405
(910) 256-1900 www.landfall.biz

© 2006 LANDFALL EXECUTIVE SUITES

LANDFALL EXECUTIVE SUITES
FIRST CLASS OFFICES FOR GROWING BUSINESSES

here. Consult the Yellow Pages of a local phone book for a larger selection.

Olsten Staffing Services
513 Market St., Wilmington
(910) 343-8763

Olsten is part of an international company that specializes in a wide variety of temporary staffing assignments, including office services, legal support, accounting services, technical services, production/distribution/assembly and office automation.

Quality Staffing Specialists
3806 Park Ave., Wilmington
(910) 793-1010

In Wilmington since November 1999, Quality Staffing Specialists is a full-service staffing agency. This agency offers temporary and temporary-to-permanent staffing in administrative, medical, legal and pharmaceutical positions as well as skilled manufacturing and trade jobs. Executive search is another aspect of the agency's services.

The Reserves Network
803 S. College Rd., Wilmington
(910) 799-8500

The Reserves Network combines over a decade of experience in the Wilmington market with the resources of a national agency. The agency offers total workforce solutions for the clients and applicants, providing services that include temporary placement, temporary-to-permanent placement, direct hire,

payrolling and executive search and recruitment. Areas of specialization are professional, administrative, clerical support, accounting and finance, engineering, technical, sales and marketing, information technology and more.

SENC Technical Services
3142 Wrightsville Ave., Wilmington
(910) 251-1925

SENC offers contract, permanent and contract-to-hire workers in technical fields such as engineering, designing/drafting, electronics, computer programming and more.

Youngblood Staffing
2517 Delaney Ave., Wilmington
(910) 799-0103

Serving southeastern North Carolina, Youngblood Staffing is a regional staffing services agency that utilizes customized staffing strategies to help companies locate and maintain a balanced and innovative work force. The agency's experienced management and staff, knowledgeable about the employment marketplace, also provide preferred employment opportunities to qualified candidates. Youngblood Medical Staffing is a medical division providing clerical staff to the region's medical community.

Office Space and Services

Because the region has a high percentage of single-staff entrepreneurs, there is a need for office space with secretarial services. Several office centers provide the individual or small company with turnkey services that include a central reception area, support staff services, use of office equipment and an opportunity to be in a professional setting. Utilities, excluding phone service, and janitorial services are included in the lease.

Landfall Executive Suites
1213 Culbreth Dr., Wilmington
(910) 256-1900, (910) 509-7250

Located in one of Wilmington's hottest growth area's, this upscale facility offers furnished and unfurnished office suites with long or short-term leases that include all utilities, high-speed Internet access, parking, use of fully equipped break rooms, a reception area and receptionist to greet guests and to provide personalized telephone answering, and support staff for secretarial services, desktop publishing and web design. Networked color copiers, video conferencing equipment and LCD projectors are also available. Landfall Executive Suites is conveniently located near the beach, Mayfaire Towncenter and the airport.

The Cotton Exchange
Executive Office Center
321 N. Front St., Wilmington
(910) 343-9896

Overlooking the Cape Fear River in Historic Downtown Wilmington, the Cotton Exchange Executive Office Center provides unfurnished offices for individuals or small companies with both long and short-term leases, as well as a corporate identity package that includes mailboxes, phone messages and receptionist answering services for businesses not physically located at the center. Professional support services are available. The Cotton Exchange Executive Office Center also handles leasing of the Cotton Exchange retail shops and restaurants. Free parking is available for tenants and their clients.

UNCW Executive Development Center
1241A Military Cutoff Rd., Wilmington
(910) 962-3578

Housed in the Northeast Regional Library adjacent to the Landfall Shopping Center, this new state-of-the-art meeting facility features

8,000 square feet of first-class training space and accommodates up to 200 participants. Seven meeting rooms offer a variety of seating options — theater, classroom and boardroom styles — and include moveable tables and high-backed ergonomic executive chairs. On-site technicians are available, and the center's large list of technical equipment includes 10' by 10' motorized screens, LCD projectors, VCR/CD/DVD equipment, ELMO document cameras, Plasma TV, overhead projectors, wireless microphones, 30 laptop computers, high-speed T-1 line wireless Internet access and more. Full-range catering is another featured service of the facility. The executive center is an extension of the University of North Carolina at Wilmington and the Division for Public Service and Continuing Studies.

Banking and Financial Services

The three major Wilmington-area counties — New Hanover, Brunswick and Pender — have been a virtual hotbed of economic activity for the past few decades. Fueled by residential and commercial construction, strong population growth (especially from retirees), ever-increasing tourism, a burgeoning health-care system and significant industrial development, the Wilmington-area financial community has grown in both strength and numbers.

The strong influx of older adults with funds to invest and manage plus homes to buy has been a major factor in the vigorous development of brokerages, financial managers and banking institutions. Concurrently, renovation, restoration and construction in the downtown and the historical district has furthered the development of financial and investment resources, as has a new convention center with its attendant commercial development planned for downtown on the river front.

With a superior quality of life attracting people seeking a better place to live, along with excellent educational facilities including the University of North Carolina at Wilmington and the outstanding Cape Fear Community College to provide skilled employees, the Wilmington area has seen the creation of a financial infrastructure that truly has become the financial center of southeastern North Carolina.

The following listings contain some of the principal financial institutions in this area. For a complete list including branch locations, addresses and phone numbers, consult our local telephone directories or contact your chamber of commerce (see the Area Overview chapter for a list of chambers of commerce).

BANKS

Among the national, regional and local banks available in the three counties are: Bank of America, Bank of Wilmington, BB&T, Carolina First, Central Carolina Bank, Coastal Federal Bank, Cooperative Bank, East Carolina Bank, First Citizens Bank, FNB Southeast, Port City Capital Bank, RBC Centura Bank and Wachovia Bank.

FINANCIAL SERVICES

Just a sampling of the many quality services available in our area are: American Express Financial Advisors, Anlyan & Hively Wealth Management, Bailey Benefits Group, Copley Investment Management, Edward Jones, Fisher & Company CPAs, Fountain Financial Associates, Jones Coggins & Co., Merrill Lynch, Morgan Keegan & Co., Charles Schwab & Co., Smith Barney, RSM McGladrey, Morgan Stanley, UBS Financial Services, Inc. and Wachovia Securities.

MORTGAGE LENDERS

In addition to banks, you can look to a wide variety of companies for assistance in obtaining funds to finance your purchase. Among the many available in our area are:

1st Consumer Mortgage, 1st Priority Mortgage, Alpha Mortgage, American Harbor Mortgage, American Home Mortgage, Atlantic Bay Mortgage Group, Countrywide Home Loans, Dover Mortgage Co., Equity One Mortgage, Family First Mortgage Corp., First Equity Mortgage, Hanover Mortgage Consultants, Lumina Mortgage Co., National City Mortgage, National Mortgage, Paragon Bank Mortgage, Stevens Mortgage Consulting, Sunset Mortgage and Wells Fargo Home Mortgage. See our Home Ownership chapter for more extensive information on mortgage lenders.

AAXA Discount Mortgage
6322 Oleander Dr., Wilmington
toll free (877) 728-3569

With corporate headquarters in Wilmington and operating in 25 states, AAXA Discount Mortgage specializes in low-cost, online lending. The company trademark is "We give you credit for your good credit," and it offers deep discounts for excellent credit. By utilizing state-of-the-art technology to improve efficiencies and smooth out the lending process, AAXA is able to drive down the cost of home financing.

Putting the customer first, AAXA seeks to provide the lowest fees possible, giving outstanding customer service while removing many of the pitfalls associated with traditional mortgages and lenders. AAXA approves most loans in-house for faster processing times. AAXA offers conventional loans, construction loans, lot loans, home equity lines of credit, 100 percent financing, commercial loans, flex-option interest-only loans, and low cost No Documentation loans.

Faith is a strong characteristic of southeastern North Carolina. The quest for religious freedom was one of the main reasons European settlers migrated to this area in the 18th century. The founding citizens of Wilmington brought their own beliefs with them, created spiritual homes for a broad spectrum of nationalities and eventually built stunning architectural monuments, many of which are on the National Historical Register.

The history of churches in the Cape Fear area could fill several books. Many of the region's larger churches were occupied by British or Union troops, and historical commentary about those episodes conjure up dramatic pictures. Imagine, if you will, the courtyards of downtown Wilmington churches populated by weary soldiers for so long that their camp fires permanently blackened the steeples.

From the beginning, settlers here established a religious environment of respect, support and tolerance of each other's rights to observe beliefs. In the entire recorded history of Wilmington, there is no evidence of religious oppression. In fact, we find many examples of a congregation of one denomination coming to the aid of another, such as when the members of Temple Israel, the first Jewish Temple in North Carolina, freely shared their building with neighboring Methodists for two years after the Methodist church was destroyed by fire in 1886. In the aftermath of the Civil War, many white congregations offered financial and moral support to newly created black churches when black members decided the time had come to create their own houses of worship.

The grander houses of worship in downtown Wilmington date from the 18th and 19th centuries and, in addition to providing opulent settings for large congregations, figure prominently on historic tours of the area. One cannot view the Wilmington skyline without being instantly struck by the profusion of spires. The tallest and oldest, the 197-foot twin spire of First Baptist Church was toppled by Hurricane Floyd in 1999. After a full year of determination to rebuild the spire in its exact authenticity, it has been restored to its former beauty.

Visitors enjoy the fascinating history and architecture of many local churches and temples, including St. James Episcopal at the corner of S. Third and Market streets; St. Mary's Catholic on Ann Street; Temple of Israel at the corner of S. Fourth and Market streets; St. Paul's Evangelical Lutheran on Market Street; First Presbyterian on S. Third Street; and St. Stephen AME on Red Cross Street. If you want to know more about these and other historic churches, see our Attractions chapter or drop by the North Carolina Room at the New Hanover County Public Library in downtown Wilmington and ask for information.

Wilmington has interdenominational, non-denominational, Full Gospel, Episcopal, Holiness, Pentecostal and AME/AME Zion houses of worship. Other religions with a presence in the area include Jewish, Roman Catholic, Jehovah's Witnesses, Greek Orthodox, Christian Science, Islam, Lutheran, Quaker, Unitarian, Seventh Day Adventist, Unity, Eckankar and United Methodist. Meditation groups meet in various spiritual centers. You can get specific information about spiritual organizations, services and locations via the Yellow Pages, the "Religion" page in Saturday's Star-News, public libraries, local chambers of commerce and visitor centers.

The Thai temple rises from the coastal forests of Brunswick County in Bolivia. The Buddhist Association of North Carolina has been building this temple for many years and has relied on community donations to complete the work. It represents an important addition to the region's religious and philosophical centers. Located on Midway Road between N.C. 211 and U.S. 17 Business,

Church of the Servant

Episcopal

4925 Oriole Dr, Wilmington NC 28403 395-0616

Church of the Servant is a Christian Community committed to the spiritual development of the individual so that each may become a responsible servant in the world

ADULT AND CHILDREN'S CHRISTIAN EDUCATION PROGRAMS
EPISCOPAL CAMPUS MINISTRY
INTEGRITY
LABYRINTH
BARGAIN BOX
COMMUNITY
OUTREACH PROGRAMS
LOBSTER FEST

SUNDAY SCHEDULE
8:30 & 11am-Holy Eucharist
Nursery is available
9:30am-Adult & Children's
Christian Education

WEDNESDAY HOLY EUCHARIST
6:00pm-Holy Eucharist (During Academic Year)

EPISCOPAL CAMPUS MINISTRY
During Academic Year
6:30pm-Dinner and Program

LABYRINTH WALK
Open the 3rd Friday 7-10pm and Saturday 9am-Noon of each month.
Contact the church office for appointments at other times.

WWW.CHURCHOFTHESERVANTNC.ORG

it's a bit difficult to locate, but you can call for directions, (910) 253-4526.

If you want to attend services while you're on vacation and you're wondering what to wear, here's some advice. Southern coast people don't dress up much for work and they love to wear casual clothes most of the time, but they generally dress for worship. Still, if casual clothes are all you brought, you will be welcome. People in our tourist-oriented communities are used to seeing visitors in vacation mode.

Wilmington and the southern coast area have an abundance of spiritual resources in terms of bookstores. Mainstream Christian shoppers will find Bibles, videos, tapes, music, gifts, books, cards and other religious items in these local shops:

Cox Christian Bookstore, 75 S. Kerr Avenue, Wilmington, (910) 762-2272

Salt Shaker Bookstore and Café, 705 S. Kerr Avenue, Wilmington, (910) 350-1753

Just Lovely Gifts & Christian Literature, 4830 Main Street, Shallotte, (910) 755-7101

INDEX

I

T

U

V

W